Focus on Personal Finance

An Active Approach to Help You Achieve Financial Literacy

SEVENTH EDITION

The McGraw Hill Series in Finance, Insurance, and Real Estate

FINANCIAL MANAGEMENT

Block, Hirt, and Danielsen
Foundations of Financial Management
Seventeenth Edition

Brealey, Myers, and Allen
Principles of Corporate Finance
Thirteenth Edition

Brealey, Myers, and Allen
Principles of Corporate Finance, Concise
Second Edition

Brealey, Myers, and Marcus
Fundamentals of Corporate Finance
Tenth Edition

Brooks
FinGame Online 5.0

Bruner, Eades, and Schill
Case Studies in Finance: Managing for Corporate Value Creation
Eighth Edition

Cornett, Adair, and Nofsinger
Finance: Applications and Theory
Fifth Edition

Cornett, Adair, and Nofsinger
M: Finance
Fifth Edition

DeMello
Cases in Finance
Third Edition

Grinblatt (editor)
Stephen A. Ross, Mentor: Influence through Generations

Grinblatt and Titman
Financial Markets and Corporate Strategy
Second Edition

Higgins
Analysis for Financial Management
Twelfth Edition

Ross, Westerfield, Jaffe, and Jordan
Corporate Finance
Thirteenth Edition

Ross, Westerfield, Jaffe, and Jordan
Corporate Finance: Core Principles and Applications
Sixth Edition

Ross, Westerfield, and Jordan
Essentials of Corporate Finance
Tenth Edition

Ross, Westerfield, and Jordan
Fundamentals of Corporate Finance
Thirteenth Edition

Shefrin
Behavioral Corporate Finance: Decisions that Create Value
Second Edition

INVESTMENTS

Bodie, Kane, and Marcus
Essentials of Investments
Twelfth Edition

Bodie, Kane, and Marcus
Investments
Twelfth Edition

Hirt and Block
Fundamentals of Investment Management
Tenth Edition

Jordan, Miller, and Dolvin
Fundamentals of Investments: Valuation and Management
Eighth Edition

Stewart, Piros, and Heisler
Running Money: Professional Portfolio Management
First Edition

Sundaram and Das
Derivatives: Principles and Practice
Second Edition

FINANCIAL INSTITUTIONS AND MARKETS

Rose and Hudgins
Bank Management and Financial Services
Ninth Edition

Rose and Marquis
Financial Institutions and Markets
Eleventh Edition

Saunders and Cornett
Financial Institutions Management: A Risk Management Approach
Tenth Edition

Saunders and Cornett
Financial Markets and Institutions
Eighth Edition

INTERNATIONAL FINANCE

Eun and Resnick
International Financial Management
Ninth Edition

REAL ESTATE

Brueggeman and Fisher
Real Estate Finance and Investments
Seventeeth Edition

Ling and Archer
Real Estate Principles: A Value Approach
Sixth Edition

FINANCIAL PLANNING AND INSURANCE

Allen, Melone, Rosenbloom, and Mahoney
Retirement Plans: 401(k)s, IRAs, and Other Deferred Compensation Approaches
Twelfth Edition

Altfest
Personal Financial Planning
Second Edition

Harrington and Niehaus
Risk Management and Insurance
Second Edition

Kapoor, Dlabay, Hughes, and Hart
Focus on Personal Finance: An Active Approach to Help You Achieve Financial Literacy
Seventh Edition

Kapoor, Dlabay, Hughes, and Hart
Personal Finance
Thirteenth Edition

Walker and Walker
Personal Finance: Building Your Future
Second Edition

Focus on Personal Finance

An Active Approach to Help You Achieve Financial Literacy

SEVENTH EDITION

Jack R. Kapoor
COLLEGE OF DUPAGE

Les R. Dlabay
LAKE FOREST COLLEGE

Robert J. Hughes
DALLAS COUNTY COMMUNITY COLLEGES

Melissa M. Hart
NORTH CAROLINA STATE UNIVERSITY

FOCUS ON PERSONAL FINANCE, SEVENTH EDITION

Published by McGraw Hill LLC, 1325 Avenue of the Americas, New York, NY 10121. Copyright © 2022 by McGraw Hill LLC. All rights reserved. Printed in the United States of America. Previous editions © 2019, 2016, and 2013. No part of this publication may be reproduced or distributed in any form or by any means, or stored in a database or retrieval system, without the prior written consent of McGraw Hill LLC, including, but not limited to, in any network or other electronic storage or transmission, or broadcast for distance learning.

Some ancillaries, including electronic and print components, may not be available to customers outside the United States.

This book is printed on acid-free paper.

2 3 4 5 6 7 8 9 LWI 24 23 22

ISBN 978-1-260-77237-1 (bound edition)
MHID 1-260-77237-3 (bound edition)
ISBN 978-1-264-11197-8 (loose-leaf edition)
MHID 1-264-11197-5 (loose-leaf edition)

Portfolio Manager: *Charles Synovec*
Product Developer: *Allison McCabe-Carroll*
Marketing Manager: *Trina Maurer*
Content Project Managers: *Pat Frederickson and Jamie Koch*
Buyer: *Susan K. Culbertson*
Designer: *Beth Blech*
Content Licensing Specialist: *Traci Vaske*
Cover Image: *YinYang/Getty Images*
Compositor: *SPi Global*

All credits appearing on page or at the end of the book are considered to be an extension of the copyright page.

Library of Congress Cataloging-in-Publication Data

Names: Kapoor, Jack R., 1937- author.
Title: Focus on personal finance : an active approach to help you achieve
    financial literacy / Jack R. Kapoor [and three others].
Description: Seventh edition. | New York, NY : McGraw Hill,
    [2022] | Series: The McGraw Hill series in finance, insurance,
    and real estate | Includes index.
Identifiers: LCCN 2020036759 | ISBN 9781260772371 (hardcover)
Subjects: LCSH: Finance, Personal. | Investments.
Classification: LCC HG179 .K368 2022 | DDC 332.024—dc23
LC record available at https://lccn.loc.gov/2020036759

mheducation.com/highered

Dedication

To my grandchildren, Joshua, Audra, and Hannah Tucker; and Veda and Asha Kapoor

To my wife, Linda Dlabay; my children, Carissa and Kyle; their spouses, Doug Erickson and Anne Jaspers; and my grandchildren Lucy Dlabay and Caleb Erickson

To my wife, Robin, and the memory of my mother, Barbara Y. Hughes

To my husband, David Hart, and my children, Alex and Madelyn

Brief Table of Contents

YinYang/Getty Images

vi

Focus on . . . the Cover

How do you feel when you look at this cover? We hope the image on the book conveys a feeling of relaxation and overall peace of mind—both achieved, in part, by developing a solid financial plan. From cover to cover, this text's goal is to help you gain the financial literacy and personal finance skills you need to make sound financial decisions for life. Use this book as a tool to help you plan for a successful financial future!

Focus on . . . the Authors

Jack R. Kapoor, EdD, *College of DuPage*

Jack Kapoor has been a professor of business and economics in the Business and Technology Division of the College of DuPage, Glen Ellyn, Illinois, where he taught Personal Finance, Introduction to Business, Marketing, Management, and Economics for more than 40 years. Professor Kapoor is a recipient of the Business and Technology Division's Outstanding Professor Award. He received his BA and MS from San Francisco State College and his EdD in Business and Economic Education from Northern Illinois University. He previously taught at Illinois Institute of Technology's Stuart School of Management, San Francisco State University's School of World Business, and other colleges. He served as an assistant national bank examiner for the U.S. Treasury Department and has been an international trade consultant to Bolting Manufacturing Co., Ltd., Mumbai, India.

Dr. Kapoor is known internationally as a co-author of several textbooks, including *Business: A Practical Approach* (Rand McNally), *Business* (Cengage Learning), *Business and Personal Finance* (Glencoe), and *Personal Finance* (McGraw Hill). He served as a content consultant for two popular national television series, *The Business File: An Introduction to Business* and *Dollars and Sense: Personal Finance for the 21st Century;* and he developed two full-length audio courses in Business and Personal Finance. He has been quoted in many national newspapers and magazines, including *USA Today, U.S. News & World Report,* the *Chicago Sun-Times, Crain's Small Business,* the *Chicago Tribune,* and other publications.

Dr. Kapoor has traveled around the world and has studied business practices in capitalist, socialist, and communist countries.

Les R. Dlabay, EdD, *Lake Forest College*

"Learning for a life worth living" is the teaching emphasis of Les Dlabay, professor of business emeritus, who taught at Lake Forest College, Lake Forest, Illinois, for 35 years. In an effort to prepare students for diverse economic settings, he makes extensive use of field research projects and interactive learning related to food, water, health care, and education. He believes our society can improve global business development through volunteering, knowledge sharing, and financial support. Dr. Dlabay has authored or has adaptations of more than 40 textbooks in the United States, Canada, India, and Singapore. He has taught more than 30 different courses during his career and has presented over 300 workshops and seminars to academic, business, and community organizations. Professor Dlabay has a collection of cereal packages from more than 100 countries and banknotes from 200 countries, which are used to teach about economic, cultural, and political elements of international business environments.

His research involves informal and alternative financial services in cross-cultural and global business settings. Dr. Dlabay serves on the board of Andean Aid (www.andeanaid. org), which provides tutoring assistance and spiritual guidance to school-age children in Colombia and Venezuela, and teaches community-based money management and workforce readiness classes for Love INC of Lake County (Illinois), which mobilizes local churches to transform lives and communities. Professor Dlabay has a BS (Accounting) from the University of Illinois, Chicago; an MBA from DePaul University; and an EdD in Business and Economic Education from Northern Illinois University. He has received The Great Teacher award at Lake Forest College three times.

Robert J. Hughes, EdD, *Dallas County Community Colleges*

Financial literacy! Only two words, but Bob Hughes, professor of business at Dallas County Community Colleges, believes that these two words can change your life. Whether you want to be rich or just manage the money you have, the ability to analyze financial decisions and gather financial information are skills that can always be improved. Dr. Hughes has taught personal finance, introduction to business, business math, small business management, small business finance, and accounting for over 35 years. In addition to *Focus on Personal Finance* and *Personal Finance,* published by McGraw Hill, he has authored college textbooks for Introduction to Business, Business Mathematics, and Small Business Management. He also served as a content consultant for two popular national television series, *Dollars & Sense: Personal Finance for the 21st Century* and *It's Strictly Business,* and he is the lead author for a business math project utilizing artificial intelligence instruction funded by the ALEKS Corporation. He received his BBA from Southern Nazarene University and his MBA and EdD from the University of North Texas. His hobbies include writing, investing, collecting French antiques, art, and travel.

Melissa M. Hart, CPA, *North Carolina State University*

Melissa Hart is a senior lecturer in the Poole College of Management at North Carolina State University. She teaches courses in personal and corporate finance. She is a member of the Academy of Outstanding Teachers. She has been nominated for the Gertrude Cox Award for Innovative Excellence in Teaching with Technology for developing unique approaches to introduce technology into the classroom and the distance education environment. Spreading the word about financial literacy has always been a passion of hers. It doesn't stop at the classroom. Each year she shares her commonsense approach of "No plan is a plan" to various student groups, clubs, high schools, and other organizations. She is a member of the North Carolina Association of Certified Public Accountants and the American Institute of Certified Public Accountants. She received her BBA from the University of Maryland and an MBA from North Carolina State University. Prior to obtaining an MBA, she worked eight years in public accounting in auditing, tax compliance, and consulting. Her hobbies include keeping up with her family's many extracurricular activities. She travels extensively with her family to enjoy the many cultures and beauty of the country and the world.

Dear Personal Finance Students and Professors

Today everyone has a story about how the coronavirus pandemic affected their life. Did you quarantine with family members, friends, or alone? Did you drive around for hours trying to get basic necessities—the last roll of toilet paper or bottle of hand sanitizer? Were you laid off from your job? Did you worry about how to pay your bills and pay for food and medicines? All good questions that describe how a pandemic can affect both your health and your financial security. For many people, it was a wake-up call that they needed money and a personal financial plan.

While there are no guarantees there won't be hardships ahead, we can provide you with the information you need to weather the next crisis. The material in this new edition of *Focus on Personal Finance* will help you answer important questions including:

- How much should you have in an emergency fund?
- Why does your ratio of cash and liquid assets to monthly expenses matter in a crisis?
- What happens if you skip a monthly payment or can't pay your bills?
- If you get sick, will your health insurance cover treatment?
- What portion of your income should you save each month?
- What is your risk tolerance for investing in a volatile market?
- Will you have to delay retirement?

What's Next?

For both students and professors, the pandemic led to new problems. Many students and professors quickly found their schedule change from on-campus classes to online delivery in a matter of days. As authors, we realized our textbook materials and our digital package were an even more important component that could help students learn. As we prepared this edition of the text and digital package, we worked hard to include important content in every chapter you can use to develop your own plan to build financial security and to weather another pandemic, an unexpected job loss, or unexpected life situations.

As we emerge from this crisis, ask yourself what financial lessons you have learned. As you think about the answer, keep in mind the decisions that we all make every day can lead to effective money management and help build financial security. That's what this course, this text, and the digital package are all about: learning how to make better financial decisions and managing your money, even in a time of crisis.

Text (Or eBook Option)

The new seventh edition of *Focus on Personal Finance* provides current content, examples, exhibits, and features in each chapter to illustrate concepts that can be used to build financial health. Our new *FinTech for Financial Literacy* feature is designed to help you use technology to improve financial decisions. Another new feature of this edition is the *Financial Literacy Portfolio* that appears at the end of each chapter. These features are designed to introduce students to the many resources that promote financial competencies, action research, and outcomes. In addition, as always, we have reviewed and revised websites and apps throughout the text to provide you with up-to-date sources of information.

Digital Package

As teachers and authors, we are acutely aware of the importance of having a robust digital package—especially now as more and more classes are taught online. We are proud of the tools we have created to facilitate student learning. For students, our digital package includes an interactive e-book, practice quizzes, and short videos along with assignable and auto-graded questions. We also offer auto-graded *Your Personal Financial Plan* sheets that are built around the cases in the text and an electronic version of the *Daily Spending Diary* sheets. For instructors, our digital resources include a comprehensive instructor manual, computerized test bank, and PowerPoint presentations for each chapter. In short, should you need digital resources at any time, we have those covered.

New Normal

While we don't know how the events surrounding coronavirus pandemic will change the future, we do believe the basic principles in a personal finance course can help your students through a crisis and beyond. We are happy to join you on this journey! We invite you to begin by reading Chapter 1, *Personal Financial Planning in Action.*

Welcome to the new, seventh edition of Focus on Personal Finance!

Jack Kapoor

kapoorj@att.net

Les Dlabay

dlabay@lakeforest.edu

Bob Hughes

Hughespublishing@outlook.com

Melissa Hart

mmhart@ncsu.edu

New to This Edition

The seventh edition of *Focus on Personal Finance* contains new and updated boxed features, exhibits and tables, articles, and end-of-chapter material. The following grid highlights just some of the significant content revisions made to *Focus on Personal Finance,* 7e.

Global changes for all chapters

- New *FinTech for Financial Literacy* margin feature.
- New *Digital Financial Literacy with. . .* feature in each chapter.
- Revised *Road Map–Dashboard* feature at the end of each chapter.
- Revised and updated problems throughout.
- New *Financial Literacy Portfolio* activity at the end of the chapter.
- Updated websites and apps on *Your Personal Financial Plan* sheets.

CHAPTER 1 Personal Financial Planning in Action	• New definition of *financial literacy*. • New **Exhibit 1-1,** Planning for Personal Financial Literacy. • New *CAUTION!* feature on avoiding lifestyle inflation. • Expanded *Financial Literacy in Practice* feature for creating financial goals. • New *FinTech for Financial Literacy* feature discussing automated systems for banking and personal finance activities. • New *Digital Financial Literacy with. . .* feature with resources available at **kiplinger.com**. • New coverage of school funding sources. • New *Financial Literacy Portfolio* feature to help students develop financial goals using the S-M-A-R-T format. • Relocation of *Daily Spending Diary* instructions and sample sheets to the end of Chapter 1.
CHAPTER 2 Money Management Skills	• New *FinTech for Financial Literacy* feature on using robo-advisors to guide financial planning. • New *CAUTION!* feature on having an accurate record of spending and reduced financial stress. • New *Money Minute Focus* feature on unused educational grants and scholarships. • New *Money Minute Focus* feature on *kakeibo*, a system used in Japan for managing personal finances. • An updated *Money Minute Focus* feature on how most households can have an additional $500 or more a month. • New *Digital Financial Literacy with. . .* feature on clark.com. • New *Financial Literacy Portfolio* feature teaching students how to effectively organize their financial records. • Relocation of *Developing a Career Search Strategy* appendix to the end of Chapter 2 with new coverage of human-centered design, the use of artificial intelligence in the hiring process, and a checklist for interview success.

CHAPTER 3 Taxes in Your Financial Plan	• New *FinTech for Financial Literacy* feature on cryptocurrency. • Coverage of TCJA tax information throughout with updated content on how to file taxes online. • Updated figures with revised tax brackets, rates, and calculations. • Revised **Exhibit 3-3,** showing up-to-date tax forms. • Revised **Exhibit 3-4,** showing up-to-date deduction schedule. • Revised **Exhibit 3-5,** showing up-to-date tax tables and rates. • New *Digital Financial Literacy with. . .* feature showing students how to use **thebalance.com** to help find the latest information to guide their financial decision making. • New *Financial Literacy Portfolio* feature guiding students on how to prepare to file a federal income tax return.
CHAPTER 4 Financial Services: Savings Plans and Payment Accounts	• New *FinTech for Financial Literacy* feature on *neobanks*. • Revised and expanded **Exhibit 4-4** for assessing and selecting a financial institution. • Updated *CAUTION!* feature on unnecessary bank fees. • New *CAUTION!* feature on potential payment deceptions. • New *Money Minute Focus* feature on education savings plans. • New *Money Minute Focus* feature on the use of varied savings accounts to effectively manage finances. • Updated *FinTech for Financial Literacy* feature on cybercurrencies. • New *Digital Financial Literacy with. . .* feature on **nerdwallet.com**. • New *Financial Literacy Portfolio* feature on potential payment deceptions.
CHAPTER 5 Consumer Credit Advantages, Disadvantages Sources, and Costs	• Updated **Exhibit 5-2** showing the volume of consumer credit. • Revised and updated **Exhibit 5-10** covering consumer bankruptcy filings in the United States. • New *Money Minute Focus* feature explaining how a security freeze on your credit report can stop identity thieves from opening new accounts in your name. • New and updated content in **What is Consumer Credit?, Credit Cards, Home Equity Loans, Applying for Credit, FICO** and **VantageScore, and Bankruptcy sections**. • New *FinTech for Financial Literacy* feature on the Fair Credit Reporting Act. • Updated Home Equity Loans example. • New *Digital Financial Literacy with. . .* feature covering selecting and using a retail credit card. • New *Smart Money Minute* feature revealing how to obtain free credit reports. • New *Financial Literacy Portfolio* feature on how to research and compare alternative credit sources.
CHAPTER 6 Consumer Purchasing and Wise Buying Strategies	• New *Money Minute Focus* feature on avoiding financial difficulties when mixing needs and wants. • New *Money Minute Focus* feature on the buying habits of minimalists and frugal people. • New *Money Minute Focus* feature on the financial benefits of driving an older car. • New *Digital Financial Literacy with. . .* feature with motor vehicle testing and product information from **consumerreports.org**.

CHAPTER 6 *(Continued)*	• New *Money Minute Focus* feature on renting or borrowing rather than owning motor vehicles, clothing, cameras, power tools, and home appliances. • Updated *Money Minute Focus* feature on common consumer complaints and scams. • New *CAUTION!* feature on avoiding scams of online used-car sellers. • New *CAUTION!* feature on scholarship and financial aid scams. • New *FinTech for Financial Literacy* feature on retail technology trends. • New *Financial Literacy Portfolio* feature guiding students on how to plan for a consumer purchase. • Relocation of **Consumer Agencies and Organizations** appendix to the end of Chapter 6 with updated links and contact information.
CHAPTER 7 Selecting and Financing Housing	• New *FinTech for Financial Literacy* feature on digital innovations connecting buyers, sellers, brokers, lenders, and landlords. • New *Digital Financial Literacy with. . .* feature with home ownership, mortgage, and other housing information at **money.com**. • Revised and updated coverage of factory-built houses, prefabricated homes, modular homes, mobile homes, and manufactured homes. • New *Money Minute Focus* feature on planning for home buying costs. • New *Money Minute Focus* feature on iBuyers. • Updated *Money Minute Focus* feature on shorter mortgages and paying an additional amount each month. • Revised *CAUTION!* feature on e-mail hacking, identity theft, and wire fraud related to home buying. • Updated **Exhibit 7-9** on common closing costs. • New *Financial Literacy Portfolio* feature on comparing housing alternatives.
CHAPTER 8 Home and Automobile Insurance	• New *Personal Finance in Practice* feature on flood facts. • New *FinTech for Financial Literacy* feature explaining InsurTech. • New *FinTech for Financial Literacy* feature covering global positioning systems and the auto insurance industry. • New *Money Minute Focus* feature on seat belt usage. • New and revised content in the **Property and Liability Insurance in Your Financial Plan** section. • New and revised content in the **Automobile Insurance Coverages** section. • New **Digital Financial Literacy with. . .** feature explaining usage-based auto insurance. • New *Financial Literacy Portfolio* feature guiding students on researching and selecting home and auto insurance coverage.
CHAPTER 9 Health and Disability Income insurance	• New *Money Minute Focus* feature on the Families First Coronavirus Response Act. • New *Money Minute Focus* feature covering COVID-19 testing coverage. • New *Money Minute Focus* feature on the Family Leave and Medical Act. • New *Money Minute Focus* feature on insuring Americans through private insurers. • New *FinTech for Financial Literacy* feature explaining crowd funding websites.

CHAPTER 9 *(Continued)*	• New *Caution!* feature on HSA contributions. • New *Digital Financial Literacy with. . .* feature covering Medicare's BlueButton and BlueButton 2.0. • Revised *Financial Literacy in Practice* feature covering HSAs. • Expanded discussion of out-of-pocket limits, dental expense insurance, and Medicare coverage in the **What Is Not Covered by Medicare** section. • New content covering health insurance options for the unemployed and a new discussion on exclusive provider organizations. • New content discussing nurse lines, virtual visits, retail clinics, and urgent care. • Updated content within the **Major Medical Expense Insurance Coverage, Health Care Costs,** and **Long-Term Care Insurance sections**. • Revised **Exhibit 9-1** outlining health insurance must-haves. • Revised **Exhibit 9-2** comparing managed health care plans. • Revised **Exhibit 9-5** examining U.S. national health expenditures. • New *Financial Literacy Portfolio* feature covering how to research and select health and disability insurance.
CHAPTER 10 Financial Planning with Life Insurance	• New *What Would You Do?* feature on choosing types of insurance. • New *What Would You Do?* feature on examining types and amounts of insurance. • New *What Would You Do?* feature on choosing the right insurance policy. • New *FinTech for Financial Literacy* feature outlining how insurers turn vision into reality. • New *FinTech for Financial Literacy* feature examining the Insurance Barometer Study. • New *Money Minute Focus* feature covering individual life insurance policies. • Revised content within the **Financial Planning with Annuities** section. • Updated discussion on the nonworking spouse method of determining life insurance needs. • Revised **How Long Will You Live?** subsection. • Updated **Exhibit 10-1** covering life expectancy across all races. • New *Digital Financial Literacy with. . .* feature with **Kiplinger.com** on how to shop for life insurance. • New *Financial Literacy Portfolio* feature guiding students on how to determine the type and amount of life insurance coverage they may need.
CHAPTER 11 Investing Basics and Evaluating Bonds	• New example of the time value of money. • New example explaining how the time value of money can help people obtain their long-term investment goals. • Many new examples highlighting financial points of interest for Coca-Cola, Amazon, Facebook, Payless ShoeSource, J. C. Penney, Walmart, McDonald's, Square Inc., and Pacific Gas & Electric. • New *Digital Financial Literacy with. . .* describing how the Motley Fool website can educate, amuse, and enrich an investor's experience. • Revised *Money Minute Focus* feature providing yields for investment-grade bonds. • New *Money Minute Focus* feature on the 50/20/30 rule. • Revised *Figure It Out* feature on determining the time value of money.

CHAPTER 11 *(Continued)*	• New risk tolerance quiz in **Exhibit 11-2** providing a way for students to measure their risk tolerance.
	• Revised **Exhibit 11-6** with up-to-date information about Treasury bills, Treasury notes, Treasury bonds, and TIPs.
	• New **Exhibit 11-7** covering bond information available by accessing the Financial Investment Regulatory Authority website.
	• Revised **Exhibit 11-8** examining the description of bond ratings provided by Moody's Investors Service and Standard & Poor's Corporation.
	• New discussion on how the business cycle and financial markets are affected by political and economic developments and pandemics such as the coronavirus.
	• New *FinTech for Financial Literacy* feature covering using an asset allocation calculator to construct an investment portfolio.
	• New *Caution!* feature pointing out questions students may want to ask in job interviews about employee health care and retirement match programs.
	• Revised *What Would You Do?* feature on preparing for a downturn in the economy or a potential job loss
	• Revised *Figure It Out* feature and tryout problem illustrating how to use a financial calculator to determine the time value of money.
	• New **Real Personal Finance** case asking students to choose between an investment in CDs or corporate bonds.
	• New *Financial Literacy Portfolio* feature guiding students to create an investment start-up plan.
CHAPTER 12 Investing in Stocks	• New examples providing information about utility firms that provide above-average dividends.
	• New example describing how Casper Sleep used an IPO to raise over $100 million.
	• New examples in the **Common and Preferred Stock, Buying Stock on Margin**, and **Selling Short** sections.
	• Revised **Exhibit 12-1** showing how the record date is determined for a Microsoft dividend payment.
	• New **Exhibit 12-2** describing how investors make money from dividends and appreciation of value.
	• New **Exhibit 12-4** providing information students can use to evaluate an investment in Walmart stock.
	• New **Exhibit 12-5** offering detailed information for Microsoft provided by Value Line.
	• Revised **Exhibit 12-6** outlining typical commission charges for stock transactions.
	• Revised **Exhibit 12-7** providing an example of dollar cost averaging for Johnson & Johnson.
	• New *FinTech for Financial Literacy* feature discussing using the Internet to obtain historical information for dividends and stock prices.
	• New *FinTech for Financial Literacy* feature describing the TD Ameritrade mobile app.
	• New *Digital Financial Literacy with. . .* feature examining information available at the Investor.gov website.
	• Revised *Money Minute Focus* feature providing current and historical data for the Dow Jones Average.

CHAPTER 12 *(Continued)*	• New *Money Minute Focus* feature revealing how students can use simulations or virtual stock market games to practice their investment skills. • New and revised calculations for companies in the **Numerical Measures That Influence Investment Decisions** section. • New and expanded discussion in the **Commission Charges** section. • New **Real Personal Finance case** asking students to use Value Line information to evaluate an investment. • New *Financial Literacy Portfolio* feature showing students how to research potential stock investments.
CHAPTER 13 Investing in Mutual Funds	• Revised definition for *mutual fund.* • New **Exhibit 13-1** detailing the type of holdings in the Fidelity Balanced Fund. • New **Exhibit 13-2** providing information about sales loads, annual fund operating expenses, and other fees. • New **Exhibit 13-4** providing data investors can use to evaluate the Fidelity Contrafund. • New **Exhibit 13-5** showing mutual fund research information for the T. Rowe Price Dividend Growth Fund. • Updated **Exhibit 13-6** providing information about Kiplinger's 25 favorite no-load funds. • Revised *Money Minute Focus* feature on why investors purchase mutual funds. • New *Money Minute Focus* feature describing the number of households that own funds in each generation. • New information about the J.P. Morgan Large Cap Growth Fund illustrating the cost of investing in a load fund. • New information about the Alger Mid-Cap Growth Fund illustrating the cost of investing in a fund with a contingent deferred sales load. • New material explaining the objective of the Dodge and Cox Stock Fund. • New data on the number and percentages of closed-end, exchange-traded, and open-end funds. • New material and statistics in the **Other Funds, Why Investors Purchase Mutual Funds,** and **Professional Advisory Services** sections. • New *Digital Financial Literacy with. . .* feature describing the type of information investors can obtain on the Kiplinger.com website. • New *FinTech for Financial Literacy* feature on using the Fund Analyzer app to analyze and compare fund costs. • New *FinTech for Financial Literacy* feature on using the Personal Capital app to track the value of investments. • New **Real Personal Finance case** asking students to use Morningstar research information to evaluate an investment in the T. Rowe Price Dividend Growth Fund. • New *Financial Literacy Portfolio* feature asking students to construct their own investment portfolio.
CHAPTER 14 Starting Early: Retirement and Estate Planning	• Updated **Exhibit 14-5** outlining various types of IRAs. • Revised *Financial Literacy in Practice* feature covering "The Psychology of Planning for Retirement While You Are Young." • New *FinTech for Financial Literacy* feature outlining **Kiplinger.com's** retiree tax map.

CHAPTER 14 *(Continued)*	• New ***Money Minute Focus*** feature discussing drawing Social Security at age 62 versus age 70.
	• Revised ***Money Minute Focus*** feature showing the average monthly Social Security benefits in 2020.
	• New ***What Would You Do?*** feature discussing what to do with lump-sum 401(k) plan money.
	• Updated IRA, Roth IRA, and SEP contribution limits for 2020 as well as the Credit Shelter Trust exemption and gift tax amounts.
	• New discussion covering the required minimum distribution and the Secure Act of 2019.
	• Expanded the **Social Security Retirement Benefits** section.
	• New ***Financial Literacy Portfolio*** feature guiding students to develop their own retirement/estate planning guide plan.

Focus on . . . Learning

3 Steps to Financial Literacy

Getting your finances in order is simpler than you think, and we're here to show students how. These chapter opening features break down key action items students need to take to address the most important personal finance issues from the chapter, as part of the book's emphasis on taking action. These steps connect with the *Road Map to Financial Literacy* and *Your Personal Finance Dashboard* at the end of each chapter.

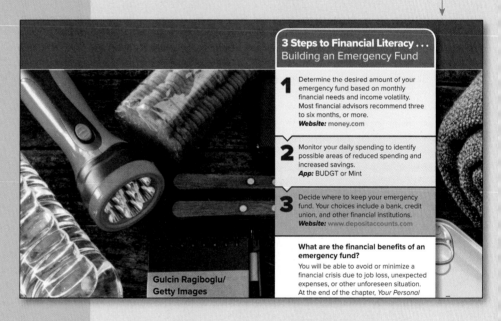

3 Steps to Financial Literacy . . .
Building an Emergency Fund

1 Determine the desired amount of your emergency fund based on monthly financial needs and income volatility. Most financial advisors recommend three to six months, or more.
Website: money.com

2 Monitor your daily spending to identify possible areas of reduced spending and increased savings.
App: BUDGT or Mint

3 Decide where to keep your emergency fund. Your choices include a bank, credit union, and other financial institutions.
Website: www.depositaccounts.com

What are the financial benefits of an emergency fund?
You will be able to avoid or minimize a financial crisis due to job loss, unexpected expenses, or other unforeseen situation. At the end of the chapter, *Your Personal*

Gulcin Ragiboglu/
Getty Images

---

ancial Decisions

money. However, the amount, along with needs, financial choices, ns, will vary from person to person. In this book, you will have the our current situation, learn about varied financial paths, and move financial security.

the use of knowledge and skills for earning, saving, spending, and ieve personal, family, and community goals. The process includes ehaviors, and competencies to meet current and future financial iteracy leads to financial well-being and a lifetime of financial secu- ng personal and economic circumstances. As shown in Exhibit 1-1, e result of information and knowledge, attitudes and abilities, and

oals may include buying a new car or a larger home, pursuing g, contributing to charity, traveling extensively, and gaining finan- o achieve these and other goals, people need to identify and set d personal satisfaction are the result of an organized process that o as *personal money management* or *personal financial planning*.

tion and Financial Planning

ning is the process of managing your money to achieve personal This planning process allows you to control your financial situation.

LO1.1
Identify social and economic influences on financial literacy and personal financial decisions.

ACTION ITEM
Do you have an emergency fund for unexpected expenses?
☐ Yes ☐ No

personal financial planning The process of managing your money to achieve personal economic satisfaction.

Learning Objective References

Citations in the margins next to the relevant text refer to corresponding chapter objectives listed at the beginning of each chapter.

Action Items

As part of the emphasis on taking action to gain financial skills, Action Items are posted at the start of each main section of a chapter. These are designed to get students thinking about what daily actions they can be taking to achieve financial literacy and independence.

An interactive and engaging chapter opener gets students organized and demonstrates the relevance of the material to their own lives.

Learning Objectives

Learning objectives highlight the goals of each chapter for easy reference. Throughout the book, in the end-of-chapter material and even in the supplement materials, these objectives provide a valuable foundation for assessment.

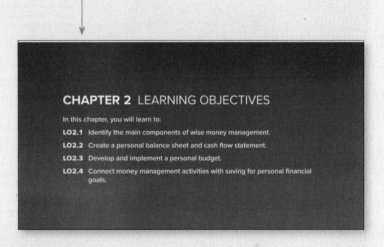

CHAPTER 2 LEARNING OBJECTIVES

In this chapter, you will learn to:

LO2.1 Identify the main components of wise money management.

LO2.2 Create a personal balance sheet and cash flow statement.

LO2.3 Develop and implement a personal budget.

LO2.4 Connect money management activities with saving for personal financial goals.

YOUR PERSONAL FINANCIAL PLAN SHEETS

5. Financial Documents and Records
6. Creating a Personal Balance Sheet
7. Creating a Personal Cash Flow Statement
8. Developing a Personal Budget

A Successful Money Management Plan

"Each month, I have too many days and not enough money. If the month were only 20 days long, budgeting would be easy."

Daily spending and saving decisions are the focus of financial planning. You must coordinate these actions with your needs, goals, and personal situation. Maintaining financial records and planning your spending are essential for successful personal financial management. The time and effort you devote to these activities will yield benefits. **Money management** refers to the day-to-day financial activities necessary to manage current personal economic resources while working toward long-term financial security.

LO2.1

Identify the main components of wise money management.

ACTION ITEM

My money management strategy involves:

☐ no spending plan

Your Personal Financial Plan Sheets

A list of the *Your Personal Financial Plan* worksheets for each chapter is presented at the start of the chapter for easy reference.

Examples

Worked-out examples featuring key concepts and calculations appear throughout the text, a valuable feature for students to see how personal finance works in practice.

SIMPLE INTEREST ON THE DECLINING BALANCE When simple interest is paid back in more than one payment, the method of computing interest is known as the declining balance method. You pay interest only on the amount of principal that you have not yet repaid. The more often you make payments, the lower the interest you'll pay. Most credit unions use this method.

> **EXAMPLE: Using the Simple Interest Formula on the Declining Balance**
>
> Using simple interest on the declining balance to compute interest charges, the interest on a 5 percent, $1,000 loan repaid in two payments, one at the end of the first half-year and another at the end of the second half-year, would be $37.50, as follows:
> First payment:
>
> $$I = P \times r \times T$$
> $$= \$1,000 \times 0.05 \times 1/2$$
> $$= \$25 \text{ interest plus } \$500, \text{ or } \$525$$
>
> Second payment:
>
> $$I = P \times r \times T$$
> $$= \$500 \times 0.05 \times 1/2$$
> $$= \$12.50 \text{ interest plus the remaining balance of } \$500, \text{ or } \$512.50$$
>
> Total payment on the loan:
>
> $$\$525 + \$512.50 = \$1,037.50$$
>
> Using the APR formula,
>
> $$\text{APR} = \frac{2 \times n \times I}{P(N+1)} = \frac{2 \times 2 \times \$37.50}{\$1,000(2+1)} = \frac{\$150}{\$3,000} = 0.05, \text{ or } 5\%$$

a periodic charge for the use of credit, or other finance option to pay the bill in full within 30 days without interest y installments based on the account balance plus interest. ace period of 20 to 25 days to pay a bill in full before you

g check credit. Also called a *bank line of credit*, this is a ed amount that you can use by writing a special check. nts over a set period. The finance charges are based on the e month and on the outstanding balance.

pular. The average cardholder has more than nine credit d gasoline cards. Cardholders who pay off their balances own as *convenience* users. Cardholders who do not pay off known as *borrowers*.
offer a grace period, a time period during which no finance count. A **finance charge** is the total dollar amount you pay ay your entire balance before the due date stated on your to pay a finance charge. Borrowers carry balances beyond ce charges. Many credit cards offer "teaser rates." These

interest A periodic charge for the use of credit.

revolving check credit A prearranged loan from a bank for a specified amount; also called a *bank line of credit*.

finance charge The total dollar amount paid to use credit.

Key Terms

Key terms appear in bold type within the text and are defined in the margins. A list of key terms and page references is located at the end of each chapter.

Your Personal Financial Plan Sheet References

The integrated use of the *Your Personal Financial Plan* sheets is highlighted with an icon. This visual helps connect this study resource into the learning process and continue to track personal financial habits.

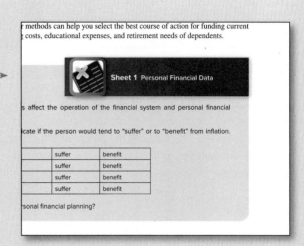

Practice Quizzes

Practice Quizzes at the end of each major section provide questions and exercises to assess knowledge of the main ideas. These will determine whether concepts have been mastered or if additional study is needed on certain topics.

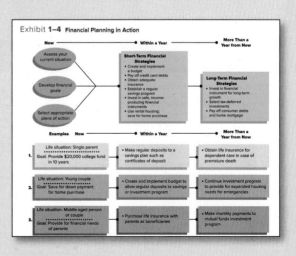

Exhibits and Tables

Throughout the text, exhibits and tables visually illustrate important personal finance concepts and processes.

Focus on . . .
Personal Finance in Real Life

Margin Features

Each chapter contains several *Money Minute Focus*, and *CAUTION!* boxes. The *Money Minute Focus* boxes contain fun facts, information, and financial planning assistance for wise personal financial actions. The *CAUTION!* boxes highlight opportunities where students should take pause and think a decision through.

money minute focus

To develop financial literacy among children:
(1) have a payday for chores, not an allowance;
(2) explain opportunity cost, needs vs. wants;
(3) start a savings jar or bank account for unexpected situations; (4) create a budgeting chart to show family spending; (5) sign an agreement with payment dates for money borrowed from parents;
(6) have them buy shampoo, toothpaste, snacks to prepare them to be on their own.

STEP 2: Develop Your Financial Goals

You should periodically analyze your financial values and goals. The purpose of this action is to clarify your needs and wants. Specific financial goals are vital to financial planning. Others can suggest financial goals for you, but *you* must decide which goals to pursue. Your financial goals can range from spending all of your current income to developing an extensive savings and investment program for your future financial security.

CAUTION !

Don't become a victim of *lifestyle inflation*. When receiving a salary increase, overspending and increased debt may occur. Maintain your existing spending at a frugal level. Instead of buying a bigger house or new car, pay off debts and save for future needs. Keep living expenses and housing costs low; upgrade, maintain, and improve your current home. Increase your automatic savings amounts.

Digital Financial Literacy

Students are both consumers and producers of digital content. This feature provides students with an opportunity to enhance their digital financial literacy skills to identify, research, and implement money decisions.

Digital Financial Literacy With. . .

Kiplinger's
Kiplinger's Personal Finance

Online resources (apps, websites, podcasts, blogs, videos, social media) are valuable for learning. As both a consumer and producer of digital content, you need to be able to locate, assess, create, and share information for wise money management. Also, online safety, privacy settings, social media sharing, and fake news can influence your financial well-being and career opportunities. Improving your *digital financial literacy* involves developing skills for using information to identify, research, and implement money decisions. Kiplinger.com and *Kiplinger's Personal Finance* magazine offer a wide variety of personal financial articles, videos, podcasts, calculators, *and* other features. A recent article in the magazine featured an individual who had a strong savings program but wanted to invest for a higher return. His goals included continuing to save for retirement and buying a car and a house. He also kept some of his savings in an account as an emergency fund.

As the years progressed, and marriage was on the horizon, consideration was given to some additional goals. These financial targets included buying a bigger house and renting out the current one. *Kiplinger's Personal Finance* staff also recommended that the couple consult a financial planner as they make plans to formally combine their finances.

ACTION STEPS FOR. . .

. . .Information Literacy

Based on your personal life situation, identify a financial goal and develop action steps to achieve that goal. Create a list of questions that might be used to validate the action steps.

. . .Financial Literacy

Locate the "Tools Gallery" at kiplinger.com and select one of the items. Prepare a visual (photo, poster) or brief video that explains how this tool might be used to achieve a personal financial goal.

. . .Digital Literacy

Select an article from kiplinger.com. Talk with others about the article. Describe how an online video or app might be used to communicate the information from these sources.

Financial Literacy in Practice

These features offer information that can assist you when faced with special situations and unique financial planning decisions. They challenge you to apply the concepts you have learned to your life and record personal responses.

Financial Literacy in Practice

Creating Goals and Assessing Financial Health

Using the S-M-A-R-T format, create a financial goal that you would like to accomplish regarding saving, spending, or sharing your time, talents, or financial resources.

Example	Your Goal
Specific . . . Create an emergency fund . . .	
Measurable . . . of $1,800 . . .	
Action-oriented . . . at a credit union . . .	
Realistic . . . by reduced spending on food away from home . . .	
Time-based . . . within the next six months.	

What are your next actions to achieve this financial goal?

(1)

(2)

(3)

Figure It Out!

This feature presents important mathematical applications relevant to personal finance situations and concepts.

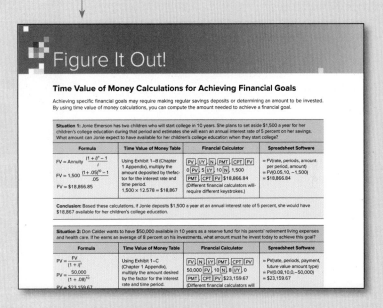

Figure It Out!

Time Value of Money Calculations for Achieving Financial Goals

Achieving specific financial goals may require making regular savings deposits or determining an amount to be invested. By using time value of money calculations, you can compute the amount needed to achieve a financial goal.

Situation 1: Jonie Emerson has two children who will start college in 10 years. She plans to set aside $1,500 a year for her children's college education during that period and estimates she will earn an annual interest rate of 5 percent on her savings. What amount can Jonie expect to have available for her children's college education when they start college?

Formula	Time Value of Money Table	Financial Calculator	Spreadsheet Software
$FV = Annuity \frac{(1+i)^n - 1}{i}$ $FV = 1,500 \frac{(1+.05)^{10} - 1}{.05}$ $FV = \$18,866.85$	Using Exhibit 1–B (Chapter 1 Appendix), multiply the amount deposited by the factor for the interest rate and time period. $1,500 \times 12.578 = \$18,867$	PV, I/Y, N, PMT, CPT, FV 0 PV, 5 I/Y, 10 N, 1,500 PMT, CPT, FV $18,866.84 (Different financial calculators will require different keystrokes.)	= FV(rate, periods, amount per period, amount) = FV(0.05,10, −1,500) = $18,866.84

Conclusion: Based these calculations, if Jonie deposits $1,500 a year at an annual interest rate of 5 percent, she would have $18,867 available for her children's college education.

Situation 2: Don Calder wants to have $50,000 available in 10 years as a reserve fund for his parents' retirement living expenses and health care. If he earns an average of 8 percent on his investments, what amount must he invest today to achieve this goal?

Formula	Time Value of Money Table	Financial Calculator	Spreadsheet Software
$PV = \frac{FV}{(1+i)^n}$ $PV = \frac{50,000}{(1+.08)^{10}}$ $PV = \$23,159.67$	Using Exhibit 1–C (Chapter 1 Appendix), multiply the amount desired by the factor for the interest rate and time period.	FV, N, I/Y, PMT, CPT, PV 50,000 FV, 10 N, 8 I/Y, 0 PMT, CPT, PV $23,159.67 (Different financial calculators will	= PV(rate, periods, payment, future value amount type) = PV(0.08,10,0,−50,000) = $23,159.67

What Would You Do?

WHAT WOULD YOU DO? You plan to spend $5,000 on a smart television and home theater system. You are willing to spend some of your $9,000 in savings. However, you want to finance the rest and pay it off in small monthly installments out of the $400 a month you earn working part-time. How might you obtain a low-interest loan and make low monthly payments?

These situations, placed in the main text throughout each chapter, are designed to engage students in decision-making relating to the topics being discussed.

FinTech for Financial Literacy

FinTech for Financial Literacy

Robo-advisors are automated programs to guide financial planning. These online financial planners may be completely autonomous or may be combined with human assistance. The process starts by responding to questions related to income, assets, debt, goals, and risk tolerance. Then, computer algorithms suggest actions for your investment portfolio and financial plan. Digital advisers have lower fees than other financial planners. Search nerdwallet.com for advice on selecting a robo-advisor.

First, *personal financial records and documents* help you plan the use of your resources. These provide evidence of business transactions and ownership of property, and are helpful in legal matters. Next, *personal financial statements* measure and guide your financial position and progress. Finally, your spending plan, or *budget,* is the basis for effective money management.

A System for Personal Financial Records

Purchase receipts, credit card statements, insurance policies, and tax forms are the basis of financial recordkeeping and personal economic choices. An organized system of financial records provides a basis for (1) handling daily business activities, such as bill paying; (2) planning and measuring financial progress; (3) completing required tax reports; (4) making effective investment decisions;

FinTech (financial technology) involves apps, software, and computers for banking and other financial activities. This margin feature highlights emerging and expanding use of FinTech, affecting various aspects of personal finance.

Focus on . . .
Practice and Assessment

Road Map to Financial Literacy and Your Personal Finance Dashboard

Having read the chapter, now consider your financial progress. The road map is designed to help you move forward in your personal financial journey. The dashboard is designed to help you monitor key performance indicators for your personal financial situation.

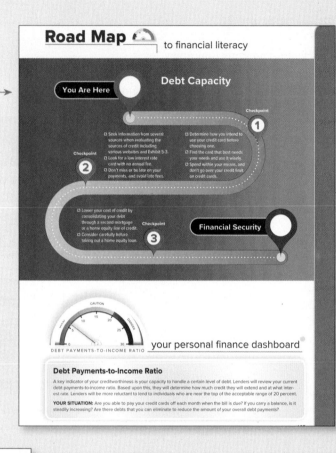

Road Map to financial literacy

You Are Here

Debt Capacity

Checkpoint 1
□ Determine how you intend to use your credit card before choosing one.
□ Find the card that best needs your needs and use it wisely.
□ Spend within your means, and don't go over your credit limit on credit cards.

Checkpoint 2
□ Seek information from several sources when evaluating the sources of credit including various websites and Exhibit 5-3.
□ Look for a low interest rate card with no annual fee.
□ Don't miss or be late on your payments, and avoid late fees.

Checkpoint 3
□ Lower your cost of credit by consolidating your debt through a second mortgage or a home equity line of credit.
□ Consider carefully before taking out a home equity loan.

Financial Security

your personal finance dashboard

DEBT PAYMENTS-TO-INCOME RATIO

Debt Payments-to-Income Ratio

A key indicator of your creditworthiness is your capacity to handle a certain level of debt. Lenders will review your current debt payments-to-income ratio. Based upon this, they will determine how much credit they will extend and at what interest rate. Lenders will be more reluctant to lend to individuals who are near the top of the acceptable range of 20 percent.

YOUR SITUATION: Are you able to pay your credit cards off each month when the bill is due? If you carry a balance, is it steadily increasing? Are there debts that you can eliminate to reduce the amount of your overall debt payments?

Chapter Summary

Organized by learning objective, this concise content summary is a great study and self-assessment tool, located conveniently at the end of chapters.

Chapter Summary

LO5.1 Consumer credit is the use of credit by individuals and families for personal needs. Among the advantages of using credit are the ability to purchase goods when needed and pay for them gradually, the ability to meet financial emergencies, convenience in shopping, and establishment of a credit rating. Disadvantages are that credit costs money, encourages overspending, and ties up future income.

LO5.2 Closed-end and open-end credit are two types of consumer credit. With closed-end credit, the borrower pays back a one-time loan in a stated period of time and with a specified number of payments. With

LO5.4 Compare the finance charge and the annual percentage rate (APR) as you shop for credit. Under the Truth in Lending Act, creditors are required to state the cost of borrowing so that you can compare credit costs and shop for credit.

LO5.5 If a billing error occurs on your account, notify the creditor in writing within 60 days. If the dispute is not settled in your favor, you can place your version of it in your credit file. You may also withhold payment on any defective goods or services you have purchased with a credit card as long as you have attempted to resolve the problem with the merchant.

Key Formulas

A list of key formulas and page references appears at the end of select chapters, grouped for easy reference.

Key Formulas

Page	Topic	Formula
183	Calculating annual percentage rate (APR)	$APR = \dfrac{2 \times \text{Number of payment periods in one year} \times \text{Dollar cost of credit}}{\text{Loan amount (Total number of payments to pay off the loan + 1)}}$ $= 2 \times n \times t/P(N+1)$
184	Calculating simple interest	Interest (in dollars) = Principal borrowed × Interest rate × Length of loan in years $I = P \times r \times T$
172	Calculating debt payments-to-income ratio	Monthly debt payments (excluding mortgage payments) divided by net monthly income
172	Calculating debt-to-equity ratio	Total liabilities (excluding mortgage) divided by net worth

Self-Test Problems

Self-test problems are worked out using step-by-step solutions so that students can see how they were solved. This user-friendly feature increases student comprehension of the material and gives confidence to solve the end-of-chapter problems.

Self-Test Problems

1. Suppose that your monthly net income is $3,000. Your monthly debt payments include your student loan payment and a gas credit card, and they total $400. What is your debt payments-to-income ratio?
2. Suppose you borrow $2,000 at 6 percent and will repay it in one payment at the end of one year. Use the simple interest formula to determine the amount of interest you will pay.

Solutions

Financial Planning Problems

A variety of problems allow students to put their quantitative analysis of personal financial decisions to work. Each problem is tagged with a corresponding learning objective for easy assessment.

Financial Literacy Portfolio

To develop competencies related to specific financial decisions, this activity asks students to conduct action research beyond the class setting. Outcomes are presented in the form of a written, visual, or other creative format.

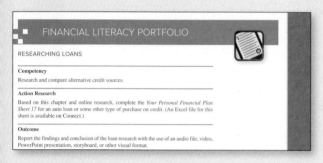

Real Life Personal Finance

Students can work through a hypothetical personal finance dilemma in order to apply concepts from the chapter. A series of questions reinforces successful mastery and application of these chapter topics.

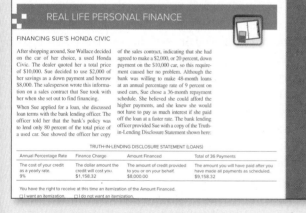

Continuing Case

This feature allows students to apply course concepts in a life situation. It encourages students to evaluate the finances that affect a household and then respond to the resulting shift in needs, resources, and priorities through the questions at the end of each case.

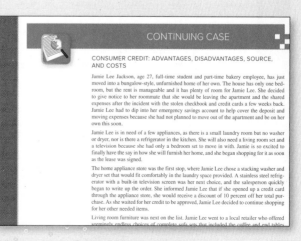

Daily Spending Diary

Do you buy a latte or juice every day before class? Do you and your friends meet for a movie once a week? How much do you spend on gas for your car each month? Do you like to donate to your favorite local charity a couple of times a year?

These everyday spending activities might go largely unnoticed, yet they have a significant effect on the overall financial health of an individual. The *Daily Spending Diary* sheets offer students a place to keep track of *every cent they spend* in any category. Careful monitoring and assessing of daily spending habits can lead to better control and understanding of your personal finances.

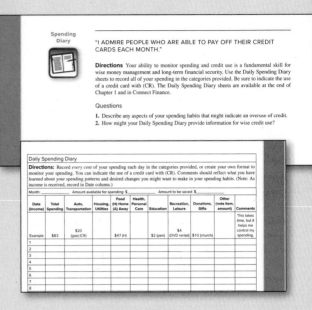

Your Personal Financial Plan

The *Your Personal Financial Plan* sheets that correlate with sections of the text are conveniently located at the end of each chapter. The perforated worksheets ask students to work through the applications and record their own personal financial plan responses. These sheets apply concepts learned to their unique situation and serve as a road map to their personal financial future. Students can fill them out, rip them out, submit them for homework, and keep them filed in a safe spot for future reference. Excel spreadsheets for each of the *Your Personal Financial Plan* sheets are available through Connect.

Key websites and apps are provided to help students research and devise their personal financial plan, and the What's Next for Your Personal Financial Plan? section at the end of each sheet challenges students to use their responses to plan the next level, as well as foreshadow upcoming concepts.

Look for one or more *Your Personal Financial Plan* icons next to most Practice Quizzes. This graphic directs students to the *Personal Financial Plan* sheet that corresponds with the preceding section.

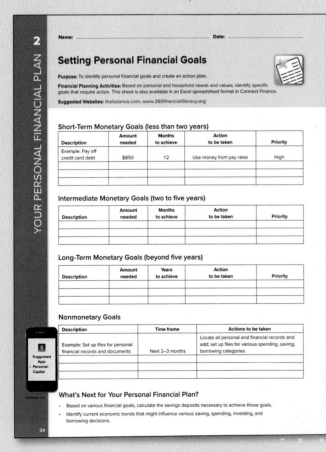

Online Support for Students and Instructors

Few textbooks provide such innovative and practical instructional resources for both students and teachers. The comprehensive teaching–learning package for *Focus on Personal Finance,* 7e, includes the following:

For Instructors

The Instructor's site, delivered through Connect, provides the instructor with one resource for all supplementary material, including:

- *Teacher's Resource Manual:* Revised by Jake Poysti and Brendon Mitschow, this supplement includes a "Course Planning Guide" with instructional strategies, course projects, and supplementary resource lists. The Chapter Teaching Materials section of the *Teacher's Resource Manual* provides a chapter overview, the chapter objectives with summaries, introductory activities, and detailed lecture outlines with teaching suggestions. This section also includes concluding activities, ready-to-duplicate quizzes, supplementary lecture materials and activities, and answers to concept checks, end-of-chapter questions, problems, and cases.

- *Test Bank,* revised by Emily Bello, consists of true–false, multiple-choice, problem-solving, and essay questions. These test items are organized by the learning objectives for each chapter. This resource also includes answers and an indication of difficulty level.

- Chapter *PowerPoint Presentations,* revised and enhanced by Courtney Baggett, offer more than 300 visual presentations that may be edited and manipulated to fit a particular course format. If you choose to customize the slides, an online digital image library allows you to pick and choose from all of the figures and tables in the book.

- The *Focus on Personal Finance* blog (https://kapoorfinancefocus.com/) offers summaries of current articles with timely, relevant information to enhance the learning environment. The articles are keyed to the appropriate chapter and topic for ease of use. Each blog post includes a link to the original source, along with discussion questions (useful for in-class or discussion boards) and teaching suggestions.

Remote Proctoring & Browser-Locking Capabilities

McGraw Hill connect + proctorio

New remote proctoring and browser-locking capabilities, hosted by Proctorio within Connect, provide control of the assessment environment by enabling security options and verifying the identity of the student.

Seamlessly integrated within Connect, these services allow instructors to control students' assessment experience by restricting browser activity, recording students' activity, and verifying students are doing their own work.

Instant and detailed reporting gives instructors an at-a-glance view of potential academic integrity concerns, thereby avoiding personal bias and supporting evidence-based claims.

Tegrity: Lectures 24/7

Tegrity in Connect is a tool that makes class time available 24/7 by automatically capturing every lecture. With a simple one-click start-and-stop process, you capture all computer screens and corresponding audio in a format that is easy to search, frame by frame. Students can replay any part of any class with easy-to-use, browser-based viewing on a PC, Mac, iPod, or other mobile device.

Educators know that the more students can see, hear, and experience class resources, the better they learn. In fact, studies prove it. Tegrity's unique search feature helps students efficiently find what they need, when they need it, across an entire semester of class recordings. Help turn your students' study time into learning moments immediately supported by your lecture. With Tegrity, you also increase intent listening and class participation by easing students' concerns about note-taking. Using Tegrity in

Connect will make it more likely you will see students' faces, not the tops of their heads.

Test Builder in Connect

Available within Connect, Test Builder is a cloud-based tool that enables instructors to format tests that can be printed or administered within a LMS. Test Builder offers a modern, streamlined interface for easy content configuration that matches course needs, without requiring a download.

Test Builder allows you to:

- access all test bank content from a particular title.
- easily pinpoint the most relevant content through robust filtering options.
- manipulate the order of questions or scramble questions and/or answers.
- pin questions to a specific location within a test.
- determine your preferred treatment of algorithmic questions.
- choose the layout and spacing.
- add instructions and configure default settings.

Test Builder provides a secure interface for better protection of content and allows for just-in-time updates to flow directly into assessments.

Assurance of Learning Ready

Assurance of learning is an important element of many accreditation standards. *Focus on Personal Finance,* 7e, is designed specifically to support your assurance of learning initiatives. Each chapter in the book begins with a list of numbered learning objectives that appear throughout the chapter, as well as in the end-of-chapter problems and exercises. Every test bank question is also linked to one of these objectives, in addition to level of difficulty, topic area, Bloom's taxonomy level, and AACSB skill area. Connect, McGraw Hill's online homework solution, and EZ Test, McGraw Hill's easy-to-use test bank software, can search the test bank by these and other categories, providing an engine for targeted assurance of learning analysis and assessment.

AACSB Statement

McGraw Hill is a proud corporate member of AACSB International. Understanding the importance and value of AACSB accreditation, *Focus on Personal Finance,* 7e, has sought to recognize the curricula guidelines detailed in the AACSB standards for business accreditation by connecting selected questions in the test bank to the general knowledge and skill guidelines found in the AACSB standards.

The statements contained in *Focus on Personal Finance,* 7e, are provided only as a guide for the users of this text. The AACSB leaves content coverage and assessment within the purview of individual schools, the mission of the school, and the faculty. While *Focus on Personal Finance,* 7e, and the teaching package make no claim of any specific AACSB qualification or evaluation, we have, within the test bank, labeled selected questions according to the six general knowledge and skills areas.

For Students (available through Connect and class instructor)

Digital Broadcasts

View chapter-related videos to see how personal finance topics are applied in everyday life.

Narrated Summary Videos

Every student learns differently, and the narrated summary videos were created with that in mind! These presentations guide students through understanding key topics and principles by presenting real-life examples based on chapter content.

And More!

Looking for more ways to study? Self-grading crossword puzzles will help students learn the material. Students can also access Excel templates for the *Your Personal Financial Plan* sheets and the *Daily Spending Diary.*

SUPPORT AT
every step

Students: Get Learning that Fits You

Effective tools for efficient studying

Connect is designed to make you more productive with simple, flexible, intuitive tools that maximize your study time and meet your individual learning needs. Get learning that works for you with Connect.

Study anytime, anywhere

Download the free ReadAnywhere app and access your online eBook or SmartBook 2.0 assignments when it's convenient, even if you're offline. And since the app automatically syncs with your eBook and SmartBook 2.0 assignments in Connect, all of your work is available every time you open it. Find out more at **www.mheducation.com/readanywhere**

> *"I really liked this app—it made it easy to study when you don't have your textbook in front of you."*
>
> - Jordan Cunningham,
>   Eastern Washington University

Calendar: owattaphotos/Getty Images

Everything you need in one place

Your Connect course has everything you need—whether reading on your digital eBook or completing assignments for class, Connect makes it easy to get your work done.

Learning for everyone

McGraw Hill works directly with Accessibility Services Departments and faculty to meet the learning needs of all students. Please contact your Accessibility Services Office and ask them to email accessibility@mheducation.com, or visit **www.mheducation.com/about/accessibility** for more information.

Thank You!

We express our deepest appreciation for the efforts of the colleagues whose extensive feedback over the years has helped to shape and create this text.

Janice Akao, *Butler Community College*

Sophia Anong, *University of Georgia*

Brenda Anthony, *Tallahassee Community College*

Anna Antus, *Normandale Community College*

Victoria Arnold, *University of Central Oklahoma*

Eddie Ary, *Ouachita Baptist University*

Chris A. Austin, *Normandale Community College*

Gail H. Austin, *Rose State College*

Kali Bard, *Crowder College*

George Bernard, *Seminole State College of Florida*

Judy Bernard, *Bluegrass Community and Technical College*

Tom Bilyeu, *Southwestern Illinois College*

Ross Blankenship, *State Fair Community College*

William F. Blosel, *California University of Pennsylvania*

John Bockino, *Suffolk County Community College*

Karen Bonding, *University of Virginia*

Lyle Bowlin, *Southeastern University*

Michael Brandl, *University of Texas–Austin*

Jerry Braun, *Daytona State College–Daytona Beach*

Darleen Braunshweiger, *Nassau Community College*

Jennifer Brewer, *Butler County Community College*

Robert Brown, *Santa Barbara City College*

Bruce Brunson, *Virginia Tech*

Peg Camp, *University of Nebraska–Kearney*

Mary Ann Campbell, *University of Central Arkansas*

Ron Cereola, *James Madison University*

Stephen Chambers, *Johnson County Community College*

It-Keong Chew, *University of Kentucky*

Marc Condos, *American River College*

Mary Emily Cooke, *Surry Community College*

Trung Dang, *Lone Star College North Harris*

Beth Deinert, *Southeast Community College—Milford*

Julie Douthit, *Abilene Christian University*

Bill Dowling, *Savannah State University*

Chip Downing, *Massasoit Community College*

Dorsey Dyer, *Davidson County Community College*

John D. Farlin, *Ohio Dominican University*

Garry Fleming, *Roanoke College*

Paula G. Freston, *Merced College*

Robert Friederichs, *Alexandria Technical College*

Mark Fronke, *Cerritos College*

Caroline S. Fulmer, *University of Alabama*

Harry Gallatin, *Indiana State University*

Dwight Giles, *Jefferson State Community College*

Terri Gonzales, *Delgado Community College*

Michael Gordinier, *Washington University*

Shari Gowers, *Dixie State College*

Michelle Grant, *Bossier Parish Community College*

Paul Gregg, *University of Central Florida*

Michael P. Griffin, *University of Massachusetts–Dartmouth*

Don Hardwick, *Bluegrass Community and Technical College*

Josh Harris, *Clemson University*

Monte Hill, *Nova Community College–Annandale*

Ward Hooker, *Orangeburg–Calhoun Tech College*

Ishappa S. Hullur, *Morehead State University*

Samira Hussein, *Johnson County Community College*

Dorothy W. Jones, *Northwestern State University*

Richard "Lee" Kitchen, *Tallahassee Community College*

Jeanette Klosterman, *Hutchinson Community College*

Robert Kozub, *University of Wisconsin–Milwaukee*

Margo Kraft, *Heidelberg College*

John Ledgerwood, *Bethune-Cookman College*

Marc LeFebvre, *Creighton University*

Eveline Lewis, *Evangel University*

Nolan Lickey, *Utah Valley State College*

Joseph T. Marchese, *Monroe Community College*

John Marcis, *Coastal Carolina University*

Kenneth L. Mark, *Kansas City Kansas Community College*

Paul S. Marshall, *Widener University*

Kera Mattes, *Liberty University*

Jennifer Morton, *Ivy Tech Community College of Indiana*

Allan O'Bryan, *Rochester Community & Tech College*

Susan Pallas-Duncan, *Southeast Community College*

Carl Parker, *Fort Hays State University*

David M. Payne, *Ohio University*

Aaron Phillips, *California State University–Bakersfield*

Padmaja Pillutla, *Western Illinois University*

Mark Pope, *University of Texas*

Tom Prusa, *Rutgers University*

Barbara Purvis, *Centura College*

Brenda Rice, *Ozarks Technical Community College*

Carla Rich, *Pensacola Junior College*

John Roberts, *Florida Metropolitan University*

Sammie Root, *Texas State University–San Marcos*

Clarence Rose, *Radford University*

Joan Ryan, *Clackamas Community College*

Martin St. John, *Westmoreland County Community College*

Tim Samolis, *Pittsburgh Technical Institute*

Todd Saville, *Kirkwood Community College*

Steven R. Scheff, *Florida Gulf Coast University*

James T. Schiermeyer, *Texas Tech University*

Beth Scull, *University of South Carolina*

Joseph Simon, *Casper College*

Vernon Stauble, *San Bernardino Valley College*

Lea Timpler, *College of the Canyons*

Michael Trohimczyk, *Henry Ford Community College*

Dick Verrone, *University of North Carolina–Wilmington*

Randall Wade, *Rogue Community College*

Shunda Ware, *Atlanta Technical College*

Kent Weilage, *McCook Community College*

Sally Wells, *Columbia College*

Micheline West, *New Hampshire Tech*

Marilyn Whitney, *University of California–Davis*

Bob Willis, *Rogers State University*

Glen Wood, *Broome Community College*

Russell Woodbridge, *Southeastern College*

Many talented professionals at McGraw Hill have contributed to the development of *Focus on Personal Finance*. We are especially grateful to Chuck Synovec, Allison McCabe-Carroll, Trina Maurer and Jamie Koch.

In addition, Jack Kapoor expresses special appreciation to Theresa and Dave Kapoor, Kathryn Thumme, and Karen and Joshua Tucker for their typing, proofreading, and research assistance. Les Dlabay expresses his thanks to Kyle Dlabay, Linda Dlabay, Anne Jaspers, Bryna Mollinger, Lu Paletta, David Pecha, Tuyen Tran, and Schuyler Vaughan for their help reviewing and updating the content. Finally, we thank our spouses and families for their patience, understanding, encouragement, and love throughout this project.

Contents

Focus on Personal Finance

1 Personal Financial Planning in Action

3 Steps to Financial Literacy . . .
Building an Emergency Fund

1 Determine the desired amount of your emergency fund based on monthly financial needs and income volatility. Most financial advisors recommend three to six months, or more.
Website: **money.com**

2 Monitor your daily spending to identify possible areas of reduced spending and increased savings.
App: BUDGT or Mint

3 Decide where to keep your emergency fund. Your choices include a bank, credit union, and other financial institutions.
Website: www.depositaccounts.com

What are the financial benefits of an emergency fund?

You will be able to avoid or minimize a financial crisis due to job loss, unexpected expenses, or other unforeseen situation. At the end of the chapter, *Your Personal Finance Road Map and Dashboard* will provide guidelines for measuring the progress of your emergency fund along with suggested actions to improve your personal financial activities.

CHAPTER 1 LEARNING OBJECTIVES

In this chapter, you will learn to:

LO1.1 Identify social and economic influences on financial literacy and personal financial decisions.

LO1.2 Develop personal financial goals.

LO1.3 Calculate time value of money situations to analyze personal financial decisions.

LO1.4 Implement a plan for making personal financial and career decisions.

YOUR PERSONAL FINANCIAL PLAN SHEETS

1. Personal Financial Data
2. Setting Personal Financial Goals
3. Achieving Financial Goals Using Time Value of Money
4. Planning Your Career

Making Financial Decisions

Every person has some money. However, the amount, along with needs, financial choices, and unexpected situations, will vary from person to person. In this book, you will have the opportunity to assess your current situation, learn about varied financial paths, and move forward toward future financial security.

Financial literacy is the use of knowledge and skills for earning, saving, spending, and investing money to achieve personal, family, and community goals. The process includes developing attitudes, behaviors, and competencies to meet current and future financial obligations. Financial literacy leads to financial well-being and a lifetime of financial security, adapting to changing personal and economic circumstances. As shown in Exhibit 1-1, financial literacy is the result of information and knowledge, attitudes and abilities, and actions and behaviors.

Typical financial goals may include buying a new car or a larger home, pursuing advanced career training, contributing to charity, traveling extensively, and gaining financial self-sufficiency. To achieve these and other goals, people need to identify and set priorities. Financial and personal satisfaction are the result of an organized process that is commonly referred to as *personal money management* or *personal financial planning.*

Your Life Situation and Financial Planning

Personal financial planning is the process of managing your money to achieve personal economic satisfaction. This planning process allows you to control your financial situation. Every person, family, or household has a unique situation; therefore, financial decisions must be planned to meet specific needs and goals.

LO1.1
Identify social and economic influences on financial literacy and personal financial decisions.

ACTION ITEM

Do you have an emergency fund for unexpected expenses?

☐ Yes ☐ No

personal financial planning The process of managing your money to achieve personal economic satisfaction.

financial plan A formalized report that summarizes your current financial situation, analyzes your financial needs, and recommends future financial activities.

A comprehensive financial program can enhance the quality of your life and increase your satisfaction by reducing future uncertainty. A **financial plan** is a formalized report that summarizes your current financial situation, analyzes your financial needs, and recommends future financial activities. You can create this document on your own (by using the Your Personal Financial Plan sheets at the end of each chapter), or you can seek assistance from a financial planner or use a money management app.

Advantages of effective personal financial planning include:

- Increased effectiveness when obtaining, using, and protecting your financial resources throughout your life.
- Expanded control of your financial affairs by avoiding excessive debt and dependence on others.
- Improved personal relationships resulting from well-planned and effectively communicated financial decisions.
- A sense of freedom from financial worries obtained by looking to the future, anticipating expenses, and achieving personal economic goals.

Many factors influence financial decisions. People in their 20s spend money differently from those in their 50s. Personal factors such as age, income, household size, and personal beliefs influence your spending and saving patterns. Your life situation or lifestyle is created by a combination of factors.

As our society changes, different types of financial needs evolve. Today people tend to get married at a later age, and more households have two incomes. Many households are headed by single parents. More than 2 million people provide care for both dependent children and elderly parents. We are also living longer, with over 80 percent of all Americans now alive expected to live well past age 65.

adult life cycle The stages in the family situation and financial needs of an adult.

The **adult life cycle**—the stages in the family situation and financial needs of an adult—is an important influence on your financial activities and decisions. The stages are affected by age, marital status, number and age of household members, and employment situation. Your life situation is also affected by events such as graduation, dependent children leaving home, changes in health, engagement and marriage, divorce, birth or adoption of a child, retirement, a career change or a move to a new area, or the death of a spouse, family member, or other dependent.

values Ideas and principles that a person considers correct, desirable, and important.

In addition to being defined by your family situation, you are defined by your **values**—the ideas and principles that you consider correct, desirable, and important. Values have a direct influence on such decisions as spending now versus saving for the future or continuing school versus getting a job.

Financial Planning in Our Economy

Daily economic transactions facilitate financial planning activities. Exhibit 1–2 shows the monetary flows among providers and users of funds that occur in a financial system. These financial activities affect personal finance decisions. Investing in a bond, which is a *debt security,* involves borrowing by a company or government. In contrast, investing in stock, called an *equity security,* represents ownership in a corporation. Other financial market activities include buying and selling mutual funds, certificates of deposit (CDs), and commodity futures.

economics The study of how wealth is created and distributed.

In most societies, the forces of supply and demand set prices for securities, goods, and services. **Economics** is the study of how wealth is created and distributed. The economic environment includes business, labor, and government working together to satisfy needs and wants. As shown in Exhibit 1–2, government agencies regulate financial activities. The Federal Reserve System, the central bank of the United States, has significant economic responsibility. The Fed, as it is often called, attempts to maintain an adequate money supply to encourage consumer spending, business growth, and job creation.

Exhibit **1–1** Planning for Personal Financial Literacy

INFORMATION AND KNOWLEDGE

Financial Planning Activities

		Information Sources
Obtaining (Chapter 1)	Spending (Chapters 6, 7)	• Textbook reading, personal study
Planning (Chapters 2, 3)	Managing Risk (Chapters 8-10)	• Friends, relatives, others
Saving (Chapters 2, 4)	Investing (Chapters 11-13)	• Online sources, apps, podcasts
Borrowing (Chapter 5)	Retirement and Estate Planning (Chapter 14)	• Financial planning specialists

Attitudes and Abilities

- A desire for ongoing learning in varied settings and from others in diverse situations
- A willingness to monitor spending and saving activities, to develop a realistic budget
- Reconciliation of varied money attitudes among family and household members
- A personal motivation to reduce or eliminate unplanned spending and credit use
- Determination and discipline for achieving long-term goals, gaining financial independence
- A commitment to share time, talents, and resources with others in need

ACTIONS AND BEHAVIORS

Short-term

- Obtain needed career training
- Create a financial document system
- Track spending; create/implement a budget
- Begin emergency fund/regular savings plan
- Reduce or eliminate existing credit balances
- Purchase appropriate insurance coverage

Long-term

- Monitor investments for changing needs
- Seek actions for beneficial tax planning
- Ongoing review of changing life situation
- Adapt budget, financial plan, as needed
- Assess changing career opportunities
- Plan retirement income, living situation

FINANCIAL LITERACY DEVELOPMENT

EXPERIENTIAL LEARNING . . .
to use interviews, observations, and market experiences for improved financial decisions.

RETENTION, REINFORCEMENT . . .
to consistently use knowledge and skills for wise money management and personal financial decisions.

CRITICAL THINKING . . .
to creatively analyze and solve problems for financial opportunities.

GLOBAL INFLUENCES The global economy influences financial activities. The U.S. economy is affected by both foreign investors and competition from foreign companies. American businesses compete against foreign companies for the spending dollars of American consumers. When the level of exports of U.S.-made goods is lower than the level of imported goods, more U.S. dollars leave the country than the dollar value of foreign currency coming into the United States. This reduces the funds available for domestic spending and investment. Also, if foreign companies decide not to invest in the United States, the domestic money supply is reduced. This reduced money supply can cause higher interest rates.

Exhibit **1–2** **The Financial System**

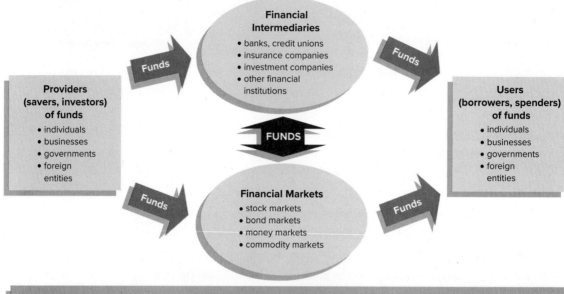

Financial Intermediaries
- banks, credit unions
- insurance companies
- investment companies
- other financial institutions

Funds

Providers (savers, investors) of funds
- individuals
- businesses
- governments
- foreign entities

Funds

FUNDS

Funds

Users (borrowers, spenders) of funds
- individuals
- businesses
- governments
- foreign entities

Funds

Financial Markets
- stock markets
- bond markets
- money markets
- commodity markets

Funds

Financial Regulators: Federal Reserve System, Federal Deposit Insurance Corporation, National Credit Union Administration, Office of the Comptroller of the Currency, Consumer Financial Protection Bureau, Securities and Exchange Commission, state banking agencies, state insurance agencies.

inflation A rise in the general level of prices.

INFLATION Most people are concerned with the buying power of their money. **Inflation** is a rise in the general level of prices. In times of inflation, the buying power of the dollar decreases. For example, if prices increased 5 percent during the last year, items that previously cost $100 would now cost $105. This means more money is needed to buy the same amount of goods and services.

Inflation is most harmful to people with fixed incomes. Due to inflation, retired people and others whose incomes do not change can only afford fewer goods and services. Inflation can also have a negative affect on lenders of money. Unless an appropriate interest rate is charged, amounts repaid by borrowers in times of inflation have less buying power than the money they borrowed.

Inflation rates vary. During the late 1950s and early 1960s, the annual inflation rate was in the 1 to 3 percent range. During the late 1970s and early 1980s, the cost of living increased 10 to 12 percent annually. At a 12 percent annual inflation rate, prices double (and the value of the dollar is cut in half) in about six years. To find out how fast prices (or your savings) will double, use the *Rule of 72:* Just divide 72 by the annual inflation (or interest) rate.

EXAMPLE: Rule of 72

An annual inflation rate of 4 percent, for example, means prices will double in 18 years (72 ÷ 4 = 18). Regarding savings, if you earn 6 percent, your money will double in 12 years (72 ÷ 6 = 12).

More recently, the reported annual price increase for goods and services as measured by the consumer price index has been in the 2 to 4 percent range. The *consumer price index (CPI),* computed and published by the Bureau of Labor Statistics, is a measure of the average change in the prices urban consumers pay for a fixed "basket" of goods and services.

Inflation rates can be deceptive since the price index is based on certain items. Many people face *hidden* inflation since the cost of necessities (food, gas, health care) on which they spend the greatest proportion of their money may rise at a higher rate than that of nonessential items, which could be dropping in price. This results in a reported inflation rate much lower than the actual cost-of-living increase being experienced by consumers.

Deflation, a decline in prices, can also have damaging economic effects. As prices drop, consumers expect they will go even lower. As a result, consumers cut their spending, which causes damaging economic conditions. While widespread deflation is unlikely, certain items may be affected and their prices will drop.

CAUTION !

Don't become a victim of *lifestyle inflation.* When receiving a salary increase, overspending and increased debt may occur. Maintain your existing spending at a frugal level. Instead of buying a bigger house or new car, pay off debts and save for future needs. Keep living expenses and housing costs low; upgrade, maintain, and improve your current home. Increase your automatic savings amounts.

INTEREST RATES In simple terms, interest rates represent the cost of money. Like everything else, money has a price. The forces of supply and demand usually influence interest rates. When consumers expand their saving and investing, the supply of money available for lending increases and interest rates tend to decrease. However, as borrowing by consumers, businesses, and government increases, interest rates are likely to rise due to an increased demand for money.

Interest rates affect your financial planning activities. The earnings you receive as a saver or an investor reflect current interest rates as well as a *risk premium* based on such factors as the length of time your funds will be used by others, expected inflation, and the extent of uncertainty about getting your money back. Risk is also a factor in the interest rate you pay as a borrower. People with poor credit ratings pay a higher interest rate than people with good credit ratings. Interest rates influence many financial decisions.

WHAT WOULD YOU DO? The future direction of interest rates is usually uncertain. You are trying to decide how interest rates might affect your savings and investing decisions. What information sources would help you better understand how changing interest rates might affect the amount saved and invested by individuals? If interest rates are expected to rise, or fall, what actions might be appropriate for your savings and investment decisions?

Financial Planning Activities

To achieve a secure financial position, you must coordinate several components through an organized plan and wise decision making.

OBTAINING (CHAPTER 1) You obtain financial resources from employment, investments, or ownership of a business. Obtaining financial resources is the foundation of financial planning.

PLANNING (CHAPTERS 2, 3) Planned spending with a budget is vital for achieving goals and future financial security. Efforts to anticipate expenses along with making certain financial decisions can reduce taxes, increase savings, and result in less financial stress.

SAVING (CHAPTERS 2, 4) Long-term financial security starts with a regular savings plan for emergencies, unexpected bills, replacement of major items, and the purchase of expensive goods and services, such as a college education, a boat, or a vacation home. Once you have established a basic savings plan, use additional money for investments that offer greater financial growth.

bankruptcy A set of federal laws allowing you to either restructure your debts or remove certain debts.

BORROWING (CHAPTER 5) Wise use of credit can contribute to your financial goals. In contrast, the overuse and misuse of credit will likely result in a person's debts exceeding the resources available to pay those debts. **Bankruptcy** is a set of federal laws allowing you to either restructure your debts or remove certain debts. The people who declare bankruptcy may have avoided this trauma with wise spending and careful borrowing decisions. Chapter 5 discusses bankruptcy in detail.

SPENDING (CHAPTERS 6, 7) Financial planning is not designed to prevent enjoyment of life but to help you obtain what you want. Too often purchases are made without considering the financial consequences. Some people shop compulsively, creating financial difficulties. Use a spending plan to control your living expenses and other financial obligations. Spending less than you earn is the only way to achieve long-term financial security.

MANAGING RISK (CHAPTERS 8, 9, 10) Adequate insurance coverage is another area for financial planning decisions. Some types of insurance are commonly overlooked. For example, the number of people who suffer disabling injuries or diseases at age 50 is greater than the number who die at that age, so people may need disability insurance more than they need life insurance. Yet research reveals that most people have adequate life insurance but few have disability insurance.

INVESTING (CHAPTERS 11, 12, 13) Although many types of investments are available, people invest for two primary reasons. Those interested in *current income* select investments that pay regular dividends or interest. In contrast, investors who desire *long-term growth* choose stocks, mutual funds, real estate, and other investments with potential for increased future value. You can achieve investment diversification by creating a *portfolio* with varied assets, such as stocks, bond mutual funds, real estate, and collectibles such as rare coins.

RETIREMENT AND ESTATE PLANNING (CHAPTER 14) Most people desire financial security upon completion of full-time employment; however, retirement planning also involves thinking about your housing situation, your recreational activities, and possible part-time work or volunteering.

Transfers of money or property to others should be timed, if possible, to minimize the taxes and maximize the benefits for those receiving the financial resources. Knowledge of property transfer methods can help you select the best course of action for funding current and future living costs, educational expenses, and retirement needs of dependents.

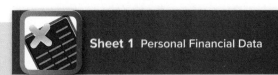

Sheet 1 Personal Financial Data

PRACTICE QUIZ 1–1

1. How do personal and economic factors affect the operation of the financial system and personal financial decisions?

2. For each of the following situations, indicate if the person would tend to "suffer" or to "benefit" from inflation. (Circle your answer)

A person with money in a savings account.	suffer	benefit
A person who is borrowing money.	suffer	benefit
A person who is lending money.	suffer	benefit
A person receiving a fixed-income amount.	suffer	benefit

3. What are the advantages of effective personal financial planning?

Developing and Achieving Financial Goals

Why do so many Americans—living in one of the richest countries in the world—have money problems? The answer is based on two main factors. The first is poor planning and weak money management habits in areas such as spending and the use of credit. The other factor is extensive advertising, selling efforts, and product availability that encourage overbuying. Achieving financial well-being starts with clear financial goals.

Types of Financial Goals

What would you like to do tomorrow? Believe it or not, that question involves goal setting, which may be viewed in three time frames:

- *Short-term goals* will be achieved within the next year or so, such as saving for a vacation or paying off small debts.
- *Intermediate goals* have a time frame of two to five years.
- *Long-term goals* involve financial plans that are more than five years off, such as retirement, money for children's college education, or the purchase of a vacation home.

ACTION ITEM

Do you have specific financial goals that you hope to achieve in the future?

☐ Yes ☐ No

Long-term goals should be planned in coordination with short-term and intermediate goals. Setting and achieving short-term goals is commonly the basis for moving toward success of long-term goals. For example, saving for a down payment to buy a house is a short-term goal that can be a foundation for a long-term goal: owning your own home.

A goal of obtaining increased career training is different from a goal of saving money to pay a semiannual auto insurance premium. *Consumable-product goals* usually occur on a periodic basis and involve items that are used up relatively quickly, such as food, clothing, and entertainment. *Durable-product goals* usually involve infrequently purchased, expensive items such as appliances, cars, and sporting equipment; these consist of tangible items.

In contrast, many people overlook *intangible-purchase, or nonfinancial, goals.* These goals relate to personal relationships, health, education, community service, and leisure. Examples include learning a new skill to expand your career, participating in community service activities, and creating art through writing, photography, drawing, or sculpture.

> **WHAT WOULD YOU DO?** Each day, people encounter various circumstances that hinder their financial goals. Personal and household situations change, or economic conditions result in unexpected consequences. What situations in your life might influence the financial goals that you decide to pursue? Describe various actions you might take to achieve your financial goals.

Goal-Setting Guidelines

An old saying goes, "If you don't know where you're going, you might end up somewhere else and not even know it." Goal setting is central to financial decision making. Your financial goals are the basis for planning, implementing, and measuring the progress of your spending, saving, and investing activities. Exhibit 1–1 offers short-term and long-term financial actions that can be the basis for your financial goals.

Your financial goals should take a SMART approach, in that they are:

- **S**—*specific,* so you know exactly what your goals are and can create a plan designed to achieve those objectives.

money minute focus

To become financially disciplined:

> Select a word or short phrase to describe your goal.
> Use a visual reminder—a photo, sticky note, or note card on your desk, computer, bathroom mirror, refrigerator, or car dashboard.
> Keep a financial diary or journal.
> Obtain support; work with a friend, roommate, spouse, or group to stay accountable.

Financial goals often lack the "why" to achieve meaningful results. If you are unable to answer "why," this may indicate a goal that is not appropriate. What is the "why" for one of your financial goals?

Creating Goals and Assessing Financial Health

Using the S-M-A-R-T format, create a financial goal that you would like to accomplish regarding saving, spending, or sharing your time, talents, or financial resources.

Example	Your Goal
Specific . . . Create an emergency fund . . .	
Measurable . . . of $1,800 . . .	
Action-oriented . . . at a credit union . . .	
Realistic . . . by reduced spending on food away from home . . .	
Time-based . . . within the next six months.	

What are your next actions to achieve this financial goal?

(1)

(2)

(3)

To evaluate your current financial activities for achieving goals, respond with a **YES** or **NO** answer to the following items:

	Yes	No
1. Do you have a budget or spending plan that guides your financial activities?		
2. Each month, do you pay your bills and credit card accounts on time?		
3. Do you maintain a record of the amount spent on various items each month?		
4. Is your monthly spending less than your income?		
5. If you had an unexpected major expense, would you have access to funds to cover this cost?		
6. Do you know the amount in the bank account you use for daily spending?		
7. Do you have money automatically set aside each month in a savings or investment program?		
8. Does your recordkeeping system allow you to quickly locate important documents?		
9. Do you know the balance of your credit card accounts and other loans?		
10. Over the past year, have you avoided late fees for credit cards, loans, and bills?		

A positive answer to eight or more of these questions indicates a strong personal financial situation.

- **M**—*measurable,* by a specific amount. For example, "Accumulate $5,000 in an investment fund within three years" is more measurable than "Put money into an investment fund."
- **A**—*action-oriented,* providing the basis for the personal financial activities you will undertake. For example, "Reduce credit card debt" will usually mean actions to pay off amounts owed.

- **R**—*realistic,* involving goals based on your income and life situation. For example, it is probably not realistic to expect to buy a new car each year if you are a full-time student.
- **T**—*time-based,* indicating a time frame for achieving the goal, such as three years. This allows you to measure your progress toward your financial goals.

Once you identify a S-M-A-R-T goal, a system is needed to achieve the goal. Actions steps along with a timeline can be the basis for achieving financial goals. The *Financial Literacy in Practice* feature "Creating Goals and Assessing Financial Health" can guide your goal-setting activities.

 Sheet 2 Setting Personal Financial Goals

PRACTICE QUIZ 1–2

1. What are examples of long-term goals?

2. What are the main characteristics of useful financial goals?

3. Match the following common goals to the life situation of the people listed.

a. Pay off student loans	_____ A young couple without children
b. Start a college savings fund	_____ An older person living alone
c. Increase retirement contributions	_____ A person who just completed college
d. Finance long-term care	_____ A single mother with a preschool daughter

Opportunity Costs and the Time Value of Money

In every financial decision, you sacrifice something to get something that you consider more desirable. For example, you might not buy an item now to save for a future purchase or long-term financial security. Or you might obtain the use of an expensive item now by making credit payments from future earnings.

   Opportunity cost is what you give up when making a choice. This cost, often referred to as a *trade-off,* cannot always be measured in dollars. Opportunity costs should be viewed in terms of both personal and financial resources.

Personal Opportunity Costs

An important personal opportunity cost is the time used for one activity cannot be used for other activities. Time used for studying, working, or shopping will not be available for other uses. Other personal opportunity costs relate to health. Poor eating habits, lack of sleep, or avoiding exercise can result in illness, time away from school or work, increased health care costs, and reduced financial security. Similar to financial resources, your personal resources (time, energy, health, abilities, knowledge) require planning and wise management.

Financial Opportunity Costs

Would you rather have $100 today or $103 a year from now? How about $120 a year from now instead of $100 today? Your choice among these alternatives will depend on several factors, including current needs, future uncertainty, and current interest rates. If you wait to receive your money in the future, you want to be rewarded for the risk. The **time value of money** involves increases in an amount of money as a result of interest earned. Saving

LO1.3

Calculate time value of money situations to analyze personal financial decisions.

ACTION ITEM

Do you set aside an amount of money on a regular basis for various financial goals?

☐ Yes   ☐ No

opportunity cost What a person gives up by making a choice.

time value of money Increase in an amount of money as a result of interest earned.

or investing a dollar instead of spending it today results in a future amount greater than a dollar. Every time you spend, save, invest, or borrow money, you should consider the time value of that money as an opportunity cost. Spending money from your savings account means lost interest earnings; however, what you buy with that money may have a higher priority than the interest earned.

> **WHAT WOULD YOU DO?** Savings is the foundation for long-term financial security. However, most people do not make saving a priority. What would you tell someone who says they do not have enough money available to save anything? Describe actions you might take to start or expand your savings program.

INTEREST CALCULATIONS Three amounts are used to calculate the time value of money for savings in the form of interest earned:

- The amount of the savings (commonly called the *principal*).
- The annual interest rate.
- The length of time the money is on deposit.

These three items are multiplied to obtain the amount of interest. Simple interest is calculated as follows:

Amount in savings × Annual interest rate × Time period = Interest

For example, $500 on deposit at 6 percent for six months would earn $15 ($500 × 0.06 × 6/12 or ½ year).

The increased value of money from interest earned involves two types of time value of money calculations, future value and present value. The amount that will be available at a later date is called the *future value*. In contrast, the current value of an amount desired in the future is the *present value*. Five methods are available for calculating time value of money:

1. *Formula calculation.* With this method, math notations are used to compute future value and present value.
2. *Time value of money tables.* In the past, before calculators and computers, future value and present value tables were used for easier computing (see Chapter 1 Appendix).
3. *Financial calculator.* Various calculators are programmed with financial functions. Both future value and present value calculations are performed using appropriate keystrokes.
4. *Spreadsheet software.* Excel and other spreadsheet programs have built-in formulas for financial calculations, including future value and present value.
5. *Websites and apps.* Many time value of money calculators are available online and through mobile devices. These programs calculate the future value of savings as well as loan payment amounts.

FUTURE VALUE OF A SINGLE AMOUNT Money deposited in a bank account earns interest. **Future value** is the amount to which current savings will grow based on a certain interest rate and a certain time period. For example, $100 deposited in a 6 percent account for one year will grow to $106. This amount is computed as follows:

$$\text{Future value} = \$100 + (\$100 \times 0.06 \times 1 \text{ year}) = \$106$$

future value The amount to which current savings will increase based on a certain interest rate and a certain time period; also referred to as *compounding.*

The same process could be continued for a second, third, and fourth year; however, the computations would be time-consuming. The previously mentioned calculation methods make the process easier.

An example of the future value of a single amount might involve an investment of $650 earning 8 percent for 10 years. This situation would be calculated as follows:

Formula	Time Value of Money Table	Financial Calculator	Spreadsheet Software
$FV = PV (1 + i)^n$ $FV = 650(1 + 0.08)^{10}$ $FV = \$1,403.30$ i—interest rate n—number of time periods	Using Exhibit 1–A in the Chapter 1 Appendix, multiply the amount deposited by the factor for the interest rate and time period. $650 \times 2.159 = \$1,403.35$ (The slight difference in this answer is the result of rounding the decimal places.)	$\boxed{PV}$, $\boxed{I/Y}$, $\boxed{N}$, $\boxed{PMT}$, $\boxed{CPT}$, $\boxed{FV}$ $650\ \boxed{PV}$, $8\ \boxed{I/Y}$, $10\ \boxed{N}$, $0\ \boxed{PMT}$, $\boxed{CPT}\ \boxed{FV}$ $\$1,403.30$ (Different financial calculators will require different keystrokes.)	=FV(rate, periods, amount per period, single amount) =FV(0.08,10,0,−650) =$1,403.30

NOTE: Expanded explanations of these time value of money calculation methods are presented in the **Chapter 1 Appendix**.

Future value computations may be referred to as *compounding,* since interest is earned on previously earned interest. Compounding allows the future value of a deposit to grow faster than it would if interest were paid only on the original deposit. The sooner you make deposits, the greater the future value will be. Depositing $1,000 in a 5 percent account at age 40 will give you $3,387 at age 65. Making the $1,000 deposit at age 25 would result in an account balance of $7,040 at age 65.

FUTURE VALUE OF A SERIES OF DEPOSITS

Many savers and investors make regular deposits. An *annuity* is a series of equal deposits or payments. To determine the future value of equal yearly savings deposits, time value of money tables can be used (see Exhibit 1–B in the Chapter 1 Appendix). For this table to be used, and for an annuity to exist, the deposits must earn a constant interest rate. For example, if you deposit $50 a year at 7 percent for six years, starting at the end of the first year, you will have $357.65 at the end of that time ($50 × 7.153). The nearby *Figure It Out!* feature presents examples of using future value to achieve financial goals.

money minute focus

If you invest $2,000 a year (at 9 percent) from ages 35 to 65 (31 years), these funds will grow to $352,427 by age 65. However, if you save $2,000 a year (at 9 percent) **for only 10 years** from ages 25 to 34, at age 65 you would have a retirement fund worth $545,344! Most important: Start investing something now!

PRESENT VALUE OF A SINGLE AMOUNT
Another aspect of the time value of money involves determining the current value of an amount desired in the future. **Present value** is the current value for a future amount based on a particular interest rate for a certain period of time. Present value computations, also called *discounting,* allow you to determine how much to deposit now to obtain a desired total in the future. For example, using the present value table (Exhibit 1–C in the Chapter 1 Appendix), if you want $1,000 five years from now and you earn 5 percent on your savings, you need to deposit $784 ($1,000 × 0.784).

present value The current value for a future amount based on a certain interest rate and a certain time period; also referred to as *discounting.*

PRESENT VALUE OF A SERIES OF DEPOSITS
You may also use present value computations to determine how much you need to deposit now so that you can take a certain amount out of the account for a desired number of years. For example, if you want to take $400 out of an investment account each year for nine years and your money is earning an annual rate of 8 percent, you can see from Exhibit 1–D (Chapter 1 Appendix) that you would need to make a current deposit of $2,498.80 ($400 × 6.247).

Additional details for the formulas, tables, and other methods for calculating time value of money are presented in the appendix at the end of this chapter.

Figure It Out!

Time Value of Money Calculations for Achieving Financial Goals

Achieving specific financial goals may require making regular savings deposits or determining an amount to be invested. By using time value of money calculations, you can compute the amount needed to achieve a financial goal.

Situation 1: Jonie Emerson has two children who will start college in 10 years. She plans to set aside $1,500 a year for her children's college education during that period and estimates she will earn an annual interest rate of 5 percent on her savings. What amount can Jonie expect to have available for her children's college education when they start college?

Formula	Time Value of Money Table	Financial Calculator	Spreadsheet Software
$FV = \text{Annuity} \dfrac{(1+i)^n - 1}{i}$ $FV = 1{,}500 \dfrac{(1+.05)^{10} - 1}{.05}$ $FV = \$18{,}866.85$	Using Exhibit 1–B (Chapter 1 Appendix), multiply the amount deposited by the factor for the interest rate and time period. $1{,}500 \times 12.578 = \$18{,}867$	PV , I/Y , N , PMT , CPT FV 0 PV , 5 I/Y , 10 N , 1,500 PMT , CPT FV $18,866.84 (Different financial calculators will require different keystrokes.)	= FV(rate, periods, amount per period, amount) = FV(0.05,10, −1,500) = $18,866.84

Conclusion: Based these calculations, if Jonie deposits $1,500 a year at an annual interest rate of 5 percent, she would have $18,867 available for her children's college education.

Situation 2: Don Calder wants to have $50,000 available in 10 years as a reserve fund for his parents' retirement living expenses and health care. If he earns an average of 8 percent on his investments, what amount must he invest today to achieve this goal?

Formula	Time Value of Money Table	Financial Calculator	Spreadsheet Software
$PV = \dfrac{FV}{(1+i)^n}$ $PV = \dfrac{50{,}000}{(1+.08)^{10}}$ $PV = \$23{,}159.67$	Using Exhibit 1–C (Chapter 1 Appendix), multiply the amount desired by the factor for the interest rate and time period. $50{,}000 \times 0.463 = \$23{,}150$	FV , N , I/Y , PMT , CPT PV 50,000 FV , 10 N , 8 I/Y , 0 PMT , CPT PV $23,159.67 (Different financial calculators will require different keystrokes.)	= PV(rate, periods, payment, future value amount type) = PV(0.08,10,0,−50,000) = $23,159.67

Conclusion: Don needs to invest approximately $23,160 today for 10 years at 8 percent to achieve the desired financial goal.

NOTE: Expanded explanations of these time value of money calculation methods are presented in the **Chapter 1 Appendix.**

Sheet 3 Achieving Financial Goals Using Time Value of Money

PRACTICE QUIZ 1–3

1. What are some examples of personal opportunity costs?

2. What does time value of money measure?

3. Use the time value of money tables in Exhibit 1–3 (or a financial calculator) to calculate the following:

   a. The future value of $100 at 7 percent in 10 years.
   b. The future value of $100 a year for six years earning 6 percent.
   c. The present value of $500 received in eight years with an interest rate of 8 percent.

A Plan for Personal Financial Planning

Everyone makes hundreds of decisions each day. Most of these choices are quite simple and have few consequences. However, some are complex and have long-term effects on our personal and financial situations, as shown here:

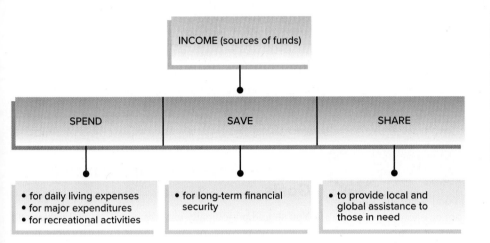

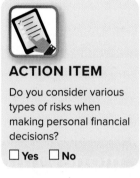

LO1.4

Implement a plan for making personal financial and career decisions.

ACTION ITEM

Do you consider various types of risks when making personal financial decisions?

☐ Yes ☐ No

While everyone makes decisions, few people consider how to make better decisions. As Exhibit 1–3 shows, the financial planning process can be viewed in six steps that can be adapted to any life situation.

STEP 1: Determine Your Current Financial Situation

In the first step, determine your current financial situation regarding income, savings, living expenses, and debts. Prepare a list of assets and debts, along with amounts spent for various items is the foundation for financial planning activities. The personal financial statements discussed in Chapter 2 will provide the information needed for this phase of financial decision making.

Exhibit **1–3** **The Financial Planning Process**

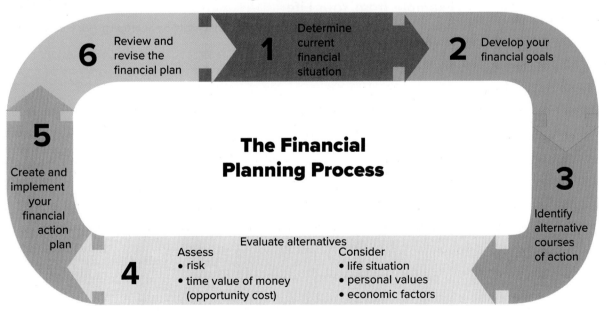

EXAMPLE: Step 1 - Determine Your Current Situation

Carla Elliot plans to complete her college degree in the next two years. She works two part-time jobs in an effort to pay her educational expenses. Currently, Carla has $700 in a savings account and existing debt that includes a $640 balance on her credit card and $2,300 in student loans. What additional information should Carla have available when planning her personal finances?

_____

Example from Your Life

What actions have you taken to determine your current financial situation?

_____

---

money minute focus

To develop financial literacy among children: (1) have a payday for chores, not an allowance; (2) explain opportunity cost, needs vs. wants; (3) start a savings jar or bank account for unexpected situations; (4) create a budgeting chart to show family spending; (5) sign an agreement with payment dates for money borrowed from parents; (6) have them buy shampoo, toothpaste, snacks to prepare them to be on their own.

STEP 2: Develop Your Financial Goals

You should periodically analyze your financial values and goals. The purpose of this action is to clarify your needs and wants. Specific financial goals are vital to financial planning. Others can suggest financial goals for you, but *you* must decide which goals to pursue. Your financial goals can range from spending all of your current income to developing an extensive savings and investment program for your future financial security.

EXAMPLE: Step 2 - Develop Financial Goals

Carla Elliot's main financial goals for the next two years are to complete her college degree and to reduce the amounts owed. What other goals might be appropriate for Carla?

_____

Example from Your Life

Describe some short-term or long-term goals that might be appropriate for your life situation.

_____

STEP 3: Identify Alternative Courses of Action

Identifying alternatives is crucial when making decisions. Although many factors can influence available alternatives, possible courses of action usually fall into these categories:

- *Continue the same course of action.* For example, you may determine that the amount you have saved each month is still appropriate.
- *Expand the current situation.* You may choose to save a larger amount each month.
- *Change the current situation.* You may decide to use a money market account instead of a regular savings account.
- *Take a new course of action.* You may decide to use your monthly saving budget to pay off credit card debts.

Not all of these categories will apply to every decision; they represent possible courses of action. For example, if you stop working full-time to go to school, you must identify several alternatives under the category "Take a new course of action." Creativity in decision making is vital. Considering all possible alternatives will help you make more effective and satisfying decisions. For instance, most people believe they must own a car to get to work or school. However, they should consider other alternatives such as public transportation, carpooling, renting a car, shared ownership of a car, or using a ride-sharing service.

Remember, when you decide not to take action, you elect to "do nothing," which can be a dangerous alternative.

EXAMPLE: Step 3 - Identify Alternatives

To achieve her goals, Carla Elliot has several options available. She could reduce her spending, seek a higher-paying part-time job, or use her savings to pay off some of her debt. What additional alternatives might she consider?

_____

Example from Your Life

List various alternatives for achieving the financial goals you identified in Step 2.

_____

STEP 4: Evaluate Your Alternatives

Next, evaluate possible courses of action, taking into consideration your life situation, personal values, and current economic conditions. How will the ages of dependents affect your saving goals? How do you like to spend leisure time? How will changes in interest rates affect your financial situation?

CONSEQUENCES OF CHOICES Every decision closes off alternatives. For example, a decision to invest in stock may mean you cannot take a vacation. A decision to go to school full-time may mean you cannot work full-time. Opportunity cost is what you give up by making a choice. These trade-offs cannot always be measured in dollars. However, the resources you give up (money or time) have a value that is lost.

EVALUATING RISK Uncertainty is also a part of every decision. Selecting a college major and choosing a career field involve risk. What if you don't like working in a field or cannot obtain employment? Other decisions involve a very low degree of risk, such as putting money in an insured savings account or purchasing items that cost only a few dollars. Your chance of losing something of great value is not present in these situations.

In many financial decisions, identifying and evaluating risk are difficult. Common risks to consider include:

- Inflation risk, due to rising or falling (deflation) prices that cause changes in buying power.
- Interest rate risk, resulting from changes in the cost of money, which can affect your costs (when you borrow) and benefits (when you save or invest).
- Income risk may result from loss of a job or encountering illness.
- Personal risk involves tangible and intangible factors that create a less than desirable situation, such as health or safety concerns.

FinTech for Financial Literacy

FinTech (financial technology) involves apps, websites, computers, and other automated systems for banking and personal finance activities. Artificial intelligence, robotics, drones, blockchain, and other innovations will influence how you earn, save, spend, and invest. Robo-advisors, for example, offer personalized, investment advice based on your income, assets, debt, financial goals, and risk tolerance. Other FinTech operations include crowdfunding, cryptocurrencies, budgeting and payment apps, and online start-ups providing insurance.

- Liquidity risk occurs when savings and investments that have potential for higher earnings are difficult to convert to cash or to sell without significant loss in value.

The best way to consider risk is to gather information based on your experience and the experiences of others, and to use financial planning information sources.

FINANCIAL PLANNING INFORMATION SOURCES Appropriate information is required at each stage of the financial planning process. In addition to this book, useful sources available to help you include (1) online sources and apps; (2) financial institutions, such as banks, credit unions, and investment companies; (3) media sources, such as newspapers, magazines, television, radio, podcasts, and online videos; and (4) financial specialists, such as financial planners, insurance agents, investment advisors, credit counselors, lawyers, and tax preparers.

EXAMPLE: Step 4 - Evaluate Alternatives

As Carla Elliot evaluates her alternative courses of action, she should consider both her short-term and long-term situations. What risks and trade-offs should Carla consider?

_____

Example from Your Life

In your life, what types of risks might be encountered when planning and implementing various personal financial activities?

_____

STEP 5: Create and Implement Your Financial Action Plan

You are now ready to develop an action plan to achieve your goals. For example, you can increase your savings by reducing your spending or by increasing your income. If you are concerned about year-end tax payments, you may increase the amount withheld from each paycheck, file quarterly tax payments, or shelter current income in a tax-deferred retirement program.

To implement your financial action plan, you may need assistance from others. For example, you may contact an insurance agent to purchase property insurance or use an investment broker to purchase stocks, bonds, or mutual funds. Exhibit 1–4 offers a framework for developing and implementing a financial plan, along with examples for several life situations. Also, the Chapter 5 Appendix provides information on financing your education.

According to *AICPA Insights,* common financial planning mistakes are:

- Unrealistic expectations. Be sure your plan is based on sensible assumptions for income, spending, and saving amounts.
- Emotional decision making. Do not let feelings and emotional reactions guide your actions.
- Inflexibility. Be ready for unexpected events with an emergency fund and a contingency plan.
- Inaction. Failing to deal with insurance needs or a tax situation will make any financial plan worthless; have an action plan.
- Unclear values and priorities. Taking the wrong path will result in an inappropriate financial destination. Have a "save-first" mindset instead of "spend-first."

The *Financial Literacy in Practice* feature "Which Path Will You Choose?" provides guidelines for choosing your financial planning direction.

Financial Literacy in Practice

Which Path Will You Choose? Only One Will Result in Financial Security

Do you feel stress when you think about money? Are your financial decisions influenced by emotions rather than valid information? Do you often have disagreements about money?

To address these and other financial concerns, two paths exist for your daily money decisions. The *easy* path involves little thinking, no planning, and minimal effort, usually resulting in wasted money and financial difficulties. In contrast, the *appropriate* path takes some time and effort but results in lower stress and personal financial security.

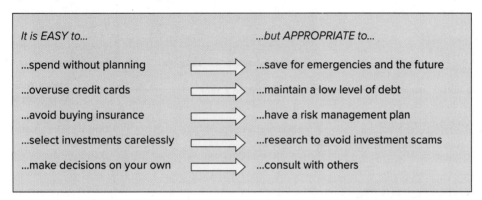

It is EASY to...	...but APPROPRIATE to...
...spend without planning	...save for emergencies and the future
...overuse credit cards	...maintain a low level of debt
...avoid buying insurance	...have a risk management plan
...select investments carelessly	...research to avoid investment scams
...make decisions on your own	...consult with others

You can easily start to move yourself from *easy mistakes* to *appropriate actions* with these steps:

1. *Do something.* Start small, such as saving a small amount each month. Or decide to reduce your credit card use.

2. *Avoid excuses.* Do not tell yourself that "I don't have time" or "It's what everyone else is doing."

3. *Rate your current situation.* Indicate on this scale where you are currently in relation to the two available paths:

Spender   Saver

Financial difficulties   Financial security

4. *Set your mission.* Create a *personal finance mission statement* to communicate your personal values, financial goals, and future vision. This paragraph (or list, diagram, or other format) will remind you and family members of your desired path. The wording describes where you want to be and how you will get there. Develop your financial mission statement by talking with those who can help guide your actions. Your personal finance mission statement may include such phrases as "My financial mission is to change my spending habits for . . . ," " . . . to better understand my insurance needs . . . ," or "donate to (or volunteer for) local community service organizations."

Choosing whether to take *easy* or *difficult* actions can result in reduced emotional stress, improved personal relationships, and enhanced financial security.

EXAMPLE: Step 5 - Create a Financial Plan

Carla has decided to reduce her course load and work longer hours in an effort both to reduce her debt level and to increase the amount she has in savings. What are the benefits and drawbacks of this choice?

_____

Example from Your Life

Describe the benefits and drawbacks of a financial situation you have encountered during the past year.

_____

Exhibit **1-4** **Financial Planning in Action**

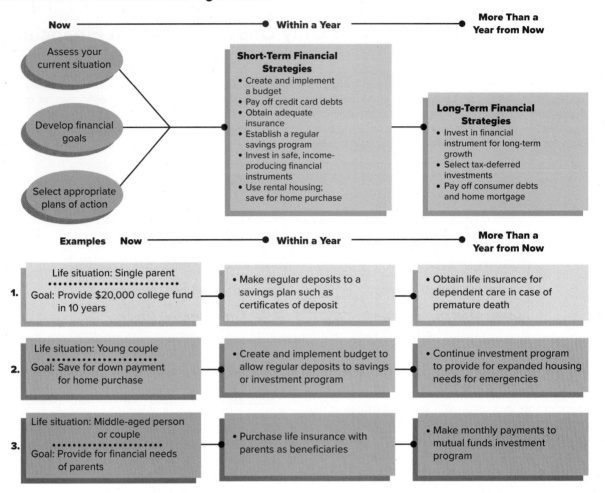

STEP 6: Review and Revise Your Plan

Financial planning is an ongoing process that does not end when you take action. You need to regularly assess your financial decisions. You should do a review of your finances at least once a year. Changing personal, social, and economic factors may require a more frequent review.

When life events affect your financial needs, this financial planning process will help you adapt to changes. A regular review of this process will help you adjust priorities to bring your financial goals and activities in line with your current life situation.

EXAMPLE: Step 6 - Review and Revise the Plan

Over the next 6 to 12 months, Carla Elliot should review her financial, personal, and educational situation. What circumstances might occur that could require that Carla take a different approach to her personal finances?

_____

Example from Your Life

What factors in your life might affect your personal financial situation and decisions in the future?

_____

Online resources (apps, websites, podcasts, blogs, videos, social media) are valuable for learning. As both a consumer and producer of digital content, you need to be able to locate, assess, create, and share information for wise money management. Also, online safety, privacy settings, social media sharing, and fake news can influence your financial well-being and career opportunities. Improving your *digital financial literacy* involves developing skills for using information to identify, research, and implement money decisions.

Kiplinger.com and *Kiplinger's Personal Finance* magazine offer a wide variety of personal financial articles, videos, podcasts, calculators, and other features. A recent article in the magazine featured an individual who had a strong savings program but wanted to invest for a higher

Kiplinger's Personal Finance

return. His goals included continuing to save for retirement and buying a car and a house. He also kept some of his savings in an account as an emergency fund.

As the years progressed, and marriage was on the horizon, consideration was given to some additional goals. These financial targets included buying a bigger house and renting out the current one. *Kiplinger's Personal Finance* staff also recommended that the couple consult a financial planner as they make plans to formally combine their finances.

ACTION STEPS FOR. . .

. . .Information Literacy

Based on your personal life situation, identify a financial goal and develop action steps to achieve that goal. Create a list of questions that might be used to validate the action steps.

. . .Financial Literacy

Locate the "Tools Gallery" at **kiplinger.com** and select one of the items. Prepare a visual (photo, poster) or brief video that explains how this tool might be used to achieve a personal financial goal.

. . .Digital Literacy

Select an article from **kiplinger. com.** Talk with others about the article. Describe how an online video or app might be used to communicate the information from these sources.

Career Choice and Financial Planning

Have you ever wondered why some people find great satisfaction in their work, while others only put in their time? As with other personal financial decisions, career selection and professional growth require planning. The lifework you select is a key to your financial well-being and personal satisfaction. The steps of the financial planning process can guide your career planning, advancement, and career change. Your career goals will affect how you use this process. If you desire more responsibility on the job, for example, you may decide to obtain advanced training or change career fields. The Chapter 2 Appendix provides guidance for obtaining employment and professional advancement.

EXAMPLE: Your Career Planning Decisions

Based on your current or future career situation, describe how you might use the financial planning process (Exhibit 1–3) to plan and implement an employment decision.

_____

_____

Your education can be a significant investment with future career and financial benefits. Alternatives to fund school costs include: (1) grants, which don't need to be repaid; (2) financial aid and work-study programs; (3) scholarships; (4) education loans; (5) tax credits; (6) personal savings; (7) lower-cost living locations; and (8) tuition reimbursement programs. For additional guidance on financing your education, see the Chapter 5 Appendix.

Sheet 4 Planning Your Career

PRACTICE QUIZ 1–4

1. What actions might a person take to identify alternatives when making a financial decision?

2. Why are career planning activities considered to be personal financial decisions?

3. For the following situations, identify the type of risk being described.

   _____ Not getting proper rest and exercise.
   _____ Not being able to obtain cash from a certificate of deposit before the maturity date.
   _____ Taking out a variable rate loan when rates are expected to rise.
   _____ Training for a career field with low potential demand in the future.

4. For the following sources of personal finance information, list a specific website, organization, or person whom you might contact in the future.

Type of information	Specific source	Contact information
Website		
App		
Financial institution		
Financial specialist		

Road Map  to financial literacy

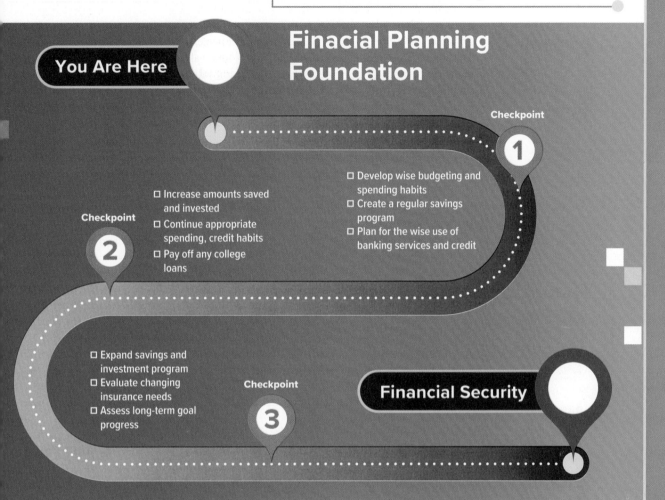

You Are Here

Finacial Planning Foundation

Checkpoint 1
- ☐ Develop wise budgeting and spending habits
- ☐ Create a regular savings program
- ☐ Plan for the wise use of banking services and credit

Checkpoint 2
- ☐ Increase amounts saved and invested
- ☐ Continue appropriate spending, credit habits
- ☐ Pay off any college loans

Checkpoint 3
- ☐ Expand savings and investment program
- ☐ Evaluate changing insurance needs
- ☐ Assess long-term goal progress

Financial Security

your personal finance dashboard

Emergency Savings Fund

A dashboard is used to monitor key performance indicators of success. You can use this tool to assess your personal financial situation. An often overlooked action is the creation of an emergency fund. Financial advisers commonly suggest saving three to six months of living expenses for unexpected situations. More may be needed if you are self-employed.

YOUR SITUATION: Have you started your emergency fund? Do you make progress each month?

LO1.1 Financial decisions are affected by a person's life situation (income, age, household size, health), personal values, and economic factors (prices, interest rates, and employment opportunities). The major elements of financial planning are obtaining, planning, saving, borrowing, spending, managing risk, investing, and retirement and estate planning.

LO1.2 Financial goals should take a S-M-A-R-T approach with goals that are: Specific, Measurable, Action-oriented, Realistic, and Time-based.

LO1.3 Every decision involves a trade-off with things given up. Personal opportunity costs include time, effort, and health. Financial opportunity costs are based on the time value of money. Future value and present value calculations enable you to measure the increased value (or lost interest) that results from a saving, investing, borrowing, or purchasing decision.

LO1.4 Personal financial planning involves these steps: (1) determine your current financial situation; (2) develop financial goals; (3) identify alternative courses of action; (4) evaluate alternatives; (5) create and implement a financial action plan; and (6) review and revise the financial plan.

Key Terms

adult life cycle 4	future value 12	present value 13
bankruptcy 8	inflation 6	time value of money 11
economics 4	opportunity cost 11	values 4
financial plan 4	personal financial planning 3	

Self-Test Problems

1. The Rule of 72 provides a guideline for determining how long it takes your money to double. This rule can also be used to determine your earning rate. If your money is expected to double in 12 years, what is your rate of return?
2. If you desire to have $10,000 in savings eight years from now, what amount would you need to deposit in an account that earns 5 percent?

Self-Test Solutions

1. Using the Rule of 72, if your money is expected to double in 12 years, you are earning approximately 6 percent (72 ÷ 12 years = 6 percent).
2. To calculate the present value of $10,000 for eight years at 5 percent, use Exhibit 1–3C (or Exhibit 1–C in the Chapter 1 Appendix): $10,000 × 0.677 = $6,770

Financial Planning Problems

(*Note:* Some of these problems require the use of the time value of money tables in the Chapter 1 Appendix, a financial calculator, or spreadsheet software.)

1. Using the Rule of 72, approximate the following amounts: (LO1.1)
   a. If the value of land in an area is increasing 6 percent a year, how long will it take for property values to double?
   b. If you earn 10 percent on your investments, how long will it take for your money to double?
   c. At an annual interest rate of 5 percent, how long will it take for your savings to double?
2. In 2019, selected automobiles had an average cost of $16,000. The average cost of those same automobiles is now $20,000. What was the rate of increase for these automobiles between the two time periods?   (LO1.1)
3. A family spends $46,000 a year for living expenses. If prices increase 3 percent a year for the next three years, what amount will the family need for their living expenses after three years?   (LO1.1)
4. Ben Collins plans to buy a house for $260,000. If the real estate in his area is expected to increase in value 2 percent each year, what will its approximate value be seven years from now?   (LO1.2)

5. What would be the yearly earnings for a person with $9,000 in savings at an annual interest rate of 1.5 percent?   (LO1.3)

6. Using a financial calculator, Excel, or the time value of money tables in the Chapter 1 Appendix, calculate the following: (LO1.3)
   a. The future value of $550 six years from now at 7 percent.
   b. The future value of $900 saved each year for 10 years at 8 percent.
   c. The amount a person would have to deposit today (present value) at a 5 percent interest rate to have $1,000 five years from now.
   d. The amount a person would have to deposit today to be able to take out $500 a year for 10 years from an account earning 8 percent.

7. If you desire to have $12,000 for a down payment for a house in five years, what amount would you need to deposit today? Assume that your money will earn 4 percent.   (LO1.3)

8. Pete Morton is planning to go to graduate school in a program of study that will take three years. Pete wants to have $8,000 available each year for various school and living expenses. If he earns 3 percent on his money, how much must he deposit at the start of his studies to be able to withdraw $8,000 a year for three years?   (LO1.3)

9. Carla Lopez deposits $2,800 a year into her retirement account. If these funds have average earnings of 7 percent over the 40 years until her retirement, what will be the value of her retirement account?   (LO1.3)

10. If a person spends $10 a week on coffee (assume $500 a year), what would be the future value of that amount over 10 years if the funds were deposited in an account earning 3 percent?   (LO1.3)

11. A financial company that advertises on television will pay you $60,000 now for annual payments of $10,000 that you are expected to receive for a legal settlement over the next 10 years. If you estimate the time value of money at 10 percent, would you accept this offer?   (LO1.3)

12. Tran Lee plans to set aside $2,600 a year for the next seven years, earning 3 percent. What would be the future value of this savings amount?   (LO1.3)

13. If you borrow $8,000 with a 5 percent interest rate to be repaid in five equal payments at the end of the next five years, what would be the amount of each payment? (*Note:* Use the present value of an annuity table in the Chapter 1 Appendix.)   (LO1.3)

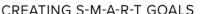 **To reinforce the content in this chapter, more problems are provided at connect.mheducation.com.**

FINANCIAL LITERACY PORTFOLIO. . .

CREATING S-M-A-R-T GOALS

Competency. . .

Develop personal financial goals.

Action Research. . .

Based on the S-M-A-R-T goal format discussed in this chapter, create three personal finance goals for your life or for someone else. Also refer to *Your Personal Financial Plan* Sheet 2 at the end of this chapter. Talk with several people about their financial goals. What are common goals for various personal situations? How have might employment situations affect financial decisions? Also, ask about potential risks involved with making financial decisions. What actions might be taken to investigate and reduce these risks?

Outcome. . .

Create three S-M-A-R-T goals: (1) one for SAVING; (2) one for SPENDING; and (3) one for SHARING, such as donating money, time, or skills to a charity or nonprofit. For each goal, develop an action plan (with three to five steps) presented in a visual format (flowchart, video, photo essay, PowerPoint presentation, or other visual format).

REAL LIFE PERSONAL FINANCE

YOU BE THE FINANCIAL PLANNER

While at some point in your life you may use the services of a financial planner, your personal knowledge should be the foundation for most financial decisions. For each of these situations, determine actions you might recommend.

Situation 1: Fran and Ed Blake, ages 43 and 47, have a daughter who is completing her first year of college and a son three years younger. Currently, they have $34,000 in various savings and investment funds set aside for their children's education. With the increasing cost of education, they are concerned about whether this amount is adequate. In recent months, Fran's mother has required extensive medical attention and personal care assistance. Unable to live alone, she is now a resident of a long-term care facility. The cost of this service is $5,600 a month, with annual increases of about 5 percent. While a major portion of the cost is covered by her Social Security and pension, Fran's mother is unable to cover the entire cost. In addition, the Blakes are concerned about saving for their own retirement. While they have consistently made annual deposits to a retirement fund, current financial demands may force them to access some of that money.

Situation 2: "While I knew it might happen someday, I didn't expect it right now." This was the reaction of Patrick Hamilton when his company merged with another business and moved its offices to another state, resulting in him losing his job. Patrick does have some

flexibility in his short-term finances since he has three months of living expenses in a savings account. However, "three months can go by very quickly," as Patrick noted.

Situation 3: Nina Resendiz, age 23, recently received an $8,000 gift from her aunt. She is considering various uses for these unexpected funds, including paying off credit card bills from her last vacation or setting aside money for a down payment on a house. Or she might invest the money in a tax-deferred retirement account. Another possibility is using the money for technology certification courses to enhance her earning power. Nina also wants to contribute some of the funds to a homeless shelter and a global organization that helps start small businesses in low-income areas. She is overwhelmed by the choices and comments to herself, "I want to avoid the temptation of wasting the money on impulse items. I want to make sure I use the money on things with lasting value."

Questions

1. In each situation, what are the main financial planning issues that need to be addressed?

2. What additional information would you like to have before recommending actions in each situation?

3. Based on the information provided, along with Exhibit 1–1 and the financial planning process, what actions would you recommend in each situation?

SETTING FINANCIAL GOALS

Jamie Lee Jackson, age 24, has recently decided to switch from attending college part-time to full-time in order to pursue her business degree, and she aims to graduate within the next three years. She has 55 credit hours remaining in order to earn her bachelor's degree and knows that it will be a challenge to complete her course of study while still working part-time in the bakery department of a local grocery store, where she earns $390 a week. Jamie Lee wants to keep her part-time job at the grocery store as she loves baking and creates very decorative cakes. She dreams of opening her own cupcake café within the next five years.

Jamie Lee currently shares a small apartment with a friend, and they split all of the associated living expenses, such as rent and utilities, although she would really like to eventually have a place of her own. Her car is still going strong, even though it is seven years old, and she has no plans to buy a new one any time soon. She is carrying a balance on her credit card and is making regular monthly payments of $50 with hopes of paying it off within a year. Jamie has also recently taken out a student loan to cover her educational costs and expenses. Jamie Lee just started depositing $1,800 a year in a savings account that earns 2 percent interest in hopes of having the $9,000 down payment needed to start the cupcake café two years after graduation.

Current Financial Situation

Checking account: $1,250

Emergency fund savings account: $3,100

Car (current value): $4,000

Student loan: $5,400

Credit card balance: $400

Gross monthly salary: $2,125

Net monthly salary: $1,560

Questions

1. Using *Your Personal Financial Plan* Sheet 2, what are Jamie Lee's short-term financial goals? How do they compare to her intermediate financial goals?
2. Assess Jamie Lee's current financial situation. Using the SMART approach, what recommendations would you make for her to achieve her long-term goals?
3. Name two opportunity costs that would be considered in Jamie Lee's situation.
4. Jamie Lee needs to save a total of $9,000 in order to start her cupcake café venture. She is presently depositing $1,800 a year in a regular savings account earning 2 percent interest. How much will she have accumulated five years from now in this regular savings account, assuming she will leave her emergency fund savings account balance untouched except for a rainy day?

Spending Diary

"I FIRST THOUGHT THIS PROCESS WOULD BE A WASTE OF TIME, BUT THE INFORMATION HAS HELPED ME BECOME MUCH MORE CAREFUL OF HOW I SPEND MY MONEY."

Nearly everyone who has made the effort to keep a daily spending diary has found it beneficial. Though at first the process may seem tedious, after a while recording this information becomes easier and faster.

Directions Using the Daily Spending Diary sheet, which follows, record *every cent* of your spending each day in the categories provided or, you may create your own format or use an app to monitor your spending. You can indicate the use of a credit card with (CR). This experience will help you better understand your spending patterns and identify desired changes you might want to make in your spending habits.

Questions

1. What did your daily spending diary reveal about your spending habits? What areas of spending might you consider changing?
2. How might your daily spending diary assist you when identifying and achieving financial goals?

A *Daily Spending Diary* sheet is located in the next section and on the library resource site within Connect.

Daily Spending Diary (Instructions and Sheets)

Effective personal financial planning depends on spending less than you earn. The use of a Daily Spending Diary will provide information to better understand your spending patterns and to help you achieve desired financial goals.

The following sheets, which are also available on the library resource site in Connect, can be used to record *every cent* of your spending each day in the categories provided. Or, you can create your own format to monitor your spending. You can indicate the use of a credit card with (CR). Various apps are also available to record and monitor your spending.

This experience will help you understand your spending habits and identify desired changes you might want to make. Your comments should reflect what you have learned about your spending and can assist with changes you might want to make. Ask yourself, "What spending amounts can I reduce or eliminate?"

Many people who take on this task find it difficult at first and may consider it a waste of time. However, nearly everyone who makes a serious effort to keep a Daily Spending Diary has found it beneficial. The process may seem tedious at first, but after a while recording this information becomes easier and faster. Most important, you will know where your money is going. Then you will be able to better decide if that is truly how you want to spend your available financial resources. A sincere effort will result in useful information for monitoring and controlling your spending, and create the foundation for long-term financial security. At the end of each chapter, questions are provided to guide your daily spending related to the topic of the chapter.

Using a Daily Spending Diary can help to:

- reveal hidden spending habits so you can better save for the future.
- create and achieve financial goals.
- revise buying habits and reduce wasteful spending.
- control credit card purchases.
- improve record-keeping for measuring your financial progress and filing your taxes.
- plan for major expenses during the year.
- start an investment program with the money you save through controlled spending.

The following Daily Spending Diary sheets are also available in an Excel format in Connect Finance.

You may also track your spending using apps, such as Spending Tracker, Track Every Coin, Mint, Level Money, and Spendee.

Daily Spending Diary

Directions: Record *every cent* of your spending each day in the categories provided, or create your own format to monitor your spending. You can indicate the use of a credit card with (CR). Comments should reflect what you have learned about your spending patterns and desired changes you might want to make in your spending habits. (Note: As income is received, record in Date column.)

Month: _____ Amount available for spending: $_____ Amount to be saved: $_____

Date (Income)	Total Spending	Auto, Transportation	Housing, Utilities	Food (H) Home (A) Away	Health, Personal Care	Education	Recreation, Leisure	Donations, Gifts	Other (note item, amount)	Comments
Example	$83	$20 (gas) (CR)		$47 (H)		$2 (pen)	$4 (DVD rental)	$10 (church)		This takes time, but it helps me control my spending.
1										
2										
3										
4										
5										
6										
7										
8										
9										
10										
11										
12										
13										
14										
Subtotal										
15										
16										
17										
18										
19										
20										
21										
22										
23										
24										
25										
26										
27										
28										
29										
30										
31										
Total										

Total Income	Total Spending	Difference(+/−)	**Actions:** amount to savings, areas for reduced spending, other actions . . . .
$_____	$_____	$_____	

Daily Spending Diary

Directions: Record *every cent* of your spending each day in the categories provided, or create your own format to monitor your spending. You can indicate the use of a credit card with (CR). Comments should reflect what you have learned about your spending patterns and desired changes you might want to make in your spending habits. (*Note:* As income is received, record in Date column.)

Month: _____ Amount available for spending: $_____ Amount to be saved: $_____

Date (Income)	Total Spending	Auto, Transportation	Housing, Utilities	Food (H) Home (A) Away	Health, Personal Care	Education	Recreation, Leisure	Donations, Gifts	Other (note item, amount)	Comments
1										
2										
3										
4										
5										
6										
7										
8										
9										
10										
11										
12										
13										
14										
Subtotal										
15										
16										
17										
18										
19										
20										
21										
22										
23										
24										
25										
26										
27										
28										
29										
30										
31										
Total										

Total Income	Total Spending	Difference(+/−)	**Actions:** amount to savings, areas for reduced spending, other actions . . . .
$_____	$_____	$_____	

Daily Spending Diary

Directions: Record *every cent* of your spending each day in the categories provided, or create your own format to monitor your spending. You can indicate the use of a credit card with (CR). Comments should reflect what you have learned about your spending patterns and desired changes you might want to make in your spending habits. (*Note:* As income is received, record in Date column.)

Month: _____ Amount available for spending: $_____ Amount to be saved: $_____

Date (Income)	Total Spending	Auto, Transportation	Housing, Utilities	Food (H) Home (A) Away	Health, Personal Care	Education	Recreation, Leisure	Donations, Gifts	Other (note item, amount)	Comments
1										
2										
3										
4										
5										
6										
7										
8										
9										
10										
11										
12										
13										
14										
Subtotal										
15										
16										
17										
18										
19										
20										
21										
22										
23										
24										
25										
26										
27										
28										
29										
30										
31										
Total										

Total Income	Total Spending	Difference(+/−)	**Actions:** amount to savings, areas for reduced spending, other actions . . . .
$_____	$_____	$_____	

Daily Spending Diary

Directions: Record *every cent* of your spending each day in the categories provided, or create your own format to monitor your spending. You can indicate the use of a credit card with (CR). Comments should reflect what you have learned about your spending patterns and desired changes you might want to make in your spending habits. (*Note:* As income is received, record in Date column.)

Month: _____ Amount available for spending: $_____ Amount to be saved: $_____

Date (Income)	Total Spending	Auto, Transportation	Housing, Utilities	Food (H) Home (A) Away	Health, Personal Care	Education	Recreation, Leisure	Donations, Gifts	Other (note item, amount)	Comments
1										
2										
3										
4										
5										
6										
7										
8										
9										
10										
11										
12										
13										
14										
Subtotal										
15										
16										
17										
18										
19										
20										
21										
22										
23										
24										
25										
26										
27										
28										
29										
30										
31										
Total										

Total Income	Total Spending	Difference(+/−)	**Actions:** amount to savings, areas for reduced spending, other actions . . . .
$_____	$_____	$_____	

Personal Financial Data

Purpose: To create a record of personal financial information.

Financial Planning Activities: Complete the information requested to provide a quick reference for vital household data. This sheet is also available in an Excel spreadsheet format in Connect Finance.

Suggested Websites: **www.money.com**, **www.kiplinger.com**, **www.20somethingfinance.com**

Name		
Birth Date		
Marital Status		
Address		
Phone		
Email		
Social Security No.		
Driver's License No.		
Place of Employment		
Address		
Phone		
Position		
Length of Service		
Checking Acct. No.		
Financial Inst.		
Address		
Phone		

Dependent Data

Name	Birth date	Relationship	Social Security No.

What's Next for Your Personal Financial Plan?

- Identify financial planning experts (insurance agent, banker, investment adviser, tax preparer, others) you might contact for financial planning information or assistance.
- Discuss with other household members various financial planning priorities.

Suggested App:
- Google Docs

McGraw Hill

Name: _____ Date: _____

Setting Personal Financial Goals

Purpose: To identify personal financial goals and create an action plan.

Financial Planning Activities: Based on personal and household needs and values, identify specific goals that require action. This sheet is also available in an Excel spreadsheet format in Connect Finance.

Suggested Websites: thebalance.com, www.360financialliteracy.org

Short-Term Monetary Goals (less than two years)

Description	Amount needed	Months to achieve	Action to be taken	Priority
Example: Pay off credit card debt	$850	12	Use money from pay raise	High

Intermediate Monetary Goals (two to five years)

Description	Amount needed	Months to achieve	Action to be taken	Priority

Long-Term Monetary Goals (beyond five years)

Description	Amount needed	Years to achieve	Action to be taken	Priority

Nonmonetary Goals

Description	Time frame	Actions to be taken
Example: Set up files for personal financial records and documents	Next 2–3 months	Locate all personal and financial records and add; set up files for various spending, saving, borrowing categories

Suggested App:
• Personal-Capital

McGraw Hill

What's Next for Your Personal Financial Plan?

- Based on various financial goals, calculate the savings deposits necessary to achieve those goals.
- Identify current economic trends that might influence various saving, spending, investing, and borrowing decisions.

Achieving Financial Goals Using Time Value of Money

Purpose: To calculate future and present value amounts related to financial planning decisions.

Financial Planning Activities: Calculate future and present value amounts related to specific financial goals using time value of money tables, a financial calculator, spreadsheet software, or an online calculator. This sheet is also available in an Excel spreadsheet format in Connect Finance.

Suggested Websites: www.moneychimp.com/calculator, www.grunderware.com, www.investopedia.com/calculator

Future Value of a Single Amount

1. To determine future value of a single amount
2. To determine interest lost when cash purchases are made

current amount	times	future value factor	equals	future value amount
$ _____	×	$ _____	=	$ _____

(Use financial calculator, Excel, or Exhibit 1–A in Chapter 1 Appendix.)

Future Value of a Series of Deposits

1. To determine future values of regular savings deposits
2. To determine future value of regular retirement deposits

regular deposit amount	times	future value of annuity factor	equals	future value amount
$ _____	×	$ _____	=	$ _____

(Use financial calculator, Excel, or Exhibit 1–B in Chapter 1 Appendix.)

Present Value of a Single Amount

1. To determine an amount to be deposited now that will grow to desired amount

future amount desired	times	present value factor	equals	present value amount
$ _____	×	$ _____	=	$ _____

(Use financial calculator, Excel, or Exhibit 1–C in Chapter 1 Appendix.)

Present Value of a Series of Deposits

1. To determine an amount that can be withdrawn on a regular basis

regular amount to be withdrawn	times	present value of annuity factor	equals	present value amount
$ _____	×	$ _____	=	$ _____

(Use financial calculator, Excel, or Exhibit 1–D in Chapter 1 Appendix.)

Suggested App:
- TVM Financial Calculator

What's Next for Your Personal Financial Plan?

- Describe some situations in which you could use time value of money calculations for achieving various personal financial goals.
- What specific actions are you taking to achieve various financial goals?

Name: _____ Date: _____

Planning Your Career

Purpose: To become familiar with work activities and career requirements for a field of employment.

Financial Planning Activities: Use various information sources (the *Career Occupational Outlook Handbook, personal contacts,* websites) to obtain information related to one or more career fields of interest to you. This sheet is also available in an Excel spreadsheet format in Connect Finance.

Suggested Websites: www.monster.com, www.rileyguide.com, www.thebalancecareers.com

Career field, job titles	
Nature of the work General activities and duties	
Working conditions Physical surroundings, hours, mental and physical demands	
Training and other qualifications	
Earnings Starting and advanced	
Additional information	
Other questions that require further research	
Sources of additional information Publications, trade associations, professional organizations, government agencies	

What's Next for Your Personal Financial Plan?

- Talk with various people who have worked in the career fields of interest to you.
- Outline a plan for long-term professional development and career advancement.

(*NOTE:* For additional career planning information, see the Chapter 2 Appendix)

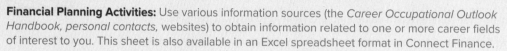

Suggested App:
- Job Search Organizer

McGraw Hill

Chapter 1 Appendix:
Time Value of Money

- "If I deposit $10,000 today, how much will I have for a down payment on a house in five years?"
- "Will $2,000 saved each year give me enough money when I retire?"
- "How much must I save today to have enough for my children's college education?"

The *time value of money,* more commonly referred to as *interest,* is the cost of money that is borrowed or lent. Interest can be compared to rent, the cost of using an apartment or other item. The time value of money is based on the fact that a dollar received today is worth more than a dollar that will be received one year from today because the dollar received today can be saved or invested and will be worth more than a dollar a year from today. Similarly, a dollar that will be received one year from today is currently worth less than a dollar today.

The time value of money has two major components: future value and present value. *Future value* computations, also referred to as *compounding,* yield the amount to which a current sum will increase based on a certain interest rate and period of time. *Present value,* which is calculated through a process called *discounting,* is the current value of a future sum based on a certain interest rate and period of time.

In future value problems, you are given an amount to save or invest and you calculate the amount that will be available at some future date. With present value problems, you are given the amount that will be available at some future date and you calculate the current value of that amount. Both future value and present value computations are based on basic interest rate calculations.

Interest Rate Basics

Simple interest is the dollar cost of borrowing or earnings from lending money. The interest is based on three elements:

- The dollar amount, called the *principal.*
- The *rate of interest.*
- The length of *time.*

The formula and financial calculator computations are as follows:

INTEREST RATE BASICS	
Formula	**Financial Calculator***
Interest = Principal × Rate of interest (annual) × Time (years)	Interest = Amount × Rate × Number of (or portion of) years

The interest rate is stated as a percentage for a year. For example, you must convert 12 percent to either 0.12 or 12/100 before doing your calculations. The time element must also be converted to a decimal or fraction. For example, three months would be shown as 0.25, or 1/4 of a year. Interest for two and a half years would involve a time period of 2.5.

Example A: Suppose you borrow $1,000 at 5 percent and will repay it in one payment at the end of one year. Using the simple interest calculation, the interest is $50, computed as follows:

INTEREST RATE BASICS	
Formula	**Financial Calculator***
$50 = $1,000 × 0.05 × 1 year	$50 = 1000 × .05 × 1

Example B: If you deposited $750 in a savings account paying 8 percent, how much interest would you earn in nine months? You would compute this amount as follows:

Interest = $750 × 0.08 × 3/4 (or 0.75 of a year) = $45	−750 PV , 8 I/Y , 9/12 = .75 N , 0 PMT , CPT
	FV 795. 795 − 750 = 45

*NOTE: These financial calculator notations may require slightly different keystrokes when using various brands and models.

Sample Problem 1

How much interest would you earn if you deposited $300 at 6 percent for 27 months? *(Answers to sample problems are given later in this appendix.)*

Sample Problem 2

How much interest would you pay to borrow $670 for eight months at 12 percent?

Future Value of a Single Amount

The future value of an amount consists of the original amount plus compound interest. This calculation involves the following elements:

$$FV = \text{Future value}$$
$$PV = \text{Present value}$$
$$i = \text{Interest rate}$$
$$n = \text{Number of time periods}$$

The formula and financial calculator computations are as follows:

FUTURE VALUE OF A SINGLE AMOUNT		
Formula	**Table**	**Financial Calculator**
$FV = PV(1 + i)^n$	FV = PV(Table factor)	PV , I/Y , N , PMT , CPT FV

Example C: The future value of $1 at 10 percent after three years is $1.33. This amount is calculated as follows:

$1.33 = $1(1.00 + 0.10)^3	Using Exhibit 1–A: $1.33 = $1.00(1.33)	1 PV , 10 I/Y , 3 N , 0 PMT , CPT FV 1.33

Future value tables are available to help you determine compounded interest amounts (see Exhibit 1–A). Looking at Exhibit 1–A for 10 percent and three years, you can see that $1 would be worth $1.33 at that time. For other amounts, multiply the table factor by the original amount. This process may be viewed as follows:

Future value (rounded)	$1		$1.10		$1.21		FV = $1.33
		Interest $0.10		Interest $0.11		Interest $0.12	
After year	0		1		2		3

FUTURE VALUE OF A SINGLE AMOUNT		
Formula	**Table**	**Financial Calculator**
Example D: If your savings of $400 earns 12 percent, compounded *monthly,* over a year and a half, use the table factor for 1 percent (the monthly rate) for 18 time periods; the future value would be:		
$478.46 = $400 (1 + 0.01)^{18}$	$478.40 = $400 (1.196)$	-400 PV, $12/12 = 1$ I/Y, $1.5 \times 12 = 18$ N, 0 PMT, CPT FV 478.46
Excel formula notation for future value of a single amount	=FV(rate, nper, pmt, pv, type)	
	Example D solution =FV(0.01,18, 0,−400) = 478.46	

Sample Problem 3

What is the future value of $800 at 8 percent after six years?

Sample Problem 4

How much would you have in savings if you kept $200 on deposit for eight years at 8 percent, compounded *semiannually?*

Future Value of a Series of Equal Amounts (an Annuity)

Future value may also be calculated for a situation in which regular additions are made to savings. The formula and financial calculator computations are as follows:

FUTURE VALUE OF A SERIES OF EQUAL AMOUNTS (ANNUITY)		
Formula	**Table**	**Financial Calculator**
$FV = \text{Annuity} \dfrac{(1 + i)^n - 1}{i}$	Using Exhibit 1–B: Annuity × Table factor	PMT, N, I/Y, PV, CPT FV
This calculation assumes that (1) each deposit is for the same amount, (2) the interest rate is the same for each time period, and (3) the deposits are made at the end of each time period.		
Example E: The future value of three $1 deposits made at the end of the next three years, earning 10 percent interest, is $3.31. This is calculated as follows:		
$3.31 = $1\dfrac{(1 + 0.10)^3 - 1}{0.10}$	Using Exhibit 1–B: $3.31 = $1 × 3.31	-1 PMT, 3 N, 10 I/Y, 0 PV, CPT FV 3.31

This may be viewed as follows:

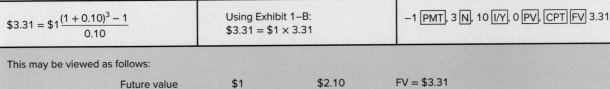

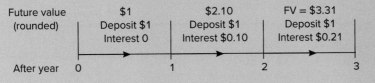

FUTURE VALUE OF A SERIES OF EQUAL AMOUNTS

Formula	Table	Financial Calculator
Example F: If you plan to deposit $40 a year for 10 years, earning 8 percent compounded annually, the future value of this amount is:		
$579.46 = \$40 \dfrac{(1 + 0.08)^{10} - 1}{0.08}$	Using Exhibit 1–B $579.48 = $40(14.487)$	-40 PMT , 10 N , 10 I/Y , 0 PV , CPT FV 579.46
Excel formula notation for future value of a series	=FV(rate, nper, pmt)	
	Example F solution =FV(0.08,10,240) = 579.46	

Sample Problem 5

What is the future value of an annual deposit of $230 earning 6 percent for 15 years?

Sample Problem 6

What amount would you have in a retirement account if you made annual deposits of $375 for 25 years earning 12 percent, compounded annually?

Present Value of a Single Amount

If you want to know how much you need to deposit now to receive a certain amount in the future, the formula and financial calculator computations are as follows:

PRESENT VALUE OF A SINGLE AMOUNT

Formula	Table	Financial Calculator
$PV? = ?\dfrac{FV}{(1 + i)^n}$	Using Exhibit 1–C: PV = FV(Table factor)	FV , N , I/Y , PMT , CPT PV
Example G: The present value of $1 to be received three years from now based on a 10 percent interest rate is calculated as follows:		
$\$0.75 = \dfrac{\$1}{(1 + 0.10)^3}$	Using Exhibit 1–C: $0.75 = $1(0.751)$	1 FV , 3 N , 10 I/Y , 0 PMT , CPT PV – .75131

This may be viewed as follows:

Present value (rounded)	$0.75		$0.83		$0.91		$1
		Discount (interest) $0.075		Discount (interest) $0.0825		Discount (interest) $0.0905	
After year	0		1		2		3

Present value tables are available to assist you in this process (see Exhibit 1–C). Notice that $1 at 10 percent for three years has a present value of $0.75. For amounts other than $1, multiply the table factor by the amount involved.

Example H: If you want to have $300 seven years from now and your savings earn 10 percent, compounded *semiannually* (which would be 5 percent for 14 time periods), finding how much you would have to deposit today is calculated as follows:

Formula	Table	Financial Calculator
$\$151.52 = \dfrac{\$300}{(1 + 0.05)^{14}}$	Using Exhibit 1–C: $151.50 = $300(0.505)$	300 FV , 7 × 2 = 14 N , 10/2 = 5 I/Y , 0 PMT , CPT PV – 151.52
Excel formula notation for present value of a single amount	=PV(rate, nper, pmt, fv, type)	
	Example H solution: =PV(0.05,14, 0,–300) = 151.52	

Sample Problem 7

What is the present value of $2,200 earning 15 percent for eight years?

Sample Problem 8

To have $6,000 for a child's education in 10 years, what amount should a parent deposit in a savings account that earns 12 percent, compounded *quarterly?*

Present Value of a Series of Equal Amounts (an Annuity)

The final time value of money situation allows you to receive an amount at the end of each time period for a certain number of periods. The formula and financial calculator computations are as follows:

PRESENT VALUE OF A SERIES OF EQUAL AMOUNTS (ANNUITY)		
Formula	**Table**	**Financial Calculator**
$PV = \text{Annuity} \times \dfrac{1 - \dfrac{1}{(1+i)^n}}{i}$	Using Exhibit 1–D: PV = Annuity(Table factor)	PMT, N, I/Y, FV, CPT PV
Example I: The present value of a $1 withdrawal at the end of the next three years would be $2.49, for money earning 10 percent. This would be calculated as follows:		
$\$2.49 = \$1\left[\dfrac{1 - \dfrac{1}{(1 + 0.10)^3}}{0.10}\right]$	Using Exhibit 1–D: $2.49 = $1(2.487)	1 PMT, 3 N, 10 I/Y, 0 FV, CPT PV – 2.48685

This may be viewed as follows:

Present value $2.49 $1.74 $0.91 $0
(fund balance)   Withdrawal – $1   Withdrawal – $1   Withdrawal – $1
                    Interest + $0.25   Interest + $0.17   Interest + $0.09

After year   0   1   2   3

This same amount appears in Exhibit 1–D for 10 percent and three time periods. To use the table for other situations, multiply the table factor by the amount to be withdrawn each year.

Example J: If you wish to withdraw $100 at the end of each year for 10 years from an account that earns 14 percent, compounded annually, what amount must you deposit now?

$\$521.61 = \$100\left(\dfrac{1 - \dfrac{1}{(1 + 0.14)^{10}}}{0.14}\right)$	Using Exhibit 1–D: $521.60 = $100(5.216)	100 PMT, 10 N, 14 I/Y, 0 FV, CPT PV – 521.61
Excel formula notation for present value of a series	=PV(rate, nper, pmt)	
	Example J solution =PV(0.14,10,–100) = 521.61	

Sample Problem 9

What is the present value of a withdrawal of $200 at the end of each year for 14 years with an interest rate of 7 percent?

Sample Problem 10

How much would you have to deposit now to be able to withdraw $650 at the end of each year for 20 years from an account that earns 11 percent?

Using Present Value to Determine Loan Payments

Present value tables (Exhibit 1–D) can also be used to determine installment payments for a loan as follows:

PRESENT VALUE TO DETERMINE LOAN PAYMENTS	
Table	**Financial Calculator**
$$\frac{\text{Amount borrowed}}{\text{Present value of a series table factor (Exhibit 1–D)}} = \text{Loan payment}$$	PV, I/Y, N, FV, CPT PMT
Example K: If you borrow $1,000 with a 6 percent interest rate to be repaid in three equal payments at the end of the next three years, the payments will be $374.11. This is calculated as follows:	
$$\frac{\$1,000}{2.673} = \$374.11$$	1000 PV, 6 I/Y, 3 N, 0 FV, CPT PMT – 374.10981
Excel formula notation for determining loan payment amount	=PMT(rate, nper, pv)
	Example K solution =PMT(.06, 3, −1000) = $374.11

Sample Problem 11

What would be the annual payment amount for a $20,000, 10-year loan at 7 percent?

Answers to Sample Problems (based on TVM tables)

1. $300 × 0.06 × 2.25 years (27 months) = $40.50.
2. $670 × 0.12 × 2/3 (of a year) = $53.60.
3. $800(1.587) = $1,269.60. (Use Exhibit 1–A, 8 percent, 6 periods.)
4. $200(1.873) = $374.60. (Use Exhibit 1–A, 4 percent, 16 periods.)
5. $230(23.276) = $5,353.48. (Use Exhibit 1–B, 6 percent, 15 periods.)
6. $375(133.33) = $49,998.75. (Use Exhibit 1–B, 12 percent, 25 periods.)
7. $2,200(0.327) = $719.40. (Use Exhibit 1–C, 15 percent, 8 periods.)
8. $6,000(0.307) = $1,842. (Use Exhibit 1–C, 3 percent, 40 periods.)
9. $200(8.745) = $1,749. (Use Exhibit 1–D, 7 percent, 14 periods.)
10. $650(7.963) = $5,175.95. (Use Exhibit 1–D, 11 percent, 20 periods.)
11. $20,000/7.024 = $2,847.38. (Use Exhibit 1–D, 7 percent, 10 periods.)

Time Value of Money Application Exercises

1. **(Present value of an annuity)** You wish to borrow $18,000 to buy a new automobile. The rate is 8.6 percent over four years with monthly payments. Find the monthly payment. (Answer: $444.52)

2. **(Present value of an annuity)** How much money must your rich uncle give you now to finance four years of college, assuming an annual cost of $48,000 and an interest rate of 6 percent (applied to the principal until disbursed)? (Answer: $166,325.07)

3. **(Present value of a single amount)** How much money must you set aside at age 20 to accumulate retirement funds of $100,000 at age 65, assuming a rate of interest of 7 percent? (Answer: $4,761.35)

4. **(Future value of a single amount)** If you deposit $2,000 in a five-year certificate of deposit at 5.2 percent, how much will it be worth in five years? (Answer: $2,576.97)

5. **(Future value of a single amount)** If you deposit $2,000 in a five-year certificate of deposit at 5.2 percent with quarterly compounding, how much will it be worth in five years? (Answer: $2,589.52)

6. **(Future value of an annuity)** You choose to invest $50 per month in a 401(k) that invests in an international stock mutual fund. Assuming an annual rate of return of 9 percent, how much will this fund be worth if you are retiring in 40 years? (Answer: $234,066.01)

7. **(Future value of an annuity)** Instead, you invest $600 per year in a 401(k) that invests in an international stock mutual fund. Assuming an annual rate of return of 9 percent, how much will this fund be worth if you are retiring in 40 years? (Answer: $202,729.47)

Time Value of Money Calculation Methods: A Summary

The time value of money may be calculated using a variety of techniques. When achieving specific financial goals requires regular deposits to a savings or investment account, the computation may occur in one of several ways. For example, Jonie Emerson plans to deposit $10,000 in an account for the next 10 years. She estimates these funds will earn an annual rate of 5 percent. What amount can Jonie expect to have available after 10 years?

Method	Process, Results
Formula Calculation The most basic method of calculating the time value of money involves using a formula.	For this situation, the formula would be: $$PV(1 + i)^n = FV$$ The result should be $$\$10,000 \, (1 + 0.05)^{10} = \$16,288.95$$
Time Value of Money Tables Instead of calculating with a formula, time value of money tables are available. The numeric factors presented ease the computational process.	Using the table in Exhibit 1–A: $10,000 Future value of $1, 5%, 10 years $10,000 × 1.629 = $16,290
Financial Calculator A variety of financial calculators are programmed with various financial functions. Both future value and present value calculations may be performed using the appropriate keystrokes.	Using a financial calculator, the keystrokes would be: Amount −10,000 $\boxed{PV}$ Time periods 10 $\boxed{N}$ Interest rate 5 $\boxed{I}$ Result $\boxed{FV}$ $16,288.94
Spreadsheet Software Excel and other software programs have built-in formulas for various financial computations, including time value of money.	When using a spreadsheet program, this type of calculation would require this format: = FV(rate, periods, amount per period, single amount) The results of this example would be: = FV(0.05, 10, 0, −10,000) = $16,288.95
Time Value of Money Websites Many time value of money calculators are available online. These web-based programs perform calculations for the future value of savings as well as determine amounts for loan payments.	Some easy-to-use calculators for computing the time value of money and other financial computations are located at • www.fncalculator.com/ • www.dinkytown.net • www.moneychimp.com/calculator • money.cnn.com/tools
Mobile Apps Financial tools on a mobile device are available for time value of money calculations.	• TVM Financial Calculator • Time Value of Money Calculator • FV & PV Calculator

NOTE: The slight differences in answers are the result of rounding.

Exhibit 1–A Future Value (Compounded Sum) of $1 after a Given Number of Time Periods

Period	1%	2%	3%	4%	5%	6%	7%	8%	9%	10%	11%
1	1.010	1.020	1.030	1.040	1.050	1.060	1.070	1.080	1.090	1.100	1.110
2	1.020	1.040	1.061	1.082	1.103	1.124	1.145	1.166	1.188	1.210	1.232
3	1.030	1.061	1.093	1.125	1.158	1.191	1.225	1.260	1.295	1.331	1.368
4	1.041	1.082	1.126	1.170	1.216	1.262	1.311	1.360	1.412	1.464	1.518
5	1.051	1.104	1.159	1.217	1.276	1.338	1.403	1.469	1.539	1.611	1.685
6	1.062	1.126	1.194	1.265	1.340	1.419	1.501	1.587	1.677	1.772	1.870
7	1.072	1.149	1.230	1.316	1.407	1.504	1.606	1.714	1.828	1.949	2.076
8	1.083	1.172	1.267	1.369	1.477	1.594	1.718	1.851	1.993	2.144	2.305
9	1.094	1.195	1.305	1.423	1.551	1.689	1.838	1.999	2.172	2.358	2.558
10	1.105	1.219	1.344	1.480	1.629	1.791	1.967	2.159	2.367	2.594	2.839
11	1.116	1.243	1.384	1.539	1.710	1.898	2.105	2.332	2.580	2.853	3.152
12	1.127	1.268	1.426	1.601	1.796	2.012	2.252	2.518	2.813	3.138	3.498
13	1.138	1.294	1.469	1.665	1.886	2.133	2.410	2.720	3.066	3.452	3.883
14	1.149	1.319	1.513	1.732	1.980	2.261	2.579	2.937	3.342	3.797	4.310
15	1.161	1.346	1.558	1.801	2.079	2.397	2.759	3.172	3.642	4.177	4.785
16	1.173	1.373	1.605	1.873	2.183	2.540	2.952	3.426	3.970	4.595	5.311
17	1.184	1.400	1.653	1.948	2.292	2.693	3.159	3.700	4.328	5.054	5.895
18	1.196	1.428	1.702	2.026	2.407	2.854	3.380	3.996	4.717	5.560	6.544
19	1.208	1.457	1.754	2.107	2.527	3.026	3.617	4.316	5.142	6.116	7.263
20	1.220	1.486	1.806	2.191	2.653	3.207	3.870	4.661	5.604	6.727	8.062
25	1.282	1.641	2.094	2.666	3.386	4.292	5.427	6.848	8.623	10.835	13.585
30	1.348	1.811	2.427	3.243	4.322	5.743	7.612	10.063	13.268	17.449	22.892
40	1.489	2.208	3.262	4.801	7.040	10.286	14.974	21.725	31.409	45.259	65.001
50	1.645	2.692	4.384	7.107	11.467	18.420	29.457	46.902	74.358	117.390	184.570

Period	12%	13%	14%	15%	16%	17%	18%	19%	20%	25%	30%
1	1.120	1.130	1.140	1.150	1.160	1.170	1.180	1.190	1.200	1.250	1.300
2	1.254	1.277	1.300	1.323	1.346	1.369	1.392	1.416	1.440	1.563	1.690
3	1.405	1.443	1.482	1.521	1.561	1.602	1.643	1.685	1.728	1.953	2.197
4	1.574	1.630	1.689	1.749	1.811	1.874	1.939	2.005	2.074	2.441	2.856
5	1.762	1.842	1.925	2.011	2.100	2.192	2.288	2.386	2.488	3.052	3.713
6	1.974	2.082	2.195	2.313	2.436	2.565	2.700	2.840	2.986	3.815	4.827
7	2.211	2.353	2.502	2.660	2.826	3.001	3.185	3.379	3.583	4.768	6.276
8	2.476	2.658	2.853	3.059	3.278	3.511	3.759	4.021	4.300	5.960	8.157
9	2.773	3.004	3.252	3.518	3.803	4.108	4.435	4.785	5.160	7.451	10.604
10	3.106	3.395	3.707	4.046	4.411	4.807	5.234	5.696	6.192	9.313	13.786
11	3.479	3.836	4.226	4.652	5.117	5.624	6.176	6.777	7.430	11.642	17.922
12	3.896	4.335	4.818	5.350	5.936	6.580	7.288	8.064	8.916	14.552	23.298
13	4.363	4.898	5.492	6.153	6.886	7.699	8.599	9.596	10.699	18.190	30.288
14	4.887	5.535	6.261	7.076	7.988	9.007	10.147	11.420	12.839	22.737	39.374
15	5.474	6.254	7.138	8.137	9.266	10.539	11.974	13.590	15.407	28.422	51.186
16	6.130	7.067	8.137	9.358	10.748	12.330	14.129	16.172	18.488	35.527	66.542
17	6.866	7.986	9.276	10.761	12.468	14.426	16.672	19.244	22.186	44.409	86.504
18	7.690	9.024	10.575	12.375	14.463	16.879	19.673	22.091	26.623	55.511	112.460
19	8.613	10.197	12.056	14.232	16.777	19.748	23.214	27.252	31.948	69.389	146.190
20	9.646	11.523	13.743	16.367	19.461	23.106	27.393	32.429	38.338	86.736	190.050
25	17.000	21.231	26.462	32.919	40.874	50.658	62.669	77.388	95.396	264.700	705.640
30	29.960	39.116	50.950	66.212	85.850	111.070	143.370	184.680	237.380	807.790	2,620.000
40	93.051	132.780	188.880	267.860	378.720	533.870	750.380	1,051.700	1,469.800	7,523.200	36,119.000
50	289.000	450.740	700.230	1,083.700	1,670.700	2,566.200	3,927.400	5,998.900	9,100.400	70,065.000	497,929.000

Exhibit 1-B   Future Value (Compounded Sum) of $1 Paid In at the End of Each Period for a Given Number of Time Periods (an Annuity)

Period	1%	2%	3%	4%	5%	6%	7%	8%	9%	10%	11%
1	1.000	1.000	1.000	1.000	1.000	1.000	1.000	1.000	1.000	1.000	1.000
2	2.010	2.020	2.030	2.040	2.050	2.060	2.070	2.080	2.090	2.100	2.110
3	3.030	3.060	3.091	3.122	3.153	3.184	3.215	3.246	3.278	3.310	3.342
4	4.060	4.122	4.184	4.246	4.310	4.375	4.440	4.506	4.573	4.641	4.710
5	5.101	5.204	5.309	5.416	5.526	5.637	5.751	5.867	5.985	6.105	6.228
6	6.152	6.308	6.468	6.633	6.802	6.975	7.153	7.336	7.523	7.716	7.913
7	7.214	7.434	7.662	7.898	8.142	8.394	8.654	8.923	9.200	9.487	9.783
8	8.286	8.583	8.892	9.214	9.549	9.897	10.260	10.637	11.028	11.436	11.859
9	9.369	9.755	10.159	10.583	11.027	11.491	11.978	12.488	13.021	13.579	14.164
10	10.462	10.950	11.464	12.006	12.578	13.181	13.816	14.487	15.193	15.937	16.722
11	11.567	12.169	12.808	13.486	14.207	14.972	15.784	16.645	17.560	18.531	19.561
12	12.683	13.412	14.192	15.026	15.917	16.870	17.888	18.977	20.141	21.384	22.713
13	13.809	14.680	15.618	16.627	17.713	18.882	20.141	21.495	22.953	24.523	26.212
14	14.947	15.974	17.086	18.292	19.599	21.015	22.550	24.215	26.019	27.975	30.095
15	16.097	17.293	18.599	20.024	21.579	23.276	25.129	27.152	29.361	31.772	34.405
16	17.258	18.639	20.157	21.825	23.657	25.673	27.888	30.324	33.003	35.950	39.190
17	18.430	20.012	21.762	23.698	25.840	28.213	30.840	33.750	36.974	40.545	44.501
18	19.615	21.412	23.414	25.645	28.132	30.906	33.999	37.450	41.301	45.599	50.396
19	20.811	22.841	25.117	27.671	30.539	33.760	37.379	41.446	46.018	51.159	56.939
20	22.019	24.297	26.870	29.778	33.066	36.786	40.995	45.762	51.160	57.275	64.203
25	28.243	32.030	36.459	41.646	47.727	54.865	63.249	73.106	84.701	98.347	114.410
30	34.785	40.588	47.575	56.085	66.439	79.058	94.461	113.280	136.310	164.490	199.020
40	48.886	60.402	75.401	95.026	120.800	154.760	199.640	259.060	337.890	442.590	581.830
50	64.463	84.579	112.800	152.670	209.350	290.340	406.530	573.770	815.080	1,163.900	1,668.800

Period	12%	13%	14%	15%	16%	17%	18%	19%	20%	25%	30%
1	1.000	1.000	1.000	1.000	1.000	1.000	1.000	1.000	1.000	1.000	1.000
2	2.120	2.130	2.140	2.150	2.160	2.170	2.180	2.190	2.200	2.250	2.300
3	3.374	3.407	3.440	3.473	3.506	3.539	3.572	3.606	3.640	3.813	3.990
4	4.779	4.850	4.921	4.993	5.066	5.141	5.215	5.291	5.368	5.766	6.187
5	6.353	6.480	6.610	6.742	6.877	7.014	7.154	7.297	7.442	8.207	9.043
6	8.115	8.323	8.536	8.754	8.977	9.207	9.442	9.683	9.930	11.259	12.756
7	10.089	10.405	10.730	11.067	11.414	11.772	12.142	12.523	12.916	15.073	17.583
8	12.300	12.757	13.233	13.727	14.240	14.773	15.327	15.902	16.499	19.842	23.858
9	14.776	15.416	16.085	16.786	17.519	18.285	19.086	19.923	20.799	25.802	32.015
10	17.549	18.420	19.337	20.304	21.321	22.393	23.521	24.701	25.959	33.253	42.619
11	20.655	21.814	23.045	24.349	25.733	27.200	28.755	30.404	32.150	42.566	56.405
12	24.133	25.650	27.271	29.002	30.850	32.824	34.931	37.180	39.581	54.208	74.327
13	28.029	29.985	32.089	34.352	36.786	39.404	42.219	45.244	48.497	68.760	97.625
14	32.393	34.883	37.581	40.505	43.672	47.103	50.818	54.841	59.196	86.949	127.910
15	37.280	40.417	43.842	47.580	51.660	56.110	60.965	66.261	72.035	109.690	167.290
16	42.753	46.672	50.980	55.717	60.925	66.649	72.939	79.850	87.442	138.110	218.470
17	48.884	53.739	59.118	65.075	71.673	78.979	87.068	96.022	105.930	173.640	285.010
18	55.750	61.725	68.394	75.836	84.141	93.406	103.740	115.270	128.120	218.050	371.520
19	63.440	70.749	78.969	88.212	98.603	110.290	123.410	138.170	154.740	273.560	483.970
20	72.052	80.947	91.025	102.440	115.380	130.030	146.630	165.420	186.690	342.950	630.170
25	133.330	155.620	181.870	212.790	249.210	292.110	342.600	402.040	471.980	1,054.800	2,348.800
30	241.330	293.200	356.790	434.750	530.310	647.440	790.950	966.700	1,181.900	3,227.200	8,730.000
40	767.090	1,013.700	1,342.000	1,779.100	2,360.800	3,134.500	4,163.210	5,529.800	7,343.900	30,089.000	120,393.000
50	2,400.000	3,459.500	4,994.500	7,217.700	10,436.000	15,090.000	21,813.000	31,515.000	45,497.000	80,256.000	165,976.000

Exhibit 1–C Present Value of $1 to Be Received at the End of a Given Number of Time Periods

Period	1%	2%	3%	4%	5%	6%	7%	8%	9%	10%	11%	12%
1	0.990	0.980	0.971	0.962	0.952	0.943	0.935	0.926	0.917	0.909	0.901	0.893
2	0.980	0.961	0.943	0.925	0.907	0.890	0.873	0.857	0.842	0.826	0.812	0.797
3	0.971	0.942	0.915	0.889	0.864	0.840	0.816	0.794	0.772	0.751	0.731	0.712
4	0.961	0.924	0.888	0.855	0.823	0.792	0.763	0.735	0.708	0.683	0.659	0.636
5	0.951	0.906	0.863	0.822	0.784	0.747	0.713	0.681	0.650	0.621	0.593	0.567
6	0.942	0.888	0.837	0.790	0.746	0.705	0.666	0.630	0.596	0.564	0.535	0.507
7	0.933	0.871	0.813	0.760	0.711	0.665	0.623	0.583	0.547	0.513	0.482	0.452
8	0.923	0.853	0.789	0.731	0.677	0.627	0.582	0.540	0.502	0.467	0.434	0.404
9	0.914	0.837	0.766	0.703	0.645	0.592	0.544	0.500	0.460	0.424	0.391	0.361
10	0.905	0.820	0.744	0.676	0.614	0.558	0.508	0.463	0.422	0.386	0.352	0.322
11	0.896	0.804	0.722	0.650	0.585	0.527	0.475	0.429	0.388	0.350	0.317	0.287
12	0.887	0.788	0.701	0.625	0.557	0.497	0.444	0.397	0.356	0.319	0.286	0.257
13	0.879	0.773	0.681	0.601	0.530	0.469	0.415	0.368	0.326	0.290	0.258	0.229
14	0.870	0.758	0.661	0.577	0.505	0.442	0.388	0.340	0.299	0.263	0.232	0.205
15	0.861	0.743	0.642	0.555	0.481	0.417	0.362	0.315	0.275	0.239	0.209	0.183
16	0.853	0.728	0.623	0.534	0.458	0.394	0.339	0.292	0.252	0.218	0.188	0.163
17	0.844	0.714	0.605	0.513	0.436	0.371	0.317	0.270	0.231	0.198	0.170	0.146
18	0.836	0.700	0.587	0.494	0.416	0.350	0.296	0.250	0.212	0.180	0.153	0.130
19	0.828	0.686	0.570	0.475	0.396	0.331	0.277	0.232	0.194	0.164	0.138	0.116
20	0.820	0.673	0.554	0.456	0.377	0.312	0.258	0.215	0.178	0.149	0.124	0.104
25	0.780	0.610	0.478	0.375	0.295	0.233	0.184	0.146	0.116	0.092	0.074	0.059
30	0.742	0.552	0.412	0.308	0.231	0.174	0.131	0.099	0.075	0.057	0.044	0.033
40	0.672	0.453	0.307	0.208	0.142	0.097	0.067	0.046	0.032	0.022	0.015	0.011
50	0.608	0.372	0.228	0.141	0.087	0.054	0.034	0.021	0.013	0.009	0.005	0.003

Period	13%	14%	15%	16%	17%	18%	19%	20%	25%	30%	35%	40%	50%
1	0.885	0.877	0.870	0.862	0.855	0.847	0.840	0.833	0.800	0.769	0.741	0.714	0.667
2	0.783	0.769	0.756	0.743	0.731	0.718	0.706	0.694	0.640	0.592	0.549	0.510	0.444
3	0.693	0.675	0.658	0.641	0.624	0.609	0.593	0.579	0.512	0.455	0.406	0.364	0.296
4	0.613	0.592	0.572	0.552	0.534	0.515	0.499	0.482	0.410	0.350	0.301	0.260	0.198
5	0.543	0.519	0.497	0.476	0.456	0.437	0.419	0.402	0.320	0.269	0.223	0.186	0.132
6	0.480	0.456	0.432	0.410	0.390	0.370	0.352	0.335	0.262	0.207	0.165	0.133	0.088
7	0.425	0.400	0.376	0.354	0.333	0.314	0.296	0.279	0.210	0.159	0.122	0.095	0.059
8	0.376	0.351	0.327	0.305	0.285	0.266	0.249	0.233	0.168	0.123	0.091	0.068	0.039
9	0.333	0.300	0.284	0.263	0.243	0.225	0.209	0.194	0.134	0.094	0.067	0.048	0.026
10	0.295	0.270	0.247	0.227	0.208	0.191	0.176	0.162	0.107	0.073	0.050	0.035	0.017
11	0.261	0.237	0.215	0.195	0.178	0.162	0.148	0.135	0.086	0.056	0.037	0.025	0.012
12	0.231	0.208	0.187	0.168	0.152	0.137	0.124	0.112	0.069	0.043	0.027	0.018	0.008
13	0.204	0.182	0.163	0.145	0.130	0.116	0.104	0.093	0.055	0.033	0.020	0.013	0.005
14	0.181	0.160	0.141	0.125	0.111	0.099	0.088	0.078	0.044	0.025	0.015	0.009	0.003
15	0.160	0.140	0.123	0.108	0.095	0.084	0.074	0.065	0.035	0.020	0.011	0.006	0.002
16	0.141	0.123	0.107	0.093	0.081	0.071	0.062	0.054	0.028	0.015	0.008	0.005	0.002
17	0.125	0.108	0.093	0.080	0.069	0.060	0.052	0.045	0.023	0.012	0.006	0.003	0.001
18	0.111	0.095	0.081	0.069	0.059	0.051	0.044	0.038	0.018	0.009	0.005	0.002	0.001
19	0.098	0.083	0.070	0.060	0.051	0.043	0.037	0.031	0.014	0.007	0.003	0.002	0
20	0.087	0.073	0.061	0.051	0.043	0.037	0.031	0.026	0.012	0.005	0.002	0.001	0
25	0.047	0.038	0.030	0.024	0.020	0.016	0.013	0.010	0.004	0.001	0.001	0	0
30	0.026	0.020	0.015	0.012	0.009	0.007	0.005	0.004	0.001	0	0	0	0
40	0.008	0.005	0.004	0.003	0.002	0.001	0.001	0.001	0	0	0	0	0
50	0.002	0.001	0.001	0.001	0	0	0	0	0	0	0	0	0

Exhibit 1–D Present Value of $1 Received at the End of Each Period for a Given Number of Time Periods (an Annuity)

Period	1%	2%	3%	4%	5%	6%	7%	8%	9%	10%	11%	12%
1	0.990	0.980	0.971	0.962	0.952	0.943	0.935	0.926	0.917	0.909	0.901	0.893
2	1.970	1.942	1.913	1.886	1.859	1.833	1.808	1.783	1.759	1.736	1.713	1.690
3	2.941	2.884	2.829	2.775	2.723	2.673	2.624	2.577	2.531	2.487	2.444	2.402
4	3.902	3.808	3.717	3.630	3.546	3.465	3.387	3.312	3.240	3.170	3.102	3.037
5	4.853	4.713	4.580	4.452	4.329	4.212	4.100	3.993	3.890	3.791	3.696	3.605
6	5.795	5.601	5.417	5.242	5.076	4.917	4.767	4.623	4.486	4.355	4.231	4.111
7	6.728	6.472	6.230	6.002	5.786	5.582	5.389	5.206	5.033	4.868	4.712	4.564
8	7.652	7.325	7.020	6.733	6.463	6.210	5.971	5.747	5.535	5.335	5.146	4.968
9	8.566	8.162	7.786	7.435	7.108	6.802	6.515	6.247	5.995	5.759	5.537	5.328
10	9.471	8.983	8.530	8.111	7.722	7.360	7.024	6.710	6.418	6.145	5.889	5.650
11	10.368	9.787	9.253	8.760	8.306	7.887	7.499	7.139	6.805	6.495	6.207	5.938
12	11.255	10.575	9.954	9.385	8.863	8.384	7.943	7.536	7.161	6.814	6.492	6.194
13	12.134	11.348	10.635	9.986	9.394	8.853	8.358	7.904	7.487	7.103	6.750	6.424
14	13.004	12.106	11.296	10.563	9.899	9.295	8.745	8.244	7.786	7.367	6.982	6.628
15	13.865	12.849	11.939	11.118	10.380	9.712	9.108	8.559	8.061	7.606	7.191	6.811
16	14.718	13.578	12.561	11.652	10.838	10.106	9.447	8.851	8.313	7.824	7.379	6.974
17	15.562	14.292	13.166	12.166	11.274	10.477	9.763	9.122	8.544	8.022	7.549	7.102
18	16.398	14.992	13.754	12.659	11.690	10.828	10.059	9.372	8.756	8.201	7.702	7.250
19	17.226	15.678	14.324	13.134	12.085	11.158	10.336	9.604	8.950	8.365	7.839	7.366
20	18.046	16.351	14.877	13.590	12.462	11.470	10.594	9.818	9.129	8.514	7.963	7.469
25	22.023	19.523	17.413	15.622	14.094	12.783	11.654	10.675	9.823	9.077	8.422	7.843
30	25.808	22.396	19.600	17.292	15.372	13.765	12.409	11.258	10.274	9.427	8.694	8.055
40	32.835	27.355	23.115	19.793	17.159	15.046	13.332	11.925	10.757	9.779	8.951	8.244
50	39.196	31.424	25.730	21.482	18.256	15.762	13.801	12.233	10.962	9.915	9.042	8.304

Period	13%	14%	15%	16%	17%	18%	19%	20%	25%	30%	35%	40%	50%
1	0.885	0.877	0.870	0.862	0.855	0.847	0.840	0.833	0.800	0.769	0.741	0.714	0.667
2	1.668	1.647	1.626	1.605	1.585	1.566	1.547	1.528	1.440	1.361	1.289	1.224	1.111
3	2.361	2.322	2.283	2.246	2.210	2.174	2.140	2.106	1.952	1.816	1.696	1.589	1.407
4	2.974	2.914	2.855	2.798	2.743	2.690	2.639	2.589	2.362	2.166	1.997	1.849	1.605
5	3.517	3.433	3.352	3.274	3.199	3.127	3.058	2.991	2.689	2.436	2.220	2.035	1.737
6	3.998	3.889	3.784	3.685	3.589	3.498	3.410	3.326	2.951	2.643	2.385	2.168	1.824
7	4.423	4.288	4.160	4.039	3.922	3.812	3.706	3.605	3.161	2.802	2.508	2.263	1.883
8	4.799	4.639	4.487	4.344	4.207	4.078	3.954	3.837	3.329	2.925	2.598	2.331	1.922
9	5.132	4.946	4.772	4.607	4.451	4.303	4.163	4.031	3.463	3.019	2.665	2.379	1.948
10	5.426	5.216	5.019	4.833	4.659	4.494	4.339	4.192	3.571	3.092	2.715	2.414	1.965
11	5.687	5.453	5.234	5.029	4.836	4.656	4.486	4.327	3.656	3.147	2.752	2.438	1.977
12	5.918	5.660	5.421	5.197	4.988	4.793	4.611	4.439	3.725	3.190	2.779	2.456	1.985
13	6.122	5.842	5.583	5.342	5.118	4.910	4.715	4.533	3.780	3.223	2.799	2.469	1.990
14	6.302	6.002	5.724	5.468	5.229	5.008	4.802	4.611	3.824	3.249	2.814	2.478	1.993
15	6.462	6.142	5.847	5.575	5.324	5.092	4.876	4.675	3.859	3.268	2.825	2.484	1.995
16	6.604	6.265	5.954	5.668	5.405	5.162	4.938	4.730	3.887	3.283	2.834	2.489	1.997
17	6.729	6.373	6.047	5.749	5.475	5.222	4.988	4.775	3.910	3.295	2.840	2.492	1.998
18	6.840	6.467	6.128	5.818	5.534	5.273	5.033	4.812	3.928	3.304	2.844	2.494	1.999
19	6.938	6.550	6.198	5.877	5.584	5.316	5.070	4.843	3.942	3.311	2.848	2.496	1.999
20	7.025	6.623	6.259	5.929	5.628	5.353	5.101	4.870	3.954	3.316	2.850	2.497	1.999
25	7.330	6.873	6.464	6.097	5.766	5.467	5.195	4.948	3.985	3.329	2.856	2.499	2.000
30	7.496	7.003	6.566	6.177	5.829	5.517	5.235	4.979	3.995	3.332	2.857	2.500	2.000
40	7.634	7.105	6.642	6.233	5.871	5.548	5.258	4.997	3.999	3.333	2.857	2.500	2.000
50	7.675	7.133	6.661	6.246	5.880	5.554	5.262	4.999	4.000	3.333	2.857	2.500	2.000

2 Money Management Skills

3 Steps to Financial Literacy . . .
Improved Cash Flow

1 Plan a system to monitor your cash inflows (income) and outflows (spending).
App: Spending Tracker

2 Identify your fixed expenses. Seek actions to take to control and reduce variable expenses.
Website: thebalance.com

3 Spend according to your plan to avoid a negative cash flow and to avoid debt problems.
App: YNAB

Why is an improved cash flow important for your financial situation?

A positive monthly cash flow will allow you to set aside funds for future financial security and avoid financial difficulties. At the end of the chapter, *Your Personal Finance Road Map and Dashboard* will provide additional information on measuring your cash flow situation.

CHAPTER 2 LEARNING OBJECTIVES

In this chapter, you will learn to:

LO2.1 Identify the main components of wise money management.

LO2.2 Create a personal balance sheet and cash flow statement.

LO2.3 Develop and implement a personal budget.

LO2.4 Connect money management activities with saving for personal financial goals.

YOUR PERSONAL FINANCIAL PLAN SHEETS

5. Financial Documents and Records
6. Creating a Personal Balance Sheet
7. Creating a Personal Cash Flow Statement
8. Developing a Personal Budget

A Successful Money Management Plan

"Each month, I have too many days and not enough money. If the month were only 20 days long, budgeting would be easy."

Daily spending and saving decisions are the focus of financial planning. You must coordinate these actions with your needs, goals, and personal situation. Maintaining financial records and planning your spending are essential for successful personal financial management. The time and effort you devote to these activities will yield benefits. **Money management** refers to the day-to-day financial activities necessary to manage current personal economic resources while working toward long-term financial security.

Components of Money Management

Three main money management activities are interrelated, as shown here:

3. BUDGETING – creating and implementing a plan for spending and saving.

2. FINANCIAL STATEMENTS – preparing a Balance Sheet and Cash Flow Statement on a regular basis.

1. FINANCIAL DOCUMENTS – storing and maintaining personal financial records and documents.

LO2.1

Identify the main components of wise money management.

ACTION ITEM

My money management strategy involves:

☐ **no spending plan.**

☐ **tracking my spending.**

☐ **using savings to pay current bills.**

Money management Day-to-day financial activities necessary to manage current personal economic resources while working toward long-term financial security.

FinTech for Financial Literacy

Robo-advisors are automated programs to guide financial planning. These online financial planners may be completely autonomous or may be combined with human assistance. The process starts by responding to questions related to income, assets, debt, goals, and risk tolerance. Then, computer algorithms suggest actions for your investment portfolio and financial plan. Digital advisers have lower fees than other financial planners. Search **nerdwallet.com** for advice on selecting a robo-advisor.

First, *personal financial records and documents* help you plan the use of your resources. These provide evidence of business transactions and ownership of property, and are helpful in legal matters. Next, *personal financial statements* measure and guide your financial position and progress. Finally, your spending plan, or *budget,* is the basis for effective money management.

A System for Personal Financial Records

Purchase receipts, credit card statements, insurance policies, and tax forms are the basis of financial recordkeeping and personal economic choices. An organized system of financial records provides a basis for (1) handling daily business activities, such as bill paying; (2) planning and measuring financial progress; (3) completing required tax reports; (4) making effective investment decisions; and (5) determining available resources for current and future spending.

As Exhibit 2–1 shows, most financial records are kept in one of three places: a home file, a safe deposit box, or a computer system or online. A home file should be used to keep records for current needs and documents with limited value. Your home file may be a series of folders, a cabinet with several drawers, or even a box. Whatever method you use, your system should be secure and organized to allow quick access to needed documents and information.

safe deposit box A private storage area at a financial institution with maximum security for valuables.

Important financial records and valuable articles should be kept in a location that provides better security than a home file. A **safe deposit box** is a private storage area at a financial institution with maximum security for valuables and difficult-to-replace documents.

The number of financial records and documents may seem overwhelming; but they can easily be organized into 10 categories (see Exhibit 2–1). These groups correspond to the major topics covered in this book. You may not need to use all of these records and documents at present. As your financial situation changes, you will add others.

How long should you keep personal finance records? Records such as birth certificates, wills, and Social Security data should be kept permanently. Records for investments should be kept as long as you own the items. Federal tax documents should be kept for three years from the date you file your return. Under certain circumstances in an audit, the Internal Revenue Service may request information from further back. As a result, consider keeping your tax records for six years. Keep documents related to the purchase and sale of real estate indefinitely.

> **WHAT WOULD YOU DO?** You are required to provide evidence of ownership of your automobile for registration and insurance for the vehicle. However, you are not able to locate the needed documents. What actions might be taken to create a system for storing your vital documents? How can your system combine physical copies of documents along with digital storage?

When storing electronic financial documents and records in the cloud, consider the following actions:

- Download copies of all statements and forms to your local storage area using a system of files and folders.
- Back up files on external media or use an online backup service.
- Secure data with complex passwords and encryption.

Exhibit 2–1 Where to Keep Your Financial Records

Home Files, Home Computer, or Online

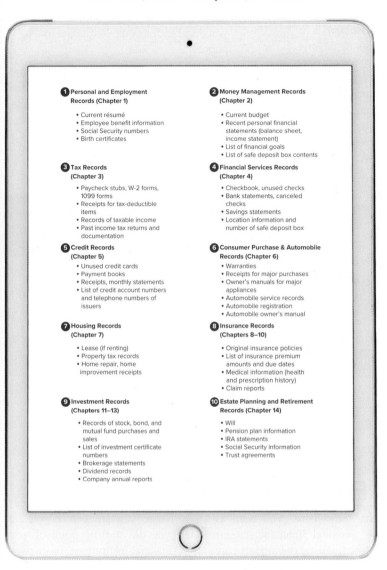

1 Personal and Employment Records (Chapter 1)
- Current résumé
- Employee benefit information
- Social Security numbers
- Birth certificates

2 Money Management Records (Chapter 2)
- Current budget
- Recent personal financial statements (balance sheet, income statement)
- List of financial goals
- List of safe deposit box contents

3 Tax Records (Chapter 3)
- Paycheck stubs, W-2 forms, 1099 forms
- Receipts for tax-deductible items
- Records of taxable income
- Past income tax returns and documentation

4 Financial Services Records (Chapter 4)
- Checkbook, unused checks
- Bank statements, canceled checks
- Savings statements
- Location information and number of safe deposit box

5 Credit Records (Chapter 5)
- Unused credit cards
- Payment books
- Receipts, monthly statements
- List of credit account numbers and telephone numbers of issuers

6 Consumer Purchase & Automobile Records (Chapter 6)
- Warranties
- Receipts for major purchases
- Owner's manuals for major appliances
- Automobile service records
- Automobile registration
- Automobile owner's manual

7 Housing Records (Chapter 7)
- Lease (if renting)
- Property tax records
- Home repair, home improvement receipts

8 Insurance Records (Chapters 8–10)
- Original insurance policies
- List of insurance premium amounts and due dates
- Medical information (health and prescription history)
- Claim reports

9 Investment Records (Chapters 11–13)
- Records of stock, bond, and mutual fund purchases and sales
- List of investment certificate numbers
- Brokerage statements
- Dividend records
- Company annual reports

10 Estate Planning and Retirement Records (Chapter 14)
- Will
- Pension plan information
- IRA statements
- Social Security information
- Trust agreements

Safe Deposit Box or Fireproof Home Safe

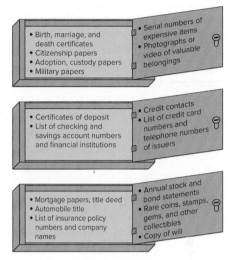

- Birth, marriage, and death certificates
- Citizenship papers
- Adoption, custody papers
- Military papers
- Serial numbers of expensive items
- Photographs or video of valuable belongings

- Certificates of deposit
- List of checking and savings account numbers and financial institutions
- Credit contacts
- List of credit card numbers and telephone numbers of issuers

- Mortgage papers, title deed
- Automobile title
- List of insurance policy numbers and company names
- Annual stock and bond statements
- Rare coins, stamps, gems, and other collectibles
- Copy of will

Computer, Tablet, Phone

- Scanned copies of documents
- Spreadsheet summaries of budgets, investment records
- Digital versions of income tax returns, wills, and estate plan
- Apps for banking activities, financial recordkeeping, and investment transactions

What Not to Keep . . .

Wastebasket

- Receipts for small, non-tax-deductible purchases
- Expired warranties

Shredder

- Quarterly investment account statements (keep the annual summary statements)
- Documents that you no longer need with personal information such as your Social Security number or account numbers

Computer Recycle Bin

Empty recycle bin on regular basis. Make sure personal data files are completely erased.

CAUTION!

Many people make the *mistake* of not having an accurate record of spending, creating financial trouble. An *action* is to use an app or a written spending record. This can result in *success* with funds for financial goals and emergencies. For reduced financial stress: (1) Have a low debt-to-income ratio. (2) Delay, reduce, or eliminate unnecessary expenses. (3) Build up emergency savings. (4) Seek additional income by selling possessions, working extra hours at your job, securing part-time work, starting a home-based or online business, turning a hobby into a business, or selling your expertise as a consultant.

- Scan copies of documents so that you no longer need to keep paper versions.
- Completely erase files when discarding items that are no longer needed or when you dispose of a computer, tablet, or phone.

Hard copies may be required for car titles, birth certificates, property deeds, and life insurance policies. Original receipts may be needed for returns or warranty service.

Sheet 5 Financial Documents and Records

PRACTICE QUIZ 2–1

1. What are the three major money management activities?
2. What are the benefits of an organized system of financial records and documents?
3. For each of the following records, check the column to indicate the length of time the item should be kept. "Short time period" refers to less than five years.

Document	Short time period	Longer time period
Credit card statements		
Mortgage documents		
Receipts for furniture, clothing		
Retirement account information		
Will		

LO2.2

Create a personal balance sheet and cash flow statement.

ACTION ITEM

My cash flow statement details are:

☐ very simple but useful.
☐ very detailed.
☐ nonexistent.

balance sheet A financial statement that reports what an individual or a family owns and owes; also called a *net worth statement* or *statement of financial position.*

Personal Financial Statements

Every journey starts somewhere. You need to know where you are before you can go somewhere else. Personal financial statements tell you the starting point of your financial journey. Most financial documents come from financial institutions, businesses, or the government. However, two records you create yourself are the personal balance sheet and the cash flow statement, also called *personal financial statements.*

These reports provide information about your current financial position and present a summary of your income and spending. The main purposes of personal financial statements are to (1) report your current financial position; (2) measure your progress toward financial goals; (3) maintain information about your financial activities; and (4) provide data for preparing tax forms or applying for credit.

Your Personal Balance Sheet: The Starting Point

The current financial position of an individual or family is the starting point for financial planning. A **balance sheet**, also called a *net worth statement* or *statement of financial position,* reports what you own and what you owe. You prepare a personal balance sheet to determine your current financial position using the following process:

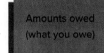

Items of value (what you own) − Amounts owed (what you owe) = Net worth (your wealth)

Exhibit 2-2 Creating a Personal Balance Sheet

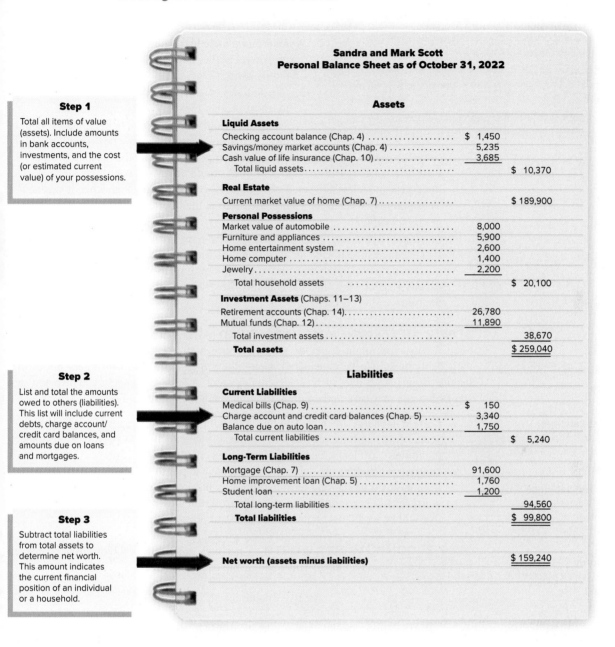

Step 1

Total all items of value (assets). Include amounts in bank accounts, investments, and the cost (or estimated current value) of your possessions.

Step 2

List and total the amounts owed to others (liabilities). This list will include current debts, charge account/credit card balances, and amounts due on loans and mortgages.

Step 3

Subtract total liabilities from total assets to determine net worth. This amount indicates the current financial position of an individual or a household.

Sandra and Mark Scott
Personal Balance Sheet as of October 31, 2022

Assets

Liquid Assets

Checking account balance (Chap. 4)	$ 1,450	
Savings/money market accounts (Chap. 4)	5,235	
Cash value of life insurance (Chap. 10)	3,685	
Total liquid assets		$ 10,370

Real Estate

Current market value of home (Chap. 7)	$ 189,900

Personal Possessions

Market value of automobile	8,000	
Furniture and appliances	5,900	
Home entertainment system	2,600	
Home computer	1,400	
Jewelry	2,200	
Total household assets		$ 20,100

Investment Assets (Chaps. 11–13)

Retirement accounts (Chap. 14)	26,780	
Mutual funds (Chap. 12)	11,890	
Total investment assets		38,670
Total assets		**$ 259,040**

Liabilities

Current Liabilities

Medical bills (Chap. 9)	$ 150	
Charge account and credit card balances (Chap. 5)	3,340	
Balance due on auto loan	1,750	
Total current liabilities		$ 5,240

Long-Term Liabilities

Mortgage (Chap. 7)	91,600	
Home improvement loan (Chap. 5)	1,760	
Student loan	1,200	
Total long-term liabilities		94,560
Total liabilities		**$ 99,800**

Net worth (assets minus liabilities)	**$ 159,240**

For example, if your possessions are worth $4,500 and you owe $800 to others, your net worth is $3,700. As shown in Exhibit 2–2, preparation of a balance sheet involves three main steps.

STEP 1: LIST ITEMS OF VALUE Money in bank accounts combined with other items of value are the foundation of your current financial position. **Assets** are cash and other tangible property with a monetary value. The balance sheet for Sandra and Mark Scott lists their assets in four categories:

1. **Liquid assets** are cash and items of value that can easily be converted to cash. Money in checking and savings accounts is *liquid* and is available to the Scott family for current spending. The cash value of their whole life insurance policy may

assets Cash and other tangible property with a monetary value.

liquid assets Cash and items of value that can easily be converted to cash.

be borrowed if needed. While assets other than liquid assets can also be converted into cash, the process is not quite as easy.

2. *Real estate* includes a home, a condominium, vacation property, or other buildings or land that a person or family owns.

3. *Personal possessions* are a major portion of assets for most people. Included in this category are automobiles and other personal belongings. Although these items have value, they may be difficult to convert to cash. You may decide to list your possessions on the balance sheet at their original cost. However, these values should be revised over time, since a three-year-old television set, for example, is worth less now than when it was new. Thus you may wish to list your possessions at their current value (also referred to as *market value*).

4. *Investment assets* are funds set aside for long-term financial needs. The Scott family will use their investments for such things as financing their children's education, purchasing a vacation home, and saving for retirement. Since investment assets usually fluctuate in value, the amounts listed should reflect their value at the time the balance sheet is prepared.

STEP 2: DETERMINE AMOUNTS OWED After looking at the total assets of the Scott family, you might conclude that they have a strong financial position. However, their debts must also be considered. **Liabilities** are amounts owed to others but do not include items not yet due, such as next month's rent. A liability is a debt you owe now, not something you may owe in the future. Liabilities fall into two categories:

1. **Current liabilities** are debts you must pay within a short time, usually less than a year. These liabilities include such things as medical bills, tax payments, insurance premiums, cash loans, and credit card balances.

2. **Long-term liabilities** are debts you do not have to pay in full until more than a year from now. Common long-term liabilities include auto loans, educational loans, and mortgages. A *mortgage* is an amount borrowed to buy a house or other real estate that will be repaid over a period of 15, 20, or 30 years.

STEP 3: COMPUTE NET WORTH A person's **net worth** is the difference between total assets and total liabilities. This relationship can be stated as

$$\text{Assets} - \text{Liabilities} = \text{Net worth}$$

Net worth is the amount you would have left if all assets were sold for the listed values and all debts were paid in full. Also, total assets equal total liabilities plus net worth. The balance sheet of a business is commonly expressed as

$$\text{Assets} = \text{Liabilities} + \text{Net worth}$$

As Exhibit 2–2 shows, Sandra and Mark Scott have a net worth of $159,240. Since very few people, if any, liquidate all assets, the amount of net worth has a more practical purpose: It provides a measurement of your current financial position.

liabilities Amounts owed to others.

current liabilities Debts that must be paid within a short time, usually less than a year.

long-term liabilities Debts that are not required to be paid in full until more than a year from now.

net worth The difference between total assets and total liabilities.

> ### EXAMPLE: Net Worth
>
> If a household has $193,000 of assets and liabilities of $88,000, the net worth would be $105,000 ($193,000 minus $88,000).

Figure It Out!

Ratios for Evaluating Financial Progress

Financial ratios are used to measure changes in your financial situation. These relationships indicate progress toward an improved financial position.

Ratio	Calculation	Example	Interpretation
Debt ratio	Liabilities divided by net worth	$25,000/$50,000 = 0.5	Shows relationship between debt and net worth; a low debt ratio is best.
Current ratio	Liquid assets divided by current liabilities	$4,000/$2,000 = 2	Indicates $2 in liquid assets for every $1 of current liabilities; a high current ratio is desirable to have cash available to pay bills.
Liquidity ratio	Liquid assets divided by monthly expenses	$10,000/$4,000 = 2.5	Indicates the number of months in which living expenses can be paid if an emergency arises; a high liquidity ratio is desirable.
Debt-payments ratio	Monthly credit payments divided by take-home pay	$540/$3,600 = 0.15	Indicates how much of a person's earnings goes for debt payments (excluding a home mortgage); most financial advisors recommend a debt-payments ratio of less than 20 percent.
Savings ratio	Amount saved each month divided by gross income	$648/$5,400 = 0.12	Financial experts recommend monthly savings of 5–10 percent.

Based on the following information, calculate the ratios requested:

- Liabilities $12,000
- Liquid assets $2,200
- Monthly credit payments $150
- Monthly savings $130

- Net worth $36,000
- Current liabilities $550
- Take-home pay $900
- Gross income $1,500

(1) Debt ratio _____
(2) Debt-payments ratio _____

(3) Current ratio _____
(4) Savings ratio _____

Analysis: How do these ratios compare with the guidelines mentioned in the "Interpretation" column above?

ANSWERS: 1. $12,000/$36,000 = 0.33; **2.** $150/$900 = 0.166; **3.** $2,200/$550 = 4.0; **4.** $130/$1,500 = 0.086, 8.67 percent.

A person may have a high net worth but still have financial difficulties. Having many assets with low liquidity means not having the cash available to pay current expenses. **Insolvency** is the inability to pay debts when they are due; it occurs when a person's liabilities far exceed available assets. The *Figure It Out!* feature ("Ratios for Evaluating Financial Progress") provides additional methods for assessing your financial situation.

Individuals and families can increase their net worth by (1) increasing their savings; (2) reducing spending; (3) increasing the value of investments and other possessions; and (4) reducing amounts owed. Remember, your net worth is *not* money available to use but an indication of your financial position on a given date.

insolvency The inability to pay debts when they are due because liabilities far exceed the value of assets.

Your Cash Flow Statement: Inflows and Outflows

Each day, financial events can affect your net worth. When you receive a paycheck or pay living expenses, your assets and liabilities change. **Cash flow** is the actual inflow and outflow of cash during a given time period. Income from employment will probably represent your most important *cash inflow;* however, other income, such as interest earned on a

cash flow The actual inflow and outflow of cash during a given time period.

cash flow statement
A financial statement that summarizes cash receipts and payments for a given period; also called a *personal income and expenditure statement.*

savings account, should also be considered. In contrast, payments for items such as rent, food, and loans are *cash outflows.*

A **cash flow statement**, also called a *personal income and expenditure statement* (Exhibit 2–3), is a summary of cash receipts and payments for a given period, such as a month or a year. This report provides information on your income and spending patterns, which will be helpful when preparing a budget.

A bank account can provide information for your cash flow statement. Deposits to the account are your *inflows;* checks written, cash withdrawals, and debit card payments are your *outflows.* Of course, in using this system, when you do not deposit entire amounts received, you must also note the spending of these other amounts on your cash flow statement.

Exhibit 2–3 Creating a Cash Flow Statement

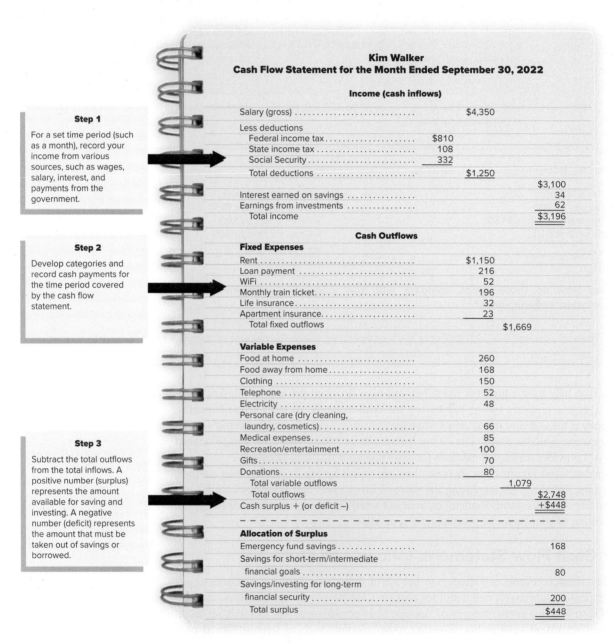

Step 1

For a set time period (such as a month), record your income from various sources, such as wages, salary, interest, and payments from the government.

Step 2

Develop categories and record cash payments for the time period covered by the cash flow statement.

Step 3

Subtract the total outflows from the total inflows. A positive number (surplus) represents the amount available for saving and investing. A negative number (deficit) represents the amount that must be taken out of savings or borrowed.

Kim Walker
Cash Flow Statement for the Month Ended September 30, 2022

Income (cash inflows)

Salary (gross)		$4,350
Less deductions		
Federal income tax	$810	
State income tax	108	
Social Security	332	
Total deductions	$1,250	
		$3,100
Interest earned on savings		34
Earnings from investments		62
Total income		$3,196

Cash Outflows

Fixed Expenses

Rent	$1,150	
Loan payment	216	
WiFi	52	
Monthly train ticket	196	
Life insurance	32	
Apartment insurance	23	
Total fixed outflows		$1,669

Variable Expenses

Food at home	260	
Food away from home	168	
Clothing	150	
Telephone	52	
Electricity	48	
Personal care (dry cleaning, laundry, cosmetics)	66	
Medical expenses	85	
Recreation/entertainment	100	
Gifts	70	
Donations	80	
Total variable outflows		1,079
Total outflows		$2,748
Cash surplus + (or deficit –)		+$448

Allocation of Surplus

Emergency fund savings	168
Savings for short-term/intermediate financial goals	80
Savings/investing for long-term financial security	200
Total surplus	$448

The process for preparing a cash flow statement involves three steps:

| Total cash received during the time period | − | Cash outflows during the time period | = | Cash surplus or deficit |

STEP 1: RECORD INCOME To create a cash flow statement, start by identifying money received. **Income** is the inflows of cash for an individual or a household. For most people, the main source of income is money received from a job. Other common income sources include commissions, self-employment income, interest, dividends, gifts, grants, scholarships, government payments, pensions, retirement income, alimony, and child support.

In Exhibit 2–3, notice that Kim Walker's monthly salary (or *gross income*) of $4,350 is her main source of income. However, she does not have use of the entire amount. **Take-home pay,** also called *net pay,* is a person's earnings after deductions for taxes and other items. Kim's deductions for federal, state, and Social Security taxes are $1,250. Her take-home pay is $3,100. This amount, plus earnings from savings and investments, is the income she has available for use during the current month. Deductions for retirement or savings would reduce funds available for current use; those amounts would be included as assets on the balance sheet.

Take-home pay is also called *disposable income,* the amount a person or household has available to spend. **Discretionary income** is money left over after paying for housing, food, and other necessities. Studies report that discretionary income ranges from less than 5 percent for people under age 25 to more than 40 percent for older people.

STEP 2: RECORD CASH OUTFLOWS Cash payments for living expenses and other items make up the second component of a cash flow statement. Kim Walker divides her cash outflows into two major categories: fixed expenses and variable expenses. Every individual and household has different cash outflows, but these main categories, along with the subcategories Kim uses, can be adapted to most situations.

1. *Fixed expenses* are payments that do not vary from month to month. Rent or mortgage payments, installment loan payments, wifi service, and a monthly train ticket for commuting to work are examples of constant or fixed cash outflows. For Kim, another type of fixed expense is the amount she sets aside each month for payments due once or twice a year. For example, Kim pays $384 every March for life insurance. Each month, she records a fixed outflow of $32 for deposit in a special savings account so that the money will be available when her insurance payment is due.
2. *Variable expenses* are flexible payments that change from month to month. Common examples of variable cash outflows are food, clothing, utilities (such as electricity and telephone), recreation, medical expenses, gifts, and donations. The use of a checkbook or some other record-keeping system is necessary for an accurate total of cash outflows.

STEP 3: DETERMINE NET CASH FLOW The difference between inflows and outflows can be either a positive (*surplus*) or a negative (*deficit*) cash flow. A deficit exists if more cash goes out than comes in during a given month. This amount must be made up by withdrawals from savings or by borrowing.

When you have a cash surplus, as Kim did (Exhibit 2–3), this amount is available for saving, investing, or paying off debts. Each month, Kim sets aside money for her *emergency fund* in a savings account that she would use for unexpected expenses or to pay living costs if she did not receive her salary. She deposits the rest of the surplus in savings and investment plans that have two purposes. The first is the achievement of short-term and intermediate financial goals, such as a new car, a vacation, or returning to school; the second is long-term financial security—her retirement.

A cash flow statement provides the foundation for preparing and implementing a spending, saving, and investment plan. The cash flow statement reports the *actual* spending of a household. In contrast, a budget, which has a similar format, documents *projected* income and spending.

income Inflows of cash to an individual or a household.

take-home pay Earnings after deductions for taxes and other items; also called *disposable income* or *net pay.*

discretionary income Money left over after paying for housing, food, and other necessities.

Sheet 6 Creating a Personal Balance Sheet

Sheet 7 Creating a Personal Cash Flow Statement

PRACTICE QUIZ 2–2

1. What are the main purposes of personal financial statements?

2. What does a personal balance sheet tell you about your financial situation?

3. For the following items, identify each as an asset (A), liability (L), cash inflow (CI), or cash outflow (CO):

_____ Monthly rent   _____ Automobile loan

_____ Interest on savings account   _____ Collection of rare coins

_____ Retirement account   _____ Mortgage amount

_____ Electric bill   _____ Market value of automobile

4. Jan Franks has liquid assets of $6,300 and monthly expenses of $2,100. Based on the liquidity ratio, she has _____ months in which living expenses could be paid if an emergency arises. How might financial ratios be used when planning and implementing financial activities?

LO2.3

Develop and implement a personal budget.

ACTION ITEM

My budgeting attitude is:

☐ **"I don't have enough money to have a budget."**

☐ **"I use an app to monitor spending."**

☐ **"My detailed plan helps me avoid money troubles."**

budget A specific plan for spending income; also called a *spending plan.*

A Plan for Effective Budgeting

A **budget,** or *spending plan,* is necessary for successful financial planning. The common financial problems of overusing credit, lacking a regular savings program, and failing to plan for future financial security can be minimized through budgeting. A budget will help you live within your income, spend your money wisely, reach your financial goals, prepare for financial emergencies, and develop wise financial management habits. With a budget, you will be in control of your life. Without a budget, others will be in control, such as those to whom you owe money. Use a budget to tell your money where to go, rather than having overspending and debt control your life.

Budgeting activities may be viewed in a seven-step process: (1) Set Financial Goals; (2) Estimate Income; (3) Budget an Emergency Fund and Savings; (4) Budget Fixed Expenses; (5) Budget Variable Expenses; (6) Record Spending Amounts; and (7) Review Spending and Savings Patterns.

In the first steps, record and review past spending, saving, and income to plan financial goals. Next, use this information to plan budgeted amounts. Then, maintain a record of spending to compare actual amounts to budgeted amounts. Finally, review and adjust future budget amounts based on changes in your household situation, finances, and goals.

Step 1: Set Financial Goals

Your future plans are the foundation for a financial direction. Financial goals are plans for your spending, saving, and investing. As discussed in Chapter 1, financial goals should take a SMART approach with goals that are **S**pecific, **M**easurable, **A**ction-oriented, **R**ealistic, and **T**ime-based. Exhibit 2–4 gives general examples of potential financial goals for different life situations. These goal areas must be put in a more specific format to be considered SMART, such as "save an amount each month to accumulate $5,000 within three years for a down payment on a townhouse."

Step 2: Estimate Income

As Exhibit 2–5 shows for the Robinson Family, after setting goals, you need to estimate available money for a given time period. A common budgeting period is a month, since many payments, such as rent or mortgage, utilities, and credit cards, are due each month. In determining available income, include only money that you are sure you'll receive. Bonuses, gifts, or unexpected income should not be considered until the money is actually

Personal Situation	Short-Term Goals (less than 2 years)	Intermediate Goals (2–5 years)	Long-Term Goals (over 5 years)
Single person	• Complete college • Pay off auto loan	• Take a vacation to Europe • Pay off education loan • Attend graduate school	• Buy a vacation home in the mountains • Provide for retirement income
Married couple (no children)	• Take an annual vacation • Buy a new car	• Remodel home • Build a stock portfolio	• Buy a retirement home • Provide for retirement income
Parent (young children)	• Increase life insurance • Increase savings	• Increase investments • Buy a new car	• Accumulate a college fund for children • Move to a larger home

Exhibit **2–4**

Common Financial Goals

received. As previously noted, any deductions for retirement savings would not be included since these funds are not available for current use.

Budgeting income may be difficult if your earnings vary by season or your income is irregular, as with sales commissions. In these situations, estimate your income on the low side to avoid overspending and other financial difficulties.

Step 3: Budget an Emergency Fund and Savings

To set aside money for unexpected expenses as well as future financial security, the Robinsons have budgeted several amounts for savings and investments (see Exhibit 2–5). Financial advisors suggest that an emergency fund representing three to six months of living expenses be established for use in periods of unexpected financial difficulty. This amount will vary based on a person's life situation and employment stability.

The Robinsons also set aside an amount each month for their automobile insurance payment, which is due every six months. Both this amount and the emergency fund are put into a savings account.

A frequent budgeting mistake is to save the amount left at the end of the month. When you do that, you often have *nothing* left for savings. Since saving is vital for long-term financial security, remember to always "pay yourself first."

money minute focus

Kakeibo, pronounced "kah-keh-boh" and translates as "household financial ledger," has been used in Japan for managing personal finances for over 100 years. This recordkeeping method emphasizes physically writing all financial inflows and outflows for awareness of bad money habits. *Kakeibo* can help you become completely honest about your spending with the use of four categories: (1) needs, (2) wants, (3) culture, such as books and museum visits, and (4) unexpected—medical expenses or car repairs.

Step 4: Budget Fixed Expenses

Definite obligations make up this portion of a budget. As Exhibit 2–5 shows, the Robinsons have *fixed expenses* for housing, taxes, and loan payments. They make a monthly payment of $29 for life insurance. The budgeted total for their fixed expenses is $806, or 28 percent of estimated available income.

Notice that a budget has a similar format to the previously discussed cash flow statement. A budget, however, involves *projected* or planned income and expenses. The cash flow statement reports the *actual* income and expenses.

Assigning amounts to spending categories requires careful consideration. The amount you budget for various items will depend on your current needs and plans for the future. A common suggestion is the 50/30/20 rule with 50 percent of income for necessities, 30 percent for wants, and 20 percent for saving and financial goals. Exhibit 2–6 suggests budget allocations for different life situations.

Exhibit 2–5 Developing a Monthly Budget

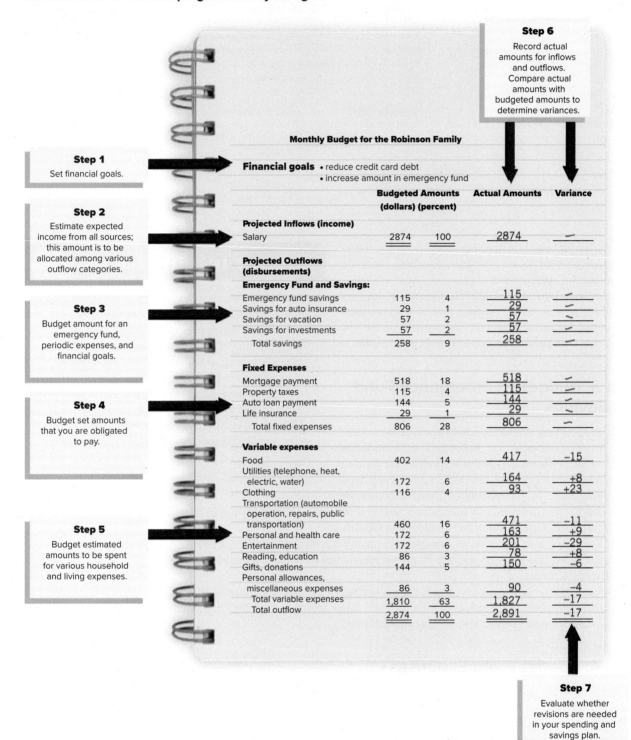

Step 6
Record actual amounts for inflows and outflows. Compare actual amounts with budgeted amounts to determine variances.

Step 1
Set financial goals.

Step 2
Estimate expected income from all sources; this amount is to be allocated among various outflow categories.

Step 3
Budget amount for an emergency fund, periodic expenses, and financial goals.

Step 4
Budget set amounts that you are obligated to pay.

Step 5
Budget estimated amounts to be spent for various household and living expenses.

Step 7
Evaluate whether revisions are needed in your spending and savings plan.

Monthly Budget for the Robinson Family

Financial goals • reduce credit card debt
• increase amount in emergency fund

	Budgeted Amounts (dollars)	Budgeted Amounts (percent)	Actual Amounts	Variance
Projected Inflows (income)				
Salary	2874	100	2874	—
Projected Outflows (disbursements)				
Emergency Fund and Savings:				
Emergency fund savings	115	4	115	—
Savings for auto insurance	29	1	29	—
Savings for vacation	57	2	57	~
Savings for investments	57	2	57	—
Total savings	258	9	258	—
Fixed Expenses				
Mortgage payment	518	18	518	—
Property taxes	115	4	115	—
Auto loan payment	144	5	144	—
Life insurance	29	1	29	~
Total fixed expenses	806	28	806	—
Variable expenses				
Food	402	14	417	−15
Utilities (telephone, heat, electric, water)	172	6	164	+8
Clothing	116	4	93	+23
Transportation (automobile operation, repairs, public transportation)	460	16	471	−11
Personal and health care	172	6	163	+9
Entertainment	172	6	201	−29
Reading, education	86	3	78	+8
Gifts, donations	144	5	150	−6
Personal allowances, miscellaneous expenses	86	3	90	−4
Total variable expenses	1,810	63	1,827	−17
Total outflow	2,874	100	2,891	−17

Although this information can be of value when creating budget categories, maintaining a detailed record of your spending for several months is a better source for your personal situation. Don't become discouraged. Use a simple system, such as a notebook or your checkbook. This "spending diary" will help you know where your money is going. (See the Spending Diary at the end of Chapter 1.)

Exhibit **2–6** **Typical After-Tax Budget Allocations for Different Life Situations**

Budget Category	Student	Working Single (no dependents)	Couple (children under 18)	Single Parent (young children)	Parents (children over 18 in college)	Couple (over 55, no dependent children)
Housing (rent or mortgage payment; utilities; furnishings and appliances)	0–25%	30–35%	25–35%	20–30%	25–30%	25–35%
Transportation	5–10	15–20	15–20	10–18	12–18	10–18
Food (at home and away from home)	15–20	15–25	15–25	13–20	15–20	18–25
Clothing	5–12	5–15	5–10	5–10	4–8	4–8
Personal and health care (including child care)	3–5	3–5	4–10	8–12	4–6	6–12
Entertainment and recreation	5–10	5–10	4–8	4–8	6–10	5–8
Reading and education	10–30	2–4	3–5	3–5	6–12	2–4
Personal insurance and pension payments	0–5	4–8	5–9	5–9	4–7	6–8
Gifts, donations, and contributions	4–6	5–8	3–5	3–5	4–8	3–5
Savings	0–10	4–15	5–10	5–8	2–4	3–5

Sources: Bureau of Labor Statistics (**http://stats.bls.gov**); *Money; The Wall Street Journal*

Step 5: Budget Variable Expenses

Planning for *variable expenses* is not as easy as budgeting for savings or fixed expenses. Variable expenses will fluctuate by household situation, time of year, health, economic conditions, and other factors. A major portion of the Robinsons' planned spending—over 60 percent of their budgeted income—is for variable living costs. They base their estimates on past spending as well as expected changes in their cost of living.

Step 6: Record Spending Amounts

After having established a spending plan, you will need to keep track of your actual income and expenses. This process is similar to preparing a cash flow statement. In Exhibit 2–5, notice that the Robinsons estimated specific amounts for income and expenses. These are presented under "Budgeted Amounts." The family's actual spending was not always the same as planned. A **budget variance** is the difference between the amount budgeted and the actual amount received or spent. The total variance for the Robinsons was a $17 **deficit**, since their actual spending exceeded their planned spending by this amount. They would have had a **surplus** if their actual spending had been less than they had planned.

budget variance
The difference between the amount budgeted and the actual amount received or spent.

deficit The amount by which actual spending exceeds planned spending.

surplus The amount by which actual spending is less than planned spending.

EXAMPLE: Budget Variance

If a family budgets $380 a month for food and spends $363, this would result in a $17 budget *surplus*. However, if the family spent $406 on food during the month, a $26 budget *deficit* would exist.

Variances for income should be viewed as the opposite of variances for expenses. Less income than expected would be a deficit, whereas more income than expected would be a surplus. Spending more than planned for an item may be justified by reducing spending for another item or putting less into savings. Revising your budget and financial goals may

Financial Literacy in Practice

A Money Management SWOT Analysis

SWOT (**s**trengths, **w**eaknesses, **o**pportunities, **t**hreats) analysis, a planning tool used by companies, can also help with money management and budgeting activities. Listed below are examples of possible items for each SWOT category. In the area provided, assess your strengths, weaknesses, opportunities, and threats related to budgeting and money management. Do online research and talk with others to get ideas for your personal SWOT items.

Internal (personal) Factors	External (economic, social) Influences
Strengths	**Opportunities**
• Saving 5–10 percent of income • Informed on personal finance topics • No credit card debt • Flexible job skills *Your strengths:* _____ _____	• Phone apps for monitoring finances • Part-time work to supplement income • Availability of no-fee bank account • Low-interest-rate education loan *Potential opportunities:* _____ _____
Weaknesses	**Threats**
• High level of credit card debt • No emergency fund • Automobile in need of repairs • Low current cash inflow *Your weaknesses:* _____ _____	• Lower market value of retirement fund • Possible reduced hours at part-time job • Reduced home market value • Increased living costs (inflation) *Potential threats:* _____ _____

Creating a money management SWOT analysis is only a start. Next, you need to select actions to build on your strengths, minimize your weaknesses, take advantage of opportunities, and avoid being a victim of threats. Through research and creative planning, weaknesses and threats can become strengths and opportunities.

money minute focus

Most households can have an additional $500 or more a month available by

- Adjusting your tax withholding.
- Cutting insurance costs.
- Wiser food shopping.
- Not eating at restaurants.
- Avoiding online shopping.
- Using less energy and a less expensive phone plan.
- Canceling subscription services and memberships.
- Avoiding bank fees.
- Not being in debt.

By clearly identifying essentials (your *needs*) and luxury items (your *wants*), wise spending and increased savings will occur.

be necessary. The nearby *Financial Literacy in Practice* feature, "A Money Management SWOT Analysis," provides an additional method to evaluate and plan your money management activities.

Step 7: Review Spending and Saving Patterns

Like most decision-making activities, budgeting is an ongoing process. You will need to review and perhaps revise your spending plan on a regular basis.

REVIEW YOUR FINANCIAL PROGRESS The results of your budget may be obvious, such as having extra cash in your bank account or falling behind in your bill payments. However, such obvious results may not always be present. Occasionally, you will have to review areas where spending has been more or less than expected. You can prepare an annual summary to compare actual spending with budgeted amounts for each month. A spreadsheet program can be useful for this purpose. This summary will help you see areas where changes in your budget may be necessary. This review process is vital to both successful short-term money management and long-term financial security.

REVISE YOUR GOALS AND BUDGET ALLOCATIONS What should you cut first when a budget shortage occurs? This question doesn't have easy answers, and answers will vary for different households. The most common overspending areas are entertainment and food, especially away-from-home meals. Purchasing less expensive brand items, buying quality used products, and avoiding credit card purchases are common budget adjustment techniques. When household budgets must be cut, spending is most frequently reduced for vacations, dining out, cleaning and lawn services, cable/Internet service, and charitable donations.

At this point in the budgeting process, you may also revise your financial goals. Are you making progress toward achieving your objectives? Have changes in personal or economic conditions affected the desirability of certain goals? Have new goals surfaced that should be given a higher priority? Addressing these issues while creating an effective saving method will help ensure accomplishment of your financial goals.

> **WHAT WOULD YOU DO?** As a result of a reduced income, you need to make some changes in your spending. What budget items might you consider reducing when faced with this situation? When would the use of your savings be appropriate? What additional sources of funds might be available?

SUCCESSFUL BUDGETING Having a spending plan will not eliminate financial worries. A budget will work only if you follow it. Changes in income, living expenses, and goals will require a revised spending plan. Successful budgets are those that are:

- *Well planned.* A good budget takes time and effort to prepare and should involve everyone affected by it.
- *Realistic.* If you have a moderate income, don't immediately expect to save enough money for an expensive car. A budget is designed not to prevent you from enjoying life but to help you achieve what you want most.
- *Flexible.* Unexpected expenses and life situation changes will require a budget that can easily be revised.
- *Clearly communicated.* Unless you and others involved are aware of the spending plan, it will not work. The budget should be visual to all household members.

SELECTING A BUDGETING SYSTEM Although your bank statement will give you a fairly complete record of expenses, it does not serve the purpose of a spending plan. A budget requires that you outline how you will spend available income. Individuals and households commonly use these types of budgeting systems:

- A *mental budget* exists only in a person's mind. This simple system may be appropriate for limited resources and minimal financial responsibilities. However, over time, this is a dangerous approach for effective money management.
- A *physical budget* involves envelopes, folders, or containers to hold money or slips of paper. Envelopes would contain the amount of cash or a note listing the amount to be used for "Food," "Rent," "Auto Payment," and other expenses.
- A *written budget* can be kept in a notebook or with multicolumn accounting paper.
- A *digital budget* may involve a spreadsheet, specialized software such as Quicken, or an app. The budget site **Mvelopes.com** makes use of virtual envelopes to track, monitor, and plan your spending.

The budgeting system you use will depend on your personal and financial situation. Most important is to select a system that best helps you achieve your financial goals.

PRACTICE QUIZ 2–3

Sheet 8 Developing a Personal Budget

1. What are the main purposes of a budget?

2. How does a person's life situation affect goal setting and amounts allocated for various budget categories?

3. For each of the following household expenses, indicate if the item is a FIXED or a VARIABLE expense.

   _____ Food away from home   _____ Cable television

   _____ Rent   _____ Electricity

   _____ Health insurance premium   _____ Auto repairs

4. The Nollin family has budgeted expenses for a month of $4,560 and actual spending of $4,480. This would result in a budget SURPLUS or DEFICIT (circle one) of $ _____.

LO2.4

Connect money management activities with saving for personal financial goals.

ACTION ITEM

My savings program is:

☐ **not started.**

☐ **a small amount.**

☐ **achieving a financial goal.**

Money Management and Achieving Financial Goals

Personal financial statements and a budget help you achieve financial goals with

1. Your balance sheet: reporting your current financial position—where you are now.
2. Your cash flow statement: telling you what you received and spent over the past month.
3. Your budget: planning spending and saving to achieve financial goals.

Many people prepare a balance sheet on a periodic basis, such as every three or six months. Between those points in time, your budget and cash flow statement help you plan and measure spending and saving activities. For example, you might prepare balance sheets on January 1, June 30, and December 31. Your budget would serve to plan your spending and saving between these points in time, and your cash flow statement of income and outflows would document your actual spending and saving. This relationship may be viewed as follows:

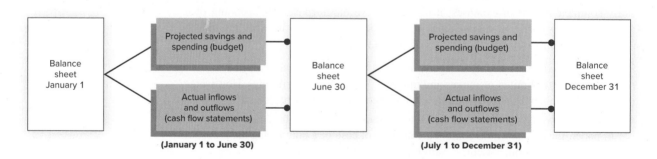

Changes in your net worth result from cash inflows and outflows. In periods when your outflows exceed your inflows, you must draw on savings or borrow (buy on credit). When this happens, lower assets (savings) or higher liabilities (due to the use of credit) result in a lower net worth. When inflows exceed outflows, putting money into savings or paying off debts results in a higher net worth.

Clark Howard encourages everyone to "save more and spend less." Through his television program, radio show, podcasts, books, app, and website (**clark.com**), this consumer expert offers advice on topics ranging from cellphone plans and the best credit cards, to product reviews and phishing scams. Howard is also very active in volunteer programs and community service that includes building homes for people in need.

Clark Howard, Inc.

In good times, prepare for difficult times. Then, when the difficult times come, you are prepared. Howard suggests the CLARK Method for budgeting:

Calculate your income

List your expenses

Analyze your spending and set goals

Record everything

Knock out debt and build your savings

While you should have an emergency fund, at some point you might encounter a larger unplanned financial need. When this occurs, Clark Howard suggests these actions to spend less money and make more money.

To spend less money:

- Cook more, eat out less
- Switch phone providers
- Cancel subscriptions
- Refinance loans/debt
- Downsize home or car
- Shop for cheaper prescription drugs
- Cut water, electricity use
- Get car insurance quotes

- Reduce entertainment
- Stop buying clothes
- Reduce charitable giving
- Cancel gym membership
- Get fewer haircuts
- Do-it-yourself repairs

To make more money:

- Find a new job
- Ask for raise/more hours
- Get a side hustle
- Sell old stuff
- Earn cash back from apps
- Switch to an online bank for more interest

The *receipt trick* is another tip to increase future savings. Many retailers display a "You Saved" amount on a receipt for items on sale and store discounts. By putting this amount in a savings account, you can avoid spending the "saved" money. Collect receipts in an envelope or scan them with an app to analyze shopping habits and make wiser future purchases. This action can result in an extra amount added to your savings for emergencies or retirement.

ACTION STEPS FOR. . .

. . . Information Literacy

Locate a recent budgeting or wise spending article on **clark. com**. What aspects of the article do you believe are most valid for your personal money management activities?

. . . Financial Literacy

Ask another person to select an article from **clark.com**. Prepare a summary of why the article was selected and how the information might be used for improved financial planning.

. . . Digital Literacy

Select an article from one of the topic categories on **clark.com**. Develop an outline of three key ideas that could be the basis for creating a podcast.

Selecting a Saving Technique

Traditionally, the United States ranked low in savings rate among economically developed countries. Low savings affect personal financial security. Studies reveal that the majority of Americans do not set aside an adequate amount for emergencies.

FinTech for Financial Literacy

Innovative apps and websites are available to assist with money management activities:

- **Albert** (albert.com) is an app to guide financial decisions.
- **SaverLife** (about.saverlife.org) helps create a habit of saving.
- **Scratch** (scratch.fi) helps borrowers repay loans.
- **Axos Invest** (axosinvest.com) suggests and manages investments for financial goals.
- **Greenlight** (greenlightcard.com) teaches financial responsibility to children.
- **gohenry** (gohenry.com) helps kids build money management skills.

Since most people find saving difficult, these methods can help make it easier:

1. Use payroll deduction or a payment app to deposit funds in a separate savings account. This can be a percentage of income, such as 5 or 10 percent, or a specific dollar amount. Remember to "pay yourself first." Also, take advantage of employer matching retirement fund contributions.

2. Enroll in a *round-up program*, in which a purchase amount or bill payment is rounded up to the nearest dollar with the difference transferred to a savings account.

3. To increase savings, cut online spending, save coins, sell unneeded items, or use library services. Bring lunch instead of buying it; avoid expensive coffee and snacks. Then, put the money saved in a container or use an app to transfer money to a savings or investment account.

How you save is not as important as making regular savings deposits that will help you achieve financial goals. Small amounts of savings can grow faster than you realize.

Calculating Savings Amounts

To achieve your financial objectives, convert savings goals into specific amounts. Your use of a savings or investment plan is vital to the growth of your money. As Exhibit 2–7 shows, time value of money calculations introduced in Chapter 1 can be used to calculate progress toward achieving different financial goals using varied savings methods.

Exhibit **2–7** Using Savings to Achieve Financial Goals

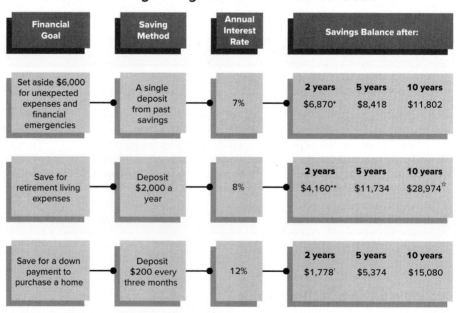

Financial Goal	Saving Method	Annual Interest Rate	Savings Balance after:		
			2 years	**5 years**	**10 years**
Set aside $6,000 for unexpected expenses and financial emergencies	A single deposit from past savings	7%	$6,870*	$8,418	$11,802
Save for retirement living expenses	Deposit $2,000 a year	8%	$4,160**	$11,734	$28,974☆
Save for a down payment to purchase a home	Deposit $200 every three months	12%	$1,778†	$5,374	$15,080

* Based on the future value of $1 tables in Chapter 1 and Chapter 1 Appendix.
** Based on the future value of a series of deposits tables in Chapter 1 and Chapter 1 Appendix.
☆ With annual $2,000 deposits, this same retirement account would grow to over $500,000 in 40 years.
† Based on quarterly compounding, explained in Chapter 4.

PRACTICE QUIZ 2–4

1. What relationship exists among personal financial statements, budgeting, and achieving financial goals?

2. What are some suggested methods to make saving easy? What are long-term effects of low savings for both individuals and the economy of a country?

3. If you wanted to obtain the following types of information, check the box for the document that you would find most useful.

Financial information needed	Balance sheet	Cash flow statement	Budget
Amounts owed for medical expenses			
Spending patterns for the past few months			
Planned spending patterns for the next month			
Current value of investment accounts			
Amounts to deposit in savings accounts			

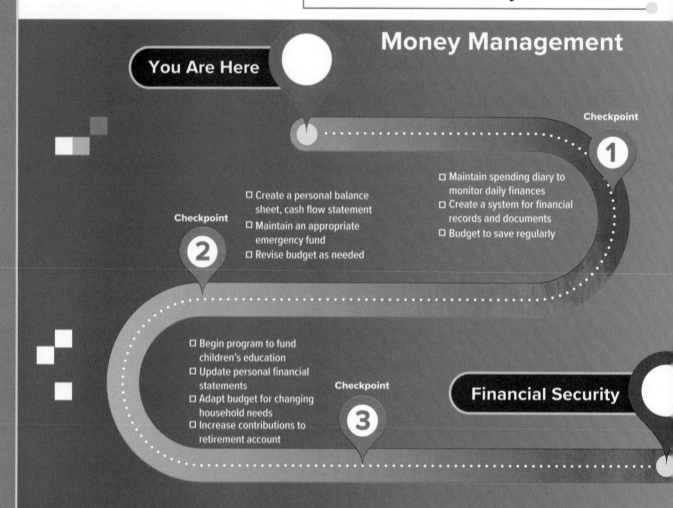

Money Management

You Are Here

Checkpoint 1
- ☐ Maintain spending diary to monitor daily finances
- ☐ Create a system for financial records and documents
- ☐ Budget to save regularly

Checkpoint 2
- ☐ Create a personal balance sheet, cash flow statement
- ☐ Maintain an appropriate emergency fund
- ☐ Revise budget as needed

Checkpoint 3
- ☐ Begin program to fund children's education
- ☐ Update personal financial statements
- ☐ Adapt budget for changing household needs
- ☐ Increase contributions to retirement account

Financial Security

MONTHLY BUDGET

your personal finance dashboard

Cash Flow Analysis

A monthly cash flow analysis will help you achieve financial goals. By comparing cash inflows (income) and cash outflows (spending), you will determine if you have a surplus or deficit. A surplus allows you to save more or pay off debts. A deficit reduces your savings or increases the amount you owe.

YOUR SITUATION: Do you maintain a record of cash inflows and outflows? How can you reduce spending to improve your cash flow situation?

LO2.1 Successful money management requires coordination of personal financial records, personal financial statements, and budgeting activities. An organized system of financial records and documents should provide ease of access as well as security for financial documents.

LO2.2 A personal balance sheet, also known as a *net worth statement,* is prepared by listing items of value (assets) and amounts owed to others (liabilities). The difference between your total assets and your total liabilities is your net worth. A cash flow statement, also called a *personal income and expenditure statement,* is a summary of cash receipts and payments for a given period, such as a month or a year.

LO2.3 The budgeting process consists of seven steps: (1) set financial goals; (2) estimate income; (3) budget an emergency fund and savings; (4) budget fixed expenses; (5) budget variable expenses; (6) record spending amounts; and (7) review spending and saving patterns.

LO2.4 The relationship among the personal balance sheet, cash flow statement, and budget provides the basis for achieving long-term financial security. Future value and present value calculations may be used to compute the increased value of savings for achieving financial goals.

assets 55	deficit 63	money management 51
balance sheet 54	discretionary income 59	net worth 56
budget 60	income 59	safe deposit box 52
budget variance 63	insolvency 57	surplus 63
cash flow 58	liabilities 56	take-home pay 59
cash flow statement 58	liquid assets 55	
current liabilities 56	long-term liabilities 56	

Page	Topic	Formula
56	Net worth	Net worth = Total assets − Total liabilities *Example:* = $125,000 − $53,000 = $72,000
57	Debt ratio	Debt ratio = Liabilities/Net worth *Example:* = $7,000/$21,000 = 0.33
57	Current ratio	Current ratio = Liquid assets/Current liabilities *Example:* = $8,500/$4,500 = 1.89
57	Liquidity ratio	Liquidity ratio = Liquid assets/Monthly expenses *Example:* = $8,500/$3,500 = 2.4
57	Debt-payments ratio	Debt-payments ratio = Monthly credit payments/Take-home pay *Example:* = $760/$3,800 = 0.20
57	Savings ratio	Savings ratio = Amount saved per month/Gross monthly income *Example:* = $460/$3,800 = 0.12
63	Cash surplus (or deficit)	Cash surplus (or deficit) = Total inflows − Total outflows *Example:* = $5,600 − $4,970 = $630 (surplus)

1. The Hamilton household has $145,000 in assets and $63,000 in liabilities. What is the family's net worth?
2. Harold Daley budgeted $210 for food for the month of July. He spent $227 on food during July. Does he have a budget surplus or deficit, and what is the amount?

Self-Test Solutions

1. Net worth is determined by assets ($145,000) minus liabilities ($63,000), resulting in a net worth of $82,000.
2. The budget *deficit* of $17 is calculated by subtracting the actual spending ($227) from the budgeted amount ($210).

**Financial Planning
Problems**

1. Based on the following data, determine the amount of total assets, total liabilities, and net worth.   (LO2.2)

   Liquid assets, $3,870   Investment assets, $8,340
   Current liabilities, $2,670   Household assets, $87,890
   Long-term liabilities, $76,230

   a. Total assets $
   b. Total liabilities $
   c. Net worth $

2. Using the following balance sheet items and amounts, calculate the total liquid assets and total current liabilities.   (LO2.2)

   Money market account, $2,600   Medical bills, $262
   Mortgage, $158,000   Checking account, $780
   Retirement account, $87,400   Credit card balance, $489

   a. Total liquid assets $
   b. Total current liabilities $

3. Use the following items to determine the total assets, total liabilities, net worth, total cash inflows, and total cash outflows.   (LO2.2)

   Rent for the month, $650   Monthly take-home salary, $2,185
   Spending for food, $345   Cash in checking account, $450
   Savings account balance, $1,890   Balance of educational loan, $2,160
   Current value of automobile, $8,800   Telephone bill paid for month, $65
   Credit card balance, $235   Loan payment, $80
   Auto insurance, $230   Household possessions, $3,400
   Video equipment, $2,350   Payment for electricity, $90
   Lunches/parking at work, $180   Donations, $160
   Personal computer, $1,200   Value of stock investment, $860
   Clothing purchase, $110   Restaurant spending, $130

   a. Total assets $
   b. Total liabilities $
   c. Net worth $
   d. Total cash inflows $
   e. Total cash outflows $

4. For each of the following situations, compute the missing amount.   (LO2.2)
   a. Assets $65,000; liabilities $18,000; net worth $
   b. Assets $86,500; liabilities $; net worth $18,700
   c. Assets $34,280; liabilities $12,965; net worth $
   d. Assets $; liabilities $38,345; net worth $52,654

5. Based on the following financial data, calculate the ratios requested.   (LO2.2)

Liabilities, $7,800

Liquid assets, $4,600

Monthly credit payments, $640

Monthly savings, $130

Net worth, $58,000

Current liabilities, $1,300

Take-home pay, $2,575

Gross income, $2,850

   a. Debt ratio

   b. Current ratio

   c. Debt-payments ratio

   d. Savings ratio

6. The Fram family has liabilities of $128,000 and a net worth of $340,000. What is their debt ratio? How would you assess this?   (LO2.2)

7. Carl Lester has liquid assets of $2,680 and current liabilities of $2,436. What is his current debt ratio? What comments do you have about this financial position?   (LO2.2)

8. For the following situations, calculate the cash surplus or deficit: (LO2.2)

Cash Inflows	Cash Outflows	Difference (surplus or deficit)
$3,460	$3,306	$_____ _____
4,693	4,803	$_____ _____
4,287	4,218	$_____ _____

9. The Brandon household has a monthly income of $5,630 on which to base their budget. They plan to save 10 percent and spend 32 percent on fixed expenses and 56 percent on variable expenses.   (LO2.3)

   a. What amount do they plan to set aside for each major budget section?

      Savings $_____

      Fixed expenses $_____

      Variable expenses $_____

   b. After setting aside these amounts, what amount would remain for additional savings or for paying off debts?

10. Fran Powers created the following budget and reported the actual spending listed. Calculate the variance for each of these categories, and indicate whether it was a *deficit* or a *surplus*.   (LO2.3)

Item	Budgeted	Actual	Variance	Deficit/Surplus
Food	$360	$298	_____	_____
Transportation	320	334	_____	_____
Housing	950	982	_____	_____
Clothing	110	134	_____	_____
Personal	275	231	_____	_____

11. Use future value and present value calculations (see tables in the Chapter 1 Appendix) to determine the following: (LO2.4)

   a. The future value of a $600 savings deposit after eight years at an annual interest rate of 6 percent.

   b. The future value of saving $1,800 a year for five years at an annual interest rate of 5 percent.

   c. The present value of a $2,000 savings account that will earn 3 percent interest for four years.

12. Brenda plans to reduce her spending by $50 a month. What would be the future value of this reduced spending over the next 10 years? (Assume an annual deposit to her savings account and an annual interest rate of 3 percent.)   (LO2.4)

13. Kara George received a $5,000 gift for graduation from her uncle. If she deposits this in an account paying 3 percent, what will be the value of this gift in 12 years?   (LO2.4)

Mc Graw Hill **connect** To reinforce the content in this chapter, more problems are provided at connect.mheducation.com.

ORGANIZING FINANCIAL RECORDS

Competencies. . .

(1) Create a system to organize personal financial documents and records. (2) Prepare personal finance statements. (3) Track spending to create a budget.

Action Research. . .

(1) Based on this chapter, the Your Personal Financial Plan Sheet 5, online research, and discussions with others, plan a system to organize your personal financial documents and records. (2) Based on the Personal Financial Statements section of this chapter and Your Personal Financial Plan Sheets 6 and 7, plan a personal balance sheet and cash flow statement. (3) Based on the budgeting section of this chapter and Your Personal Financial Plan Sheet 8: (a) talk with two to three others about how they track their spending, and research spending apps; (b) locate an online photo or format for an envelope budgeting system that you might consider using.

Outcomes. . .

(1) Create a visual (PowerPoint presentation, photo essay, smartphone app prototype, or other format) with a system to organize your personal financial documents and records. (2) Present a simple personal balance sheet and cash flow statement (8 to 10 items each) based on your current life situation or for a hypothetical situation. (3) Prepare a written summary with visuals describing your spending tracking system and your preliminary budget.

REAL LIFE PERSONAL FINANCE

ADJUSTING THE BUDGET

In a recent month, the Constantine family had a budget deficit, which is something they want to avoid so they do not have future financial difficulties. Jason and Karen Constantine and their children (ages 10 and 12) plan to discuss the situation after dinner this evening.

While at work, Jason was talking with his friend Ken Lopez. Ken had been a regular saver since he was very young, starting with a small savings account. Those funds were then invested in various stocks and mutual funds. While in college, Ken was able to pay for his education while continuing to save between $50 and $100 a month. He closely monitored his spending. Ken realized that the few dollars here and there for snacks and other minor purchases quickly add up.

Today, Ken works as a customer service manager for the online division of a retailing company. He lives with his wife and their two young children. The family's spending plan allows for all their needs and also includes regularly saving and investing for the children's education and for retirement.

Jason asked Ken, "How come you never seem to have financial stress in your household?"

Ken replied, "Do you know where your money is going each month?"

"Not really" was Jason's response.

"You'd be surprised by how much is spent on little things you might do without," Ken responded.

"I guess so. I just don't want to have to go around with a notebook writing down every amount I spend," Jason said in a troubled voice.

"Well, you have to take some action if you want your financial situation to change," Ken countered.

That evening, the Constantine family met to discuss their budget situation:

Current Spending		Suggested Budget	
Rent	$950	Rent	$ ____
Electricity, water	120	Electricity, water	____
Telephone	55	Telephone	____
Cable, internet	125	Cable, internet	____
Food (at home)	385	Food (at home)	____
Food (away)	230	Food (away)	____
Auto payment	410	Auto payment	____
Gas, oil changes	140	Gas, oil changes	____
Insurance	125	Insurance	____
Clothing	200	Clothing	____
Personal, gifts	185	Personal, gifts	____
Donations	50	Donations	____
Savings	35	Savings	____
Total spending	$3,010	Total budgeted	$
Total monthly amount available.................	$2,800	Total monthly amount available.................	$2,800
Surplus (deficit)	($210)	Surplus (deficit)	$

Questions

1. What situations might have created the budget deficit for the Constantine family?
2. What amounts would you suggest for the various categories for the family budget?
3. Describe additional actions the Constantine family might consider related to their budget and other money management activities.

MANAGING A BUDGET

Jamie Lee Jackson, age 24, a busy full-time college student and part-time bakery clerk, has been trying to organize all of her priorities, including her budget. She has been wondering if she is allocating enough of her income toward savings, which includes accumulating enough money toward the $9,000 down payment she needs to open her dream cupcake café.

Jamie Lee has been making regular deposits to both her regular and her emergency savings accounts. She would really like to sit down and get a clearer picture of how much she is spending on various expenses, including rent, utilities, and entertainment, and how her debt compares to her savings and assets. She realizes that she must stay on track and keep a detailed budget if she is to realize her dream of being self-employed after college graduation.

Current Financial Situation

Assets:
Checking account: $1,250
Emergency fund savings account: $3,100
Car: $4,000

Liabilities:
Student loan: $5,400
Credit card balance: $400

Savings:
Regular savings: $150
Emergency savings: $25

Income:
Gross monthly salary: $2,125
Net monthly salary: $1,560

Monthly Expenses:
Rent obligation: $275
Utilities obligation: $125
Food: $120
Gas/Maintenance: $100
Credit card payment: $50

Entertainment:
Cake decorating class: $35
Movies with friends: $50

Questions

1. According to the text, a personal balance sheet is a statement of your net worth. It is an accounting of what you own as well as what you owe. Using the information provided, prepare a personal balance sheet for Jamie Lee.
2. Using the "Ratios for Evaluating Financial Progress" feature earlier in the chapter, what is Jamie Lee's debt ratio? When comparing Jamie Lee's liabilities and her net worth, is the relationship a favorable one?
3. Using the "Ratios for Evaluating Financial Progress" feature earlier in the chapter, what is Jamie Lee's savings ratio? Using the rule of thumb recommended by financial experts, is she saving enough?
4. Using Exhibit 2–6, Typical After-Tax Budget Allocations for Different Life Situations, calculate the budget allocations for Jamie Lee using her net monthly salary (or after-tax salary) amount. Is she within the recommended parameters for a student?

Spending Diary

"I AM AMAZED HOW LITTLE THINGS CAN ADD UP. . . . HOWEVER, SINCE KEEPING TRACK OF ALL MY SPENDING, I REALIZE THAT I NEED TO CUT DOWN ON SOME ITEMS SO I CAN PUT SOME MONEY AWAY INTO SAVINGS."

Directions Continue or start using the Daily Spending Diary sheets or create your own format to record *every cent* of your spending in the categories provided. This experience will help you better understand your spending patterns and help you plan for achieving financial goals. The Daily Spending Diary sheets are located at the end of Chapter 1 and in Connect Finance.

Questions

1. What information from your daily spending diary might encourage you to reconsider various money management actions?
2. How can your daily spending diary assist you when planning and implementing a budget?

Financial Documents and Records

Purpose: To develop a system for maintaining and storing personal documents and records.

Financial Planning Activities: Indicate the location of the following records, and create files for the eight major categories of financial documents. This sheet is also available in an Excel spreadsheet format in Connect Finance.

Suggested Websites: money.cnn.com, www.kiplinger.com, www.usa.gov

Item	Home file	Safe deposit box	Other (specify location—computer file, app, online)
1. Money management records			
• Budget, financial statements			
2. Personal/employment records			
• Current résumé, Social Security card			
• Educational transcripts			
• Birth, marriage, divorce certificates			
• Citizenship, military papers			
• Adoption, custody papers			
3. Tax records			
4. Financial services/consumer credit records			
• Unused or canceled checks			
• Savings, passbook statements			
• Credit card information, statements			
• Credit contracts			
5. Consumer purchase, housing, and automobile records			
• Warranties, receipts			
• Owner's manuals			
• Lease or mortgage papers, title deed, property tax info			
• Automobile title			
• Auto registration			
• Auto service records			
6. Insurance records			
• Insurance policies			
• Home inventory			
• Medical information (health history)			
7. Investment records			
• Broker statements			
• Dividend reports			
• Stock/bond records			
• Rare coins, stamps, and collectibles			
8. Estate planning and retirement			
• Will			
• Pension, Social Security info			

Suggested App:
• FileThis
• DropBox

McGraw Hill

What's Next for Your Personal Financial Plan?

• Plan a physical or online program for storing your financial documents and records.

• Decide if various documents may no longer be needed; plan to shred or dispose.

Name: _____ **Date:** _____

Creating a Personal Balance Sheet

Purpose: To determine your current financial position.

Financial Planning Activities: List current values of the assets; list amounts owed for liabilities; subtract total liabilities from total assets to determine net worth. This sheet is also available in an Excel spreadsheet format in Connect Finance.

Suggested Websites: www.kiplinger.com, money.com, www.thebalance.com

Balance sheet as of	_____	
Assets		
Liquid assets		
Checking account balance	_____	
Savings/money market accounts, funds	_____	
Cash value of life insurance	_____	
Other _____	_____	
Total liquid assets		_____
Household assets and possessions		
Current market value of home	_____	
Market value of automobiles	_____	
Furniture	_____	
Stereo, video, phone, computer equipment	_____	
Jewelry	_____	
Other _____	_____	
Other _____	_____	
Total household assets		_____
Investment assets		
Savings certificates	_____	
Stocks and bonds	_____	
Individual retirement accounts	_____	
Mutual funds	_____	
Other _____	_____	
Total investment assets		_____
Total assets	··	_____
Liabilities		
Current liabilities		
Charge account and credit card balances	_____	
Loan balances	_____	
Other _____	_____	
Other _____	_____	
Total current liabilities		_____
Long-term liabilities		
Mortgage	_____	
Other _____	_____	
Total long-term liabilities		_____
Total liabilities	··	_____
Net worth (assets minus liabilities)	··	_____

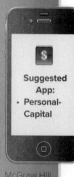

Suggested App:
• Personal-Capital

McGraw Hill

What's Next for Your Personal Financial Plan?

• Compare your net worth to previous balance sheets.

• Decide how often you will prepare a balance sheet.

Name: _____ Date: _____

Creating a Personal Cash Flow Statement

Purpose: To maintain a record of cash inflows and outflows for a month (or three months).

Financial Planning Activities: Record inflows and outflows of cash for a one- (or three-) month period. This sheet is also available in an Excel spreadsheet format in Connect Finance.

Suggested Websites: www.americasaves.org, money.com

For month ending	_____
Cash inflows	
Salary (take-home)	_____
Other income	_____
Other income	_____
Total income	.... _____
Cash outflows	
Fixed expenses	
Mortgage or rent	_____
Loan payments	_____
Insurance	_____
Other _____	_____
Other _____	_____
Total fixed outflows	.... _____
Variable expenses	_____
Food	_____
Clothing	_____
Electricity	_____
Telephone/cable/internet	_____
Water	_____
Transportation	_____
Personal care	_____
Medical expenses	_____
Recreation/entertainment	_____
Gifts	_____
Donations	_____
Other _____	_____
Other _____	_____
Total variable outflows	.... _____
Total outflows	.... _____
Surplus/Deficit	.... _____
Allocation of surplus	
Emergency fund savings	_____
Financial goal savings	_____
Other savings _____	_____

Suggested App:
• Spending-Tracker
• EveryDollar

McGraw Hill

What's Next for Your Personal Financial Plan?

- Decide which areas of spending need to be revised.
- Evaluate your spending patterns for preparation of a budget.

Name: _____   Date: _____

Developing a Personal Budget

Purpose: To compare projected and actual spending for a one- (or three-) month period.

Financial Planning Activities: Estimate projected spending based on your cash flow statement, and maintain records for actual spending for these same budget categories. This sheet is also available in an Excel spreadsheet format in Connect Finance.

Suggested Websites: www.betterbudgeting.com, www.asec.org, www.mymoney.gov

	Budgeted amounts		Actual amounts	Variance
Income	**Dollar**	**Percent**		
Salary				
Other _____				
Total income		**100%**		
Expenses				
Fixed expenses Mortgage or rent				
Property taxes				
Loan payments				
Insurance				
Other _____				
Total fixed expenses				
Emergency fund/savings Emergency fund				
Savings for _____				
Savings for _____				
Total savings				
Variable expenses Food				
Utilities				
Clothing				
Transportation costs				
Personal care				
Medical and health care				
Entertainment				
Education				
Gifts/donations				
Miscellaneous				
Other _____				
Other _____				
Total variable expenses				
Total expenses		**100%**		

Suggested App:
• Mint
• YNAB

McGraw Hill

What's Next for Your Personal Financial Plan?

• Evaluate the appropriateness of your budget for your current life situation.

• Assess whether your budgeting activities are helping you achieve your financial goals.

Chapter 2 Appendix: Developing a Career Strategy

....

"Only two days until the weekend." "Just 10 more minutes of sleep!" "Oh, no!" "Excellent!" These are some common responses to "It's time to get up for work."

Have you ever wondered why some people find great satisfaction in their work, while others only put in their time? As with other personal financial decisions, career selection and professional growth require planning. Most people will change jobs, and even careers, several times during a lifetime. Be ready to reevaluate your choice of work on a regular basis.

The Career Planning Process

Career planning activities may be implemented using the following steps:

1. *Personal assessment*—to determine interests and values, and to identify talents and abilities.
2. *Employment market analysis*—to assess geographic, economic, technological, and social influences on employment opportunities.
3. *Application process*—in which you prepare a résumé and create a cover letter.
4. *Interview process*—in which you practice your interview skills, research the organization, and send a follow-up message to the organization.
5. *Employment acceptance*—when you assess the salary and other financial factors as well as the organizational environment of your potential employer.
6. *Career development and advancement*—in which you develop plans to enhance career success behaviors and build strong work relationships.

> **CAREER ACTION ACTIVITY 1**
>
> For each step of the career planning process, write: (*a*) a goal you have now or might have in the future and (*b*) an action you might take regarding this element of career planning.

Information Sources for Career Trends

While careers have dwindled in some sectors of our economy, opportunities in other sectors have grown. Service industries that are expected to have the greatest employment potential include information and computer technology, health care, social and government services, technical sales, transportation and logistics, hospitality and food services, management and human resources, education and training, and financial services.

Many career information sources are available; these include:

1. *Career development office,* which offers many on-campus services, including career exploration and assistance with résumés, cover letters, and interview preparation.

money minute focus

An *elevator speech* is a short, persuasive, focused summary of your experiences and skills used when networking and in other settings. This talk should be conversational (not forced), memorable, and sincere. The use of an engaging idea or question can help keep the conversation going.

Networking and mentor programs provide connections to alumni, employers, and internships.

2. *Online sources* can assist with all aspects of career planning. Consider a web search to gather information about résumés, effective interviewing, or creating a career portfolio. Also available is the *Occupational Outlook Handbook* (**www.bls.gov/ooh/**), which provides detailed information on most careers.

3. *Informational interviews* are very effective for obtaining career information. A planned discussion with a person in a field of interest to you will help you learn about the job duties, required training, and the person's feelings about the career. Most people like to talk about their work experiences. Before the interview, plan your questions, which may include:

- How did you get your current position? Did other jobs lead to this one?
- In what ways do you find your work most satisfying? What are your main frustrations?
- What tasks and activities are required in your work?
- What are the most important qualifications, training, and education?
- What advice would you give a person who is considering this type of work?

CAREER ACTION ACTIVITY 2

Using an online career information source, prepare a brief summary of key ideas that might be of value to you in the future.

money minute focus

A valuable career skill for creative problem solving is *human-centered design* (HCD), also called *design thinking*. HCD is a three-step process: (1) **HEAR** (also called *inspiration*) involves immersion in the lives of people to listen and understand their needs. (2) **CREATE** (*ideation*) identifies business opportunities and develops prototypes based on the needs. (3) **DELIVER** (*implementation*) involves a market solution to serve identified needs. Successful human-centered design requires deep empathy with people, generating many ideas, building credible prototypes, seeking feedback, and putting an innovative solution into use.

Obtaining Employment Experience

Most people possess more career skills than they realize. Your involvement in school, community, and work activities provides a foundation for employment experiences. The following opportunities offer work-related training:

1. *Part-time employment* can provide experience and knowledge for a career field.
2. *Volunteer work* in community organizations or agencies can help you acquire skills, establish good work habits, and make contacts.
3. *Internships* allow you to gain experience needed to obtain employment in a field.
4. *Campus projects* offer work-related experiences to help you obtain career skills through campus organizations, course assignments, and research projects.

CAREER ACTION ACTIVITY 3

Create a list of your work, volunteer, and school activities. Describe how each could apply to a future work situation.

Identifying Job Opportunities

Some of the most valuable sources of job information are presented in this list.

1. *Job advertisements* posted online, in newspapers, and in professional periodicals are a common source. However, many available jobs may not be advertised to the general public, so consider other job search activities.

2. *Personal and business contacts* are available to advise people about careers. Friends, relatives, and others are potential contacts. *Networking* is the process of making and using contacts to obtain and update career information.

3. *Career fairs,* on campus and at convention centers, allow you to contact several firms with one visit. At a career fair, you will be asked questions to determine if you qualify for a longer interview. Prepare for job fairs by being ready to quickly communicate your potential contributions to an organization. Knowing something about the organization can distinguish you from other applicants.

4. *Employment agencies* match job hunters with employers. Often the hiring company pays the fee. Be wary when asked to pay a fee in advance. Government employment services are available through your state employment service or state department of labor.

5. *Job creation* involves developing a position that matches your skills with organizational needs. Your abilities and interests may allow you to create a demand for your services as a consultant or by starting your own business.

6. *Other job search sources* include (*a*) visits to companies to make face-to-face contacts; (*b*) business directories and websites to obtain names of organizations that employ people with your qualifications; and (*c*) alumni who work in your field.

CAREER ACTION ACTIVITY 4

Using a source of available jobs, select a position that you might apply for in the future. How well do your current and future qualifications match those required for the job?

Developing a Résumé

Marketing yourself to prospective employers usually requires a résumé, or personal information sheet.

Résumé Elements

A résumé is a summary of your education, training, experience, and other qualifications with these main components:

1. The *personal data section* presents your name, telephone number, and e-mail address. Do not include your birth date, sex, height, and weight unless this information applies to a specific job qualification.

2. A *career summary* is designed to clearly communicate the unique skills and competencies you possess for the career field to which you are applying.

3. The *education section* should include dates, schools attended, fields of study, and degrees earned.

4. The *experience section* lists organizations, dates of involvement, responsibilities in previous positions, relevant school activities, and community service.

money minute focus

Résumés often include vague words such as *competent, creative, flexible, motivated,* or *team player.* Instead, give specific examples of your experiences and achievements to better communicate these capabilities.

Highlight computer skills, technical abilities, and other specific competencies.
Use action verbs to connect your experience to the needs of the organization.
Focus this information on results and accomplishments.

5. The *related information section* may include honors, awards, certifications, memberships, and other activities related to your career field.

References are not included in a résumé; however, have this information available when requested. Contact people who are willing to verify your skills and experiences. These individuals may be teachers, past employers, supervisors, or business colleagues.

Résumé Preparation

No exact formula exists; however, a résumé must be presented in a professional manner. Many candidates are disqualified by poor résumés. The use of bulleted items, bold type, and short sentences improves readability. Be sure to view your résumé on a smartphone or tablet since many hiring managers review applications on a mobile device. Limit your résumé to one page. Send a two-page résumé only if you have enough material to fill three pages; then use the most relevant information to prepare an impressive two-page presentation.

One key to successful résumé writing is the use of action words to demonstrate what you have accomplished or achieved. Examples of strong action words include:

• *Accomplished*	• *Directed*	• *Organized*
• *Achieved*	• *Edited*	• *Planned*
• *Administered*	• *Facilitated*	• *Produced*
• *Coordinated*	• *Initiated*	• *Researched*
• *Created*	• *Implemented*	• *Supervised*
• *Designed*	• *Managed*	• *Trained*
• *Developed*	• *Monitored*	• *Updated*

Other words and phrases that can impress prospective employers include *foreign language skills, computer experience, achievement, research experience, flexible, team projects,* and *overseas study/experience.* Instead of just listing your ability to use various software (such as Excel or PowerPoint), describe how these tools were used to research information or to present findings for a specific project. For best results, seek assistance from counselors, the campus career development office, and friends to find errors and suggest improvements (see Exhibit 2-A).

When preparing a résumé, consider using the STAR principle to communicate your experiences and achievements:

S	Situation, or the setting	*Example:* Fundraising coordinator for campus organization
T	Task, your duties	*Example:* Prepared a plan to raise funds for social service agency
A	Actions you took	*Example:* Administered a team that solicited donations on campus
R	Result, the outcome	*Example:* Resulted in donating over $2,000 to a homeless shelter

On your résumé, this experience could be presented in this manner:

• Coordinated fundraising campaign for campus organization to raise funds for social service agency, resulting in soliciting and donating over $2,000 to a homeless shelter.

The STAR principle is also useful when communicating your background in an interview.

Exhibit 2-A Résumé Makeover

BEFORE:
CAREER OBJECTIVE
An entry-level position in medical or health care administration.

BEFORE:
Researched overdue accounts, created collection method for faster accounts receivable turnover, assisted in training billing clerks.

...also consider including relevant class experiences, such as:
• Coordinated team research project to identify health care opportunities in Asian markets.

BEFORE:
Newsletter editor, University of South Arkansas chapter of Financial Management Association, January–June 2022.

CHAD BOSTWICK

bostwc@unsoark.edu   Phone: (407)555-1239

CAREER SUMMARY

Customer service specialist in health care industry. Effective training, technology capabilities. Qualified in team building and innovation development. Planned and implemented strategies to increase customer satisfaction by over 20 percent.

EDUCATION

Bachelor of Science in Business Administration and Health Care Marketing, University of South Arkansas, June 2022.

Associate of Arts, Medical Technician Assistant, Arrow Valley Community College, Arlington, Kansas, June 2020.

ORGANIZATIONAL EXPERIENCE

Patient account clerk, University Hospital, Jasper, Missouri, November 2020 – present
• Researched accounts to reduce uncollectible amounts by 12 percent
• Created collection method to improve accounts receivable turnover
• Trained newly hired billing clerks in database applications

Sales data clerk, Jones Medical Supply Company, Benton, Kansas, January–August 2020
• Maintained inventory records, processed customer records
• Supervised quality control of entry-level data clerks

CAMPUS ACTIVITIES

Newsletter editor, University of South Arkansas chapter of Financial Management Association, January–June 2022
• Managed editorial staff to research, design, and publish online newsletter
• Researched and prepared news stories on financial industry trends

Tutor for business statistics and computer lab, 2020–2022
• Coordinated review sessions for exams and homework assignments
• Developed problems and case studies to supplement course materials

HONORS

College of Business Community Service Award, University of South Arkansas, June 2022

Arrow Valley Health Care Society Scholarship, June 2020

EXAMPLE: Your Social Résumé Strategy

Résumés have become online "living entities" through social media networks. Your interactions with hiring managers may include:

- A LinkedIn profile highlighting career achievements and competencies to enhance your employment potential. Links to photos, videos, and presentations can showcase your skills. Recommendations on LinkedIn can help you move forward in the job application process
- Twitter to communicate unique skills and a personal brand by linking prospective employers to your website.
- Instagram, Facebook, and Pinterest to present your personal brand, résumé, photos, videos, and other visuals related to career competencies, expertise, and achievements.
- A video résumé to communicate distinctive qualities and potential contributions to the organization.

Be careful with your social media life since aspects of your private life become public. Employers use social media to screen candidates. Avoid negative comments, inappropriate photos, and too much personal information. Also, beware of an incomplete or outdated profile, and not having appropriate connections in your network.

CAREER ACTION ACTIVITY 5

Outline the main sections of a résumé that you might use in the future. Conduct an online search to locate a résumé format.

Résumé Submission

Traditionally, résumés have been mailed or hand delivered. When presenting a résumé in person, you have an opportunity to observe the company environment and make a positive impression about your career potential. Today, most companies and recruiters request online submission of résumés by email or through a website.

Most résumé posting sites are free. Never pay a large fee; scam artists have set up phony websites with online payment systems to defraud people. Only post to sites with jobs in the geographic region of interest to you and for which you qualify.

Résumés sent by e-mail should be addressed to a specific person with a subject line referencing the specific job. Your e-mail should include a cover letter to introduce yourself and to encourage the recipient to read your résumé. Properly format your résumé and include it in the body of the e-mail or attach it as a PDF.

Follow up with a call or e-mail to reinforce your qualifications and interest. Ask about how and when to follow up on your status in the job search process.

Most important, your résumé and cover letter should have F-O-C-U-S:

- **F**it—communicate your suitability for the company culture and specific position.
- **O**bjective—present a goal of your desire to work in the industry.
- **C**onnect—provide examples of accomplishments that will benefit the company.
- **U**nique—emphasize your distinctive qualities and campus experiences.
- **S**kills—relate your abilities to company needs and industry trends.

CAREER ACTION ACTIVITY 6

Go to a website that posts résumés. Obtain information on the process involved in posting a résumé online.

Creating a Cover Letter

A *cover letter,* designed to express your interest in a specific job, accompanies your résumé and consists of three main sections:

1. The *introductory paragraph* gets the reader's attention. Indicate your reason for writing by referring to the employment position. Communicate what you have to offer the organization. If applicable, mention the person who referred you.
2. The *development paragraphs* highlight aspects of your background that specifically qualify you for the position. At this point, elaborate on experiences and training. Connect your skills and competencies to specific organizational needs.
3. The *concluding paragraph* should request action. Ask for an interview to discuss your qualifications in detail. Include your contact information, such as telephone numbers and the times when available. Close your letter by summarizing how you can provide benefit to the organization.

money minute focus

The *Q letter* (Q for qualifications) provides a side-by-side comparison of your experiences and abilities with the job requirements. The two coordinated lists allow you to be quickly rated as a viable candidate for the position.

Exhibit **2-B** **Sample Cover Letter**

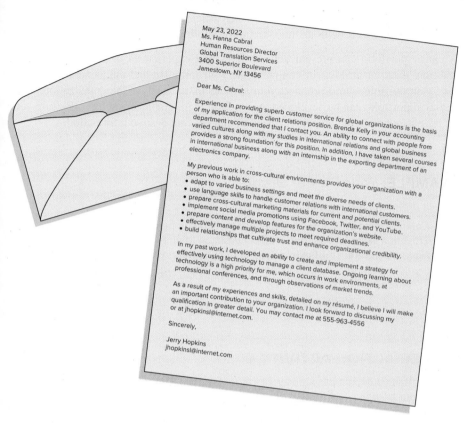

May 23, 2022
Ms. Hanna Cabral
Human Resources Director
Global Translation Services
3400 Superior Boulevard
Jamestown, NY 13456

Dear Ms. Cabral:

Experience in providing superb customer service for global organizations is the basis of my application for the client relations position. Brenda Kelly in your accounting department recommended that I contact you. An ability to connect with people from varied cultures along with my studies in international relations and global business provides a strong foundation for this position. In addition, I have taken several courses in international business along with an internship in the exporting department of an electronics company.

My previous work in cross-cultural environments provides your organization with a person who is able to:
- adapt to varied business settings and meet the diverse needs of clients.
- use language skills to handle customer relations with international customers.
- prepare cross-cultural marketing materials for current and potential clients.
- implement social media promotions using Facebook, Twitter, and YouTube.
- prepare content and develop features for the organization's website.
- effectively manage multiple projects to meet required deadlines.
- build relationships that cultivate trust and enhance organizational credibility.

In my past work, I developed an ability to create and implement a strategy for effectively using technology to manage a client database. Ongoing learning about technology is a high priority for me, which occurs in work environments, at professional conferences, and through observations of market trends.

As a result of my experiences and skills, detailed on my résumé, I believe I will make an important contribution to your organization. I look forward to discussing my qualification in greater detail. You may contact me at 555-963-4556 or at jhopkinsl@internet.com.

Sincerely,

Jerry Hopkins
jhopkinsl@internet.com

Create a personalized cover letter for each position addressed to the appropriate person in the organization. A poorly prepared cover letter guarantees rejection (see Exhibit 2-B).

In recent years, job applicants are increasingly using a *targeted application letter* instead of a résumé and cover letter. After researching a position and company, you can communicate how your specific skills and experiences will benefit the organization. Once again, your goal is to emphasize achievements and accomplishments so you will be invited for an interview.

CAREER ACTION ACTIVITY 7

Select a potential employment position. Create a cover letter for that position. Conduct an online search to obtain additional suggestions for effective cover letters.

Career Portfolios

In addition to a résumé, you may prepare a *career portfolio.* This collection of documents and other items provides tangible evidence of your abilities and skills. A career portfolio may include the following items:

1. *Documentation*—a résumé, sample interview answers, a competency summary, and letters of recommendation.
2. *Creative works*—ads, product designs, packages, brand promotions, and video clips on a DVD, USB drive, or personal website.

3. *Research project samples*—research findings, PowerPoint presentations, website designs, marketing plans, and photos of project activities.
4. *Employment accomplishments*—published articles, sales results data, financial charts, and news articles about community activities.

A career portfolio can present your abilities and experiences in a tangible manner. In addition, these materials will communicate your initiative and uniqueness. The cover page of your portfolio should connect your abilities to the needs of the organization.

A digital portfolio can be developed on a website with graphics and links. Be sure your home page is not cluttered and is organized to quickly find desired information.

EXAMPLE: Your Career Brand

Your professional image, or "brand," should:

- Communicate unique skills, experiences, and competencies.
- Provide a vision of your potential contribution to an employer.
- Have a consistent message online, in print, and elsewhere.
- Involve ongoing actions that communicate your image, such as "collaborator" or "international expert."

CAREER ACTION ACTIVITY 8

List items that you might include in your career portfolio. Describe the format for presenting your portfolio.

The Job Interview

The interview phase is limited to candidates who possess the desired qualifications.

Preparing for the Interview

Prepare by obtaining additional information about the organization. The best sources include the library, websites, observations during company visits, analysis of company products, informal conversations with current employees, and discussions with people knowledgeable about the company or industry. Research the company's operations, competitors, recent successes, future plans, and personnel policies to help you discuss your potential contributions to the company.

Conduct an online search for questions to ask during the interview; these can include:

- What do employees like most about your organization's working environment?
- What challenges are most often encountered by new employees?
- What training opportunities are available to employees who desire advancement?
- What qualities do your most successful employees possess?
- What actions of competitors might affect the company in the near future?

Successful interviewing requires practice. Use a video or work with friends to develop confidence when interviewing. Organize ideas, speak clearly and calmly, and communicate enthusiasm. Prepare specific answers regarding your strengths. Campus organizations and career development offices may offer opportunities for interview practice.

Forbes.com reports that executive recruiters agree on the three vital job interview questions: (1) Can you do the job? (to assess your strengths); (2) Will you love the job?

Exhibit 2-C
Common Interview Questions

EDUCATION AND TRAINING QUESTIONS

What education and training qualify you for this job?

Why are you interested in working for this organization?

In addition to going to school, what activities have helped you expand your interests and knowledge?

WORK AND OTHER EXPERIENCE QUESTIONS

In what types of situations have you done your best work?

Describe the supervisors who motivated you most.

Which of your past accomplishments are you most proud of?

Describe your experiences in working on a team and coordinating the activities of several people.

Describe some people whom you have found difficult to work with.

Describe a situation in which your determination helped you achieve a specific goal.

Describe situations in which you demonstrated creative problem solving.

PERSONAL QUALITIES QUESTIONS

What are your major strengths?

What are your major weaknesses?

What have you done to overcome your weaknesses?

What do you plan to be doing three to five years from now?

Which individuals have had the greatest influence on you?

What traits make a person successful?

How well do you communicate your ideas orally and in writing?

How did you prepare for this interview?

(*NOTE:* Also, search online for sample interview questions for your specific industry such as engineering, finance, health care, hospitality, information technology, medical technology, sales, or social services.)

(to assess your motivation); and (3) Can we tolerate working with you? (to assess your organizational fit). In addition, Exhibit 2-C presents other common interview questions.

When interviewing, keep in mind that proper dress and grooming are vital. Dress more conservatively than current employees. A business suit is usually appropriate. Avoid trendy and casual styles, and don't wear too much jewelry.

Confirm the time and location of the interview. Take copies of your résumé, your reference list, and paper for notes. Arrive about 10 minutes earlier than your appointed time.

EXAMPLE: Preparing for a Virtual Interview

1. Prepare as you would for any other interview; dress appropriately.
2. Test your computer connection in advance; plan a quiet environment.
3. Eliminate visual distractions; select an appropriate background.
4. Place the camera at eye level to avoid distorted face angles.
5. Go online early to communicate punctuality; check the time, time zone.
6. Maintain eye contact with the camera to project confidence and professionalism.
7. Tape notes and questions on a wall behind the camera to avoid looking down.

The Interview Process

Interviews may include situations or questions to determine how you react under pressure. Answer clearly in a controlled manner. Career counselors suggest having a "theme" for interview responses to focus on your key qualifications. Throughout the interview, come back to the central idea that communicates your potential contributions to the organization.

Behavioral interviewing, also called *competency-based interviewing,* is frequently used to evaluate an applicant's on-the-job potential. In these questions, you might be asked how you would handle various work situations. Behavioral interview questions typically begin with "Describe . . ." or "Tell me about . . ." to encourage interviewees to better explain their work style.

In *situational interviewing,* you are asked to participate in role-playing, similar to what may be encountered on the job. For example, you might be asked to resolve a complaint with a customer or negotiate with a supplier. This interview experience is used to evaluate your ability to work in various organizational environments.

The *case interview* gives prospective employees an opportunity to demonstrate their ability to think in a structured, creative manner when presented with a real-world problem. These case situations may cover topics such as competition, joint ventures, raising capital, or supply chain management. When involved in a case interview, be sure to listen and read carefully to understand the background and main problem. Organize your analysis and consider alternative courses of action. Use evidence to support your suggested actions. Clearly communicate your analysis process, conclusions, and recommendations. To find sample cases and suggestions, search online for "preparing for case interviews." Most important in a case interview is emphasis on the process, analysis, and actions rather than finding the "right" answer.

When encountering a *panel interview* with several people asking questions, make eye contact and engage all participants as you answer a question. In a *group interview,* be ready to answer a question with a slightly different response than the other job candidates.

Avoid talking too much, but answer each question completely, maintaining good eye contact. Stay calm during the interview. Remember, you are being asked questions about a subject about which you are the world's expert—YOU! Finally, thank the interviewer for the opportunity to discuss the job and your qualifications.

EXAMPLE: Asking for the Job

Near the conclusion of an interview, show your enthusiasm and desire for the position by asking for the job:

- "I believe my experiences would contribute to the continued success of your organization. Is there any additional information you need for making me an offer for the job?"
- "Based on my abilities in the area of _____, am I the appropriate fit for this position?"
- "This job is of great interest to me. What additional information would convince you that I'm the right person?"
- "Since my background and skills seem appropriate for the position, what is the next step in the hiring process?"

After the Interview

Most interviewers conclude by telling you when you can expect to hear from them. While waiting, do two things. First, within a day, send an e-mail to every person you met to express appreciation for the opportunity to interview. Also, reinforce your skills and interest in the job. If you don't get the job, this connection can make a positive impression for future consideration.

Second, do a self-evaluation of your interview performance. Write down the areas to improve. Try to remember the questions you were asked that differed from the questions you expected. Remember, the more interviews you have, the better you will present yourself and the better the chance of being offered a job.

EXAMPLE: A Checklist for Interview Success

To enhance your interview success, **theladders.com** suggests these actions:

- Don't arrive late . . . or too early.
- Show respect to the receptionist and all others with whom you interact.
- While waiting, don't be on your phone; review notes, and be ready to shake hands.
- Have a confident handshake and a pleasant smile; don't sit before you are asked.
- If offered a drink, accept water but not coffee. A drink of cold water can help reduce sweating, and spilling it won't lead to pain or stains!
- Connect with the interviewer through common interests and background; adapt responses to questions based on the age of the interviewer.
- Avoid looking at your watch or cell phone during the interview.
- Maintain good eye contact, an appropriate posture, proper hand positions, and professional body language.
- Make sure your voice and tone are engaging and calming.
- Communicate competency with confidence, but don't oversell yourself.
- Ask well-prepared questions that reflect company and industry knowledge as well as your vision for the job position.
- Be prepared for strange questions designed to assess your ability to respond under pressure and determine your creative problem solving.
- Clothing color should be conservative, such as black, blue, gray, and brown.
- Within a day, send a thank-you e-mail, and maybe a handwritten note, to all people involved in the interview.
- If you don't hear back within the time they set, contact the organization to express your continued interest.

CAREER ACTION ACTIVITY 9

Have someone ask you sample interview questions, and have them point out the strengths and weaknesses of your interview skills.

Job Offer Comparison

The financial aspects of a job should be assessed along with some organization factors.

1. *Salary and financial factors*—Your rate of pay will be affected by the type of work and your experience. The position may also include employee

FinTech for Financial Literacy

Artificial intelligence (AI) is used to identify and hire. Computer-based matching of job descriptions with résumés can discover the candidates with the best fit. Algorithms are AI programs used to post openings on the job boards that attract the most qualified applicants. Chatbots are used to analyze word choice, tone of voice, and eye contact during a video interview. *Voice masking* helps to eliminate bias against a foreign accent. However, concerns exist that some desirable candidates may not be comfortable interacting with automated systems.

benefits. These include insurance, retirement plans, vacation time, and other benefits for employees. Many organizations offer recreational facilities, discounts, and other advantages for workers.

2. *Organizational environment*—While the financial elements of a job are very important, also consider the working environment. Leadership style, dress code, and the social atmosphere should be investigated. Talk with people who have worked in the organization. Advancement potential might also be evaluated. Training programs may be available. These opportunities can be very beneficial for your long-term career success.

CAREER ACTION ACTIVITY 10

Prepare a list of the factors that you would consider when accepting a job. Talk to other people about what they believe to be important when accepting a job.

Career Strategies in a Weak Job Market

In times of weak economic conditions, obtaining employment can be difficult. Certain actions could be useful when attempting to seek employment or maintain your current position. Consider the following:

- Acknowledge stress, anxiety, frustration, and fear. Eat properly and exercise to avoid health problems.
- Assess your financial situation. Determine sources of emergency funds to pay needed expenses. Cut unnecessary spending.
- Evaluate your current and future employment potential. Consider work and community experiences that you have but are not on your résumé.
- Maintain a focus with a positive outlook. Your ability to communicate confidence and competency will result in more job offers.
- Connect with others in professional and social settings.
- Consider part-time work, consulting, and volunteering to exercise your skills, develop new contacts, and expand your career potential.

An ability to obtain and maintain employment in difficult economic times will serve you in every type of job market.

Exhibit 2-D provides a summary of suggestions for your career planning activities.

CAUTION!

Beware of these warning signs for fraudulent online job opportunities:

- Offers to access exclusive government job listings.
- A guaranteed job for a fee.
- Being offered a job without any type of screening or interview.
- Requiring you to provide a credit card or bank account information.

Exhibit **2-D** Creating a Focused Career Planning Strategy

While planning a career can be overwhelming, a few simple actions are available to help adapt to a changing employment market.

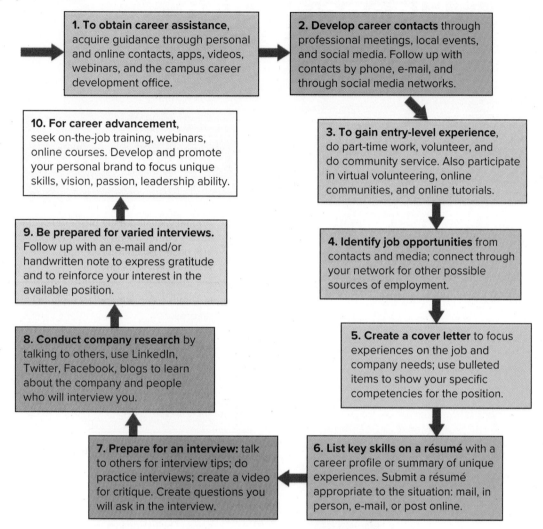

1. To obtain career assistance, acquire guidance through personal and online contacts, apps, videos, webinars, and the campus career development office.

2. Develop career contacts through professional meetings, local events, and social media. Follow up with contacts by phone, e-mail, and through social media networks.

10. For career advancement, seek on-the-job training, webinars, online courses. Develop and promote your personal brand to focus unique skills, vision, passion, leadership ability.

3. To gain entry-level experience, do part-time work, volunteer, and do community service. Also participate in virtual volunteering, online communities, and online tutorials.

9. Be prepared for varied interviews. Follow up with an e-mail and/or handwritten note to express gratitude and to reinforce your interest in the available position.

4. Identify job opportunities from contacts and media; connect through your network for other possible sources of employment.

8. Conduct company research by talking to others, use LinkedIn, Twitter, Facebook, blogs to learn about the company and people who will interview you.

5. Create a cover letter to focus experiences on the job and company needs; use bulleted items to show your specific competencies for the position.

7. Prepare for an interview: talk to others for interview tips; do practice interviews; create a video for critique. Create questions you will ask in the interview.

6. List key skills on a résumé with a career profile or summary of unique experiences. Submit a résumé appropriate to the situation: mail, in person, e-mail, or post online.

Enhance career planning activities with an online presence. Avoid actions that might present you in less than a professional manner. To communicate an appropriate online image, consider these actions:

- DO get connected to LinkedIn and other professional networking sites.
- DON'T put items online that create an inappropriate image; search your name to assess online presence.
- DO use keywords for capabilities and experiences expected in the industry in which you work.
- DON'T post your résumé online arbitrarily; select websites appropriate for your specific job search.
- DO regular follow-ups with online contacts; share current news and ideas on industry trends.
- DON'T join online groups in which you will not be an active participant.
- DO create a blog to enhance your online image and communicate areas of expertise.

Continually search online and use apps to update career planning activities.

3

Taxes in Your Financial Plan

3 Steps to Financial Literacy . . .
Taxes in Your Financial Plan

1 Annually, estimate the proper tax withholding and other tax payments (as appropriate) based on current tax rates.
Website: www.irs.gov

2 Maintain complete and accurate tax records.
App: Expensify

3 Each year, review tax resources to ensure that you understand tax law changes for your financial situation.
Website: taxtopics.net

What's wrong with a large tax refund?

Each year, millions of American households receive federal tax refunds totaling over $260 billion, which represents several billion dollars in lost earnings from investing and saving. By not receiving a large tax refund, you can use the money during the year for saving or other financial needs. Monitoring your taxes throughout the year, rather than waiting until April 15, is a vital component of financial planning. At the end of the chapter, *Your Personal Finance Road Map and Dashboard* will help you measure how well you have planned for your tax situation.

CHAPTER 3 LEARNING OBJECTIVES

In this chapter, you will learn to:

LO3.1 Identify the major tax types in our society.

LO3.2 Calculate taxable income and the amount owed for federal income tax.

LO3.3 Prepare a federal income tax return.

LO3.4 Select appropriate tax strategies for various life situations.

YOUR PERSONAL FINANCIAL PLAN SHEETS

9. Federal Income Tax Estimate
10. Tax Planning Activities

Taxes in Your Financial Plan

Taxes are an everyday financial fact of life. You pay taxes when you get a paycheck or make a purchase. However, most people concern themselves with taxes only immediately before April 15. Tax planning should be an ongoing process throughout the year.

Planning Your Tax Strategy

Each year, the Tax Foundation determines how long the average person works to pay taxes. In recent years, "Tax Freedom Day" came in mid-April. This means that the time that elapsed from January 1 until mid-April represents the portion of the year people work to pay their taxes.

Tax planning starts with knowing current tax laws, maintaining complete and appropriate tax records, then making purchase and investment decisions that can reduce your tax liability. Your primary goal should be to pay your fair share of taxes while taking advantage of appropriate tax benefits.

Types of Tax

Most people pay taxes in four major categories: taxes on purchases, taxes on property, taxes on wealth, and taxes on earnings.

TAXES ON PURCHASES You probably pay *sales tax* on many purchases. Many states exempt food and drugs from sales tax to reduce the financial burden on low-income households. In recent years, all but five states (Alaska, Delaware, Montana, New Hampshire, and Oregon) had a general sales tax. An **excise tax** is imposed by the federal and state

LO3.1

Identify the major tax types in our society.

ACTION ITEM

I understand the various types of taxes I pay.

☐ Yes ☐ No

excise tax A tax imposed on specific goods and services, such as gasoline, cigarettes, alcoholic beverages, tires, and air travel.

governments on specific goods and services, such as gasoline, cigarettes, alcoholic beverages, tires, air travel, hotels, and phone service.

TAXES ON PROPERTY *Real estate property tax* is a major source of revenue for local governments. This tax is based on the value of land and buildings. Many people have seen significant increases in property taxes in the last decade. Some areas also impose a *personal property tax* on the value of automobiles, boats, furniture, farm equipment, and even livestock.

estate tax A tax imposed on the value of a person's property at the time of death.

inheritance tax A tax levied on the value of property bequeathed by a deceased person.

TAXES ON WEALTH An estate tax is imposed on the value of a person's property at the time of death. This federal tax is based on the fair market value of the deceased person's investments, property, and bank accounts less allowable deductions and other taxes.

Money and property passed on to heirs may be subject to a state tax. An inheritance tax is levied on the value of property bequeathed by a deceased person. This tax is paid for the right to acquire the inherited property.

Individuals are allowed to give money or items valued at $15,000 or less in a year (as of 2020) to a person without being subject to taxes. Gift amounts greater than $15,000 may have estate tax implications later. Amounts given for tuition payments or medical expenses are not subject to gift taxes as long as they are paid directly to the institution.

TAXES ON EARNINGS The two main taxes on wages and salaries are Social Security and income taxes. The Federal Insurance Contributions Act (FICA) created the Social Security tax to fund the old-age, survivors, and disability insurance portion of the Social Security system and the hospital insurance portion (Medicare).

For most people, the Social Security tax is 6.2 percent, and the Medicare tax is an additional 1.45 percent, for a total of 7.65 percent. Your employer must also pay an equal amount. If you are self-employed, you must pay both of these parts, for a total of 15.3 percent. There are some limitations and additional surcharges owed. Each year there is a cap on the maximum amount of wages subject to Social Security; in 2020, the amount is $137,700. There is no wage cap for the Medicare tax. In fact, if your wages are more than $200,000 (individual) or $250,000 (married filing jointly), there is an additional Medicare surtax of 0.9 percent, payable only by the employee.

Income tax is a major financial planning factor for most people. Some workers are subject to federal, state, and local income taxes. Currently, only seven states do not have a state income tax. Additionally, two states, New Hampshire and Tennessee, tax only dividend and interest income.

Throughout the year, your employer will withhold income tax payments from your paycheck, or you may be required to make estimated tax payments if you own your own business. Both types of payments are only estimates; you may need to pay an additional amount, or you may get a tax refund. The following sections will assist you in preparing your federal income tax return and planning your future tax strategies.

PRACTICE QUIZ 3–1

1. What are the four major categories of taxes?

2. For each of the following financial planning situations, list the type of tax that is being described.

    a. A tax on the value of a person's house.
    b. The additional charge for gasoline and hotels.
    c. Payroll deductions for federal government retirement benefits.
    d. Amount owed on property received from a deceased person.
    e. Payroll deductions for a direct tax on earnings.

The Basics of Federal Income Tax

On December 22, 2017, the Tax Cuts and Jobs Act (TCJA) was signed into law. It included reductions in tax rates for individuals, larger standard deductions for all taxpayers, as well as limits to other more commonly used deductions. These changes have been incorporated into this chapter. It is important to note than many of the changes are not considered permanent and could expire on December 31, 2025, if not extended.

Each year, millions of Americans are required to pay their share of income taxes to the federal government. As shown in Exhibit 3–1, this process involves several steps.

Step 1: Determining Adjusted Gross Income

This process starts with steps to determine **taxable income,** which is the net amount of income, after allowable deductions, on which income tax is computed.

TYPES OF INCOME Most, but not all, income is subject to taxation. Your gross, or total, income can consist of three main components:

1. **Earned income** is usually in the form of wages, salary, commission, fees, tips, or bonuses.
2. **Investment income** (sometimes referred to as *portfolio income*) is money received in the form of dividends, interest, or rent from investments.
3. **Passive income** results from business activities in which you do not actively participate, such as a limited partnership, or rental property that you do not actively manage.

Other types of income subject to federal income tax include alimony (per divorce decree before December 31, 2018), awards, lottery winnings, credit card sign-up bonuses, and prizes. For example, cash and prizes won on television game shows are subject to both federal and state taxes.

Total income is also affected by exclusions. An **exclusion** is an amount not included in gross income. For example, the foreign income exclusion allows U.S. citizens working and living in another country to exclude a certain portion ($107,600 in 2020, adjusted each year for inflation) of their income from federal income taxes.

Exclusions may also be referred to as **tax-exempt income,** or income that is not subject to tax. For example, interest earned on most state and city bonds is exempt from federal income tax. **Tax-deferred income** is income that will be taxed at a later date. For example, amounts invested in a retirement account will be taxed when it is withdrawn in the future.

ADJUSTMENTS TO INCOME **Adjusted gross income (AGI)** is gross income after certain reductions have been made. These reductions, called *adjustments to income,* include contributions to an individual retirement account (IRA) or a Keogh retirement plan, penalties for early withdrawal of savings, and alimony payments (per divorce decree before December 31, 2018). Adjusted gross income is used as the basis for computing various income tax deductions, such as medical expenses.

Certain adjustments to income, such as tax-deferred retirement plans, are a type of tax shelter. **Tax shelters** are investments that provide immediate tax benefits and a reasonable expectation of a future financial return. In recent years, tax court rulings and changes in the tax code have disallowed various types of tax shelters that were considered excessive.

Step 2: Computing Taxable Income

DEDUCTIONS A **tax deduction** is an amount subtracted from adjusted gross income to arrive at taxable income. Every taxpayer receives at least the **standard deduction**, a set amount on which no taxes are paid. As of 2020, single people receive a standard deduction of $12,400 (married couples filing jointly receive $24,800). Blind people and individuals 65 and older receive higher standard deductions.

LO3.2

Calculate taxable income and the amount owed for federal income tax.

ACTION ITEM

I understand how to calculate taxable income and federal tax owed.

☐ Yes   ☐ No

taxable income The net amount of income, after allowable deductions, on which income tax is computed.

earned income Money received for personal effort, such as wages, salary, commission, fees, tips, or bonuses.

investment income Money received in the form of dividends, interest, or rent from investments; also called *portfolio income.*

passive income Income resulting from business activities in which you do not actively participate.

exclusion An amount not included in gross income.

tax-exempt income Income that is not subject to tax.

tax-deferred income Income that will be taxed at a later date.

adjusted gross income (AGI) Gross income reduced by certain adjustments, such as contributions to an individual retirement account (IRA) and alimony payments.

tax shelter An investment that provides immediate tax benefits and a reasonable expectation of a future financial return.

tax deduction An amount subtracted from adjusted gross income to arrive at taxable income.

Exhibit **3–1** Computing Taxable Income and Your Tax Liability

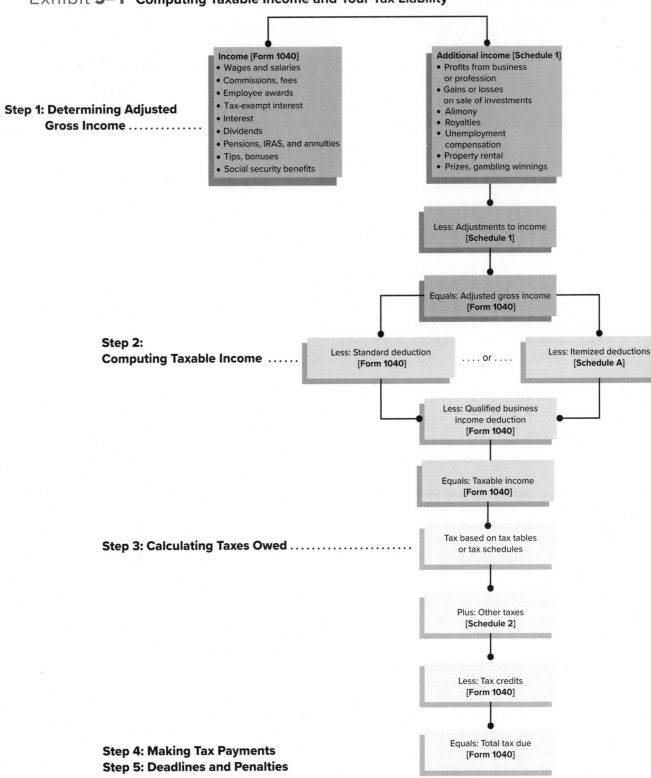

Step 1: Determining Adjusted Gross Income . . . .

Income [Form 1040]
- Wages and salaries
- Commissions, fees
- Employee awards
- Tax-exempt interest
- Interest
- Dividends
- Pensions, IRAS, and annuities
- Tips, bonuses
- Social security benefits

Additional income [Schedule 1]
- Profits from business or profession
- Gains or losses on sale of investments
- Alimony
- Royalties
- Unemployment compensation
- Property rental
- Prizes, gambling winnings

Less: Adjustments to income [Schedule 1]

Equals: Adjusted gross income [Form 1040]

Step 2: Computing Taxable Income . . . . . .

Less: Standard deduction [Form 1040]   . . . . or . . . .   Less: Itemized deductions [Schedule A]

Less: Qualified business income deduction [Form 1040]

Equals: Taxable income [Form 1040]

Step 3: Calculating Taxes Owed . . . .

Tax based on tax tables or tax schedules

Plus: Other taxes [Schedule 2]

Less: Tax credits [Form 1040]

Equals: Total tax due [Form 1040]

Step 4: Making Tax Payments
Step 5: Deadlines and Penalties

standard deduction A set amount on which no taxes are paid.

Some people may qualify for more than the standard deduction. **Itemized deductions** are expenses a taxpayer is allowed to deduct from adjusted gross income. These deductions must be reported on a Form 1040, Schedule A form. Common itemized deductions include:

- *Medical and dental expenses*—physician fees, prescription medications, hospital expenses, medical insurance premiums, hearing aids, eyeglasses, and medical travel

Financial Literacy in Practice

Is It Taxable Income? Is It Deductible?

Certain financial benefits individuals receive are not subject to federal income tax. Indicate whether each of the following items would or would not be included in taxable income when you compute your federal income tax.

Indicate whether each of the following items would or would not be deductible when you compute your federal income tax.

Is it taxable income . . . ?	Yes	No	Is it deductible . . . ?	Yes	No
1. Lottery winnings	____	____	7. Life insurance premiums	____	____
2. Child support received	____	____	8. Smoking cessation program fees	____	____
3. Worker's compensation benefits	____	____	9. Fees for traffic violations	____	____
4. Life insurance death benefits	____	____	10. Mileage for driving to volunteer work	____	____
5. Municipal bond interest earnings	____	____	11. An attorney's fee for preparing a will	____	____
6. Unemployment income	____	____	12. Income tax preparation fee	____	____

NOTE: These taxable income items and deductions are based on the 2019 tax year and may change due to changes in the tax code.

ANSWERS: 1, 6, 8, 10—yes; 2, 3, 4, 5, 7, 9, 11, 12—no.

that has not been reimbursed or paid by others. Starting in 2021, the amount of this deduction is the medical and dental expenses that exceed 10 percent of adjusted gross income. For many prior years, it has been 7.5 percent of AGI.

- *Taxes*—state and local income tax, real estate property tax, and state or local personal property tax. This deduction is limited to $10,000 beginning in the 2018 tax year.
- *Interest*—as of 2020, mortgage interest (up to $750,000 loan amount), home equity loan interest (up to $100,000 if used for the home), and investment interest expense up to an amount equal to investment income.
- *Contributions*—cash or property donated to qualified charitable organizations. Contribution totals greater than 20 percent of adjusted gross income are subject to limitations.
- *Casualty and theft losses*—financial losses resulting from federally declared disasters only.

The standard deduction *or* total itemized deductions are subtracted from adjusted gross income to obtain your taxable income. In past years, there were limitations on the amount of itemized deductions for high-income taxpayers. The limitation was removed in 2018 as part of the TCJA.

You are required to maintain records to document tax deductions, such as a home filing system (Exhibit 3–2). Canceled checks and receipts serve as proof of payment for deductions such as charitable contributions, medical expenses, and business-related expenses. Travel expenses can be documented in a daily log with records of mileage, tolls,

itemized deductions Expenses that can be deducted from adjusted gross income, such as medical expenses, real estate property taxes, home mortgage interest, charitable contributions, casualty losses, and certain work-related expenses.

CAUTION!

Watch out for IRS agent impersonators. It has been reported that thousands of people have been contacted and lost millions due to these scams. Most of these scams have occurred over the phone. The IRS will contact you by mail, not phone, regarding unpaid taxes. Information on these and other tax frauds is available at **www.treasury.gov/tigta/**.

WHAT WOULD YOU DO? Each year, people begin the arduous task of collecting their tax records to begin preparing their tax return. Imagine for a moment that you could save yourself time by creating an orderly system to use in the coming year. Describe actions you might take now to create a tax recordkeeping system.

Exhibit **3-2** **A Tax Recordkeeping System**

Tax Forms and Filing Information	Income Records	Expense Records
☐ Current tax forms and instruction booklets and online resources ☐ Reference books on current tax laws and tax-saving techniques ☐ Social Security numbers of household members ☐ Copies of federal tax returns from previous years	☐ W-2 forms reporting salary, wages, and taxes withheld ☐ W-2P forms reporting pension income ☐ 1099 forms reporting interest, dividends, and capital gains and losses from savings and investments ☐ 1099 forms for self-employment income, royalty income, and lump-sum payments from pension or retirement plans	☐ Receipts for medical, dependent care, charitable donations, and job-related expenses ☐ Mortgage interest (Form 1098) and other deductible interest ☐ Business, investment, and rental-property expense documents

exemption A deduction from adjusted gross income for yourself, your spouse, and qualified dependents.

parking fees, and away-from-home costs. See the nearby *Financial Literacy in Practice* feature to review common items that may be taxable or deductible.

Generally, you should keep tax records for three years from the date you file your return. However, you may be held responsible for providing back documentation for up to six years. Records such as past tax returns and housing documents should be kept indefinitely.

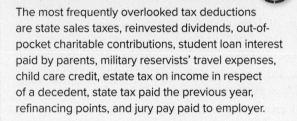

money minute focus

The most frequently overlooked tax deductions are state sales taxes, reinvested dividends, out-of-pocket charitable contributions, student loan interest paid by parents, military reservists' travel expenses, child care credit, estate tax on income in respect of a decedent, state tax paid the previous year, refinancing points, and jury pay paid to employer.

EXEMPTIONS For tax years prior to 2018, an **exemption** was allowed as a deduction from adjusted gross income for yourself, your spouse, and qualified dependents. These were eliminated with the TCJA, and the standard deductions were increased significantly instead.

QUALIFIED BUSINESS INCOME The TCJA provided significant cuts to corporate and individual tax rates. To provide a benefit to small business owners, a new provision called Section 199A permits owners of sole proprietorships, S corporations, or partnerships to deduct up to 20 percent of the income earned by the business from their individual return to arrive at taxable income.

Step 3: Calculating Taxes Owed

Your taxable income is the basis for computing the amount of tax owed.

TAX RATES Use your taxable income in conjunction with the appropriate tax table or tax schedule. For 2020, the seven-rate system for federal income tax was as follows:

Rate on Taxable Income	Single Taxpayers	Married Taxpayers Filing Jointly	Heads of Household
10%	Up to $9,875	Up to $19,750	Up to $14,100
12%	$9,876–$40,125	$19,751–$80,250	$14,101–$53,700
22%	$40,126–$85,525	$80,251–$171,050	$53,701–$85,500
24%	$85,526–$163,300	$171,051–$326,600	$85,501–$163,300
32%	$163,301–$207,350	$326,601–$414,700	$163,301–$207,350
35%	$207,351–$518,400	$414,701–$622,050	$207,351–$518,400
37%	Over $518,401	Over $622,051	Over $518,401

A separate tax rate schedule also exists for married persons who file separate income tax returns.

Tax Credits versus Tax Deductions

Many people confuse *tax credits* with *tax deductions.* Is one better than the other? A tax *credit,* such as eligible child care or dependent care expenses, results in a dollar-for-dollar reduction in the amount of taxes owed. A *tax deduction,* such as an itemized deduction in the form of medical expenses, mortgage interest, or charitable contributions, reduces the taxable income on which your taxes are based.

Here is how a $100 tax credit compares with a $100 tax deduction:

As you might expect, tax credits are less readily available than tax deductions. To qualify for a $100 child care tax credit, you may have to spend $500 in child care expenses. In some situations, spending on deductible items may be more beneficial than qualifying for a tax credit. A knowledge of tax law and careful financial planning will help you use both tax credits and tax deductions to maximum advantage.

TAX CREDIT

$100 TAX CREDIT

Reduces your taxes by $100

andreynekrasov/123RF
Brian McEntire/Shutterstock

TAX DEDUCTION

$100 TAX DEDUCTION

Reduces your taxable income by $100. The amount of your tax reduction depends on your tax bracket. Your taxes will be reduced by $12 if you are in the 12 percent tax bracket and by $24 if you are in the 24 percent tax bracket.

12% tax bracket =

CALCULATIONS

1. If a person in a 24 percent tax bracket received a $2,000 tax *deduction,* by how much would the person's taxes be reduced?

2. If a person in a 32 percent tax bracket received a $300 tax *credit,* by how much would the person's taxes be reduced?

The 10, 12, 22, 24, 32, 35 and 37 percent rates are referred to as **marginal tax rates.** Your marginal tax rate is the highest bracket and associated rate that applies to your income. After deductions, a person in the 35 percent tax bracket pays 35 cents in taxes for the next dollar of taxable income in that bracket.

In contrast, the **average tax rate** is based on the total tax due divided by taxable income. Except for taxpayers in the 10 percent bracket, this rate is less than a person's marginal tax rate. For example, a person with taxable income of $50,000 and a total tax bill of $6,790 would have an average tax rate of 13.6 percent ($6,790 ÷ $50,000).

marginal tax rate The rate used to calculate tax on the last (and next) dollar of taxable income.

average tax rate Total tax due divided by taxable income.

CALCULATING YOUR TAX Each of the tax rates represents a range of income levels. These are often referred to as "brackets." Thus, if you are married filing jointly and have a taxable income of $95,000, you and your spouse are in the 22 percent tax bracket.

Tax Due for Married Filing Jointly ($95,000 taxable income)

10% Bracket	• Range of income ($0 – $19,750) • $19,750 × 10% = $1,975
12% Bracket	• Range of income ($19,751– $80,250) • $60,499 × 12% = $7,260
22% Bracket	• Range of income ($80,251– $95,000) • $14,749 × 22% = $3,245
Total Tax Due	• Total tax due (all brackets) • $1,975 + $7,260 + $3,245 = $12,480

Although most computer programs will automatically calculate the tax owed, it is helpful to understand the process to calculate the tax due. (*Note:* For this example, we assume that you received no other income at different rates, such as capital gains.)

To calculate the tax on a specific amount of income, you must calculate the tax from each of the brackets as you progress up to your taxable income. (*Note:* This is the tax calculated prior to additional credits or other taxes, such as self-employment tax.)

ALTERNATIVE MINIMUM TAX Taxpayers with high amounts of certain deductions and various types of income may be subject to an additional tax. The *alternative minimum tax (AMT)* is designed to ensure that those who receive tax breaks also pay their fair share of taxes. The AMT was originally designed to prevent those with high incomes from using special tax breaks to pay little in taxes. However, in recent years, this tax is affecting increasing numbers of taxpayers. Some of the tax situations that can result in a person paying the AMT include high levels of deductions for state and local taxes, interest on second mortgages, medical expenses, and other deductions. Income items that can trigger the AMT are incentive stock options, long-term capital gains, and tax-exempt interest. Additional information about the AMT may be obtained at www.irs.gov.

tax credit An amount subtracted directly from the amount of taxes owed.

TAX CREDITS The tax owed may be reduced by a **tax credit**, an amount subtracted directly from the amount of taxes owed. One example of a tax credit is the credit given for child care and dependent care expenses. Another tax credit for low-income workers is the *earned-income credit (EIC)* for working parents with taxable income under a certain amount. Families that do not earn enough to owe federal income taxes are also eligible for the EIC and receive a check for the amount of their credit. A *tax credit* differs from a deduction in that a tax credit has a full dollar effect in lowering taxes, whereas a *deduction* reduces the taxable income on which the tax liability is computed.

Recent tax credits also included:

- Child tax credit up to $2,000 for each dependent under the age of 17.
- Foreign tax credit to avoid double taxation on income taxes paid to another country.
- Saver's credit (formerly the retirement tax credit) to encourage investment contributions to individual and employer-sponsored retirement plans by low- and middle-income taxpayers.
- Adoption tax credit to cover expenses when adopting a child under age 18.
- Education credits to help offset college education expenses.

See the nearby *Figure It Out!* feature to review the difference between tax deductions and tax credits.

Step 4: Making Tax Payments

You pay federal income taxes through either payroll withholding or estimated tax payments.

WITHHOLDING The pay-as-you-go system requires an employer to deduct federal income tax from your pay. The with-held amount is based on the number of exemptions and the expected deductions claimed. For example, a married person with children would have less withheld than a single person with the same salary since the married person will owe less tax.

After the end of the year, you will receive a W-2 form, which reports your annual earnings and the amounts deducted for taxes. The difference between the amount withheld and the tax owed is either the additional amount to pay or your refund. Students and low-income individuals may file for exemption from withholding if they paid no federal income tax last year and do not expect to pay any in the current year.

Many taxpayers view an annual tax refund as a "windfall," extra money they count on each year. These taxpayers are forgetting the opportunity cost of withholding excessive amounts. Others view their extra tax withholding as "forced savings." This is giving the government a free loan. A payroll deduction plan for savings could serve the same purpose while also earning interest on your funds.

ESTIMATED PAYMENTS Income from savings, investments, independent contracting, royalties, and pension payments is reported on Form 1099. People who receive such income may be required to make tax payments during the year (April 15, June 15, September 15, and January 15 as the last payment for the previous tax year). These payments are based on an estimate of taxes due at year-end. Underpayment or failure to make estimated payments can result in penalties and daily interest charges.

Step 5: Deadlines and Penalties

Most people are required to file a federal income tax return by April 15. If you are not able to file on time, you can use Form 4868 to obtain an automatic six-month extension.

This extension is for the 1040 form and other documents, but it does not delay your payment liability. You must submit the estimated amount owed along with Form 4868 by April 15. Failure to file on time can result in a penalty for being just one day late. Underpayment of quarterly estimated taxes may require paying interest on the amount you should have paid. Underpayment due to negligence or fraud can result in penalties of 50 to 75 percent.

The good news is that if you claim a refund several months or years late, the IRS will pay you interest. However, refunds must be claimed within three years of filing the return or within two years of paying the tax.

money minute focus

Each year, more than 90,000 taxpayers do not receive their refunds. The undeliverable checks total over $60 million, an average of more than $600 per check. These refund checks were returned by the post office because it was unable to deliver them. Taxpayers due a refund may contact the IRS at 1-800-829-1040 or go to www.irs.gov and click on the "Where's my refund?" link.

Sheet 9 Federal Income Tax Estimate

PRACTICE QUIZ 3–2

1. How does tax-exempt income differ from tax-deferred income?

2. When would you use the standard deduction instead of itemized deductions?

3. What is the difference between your marginal tax rate and your average tax rate?

4. For each of the following, indicate if the item is a *tax deduction* or a *tax credit*.
   a. State personal income taxes paid of $5,000
   b. Charitable donations
   c. Expenses for adopting a baby
   d. Mortgage interest on a home loan of $300,000

LO3.3

Prepare a federal income tax return.

ACTION ITEM

I know the basics of preparing a federal income tax return.

☐ Yes ☐ No

Filing Your Federal Income Tax Return

As you prepare to do your taxes, you must first determine whether you are required to file a return. Next, you need to decide which tax form best serves you and if you are required to submit supplementary schedules or forms.

Who Must File?

Every citizen or resident of the United States and every U.S. citizen who is a resident of Puerto Rico is required to file a federal income tax return if his or her income is above a certain amount. The amount is based on the person's *filing status* and other factors such as age. For example, single persons under 65 would file a return on April 15, 2020, (for tax year 2019) if their gross income exceeded $12,200. If your gross income is less than this amount but taxes were withheld, you should file a return to obtain your refund. Also, if you can be claimed as a dependent, the income limits are lower.

Your filing status is affected by marital status and dependents. The five filing status categories are:

- *Single*—never-married, divorced, or legally separated individuals with no dependents.
- *Married, filing joint return*—combines the spouses' incomes.
- *Married, filing separate returns*—each spouse is responsible for his or her own tax; under certain conditions, a married couple can benefit from this filing status.
  - *Head of household*—an unmarried individual or a surviving spouse who maintains a household (paying for more than half of the costs) for a child or a dependent relative.
  - *Qualifying widow or widower*—an individual whose spouse died within the past two years and who has a dependent; this status is limited to two years after the death of the spouse.

In some situations, you may have a choice of filing status. In such cases, compute your taxes under the alternatives to determine the most advantageous filing status.

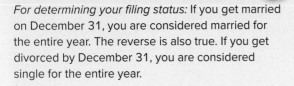

money minute focus

For determining your filing status: If you get married on December 31, you are considered married for the entire year. The reverse is also true. If you get divorced by December 31, you are considered single for the entire year.

Which Tax Forms and Schedules Should You Use?

The Tax Cuts and Jobs Act (TCJA) simplified the basic form used when filing your taxes. In the past, there were three basic forms—Form 1040, Form 1040EZ, and Form 1040A—to choose from. Now there is only one basic form, Form 1040, to report your income. If you are 65 or older, you may also use the Form 1040-SR. This form is the same as Form 1040 but with larger print and a standard deduction chart for seniors and those with blindness. There are still about 800 additional federal tax forms and schedules that are used to report additional income, deductions, extra taxes, and more complex tax situations. Most tax preparation software programs will guide you in selecting the appropriate tax forms for your situation.

Completing the Federal Income Tax Return

The major sections of Form 1040 (see Exhibit 3–3) correspond to tax topics discussed in the previous sections of this chapter:

1. *Filing status.* Your tax rate is determined by your filing status.
2. *Income.* Earnings from your employment (as reported by your W-2 form) and other income, such as savings and investment income, are reported in this section of Form 1040.
3. *Additional (other) income.* Business income, rental real estate income, and unemployment benefit income is reported on Schedule 1 and transferred to Form 1040.

Looking for the latest information to plan your saving and investing? What about guidance on banking and taxes? A valuable source is **thebalance.com** with these main information categories:

the balance

The Balance

- Investing, covering stocks, 401(k) plans, IRAs, and mutual funds.
- Credit cards, suggesting the best cards, best reward programs, and wise credit use.
- Taxes, explaining how to file along with state tax information and tax tools.
- Banking and loans with banking basics, best savings accounts, loans, and online banking.

The Tax section is broken down into the following sub-categories:

- Tax Basics: Information on tax changes for the current year, deadlines to file, and recommended tax software.
- Filing Your Return: Information on mailing your return, filing online, and choosing software to complete your return.

- Tax Filing Status: Guidance to help you choose the best filing status.
- Taxable Income: What's included in Income?
- Tax Deductions: What deductions should not be overlooked?
- Tax Credits: What tax credits might help you this year?

A recent article from **thebalance.com** discussed how selling stock affects your taxes including:

- Reporting capital gains & paying tax
- Reporting capital losses to offset capital gains.
- Why holding a stock for more than a year might be beneficial.
- The importance of keeping accurate records for stock purchases and sales.

ACTION STEPS FOR. . .

. . .Information Literacy

Locate a recent tax article on thebalance.com. What aspects of the article do you believe are most valid for your tax situation?

. . .Financial Literacy

Select a tax article from thebalance.com. Develop an outline of three key ideas that might be the basis for creating a visual (poster, document) or brief video to explain the article.

. . .Digital Literacy

Research other online tools/apps that might be helpful for you to prepare your tax return in the future.

4. *Adjustments to income.* If you qualify, you may deduct contributions (up to a certain amount) to an individual retirement account (IRA) or other qualified retirement program which is reported on Schedule 1 and transferred to Form 1040.

5. *Tax computation.* In this section, your adjusted gross income is reduced by your itemized deductions (see Exhibit 3–4) or by the standard deduction for your tax situation. In addition, an amount is deducted for each exemption to arrive at your taxable income. That income is the basis for determining the amount of your tax (see Exhibit 3–5).

6. *Other taxes.* Any special taxes, such as alternative minimum tax or self-employment tax is reported on Schedule 2 and transferred to Form 1040.

7. *Payments.* Your total withholding and other payments are indicated in this section.

8. *Tax credits.* Any additional tax credits for which you qualify are reported on Schedule 3 and transferred to Form 1040 to be subtracted.

9. *Refund or amount you owe.* If your payments exceed the amount of income tax you owe, you are entitled to a refund. If the opposite is true, you must make an additional payment. Taxpayers who want their refunds sent directly to a bank can provide the necessary account information directly on Form 1040.

Changing economic and political environments often result in new tax regulations, some of which may be favorable for you while others may not be. An important element of tax planning is your refund. Each year, more than 90 million American households receive an average tax refund of over $2,500 for a total of over $225 billion. Invested at 5 percent for a year, these refunds represent about $11.25 billion in lost earnings. By having less withheld and obtaining a smaller refund, you can save and invest these funds for your benefit during the year.

10. *Your signature.* Forgetting to sign a tax return is one of the most frequent filing errors.

What If I Made an Error on My Federal Tax Return?

Form 1040X is used to amend a previously filed tax return. If you discover income that was not reported or if you find additional deductions that will change your taxable income, you should file Form 1040X to pay the additional tax or obtain a refund. It is not recommended that you wait for the IRS to notify you that they found a difference. This could cost you penalties and interest.

Exhibit 3–3 Federal Income Tax Return—Form 1040

1. Your marriage and household situation will affect your taxable income and tax rate.

Form 1040 Department of the Treasury—Internal Revenue Service (99)
U.S. Individual Income Tax Return
OMB No. 1545-0074 IRS Use Only—Do not write or staple in this space.

Filing Status ☐ Single ☐ Married filing jointly ☐ Married filing separately (MFS) ☐ Head of household (HOH) ☐ Qualifying widow(er) (QW)
Check only one box. If you checked the MFS box, enter the name of spouse. If you checked the HOH or QW box, enter the child's name if the qualifying person is a child but not your dependent. ▶

Your first name and middle initial	Last name	Your social security number
Matthew H.	Burks	6 7 8 9 0 1 2 3 4
If joint return, spouse's first name and middle initial	Last name	Spouse's social security number
Katelyn A.	Burks	3 4 5 6 7 8 9 0 1

Home address (number and street). If you have a P.O. box, see instructions. Apt. no.
8924 Willow Lane
City, town or post office, state, and ZIP code. If you have a foreign address, also complete spaces below (see instructions).
Denver, CO 80221
Presidential Election Campaign: Check here if you, or your spouse if filing jointly, want $3 to go to this fund. Checking a box below will not change your tax or refund. ☐ You ☐ Spouse
Foreign country name | Foreign province/state/county | Foreign postal code | If more than four dependents, see instructions and ✓ here ▶ ☐

Standard Deduction: Someone can claim: ☐ You as a dependent ☐ Your spouse as a dependent
☐ Spouse itemizes on a separate return or you were a dual-status alien

Age/Blindness You: ☐ Were born before January 2, 1955 ☐ Are blind Spouse: ☐ Was born before January 2, 1955 ☐ Is blind

Dependents (see instructions): (1) First name / Last name	(2) Social security number	(3) Relationship to you	(4) ✓ if qualifies for: Child tax credit	Credit for other dependents
Brody Burks	5 6 4 8 9 7 3 2 1	Son	☑	☐
Halley Burks	5 6 4 1 2 4 5 6 7	Daughter	☑	☐
Noah Burks	5 6 4 5 6 1 2 3 4	Son	☑	☐
			☐	☐

Standard Deduction for— • Single or Married filing separately, $12,200 • Married filing jointly or Qualifying widow(er), $24,400 • Head of household, $18,350 • If you checked any box under Standard Deduction, see instructions.

Line	Item		Line	Amount
1	Wages, salaries, tips, etc. Attach Form(s) W-2		1	112,890
2a	Tax-exempt interest	b Taxable interest. Attach Sch. B if required	2b	345
3a	Qualified dividends	b Ordinary dividends. Attach Sch. B if required	3b	287
4a	IRA distributions	b Taxable amount	4b	
c	Pensions and annuities	d Taxable amount	4d	
5a	Social security benefits	b Taxable amount	5b	
6	Capital gain or (loss). Attach Schedule D if required. If not required, check here ▶ ☐		6	
7a	Other income from Schedule 1, line 9		7a	
b	Add lines 1, 2b, 3b, 4b, 4d, 5b, 6, and 7a. This is your **total income** ▶		7b	113,522
8a	Adjustments to income from Schedule 1, line 22		8a	
b	Subtract line 8a from line 7b. This is your **adjusted gross income** ▶		8b	113,522
9	**Standard deduction or itemized deductions** (from Schedule A)	9: 24,400		
10	Qualified business income deduction. Attach Form 8995 or Form 8995-A	10		
11a	Add lines 9 and 10		11a	24,400
b	**Taxable income.** Subtract line 11a from line 8b. If zero or less, enter -0-		11b	89,122

For Disclosure, Privacy Act, and Paperwork Reduction Act Notice, see separate instructions. Cat. No. 11320B Form 1040

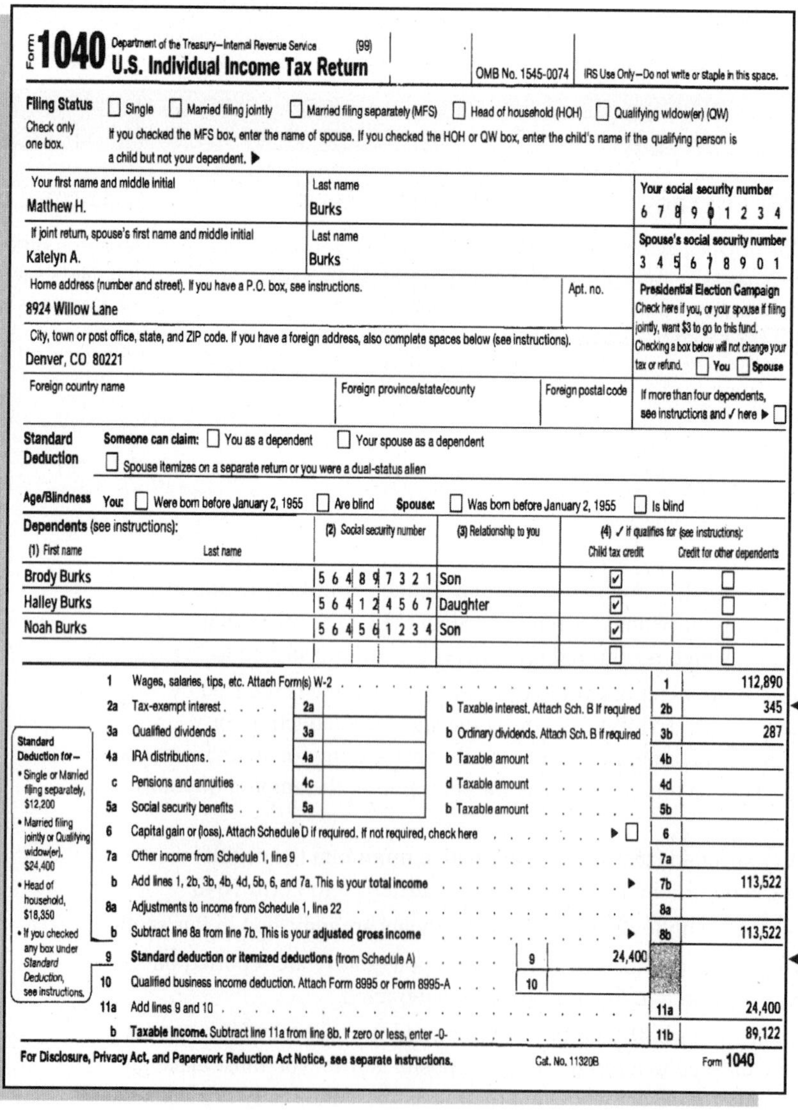

2. Your earnings and other sources of income will be reported in this section.

3. Additional income from business, rental income or unemployment.

4. Adjusted gross income results from certain deductions and will be used as a basis for computing other deductions.

5. In this section, you subtract your itemized deductions or the standard deduction to obtain taxable income; your tax is based on the tax tables or schedule.

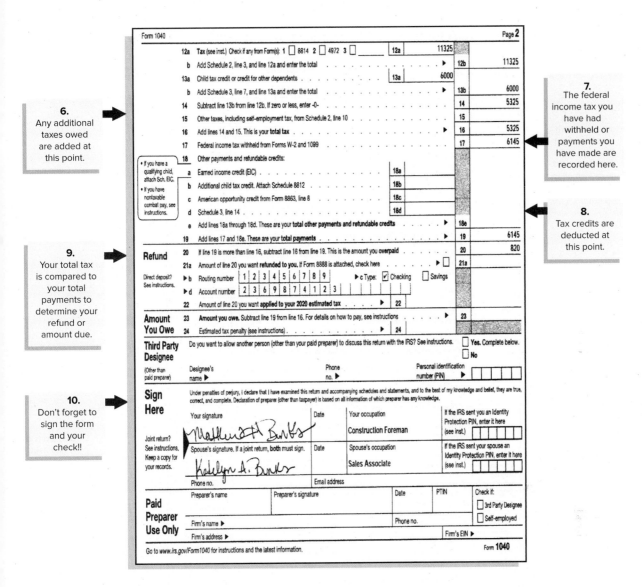

6. Any additional taxes owed are added at this point.

7. The federal income tax you have had withheld or payments you have made are recorded here.

8. Tax credits are deducted at this point.

9. Your total tax is compared to your total payments to determine your refund or amount due.

10. Don't forget to sign the form and your check!!

NOTE: These forms were used in a recent year; the current forms may not be exactly the same. Obtain current income tax forms and current tax information from your local IRS office, select post offices and libraries, or at **www.irs.gov**.

Source: Form 1040, Department of the Treasury.

How Do I File My State Tax Return?

All but seven states (Alaska, Florida, Nevada, South Dakota, Texas, Washington, and Wyoming) have some type of state income tax. In most states, the tax rate ranges from 1 to 10 percent. For further information about the income tax in your state, contact the state department of revenue. States usually require income tax returns to be filed when the federal income tax return is due. For planning your tax activities, see Exhibit 3–6.

How Do I File My Taxes Online?

Today, it is more common to electronically file (e-file) than send in a paper return. The IRS has reported that electronic filing of federal taxes now exceeds 138 million returns annually, which is over 90 percent of total tax returns. With e-file, taxpayers usually receive their refunds within three weeks. The cost for this service is usually between $15 and $40, with no fee in some cases.

FREE FILE ALLIANCE In recent years, the IRS has made online filing easier and less expensive. Through the Free File Alliance, online tax preparation and e-filing are available

Exhibit 3–4 Schedule A for Itemized Deductions—Form 1040

Health care expenses (not covered by insurance) are listed here, but must exceed 10% of adjusted gross income to be deductible.

Deductible interest payments are listed here.

A variety of other expenses may qualify under these deduction categories.

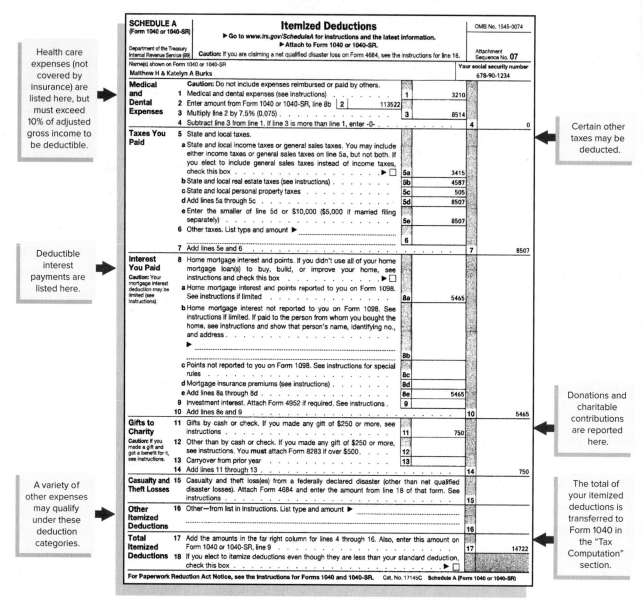

Certain other taxes may be deducted.

Donations and charitable contributions are reported here.

The total of your itemized deductions is transferred to Form 1040 in the "Tax Computation" section.

Source: Schedule A Form 1040, Department of the Treasury.

free to millions of taxpayers. This partnership between the IRS and the tax software industry has encouraged more e-filing. The IRS has reported that 50 million taxpayers have used this service and potentially saved $1.5 billion on tax preparation. The online filing process involves the following steps:

Step 1 Go to **www.irs.gov** and click "Do Your Taxes For Free."

Step 2 The initial IRS webpage gives guidance regarding the process. Your eligibility for Free File is based on your income level. You can click on a Free File company to begin your tax return. You should determine your eligibility with a particular company. A brief description of the criteria for each is provided. A "How to use Free File" option is also available to help you understand the process.

Step 3 Next, connect to the chosen company's website to begin the preparation of your tax return.

Step 4 Finally, use the company's online software to prepare your return. Your federal tax return is then filed electronically, and your tax data are stored at the vendor's site. Taxpayers who do not qualify for the Free File Alliance program may still be able to file

Exhibit **3–5** **Tax Tables and Tax Rate Schedules**

Tax Table

If line11b (taxable income) is—		And you are—			
At least	But less than	Single	Married filing jointly*	Married filing separately	Head of a household
			Your tax is—		

89,000

89,000	89,050	15,541	11,303	15,541	14,120
89,050	89,100	15,553	11,314	15,553	14,132
89,100	89,150	15,565	11,325	15,565	14,144
89,150	89,200	15,577	11,336	15,577	14,156
89,200	89,250	15,589	11,347	15,589	14,168
89,250	89,300	15,601	11,358	15,601	14,180
89,300	89,350	15,613	11,369	15,613	14,192
89,350	89,400	15,625	11,380	15,625	14,204
89,400	89,450	15,637	11,391	15,637	14,216
89,450	89,500	15,649	11,402	15,649	14,228
89,500	89,550	15,661	11,413	15,661	14,240
89,550	89,600	15,673	11,424	15,673	14,252
89,600	89,650	15,685	11,435	15,685	14,264
89,650	89,700	15,697	11,446	15,697	14,276
89,700	89,750	15,709	11,457	15,709	14,288
89,750	89,800	15,721	11,468	15,721	14,300
89,800	89,850	15,733	11,479	15,733	14,312
89,850	89,900	15,745	11,490	15,745	14,324
89,900	89,950	15,757	11,501	15,757	14,336
89,950	90,000	15,769	11,512	15,789	14,348

* This column must also be used by a qualifying widow(er).

Federal Tax Rate schedules

Married Filing Jointly or Qualifying (Widower)

If taxable income is over	but not over	the tax is
$0	$19,400	10% of the amount over $0
$19,400	$78,950	$1,940 plus 12% of the amount over $19,400
$78,950	$168,400	$9,086 plus 22% of the amount over $78,950
$168,400	$321,450	$28,765 plus 24% of the amount over $168,400
$321,450	$408,200	$65,497 plus 32% of the amount over $321,450
$408,200	$612,350	$93,257 plus 35% of the amount over $408,200
$612,350	no limit	$164,709 plus 37% of the amount over $612,350

NOTE: These were the federal income tax rates for 2019 that are used for illustrative purposes for the tax return included in the chapter exhibits. Current rates may vary due to changes in the tax code and adjustments for inflation. Obtain current income tax booklets from **www.irs.gov**.

Source: Internal Revenue Service

online for a nominal fee or use fillable forms. You don't have to purchase the software; simply go to the software company's Internet site and pay a fee to use the tax program.

Taxpayers who use the Free File Alliance are cautioned to be careful consumers. A company may attempt to sell other financial products to inexperienced taxpayers, such as expensive refund anticipation loans. Also, taxpayers using the Free File service must be aware that their state tax return might not be included in the free program.

TAX PREPARATION SOFTWARE Software packages such as H&R Block At Home and TurboTax allow you to complete needed tax forms and schedules and either print them for mailing or file online. Today, most taxpayers use computers or online products for tax recordkeeping, tax form preparation, and electronic filing.

Using tax software can save you time when preparing your Form 1040 and accompanying schedules. When selecting tax software, consider the following factors:

money minute focus

Electronically filed federal income tax returns have an accuracy rate of 99 percent, compared to 81 percent for paper returns. Most electronic filing programs do your calculations and signal potential errors before you file.

1. Your personal situation—are you employed, do you have rental property, or do you operate your own small business?
2. Special tax situations with regard to types of income, unusual deductions, and various tax credits.
3. Features in the software, such as "audit check," future tax planning, and filing your federal and state tax forms online.
4. Technical aspects, such as the hardware and operating system requirements, and online support that is provided.

What Tax Assistance Sources Are Available?

As with other aspects of personal financial planning, many tax resources are available to assist you.

Exhibit 3–6 Tax-Planner Calendar

January
- Establish a recordkeeping system for your tax information.
- If you expect a refund, file your tax return for the previous year.
- Make your final estimated quarterly payment for the previous year for income not covered by withholding.

February
- Check to make sure you received W-2 and 1099 forms from all organizations from which you had income during the previous year; these should have been received by January 31. If not, contact the organization.

March
- Organize your records and tax information in preparation for filing your tax return; if you expect a refund, file as soon as possible.

April
- April 15 is the deadline for filing your federal tax return; if it falls on a weekend, you have until the next business day (usually Monday).
- If necessary, file for an automatic extension for filing your tax forms.

May
- Review your tax return to determine whether any changes in withholding, exemptions, or marital status have not been reported to your employer.

June
- The second installment for estimated tax is due June 15 for income not covered by withholding.

July
- With the year half over, consider or implement plans for a personal retirement program such as an IRA or a Keogh plan.

August
- Tax returns are due August 15 for those who received the automatic four-month extension.
- Determine if you qualify for an IRA; if so, consider opening one.

September
- The third installment for estimated tax is due September 15 for income not covered by withholding.

October
- Determine the tax benefits of selling certain investments by year-end.
- Prepare a preliminary tax form to determine the most advantageous filing status.
- Tax returns are due October 15 for those who received the automatic six-month extension.

November
- Make any last-minute changes in withholding by your employer to avoid penalties for too little withholding.
- Determine if you qualify for an IRA; if so, consider opening one.

December
- Determine if it would be to your advantage to make payments for next year before December 31 of the current year.
- Decide if you can defer income for the current year until the following year.

NOTE: Children born before the end of the year give you a full-year exemption, so plan accordingly!

IRS SERVICES If you prepare your own tax return or desire tax information, the IRS can assist in seven ways:

1. *Publications.* The IRS offers hundreds of free booklets and pamphlets that can be obtained at a local IRS office, by mail request, by telephone, or downloaded. Especially helpful is *Your Federal Income Tax* (IRS Publication 17). IRS publications and tax forms are available by phone at 1-800-TAX-FORM or online at www.irs.gov.

2. *Recorded messages.* The IRS Tele-Tax system gives you 24-hour access to about 150 recorded tax tips at 1-800-829-4477.

3. *Phone hotline.* Information about specific problems is available through an IRS-staffed phone line at 1-800-829-1040.

4. *Walk-in service.* You can visit a local IRS office (400 are available) to obtain tax assistance.

5. *Interactive tax assistant.* The IRS has developed a query-based interactive tool that allows taxpayers to get answers for basic and advanced questions.

6. *DVD.* The IRS also sells a DVD with over 2,000 tax forms, publications, and FAQs.

7. *IRS2Go App.* This tool provides options for checking your refund status, requesting tax records, locating free tax prep help, and accessing other interactive tools.

TAX PUBLICATIONS Each year, several tax guides are published and offered for sale. Publications such as *J.K. Lasser's Your Income Tax* and *The Ernst & Young Tax Guide* can be purchased online or at local stores. The IRS also offers Publication 17, *Your Federal Income Tax (for Individuals),* which is a free resource.

ONLINE RESOURCES As with other personal finance topics, extensive information may be found on websites such as those mentioned earlier. Be sure to access reliable websites and print information for your records.

> **WHAT WOULD YOU DO?** Understanding your tax situation is critical. Most people wait until right before the tax filing deadline to research relevant tax topics. When is the best time to research tax topics? Describe actions and materials that you will utilize for your research.

Tax Preparation Services

Over 40 million U.S. taxpayers pay someone to do their income taxes. The fee for this service can range from $40 at a tax preparation service for a simple return to more than $2,000 to a certified public accountant for a complicated return.

TYPES OF TAX SERVICES Doing your own taxes may not be desirable, especially if you have sources of income other than salary. The sources available for tax assistance include the following:

- Tax services range from local, one-person operations to national firms with thousands of offices, such as H&R Block.
- Enrolled agents—government-approved tax experts—prepare returns and provide tax advice. You may contact the **National Association of Enrolled Agents** at 1-800-424-4339 for information about enrolled agents in your area.
- Many accountants offer tax assistance along with other business services. A certified public accountant (CPA) with special training in taxes can help with tax planning and the preparation of your annual tax return.
- Attorneys usually do not complete tax returns; however, you can use an attorney's services when you are involved in a tax-related transaction or when you have a difference of opinion with the IRS.
- Volunteer Income Tax Assistance (VITA) offers free tax help to low- and moderate-income taxpayers who cannot prepare their own tax returns. Certified volunteers provide this service at community centers, libraries, schools, malls, and other locations. To locate the nearest VITA site, call 1-800-906-9887.

EVALUATING TAX SERVICES When planning to use a tax preparation service, consider these factors:

- What training and experience does the tax professional possess?
- How will the fee be determined? (Avoid preparers who earn a percentage of your refund.)
- Does the preparer suggest you report various deductions that might be questioned?
- Will the preparer represent you if your return is audited?
- Is tax preparation the main business activity, or does it serve as a front for selling other financial products and services?

FinTech for Financial Literacy

The IRS now requires taxpayers to report whether they have profited by buying a cryptocurrency and then used the cryptocurrency to buy goods priced in any other currency. Any profit would be treated as a capital gain.

Additional information about tax preparers may be obtained at the websites for the National Association of Enrolled Agents (www.naea.org) and the National Association of Tax Professionals (www.natptax.com).

TAX SERVICE WARNINGS   Even if you hire a professional tax preparer, you are responsible for supplying accurate and complete information. Hiring a tax preparer will not guarantee that you pay the *correct* amount. A study conducted by *Money* magazine of 41 tax preparers reported fees ranging from $375 to $3,600, with taxes due ranging from $31,846 to $74,450 for the same fictional family. If you owe more tax because your return contains errors or you have made entries that are not allowed, you are responsible for paying that additional tax, plus any interest and penalties.

Beware of tax preparers and other businesses that offer your refund in advance. These "refund anticipation loans" frequently charge very high interest rates for this type of consumer credit. Studies reveal interest rates sometimes exceeding 300 percent (on an annualized basis).

What If Your Return Is Audited?

tax audit A detailed examination of your tax return by the Internal Revenue Service.

The Internal Revenue Service reviews all returns for completeness and accuracy. If you make an error, your tax is automatically refigured, and you receive either a bill or a refund. If you make an entry that is not allowed, you will be notified by mail. A **tax audit** is a detailed examination of your tax return by the IRS. In most audits, the IRS requests more information to support your tax return. Be sure to keep accurate records. Receipts, canceled checks, and other evidence can verify amounts that you claim. Avoiding common filing mistakes helps to minimize your chances of an audit (see Exhibit 3–7).

WHO GETS AUDITED?   Less than 1 percent of all tax filers—fewer than 1.5 million people—are audited each year. Although the IRS does not reveal its basis for auditing returns, several indicators are evident. People who claim large or unusual deductions increase their chances of an audit. Tax advisors suggest including a brief explanation or a copy of receipts for deductions that may be questioned.

TYPES OF AUDITS   The simplest and most frequent type of audit is the *correspondence audit*. This mail inquiry requires you to clarify or document minor questions. The *office audit* requires you to visit an IRS office to clarify some aspect of your tax return.

The *field audit* is more complex. An IRS agent visits you at your home, your business, or the office of your accountant to have access to your records. A field audit may be done to verify whether an individual has a home office if this is claimed.

The IRS also conducts more detailed audits for about 50,000 taxpayers. These range from random requests to document various tax return items to line-by-line reviews by IRS employees.

YOUR AUDIT RIGHTS   When you receive an audit notice, you have the right to request time to prepare. Also, you can ask the IRS for clarification of items being questioned. When audited, follow these suggestions:

- Decide whether you will bring your tax preparer, accountant, or lawyer.
- Be on time for your appointment; bring only relevant documents.
- Present tax evidence in a logical, calm, and confident manner; maintain a positive attitude.
- Make sure the information you present is consistent with the tax law.

Exhibit **3–7** **How to Avoid Common Filing Errors**

For All Returns
- Organize all tax-related information for easy access.
- Be sure to include the correct Social Security number(s).
- Follow instructions carefully. Many people deduct total medical and dental expenses rather than the amount of these expenses that exceeds 10 percent of adjusted gross income.
- Use the proper tax rate schedule or tax table column.
- Be sure to claim the correct amounts for standard deductions for your filing status.
- Consider the alternative minimum tax that may apply to your situation. Be sure to pay self-employment tax and tax on early IRA withdrawals.
- Check your math several times. Also spot-check the tax software to ensure accuracy.
- Keep a copy of your return.
- Check everything again—and file on time!

For Paper Returns
- Sign your return (both spouses must sign a joint return) or the IRS won't process it.
- Be sure to record amounts on the correct lines.
- Attach necessary documentation such as your W-2 forms and required supporting schedules.
- Make the check payable to "United States Treasury."
- Put your Social Security number, the tax year, and a daytime telephone number on your check—and be sure to sign the check!
- Put the proper postage on your mailing envelope.

- Keep your answers aimed at the auditor's questions. Answer questions clearly and completely. Be as brief as possible. The five best responses to questions during an audit are "Yes," "No," "I don't recall," "I'll have to check on that," and "What specific items do you want to see?"

If you disagree with the results of an audit, you may request a conference at the Regional Appeals Office. Although most differences of opinion are settled at this stage, some taxpayers take their cases further. A person may go to a U.S. tax court, a U.S. claims court, or a U.S. district court. Some tax disputes have gone to the U.S. Supreme Court.

PRACTICE QUIZ 3–3

1. In what ways does your filing status affect preparation of your federal income tax return?
2. What are the main sources available to help people prepare their taxes?
3. What actions can reduce the chances of an IRS audit?
4. Using your Personal Financial Plan Sheet 9, calculate your federal income tax estimate.

Tax Planning Strategies

For people to pay their fair share of taxes—no more, no less—they should practice **tax avoidance**, the use of legitimate methods to reduce one's taxes. In contrast, **tax evasion** is the use of illegal actions to reduce one's taxes. To minimize taxes owed, follow these guidelines:

- If you expect to have the *same* or a *lower* tax rate next year, *accelerate deductions* into the current year. Pay real estate property taxes or make charitable donations by December 31.

LO3.4

Select appropriate tax strategies for various life situations.

tax avoidance The use of legitimate methods to reduce one's taxes.

ACTION ITEM

I understand current tax strategies for my tax situation.

☐ **Yes**   ☐ **No**

tax evasion The use of illegal actions to reduce one's taxes.

- If you expect to have a *lower* or the *same* tax rate next year, *delay the receipt of income* until next year so the funds will be taxed at a lower rate or at a later date.
- If you expect to have a *higher* tax rate next year, consider *delaying deductions,* since they will have a greater benefit. A $1,000 deduction at 22 percent lowers your taxes $220; at 32 percent, your taxes are lowered $320.
- If you expect to have a *higher* tax rate next year, *accelerate the receipt of income* to have it taxed at the current lower rate.

Education Deduction or Tax Credit?

If you have paid higher education expenses this year, you should consider whether the Tuition and Fees deduction or one of the two Education credits are best for your tax situation.

- The Tuition and Fees deduction allows you to reduce your adjusted gross income by as much as $4,000 for expenses paid in the current year. This is available through tax year 2020.
- The American Opportunity Credit allows a credit of up to $2,500 (100 percent of the first $2,000 of qualified expenses and 25 percent of the next $2,000). This credit is limited to the first four years of postsecondary education and the student must be enrolled at least half-time.
- The Lifetime Learning Credit is limited to $2,000, which is 20 percent of up to $10,000 of qualified education expenses. This credit can be used for part-time education and graduate school funds, as well as for postsecondary education beyond the first four years.

You must choose between the Tuition and Fees deduction and one of the two credits. In addition, the taxpayer claiming the deduction or credit must be able to claim the student as a dependent or have qualified expenses for themselves or their spouse.

When considering financial decisions in relation to your taxes, remember that purchasing, investing, and retirement planning are the areas most heavily affected by tax laws.

Consumer Purchasing

The buying decisions most directly affected by taxes are the purchase of a residence, the use of credit, job-related expenses, and health care expenses.

PLACE OF RESIDENCE Owning a home is one of the best tax shelters. Both real estate property taxes and interest on the mortgage (up to $750,000 of the debt) are deductible (as itemized deductions) and thus reduce your taxable income.

CONSUMER DEBT Current tax laws allow homeowners to borrow for consumer purchases. You can deduct interest on loans (of up to $100,000) secured by your primary or secondary home up to the actual dollar amount you have invested in it—the difference between the market value of the home and the amount you owe on it. These *home equity loans,* which are *second mortgages,* must be used to invest in improvements or other expenses associated with the home.

HEALTH CARE EXPENSES *Flexible spending accounts, health savings accounts,* and expense reimbursement accounts allow you to reduce your taxable income when paying for medical expenses or child care costs. Workers are allowed to put pretax dollars into these employer & government (marketplace) sponsored programs. These "deposits" result in a lower taxable income. Then, the funds in the accounts may be used to pay for various medical expenses and dependent care costs.

Figure It Out!

Short-Term and Long-Term Capital Gains

You will pay a lower tax rate on the profits from stocks and other investments if you hold the asset for more than 12 months. As of 2020, a single taxpayer with $100,000 of taxable income would be in the 24 percent tax bracket and would pay $720 in taxes on a $3,000 short-term capital gain (assets held for less than a year). However, that same taxpayer would pay only $450 on the $3,000 (a 15 percent capital gains tax) if the investment were held for more than a year.

	Short-Term Capital Gain (assets held less than a year)	Long-Term Capital Gain (assets held a year or more)
Capital gain	$3,000	$3,000
Capital gains tax rate	24%	15%
Capital gains tax	$720	$450
Tax savings	$270 ($720 − $450)	

WHAT WOULD YOU DO? Each year, millions of taxpayers use itemized deductions and claim over $1 trillion worth of tax deductions. Remember: The IRS allows the larger of the standard or the itemized deductions. What are some actions that you might be able to take to increase your available deductions?

Investment Decisions

A major area of tax planning involves decisions related to investing.

TAX-EXEMPT INVESTMENTS Interest income from municipal bonds, which are issued by state and local governments, and other tax-exempt investments is not subject to federal income tax. Although municipal bonds have lower interest rates than other investments, the *tax-equivalent* income may be higher. For example, if you are in the 35 percent tax bracket, earning $100 of tax-exempt income would be worth more to you than earning $150 in taxable investment income. The $150 would have an after-tax value of $97.50—$150 less $52.50 (35 percent of $150) for taxes.

TAX-DEFERRED INVESTMENTS Although tax-deferred investments, with income taxed at a later date, are less beneficial than tax-exempt investments, they give you the advantage of paying taxes in the future rather than now. Examples of tax-deferred investments include:

- *Tax-deferred annuities,* usually issued by insurance companies. These investments are discussed in Chapter 10.
- *Health savings accounts,* available with high-deductible health insurance policies, may be utilized for current health care expenses or for retirement in future years. These investments are discussed in Chapter 9.
- *Retirement plans* such as IRA, SEP-IRA, or 401(k) plans. The next section discusses the tax implications of these plans.

capital gains Profits from the sale of a capital asset such as stocks, bonds, or real estate.

Capital gains, profits from the sale of a capital asset such as stocks, bonds, or real estate, are also tax-deferred; you do not have to pay the tax on these profits until the asset is sold. In recent years, *long-term* capital gains (on investments held more than a year) have been taxed at a lower rate. See the nearby *Figure It Out!* feature for an example.

The sale of an investment for less than its purchase price is, of course, a *capital loss.* Capital losses can be used to offset capital gains and up to $3,000 of ordinary income. Unused capital losses may be carried forward into future years to offset capital gains or ordinary income up to $3,000 per year.

SELF-EMPLOYMENT Owning your own business can have tax advantages. Self-employed persons may deduct expenses such as health and certain life insurance as business costs. In addition, the TCJA may allow you to deduct up to 20 percent of the income due to the Qualified Business Income deduction. Remember, business owners also have to pay self-employment tax (Social Security and Medicare) in addition to the regular tax rate.

CHILDREN'S INVESTMENTS A child under 18 or a full-time student under 24 with investment income of more than $2,200 is taxed at the parent's top rate. For investment income under $2,200, the child receives a deduction of $1,100, and the next $1,100 is taxed at his or her own rate, which is probably lower than the parent's rate.

Retirement and Education Plans

A major tax strategy for working people is the use of tax-deferred retirement plans such as individual retirement accounts (IRAs), Keogh plans, and 401(k) plans. Another tax strategy involves the use of education savings plans such as Coverdell Education Savings Accounts or 529 plans.

TRADITIONAL IRA The regular IRA deduction is available only to people who do not participate in employer-sponsored retirement plans or who have an adjusted gross income under a certain amount. As of 2020, the IRA contribution limit was $6,000. Workers age 50 and over were allowed to contribute up to $7,000 as a "catch up" to make up for lost time saving for retirement.

In general, amounts withdrawn from deductible IRAs are included in gross income. An additional 10 percent penalty is usually imposed on withdrawals made before age 59½ unless the withdrawn funds are on account of death or disability, for medical expenses, or for qualified higher education expenses.

ROTH IRA The Roth IRA also allows a $6,000 (2020) annual contribution, which is not tax-deductible; however, the earnings on the account are tax-free after five years. The funds from the Roth IRA may be withdrawn before age 59½ if the account owner is disabled or for the purchase of a first home ($10,000 maximum). Like the regular IRA, the Roth IRA is limited to people with an adjusted gross income under a certain amount.

Deductible IRAs provide tax relief up front as contributions reduce current taxes. However, taxes must be paid when the withdrawals are made from the deductible IRA. In contrast, the Roth IRA does not have immediate benefits, but the investment grows in value on a tax-free basis. Withdrawals from the Roth IRA are exempt from federal and state taxes.

SEP-IRA PLAN If you are self-employed and own your own business, you can establish a SEP-IRA (Simplified Employee Pension) plan. This retirement plan only allows contributions by the employer for employees that are at least 21 and have worked at least three of the last five years. In general, with a SEP-IRA, people may contribute 25 percent of their annual income, up to a maximum of $57,000 (in 2020), to this tax-deferred retirement plan.

401(K) PLAN The part of the tax code called 401(k) authorizes a tax-deferred retirement plan sponsored by an employer. This plan allows you to contribute a greater tax-deferred amount ($19,500 in 2020) than you can contribute to an IRA. Workers age 50 and over may be allowed to contribute an additional $6,500 if their employer allows. However, most companies set a limit on your contribution, such as 15 percent of your salary. Some employers provide a matching contribution in their 401(k) plans. For example, a company may contribute 50 cents for each $1 contributed by an employee. This results in an immediate 50 percent return on your investment.

Tax planners advise people to contribute as much as possible to a SEP-IRA or 401(k) plan since (1) the increased value of the investment accumulates on a tax-free basis until the funds are withdrawn, and (2) contributions reduce your adjusted gross income for computing your current tax liability.

COVERDELL EDUCATION SAVINGS ACCOUNT This account is designed to assist parents in saving for the education of their children. Withdrawals can be used for a variety of educational uses for kindergarten through college-age students. The annual contribution, limited to $2,000, is not tax-deductible and is limited to taxpayers with an adjusted gross income under a certain amount. However, as with the Roth IRA, the earnings accumulate tax-free.

529 PLAN The 529 plan is another education savings plan that helps parents save for the education of their children. Almost every state has a 529 plan available. There is no federal tax deduction, but the earnings grow tax-free, and there are no taxes when the money is taken out of the account for qualified education expenses. In addition, many states allow their residents to deduct contributions to their state plans up to a specified maximum.

Changing Tax Strategies

Each year, the tax code includes a myriad of changes. The Tax Cuts and Jobs Act (TCJA) discussed at the beginning of the chapter included many changes. Congress frequently passes legislation that changes the tax code. These changes require that you regularly determine how to best take advantage of the tax laws for personal financial planning.

Recent tax changes have included the following:

- Employers now allow employees with health care flexible spending accounts to carry over up to $500 of unused funds.
- Streamlined options are available for the home office deduction for small businesses.
- Qualified Business Income, also known as Section 199A, allows owners of pass-through businesses to claim a tax deduction worth up to 20% of the qualified business income. Note: Certain types of businesses are excluded from this deduction, such as engineering and architecture firms.

In addition to these and other recent tax changes, the IRS usually modifies the tax form and filing procedures yearly, so be sure to carefully consider changes in your personal situation and your income level. Well-informed taxpayers monitor their personal tax strategies to best serve daily living needs and to achieve long-term financial goals.

Flat or VAT Tax?

For many years, politicians have used tax reform as a platform to run for office. Some want to increase tax deductions to provide for certain segments, while others want to find ways to simplify the tax code. There is no denying that the tax code has become increasingly complex. The number of words in the tax code has reportedly grown from 1.4 million to more than 4 million in the last decade!

What are some options that are being proposed? First, a *flat tax* proposal has been around for many years. This would require that all taxpayers, regardless of income level and type, pay the same percentage. While seemingly relatively easy to implement, the reality is that this would be an increase in overall tax for quite a few people. The other alternative, a *value-added tax (VAT),* would add a tax to a product for each stage in the manufacturing process. It is believed that higher-income individuals would pay higher taxes since they are typically the larger consumers of goods. This has been implemented in other countries. That said, the administrative process can be a challenge for each of the companies involved in the process to remit the tax.

What do you think will happen to the tax code in five years? 10 years? 20 years?

Sheet 10 Tax Planning Activities

PRACTICE QUIZ 3–4

1. How does tax avoidance differ from tax evasion?

2. What common tax-saving methods are available to most individuals and households?

3. For the following tax situations, indicate if the item refers to tax-exempt income or tax-deferred income.

   a. Interest earned on municipal bonds
   b. Earnings on a traditional individual retirement account
   c. Education IRA earnings used for college expenses
   d. Earnings on a Roth individual retirement account

4. Using your Personal Financial Plan Sheet 10, evaluate your actions to prepare for this tax year.

Road Map

to financial literacy

You Are Here

Managing Your Tax Payments

Checkpoint

1

- ☐ Reconsider your responses to the "Action Items" for this chapter to determine actions you might consider related to your tax planning activities.
- ☐ Establish a system for organizing your tax records.
- ☐ Estimate your proper withholding amounts.

Checkpoint

2

- ☐ Participate in a tax-deferred retirement plan.
- ☐ Consider buying a home for possible tax savings.
- ☐ Revise withholding based on family changes.

Checkpoint

3

- ☐ Investigate tax-exempt investments.
- ☐ Increase contributions to tax deferred retirement plans.
- ☐ Research tax credits.

Checkpoint

4

- ☐ Continue to save and invest.
- ☐ Determine age when Social Security benefits will start.
- ☐ Continue to update your knowledge of income tax changes to help you make better informed financial decisions.

Financial Security

SMALL REFUND/SMALL AMOUNT OWED

LARGE REFUND

LARGE AMOUNT OWED

$500 $0 $500
$1000 $1000
$1500 $1500
$2000 $2000
$2500 $2500

your personal finance dashboard

TAX REFUND OR UNDERPAYMENT?

Tax Refunds

Another indicator of your financial health is your ability to organize and prepare key documents to maximize your tax situation. Whether you prepare your tax return or take it to someone to prepare, you need to have all of the key documents to pay your "fair share." You also need to monitor your tax situation throughout the year. This means understanding your tax situation and being aware of any changes.

YOUR SITUATION: Do you owe taxes each year? Do you receive an excessive tax refund? Owing taxes each year could lead to underpayment penalties. Receiving a large tax refund could be hampering your savings ability. Paying your "fair share" in a timely manner is one of the foundations for progress toward financial independence.

LO3.1 Tax planning can influence spending, saving, borrowing, and investing decisions. An awareness of income taxes, sales taxes, excise taxes, property taxes, estate taxes, inheritance taxes, gift taxes, and Social Security taxes is vital for successful financial planning.

LO3.2 Taxable income is determined by subtracting adjustments to income and deductions from gross income. Your total tax liability is based on the published tax tables or tax schedules, less any tax credits.

LO3.3 The major sections of Form 1040 provide the basic framework for filing your federal income tax return. The main sources of tax assistance are IRS services and publications, other publications, the Internet, computer software, and professional tax preparers such as commercial tax services, enrolled agents, accountants, and attorneys.

LO3.4 You may reduce your tax burden through careful planning and making financial decisions related to consumer purchasing and the use of debt, investments, and retirement planning.

adjusted gross income (AGI) 97	exemption 100	tax audit 112
average tax rate 101	inheritance tax 96	tax avoidance 113
capital gains 116	investment income 97	tax credit 102
earned income 97	itemized deductions 99	tax deduction 97
estate tax 96	marginal tax rate 101	tax-deferred income 97
excise tax 95	passive income 97	tax evasion 114
exclusion 97	standard deduction 98	tax-exempt income 97
	taxable income 97	tax shelter 97

1. A person had $4,102 withheld for federal income taxes and had a tax liability of $3,345. Would the difference be a refund or an additional amount due, and what would the amount be?

2. Based on the following information, what is the amount of taxable income?

Gross salary, $56,900   Dividend income, $160
Itemized deductions, $14,200   Interest earnings, $65

Solutions

1. To determine the amount of refund or additional tax due, compare the amount of tax liability with the amount withheld. The $3,345 tax liability minus the $4,102 would result in an amount refunded of $757.

2. Taxable income is calculated by adding salary, interest earned, and dividends, and then subtracting itemized deductions:

$$\$56,900 + \$65 + \$160 - \$14,200 = \$42,925$$

1. Daniel Simmons arrived at the following tax information:
   Gross salary, $62,250   Interest earnings, $75
   Dividend income, $140   Adjustments to income, $850
   Standard deduction, $12,400

   What amount would Daniel report as taxable income? (LO3.2)

2. If Samantha Jones had the following itemized deductions, should she use Schedule A or the standard deduction? The standard deduction for her tax situation is $12,400. (LO3.2) Donations to church and other charities, $5,050

   Medical and dental expenses exceeding 10 percent of adjusted gross income, $2,450

   Mortgage interest, $3,100

   State income tax, $2,920

3. What would be the average tax rate for a person who paid taxes of $4,706 on taxable income of $40,780? (LO3.2)

4. Based on the following data, would Beth and Roger Simmons receive a refund or owe additional taxes? (LO3.2)

Adjusted gross income, $42,140	Standard deduction, $24,800
Credit for child and dependent care expenses, $400	Federal income tax withheld, $2,017
	Tax rate on taxable income, 10 percent

5. If $4,323 were withheld during the year and taxes owed were $4,122, would the person owe an additional amount or receive a refund? What is the amount? (LO3.2)

6. Noor Patel has had a busy year! She decided to take a cross-country adventure. Along the way, she won a new car on *The Price Is Right* (valued at $15,500) and $500 on a scratch-off lottery ticket (the first time she ever played). She also signed up for a credit card to start the trip and was given a sign-up bonus of $100. How much from these will she have to include in her federal taxable income? (LO3.2)

7. Using the tax table on page 100, determine the amount of taxes for the following situations: (LO3.3)
   a. A head of household with taxable income of $55,000.
   b. A single person with taxable income of $35,000.
   c. Married taxpayers filing jointly with taxable income of $72,000.

8. If 300,000 people each receive an average refund of $2,500, based on an annual interest rate of 3 percent, what would be the lost annual income from savings on those refunds? (LO3.2)

9. Using the tax table in Exhibit 3–5, determine the amount of taxes for the following situations: (LO3.3)
   a. A head of household with taxable income of $89,525.
   b. A single person with taxable income of $89,001.
   c. A married person filing a separate return with taxable income of $89,365.

10. Wendy Brooks prepares her own income tax return each year. A tax preparer would charge her $75 for this service. Over a period of 10 years, how much does Wendy gain from preparing her own tax return? Assume she can earn 3 percent on her savings. (LO3.3)

11. Julia Sims has $30,000 of adjusted gross income and $5,000 of medical expenses. She expects to itemize her tax deductions this year. The most recent tax year has a medical expenses floor of 10 percent. How much of a tax deduction for medical expenses will Julia be able to take? (LO3.3)

12. Allison has returned to school after five years out of the work force. She is taking one course at the local university for a cost of $1,500. To minimize her taxes, should she take a tuition and fees deduction or an education credit? (Assume a 15 percent tax rate.) (LO3.4)

13. Would you prefer a fully taxable investment earning 10 percent or a tax-exempt investment earning 8.25 percent? (Assume a 24 percent tax rate.) Why? (LO3.4)

14. On December 30, you make a $3,000 charitable donation. (LO3.4)
   a. If you are in the 24 percent tax bracket, how much will you save in taxes for the current year?
   b. If you deposit that tax savings in a savings account for the next five years at 8 percent, what will be the future value of that account?

15. Reginald Sims deposits $5,500 each year in a tax-deferred retirement account. If he is in a 22 percent tax bracket, by what amount would his tax be reduced over a 20-year time period? (LO3.4)

16. If a person in a 32 percent tax bracket makes a deposit of $5,000 to a tax-deferred retirement account, what amount would be saved on current taxes? (LO3.4)

 To reinforce the content in this chapter, more problems are provided at connect.mheducation.com.

121

Competency...

Prepare to file a federal income tax return.

Action Research...

Based on this chapter and the Your Personal Financial Plan Sheet 9: (a) Prepare a flow-chart that communicates the steps you would take to file your federal income taxes. (b) Explain these steps in relation to: (1) if you have or will in the future prepare your own taxes, or (2) if you have had or will have in the future someone else prepare your taxes. (c) Research the tax deductions and credits for which you may be eligible for the current year.

Outcome...

Present a tax filing flowchart in a photo essay, PowerPoint presentation, video, or other creative format. Explain how these actions might need to be adapted as tax regulations change.

REAL LIFE PERSONAL FINANCE

A SINGLE FATHER'S TAX SITUATION

Ever since his wife's death, Eric Stanford has faced difficult personal and financial circumstances. His job provides him with a fairly good income but keeps him away from his daughters, ages 8 and 10, nearly 20 days a month. This requires him to use in-home child care services that consume a major portion of his income. Since the Stanfords live in a small apartment, this arrangement has been very inconvenient.

Due to the costs of caring for his children, Eric has only a minimal amount withheld from his salary for federal income taxes. Thus, more money is available during the year, but for the last few years, he has had to make a payment in April—another financial burden.

Although Eric has created an investment fund for his daughters' college education and for his retirement, he has not sought investments that offer tax benefits. Overall, he needs to look at several aspects of his tax planning activities to find strategies that will best serve his current and future financial needs.

Eric has assembled the following information for the current tax year:

Earnings from wages, $114,241

Interest earned on savings, $65

IRA deduction, $6,500

Checking account interest, $45

Current standard deduction for filing status, $18,350

Amount withheld for federal income tax, $8,825

Tax credit for child care, $1,200

Child tax credit, $4,000

Filing status: head of household

Questions

1. What are Eric's major financial concerns in his current situation?
2. In what ways might Eric improve his tax planning efforts?
3. Calculate the following:
   a. What is Eric's taxable income? (Refer to Exhibit 3–1.)
   b. What is his total tax liability? (Use tax table, Exhibit 3-5.) What is his average tax rate?
   c. Based on his withholding, will Eric receive a refund or owe additional tax? What is the amount?

FINANCIAL SERVICES: SAVINGS PLANS AND ACCOUNTS

Jamie Lee Jackson, age 26, is in her last semester of college, and graduation day is just around the corner! It is the time of year again when Jamie Lee must file her annual federal income taxes. Last year, she received an increase in salary from the bakery, which brought her gross monthly earnings to $2,550, and she also opened up an IRA, to which she contributed $300. Her savings accounts earn 2 percent interest per year, and she also received an unexpected $1,000 gift from her great aunt. Jamie was also lucky enough last year to win a raffle prize of $2,000, most of which was deposited into her regular savings account after paying off her credit card balance.

Current Financial Situation

Assets:

Checking account, $2,250

Savings account, $6,900 (interest earned last year: $125)

Emergency fund savings account, $3,900 (interest earned last year: $75)

IRA balance, $350 ($300 contribution made last year)

Car, $3,000

Liabilities:

Student loan, $10,800

Credit card balance, $0 (interest paid last year: $55)

Income:

Gross monthly salary, $2,550

Monthly Expenses:

Rent obligation, $275

Utilities obligation, $135

Food, $130

Gas/Maintenance, $110

Credit card payment, $0

Savings:

Regular savings monthly deposit, $175

Rainy day savings monthly deposit, $25

Entertainment:

Cake decorating class, $40

Movies with friends, $60

Questions

1. What impact on Jamie Lee's income will the gift of $1,000 from her great aunt have on her adjusted gross income? Will there be an impact on the adjusted gross income with her $2,000 raffle prize winnings? Explain your answer.

2. Using Exhibit 3–1 as a guide, calculate Jamie Lee's adjusted gross income amount by completing the table below:

Gross income	
(−) Adjustments to income	
= Adjusted gross income	

3. What would Jamie Lee's filing status be considered?

4. Jamie Lee has a marginal tax rate of 15 percent and an average tax rate of 11 percent. Explain why there is a difference between the two rates.

Spending Diary

"SALES TAX ON VARIOUS PURCHASES CAN REALLY INCREASE THE AMOUNT OF MY TOTAL SPENDING."

Directions Continue your Daily Spending Diary to record and monitor your spending in various categories. Your comments should reflect what you have learned about your spending patterns and help you consider possible changes you might want to make in your spending habits. The Daily Spending Diary sheets are located at the end of Chapter 1 and in Connect Finance.

Questions

1. What taxes do you usually pay that are reflected (directly or indirectly) in your daily spending diary?

2. How might your spending habits be revised to better control or reduce the amount you pay in taxes?

Name: _____   **Date:** _____

Federal Income Tax Estimate

Purpose: To estimate your current federal income tax liability.

Financial Planning Activities: Based on last year's tax return, estimates for the current year, and current tax regulations and rates, estimate your current tax liability. This sheet is also available in an Excel spreadsheet format in Connect Finance.

Suggested Websites: www.irs.gov, www.taxlogic.com

Gross income (wages, salary, investment income, and other ordinary income)		$
Less Adjustments to income (see current tax regulations)	−$	
Equals Adjusted gross income	=$	
Less Standard deduction **or** Itemized deduction		
Medical expenses (exceeding 10% of AGI)		$
State/local income, property taxes		$
Mortgage, home equity loan, interest		$
Charitable contributions		$
Casualty and theft losses (federally declared disaster areas only)		$
Amount −$ **Total**		−$
Equals Taxable income	=$	
Estimated tax (based on current tax tables or tax schedules)	$	
Less Tax credits	−$	
Plus Other taxes (AMT/Self-Employment Tax)	+$	
Equals Total tax liability	=$	
Less Estimated withholding and payments	−$	
Equals Tax due (or refund)	=$	

What's Next for Your Personal Financial Plan?

- Develop a system for filing and storing various tax records related to income, deductible expenses, and current tax forms.
- Using the IRS and other websites, identify recent changes in tax laws that may affect your financial planning decisions.

McGraw Hill

Name: _____ Date: _____

Tax Planning Activities

Purpose: To consider actions that can prevent tax penalties and may result in tax savings.

Financial Planning Activities: Consider which of the following actions are appropriate to your tax situation. This sheet is also available in an Excel spreadsheet format in Connect Finance.

Suggested Websites: www.turbotax.com, taxes.about.com

	Action to be taken (if applicable)	Completed
Filing status/withholding		
• Change filing status or exemptions due to changes in life situation.		
• Change amount of withholding due to changes in tax situation.		
• Plan to make estimated tax payments (due the 15th of April, June, September, and January).		
Tax records/documents		
• Organize home files for ease of maintaining and retrieving data.		
• Send current mailing address and correct Social Security number to IRS, place of employment, and other income sources.		
Annual tax activities		
• Be certain all needed data and current tax forms are available well before deadline.		
• Research tax code changes and uncertain tax areas.		
Tax-savings actions		
• Consider tax-exempt and tax-deferred investments.		
• If you expect to have the same or a lower tax rate next year, accelerate deductions into the current year.		
• If you expect to have the same or a lower tax rate next year, delay the receipt of income until next year.		
• If you expect to have a higher tax rate next year, delay deductions since they will have a greater benefit.		
• If you expect to have a higher tax rate next year, accelerate the receipt of income to have it taxed at the current lower rate.		
• Start or increase use of tax-deferred retirement plans.		
• Other		

What's Next for Your Personal Financial Plan?

- Identify saving and investing decisions that would minimize future income taxes.
- Develop a plan for actions to take related to your current and future tax situation.

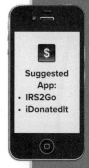

Suggested App:
- IRS2Go
- iDonatedIt

McGraw Hill

4 Financial Services: Savings Plans and Payment Accounts

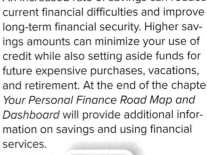

3 Steps to Financial Literacy . . .
An Increased Savings Rate

1 Identify areas in your budget that might be reduced or eliminated to save money.
App: MoneyBook

2 Determine the amount that you save each month from the reduced budget amounts.
Website: www.bankrate.com

3 Deposit your increased savings amount in an account in a bank or credit union.
Website: www.mycreditunion.gov

An increased rate of savings can reduce current financial difficulties and improve long-term financial security. Higher savings amounts can minimize your use of credit while also setting aside funds for future expensive purchases, vacations, and retirement. At the end of the chapter, *Your Personal Finance Road Map and Dashboard* will provide additional information on savings and using financial services.

TZIDO SUN/Shutterstock

CHAPTER 4 LEARNING OBJECTIVES

In this chapter, you will learn to:

LO4.1 Identify commonly used financial services.

LO4.2 Compare the types of financial institutions.

LO4.3 Assess various types of savings plans.

LO4.4 Evaluate different types of payment methods.

YOUR PERSONAL FINANCIAL PLAN SHEETS

11. Planning the Use of Financial Services
12. Comparing Savings Plans
13. Using Savings Plans to Achieve Financial Goals
14. Comparing Payment Methods; Bank Reconciliation

Planning Your Use of Financial Services

Over the years, banking activities have changed:

- from talking with a human teller. . .to connecting with a video teller at a bank cafe.
- from writing a check. . .to transferring money with an app.
- from sending in a deposit by mail. . .to clicking a picture for a remote check deposit.
- from obtaining a loan from a bank. . .to borrowing from a peer-to-peer lender.

Banks, savings and loan associations, credit unions, and other financial institutions process most payment, savings, and credit transactions. However, a growing number of nonbank and FinTech businesses are offering financial services. Tech companies such as Amazon, Apple, and Google are expanding their digital and mobile financial service activities. Exhibit 4–1 is an overview of financial services and institutions for managing cash flows and achieving financial goals.

Managing Daily Money Needs

Buying groceries, paying rent, and other spending require a cash management plan. Cash, check, credit card, debit card, and online/mobile transfer are common payment choices. With cash transactions declining, some stores are becoming *cashless* enterprises. However, a backlash has surfaced among segments of society dependent on cash business activities.

Frequent mistakes when managing current cash needs include (1) overspending due to impulse buying and overusing credit; (2) having insufficient liquid assets to pay current bills; (3) using savings or borrowing to pay for current expenses; and (4) failing to place funds not needed for current expenses in a savings account or investment plan.

LO4.1

Identify commonly used financial services.

ACTION ITEM

I am least informed about:

☐ online banking.

☐ certificates of deposit.

☐ prepaid debit cards.

Exhibit **4–1**

Financial Institutions and Banking Services

DEPOSIT INSTITUTIONS
- Commercial bank
- Credit union
- Savings and loan association
- Mutual savings bank

NON-DEPOSIT INSTITUTIONS

- Life insurance company
- Investment company
- Brokerage firm
- Credit card company
- Finance company
- Mortgage company

TYPES OF FINANCIAL SERVICES

Cash Availability	**Payment Services**
• Check cashing • ATM/debit cards • Traveler's checks • Foreign currency exchange	• Checking account • Online payments • Cashier's checks • Money orders
Savings Services	**Credit Services**
• Regular savings account • Money market account • Certificates of deposit • U.S. savings bonds	• Credit cards, cash advances • Auto loans, education loans • Mortgages • Home equity loans
Investment Services	**Other Services**
• Individual retirement accounts (IRAs) • Brokerage service • Investment advice • Mutual funds	• Insurance; trust service • Tax preparation • Safe deposit boxes • Budget counseling • Estate planning

OTHER FINANCIAL SERVICE PROVIDERS

- Pawnshop
- Check-cashing outlet
- Payday loan company
- Rent-to-own center
- Car title loan company

NON-BANK FINANCIAL SERVICE PROVIDERS
- Retailer stores (prepaid debit cards, other services)
- Online, mobile banks (E*Trade Bank, Varo Money)
- Online payment services (PayPal)
- P2P (peer-to-peer) lending intermediaries

Sources of Quick Cash

No matter how carefully you manage your money, at some time you might need more cash than you have available. To cope in that situation, you have three choices. First, you could reduce current spending or reduce amounts saved. Second, for needed funds, you could withdraw money from a savings or investment account. Finally, you might obtain a credit card cash advance or a personal loan. Remember that the use of savings and increased borrowing reduce your net worth and your potential for long-term financial security.

Types of Financial Services

Banks and other financial institutions offer services to meet your needs for achieving financial goals. These services may be viewed in four categories:

1. *Savings* provides safe storage of funds for future use. Commonly referred to as *time deposits,* money in savings accounts and certificates of deposit are examples of savings plans.
2. *Payment services* allow you to transfer money to pay expenses and for other business activities. Checking accounts and other payment methods are generally called *demand deposits.*
3. *Borrowing* is used by most people at some time during their lives. Credit alternatives range from short-term accounts, such as credit cards and cash loans, to long-term borrowing, such as a home mortgage.

4. *Other financial services* include insurance, investments, tax assistance, and financial planning. A **trust** is a legal agreement that provides for the management and control of assets by one party for the benefit of another. This type of arrangement is usually created through a commercial bank or a lawyer. Parents who want to set aside certain funds for their children's education may use a trust. Additional information on trusts is presented in Chapter 14.

To simplify financial services, many financial businesses offer consolidated accounts. An **asset management account**, also called a *cash management account,* provides a complete financial services program for a single fee. Investment companies and others offer this type of account, with checking, a debit card, an app, a credit card, online banking, and a line of credit as well as access for buying stocks, bonds, mutual funds, and other investments.

trust A legal agreement that provides for the management and control of assets by one party for the benefit of another.

asset management account An all-in-one account that includes savings, checking, borrowing, investing, and other financial services for a single fee; also called a *cash management account.*

Online and Mobile Banking

Banking online and through mobile systems are used for most financial services (see Exhibit 4–2). While traditional financial institutions offer online banking services, web-only banks, FinTechs, and *neobanks* play a significant role in this marketplace.

Mobile and online banking provide the benefits of convenience and saving time along with instant information access. Concerns of privacy, security of data, ease of overspending, costly fees, and online scams must also be considered.

More traditional electronic banking occurs through an **automatic teller machine (ATM)**, also called a *cash machine,* to facilitate transactions. To minimize ATM fees, compare several financial institutions. Use your own bank's ATM to avoid surcharges, and withdraw larger amounts to avoid fees on several small transactions. When using a non-network ATM, you might be charge twice; once by the ATM owner and once by your bank. Also beware of independent ATMs with *skimmers* used by crooks to swipe your card information. *Skimmers* are more difficult to detect since they are placed inside the ATM.

automatic teller machine (ATM) A computer terminal used to conduct banking transactions; also called a *cash machine.*

Exhibit **4–2** **Mobile Banking Services**

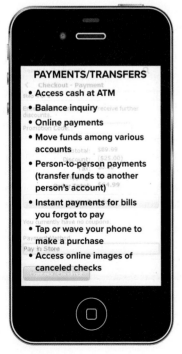

PAYMENTS/TRANSFERS
- Access cash at ATM
- Balance inquiry
- Online payments
- Move funds among various accounts
- Person-to-person payments (transfer funds to another person's account)
- Instant payments for bills you forgot to pay
- Tap or wave your phone to make a purchase
- Access online images of canceled checks

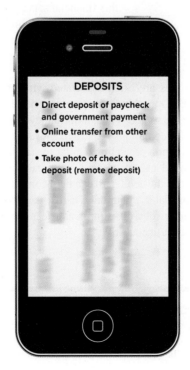

DEPOSITS
- Direct deposit of paycheck and government payment
- Online transfer from other account
- Take photo of check to deposit (remote deposit)

OTHER SERVICES
- Direct deposit, transfers to savings accounts
- Text alerts for balances, payments, deposits
- Apply and receive approval for loans
- Compare current interest rates for loans
- Check rates, apply for insurance
- Buy, sell, monitor investments
- Locate ATM and bank branches using GPS
- Access or shoot photo of store, online coupons

debit card A plastic access card used in computerized banking transactions; also called a *cash card.*

The **debit card**, or *cash card,* that activates ATM transactions is also used for purchases. A debit card is in contrast to a *credit card,* since you are spending your own funds rather than borrowing money. A lost or stolen debit card can be expensive. If you notify the financial institution within two days of the lost card, your liability for unauthorized use is $50. You can be liable for up to $500 of unauthorized use if you wait up to 60 days to notify your bank. After 60 days, your liability can be the total amount in your account and even more if your card is linked to other bank accounts. To prevent this, consider opening a separate account for using your debit card; then your main checking account won't be at risk.

Some card issuers use the same rules for lost or stolen debit cards as for credit cards: a $50 maximum. Of course, you are not liable for unauthorized use, such as a con artist using your account number to make a purchase. Remember to report the fraud within 60 days of your statement to protect your right not to be charged for the transaction.

Wireless transactions will likely reduce debit and credit card use with cardless ATM access and in-store purchases. A smartphone, cash code, and PIN will be required. App customers may authorize cash to a phone contact. Recipients are sent a code to withdraw the approved amount. A credit card "lock and limit" app to control spending and block unauthorized transactions will also be available.

FinTech for Financial Literacy

Neobanks are FinTech start-ups that appeal to technology-oriented consumers, offering financial services through digital channels and mobile apps. Benefits of neobanks include:

- lower costs than traditional financial institutions.
- access to large ATM networks with no fees.
- serving "underbanked" and "unbanked" consumers.
- usually no overdraft fees since you only spend what is in your account.
- guidance with budgeting, money management, and spending.
- ease of loan approval with technology-based decisions.

Concerns are a lack of physical bank branches; neobanks may not be government regulated; and there may be no recourse when an app malfunctions. Online and emerging financial institutions that seek to serve the connected customer segment include GoBank, SoFi Money, Varo Money, and Wells Fargo's Greenhouse.

Prepaid Debit Cards

Prepaid debit cards have become very popular for payments. For many consumers, these cards replace traditional banking services. Prepaid debit cards are issued by many financial service providers including banks, credit card companies, retailers (such as Walmart), and nonbank companies created to provide this financial service.

"Loading" (adding funds to) prepaid debit cards may occur by cash, check, direct deposit, online transfer, app check photo, or credit card cash advance. Common uses include in-store and online purchases as well as person-to-person payments. A savings account feature may also be connected to the card.

Extensive fees are often associated with prepaid debit cards. These may include an activation fee, a monthly fee, a transaction fee, a cash-withdrawal (ATM) fee, a balance-inquiry fee, a fee to add funds, a dormancy fee, a decline fee, a card replacement fee, and others. Federal regulations require disclosure of prepaid debit card fees, along with fraud and error-resolution protection similar to standard debit cards.

The expanded use of prepaid cards has resulted in lower consumer debt with some consumers since the debit card can help control spending and buying on credit. With credit cards, you "pay later"; with debit cards, you "pay now"; and with prepaid cards, you "pay before." Comparisons of features and fees for prepaid debit cards are available at **www.nerdwallet.com/prepaid**.

WHAT WOULD YOU DO? Expanded use of prepaid debit cards creates many opportunities for businesses to meet consumer demand. The fees on a prepaid debit card can be high. To avoid these fees, what actions would you take when selecting and using a prepaid debit card?

When interest rates are rising...

- Use long-term loans to take advantage of current low rates.
- Select short-term savings instruments to take advantage of higher rates when they mature.

- Use short-term loans to take advantage of lower rates when you refinance the loans.
- Select long-term savings instruments to "lock in" earnings at current high rates.

When interest rates are falling...

Exhibit **4–3**

Changing Interest Rates and Financial Service Decisions

Financial Services and Economic Conditions

Changing interest rates, rising consumer prices, and other economic factors influence financial services. For successful financial planning, be aware of current economic trends and future prospects (see Exhibit 4–3). You can learn about current interest rates with an online search as well as the business section of newspapers and financial news television programs.

Sheet 11 Planning the Use of Financial Services

PRACTICE QUIZ 4–1

1. What are the major categories of financial services?

2. What financial services are available through online and mobile systems?

3. How do changing economic conditions affect the use of financial services?

Sources of Financial Services

Many types of businesses offer financial services that were once exclusive to banks.

Comparing Financial Institutions

The basic questions to ask when selecting a financial service provider are simple:

- Where can I get the best return on my savings?
- How can I minimize the cost of checking, payments services, and other fees?
- Will I be able to borrow money if I need to?

As you use financial services, decide what you want from the organization that will serve your needs (see Exhibit 4–4). With the financial marketplace constantly changing, consider various factors before selecting your financial service provider.

The services offered will likely be a major factor. In addition, personal service may be important. Convenience may take the form of branch office and ATM locations as well as online services and mobile apps. Remember, convenience and service have a cost; compare fees and other charges at several financial institutions.

Finally, also consider safety and rates. While most financial institutions have deposit insurance to protect customers, many emerging financial service providers are not insured by federal government programs. Obtain information about earnings on savings and checking accounts and the rate you will pay for borrowed funds.

LO4.2

Compare the types of financial institutions.

ACTION ITEM

My primary financial service activities involve:

☐ a bank or credit union.

☐ online payment or app.

☐ a prepaid debit card.

Exhibit **4–4** **Selecting a Financial Institution**

STEP 1. Identify your most important featues for a financial institution, related to:

Services	Fees, earnings	Convenience	Online, mobile

• types of accounts
• deposit insurance
• loans; investments
• app/online service
	• account minimum
	  balance, ATM fees
	• loans rates
	• savings rates
		• branch, ATM
		  locations, hours
		• customer service
		• rewards program
			• ease of operation
			• services
			• privacy, security
			• app features

STEP 2. Rank the top features based on importance and your lifesituation:

College student	Young family	Older consumer
• low minimum balance • ATM access; app features • waived monthly fee	• low fee, minimum balance • savings plans for future • low-cost auto, home loans	• cash withdrawal limit and fraud detection notifications • large-font documents

STEP 3. Prepare a list of local, national, and online banks and credit unions (include the name, address, phone, website, services offered).

STEP 4. Conduct online and in-person research:
• talk with people who have used various financial institutions
• search online for services, policies, fees, and customer reviews
• if appropriate, visit the financial institution to observe and talk with staff members
• obtain a fee disclosure statement, savings rate sheet, and sample loan application

STEP 5. Based on the information collected:
• decide where to do business; you may use more than one financial institution
• take advantage of the best services at several (possibly "institutions"?) for flexibility in the future
• before changing banks, ask about fees and charges you consider unfair
• use a "switch kit" (available online) with letters and forms to change banks

The following comparison of financial service providers can guide your decision:

Financial Institution	Benefits	Drawbacks
Large-scale bank	• Many branches, fee-free ATMs • Latest digital banking services	• Limited personal service, higher fees • Potential security concerns
Regional, community bank	• High customer satisfaction • Strong personal service	• Limited numbers of branches • May not be in ATM network
Credit union	• Strong personal service • Higher savings rates, lower fees	• Few branches, limited fee-free ATMs • May have membership eligibility
Online bank, FinTech company, neobank	• High customer satisfaction • Higher yields on savings	• Limited personal contact; no branches • May lack regulation; security concerns

NOTE: Your Personal Financial Plan sheets 11, 12, and 14 at the end of the chapter can be used for this process.

Types of Financial Institutions

Despite changes in the banking environment, many familiar financial institutions still serve your needs. As shown in Exhibit 4–1, some organizations (such as banks and credit unions) offer a wide range of services, while others provide specialized assistance, such as home loans. Distinctions among the various types of financial institutions are disappearing. For example, today people can buy investments through their bank and credit union as well as from an investment company or brokerage firm.

Deposit institutions serve as intermediaries between suppliers (savers) and users (borrowers) of funds. The most common of these traditional organizations are:

- **Commercial banks** offer a full range of financial services, including checking, savings, lending, and most other services. Commercial banks, organized as corporations with investors (stockholders) contributing the needed capital to operate, exist in several types: national banks, regional banks, community banks, and online-only banks.

- **Savings and loan associations (S&Ls)** traditionally specialized in savings accounts and mortgages. Today, these organizations have expanded to offer financial services comparable to those of a bank.

- **Mutual savings banks**, owned by depositors, also specialize in savings accounts and mortgages. Located mainly in the northeastern United States, the profits of a mutual savings bank are shared by depositors usually through higher earnings on savings.

- **Credit unions** are user-owned, nonprofit, cooperative organizations. Although members traditionally had a common bond such as work location, church, or community affiliation, credit union membership today is more flexible, with more than 100 million people in the United States belonging to one. Annual banking studies consistently report lower fees and lower loan rates with higher customer satisfaction levels for credit unions compared to other financial institutions.

Nondeposit institutions offer various financial services. These nonbank institutions include:

- Life insurance companies, discussed in Chapter 10, which provide financial security for dependents with various insurance policies, some containing savings and investment features. Additional financial activities of life insurance companies include investment and retirement planning services.

- Investment companies, also called *mutual funds,* which offer a **money market fund**—a combination savings–investment plan. The company uses the money from many investors to purchase a variety of short-term financial instruments. Unlike accounts at most deposit institutions, investment company accounts are not covered by federal deposit insurance. Additional information on mutual funds is presented in Chapter 13.

- Brokerage firms, which employ investment advisers and financial planners, and serve as an agent for buying and selling stocks, bonds, and other investment securities. These companies earn commissions and fees (see Chapter 12). Expanded financial services are available from brokerage organizations, including checking accounts and online banking.

- Credit card companies, discussed in Chapter 5, which specialize in funding short-term retail lending. These networks, including VISA, MasterCard, and Discover, have also expanded into other banking and investing services.

- Finance companies, which provide loans to consumers and small businesses. These loans have short and intermediate terms with higher rates than most other lenders charge. Most finance companies also offer other financial planning services.

- Mortgage companies, which are organized primarily to provide loans for home purchases. The services of mortgage companies are presented in Chapter 7.

These and other financial institutions compete for your business. More and more of these companies are offering a combination of services (savings, checking, credit, insurance, investments) from one source.

CAUTION!

Beware of unnecessary bank fees. Actions include: (1) avoid overdraft charges by linking your checking account to savings; (2) use ATMs in your bank's network; apps are available to guide you to fee-free ATMs; (3) search for no- or low-minimum balance checking accounts; (4) consider banking at a credit union; and (5) beware of "inactivity" or "dormant account" fees, which can range from $5 to $15 per month. The account may also be "frozen" after a certain period. Be sure to check out all fees when opening an account.

commercial bank A financial institution that offers a full range of financial services to individuals, businesses, and government agencies.

savings and loan association (S&L) A financial institution that traditionally specialized in savings accounts and mortgage loans.

mutual savings bank A financial institution that is owned by depositors and specializes in savings accounts and mortgage loans.

credit union A user-owned, nonprofit, cooperative financial institution that is organized for the benefit of its members.

money market fund A savings–investment plan offered by investment companies, with earnings based on investments in various short-term financial instruments.

FinTech for Financial Literacy

What if you got paid each day you work? Instant Financial's app allows employees to take 50 percent of their pay each day in an *instant account;* the other half is paid at the end of the pay period. A concern is this app can discourage saving and result in increased debt.

Problematic Financial Businesses

Would you pay $3 to cash a $100 check? Or pay $15 to borrow $100 for two weeks? Many people who do not have bank accounts (especially low-income consumers) make use of financial service companies that charge very high fees and excessive interest rates. Over 10 million people in the United States are "unbanked," using a variety of "shadow" financial services rather than having a bank account. Another 20 percent of the population are "underbanked" and make use of many of these services in addition to having a bank account. An unbanked or underbanked person may pay over $2,000 a year in interest and other fees.

PAWNSHOPS Loans from a pawnshop are based on a proportional value of a tangible item such as jewelry, antiques, tools, or musical instruments. Many low- and moderate-income families use these organizations to obtain cash loans quickly. Pawnshops charge higher fees than other financial institutions to consumers in need of small loans—usually $50 to $75, to be repaid in 30 to 45 days. Pawnshops are often viewed as "neighborhood bankers" and "local shopping malls," since they provide both lending and retail shopping services, selling items that borrowers do not redeem. While states regulate pawnshops, the interest rates charged can range from 3 percent a month to over 100 percent annually.

CHECK-CASHING OUTLETS Most financial institutions will not cash a check unless you have an account. The more than 6,000 check-cashing outlets (CCOs) charge anywhere from 1 to 20 percent of the face value of a check; the average cost is 2 to 3 percent. For a low-income family, that can be a significant portion of the total household budget. CCOs, sometimes called *currency exchanges,* also offer services, including electronic tax filing, money orders, private postal boxes, utility bill payment, and prepaid debit cards. A person may be able to obtain these services at a lower cost at other locations.

PAYDAY LOAN COMPANIES Many consumer organizations caution against using payday loans, also referred to as *cash advances, check advance loans, postdated check loans,* and *delayed deposit loans.* Desperate borrowers pay annual interest rates of as much as 780 percent and more to obtain needed cash from payday loan companies. The most frequent users of payday loans are workers who have become trapped by debts or poor financial decisions. Some state and federal regulations exist to reduce the potential exploitation of payday loan clients.

In a typical payday loan, a consumer writes a personal check for $115 to borrow $100 for 14 days. The payday lender agrees to hold the check until the next payday. This $15 finance charge for the 14 days translates into an annual percentage rate of 391 percent. Some consumers "roll over" their loans, paying another $15 for the $100 loan for the next 14 days. After a few rollovers, the finance charge can exceed the amount borrowed. To prevent this exploitation, some employers are offering pay advances through payroll provider services. The loans have rates in the 9 to 18 percent range.

RENT-TO-OWN CENTERS Rental businesses offer big-screen televisions, computers, bedroom sets, and kitchen appliances. The rent-to-own (RTO) industry is defined as stores that lease products to consumers who can own the item if they complete a certain number of monthly or weekly payments. A $600 computer can result in $1,900 of payments. Many RTO purchases can result in annual interest rates of over 300 percent. And the item may be repossessed if a payment is late or missed.

CAR TITLE LOAN COMPANIES When in need of money, people with poor credit ratings might obtain a cash advance using their automobile title as security for a high-interest loan. These loans, usually due in 30 days, typically have a cost similar to payday loans, often exceeding 200 percent. While the process is simple, the consequences can be devastating with the repossession of your car.

These expensive, high-risk financial service providers should be avoided. Instead, properly manage your money and use the services of a reputable financial institution, such as a credit union.

PRACTICE QUIZ 4–2

1. What factors do consumers usually consider when selecting a financial institution to meet their saving and checking needs?

2. What are examples of deposit-type financial institutions?

3. Match the following descriptions with the appropriate financial institution:

a. commercial bank	_____ Commonly used by people without a bank account.
b. credit union	_____ Investment services accompany main business focus.
c. life insurance company	_____ Traditionally provides widest range of financial services.
d. check-cashing outlet	_____ Offers lower fees for members.

Comparing Savings Plans

A savings plan is vital for achieving financial goals. A range of savings alternatives exist (Exhibit 4–5). The various savings plans can be grouped into the following main categories.

Regular Savings Accounts

Regular savings accounts usually involve a low or no minimum balance and allow you to withdraw money as needed. Savers can access a summary of transactions. Banks, savings and loan associations, and other financial institutions offer regular savings accounts. At a credit union, these savings plans are called *share accounts*. High-yield savings accounts are available with restrictions that might include an initial deposit requirement, changing interest rates, a minimum balance amount, and other fees.

Certificates of Deposit

Higher earnings are available to savers when they leave money on deposit for a set time period. A **certificate of deposit (CD)** is a savings plan requiring that a certain amount be left on deposit for a stated time period (ranging from 30 days to five or more years) to earn a specific rate of return.

These time deposits can be an attractive and safe savings alternative. However, most financial institutions impose a penalty for early withdrawal of CD funds. For CDs of one year or less, the penalty is usually three months of interest. CDs of more than a year will likely have a fine of six months' interest, while a five-year CD can result in a penalty as high as 20 to 25 percent of the total interest to maturity on the account.

TYPES OF CDS While traditional certificates of deposit continue to be the most popular, financial institutions offer other types of CDs:

- *Rising-rate* or *bump-up CDs* may have higher rates at various intervals, such as every six months. Beware of ads that highlight a higher rate in the future. This rate may be in effect only for the last few months of an 18- or 24-month CD.

LO4.3

Assess various types of savings plans.

ACTION ITEM

When selecting a savings plan, most important to me is:

☐ **bank location.**

☐ **federal deposit insurance.**

☐ **rate of return.**

certificate of deposit (CD) A savings plan requiring that a certain amount be left on deposit for a stated time period to earn a specified interest rate.

Exhibit 4–5
Savings Alternatives

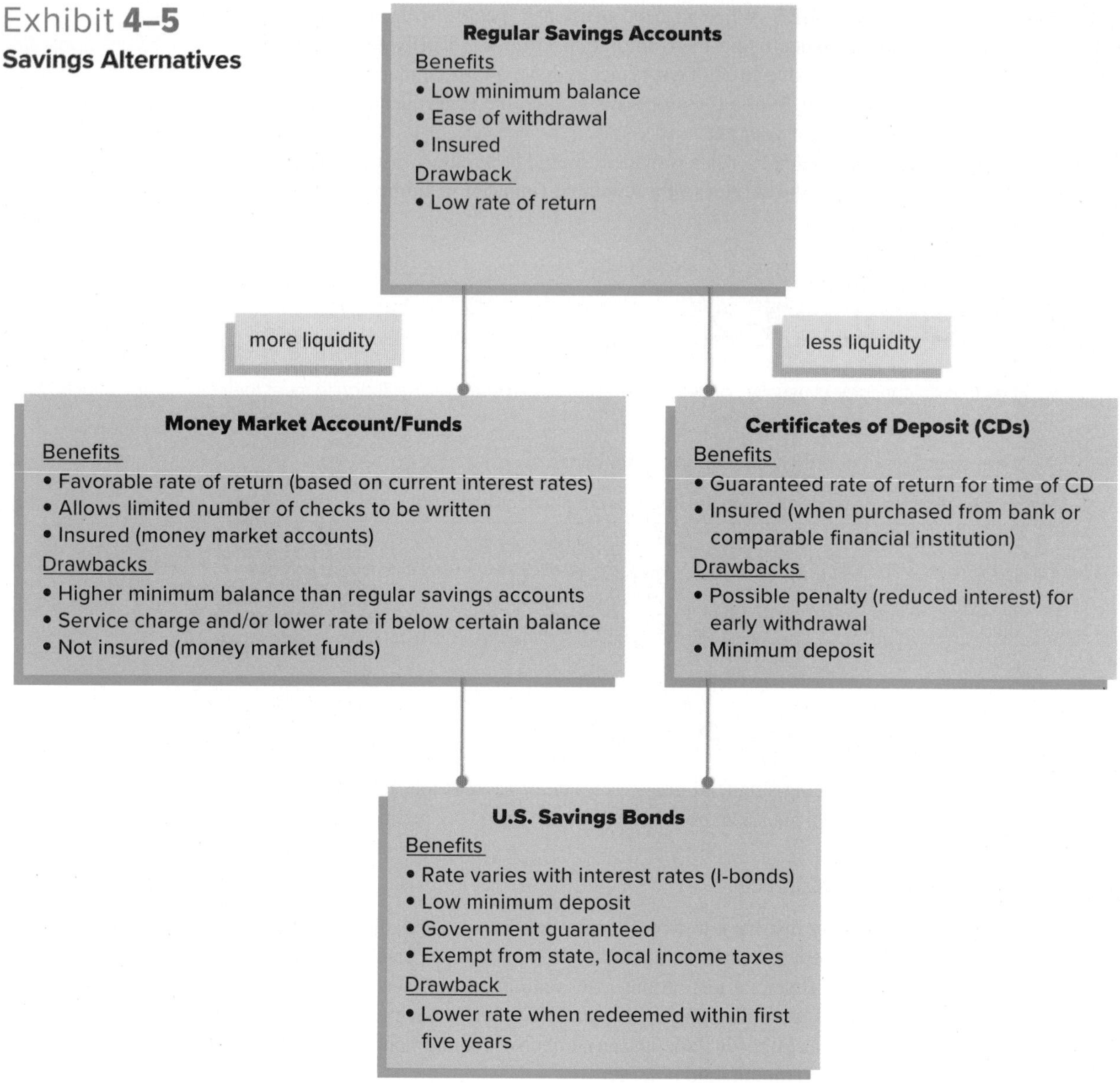

Regular Savings Accounts

Benefits
- Low minimum balance
- Ease of withdrawal
- Insured

Drawback
- Low rate of return

more liquidity

less liquidity

Money Market Account/Funds

Benefits
- Favorable rate of return (based on current interest rates)
- Allows limited number of checks to be written
- Insured (money market accounts)

Drawbacks
- Higher minimum balance than regular savings accounts
- Service charge and/or lower rate if below certain balance
- Not insured (money market funds)

Certificates of Deposit (CDs)

Benefits
- Guaranteed rate of return for time of CD
- Insured (when purchased from bank or comparable financial institution)

Drawbacks
- Possible penalty (reduced interest) for early withdrawal
- Minimum deposit

U.S. Savings Bonds

Benefits
- Rate varies with interest rates (I-bonds)
- Low minimum deposit
- Government guaranteed
- Exempt from state, local income taxes

Drawback
- Lower rate when redeemed within first five years

- *Liquid CDs* offer an opportunity to withdraw money without a penalty. You will likely be required to maintain a minimum balance in the account. This CD may have other restrictions such as a waiting period, a lower rate, or a limit on the number of withdrawals allowed.

- *A zero-coupon CD* is purchased at a deep discount (a small portion of the face value) with no interest payments. Your initial small deposit ($5,000, for example) grows to the maturity value of the CD ($10,000) in 10 years, which is approximately a 7.2 percent annual return.

- *Indexed CDs* have earnings based on the stock market. In times of strong stock performance, your earnings can be higher than those on other CDs. At other times, you may earn no interest and may even lose part of your savings. A CD based on the consumer price index can result in higher returns as inflation increases.

- *Callable CDs* start with higher rates and usually have long maturities, as high as 10 to 15 years. With this savings option, if interest rates drop, the bank may "call" (close) the account after a set period, such as one or two years. When the call option is exercised, the saver receives the original deposit amount and any interest that has been earned.

Beware of *promotional CDs* that attempt to attract savers with gifts or special rates. These "too good to be true" rates may actually be marketing efforts to sell you high-cost financial products. Always obtain a CD from a reputable bank or credit union.

MANAGING CDS When first buying or *rolling over* a CD (buying a new one at maturity), investigate potential earnings and costs. Do not allow your financial institution to automatically roll over your money into another CD for the same term. If interest rates have dropped, you might consider a shorter maturity. Or if you believe rates are at a peak and you won't need the money for some time, obtain a CD with a longer term.

Consider creating a CD *portfolio* with CDs maturing at different times; for example, $2,000 in a three-month CD, $2,000 in a six-month CD, $2,000 in a one-year CD, and $2,000 in a two-year CD. This will give you some degree of liquidity and flexibility when you reinvest your funds.

Buying CDs from an online financial institution may earn you a higher rate than from a local bank. Also, when interest rates stay low, consider other savings alternatives such as savings bonds, mutual funds, and government securities. Current information about CD rates are available at **www.bankrate.com**, **www.nerdwallet.com**, and **www.depositaccounts.com**.

> **WHAT WOULD YOU DO?** Describe situations and financial goals in which you might choose a five-year CD paying 2.67 percent instead of an 18-month savings certificate paying 1.89 percent.

Money Market Accounts and Funds

A **money market account** is a savings account that requires a minimum balance with earnings based on the changing market level of interest rates. Money market accounts may allow a limited number of checks and transfers, and may impose a fee when the account balance goes below the required minimum, usually $1,000.

Both money market accounts and money market funds offer earnings based on current interest rates, and both have minimum-balance restrictions and allow check writing. The major difference is in safety. Money market *accounts* at banks and credit unions are covered by federal deposit insurance. This is not true of money market *funds*, which are a product of investment companies. Since money market funds invest mainly in short-term (less than a year) government and corporate securities, as savings, they are usually fairly safe.

money market account A savings account offered by banks, savings and loan associations, and credit unions that requires a minimum balance and has earnings based on market interest rates.

U.S. Savings Bonds

U.S. savings bonds are a low-risk savings program guaranteed by the federal government, used to achieve financial goals. The Treasury Department offers different types of savings bonds.

Series EE bonds are the most common, involving amounts greater than $25. These bonds were originally in a paper format and purchased for set values ranging from $25 to $5,000, with maturity values of $50 to $10,000. Today, EE bonds are bought and managed online, and may be purchased for any amount.

EE bonds increase in value as interest is earned monthly and compounds semiannually. If you redeem the bonds before five years, you forfeit the latest three months of interest; after five years, you are not penalized. A bond must be held for one year before it can be cashed. Series EE bonds continue to earn interest for 30 years.

The tax advantages of series EE bonds are (1) the interest earned is exempt from state and local taxes and (2) federal income tax on earnings is not due until the bonds are redeemed. Redeemed series EE bonds may be exempt from federal income tax if the funds are used to pay tuition and fees at a college, university, or qualified technical school for yourself or

money minute focus

To encourage saving for education, a 529 plan is a qualified tuition plan with tax advantages. These programs are sponsored by state agencies and educational institutions. *Prepaid tuition plans* allow the purchase of future college credits at current prices. *Education savings plans* are investment accounts to save for future higher education expenses, such as tuition, fees, and room and board. For additional guidance on financing your education, see the Chapter 5 Appendix.

a dependent. The bonds must be purchased by an individual who is at least 24 years old, and they must be issued in the names of one or both parents. This provision is designed to assist low- and middle-income households; people whose incomes exceed a certain amount do not qualify for this tax exemption.

With the *I bond,* you earn interest based on a fixed rate and an inflation rate. Every six months, a new rate is set. I bonds are purchased at face value for an amount starting at $25. As with EE bonds, the minimum holding period is one year. Interest earned on I bonds is added to the value of the bond and received when you redeem your bond. I bonds have the same tax and education benefits as EE bonds.

A person may purchase up to $10,000 worth of savings bonds of each series (EE and I bonds) a year, for a total of $20,000. This amount applies to any person, so parents may buy an additional $20,000 in each child's name. A Treasury Direct account at **www.treasurydirect.gov** allows you 24-hour access to buy, manage, and redeem savings bonds. You can also invest in other Treasury securities such as bills, notes, bonds, and TIPS (Treasury inflation-protected securities), which are discussed in Chapter 11.

Evaluating Savings Plans

Selection of a savings plan is most often influenced by the rate of return, inflation, tax considerations, liquidity, safety, restrictions, and fees (see Exhibit 4–6).

rate of return The percentage of increase in the value of savings as a result of interest earned; also called *yield.*

RATE OF RETURN Earnings on savings are measured by the **rate of return,** or *yield,* the percentage of increase in the value of your savings from earned interest. For example, a $100 savings account that earned $5 after a year would have a rate of return, or yield, of 5 percent. This rate of return was determined by dividing the interest earned ($5) by the

Exhibit 4–6
Selecting a Savings Plan

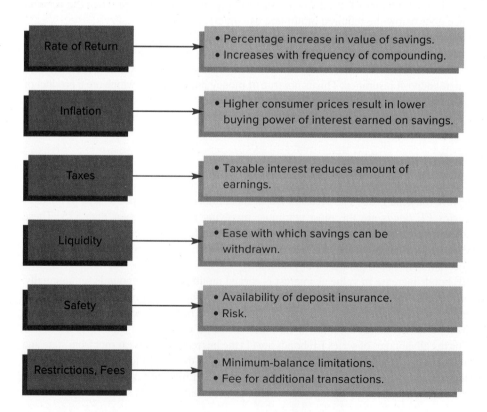

Rate of Return	• Percentage increase in value of savings. • Increases with frequency of compounding.
Inflation	• Higher consumer prices result in lower buying power of interest earned on savings.
Taxes	• Taxable interest reduces amount of earnings.
Liquidity	• Ease with which savings can be withdrawn.
Safety	• Availability of deposit insurance. • Risk.
Restrictions, Fees	• Minimum-balance limitations. • Fee for additional transactions.

Shorter compounding periods result in higher yields. This chart shows the growth of $10,000, earning a rate of 4 percent, but with different compounding methods.

	COMPOUNDING METHOD			
End of year	**Daily**	**Monthly**	**Quarterly**	**Annually**
1	$10,408	$10,407	$10,406	$10,400
2	10,833	10,831	10,829	10,816
3	11,275	11,273	11,268	11,249
4	11,735	11,732	11,726	11,699
5	12,214	12,210	12,202	12,167
10	14,918	14,908	14,889	14,802
15	18,221	18,203	18,167	18,009
20	22,254	22,203	22,167	21,911
Annual yield	4.08%	4.07%	4.05%	4.00%

Exhibit **4–7**
Compounding Frequency Affects the Savings Yield

amount in the savings account ($100). The yield on your savings usually will be greater than the stated interest rate.

Compounding refers to interest that is earned on previously earned interest. Each time interest is added to your savings, the next interest amount is computed on the new balance in the account. The more frequent the compounding, the higher your rate of return will be. For example, $100 in a savings account that earns 6 percent compounded annually will increase $6 after a year. But the same $100 in a 6 percent account compounded daily will earn $6.18 for the year. Although this difference may seem slight, large amounts held in savings for long periods of time will result in greater earnings (see Exhibit 4–7).

compounding A process that calculates interest based on previously earned interest.

The *Truth in Savings Act* requires financial institutions to disclose the following information on savings accounts: (1) fees on deposit accounts; (2) the interest rate; (3) the annual percentage yield (APY); and (4) other terms and conditions of the savings plan. The Truth in Savings Act defines **annual percentage yield (APY)** as the percentage rate expressing the total amount of interest that would be received on a $100 deposit based on the annual rate and frequency of compounding for a 365-day period. APY reflects the amount of interest a saver should expect to earn.

annual percentage yield (APY) The percentage rate expressing the total amount of interest that would be received on a $100 deposit based on the annual rate and frequency of compounding for a 365-day period.

EXAMPLE: Annual Percentage Yield

When the number of days in the term is 365 (that is, where the stated maturity is 365 days) or where the account does not have a stated maturity, the APY formula is simply

$$APY = 100 \left(\frac{Interest}{Principal} \right)$$

$$= 100 \left(\frac{66}{1,200} \right)$$

$$= 100 \, (0.055) = 0.55, \textit{ or } 5.5\%$$

INFLATION The rate of return you earn on your savings should be compared with the inflation rate. When inflation was over 10 percent, people with money in savings accounts earning 5 or 6 percent were experiencing a loss in the buying power of that money. In general, as the inflation rate increases, the interest rate earned also increases.

Figure It Out!

After-Tax Savings Rate of Return

The taxability of interest on your savings reduces your real rate of return. In other words, you lose some portion of your interest to taxes. This calculation consists of the following steps:

1. Determine your top tax rate for federal income taxes.

2. Subtract this rate, expressed as a decimal, from 1.0.

3. Multiply the result by the yield on your savings account.

4. This number, expressed as a percentage, is your after-tax rate of return.

For example,

1. You are in the 28 percent tax bracket.

2. 1.0 − 0.28 = 0.72.

3. If the yield on your savings account is 6.25 percent, 0.0625 × 0.72 = 0.045.

4. Your after-tax rate of return is 4.5 percent.

You may use the same procedure to determine the *real rate of return* on your savings based on inflation. For example, if you are earning 6 percent on savings and inflation is 5 percent, your real rate of return (after inflation) is 5.7 percent: 0.06 × (1 − 0.05) = 0.057.

CALCULATION EXAMPLES:

1. What would be the after-tax return for a person who is receiving 4 percent on savings and is in a 15 percent tax bracket? _____ percent

2. What would be the after-tax value of $100 earned in interest for a person who is in a 31 percent tax bracket? $ _____

ANSWERS 1. 3.4 percent = 0.04 × (1 − 0.15); 2. $69 = $100 × (1 − 0.31)

---

money minute focus

To effectively manage your finances, consider these accounts:

- An emergency savings account for when you face financial difficulties.
- A regular savings account for short-term needs, such as home repairs, vacation, auto maintenance, or new furniture.
- A household checking account for paying current bills with extra funds going to a savings fund.
- A spouse checking account for expenses for which each person has responsibility.
- A health savings account (HSA) for tax-free payments of medical-related expenses.
- An extra fund with "fun money" leftover after all bills are paid, savings are under control, and all accounts have an appropriate balance.

If all your accounts are at the same financial institution, use the online dashboard to monitor your balances. If you use different banks, use a website or app to view your overall financial situation.

TAXES Like inflation, taxes reduce interest earned on savings. For example, a 10 percent return for a saver in a 28 percent tax bracket means a real return of 7.2 percent (the *Figure It Out!* feature shows how to compute the after-tax savings rate of return). As discussed in Chapter 3, several tax-exempt and tax-deferred savings plans and investments can increase your real rate of return.

LIQUIDITY *Liquidity* allows you to withdraw money on short notice without a loss of value or payment of fees. Some savings plans impose penalties for early withdrawal or have other restrictions. With certain savings certificates and accounts, early withdrawal may be penalized by a loss of earnings or a lower interest rate. Consider the degree of liquidity you desire for your savings goals. To achieve long-term financial goals, many people trade off liquidity for a higher return.

SAFETY Most savings plans at banks, savings and loan associations, and credit unions are insured by agencies affiliated with the federal government. Federal Deposit Insurance Corporation (FDIC) coverage prevents a loss of money due to the failure of the insured institution. Credit unions may obtain deposit insurance through the National Credit Union Association (NCUA). Some state-chartered credit unions have opted for a private insurance program. While a few financial institutions have failed in recent years, savers with deposits covered by federal insurance have not lost any money. Depositors have either been paid or have had the accounts taken over by a financially stable institution.

The FDIC insures amounts up to $250,000 per depositor per insured financial institution. Coverage amounts that exceed the limit are possible by using different ownership categories, such as individual, joint, and trust ownership accounts. For example, a joint account, held by two people, would be covered up to $500,000, with each account owner having $250,000 of coverage. Remember, different branch offices count as the same institution, and business mergers may bring accounts from different banks together.

The FDIC and NCUA also provide deposit insurance for certain retirement accounts, up to $250,000, including traditional IRAs, Roth IRAs, Simplified Employee Pension (SEP) IRAs, and Savings Incentive Match Plans for Employees (SIMPLE) IRAs as well as self-directed Keogh accounts and various plans for state government employees. Of course, this coverage applies only to retirement accounts in financial institutions insured by the FDIC and NCUA.

To determine if all of your deposits are insured, use the Electronic Deposit Insurance Estimator (EDIE) at **www.fdic.gov/edie/**. This site includes a step-by-step tutorial with depositor situations for different types of accounts and different ownership. Information about credit union deposit coverage is available at **www.mycreditunion.gov**. Since some financial institutions may not have federal deposit insurance, investigate this matter when you are selecting a savings plan. Additional information on the regulation and consumer protection aspects of financial institutions is included in the Chapter 6 Appendix.

EXAMPLE: Deposit Insurance

If you have a $562,000 joint account with a relative in an FDIC-insured financial institution, $31,000 of your savings will not be covered by federal deposit insurance. One-half of the $562,000 exceeds the $250,000 limit by $31,000.

RESTRICTIONS AND FEES Other limitations can affect your choice of a savings program. Government regulations may limit the number of transfers and withdrawals you can make each month from a savings or money market account. After six transactions, you may be subject to a fee; ATM withdrawals do not count. Also, a delay may exist between the time interest is earned and the time it is added to your account.

Sheet 12 Comparing Savings Plans
Sheet 13 Using Savings Plans to Achieve Financial Goals

PRACTICE QUIZ 4–3

1. What are the main types of savings plans offered by financial institutions?

2. How does a money market *account* differ from a money market *fund*?

3. How do inflation and taxes affect earnings on savings?

4. In the following financial situations, put a check in the column of the major influence for the person when selecting a savings plan:

Financial Planning Situation	Rate of Return	Inflation	Taxes	Liquidity	Safety
A. An older couple needs easy access to funds for living expenses.					
B. A person is concerned with loss of buying power of funds on deposit.					
C. A saver desires to maximize earnings from the savings plan.					
D. A middle-aged person wants assurance that the funds are safe.					

After losing his job during the financial crisis of 2008, Tim Chen was asked by a family member to recommend a credit card with low foreign transaction fees. The spreadsheet he created was the start for what become **nerdwallet.com**, which today provides guidance on checking, savings, credit cards, loans, and other financial services to 100 million people.

Peer-to-peer, or person-to-person, (P2P) payment apps are replacing cash and checks to send money to friends and family. These services allow quick transfer of funds to others, usually for free or with a small fee. Some of the most common P2P services are:

- Zelle, which allows instant money transfers directly to another person's bank or credit union account using email or a text message.
- Venmo has a wide following of users for money transfers, and offers a free debit card. A fee is charged for sending money with a credit card.
- Cash App includes features for savings and making stock investments.
- PayPal is especially useful for online shopping as well as P2P money transfers.

- Google Pay users make payments and purchases with a digital wallet.
- Apple Pay Cash allows Apple users to send money by a messaging app.

Since not all apps allow sending money to other countries, overseas transfers may be done with Transfer Wise, MoneyGram, and Western Union. Social media money transfers may occur through Facebook Messenger and Skype when linked to a bank account, debit card, or PayPal account. Be aware that social network money transfers are often susceptible to scams.

Today, most money transfers are screen based. Future developments are expected to involve artificial intelligence personal assistants, voice commands, facial recognition, and virtual reality interfaces.

ACTION STEPS FOR. . .

. . .Information Literacy

Select a recent article from **nerdwallet.com** and create a list of questions that indicate a need for additional information.

. . .Financial Literacy

Describe a life situation for a single person or family. Search **nerdwallet.com** and present suggestions for budgeting, banking, saving, and other personal financial activities.

. . .Digital Literacy

Based on an article from **nerdwallet.com**, describe the features of an app that might be the basis for the information presented.

LO4.4

Evaluate different types of payment methods.

ACTION ITEM

My payment account balance is:

☐ **updated regularly.**

☐ **based on a rough estimate.**

☐ **only known by my financial institution.**

Comparing Payment Methods

Each year, paper checks become a smaller portion of payments made. While check writing is declining, checking accounts are still the main source for most debit card and online payments. As shown in Exhibit 4–8, payment alternatives have three main categories.

Digital Payments

Transactions not involving cash, checks, or credit cards have expanded with technology, improved security, and increased consumer acceptance.

DEBIT CARD TRANSACTIONS Purchases made with a debit card involve an amount deducted from your checking or other bank account. Most debit cards can be used: (1) with your signature, like a credit card, and (2) with your personal identification number (PIN), like an ATM card. When the debit card is processed like a credit card, you have more

Digital Payments	Checking Accounts	Other Payment Methods
Debit (cash) and credit cards	Regular checking account	Certified check
Online, mobile transfers	Activity checking account	Cashier's check
Stored-value (prepaid) cards	Interest-earning checking account	Money order
Smart cards ("digital wallet")		Money transfer service
		Traveler's checks

Exhibit 4–8
Payment Alternatives

security in case of fraud or a purchase dispute. However, when using a debit card to check into a hotel, buy gas, or rent a car, the business may *freeze* an amount in your bank account above what you actually spend. This hold on your funds could result in an overdrawn account. Also, remember when using a debit card, you may not have any recourse in the event of a disputed transaction.

Use a credit card to . . .
. . . delay the payment for a purchase.
. . . build a credit history with wise buying.
. . . buy online or for major purchases.
. . . earn more rewards points for spending.

Use a debit card to . . .
. . . limit your spending to available money.
. . . avoid bills that will be paid in the future.
. . . avoid interest payment or an annual fee.
. . . obtain better protection by processing a debit card transaction as a credit card.

ONLINE PAYMENTS Banks and online companies serve as third parties to facilitate online bill payments. Some online payment services give you a choice of using a credit card or a bank account, while others require one or the other. Linking a transaction to your checking account, rather than to a credit card, may not give you as much leverage when disputing a transaction.

People without a credit or debit card can use **PayNearMe .com** for online buying and other transactions. This service allows buyers to make a purchase and then pay cash at a local store. The consumer receives a receipt, and the seller is notified of the payment. This cash transaction network may be used for online purchases, telephone orders, loan repayments, money transfers, and other transactions that might require a credit card. When using these services, be sure to consider all fees, online security, and customer service availability.

MOBILE TRANSFERS Apps for mobile payments through smartphones, tablets, and other wireless devices are replacing debit and credit cards. A tap or wave of your phone at the point-of-sale terminal sensor completes the purchase. Mobile services allow you to transfer money to another person. Most require registering debit card, credit card, or bank account information; some peer-to-peer (P2P) payments are conducted by e-mail or with an app such as PayPal, Square Cash, Venmo, and Zelle. Fees for using a P2P service can range from less than a dollar per transaction to a percentage of the amount transferred.

Money transfer services are a fast, convenient, and safe way to send funds across the country or around the world. For a fee, companies such as MoneyGram, TransferWise, Western Union, and Xoom use highly secure systems to electronically deliver money to another person within a day or two.

FinTech for Financial Literacy

While cyber currencies such as Bitcoin, Tether, Ripple, and Libra gain popularity, users must understand potential concerns. Also called a *cryptocurrency* or a *virtual currency,* the main benefits of these digital assets are flexibility when making payments along with control and security. Drawbacks include: (1) a lack of awareness and understanding among users and merchants; (2) the changing value of the currency unit; (3) risks of ongoing development as new features attempt to make the digital currency more secure and accessible.

STORED-VALUE CARDS Prepaid cards for telephone service, transit fares, highway tolls, laundry service, and school lunches are common. While some of these stored-value cards are disposable, others can be reloaded with an additional amount. Also called *prepaid debit cards,* some stored-value cards may have activation charges, ATM fees, and other transaction costs. Recipients of government benefits may receive Social Security and other payments on a prepaid debit card, which is practical for people without a bank account. Some states offer the option of receiving your tax refund on a debit card.

SMART CARDS These "digital wallets" are similar to other ATM cards with an embedded microchip. In addition to banking activities, the card may also store past purchases, insurance information, and your medical history.

Checking Accounts

Even as mobile and online payments expand, a checking account is still necessary for most people. Checking accounts fall into three major categories: regular checking accounts, activity accounts, and interest-earning checking accounts.

REGULAR CHECKING ACCOUNTS *Regular checking accounts* usually have a monthly service charge that you may avoid by keeping a minimum balance in the account. Some financial institutions will waive the monthly fee if you keep a certain amount in savings. Avoiding the monthly service charge can be beneficial. For example, a monthly fee of $7.50 results in $90 a year. But, you lose interest on the minimum-balance amount in a noninterest-earning account.

ACTIVITY ACCOUNTS *Activity accounts* charge a fee for each check written and sometimes a fee for each deposit in addition to a monthly service charge. However, no minimum balance is required. An activity account is appropriate for people who write a few checks each month or are unable to maintain the required minimum balance.

INTEREST-EARNING CHECKING *Interest-earning checking accounts* usually have a minimum balance. If the account balance goes below that amount, you may not earn interest and will likely incur a service charge. These are called *share draft accounts* at credit unions. Some institutions offer high-rate checking accounts with specific requirements. For example, a higher interest rate is earned if you have a certain number of debit card transactions, pay a bill online, and have a direct deposit each month.

Evaluating Checking and Payment Accounts

Would you rather have a checking account that pays interest and requires a $1,000 minimum balance or an account that doesn't pay interest and requires a $300 minimum balance? This decision requires evaluating factors such as restrictions, fees and charges, interest, and special services (see Exhibit 4–9).

RESTRICTIONS The most common limitation on a checking account is the minimum balance to earn interest or avoid a service charge. In the past, financial institutions placed restrictions on the holding period for deposited checks. A waiting period was usually required before you could access the funds. The Check Clearing for the 21st Century Act (known as Check 21) shortens the processing time. This law establishes the *substitute check,* which is a digital reproduction of the original paper check, and is considered a legal equivalent of the original check.

FEES AND CHARGES Nearly all financial institutions require a minimum balance or impose service charges for checking accounts. When using an interest-bearing checking

Exhibit **4–9**
Checking Account Selection Factors

CHECKING ACCOUNT SELECTION FACTORS

Restrictions	**Fees and Charges**
• Minimum balance	• Monthly fee
• Federal deposit insurance	• Fees for each check or deposit
• Hours and location of branch offices	• Fee for printing of checks
• Holding period for deposited checks	• Fee to obtain canceled check copy
	• Overdraft, stop-payment order, certified check fee
	• Fees for online banking

Special Services	**Interest**
• Direct deposit	• Interest rate
• Availability of ATMs	• Minimum deposit to earn interest
• Overdraft protection	• Method of compounding
• Discounts or free checking for certain groups (students, senior citizens)	• Portion of balance for computing interest
• Free or discounted services	• Fee charged for falling below necessary balance to earn interest

account, compare your earnings with any monthly service charge. Also, consider the cost of lost or reduced interest resulting from maintaining the minimum balance. Checking account fees have increased in recent years. Items such as check printing, overdraft fees, and stop-payment orders have doubled or tripled at some financial institutions.

INTEREST The interest rate, the frequency of compounding, and the interest computation method will affect the earnings on your checking account.

SPECIAL SERVICES As financial institutions attempt to reduce paper and postage costs, canceled checks are no longer returned. Bank customers are provided with more detailed monthly statements and will likely have online access to view and print checks that have been paid.

Overdraft protection is an automatic loan made for checks written in excess of the available balance. An overdrawn account results in a *bounced check*. This service is convenient but costly. Most overdraft plans make loans in $50 or $100 increments. An overdraft of $1 might trigger a $50 loan, with a high interest rate. But overdraft protection can be less costly than the $30 or more fee charged for an overdrawn account. Federal regulations require that customers agree to overdraft protection. Many banks and credit unions allow you to cover overdrafts with an automatic transfer from a savings account for a nominal fee.

overdraft protection An automatic loan made to cover the amount of checks written in excess of the available balance in the checking account.

WHAT WOULD YOU DO? You are considering these two checking accounts: Account 1: A regular checking account with a monthly fee of $6 when the balance goes below $300. Account 2: An interest-earning checking account (paying 0.6 percent) with a monthly charge of $3 if the balance goes below $100. List the costs and benefits of these two checking accounts. Which account would you select?

Other Payment Methods

A *certified check* is a personal check with guaranteed payment. The amount of the check is deducted from your balance when the financial institution certifies the check. A *cashier's check* is a check issued by a financial institution. You may purchase one by paying the amount of the check plus a fee. You may purchase a *money order* in a similar manner from financial institutions, post offices, and stores. Certified checks, cashier's checks, and money orders allow payments that the recipient knows is valid, which, for example, would be useful when buying a used car from someone who doesn't know you.

Traveler's checks, popular before ATMs, allowed payments when away from home. This document required you to sign each check twice. First, you signed the traveler's checks when purchased. Then, as identification, you signed again as you used them. Electronic traveler's checks, in the form of a prepaid travel card, have become more common. The card allows travelers visiting other nations to obtain local currency from an ATM.

Managing Your Checking Account

Obtaining and using a checking account involve several activities.

OPENING A CHECKING ACCOUNT First, decide who the owner of the account is. Only one person is allowed to write checks on an *individual account.* A *joint account* has two or more owners. Both an individual account and a joint account require a signature card. This document is a record of the official signatures of the person or persons authorized to write checks on the account.

MAKING DEPOSITS A *deposit ticket* is used for adding funds to your checking account. On this document, you list the amounts of cash and checks being deposited. Each check you deposit requires an *endorsement*—your signature on the back of the check—to authorize the transfer of the funds into your account. The common endorsement forms are:

- A *blank endorsement* is just your signature, which should be used only when you are actually depositing or cashing a check, since a check may be cashed by anyone once it has been signed.
- A *restrictive endorsement* consists of the words *for deposit only,* followed by your signature, which is especially useful when you are depositing checks.
- A *special endorsement* allows you to transfer a check to someone else with the words *pay to the order of* followed by the name of the other person and then your signature.
- A *remote deposit capture* allows you to deposit a check with an app photo and may require the words *for remote deposit* followed by your signature and account number. Keep the check to make sure it is deposited correctly; then it can be shredded.

WRITING CHECKS Before writing a check, record the information in your check register and deduct the amount of the check from your balance. Many checking account customers use duplicate checks to maintain a record of their current balance.

The procedure for proper check writing has the following steps: (1) record the date; (2) write the name of the person or organization receiving the payment; (3) record the amount of the check in numerals; (4) write the amount of the check in words;

CAUTION!

Be aware of these potential payment deceptions:

- Store your "tap and pay" card in an RFID-blocking wallet or sleeve to prevent thieves from accessing personal data (RFID is "radio-frequency identification"). Wrapping your card in foil can also provide security.
- Each year, millions of dollars are lost by phony checks, fake money orders, and wire transfer fraud. Information on check scams is available at **www.fakechecks.org**.
- Third-party payment services often charge a fee and may send in your payment late, resulting in another fee and possible interruption of service for utilities or a poor credit report.

See the *Financial Literacy in Practice* feature for more information on avoiding scams and identity theft.

Are You Avoiding Identity Theft?

An attorney had his wallet stolen. Within a week, the thieves ordered an expensive monthly cell phone package, applied for a Visa credit card, had a credit line approved to buy a computer, and received a PIN number from the Department of Motor Vehicles to change his online driving information.

In the past, people put their Social Security and driver's license numbers on their checks, making identity theft fairly easy. With one check, a con artist could know a person's Social Security, driver's license, and bank account numbers as well as address, phone number, and perhaps even a signature sample. Identity fraud can range from passing bad checks and using stolen credit cards to theft of another person's total financial existence.

The following quiz can help you avoid becoming one of the thousands of people who have their identities stolen each day.

If you are a victim of identity theft, take the following actions:

- File a police report immediately in the area where the item was stolen. This proves you were diligent and is a first step toward an investigation (if there ever is one).
- Call the three national credit reporting organizations *immediately* to place a fraud alert on your name and Social Security number. The numbers are: Equifax, 1-800-525-6285; Experian (formerly TRW), 1-888-397-3742; and TransUnion, 1-800-680-7289.
- Complete an ID Theft Affidavit, available online.
- Contact the Social Security Administration fraud line at 1-800-269-0271.
- Check with your post office to determine if a fraudulent change-of-address order was submitted.
- Maintain a record of your actions—people you contacted, dates, and reports filed.

Additional information on financial privacy and identity theft is available at **www.identitytheft.gov**, **www.ftc.gov/idtheft**, **www.privacyrights.org**, and **www.idtheftcenter.org**.

Which of the following actions have you taken to avoid identity theft?	Yes	No	Action needed
1. I have only my initials and last name on checks so others will not know how I sign my checks. I only put the last four digits of my account number on checks when paying a bill.			
2. I download apps only from an official app store. I use security features on mobile devices, and I avoid sharing personal data on social media.			
3. I don't provide my Social Security number unless it is legally required.			
4. I keep personal documents in a locked area and shred or burn unneeded documents and delete files containing account or Social Security numbers.			
5. I change passwords and PINs often. I do not keep a list of these in my wallet, and I guard them when using them in a public place.			
6. I promptly collect my mail with account numbers, and I send bill payments from a post office or a public mailbox.			
7. I check my credit report regularly with all three credit reporting agencies to make sure it is correct. I have my name removed from mailing lists of credit agencies and companies offering credit promotions.			
8. I have a photocopy of the contents of my wallet (both sides of each item) as a record if I need to cancel accounts.			
9. I am suspicious of requests for personal or financial information by e-mail ("phishing"), phone ("vishing"), or text message ("smishing"), and avoid clicking on links.			
10. I use only secured, trusted websites when making purchases or when storing personal information online, and avoid public Wi-Fi networks.			
11. I review my bank and credit card statements each month for questionable transactions.			
12. I have a secured home wireless network with a password and personal firewall, up-to-date antivirus software with antispam, a locked router, and encrypted information.			

checks for less than a dollar should be written as "only 79 cents," for example, and cross out the word *dollars* on the check; (5) sign the check; (6) note the reason for payment. Writing a check with a pencil or red ink pen is not recommended.

A *stop-payment order* may be necessary if a check is lost or stolen. Most banks do not honor checks with "stale" dates, usually six months old or older. The fee for a stop-payment commonly ranges from $20 to more than $30. If several checks are missing or you lose your checkbook, closing the account and opening a new one is likely to be less costly than paying several stop-payment fees.

RECONCILING YOUR CHECKING ACCOUNT Online you will be able to access your a *bank statement* summarizing deposits, checks paid, ATM withdrawals, interest earned, and fees such as service charges and printing of checks. The balance reported on the statement will usually differ from the balance in your checkbook. Reasons for a difference may include checks that have not yet cleared, deposits not received by the bank, and interest earned.

To determine the correct balance, prepare a *bank reconciliation* to account for differences between the bank statement and your checkbook balance. This process involves the following steps:

1. Compare the checks written with those reported as paid on the statement. Use the canceled checks, or compare your check register with the check numbers reported on the bank statement. *Subtract* from the *bank statement balance* the total of the checks written but not yet cleared.
2. Determinewhether any deposits made are not on the statement; *add* the amount of the outstanding deposits to the *bank statement balance.*
3. *Subtract* fees or charges on the bank statement and ATM withdrawals from your *checkbook balance.*
4. *Add* any interest earned to your*checkbook balance.*

At this point, the revised balances for both the checkbook and the bank statement should be the same. If the two do not match, check your math; make sure every check and deposit was recorded correctly.

EXAMPLE: Bank Reconciliation

To determine the true balance in your checking account:

Bank Statement		Your Checkbook	
Bank balance	$920	Checkbook balance	$1,041
Subtract: Outstanding checks	−187	**Subtract:** Fees, ATM withdrawals	−271
Add: Deposit in transit	+200	**Add:** Interest earned, direct deposits	+163
Adjusted bank statement balance	933	**Adjusted checkbook balance**	933

A failure to reconcile your bank account each month can result in **not** knowing:

- Your exact spending habits for wise money management.
- If the correct deposit amounts have been credited to your account.
- Any unauthorized ATM withdrawals.
- If your bank is overcharging you for fees.
- Errors that your bank may have made in your account.

Sheet 14 Comparing Payment Methods; Bank Reconciliation

PRACTICE QUIZ 4–4

1. What factors are commonly considered when selecting a checking account?

2. Describe situations in which you might use a certified check, cashier's check, or money order.

3. Based on the following information, determine the true balance in your checking account.

Balance in your checkbook, $356	Balance on bank statement, $472
Service charge and other fees, $15	Interest earned on the account, $4
Total of outstanding checks, $187	Deposits in transit, $60

Road Map

to financial literacy

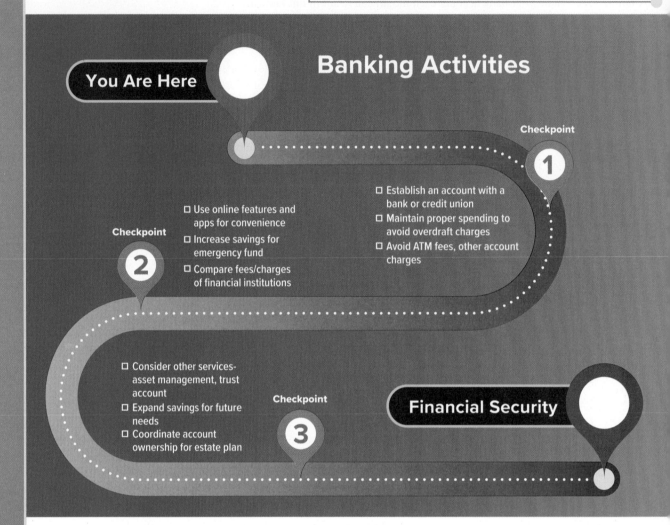

Banking Activities

You Are Here

Checkpoint 1

- ☐ Establish an account with a bank or credit union
- ☐ Maintain proper spending to avoid overdraft charges
- ☐ Avoid ATM fees, other account charges

Checkpoint 2

- ☐ Use online features and apps for convenience
- ☐ Increase savings for emergency fund
- ☐ Compare fees/charges of financial institutions

Checkpoint 3

- ☐ Consider other services-asset management, trust account
- ☐ Expand savings for future needs
- ☐ Coordinate account ownership for estate plan

Financial Security

PERCENT SAVINGS RATE

your personal finance dashboard

Savings Rate Percentage

A key indicator of financial success is the percentage saved each month. Various savings plans can be used. While most people save nothing or very little, financial experts recommend a savings rate of 5 to 10 percent. These funds might be used for emergencies, short-term goals, or long-term financial security.

YOUR SITUATION: Do you automatically set aside an amount for savings each month? How can you reduce expenses or increase income for expanded savings?

LO4.1 Financial products such as savings plans, checking accounts, loans, trust services, and electronic banking are used for managing daily financial activities.

LO4.2 Commercial banks, savings and loan associations, mutual savings banks, credit unions, life insurance companies, investment companies, finance companies, mortgage companies, pawnshops, and check-cashing outlets may be compared on the basis of services offered, rates and fees, safety, convenience, and special programs available to customers.

LO4.3 Commonly used savings plans include regular savings accounts,

certificates of deposit, interest-earning checking accounts, money market accounts, money market funds, and U.S. savings bonds. Savings plans may be evaluated on the basis of rate of return, inflation, tax considerations, liquidity, safety, restrictions, and fees.

LO4.4 Debit cards, online and mobile payment systems, and stored-value cards are increasing in use for payment activities. Regular checking accounts, activity accounts, and interest-earning checking accounts can be compared with regard to restrictions (such as a minimum balance), fees and charges, interest, and special services.

annual percentage yield (APY) 139

asset management account 129

automatic teller machine (ATM) 129

certificate of deposit (CD) 135

commercial bank 133

compounding 139

credit union 133

debit card 130

money market account 137

money market fund 133

mutual savings bank 133

overdraft protection 145

rate of return 138

savings and loan association (S&L) 133

trust 129

Page	Topic	Formula
139	Annual percentage yield (APY)	$APY = 100\left[\left(1 + \frac{Interest}{Principal}\right)^{365/days\ in\ term} - 1\right]$
		Principal = Amount of funds on deposit
		Interest = Total dollar amount earned on the principal
		Days in term = Actual number of days in the term of the account
139	When the number of days in the term is 365 or where the account does not have a stated maturity, the APY formula is simply	$APY = 100\left(\frac{Interest}{Principal}\right)$
		Example:
		$100\left[\left(1 + \frac{\$56.20}{\$1,000}\right)^{\frac{365}{365}} - 1\right] = 5.62\%$
140	After-tax rate of return	Interest rate $\times$ (1 – Tax rate)

1. What would be the annual percentage yield (APY) for a savings account that earned $174 on a balance of $3,250 over the past 365 days?
2. If you earned a 4.2 percent return on your savings, with a 15 percent tax rate, what is the after-tax rate of return?

1. To calculate the APY when the number of days in the term is 365, use this formula:

$$APY = 100 \left(\frac{\text{Interest}}{\text{Principal}} \right)$$

$$= 100 \left(\frac{174}{3250} \right)$$

$$= 100 \,(0.0535) = 5.35\%$$

2. To calculate the after-tax rate of return use

Interest rate $\times$ (1 − Tax rate)

$0.042 \times (1 - 0.15) = 0.042 \,(0.85) = 0.0357 = 3.57\%$

Financial Planning Problems

1. An ATM with a service fee of $2 is used by a person 100 times in a year. What would be the future value in 10 years (use a 2 percent rate) of the annual amount paid in ATM fees? (LO4.1)

2. If a person has ATM fees each month of $16 for six years, what would be the total cost of those banking fees? (LO4.1)

3. A payday loan company charges 6 percent interest for a two-week period. What would be the annual interest rate from that company? (LO4.2)

4. For each of these situations, determine the savings amount. Use a financial calculator or the time value of money tables in the Chapter 1 appendix. (LO4.3)

    a. What would be the value of a savings account started with $700, earning 4 percent (compounded annually) after 10 years?

    b. Brenda Young desires to have $15,000 eight years from now for her daughter's college fund. If she will earn 5 percent (compounded annually) on her money, what amount should she deposit now? Use the present value of a single amount calculation.

    c. What amount would you have if you deposited $1,800 a year for 30 years at 7 percent (compounded annually)?

5. What would be the annual percentage yield for a savings account that earned $56 in interest on $800 over the past 365 days? (LO4.3)

6. With a 28 percent marginal tax rate, would a tax-free yield of 7 percent or a taxable yield of 9.5 percent give you a better return on your savings? Why? (LO4.3)

7. Janie has a joint account with her mother with a balance of $562,000. Based on $250,000 of Federal Deposit Insurance Corporation coverage, what amount of Janie's savings would not be covered by deposit insurance? (LO4.3)

8. A certificate of deposit often charges a penalty for withdrawing funds before the maturity date. If the penalty involves two months of interest, what would be the amount for early withdrawal on a $20,000, 5 percent CD? (LO4.3)

9. What is the annual *opportunity cost* of a checking account that requires a $300 minimum balance to avoid service charges? Assume an interest rate of 3 percent. (LO4.4)

10. A bank that provides overdraft protection charges 12 percent for each $100 (or portion of $100) borrowed when an overdraft occurs. (LO4.4)

    a. What amount of interest would the customer pay for a $188 overdraft? (Assume the interest is for the full amount borrowed for a whole year.)

    b. How much would be saved by using the overdraft protection loan if a customer has three overdraft charges of $30 each during the year?

11. What would be the net *annual* cost of the following checking accounts? (LO4.4)

    a. Monthly fee, $3.75; processing fee, 25 cents per check; checks written, an average of 14 a month.

    b. Interest earnings of 4 percent with a $500 minimum balance; average monthly balance, $600; monthly service charge of $15 for falling below the minimum balance, which occurs three times a year (no interest earned in these months).

12. Based on the following information, prepare a bank reconciliation to determine the adjusted (corrected) balance: (LO4.4)

Bank balance, $680   Account fees, $12

Checkbook balance, $642   ATM withdrawals, $80

Outstanding checks, $112   Deposit in transit, $60

Direct deposits, $70   Interest earned, $8

 To reinforce the content in this chapter, more problems are provided at connect.mheducation.com.

FINANCIAL LITERACY PORTFOLIO . . .

SELECTING A FINANCIAL INSTITUTION

Competency

Research, compare, and select a financial institution.

Action Research

Based on Exhibit 4-4, identify three factors that are most important to you for selecting a financial institution. Using the websites of three different financial institutions, prepare a comparison of the three organizations based on the three factors you identified. Which of the three financial institutions would you use? Why?

Outcome

Create a visually appealing comparison of the three organizations based on the three factors you identified.

REAL LIFE PERSONAL FINANCE

EVALUATING BANKING SERVICES

"Wow! My account balance is a little lower than I expected," commented Melanie Harper as she reviewed her bank statement. "Wait a minute! There's nearly $20 in fees for ATM withdrawals and other service charges. Oh no! I also went below the minimum balance required for my *free* checking account," Melanie groaned. "That cost me $7.50!"

Melanie is not alone in her frustration with fees paid for financial services. While careless money management caused many of these charges, others could have been reduced or eliminated by comparing costs at various financial institutions.

Melanie has decided to investigate various alternatives to her current banking services. Her preliminary research provided the following:

Mobile banking—allows faster access to account information to quickly transfer funds and make payments and purchases. May include access to expanded financial services, such as low-cost, online investment trading and instant loan approval.

Prepaid debit card—would prevent overspending and require staying within the budgeted amount loaded on the card. Cards are usually accepted in most retail locations and online. A variety of fees might be associated with the card.

Check-cashing outlet—would result in fees only when services are used, such as buying money orders, cashing a check, obtaining a prepaid cash card, or paying bills online.

Many people do not realize the amount they pay each month for various bank fees. Some basic research can result in saving several hundred dollars a year.

Questions

1. What benefits and drawbacks might Melanie encounter when using each of these financial services: mobile banking, prepaid debit card, and check-cashing outlet?

2. What factors should Melanie consider when selecting among these various banking services?

3. What actions might you take to better understand the concerns associated with using various banking services?

CONTINUING CASE

FINANCIAL SERVICES: SAVINGS PLANS AND PAYMENT ACCOUNTS

Jamie Lee Jackson, age 26, is in her last semester of college and is anxiously awaiting graduation day, which is just around the corner! She still works part-time as a bakery clerk, has been sticking to her budget the past two years, and is on track to accumulate enough money for the $9,000 down payment she needs to open her cupcake café within the next two years.

Jamie Lee is still single, shares a small apartment with a friend, and continues to split all of the associated living expenses, such as rent and utilities. She now wants to find a place of her own.

One evening, after returning to the apartment after a long shift at the bakery, Jamie learned that her roommate had a couple of friends over earlier in the evening. As Jamie went to her room, she noticed that her top desk drawer had been left open and her debit/ATM card, as well as her checkbook and Social Security card, were missing. She immediately contacted the authorities, and the police instructed her to notify her financial institution immediately. But it was late Saturday night, and Jamie thought she had to now wait until Monday morning. Unfortunately, within no time, Jamie found that her checking account had been emptied!

Jamie Lee's luck worsened, as she had paid many of her monthly bills late last week. Her automobile insurance, two utility bills, and a layaway payment had all been paid for by check. Her bank almost immediately began sending overdraft alerts through her smartphone for the emptied checking account.

Current Financial Situation

Bank Accounts:

Checking account, $2,250 (before the theft)

Savings account, $6,900

Emergency fund savings account, $3,900

401(k) balance, $350

Questions

1. Jamie Lee is beside herself knowing that the thieves had unauthorized use of her debit/ATM card. What is Jamie's financial responsibility for the unauthorized use?

2. What would have been Jamie Lee's financial liability had she waited more than two days to report the debit/ATM card lost or stolen?

3. Using *Your Personal Financial Plan* Sheet 11, what financial service would benefit Jamie Lee now, as she had legitimate checks written to cover her monthly bills that are now in excess of the available checking account balance due to the theft?

"MY CASH WITHDRAWALS HAVE RESULTED IN MANY ATM FEES THAT TAKE AWAY MONEY FROM OTHER BUDGET ITEMS."

Spending Diary

Directions Start (or continue) your Daily Spending Diary or use your own format to record and monitor spending in various categories. Your comments should reflect what you have learned about your spending patterns and help you consider possible changes you might make. The Daily Spending Diary sheets are located at the end of Chapter 1 and in Connect Finance.

Questions

1. Are there any banking fees that you encounter each month? What actions might be taken to reduce or eliminate these cash outflows?

2. What other areas of your daily spending might be reduced or revised?

Name: _____ Date: _____

Planning the Use of Financial Services

Purpose: To report currently used financial services and to determine services that may be needed in the future.

Financial Planning Activities: List (1) currently used services with financial institution information (name, address, phone, website), and (2) services that are likely to be needed in the future. This sheet is also available in an Excel spreadsheet format in Connect Finance.

Suggested Websites: www.bankrate.com, www.consumerfinance.gov

Types of financial services	Current financial services used	Additional financial services needed
Payment services (checking, ATM, online bill payment, payments apps, money orders)	Financial institution	
Savings services (savings account, money market account, certificate of deposit, savings bonds)	Financial institution	
Credit services (credit cards, personal loans, mortgage)	Financial institution	
Other financial services (investments, trust account, tax planning)	Financial institution	

What's Next for Your Personal Financial Plan?

- Assess whether the current types and sources of your financial services are appropriate.
- Determine additional financial services you may wish to use in the future.

Name: _____   **Date:** _____

Comparing Savings Plans

Purpose: To compare the costs and benefits of different savings plans.

Financial Planning Activities: Analyze online information and contact various financial institutions to obtain the information requested below. This sheet is also available in an Excel spreadsheet format in Connect Finance.

Suggested Websites: www.bankrate.com, www.nerdwallet.com, www.depositaccounts.com/savings/

Type of savings plan (regular savings account, certificates of deposit, interest-earning checking accounts, money market accounts and funds, U.S. savings bonds)			
Financial institution			
Address/phone			
Website			
Annual interest rate			
Annual percentage yield (APY)			
Frequency of compounding			
Insured by FDIC, NCUA, other			
Maximum amount insured			
Minimum initial deposit			
Minimum time period savings that must be on deposit			
Penalties for early withdrawal			
Service charges/transaction fees, other costs/fees; limit on number of transactions a month			
Additional services, other information			

Suggested App:
• Digit

McGraw Hill

What's Next for Your Personal Financial Plan?

• Based on this savings plan analysis, determine the best types of savings plans for your current and future financial situation.

• When analyzing savings plans, what factors should you carefully investigate?

Name: _____   **Date:** _____

Using Savings Plans to Achieve Financial Goals

Purpose: Monitor savings for achieving financial goals.

Financial Planning Activities: Record savings plan information along with the amount of your balance or income on a periodic basis. This sheet is also available in an Excel spreadsheet format in Connect Finance.

Suggested Websites: www.savingsbonds.gov, www.fdic.gov

Regular savings account	Savings goal/Amount needed/Date needed
Acct. no. _____	
Financial	Savings goal: Date _____ $ _____
institution _____	Balance: Date _____ $ _____
Address _____	Date _____ $ _____
_____	Date _____ $ _____
Phone _____	Date _____ $ _____
Website _____	

Certificate of deposit	Savings goal/Amount needed/Date needed
Acct. no. _____	
Financial	Savings goal: Date _____ $ _____
institution _____	Balance: Date _____ $ _____
Address _____	Date _____ $ _____
_____	Date _____ $ _____
Phone _____	Date _____ $ _____
Website _____	

Money market fund/acct.	Savings goal/Amount needed/Date needed
Acct. no. _____	
Financial	Savings goal: Date _____ $ _____
institution _____	Balance: Date _____ $ _____
Address _____	Date _____ $ _____
_____	Date _____ $ _____
Phone _____	Date _____ $ _____
Website _____	

U.S. savings bonds	Savings goal/Amount needed/Date needed
Purchase	
location _____	Purchase date: _____ Maturity date: _____
_____	Amount: _____
Address _____	Purchase date: _____ Maturity date: _____
_____	Amount: _____
Phone _____	
Website _____	

Other savings	Savings goal/Amount needed/Date needed
Acct. no. _____	
Financial	Initial deposit: Date _____ $ _____
institution _____	Balance: Date _____ $ _____
Address _____	Date _____ $ _____
_____	Date _____ $ _____
Phone _____	Date _____ $ _____
Website _____	

Suggested App:
- Qapital

McGraw Hill

What's Next for Your Personal Financial Plan?

- Assess your current progress toward achieving various savings goals. Evaluate existing and new savings goals.
- Plan actions to expand the amount you are saving toward various savings goals.

Comparing Payment Methods; Bank Reconciliation

Purpose: (1) To compare different payment accounts. (2) To determine the adjusted cash balance for your checking account.

Financial Planning Activities: (1) Compare checking accounts and payment services at various financial institutions (banks, savings and loan associations, credit unions, online banks). (2) Enter data from your bank statement and checkbook for the amounts requested. This sheet is also available in an Excel spreadsheet format in Connect Finance.

Suggested Websites: www.bankrate.com, www.kiplinger.com, www.findabetterbank.com

Institution name			
Address			
Phone			
Website			
Type of account (regular checking, activity account, bill payment service)			
Minimum balance			
Monthly charge below balance			
"Free" checking for students?			
Online banking services, mobile app banking			
Branch/ATM locations			
Banking hours			
Other fees/costs			
Printing of checks			
Stop-payment order			
Overdrawn account			
Certified check			
ATM, other charges			
Other information			

Checking Account Reconciliation

Statement date:			
	Statement Balance		$_____
Step 1: Compare the checks written with those paid on statement. *Subtract* the total of the checks written but not cleared from the bank balance.	Check no.	Amount	−$_____
Step 2: Determine whether any deposits made are not on the statement; *add* the amount of the outstanding deposits to the *bank statement balance*.	Deposit date	Amount	+$_____
	Adjusted Balance		=$_____

	Checkbook Balance		
Step 3: *Subtract* fees or charges on the bank statement and ATM withdrawals from your *checkbook balance*.	Item	Amount	−$_____
Step 4: *Add* interest or direct deposits earned to your *checkbook balance*.			+$_____
Note: At this point, the two adjusted balances should be the same. If not, carefully check your math and make sure that deposits and checks recorded in your checkbook and on your statement are for the correct amounts.	**Adjusted Balance**		=$_____

Suggested App:
• MoneyPass (ATM locator)

McGraw Hill

5 Consumer Credit: Advantages, Disadvantages, Sources, and Costs

3 Steps to Financial Literacy . . . Reducing Your Debt Ratio

1. Determine the current amount owed for various debts, loans, and other credit accounts.
Website: www.budgetwise.net

2. Assess your daily spending habits to reduce your use of credit and to pay off current loans and credit balances.
App: Mint

3. Avoid using credit for current expenses. Make extra payments to reduce amounts owed.
Website: www.bankrate.com

Why is a low debt-to-income ratio important?

This ratio is an indicator of current money troubles and potential long-term financial disaster. Make every effort to reduce your current debt load. At the end of the chapter, *Your Personal Finance Road Map and Dashboard* will provide guidelines for measuring your debt-to-income ratio.

CHAPTER 5 LEARNING OBJECTIVES

In this chapter, you will learn to:

LO5.1 Analyze advantages and disadvantages of using consumer credit.

LO5.2 Assess the types and sources of consumer credit.

LO5.3 Determine whether you can afford a loan and how to apply for credit.

LO5.4 Determine the cost of credit by calculating interest using various interest formulas.

LO5.5 Develop a plan to protect your credit and manage your debts.

YOUR PERSONAL FINANCIAL PLAN SHEETS

What Is Consumer Credit?

You hear a lot about credit—credit reports, credit scores, credit freezes, and credit monitoring. What does it all mean for you? Your credit matters because if affects your ability to get a loan, a job, housing, insurance, and more. It is important to understand what credit is and how to protect it.

Credit is an arrangement to receive cash, goods, or services now and pay for them in the future. **Consumer credit** refers to the use of credit for personal needs (except a home mortgage) by individuals and families, in contrast to credit used for business purposes. Many people use credit to live beyond their means, largely because of a change in perception about credit. Past generations viewed credit as a negative and used it very sparingly. Society today has popularized credit with phrases such as "Life takes Visa" and "Priceless" campaigns, and even references to a "Plunk factor" when using a sought-after credit card. That said, used appropriately, credit can be a very useful tool.

Consumer credit is based on trust in people's ability and willingness to pay bills when due. It works because people by and large are honest and responsible. But how does consumer credit affect our economy, and how is it affected by our economy?

The Importance of Consumer Credit in Our Economy

Consumer credit dates back to colonial times. Although credit was originally a privilege of the affluent, farmers came to use it extensively. No direct finance charges were imposed; instead, the cost of credit was added to the prices of goods. With the advent of the automobile in the early 1900s, installment credit, in which the debt is repaid in equal installments over a specified period of time, exploded on the American scene.

LO5.1

Analyze advantages and disadvantages of using consumer credit.

ACTION ITEM

I pay any bills I have when they are due.

☐ Always

☐ Most of the time

☐ Sometimes

credit An arrangement to receive cash, goods, or services now and pay for them in the future.

consumer credit The use of credit for personal needs (except a home mortgage).

All economists now recognize consumer credit as a major force in the American economy. Any forecast or evaluation of the economy includes consumer spending trends and consumer credit as a sustaining force.

Uses and Misuses of Credit

Using credit to purchase goods and services may allow consumers to be more efficient or more productive, or it may lead to more satisfying lives. Many valid reasons can be found for using credit. A medical emergency may leave a person strapped for funds. A homemaker returning to the workforce may need a car. An item may cost less money now than it will cost later. Borrowing for a college education may be another valid reason. But borrowing for everyday living expenses or financing a Corvette on credit when a Ford Fiesta is all your budget allows is probably not reasonable.

Using credit increases the amount of money a person can spend to purchase goods and services now. But the trade-off is that it decreases the amount of money that will be available to spend in the future. However, many people expect their incomes to increase and therefore expect to be able to make payments on past credit purchases and still make new purchases. This should be carefully considered.

Here are some questions you should consider before you decide how and when to make a major purchase, for example, a car:

- Do I have the cash I need for the down payment?
- Do I want to use my savings for this purchase?
- Does the purchase fit my budget?
- Could I use the credit I need for this purchase in some better way?
- Could I postpone the purchase?
- What are the opportunity costs of postponing the purchase (alternative transportation costs, a possible increase in the price of the car)?
- What are the dollar costs and the psychological costs of using credit (interest, other finance charges, being in debt and responsible for making a monthly payment)?

If you decide to use credit, make sure the benefits of purchasing now (increased efficiency or productivity, a more satisfying life, etc.) outweigh the costs (financial and psychological) of using credit. Thus, credit, when effectively used, can help you have more and enjoy more. When misused, credit can result in default, bankruptcy, and loss of creditworthiness.

Advantages of Credit

Consumer credit enables people to enjoy goods and services now—a car, a home, an education—or it can provide for emergencies, and it can pay for them all through payment plans based on future income.

Credit cards permit the purchase of goods even when funds are low. Customers with previously approved credit may receive other extras, such as advance notice of sales and the right to order by phone or to buy on approval. Many retailers will accept returned merchandise without a receipt because they can look up the purchase made by a credit card. Credit cards also provide shopping convenience and the efficiency of paying for several purchases with one monthly payment.

Credit is more than a substitute for cash. Many of the services it provides are taken for granted. Every time you turn on the water tap, click the light switch, or telephone a friend, you are using credit.

Using credit is safe, since charge accounts and credit cards let you shop and travel without carrying a large amount of cash. It offers convenience, since you need a credit card to make a hotel reservation, rent a car, and shop by phone or online. You may also use credit cards for identification when cashing checks, and the use of credit provides you with a record of expenses.

The use of credit cards can provide up to a 50-day "float," the time lag between when you make the purchase and when the lender deducts the balance from your checking account when payment is due. This float, offered by many credit card issuers, includes a grace period of 20 to 25 days. During the grace period, no finance charges are assessed on current purchases if the balance is paid in full each month within 25 days after billing.

In addition, many major credit cards provide the following benefits to their customers at no extra cost:

- Accidental death and dismemberment insurance when you travel on a common carrier (train, plane, bus, or ship), up to $250,000.
- Auto rental collision damage waiver for damage due to collision or theft for $50,000 or more.
- Roadside dispatch referral service for emergency roadside assistance, such as towing, locksmith services, and more.
- Redemption of your points or miles for gift cards or cash, or to book travel—from airfare, hotels, and rental cars to vacation packages.
- No foreign transaction fees for some cards, such as Capital One.

Finally, credit indicates stability. The fact that lenders consider you a good risk usually means you are a responsible individual. However, if you do not repay your debts in a timely manner, you will find that credit has many disadvantages.

Disadvantages of Credit

Perhaps the greatest disadvantage of using credit is the temptation to overspend, especially during periods of inflation. Buying today and paying tomorrow, using cheaper dollars, seems ideal, but continual overspending can lead to serious trouble.

Whether or not credit involves *security* (or collateral)—something of value to back the loan—failure to repay a loan may result in loss of income, valuable property, and your good reputation. It can even lead to court action and bankruptcy. Misuse of credit can create serious long-term financial problems, damage family relationships, and delay progress toward financial goals. Therefore, you should approach credit with caution and avoid using it more than your budget permits.

Although credit allows immediate satisfaction of needs and desires, it does not increase total purchasing power. Credit purchases must be paid out of future income; therefore, credit ties up the use of future income. Furthermore, if your income does not increase to cover rising costs, your ability to repay credit commitments will diminish. Before buying goods and services on credit, consider whether they will have lasting value, whether they will increase your personal satisfaction during present and future income periods, and whether your current income will continue or increase.

Finally, credit costs money. It is a service for which you must pay. Paying for purchases over a period of time is more costly than paying for them with cash. Purchasing with credit rather than cash involves one obvious trade-off: The items purchased may cost more due to monthly finance charges and the compounding effect of interest on interest.

Summary: Advantages and Disadvantages of Credit

The use of credit provides immediate access to goods and services, flexibility in money management, safety and convenience, a cushion in emergencies, a means of increasing resources, and a good credit rating if you pay back your debts in a timely manner. But remember, the use of credit is a two-sided coin. An intelligent decision as to its use demands careful evaluation of your current debt, your future income, the added cost, and the consequences of overspending.

PRACTICE QUIZ 5–1

1. What is consumer credit?

2. Why is consumer credit important to our economy?

3. List two good reasons to borrow and two unnecessary reasons to borrow.

LO5.2

Assess the types and sources of consumer credit.

ACTION ITEM

If I need more money for my expenses, I borrow it.

☐ **Never**

☐ **Sometimes**

☐ **Often**

closed-end credit One-time loans that the borrower pays back in a specified period of time and in payments of equal amounts.

open-end credit A line of credit in which loans are made on a continuous basis and the borrower is billed periodically for at least partial payment.

line of credit A short-term loan that is approved before you actually need the money.

Types of Credit

Two basic types of consumer credit exist: closed-end and open-end credit. With **closed-end credit**, you pay back one-time loans in a specified period of time and in payments of equal amounts. With **open-end credit**, loans are made on a continuous basis and you are billed periodically for at least partial payment. Exhibit 5–1 shows examples of closed-end and open-end credit.

Closed-End Credit

Closed-end credit is used for a specific purpose and involves a specified amount. Mortgage loans, automobile loans, and installment loans for purchasing furniture or appliances are examples of closed-end credit. Generally, the seller holds title to the merchandise until the payments have been completed and can take possession of the item if the bill is unpaid.

The three most common types of closed-end credit are installment sales credit, installment cash credit, and single lump-sum credit. *Installment sales credit* is a loan that allows you to receive merchandise, usually high-priced items such as large appliances or furniture. You make a down payment and usually sign a contract to repay the balance, plus interest and service charges, in equal installments over a specified period.

Installment cash credit is a direct loan of money for personal purposes, home improvements, or vacation expenses. You make no down payment and make payments in specified amounts over a set period.

Single lump-sum credit is a loan that must be repaid in total on a specified day, usually within 30 to 90 days. Lump-sum credit is generally, but not always, used to purchase a single item. As Exhibit 5–2 shows, consumer installment credit reached a peak of over $4.1 trillion in 2019.

Open-End Credit

Using a credit card issued by a department store, using a bank credit card (Visa, MasterCard) to make purchases at different stores, charging a meal at a restaurant, and using overdraft protection are examples of open-end credit. As you will soon see, you do not apply for open-end credit to make a single purchase, as you do with closed-end credit. Rather, you can use open-end credit to make any purchases you wish if you do not exceed your **line of credit**, the maximum dollar amount of credit the lender has made available to you.

Exhibit **5–1**

Examples of Closed-End and Open-End Credit

Closed-End Credit	**Open-End Credit**
• Mortgage loans • Automobile loans • Installment loans (installment sales contract, installment cash credit, single lump-sum credit)	• Cards issued by department stores, bank cards (Visa, MasterCard) • Travel and entertainment (T&E) (American Express, Diners Club) • Overdraft protection

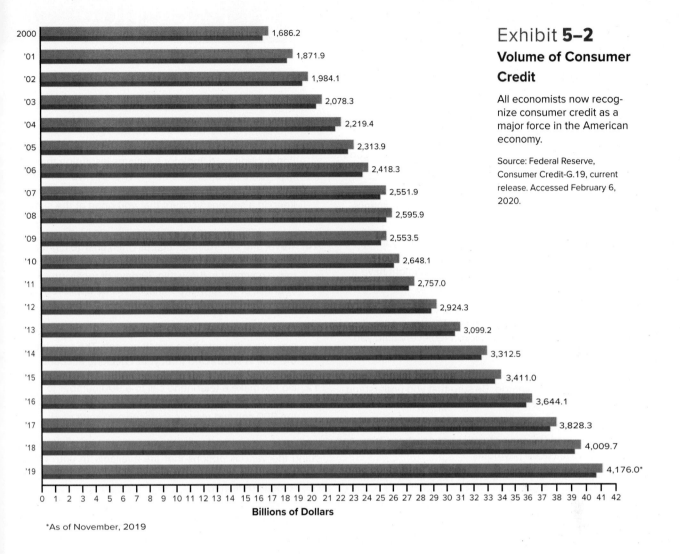

Exhibit **5–2**

Volume of Consumer Credit

All economists now recognize consumer credit as a major force in the American economy.

Source: Federal Reserve, Consumer Credit-G.19, current release. Accessed February 6, 2020.

Year	Billions of Dollars
2000	1,686.2
'01	1,871.9
'02	1,984.1
'03	2,078.3
'04	2,219.4
'05	2,313.9
'06	2,418.3
'07	2,551.9
'08	2,595.9
'09	2,553.5
'10	2,648.1
'11	2,757.0
'12	2,924.3
'13	3,099.2
'14	3,312.5
'15	3,411.0
'16	3,644.1
'17	3,828.3
'18	4,009.7
'19	4,176.0*

Billions of Dollars

*As of November, 2019

You may have to pay **interest**, a periodic charge for the use of credit, or other finance charges. Usually, you have the option to pay the bill in full within 30 days without interest charges or to make set monthly installments based on the account balance plus interest. Some creditors allow you a grace period of 20 to 25 days to pay a bill in full before you incur any interest charges.

Many banks extend **revolving check credit**. Also called a *bank line of credit,* this is a prearranged loan for a specified amount that you can use by writing a special check. Repayment is made in installments over a set period. The finance charges are based on the amount of credit used during the month and on the outstanding balance.

interest A periodic charge for the use of credit.

revolving check credit A prearranged loan from a bank for a specified amount; also called a *bank line of credit.*

Credit Cards

Credit cards are extremely popular. The average cardholder has more than nine credit cards, including bank, retail, and gasoline cards. Cardholders who pay off their balances in full each month are often known as *convenience* users. Cardholders who do not pay off their balances every month are known as *borrowers.*

Most credit card companies offer a grace period, a time period during which no finance charges will be added to your account. A **finance charge** is the total dollar amount you pay to use credit. Usually, if you pay your entire balance before the due date stated on your monthly bill, you will not have to pay a finance charge. Borrowers carry balances beyond the grace period and pay finance charges. Many credit cards offer "teaser rates." These

finance charge The total dollar amount paid to use credit.

Financial Literacy in Practice

Choosing a Credit Card

When you choose a credit card, shopping around can yield big returns. Follow these suggestions to find the card that best meets your needs and help you to use it wisely:

1. Department stores and gasoline companies are good places to obtain your first credit card.

2. Bank credit cards are offered through banks and savings and loan associations. Annual fees and finance charges vary widely, so shop around.

3. If you plan on paying off your balance every month, look for a card that has a grace period and carries no annual fee or a low annual fee. You might have a higher interest rate, but you plan to pay little or no interest anyway.

4. Watch out for creditors that offer low or no annual fees but instead charge a transaction fee every time you use the card.

5. If you plan to carry a balance, look for a card with a low monthly finance charge. Be sure that you understand how the finance charge is calculated.

6. To avoid delays that may result in finance charges, follow the card issuer's instructions as to where, how, and when to make bill payments.

7. Beware of offers of easy credit. No one can guarantee to get you credit.

8. If your card offers a grace period, take advantage of it by paying off your balance in full each month. With a grace period of 25 days, you actually get a free loan when you pay bills in full each month.

9. If you have a bad credit history and have trouble getting a credit card, look for a savings institution that will give you a secured credit card. With this type of card, your line of credit depends on how much money you keep in a savings account that you open at the same time.

10. Travel and entertainment cards often charge higher annual fees than most credit cards. Usually, you must make payment in full within 30 days of receiving your bill, or no further purchases will be approved on the account.

11. Be aware that debit cards are not credit cards but simply a substitute for a check or cash. The amount of the sale is subtracted from your checking account.

12. Do not make a telephone call to a 900 number to request a credit card. You will pay from $2 to $50 for the 900 call and may never receive a credit card.

Before you enter the world of credit, you need to understand the various options that are available to you. Which of the preceding factors would be most important in your choice of a credit card?

Sources: American Institute of Certified Public Accountants, U.S. Office of Consumer Affairs, and Federal Trade Commission.

introductory rates are good for a short period of time, typically 6 to 12 months. The rates may rise significantly after the introductory period. These should be carefully considered before transferring a balance or making significant purchases that you may not be able to repay during the introductory period.

Many credit card companies now offer reward programs that provide cash, rebates, or airline tickets. These types of cards usually have higher finance charges, and the value of the reward should be compared to the cost of the card if you do not intend to pay off the balance monthly.

The cost of a credit card depends on the type of credit card you have and the terms set forth by the lender. As a cardholder, you may have to pay interest or other finance charges. Some credit card companies charge cardholders an annual fee, usually about $95. However, many companies have eliminated annual fees in order to attract more customers. If you are looking for a credit card, be sure to shop around for one with no annual fee. The nearby *Financial Literacy in Practice* feature offers other helpful hints for choosing a credit card. Also, read the *Digital Financial Literacy* feature to understand the advantages and disadvantages of retail store credit cards.

money minute focus

Credit cards offer better consumer protections than debit cards against fraud, and your maximum liability is $50 if you report a card stolen or lost. Some credit cards have zero liability. Debit cards have the same protections against loss or theft if you report the incident within 48 hours. After 48 hours, your liability increases to $500; after 60 days, there is no limit.

Want a retail store credit card?

If you want to take advantage of holiday sales, many department stores and large retailers offer their own credit cards. These cards typically provide additional discounts and frequent shopper rewards when used exclusively at their stores or with affiliate retailers. Many cards may also include special no-interest or deferred-interest offers on purchases made during a promotional period. Like other **credit cards**, a retail store card will show as a line of credit on your **credit report**.

One advantage of these cards is that they tend to be easier to get, even if you have a poor or limited credit history. If you're able to make consistent and on-time payments, a retail store card can be one way to help you build or improve your credit.

The disadvantage is that retail store cards may carry higher interest rates than traditional credit cards. Also, if the card has a deferred-interest promotion, you could end up paying even more in interest if your balance isn't fully paid off by the end of the promotional period.

Six rules for using your store credit card wisely

When choosing whether to sign up for a retail store credit card, you should consider all of the factors you would consider with any other credit card:

- Will you be able to pay off your balance in full every month?
- If there is a deferred-interest promotion, will you be able to pay off your deferred balance in full before the end of the promotion period? If not, how much will the credit cost you and does it fit your budget?
- Are you already managing a number of other credit cards, and if so, do you want to keep track of one more card?

Here are tips and guidelines to remember so you can both enjoy the benefits and reduce risky credit card debt.

1. **Watch your overall spending during the holidays.** Before you buy something, check to make sure you're still within your budget.

cfpb Consumer Financial Protection Bureau

2. **Pay your bill on time.** A missed payment can mean late fees and interest charges—and it can hurt your credit record.

3. **Understand the differences between zero-interest and deferred-interest promotions.** These offers may sound similar, but one could have a bigger impact on your wallet.

   Retailers commonly offer "zero interest" or "deferred interest" promotions with their store credit cards. If you're considering taking advantage of one of these promos, especially to finance a large purchase such as a TV or appliance, it's important to fully understand the distinctions between the two and how they could impact your wallet once the promotion ends.

   Essentially, a zero-interest promotion means that interest will not be added to the balance of your purchase during the promotional period, and you'll only start to pay interest on the remaining balance after the promotional period ends. A deferred-interest promotion, however, is generally phrased as "no interest if paid in full in 12 months." This "if" clause generally means that if you haven't paid off your full balance by the end of the promotional period, interest going back to the date of the purchase will be added to your remaining balance.

4. **Limit the number of cards you apply for.** Too many credit applications can signal to potential creditors that there's been a negative change in your financial situation.

5. **Don't get close to your credit limit.** Getting too close to the card's credit limit can reduce your credit score.

6. **Act fast if you can't pay your bills.** Your creditors may be able to help.

Source: https://www.consumerfinance.gov/about-us/blog/six-tips-when-offered-retail-store-credit-card/

ACTION STEPS FOR. . .

. . .Information Literacy

Based on the **article**, what might be financial and psychological costs of retail credit cards? What might be alternative methods of financing a current purchase?

. . .Financial Literacy

Prepare a visual (chart, table) that presents possible advantages and disadvantages of a retail store credit card. What types of activities and purchases would be restricted without a store credit card?

. . .Digital Literacy

Based on an article from the **Consumer Financial Protection Bureau** about retail store credit cards, describe how the information might be communicated to others with an online video or app.

DEBIT CARDS Don't confuse credit cards with debit cards. Although they may look alike, they're very different. A debit card electronically subtracts money from your savings or checking account to pay for goods and services. A credit card extends credit and delays your payment. Debit cards are most frequently used at automatic teller machines (ATMs). More and more, however, they are also used to purchase goods in stores and to make other types of payments.

Raquel Garcia is serious about avoiding debt. The 18-year-old customer representative for U-Haul recently canceled her credit card. Now she gets her entire paycheck deposited onto a prepaid debit card, which she uses for all her purchases. Since she can access only what's in the account, Garcia no longer worries about breaking her budget and reports: "I'm spending just what I need."

STORED VALUE (OR GIFT) CARDS Stored-value cards, gift cards, or prepaid cards resemble a typical debit card, using magnetic stripe technology to store information and track funds. However, unlike traditional debit cards, stored value cards are prepaid, providing you with immediate money. Gift card sales have exploded over the last few years. The convenience factor for the gift giver is huge. Substantial growth has also occurred in the area of digital gift cards. These cards are sent via e-mail to recipients, who will receive an access code to activate and use their e-cards online to make purchases.

Bankruptcy courts treat gift cards the same way they handle unsecured debt: If a retailer goes bankrupt, holders get pennies on the dollar at most—and in many cases, nothing. One market research firm estimates that holders of gift cards recently lost more than $75 million when the number of retailer bankruptcies increased sharply.

SMART CARDS A smart card is a plastic card equipped with a computer chip that can store 500 times as much data as a normal credit card. Smart cards can combine credit card balances, a driver's license, health care identification, medical history, and other information all in one place. A smart card, for example, can be used to buy an airline ticket and store it digitally, and track frequent flyer miles.

TRAVEL AND ENTERTAINMENT CARDS Travel and entertainment (T&E) cards are really not credit cards because the balance is due in full each month. However, most people think of T&E cards—such as Diners Club or American Express cards—as credit cards because they don't pay for goods or services when they purchase them.

SMARTPHONES Some phones are now equipped to make purchases. This concept, called **mobile commerce**, has seen a significant increase in interest from consumers, retailers, and finance companies. For example, some credit card companies, instead of providing a physical credit card, provide stickers that attach to a phone that will allow the customer to scan the code. In addition, retailers such as Starbucks have apps that are scannable barcodes to allow quick payment using a mobile phone.

mobile commerce The ability to purchase using a mobile device.

Sources of Consumer Credit

Many sources of consumer credit are available, including commercial banks and credit unions. Exhibit 5–3 summarizes the major sources of consumer credit. Study and compare the differences to determine which source might best meet your needs and requirements.

Loans

Loans involve borrowing money with an agreement to repay it, as well as interest, within a certain amount of time. If you were considering taking out a loan, your immediate thought might be to go to your local bank. However, you might want to explore some other options first.

Exhibit **5–3** Sources of Consumer Credit

Credit Source	Type of Loan	Lending Policies
Commercial banks	Single-payment loan Personal installment loans Passbook loans Check-credit loans Credit card loans Primary mortgages Second mortgages	• Seek customers with established credit history • Often require collateral or security • Prefer to deal in large loans, such as vehicle, home improvement, and home modernization, with the exception of credit card and check-credit plans • Determine repayment schedules according to the purpose of the loan • Vary credit rates according to the type of credit, time period, customer's credit history, and the security offered • May require several days to process a new credit application
Consumer finance companies	Personal installment loans Primary mortgages Second mortgages	• Often lend to consumers without established credit history • Often make unsecured loans • Often vary rates according to the size of the loan balance • Offer a variety of repayment schedules • Make a higher percentage of small loans than other lenders • Maximum loan size limited by law • Process applications quickly, frequently on the same day the application is made
Credit unions	Personal installment loans Share draft-credit plans Credit card loans Primary mortgages Second mortgages	• Lend to members only • Make unsecured loans • May require collateral or cosigner for loans over a specified amount • May require payroll deductions to pay off loan • May submit large loan applications to a committee of members for approval • Offer a variety of repayment schedules
Life insurance companies	Single-payment or partial-payment loans	• Lend on cash value of life insurance policy • No date or penalty on repayment • Deduct amount owed from the value of policy benefit if death or other maturity occurs before repayment
Federal savings banks (savings and loan associations)	Personal installment loans (generally permitted by state-chartered savings associations) Home improvement loans Education loans Savings account loans Primary mortgages Second mortgages	• Will lend to all creditworthy individuals • Often require collateral • Loan rates vary depending on size of loan, length of payment, and security involved

Consumer credit is available from several types of sources. Which sources seem to offer the widest variety of loans?

INEXPENSIVE LOANS Parents or other family members are often the source of the least expensive loans—loans with low interest. They may charge only interest they would have earned on the money if they had deposited it in a savings account. They may even give you a loan without interest. Be aware, however, that loans can complicate family relationships. You can borrow (or invest) money with microlending organizations, such as **kiva.org**. Borrowers with good credit can borrow at interest rates lower than those charged by banks and credit unions.

Figure It Out!

Cash Advances

A cash advance is a loan billed to your credit card. You can obtain a cash advance with your credit card at a bank or an ATM or by using checks linked to your credit card account.

Most cards charge a special fee when a cash advance is taken out. The fee is based on a percentage of the amount borrowed, usually about 2 or 3 percent.

Some credit cards charge a minimum cash advance fee, as high as $5. You could get $20 in cash and be charged $5, a fee equal to 25 percent of the amount you borrowed.

Most cards do not have a grace period on cash advances. This means you pay interest every day until you repay the cash advance, even if you do not have an outstanding balance from the previous statement.

On some cards, the interest rate on cash advances is higher than the rate on purchases. Be sure to check the details on the contract sent to you by the card issuer.

Here is an example of charges that could be imposed for a $300 cash advance that you pay off when the bill arrives:

Cash advance fee = $6(2% of $300)

Interest for one month = $5(20% APR on $300)

Total cost for one month = $11($6 + $5)

In comparison, a $300 purchase on a card with a grace period could cost $0 if paid off promptly in full.

The bottom line: It is usually much more expensive to take out a cash advance than to charge a purchase to your credit card. Use cash advances only for real emergencies.

MEDIUM-PRICED LOANS Often you can obtain medium-priced loans—loans with moderate interest—from commercial banks, savings and loan associations, and credit unions. Borrowing from credit unions has several advantages. They provide personalized service, and usually they're willing to be patient with borrowers who can provide good reasons for late or missed payments. However, you must be a member of a credit union in order to get a loan.

EXPENSIVE LOANS The easiest loans to obtain are also the most expensive. Finance companies and retail stores that lend to consumers will frequently charge high interest rates, ranging from 12 to 25 percent. Banks also lend money to their credit card holders through cash advances—loans that are billed to the customer's credit card account. Most cards charge higher interest for a cash advance and charge interest from the day the cash advance is made. As a result, taking out a cash advance is much more expensive than charging a purchase to a credit card. Read the nearby *Figure It Out!* box to learn why you should avoid such cash advances.

HOME EQUITY LOANS A home equity loan is a loan based on your home equity—the difference between the current market value of your home and the amount you still owe on the mortgage.

EXAMPLE: Home Equity Loans

Depending on your income and the equity in your home, you can apply for a line of credit for anywhere from $10,000 to $250,000 or more.

Some lenders let you borrow only up to 75 percent of the value of your home, less the amount of your first mortgage. At some banks, you may qualify to borrow up to 85 percent! This higher lending limit may make the difference in your ability to get the money you need for home improvements, education, or other expenses.

Use the following chart to calculate your home loan value, which is the approximate amount of your home equity line of credit.

	Example	Your Home
Approximate market value of your home	$ 200,000	$ _____
Multiply by 0.75	× 0.75	× 0.75
Approximate loan value	150,000	_____
Subtract balance due on mortgage(s)	100,000	_____
Approximate credit limit available	$ 50,000	$ _____

Unlike interest on most other types of credit, the interest you pay on a home equity loan is tax-deductible. You should use these loans only for major items such as education, home improvements, or medical bills, and you must use them with care. If you miss payments on a home equity loan, the lender can take your home.

> **WHAT WOULD YOU DO?** You plan to spend $5,000 on a smart television and home theater system. You are willing to spend some of your $9,000 in savings. However, you want to finance the rest and pay it off in small monthly install- ments out of the $400 a month you earn working part-time. How might you obtain a low-interest loan and make low monthly payments?

PRACTICE QUIZ 5–2

1. What are two types of consumer credit?

2. Define the following key terms:
   a. Closed-end credit
   b. Open-end credit
   c. Line of credit
   d. Interest
   e. Finance charge

3. What are the major sources of:
   a. Inexpensive loans
   b. Medium-priced loans
   c. Expensive loans

4. What is the difference between a credit and a debit card?

Applying for Credit

When you are ready to apply for credit, you should know what creditors think is important in deciding whether you are creditworthy. You should also know what they cannot legally consider in their decisions. The Equal Credit Opportunity Act (ECOA) starts all credit applicants off on the same footing. It states that race, color, age, sex, marital status, and certain other factors may not be used to discriminate against you in any part of a credit dealing.

LO5.3

Determine whether you can afford a loan and how to apply for credit.

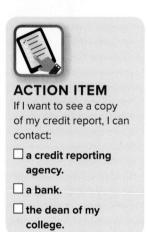

ACTION ITEM

If I want to see a copy of my credit report, I can contact:

☐ a credit reporting agency.

☐ a bank.

☐ the dean of my college.

Can You Afford a Loan?

The only way to determine how much credit you can assume is to first learn how to make an accurate and sensible personal or family budget (see Chapter 2).

Before you take out a loan, ask yourself whether you can meet all of your essential expenses and still afford the monthly loan payments. You can make this calculation in two ways. One is to add up all your basic monthly expenses and then subtract this total from your take-home pay. If the difference will not cover the monthly payment and still leave funds for other expenses, you cannot afford the loan.

A second and more reliable method is to ask yourself what you plan to give up to make the monthly loan payment. If you currently save a portion of your income that is greater than the monthly payment, you can use these savings to pay off the loan. However, if you do not, you will have to forgo spending on entertainment, new appliances, or perhaps even necessities. Are you prepared to make this trade-off? Although precisely measuring your credit capacity is difficult, you can follow certain rules of thumb.

General Rules of Credit Capacity

DEBT PAYMENTS-TO-INCOME RATIO The debt payments-to-income ratio is calculated by dividing your monthly debt payments (not including house payment, which is a long-term liability) by your net monthly income. Experts suggest that you spend no more than 20 percent of your net (after-tax) income on consumer credit payments. Thus, as Exhibit 5–4 shows, a person making $2,500 per month after taxes should spend no more than $500 on credit payments per month.

The 20 percent is the maximum; however, 15 percent or less is much better. The 20 percent estimate is based on the average family, with average expenses; it does not take major emergencies into account. If you are just beginning to use credit, you should not consider yourself safe if you are spending 20 percent of your net income on credit payments.

DEBT-TO-EQUITY RATIO The debt-to-equity ratio is calculated by dividing your total liabilities by your net worth. In calculating this ratio, do not include the value of your home

Exhibit **5–4** **How to Calculate Debt Payments-to-Income Ratio**

Spend no more than 20 percent of your net (after-tax) income on credit payments.

Monthly gross income	$3,364
Less:	
All taxes	540
Social Security	224
Monthly IRA contribution	100
Monthly net income	$2,500
Monthly installment credit payments:	
Visa	50
MasterCard	70
Discover	30
Education loan	—
Personal bank loan	—
Auto loan	350
Total monthly payments	$ 500
Debt payments-to-income ratio ($500/$2,500)	20.00%

and the amount of its mortgage. If your debt-to-equity ratio is about 1—that is, if your consumer installment debt roughly equals your net worth (not including your home or the mortgage)—you have probably reached the upper limit of debt obligations.

None of the above methods is perfect for everyone; the limits given are only guidelines. Only you, based on the money you earn, your obligations, and your financial plans for the future, can determine the exact amount of credit you need and can afford. You must be your own credit manager.

The Five Cs of Credit

When you're ready to apply for a loan or a credit card, you should understand the factors that determine whether a lender will extend credit to you.

When a lender extends credit to consumers, it takes for granted that some people will be unable or unwilling to pay their debts. Therefore, lenders establish policies for determining who will receive credit. Most lenders build such policies around the "five Cs of credit": character, capacity, capital, collateral, and conditions.

CHARACTER: WILL YOU REPAY THE LOAN? Creditors want to know your character—what kind of person they are lending money to. They want to know that you're trustworthy and stable. They may ask for personal or professional references, and they may check to see whether you have a history of trouble with the law. Some questions a lender might ask to determine your character are:

- Have you used credit before?
- How long have you lived at your present address?
- How long have you held your current job?

character The borrower's attitude toward his or her credit obligations.

CAPACITY: CAN YOU REPAY THE LOAN? Your income and the debts you already have will affect your capacity—your ability to pay additional debts. If you already have a large amount of debt in proportion to your income, lenders probably won't extend more credit to you. Some questions a creditor may ask about your income and expenses are:

- What is your job, and how much is your salary?
- Do you have other sources of income?
- What are your current debts?

capacity The borrower's ability to pay additional debts.

CAPITAL: WHAT ARE YOUR ASSETS AND NET WORTH? Assets are any items of value that you own, including cash, property, personal possessions, and investments. Your capital is the amount of your assets that exceed your liabilities, or the debts you owe. Lenders want to be sure that you have enough capital to pay back a loan. That way, if you lost your source of income, you could repay your loan from your savings or by selling some of your assets. A lender might ask:

- What are your assets?
- What are your liabilities?

capital The borrower's assets or net worth.

COLLATERAL: WHAT IF YOU DON'T REPAY THE LOAN? Creditors look at what kinds of property or savings you already have because these can be offered as collateral to secure the loan. If you fail to repay the loan, the creditor may take whatever you pledged as collateral. A creditor might ask:

- What assets do you have to secure the loan (such as a vehicle, your home, or furniture)?
- Do you have any other valuable assets (such as bonds or savings)?

collateral A valuable asset that is pledged to ensure loan payments.

conditions The general economic conditions that can affect a borrower's ability to repay a loan.

CONDITIONS: WHAT IF YOUR JOB IS INSECURE?   General economic **conditions**, such as unemployment and recession, can affect your ability to repay a loan. The basic question focuses on security—of both your job and the firm that employs you.

The information gathered from your application and the credit bureau establishes your credit rating. A *credit rating* is a measure of a person's ability and willingness to make credit payments on time. The factors that determine a person's credit rating are income, current debt, information about character, and how debts have been repaid in the past. If you always make your payments on time, you will probably have an excellent credit rating. If not, your credit rating will be poor, and a lender probably won't extend credit to you. A good credit rating is a valuable asset that you should protect.

Creditors use different combinations of the five Cs to reach their decisions. Some creditors set unusually high standards, and others simply do not offer certain types of loans. Creditors also use various rating systems. Some rely strictly on their own instincts and experience. Others use a credit scoring or statistical system to predict whether an applicant is a good credit risk. When you apply for a loan, the lender is likely to evaluate your application by asking questions such as those included in the checklist in the nearby *Financial Literacy in Practice* feature.

Your Credit Report

When you apply for a loan, the lender will review your credit history very closely. The record of your complete credit history is called your *credit report,* or *credit file.* Your credit records are collected and maintained by credit bureaus. Most lenders rely heavily on credit reports when they consider loan applications. Exhibit 5–5 provides a checklist for building and protecting your credit history.

CREDIT BUREAUS   A credit bureau is an agency that collects information on how promptly people and businesses pay their bills. The three major credit bureaus are Experian,

Exhibit **5–5**
Checklist for Building and Protecting Your Credit History

It is simple and sensible to build and protect your own credit history. Here are some steps to get you started:

- Open a checking or savings account, or both.
- Apply for a local department store credit card.
- Take out a small loan from your bank. Make payments on time.

A Creditor Must . . .	Remember That a Creditor Cannot . . .
1. Evaluate all applicants on the same basis.	1. Refuse you individual credit in your own name if you are creditworthy.
2. Consider income from part-time employment.	2. Require your spouse to cosign a loan. Any creditworthy person can be your cosigner if one is required.
3. Consider the payment history of all joint accounts, if this accurately reflects your credit history.	3. Ask about your family plans or assume that your income will be interrupted to have children.
4. Disregard information on accounts if you can prove that it doesn't affect your ability or willingness to repay.	4. Consider whether you have a telephone listing in your name.

If you want a good credit rating, you must use credit wisely. Why is it a good idea to apply for a local department store credit card or a small loan from your bank?

Reprinted courtesy of Office of Public Information, Federal Reserve Bank of Minneapolis, Minneapolis, MN 55480.

The Five Cs of Credit

Here is what lenders look for in determining your credit-worthiness.

CREDIT HISTORY

1. Character: Will you repay the loan?   Yes   No

Do you have a good attitude toward
credit obligations?   _____ _____

Have you used credit before?   _____ _____

Do you pay your bills on time?   _____ _____

Have you ever filed for bankruptcy?   _____ _____

Do you live within your means?   _____ _____

STABILITY

How long have you lived at your
present address?   _____yrs.

Do you own your home?   _____

How long have you been employed
by your present employer?   _____yrs.

INCOME

2. Capacity: Can you repay the loan?

Your salary and occupation? $_____ ; _____
Place of occupation?   _____

How reliable is your
income?   Reliable _____ ;   Not reliable _____

Any other sources of income? $_____

EXPENSES

Number of dependents?   _____

Do you pay any alimony or
child support?   Yes _____ ; No _____

Current debts? $_____

NET WORTH

3. Capital: What are your assets and net worth?

What are your assets? $_____

What are your liabilities? $_____

What is your net worth? $_____

LOAN SECURITY

4. Collateral: What if you don't repay the loan?

What assets do you have to secure
the loan? (Car, home, furniture?)   _____

What sources do you have besides
income? (Savings, stocks, bonds,
insurance?)   _____

JOB SECURITY

**5. Conditions: What general economic conditions can
   affect your repayment of the loan?**

How secure is
your job?   Secure _____ ; Not secure _____

How secure is the
firm you work for?   Secure _____ ; Not secure _____

SOURCE: Adapted from William M. Pride, Robert J. Hughes, and Jack R. Kapoor, *Business*, 12th ed. (Mason, OH: South-Western Cengage Learning, 2014), p. 541.

TransUnion, and Equifax. Each of these bureaus maintains millions of credit files on individuals, based on information they receive from lenders. Several thousand smaller credit bureaus also collect credit information about consumers. These firms make money by selling the information they collect to creditors who are considering loan applications.

Credit bureaus get their information from banks, finance companies, stores, credit card companies, and other lenders. These sources regularly transmit information about the types of credit they extend to customers, the amounts and terms of the loans, and the customers' payment habits. Credit bureaus also collect some information from other sources, such as court records.

ORDER YOUR FREE CREDIT REPORTS   You can request a free credit report once a year from each of the three major credit reporting agencies: Equifax, Experian, and TransUnion. If you ask the credit bureaus directly, they will charge you a fee to obtain your report. You may want to request your credit reports one at a time, every four months, so you can monitor your credit throughout the year without having to pay for a report. Order

Smart Money Minute

In addition to your free annual credit reports, all U.S. consumers are entitled to six free credit reports every 12 months from Equifax through December 2026. All you have to do is get a "myEquifax" account at **equifax.com/personal/credit-report-services/free-credit-reports/** or call Equifax at 866-349-5191.

your free report through **www.annualcreditreport.com** or call 1-877-322-8228. Check the accuracy of your credit report when you get it.

- Is your full name, Social Security number, birth date, and address correct?
- Are employers, creditors, or home addresses listed that don't belong to you?
- Are account statuses correctly reported as open, closed, or delinquent?
- Do judgments, such as liens or bankruptcies, appear correctly? If there are any inaccuracies, contact the credit reporting agency and creditor that furnished that information to get it corrected. If they don't fix your report, you can file a complaint with the Consumer Financial Protection Bureau.

WHAT'S IN YOUR CREDIT FILES? A typical credit bureau file contains your name, address, Social Security number, and birth date. It may also include the following information:

- Your employer, position, and income
- Your previous address
- Your previous employer
- Your spouse's name, Social Security number, employer, and income
- Whether you rent or own your home
- Checks returned for insufficient funds

CAUTION!

Are you impatient? Researchers have discovered a link between credit scores and impatience.

In addition, your credit file contains detailed credit information. Each time you use credit to make a purchase or take out a loan of any kind, a credit bureau is informed of your account number and the date, amount, terms, and type of credit. Your file is updated regularly to show how many payments you've made, how many payments were late or missed, and how much you owe. Any lawsuits or judgments against you may appear as well. Federal law protects your rights if the information in your credit file is incorrect.

FinTech for Financial Literacy

The Fair Credit Reporting Act requires each of the nationwide consumer reporting companies— Experian, Equifax, and TransUnion—to provide you with a free copy of your credit report annually. Go to **www.annualcreditreport.com**. Beware of other sites that may look and sound similar.

FAIR CREDIT REPORTING Fair and accurate credit reporting is vital to both creditors and consumers. In 1971, the U.S. Congress enacted the Fair Credit Reporting Act, which regulates the use of credit reports. This law requires the deletion of out-of-date information and gives consumers access to their files as well as the right to correct any misinformation that the files may include. The act also places limits on who can obtain your credit report.

WHO CAN OBTAIN A CREDIT REPORT? Your credit report may be issued only to properly identified persons for approved purposes. It may be supplied in response to a court order or by your own written request. A credit report may also be provided for use in connection with a credit transaction, underwriting of insurance, or some legitimate business need. Friends, neighbors, and other individuals cannot be given access to credit information about you. In fact, if they even request such information, they may be subject to a fine, imprisonment, or both.

TIME LIMITS ON UNFAVORABLE DATA Most of the information in your credit file may be reported for only seven years. However, if you've declared personal bankruptcy, that fact may be reported for 10 years. A credit reporting agency can't disclose information in your credit file that's more than 7 or 10 years old unless you're being reviewed for a credit application of $75,000 or more, or unless you apply to purchase life insurance of $150,000 or more.

INCORRECT INFORMATION IN YOUR CREDIT FILE Credit bureaus are required to follow reasonable procedures to ensure that the information in their files is correct. Mistakes can and do occur, however. If you think that a credit bureau may be reporting incorrect data from your file, contact the bureau to dispute the information. The credit bureau must check its records and change or remove the incorrect items. If you challenge the accuracy of an item on your credit report, the bureau must remove the item unless the lender can verify that the information is accurate.

If you are denied credit, insurance, employment, or rental housing based on the information in a credit report, you can get a free copy of your report. Remember to request it within 60 days of notification that your application has been denied.

WHAT ARE YOUR LEGAL RIGHTS? You have legal rights to sue a credit bureau or creditor that has caused you harm by not following the rules established by the Fair Credit Reporting Act.

Credit Scores

A credit score is a number that reflects the information in your credit report. The score summarizes your credit history and helps creditors predict how likely it is that you will repay a loan and make timely payments. Lenders use credit scores in deciding whether to grant you credit, what terms you are offered, or the interest rate you will pay on a loan.

Information used to calculate your credit score usually includes the following:

- The number and types of accounts you have (credit cards, auto loans, mortgages, etc.);
- Whether you pay your bills on time;
- How much of your available credit you are currently using;
- Whether you have any collection actions against you;
- The amount of your outstanding debt; and
- The age of your accounts.

FICO® AND VANTAGESCORE Typical questions in a credit application appear in Exhibit 5–6. The information in your credit report is used to calculate your FICO®credit score—a number generally between 300 and 850—that rates how risky a borrower is. The higher the score, the less risk you pose to creditors. Your FICO® score is available from **www.myfico.com** for a fee. Free credit reports do not provide your credit score.

According to Anthony Sprauve, senior consumer credit specialist at FICO®, "The consequences of not maintaining a sound credit score can be very costly. A low score can bar you from getting a new loan, doom you to a higher interest rate, and even cost you a new job or apartment."

VantageScore is a scoring technique, the first to be developed collaboratively by the three credit reporting companies. This model allows for a more predictive score for consumers,

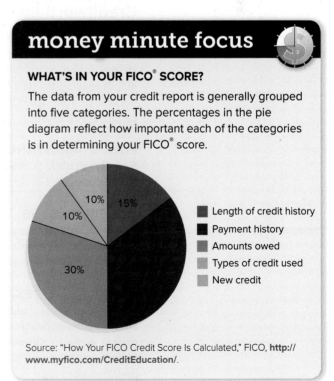

money minute focus

WHAT'S IN YOUR FICO® SCORE?

The data from your credit report is generally grouped into five categories. The percentages in the pie diagram reflect how important each of the categories is in determining your FICO® score.

- Length of credit history
- Payment history
- Amounts owed
- Types of credit used
- New credit

Source: "How Your FICO Credit Score Is Calculated," FICO, **http://www.myfico.com/CreditEducation/**.

Exhibit **5–6**

Sample Credit Application Questions

- Amount of loan requested
- Proposed use of the loan
- Your name and birth date
- Social Security and driver's license numbers
- Present and previous street addresses
- Present and previous employers and their addresses
- Present salary
- Number and ages of dependents
- Other income and sources of other income

- Have you ever received credit from us? If so, when and at which office?
- Checking account number, institution, and branch
- Savings account number, institution, and branch
- Name of nearest relative not living with you
- Relative's address and telephone number
- Your marital status
- Information regarding joint applicant: same questions as above

even for those with limited credit histories, reducing the need for creditors to manually review credit information. VantageScore features a common score range of 501 to 990 (higher scores represent lower likelihood of risk). A key benefit of VantageScore is that as long as the three major credit bureaus have the same information regarding your credit history, you will receive the same score from each of them. A different score alerts you that there are discrepancies in your report.

In late 2020, FICO® rolled out the FICO® Score 10 Suite, a new model that treats late payments and debt more severely but also now considers historical information about your credit card balances and payment amounts. If you already have a good FICO®score, your score may increase, but for many other consumers who have below average scores, the new model may mean more trouble getting loans and paying higher interest.

Other Factors Considered in Determining Creditworthiness

AGE The Equal Credit Opportunity Act is very specific about how a person's age may be used as a factor in credit decisions. A creditor may request that you state your age on an application, but if you're old enough to sign a legal contract (usually 18 to 21 years old, depending on state law), a creditor may not turn you down or decrease your credit because of your age. Creditors may not close your credit account because you reach a certain age or retire.

PUBLIC ASSISTANCE You may not be denied credit because you receive Social Security or public assistance. However, certain information related to this source of income can be considered in determining your creditworthiness.

HOUSING LOANS The ECOA also covers applications for mortgages or home improvement loans. In particular, it bans discrimination against you based on the race or nationality of the people in the neighborhood where you live or want to buy your home, a practice called *redlining*.

WHAT IS THE BEST INTEREST RATE? Effective January 1, 2011, lenders that provide mortgages, credit cards, auto loans, and most other financial products must disclose important details to their customers if they utilize risk-based pricing. Risk-based pricing seeks to differentiate consumers based on their credit information and charge higher rates for more risky customers. Customers who do not receive the best possible (or preferred rate) must be informed of their current credit score or the fact that risk-based pricing was used and the fact that other customers received better rates. Customers may also be entitled to be told what the negative factors were as well as be provided with a scale of their ranking based upon credit score. This may allow customers an opportunity to review their credit report and ensure accuracy prior to paying an unnecessarily higher interest rate.

What If Your Application Is Denied?

If your credit application is denied, the ECOA gives you the right to know the reasons. If the denial is based on a credit report from the credit bureau, you're entitled to know the specific information in the report that led to the denial. After you receive this information, you can contact the credit bureau and ask for a copy of your credit report. The bureau cannot charge a fee for this service as long as you ask to see your files within 60 days of notification that your credit application has been denied. You're entitled to ask the bureau to investigate any inaccurate or incomplete information and correct its records (see Exhibit 5–7).

What Can You Do to Improve Your Credit Score?

A credit score is a snapshot of the contents of your credit report at the time it is calculated. The first step in improving your score is to review your credit report to ensure it

Exhibit **5–7** **What If You Are Denied Credit?**

Steps you can take if you are denied credit

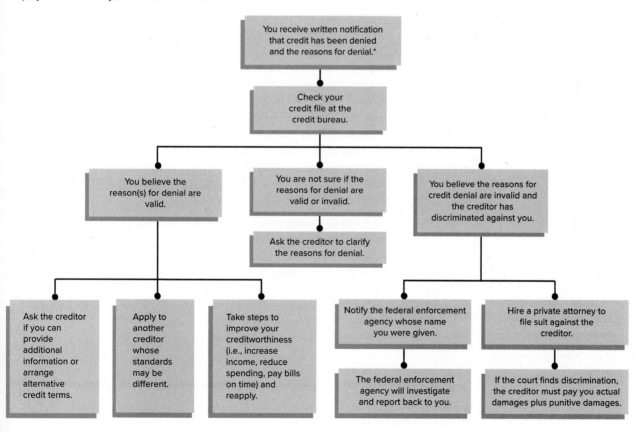

*If a creditor receives no more than **150** applications during a calendar year, the disclosures may be oral.

Reprinted courtesy of Office of Public Information, Federal Reserve Bank of Minneapolis, Minneapolis, MN 55480.

is accurate. Long-term responsible credit behavior is the most effective way to improve future scores. Pay bills on time, lower balances, and use credit wisely to improve your score over time.

1. **Get copies of your credit report—then make sure information is correct.** Go to **www.annualcreditreport.com**. This is the only authorized online source for a free credit report. Under federal law, you can get a free report from each of the three national credit reporting companies every 12 months. You can also call 877-322-8228 or complete the Annual Credit Report Request Form and mail it to Annual Credit Report Request Service, P.O. Box 105281, Atlanta, GA 30348-5281.

2. **Pay your bills on time.** One of the most important steps you can take to improve your credit score is to pay your bills by the due date. You can set up automatic payments from your bank account to help you pay on time, but be sure you have enough money in your account to avoid overdraft fees.

3. **Understand how your credit score is determined.** Your credit score is usually based on the answers to these questions:

    *   **Do you pay your bills on time?** The answer to this question is very important. If you have paid bills late, had an account referred to a collection agency, or have ever declared bankruptcy, this history will show up in your credit report.
    *   **What is your outstanding debt?** Many scoring models compare the amount of debt you have and your credit limits. If the amount you owe is close to your credit limit, it is likely to have a negative effect on your score.
    *   **How long is your credit history?** A short credit history may have a negative effect on your score, but a short history can be offset by other factors, such as timely payments and low balances.
    *   **Have you applied for new credit recently?** If you have applied for too many new accounts recently, that may negatively affect your score. However, if you request a copy of your own credit report or if creditors are monitoring your account or looking at credit reports to make prescreened credit offers, these inquiries about your credit history are not counted as applications for credit.
    *   **How many and what types of credit accounts do you have?** Many credit-scoring models consider the number and type of credit accounts you have. A mix of installment loans and credit cards may improve your score. However, too many finance company accounts or credit cards might hurt your score. To learn more about credit scoring, see the Federal Trade Commission's website, *Facts for Consumers,* at **www.ftc.gov**.

4. **Learn the legal steps to take to improve your credit report.** The Federal Trade Commission's *Building a Better Credit Report* has information on correcting errors in your report, tips on dealing with debt and avoiding scams—and more.

5. **Beware of credit-repair scams.** Sometimes doing it yourself is the best way to repair your credit. The Federal Trade Commission's *Credit Repair: How to Help Yourself* explains how you can improve your creditworthiness and lists legitimate resources for low-cost or no-cost help.

WHAT WOULD YOU DO? You recently got married and want to purchase a home in the next five years. You know how important a good credit score is for getting a lower interest rate. What are some ways you can continue to improve your credit score over the next few years?

PRACTICE QUIZ 5–3

1. What are the two general rules of measuring credit capacity? How is credit capacity calculated?

2. Define the following key terms:

    a. character
    b. capacity
    c. capital
    d. collateral
    e. conditions

3. What are the factors a lender cannot consider according to the law when offering credit?

4. What is a credit bureau?

5. Write the steps you should take if you are denied credit.

The Cost of Credit

If you are thinking of borrowing money or opening a credit account, your first step should be to figure out how much it will cost you and whether you can afford it. Then you should shop for the best terms. Two key concepts that you should remember are the finance charge and the annual percentage rate.

Finance Charge and Annual Percentage Rate

Credit costs vary. If you know the finance charge and the annual percentage rate, you can compare credit prices from different sources. The *finance charge* is the total dollar amount you pay to use credit. It includes interest costs and sometimes other costs such as service charges, credit-related insurance premiums, or appraisal fees.

For example, borrowing $100 for a year might cost you $10 in interest. If there is also a service charge of $1, the finance charge will be $11. The **annual percentage rate (APR)** is the percentage cost (or relative cost) of credit on a yearly basis. The APR is your key to comparing costs, regardless of the amount of credit or how much time you have to repay it.

Suppose you borrow $100 for one year and pay a finance charge of $10. If you can keep the entire $100 for one year and then pay it all back at once, you are paying an APR of 10 percent.

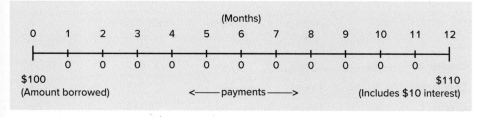

On average, you had full use of $100 throughout the year. To calculate the average use, add the loan balance during the first and last month, and then divide by 2:

$$\text{Average balance} = \frac{\$100 + \$100}{2} = \$100$$

LO5.4

Determine the cost of credit by calculating interest using various interest formulas.

ACTION ITEM
If I know the finance charge and the annual percentage rate, I can compare credit prices.

☐ **Always**

☐ **Most of the time**

☐ **Sometimes**

annual percentage rate (APR) The percentage cost (or relative cost) of credit on a yearly basis. The APR yields a true rate of interest for comparisons with other sources of credit.

But if you repay the $100 and the finance charge (a total of $110) in 12 equal monthly payments, you don't get use of $100 for the whole year. In fact, as is shown next, you get use of increasingly less of that $100 each month. In this case, the $10 charge for credit amounts to an APR of 18.5 percent.

Amount Borrowed	Month Number	Payment Made	Loan Balance
$100	1	$ 0	$100.00
	2	8.33	91.67
	3	8.33	83.34
	4	8.33	75.01
	5	8.33	66.68
	6	8.33	58.35
	7	8.33	50.02
	8	8.33	41.69
	9	8.33	33.36
	10	8.33	25.03
	11	8.33	16.70
	12	8.33	8.37

Note that you are paying 10 percent interest even though you had use of only $91.67 during the second month, not $100. During the last month, you owed only $8.37 (and had use of $8.37), but the $10 interest is for the entire $100. As calculated in the previous example, the average use of the money during the year is ($100 + $8.37) ÷ 2, or $54.19. The nearby *Figure It Out!* box shows how to calculate the APR.

Tackling the Trade-Offs

When you choose your financing, there are trade-offs between the features you prefer (term, size of payments, fixed or variable interest, or payment plan) and the cost of your loan. Here are some major trade-offs you should consider.

TERM VERSUS INTEREST COSTS Many people choose longer-term financing because they want smaller monthly payments, but the longer the term for a loan at a given interest rate, the greater the amount you must pay in interest charges. Consider the following analysis of the relationship between the term and interest costs.

Suppose you're buying a $10,000 used car. You put $2,000 down, and you need to borrow $8,000. Compare the following four credit arrangements:

	APR	Length of Loan	Monthly Payment	Total Finance Charge	Total Cost
Creditor A	5%	3 years	$240	$ 632	$8,640
Creditor B	5	4 years	184	843	8,832
Creditor C	6	4 years	188	1,018	9,024
Creditor D	6	5 years	155	1,280	9,300

How do these choices compare? The answer depends partly on what you need. The lowest-cost loan is available from creditor A. If you are looking for lower monthly payments, you could repay the loan over a longer period of time. However, you would have to pay

The Arithmetic of the Annual Percentage Rate (APR)

There are two ways to calculate the APR: using an APR formula and using the APR tables. The APR tables are more precise than the formula. The formula, given below, only approximates the APR:

$$r = \frac{2 \times n \times I}{P(N + 1)}$$

where:

    r = Approximate APR

    n = Number of payment periods in one year (12, if payments are monthly; 52, if weekly)

    I = Total dollar cost of credit

    P = Principal, or net amount of loan

    N = Total number of payments scheduled to pay off the loan

Let us compare the APR when a $100 loan is paid off in one lump sum at the end of the year and when the same loan is paid off in 12 equal monthly payments. The stated annual interest rate is 10 percent for both loans.

Using the formula, the APR for the lump-sum loan is

$$r = \frac{2 \times 1 \times \$10}{\$100(1 + 1)} = \frac{\$20}{\$100(2)} = \frac{\$20}{\$200} = 0.10, \text{or } 10\%$$

Using the formula, the APR for the monthly payment loan is

$$r = \frac{2 \times 12 \times \$10}{\$100(12 + 1)} = \frac{\$240}{\$100(13)} = \frac{\$240}{\$1,300}$$

$$= 0.1846, \text{or } 18.46\% \text{ (rounded to 18.5\%)}$$

---

more in total costs. A loan from creditor B—also at a 5 percent APR but for four years—would add about $192 to your finance charge.

If that four-year loan were available only from creditor C, the APR of 6 percent would add another $192 to your finance charges. The lowest payment—but the most costly—would be the five-year loan. Other terms, such as the size of the down payment, will also make a difference. Be sure to look at all the terms before you make your choice.

LENDER RISK VERSUS INTEREST RATE You may prefer financing that requires low fixed payments with a large final payment or only a minimum of up-front cash. But both of these requirements can increase your cost of borrowing because they create more risk for your lender.

If you want to minimize your borrowing costs, you may need to accept conditions that reduce your lender's risk. Here are a few possibilities:

- *Variable interest rate.* A variable interest rate is based on fluctuating rates in the banking system, such as the prime rate. With this type of loan, you share the interest rate risks with the lender. Therefore, the lender may offer you a lower initial interest rate than it would with a fixed-rate loan.

- *A secured loan.* If you pledge property or other assets as collateral, you'll probably receive a lower interest rate on your loan.

- *Up-front cash.* Many lenders believe you have a higher stake in repaying a loan if you pay cash for a large portion of what you are financing. Doing so may give you a better chance of getting the other terms you want.

- *A shorter term.* As you have learned, the shorter the period of time for which you borrow, the smaller the chance that something will prevent you from repaying and the lower the risk to the lender. Therefore, you may be able to borrow at a lower interest rate if you accept a shorter-term loan, but your payments will be higher.

Calculating the Cost of Credit

The most common method of calculating interest is the simple interest formula. Other methods, such as simple interest on the declining balance and add-on interest, are variations of this formula.

simple interest Interest computed on principal only and without compounding.

SIMPLE INTEREST Simple interest is the interest computed on principal only and without compounding; it is the dollar cost of borrowing money. This cost is based on three elements: the amount borrowed, which is called the *principal;* the rate of interest; and the amount of time for which the principal is borrowed.

You can use the following formula to find simple interest:

$$\text{Interest} = \text{Principal} \times \text{Rate of interest} \times \text{Time}$$
$$\text{or}$$
$$I = P \times r \times T$$

EXAMPLE: Using the Simple Interest Formula

Suppose you have persuaded a relative to lend you $1,000 to purchase a laptop computer. Your relative agreed to charge only 5 percent interest, and you agreed to repay the loan at the end of one year. Using the simple interest formula, the interest will be 5 percent of $1,000 for one year, or $50, since you have the use of $1,000 for the entire year:

$$I = \$1,000 \times 0.05 \times 1$$
$$= \$50$$

Using the APR formula discussed earlier,

$$\text{APR} = \frac{2 \times n \times I}{P(N + 1)} = \frac{2 \times 1 \times \$50}{\$1,000(1 + 1)} = \frac{\$100}{\$2,000} = 0.05, \text{ or } 5\%$$

Note that the stated rate, 5 percent, is also the annual percentage rate.

SIMPLE INTEREST ON THE DECLINING BALANCE When simple interest is paid back in more than one payment, the method of computing interest is known as the declining balance method. You pay interest only on the amount of principal that you have not yet repaid. The more often you make payments, the lower the interest you'll pay. Most credit unions use this method.

EXAMPLE: Using the Simple Interest Formula on the Declining Balance

Using simple interest on the declining balance to compute interest charges, the interest on a 5 percent, $1,000 loan repaid in two payments, one at the end of the first half-year and another at the end of the second half-year, would be $37.50, as follows:

First payment:

$$I = P \times r \times T$$
$$= \$1,000 \times 0.05 \times 1/2$$
$$= \$25 \text{interest plus } \$500, \text{ or } \$525$$

Second payment:

$$I = P \times r \times T$$
$$= \$500 \times 0.05 \times 1/2$$
$$= \$12.50 \text{interest plus the remaining balance of } \$500, \text{ or } \$512.50$$

Total payment on the loan:

$$\$525 + \$512.50 = \$1,037.50$$

Using the APR formula,

$$\text{APR} = \frac{2 \times n \times I}{P(N + 1)} = \frac{2 \times 2 \times \$37.50}{\$1,000(2 + 1)} = \frac{\$150}{\$3,000} = 0.05, \text{ or } 5\%$$

ADD-ON INTEREST With the add-on interest method, interest is calculated on the full amount of the original principal, no matter how frequently you make payments. When you pay off the loan with one payment, this method produces the same annual percentage rate as the simple interest method. However, if you pay in installments, your actual rate of interest will be higher than the stated rate. Interest payments on this type of loan do not decrease as the loan is repaid. The longer you take to repay the loan, the more interest you'll pay.

COST OF OPEN-END CREDIT The Truth in Lending Act requires that open-end creditors inform consumers as to how the finance charge and the APR will affect their costs. For example, they must explain how they calculate the finance charge. They must also inform you when finance charges on your credit account begin to accrue, so that you know how much time you have to pay your bills before a finance charge is added.

CAUTION!

Many banks will increase the interest rate because of one late payment. They'll also slap on a penalty fee, which can run as high as $50 a pop.

COST OF CREDIT AND EXPECTED INFLATION Inflation reduces the buying power of money. Each percentage point increase in inflation means a decrease of about 1 percent in the quantity of goods and services you can buy with the same amount of money. Because of this, lenders incorporate the expected rate of inflation when deciding how much interest to charge.

Remember the earlier example in which you borrowed $1,000 from your relative at the bargain rate of 5 percent for one year? If the inflation rate was 4 percent that year, your relative's actual rate of return on the loan would have been only 1 percent (5 percent stated interest minus 4 percent inflation rate). A professional lender who wanted to receive 5 percent interest on your loan might have charged you 9 percent interest (5 percent interest plus 4 percent anticipated inflation rate).

AVOID THE MINIMUM MONTHLY PAYMENT TRAP On credit card bills and with certain other forms of credit, the *minimum monthly payment* is the smallest amount you can pay and remain a borrower in good standing. Lenders often encourage you to make the minimum payment because it will then take you longer to pay off the loan. However, if you are paying only the minimum amount on your monthly statement, you need to plan your budget more carefully. The longer it takes for you to pay off a bill, the more interest you pay. The finance charges you pay on an item could end up being more than the item is worth.

Consider the following examples. In each example, the minimum payment is based on 1/36 of the outstanding balance or $20, whichever is greater.

Original Balance	Interest Rate	Years to Repay	Interest Paid	Total Interest Paid as Percentage of Original Balance
$500*	19.8%	2.5 years	$ 150	30%
$500*	12	2.5 years	78	16
$2,000**	19	22 years	4,800	240
$2,000***	19	7 years	1,120	56

*Minimum payment is 1/36 of the outstanding balance or $20, whichever is greater.
**2% minimum payment.
***4% minimum payment.

Sheet 16 Credit Card/Charge Account Comparison

Sheet 17 Consumer Loan Comparison

PRACTICE QUIZ 5-4

1. What are the two key concepts to remember when you borrow money?

2. What are the three major trade-offs you should consider as you take out a loan?

3. Using terms from the following list, complete the sentences below. Write the term you have chosen in the space provided.

finance charge	minimum monthly payment
annual percentage rate	add-on interest method
simple interest	

   a. The _____ is the cost of credit on a yearly basis expressed as a percentage.
   b. The total dollar amount paid to use credit is the _____.
   c. The smallest amount a borrower can pay on a credit card bill and remain a borrower in good standing is the _____.
   d. With the _____, interest is calculated on the full amount of the original principal, no matter how often you make payments.
   e. _____ is the interest computed only on the principal, or the amount that you borrow.

LO5.5

Develop a plan to protect your credit and manage your debts.

Protecting Your Credit

Have you ever received a bill for merchandise you never bought or that you returned to the store or never received? Have you ever made a payment that was not credited to your account or been charged twice for the same item? If so, you are not alone.

Billing Errors and Disputes

The **Fair Credit Billing Act (FCBA)**, enacted in 1975, sets procedures for promptly correcting billing mistakes, refusing to make credit card or revolving credit payments on defective goods, and promptly crediting your payments. This act is one of the main reasons why it is more advantageous to buy higher dollar value items with a credit card than a debit card. This act provides the consumer recourse against the retailer.

Follow these steps if you think that a bill is wrong or want more information about it. First notify your creditor in writing and include any information that might support your case. (A telephone call is not sufficient and will not protect your rights.) Then pay the portion of the bill that is not in question.

Your creditor must acknowledge your letter within 30 days. Then, within two billing periods (but not longer than 90 days), the creditor must adjust your account or tell you why the bill is correct. If the creditor made a mistake, you don't have to pay any finance charges on the disputed amount. If no mistake is found, the creditor must promptly send you an explanation of the situation and a statement of what you owe, including any finance charges that may have accumulated and any minimum payments you missed while you were questioning the bill.

PROTECTING YOUR CREDIT RATING According to law, a creditor may not threaten your credit rating or do anything to damage your credit reputation while you're negotiating a billing dispute. In addition, the creditor may not take any action to collect the amount in question until your complaint has been answered.

DEFECTIVE GOODS AND SERVICES Theo used his credit card to buy a new mountain bike. When it arrived, he discovered that some of the gears didn't work properly. He tried to return it, but the store would not accept a return. He asked the store to repair or

ACTION ITEM

If I have serious credit problems, I should:

☐ **contact my creditors to explain the problems.**

☐ **contact only the most persistent creditors.**

☐ **not contact my creditors and hope they will forget about me.**

Fair Credit Billing Act (FCBA) Sets procedures for promptly correcting billing mistakes, refusing to make credit card payments on defective goods, and promptly crediting payments.

replace the bike, but still he had no luck. According to the Fair Credit Billing Act, he may tell his credit card company to stop payment for the bike because he has made a sincere attempt to resolve the problem with the store.

Identity Crisis: What to Do If Your Identity Is Stolen

"I don't remember charging those items. I've never been in that store." Maybe you never charged those goods and services, but someone else did—someone who used your name and personal information to commit fraud. When imposters use your personal information for their own purposes, they are committing a crime.

The biggest problem? You may not know that your identity has been stolen until you notice that something is wrong: You may get bills for a credit card account you never opened, or you may see charges to your account for things that you didn't purchase.

CAUTION!

If you see an error on your credit report, contact the three major credit bureaus immediately: Equifax (1-800-685-1111), Experian (1-888-397-3742), and TransUnion (1-800-916-8800).

If you think that your identity has been stolen and that someone is using it to charge purchases or obtain credit in some other way, the Federal Trade Commission recommends that you take the following three actions immediately:

1. *Contact the credit bureaus.* Tell them to flag your file with a fraud alert, including a statement that creditors should call you for permission before they open any new accounts in your name.
2. *Contact the creditors.* Contact the creditors for any accounts that have been tampered with or opened fraudulently. Follow up in writing.
3. *File a police report.* Keep a copy of the police report in case your creditors need proof of the crime. If you're still having identity problems, stay alert to new instances of identity theft. You can also contact the Privacy Rights Clearinghouse at 1-619-298-3396.

Protecting Your Credit from Theft or Loss

Some thieves will pick through your trash in the hope of coming across your personal information. You can prevent this from happening by tearing or shredding any papers that contain personal information before you throw them out. Another tactic that an identity thief may use is *skimming*. Skimming involves the recording of the data on the magnetic strip of a credit or debit card. Thieves also target ATM machines by adding a device on the machine that will capture your personal identification number (PIN). This allows them to make fake cards and have access to your account. The best way to avoid falling victim is to carefully look at the machine to see if there are extra wires, strings, or cords that should not be there. Notify the bank immediately if your card is not returned.

According to a recent survey by American Consumer Credit Counseling, 64 percent of Americans do not trust retailers with their credit and debit card information. Due to recent data breaches at Target and Neiman Marcus, 42 percent of respondents are more likely to pay with cash or check.

If you believe that an identity thief has accessed your bank accounts, close the accounts immediately. If your checks have been stolen or misused, stop payment on them. If your debit card has been lost or stolen, cancel it and get another with a new PIN.

Lost credit cards are a key element in credit card fraud. To protect your card, you should take the following actions:

FinTech for Financial Literacy

Opting out may reduce identify theft. You can stop preapproved credit card offers by logging on to **www.optoutprescreen.com.**

- Be sure that your card is returned to you after a purchase. Unreturned cards can find their way into the wrong hands.

- Keep a record of your credit card number. You should keep this record separate from your card.
- Notify the credit card company immediately if your card is lost or stolen. Under the Consumer Credit Protection Act, the maximum amount that you must pay if someone uses your card illegally is $50. However, if you manage to inform the company before the card is used illegally, you have no obligation to pay at all.

money minute focus

Security Freeze

A security freeze on your credit report prevents new creditors from accessing your credit file and others from opening accounts in your name until you lift the freeze. Because most creditors will not open credit accounts without checking your credit report, a freeze can stop identity thieves from opening new accounts in your name.

Protecting Your Credit Information on the Internet

The Internet is becoming almost as important to daily life as the telephone and television. Increasing numbers of consumers use the Internet for financial activities, such as investing, banking, and shopping.

When you make purchases online, make sure that your transactions are secure, that your personal information is protected, and that your "fraud sensors" are sharpened. Although you can't control fraud or deception on the Internet, you can take steps to recognize it, avoid it, and report it. Here's how:

- Use a secure browser.
- Keep records of your online transactions.
- Review your monthly bank and credit card statements.
- Read the privacy and security policies of websites you visit.
- Keep your personal information private.
- Never give your password to anyone online.
- Don't download files sent to you by strangers.

Cosigning a Loan

If a friend or relative ever asks you to cosign a loan, think twice. *Cosigning* a loan means that you agree to be responsible for loan payments if the other party fails to make them. When you cosign, you're taking a chance that a professional lender will not take. The lender would not require a cosigner if the borrower were considered a good risk.

If you cosign a loan and the borrower does not pay the debt, you may have to pay up to the full amount of the debt as well as any late fees or collection costs. The creditor can even collect the debt from you without first trying to collect from the borrower. The creditor can use the same collection methods against you that can be used against the borrower. If the debt is not repaid, that fact will appear on your credit record.

Most private student loans today have a cosigner, typically a parent or a grandparent. Your loan may contain provisions that allow the creditor to put you in default, even if you've been making your payments on time. The Consumer Financial Protection Bureau receives complaints that private lenders place borrowers into default and make balance due all at once when the cosigner dies or files for bankruptcy.

Complaining about Consumer Credit

If you believe that a lender is not following the consumer credit protection laws, first try to solve the problem directly with the lender. If that fails, use formal complaint procedures. This section describes how to file a complaint with the federal agencies that administer credit protection laws. Exhibit 5–8 provides contact information for the various federal agencies.

Exhibit **5–8** **Federal Government Agencies That Enforce the Consumer Credit Laws**

If you think you've been discriminated against by:	You may file a complaint with the following agency:	
Consumer reporting agencies, creditors, and others not listed below	Federal Trade Commission: Consumer Response Center - FCRA Washington, DC 20580	1-877-382-4357
National banks, federal branches/agencies of foreign banks (word *National* or initials *N.A.* appear in or after bank's name)	Office of the Comptroller of the Currency Compliance Management, Mail Stop 6-6 Washington, DC 20219	1-800-613-6743
Federal Reserve System member banks (except national banks and federal branches/agencies of foreign banks)	Federal Reserve Board Division of Consumer & Community Affairs Washington, DC 20551	1-202-452-3693
Federal credit unions (words *Federal Credit Union* appear in institution's name)	National Credit Union Administration 1775 Duke Street Alexandria, VA 22314	1-703-519-4600
State-chartered banks that are not members of the Federal Reserve System	Federal Deposit Insurance Corporation Consumer Response Center, 2345 Grand Avenue, Suite 100 Kansas City, MO 64108-2638	1-877-275-3342

The law gives you certain rights as a consumer of credit. What types of complaints about a creditor might you report to these government agencies?

Consumer Credit Protection Laws

If you have a particular problem with a bank in connection with any of the consumer credit protection laws, you can get advice and help from the Federal Reserve System. You don't need to have an account at the bank to file a complaint. You may also take legal action against a creditor. If you decide to file a lawsuit, you should be aware of the various consumer credit protection laws described below.

TRUTH IN LENDING AND CONSUMER LEASING ACTS If a creditor fails to disclose information as required under the Truth in Lending Act or the Consumer Leasing Act, or gives inaccurate information, you can sue for any monetary loss you suffer. You can also sue a creditor that does not follow rules regarding credit cards. In addition, the Truth in Lending Act and the Consumer Leasing Act permit class action of all the people who have suffered the same injustice.

FAIR CREDIT AND CHARGE CARD DISCLOSURE ACT This act was initially written as an amendment to the Truth in Lending Act. This act requires that solicitations for credit cards in the mail, over the phone, in print, or online must provide the necessary terms of the account. This includes finance charges as well as cash advance or annual fees. This also includes any changes to the account.

EQUAL CREDIT OPPORTUNITY ACT (ECOA) If you think that you can prove that a creditor has discriminated against you for any reason prohibited by the ECOA, you may sue for actual damages plus punitive damages—a payment used to punish the creditor who has violated the law—up to $10,000.

FAIR CREDIT BILLING ACT A creditor that fails to follow the rules that apply to correcting any billing errors will automatically give up the amount owed on the item in question and any finance charges on it, up to a combined total of $50. This is true even if the bill was correct. You may also sue for actual damages plus twice the amount of any finance charges.

FAIR CREDIT REPORTING ACT You may sue any credit bureau or creditor that violates the rules regarding access to your credit records or that fails to correct errors in your credit file. You're entitled to actual damages plus any punitive damages the court allows if the violation is proven to have been intentional.

CONSUMER CREDIT REPORTING REFORM ACT The Consumer Credit Reporting Reform Act of 1977 places the burden of proof for accurate credit information on the credit bureau, rather than on you. Under this law, the creditor must prove that disputed information is accurate. If a creditor or the credit bureau verifies incorrect data, you can sue for damages.

ELECTRONIC FUND TRANSFER ACT If a financial institution does not follow the provisions of the Electronic Fund Transfer Act, you may sue for actual damages plus punitive damages of not less than $100 or more than $1,000. You are also entitled to court costs and attorney fees in a successful lawsuit. Class-action suits are also permitted.

CREDIT CARD ACCOUNTABILITY RESPONSIBILITY AND DISCLOSURE ACT OF 2009 (CARD ACT) This act became effective in February 2010. It changed many of the rules by which the credit card companies could provide credit and administer accounts. Credit card companies must now provide 45 days' notice of rate increases. Also, the time between receiving the statement and the payment due date has been extended to 21 days. Additionally, the credit card companies must apply payments first to the debts that carry the higher interest rates, such as cash advances. They must also provide a more detailed statement that includes the time and total interest amount to pay off the balance if only the minimum payment is made. The rules by which the credit card companies can extend credit to persons under the age of 21 have also changed. Young people must be able to show proof of income or have a signature by a person willing to accept responsibility for the account.

Consumer Financial Protection Bureau

If you are unable to find a resolution to a credit card situation, you may still have one more option. The Consumer Financial Protection Bureau (CFPB) has created a one-stop complaint website for credit card issues. You must visit the website, describe the circumstances of your complaint, and indicate any monies lost due to the issue. You can continue to check back on the website to monitor the progress of your complaint as the CFPB investigates. The website is **https://www.consumerfinance.gov/complaint/**.

Managing Your Debts

A sudden illness or the loss of your job may prevent you from paying your bills on time. If you find you cannot make your payments, contact your creditors at once and try to work out a modified payment plan with them.

Warning Signs of Debt Problems

Chris is in his late 20s. A college graduate, he has a steady job and earns an annual income of $55,000. With the latest model sports car parked in the driveway of his new home, it would appear that Chris has the ideal life.

However, Chris is deeply in debt. He is drowning in a sea of bills. Almost all his income is tied up in debt payments. The bank has already begun foreclosure proceedings on his home, and several stores have court orders to repossess practically all of his new furniture and electronic gadgets. His current car payment is overdue, and he is behind in payments on all his credit cards. If he doesn't come up with a plan of action, he'll lose everything.

Chris' situation is all too common. Some people who seem to be wealthy are just barely keeping their heads above water financially. Generally, the problem they share is financial immaturity. They lack self-discipline and don't control their impulses. They use poor judgment or fail to accept responsibility for managing their money.

Chris and others like him aren't necessarily bad people. They simply haven't thought about their long-term financial goals. Someday you could find yourself in a situation similar to Chris'. Here are some warning signs that you may be in financial trouble:

- You make only the minimum monthly payment on credit cards.
- You're having trouble making even the minimum monthly payment on your credit card bills.
- The total balance on your credit cards increases every month.
- You miss loan payments or often pay late.
- You use savings to pay for necessities such as food and utilities.
- You receive second and third payment due notices from creditors.
- You borrow money to pay off old debts.
- You exceed the credit limits on your credit cards.
- You've been denied credit because of a bad credit bureau report.

If you are experiencing two or more of these warning signs, it's time for you to rethink your priorities before it's too late.

Debt Collection Practices

The Federal Trade Commission enforces the Fair Debt Collection Practices Act. This act prohibits certain practices by debt collectors—businesses that collect debts for creditors. The act does not erase the legitimate debts that consumers owe, but it does control the ways in which debt collection agencies may do business.

Financial Counseling Services

If you're having trouble paying your bills and need help, you have several options. You can contact your creditors and try to work out an adjusted repayment plan, or you can contact a nonprofit financial counseling program.

CONSUMER CREDIT COUNSELING SERVICES The Consumer Credit Counseling Service (CCCS) is a nonprofit organization affiliated with the National Foundation for Consumer Credit (NFCC). Local branches of the CCCS provide debt counseling services for families and individuals with serious financial problems. The CCCS is not a charity, a lending institution, or a government agency. CCCS counseling is usually free. However, when the organization supervises a debt repayment plan, it sometimes charges a small fee to help pay administrative costs.

According to the NFCC, millions of consumers contact CCCS offices each year for help with their personal financial problems. To find an office near you, call 1-800-388-CCCS or go to **www.nfcc.org**. All information is kept confidential.

Credit counselors know that most individuals who are overwhelmed with debt are basically honest people who want to clear up their unmanageable *indebtedness,* the condition of being deeply in debt. Too often, such problems arise from a lack of planning or a miscalculation of earnings. The CCCS is concerned with preventing problems as much as it is with solving them. As a result, its activities are divided into two parts:

- Aiding people with serious debt problems by helping them to manage their money better and set up a realistic budget.
- Helping people prevent indebtedness by teaching them the importance of budget planning, educating them about the pitfalls of unwise credit buying, and encouraging credit institutions to withhold credit from people who cannot afford it.

Financial Literacy in Practice

Choosing a Credit Counselor

Reputable credit counseling organizations employ counselors who are certified and trained in consumer credit, debt management, and budgeting. Here are a few important questions to ask when choosing a credit counselor:

1. **What services do you offer?** Look for an organization that offers a range of services, including budget counseling, savings and debt management classes, and trained certified counselors.

2. **Are you licensed to offer services in my state?** Many states require that credit counseling agencies register or obtain a license before offering their services.

3. **Do you offer free information?** Avoid organizations that charge for information about the nature of their services.

4. **Will I have a formal written agreement or contract with you?** Don't commit to participate in a debt management program over the telephone. Get all verbal promises in writing. Read all documents carefully before you sign them. If you are told you need to act immediately, consider finding another organization.

5. **What are the qualifications of your counselors?** Are they accredited or certified by an outside organization? Which one? If not, how are they trained? Try to use an organization whose counselors are trained by an outside organization that is not affiliated with creditors.

6. **Have other consumers been satisfied with the service they received?** Once you have identified credit counseling organizations that suit your needs, check them out with your state attorney general, local consumer protection agency, and Better Business Bureau.

7. **What are your fees? Are there setup and/or monthly fees?** Get a detailed quote in writing, and specifically ask whether all fees are covered in the quote. If an organization won't help you because you can't afford to pay, look elsewhere for help.

8. **How are your employees paid? Are the employees or the organization paid more if I sign up for certain services, pay a fee, or make a contribution to your organization?** Employees who are counseling you to purchase certain services may receive a commission if you choose to sign up for those services. Many credit counseling organizations receive additional compensation from creditors if you enroll in a debt management program.

9. **What do you do to keep personal information about your clients (for example, name, address, phone number, financial information) confidential and secure?** Credit counseling organizations handle your most sensitive financial information. The organization should have safeguards in place to protect the privacy of this information and prevent misuse.

See the nearby *Financial Literacy in Practice* feature for help in choosing a credit counselor.

OTHER COUNSELING SERVICES In addition to the CCCS, universities, credit unions, military bases, and state and federal housing authorities sometimes provide nonprofit credit counseling services. These organizations usually charge little or nothing for their assistance. You can also check with your bank or local consumer protection office to see whether it has a listing of reputable financial counseling services, such as the Debt Counselors of America.

Declaring Personal Bankruptcy

What if a debtor suffers from an extreme case of financial woes? Can there be any relief? The answer is bankruptcy proceedings. *Bankruptcy* is a legal process in which some or all of the assets of a debtor are distributed among the creditors because the debtor is unable to pay his or her debts. Bankruptcy may also include a plan for the debtor to repay creditors on an installment basis. Declaring bankruptcy is a last resort because it severely damages your credit rating.

Anita Singh illustrates the face of bankruptcy. A 43-year-old freelance photographer from California, she was never in serious financial trouble until she began running up big medical costs. She reached for her credit cards to pay the bills. Because Anita didn't have health insurance, her debt quickly mounted and soon reached $23,000—too much to pay off with her $45,000-a-year income. Her solution was to declare personal bankruptcy to get relief from creditors' demands. Medical bills are the leading cause of bankruptcy.

THE U.S. BANKRUPTCY ACT OF 1978 Exhibit 5–9 illustrates the rate of personal bankruptcy in the United States. The vast majority of bankruptcies in the United States, like Anita Singh's, are filed under a part of U.S. bankruptcy code known as Chapter 7. You have two choices in declaring personal bankruptcy: Chapter 7 (a straight bankruptcy) and Chapter 13 (a wage earner plan bankruptcy). Both choices are undesirable, and neither should be considered an easy way to get out of debt.

CHAPTER 7 BANKRUPTCY In a Chapter 7 bankruptcy, an individual is required to draw up a petition listing his or her assets and liabilities. A person who files for relief under the bankruptcy code is called a *debtor*. The debtor submits the petition to a U.S. district court and pays a filing fee.

Chapter 7 is a straight bankruptcy in which many, but not all, debts are forgiven. Most of the debtor's assets are sold to pay off creditors. Certain assets, however, receive some protection. Among the assets usually protected are Social Security payments, unemployment compensation, and the net value of your home, vehicle, household goods and appliances, tools used in your work, and books.

The courts must charge a $350 case filing fee; it includes a $75 miscellaneous administrative fee, and a $15 trustee fee. If the debtor is unable to pay the fees even in installments, the court may waive the fees.

In filing a petition, a debtor must provide the following information:

- A list of all creditors and the amount and nature of their claims.
- The source, amount, and frequency of the debtor's income.
- A list of all the debtor's property.
- A detailed list of the debtor's monthly expenses.

The release from debt does not affect alimony, child support, certain taxes, fines, certain debts arising from educational loans, or debts that you fail to disclose properly to the bankruptcy court. Furthermore, debts arising from fraud, driving while intoxicated, or certain other acts or crimes may also be excluded.

Exhibit **5–9** U.S. Consumer Bankruptcy Filings, 1980–2019

Consumer bankruptcies have increased significantly over the past 40 years. Consumer bankruptcy filings rose from about 288,000 in 1980 to over 2 million in 2005. Bankruptcies decreased after the Bankruptcy Abuse Prevention and Consumer Protection Act was passed. However, poor economic conditions between 2006 and 2010 caused the numbers to increase yet again, despite the legislation. However, the level of filings is still 51 percent below the 1.54 million reached in 2010.

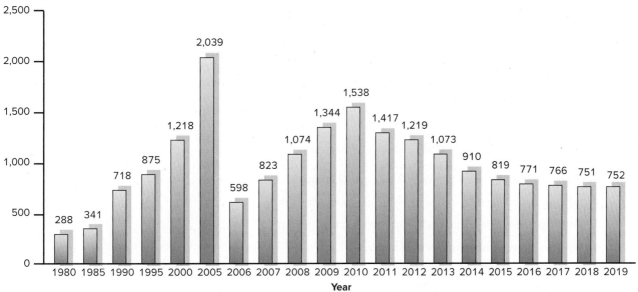

Source: Administrative Office of the U.S. Courts, http://www.uscourts.gov, accessed January 31, 2020.

THE BANKRUPTCY ABUSE PREVENTION AND CONSUMER PROTECTION ACT OF 2005 On April 20, 2005, President George W. Bush signed the Bankruptcy Abuse Prevention and Consumer Protection Act, which is perhaps the largest overhaul of the Bankruptcy Code since it was enacted in 1978. Signing the bill, the president declared, "Bankruptcy should always be the last resort in our legal system. In recent years, too many people have abused the bankruptcy laws. Under this law, Americans who have the ability to pay will be required to pay back at least a portion of their debts. The law will help make credit more affordable, because when bankruptcy is less common, credit can be extended to more people at better rates. Debtors seeking to erase all debts will now have to wait eight years from their last bankruptcy before they can file again. The law will also allow us to clamp down on bankruptcy mills that make their money by advising abusers on how to game the system."

Among other provisions, the law requires that:

- The director of the Executive Office for U.S. Trustees develop a financial management training curriculum to educate individual debtors on how to better manage their finances, and test, evaluate, and report to Congress on the curriculum's effectiveness.
- Debtors complete an approved instructional course in personal financial management.
- The clerk of each bankruptcy district maintain a list of credit counseling agencies and instructional courses on personal financial management.

Furthermore, the law may require that states should develop personal finance curricula designed for use in elementary and secondary schools.

The bottom line: The new law made it more difficult for consumers to file a Chapter 7 bankruptcy and forces them into a Chapter 13 repayment plan.

CHAPTER 13 BANKRUPTCY In Chapter 13 bankruptcy, a debtor with a regular income proposes a plan for using future earnings or assets to eliminate his or her debts over a period of time. In such a bankruptcy, the debtor normally keeps all or most of his or her property. A debtor must provide the same information that is required to file a Chapter 7 bankruptcy.

During the period when the plan is in effect, which can be as long as five years, the debtor makes regular payments to a Chapter 13 trustee, or representative, who then distributes the money to the creditors. Under certain circumstances, the bankruptcy court may approve a plan that permits the debtor to keep all property, even though he or she repays less than the full amount of the debts.

EFFECTS OF BANKRUPTCY People have varying experiences in obtaining credit after they file for bankruptcy. Some find the process more difficult, whereas others find it easier because they have removed the burden of prior debts or because creditors know that they cannot file another bankruptcy case for a certain period of time. Obtaining credit may be easier for people who file a Chapter 13 bankruptcy and repay some of their debts than for those who file a Chapter 7 bankruptcy and make no effort to repay any of their debts.

PRACTICE QUIZ 5–5

1. What steps might you take if there is a billing error in your monthly statement?
2. What steps would you take if someone stole your identity?
3. How might you protect your credit information on the Internet?
4. What are some warning signs of debt problems?
5. Distinguish between Chapter 7 and Chapter 13 bankruptcy.

Debt Capacity

You Are Here

Checkpoint 1

☐ Determine how you intend to use your credit card before choosing one.
☐ Find the card that best needs your needs and use it wisely.
☐ Spend within your means, and don't go over your credit limit on credit cards.

☐ Seek information from several sources when evaluating the sources of credit including various websites and Exhibit 5-3.
☐ Look for a low interest rate card with no annual fee.
☐ Don't miss or be late on your payments, and avoid late fees.

Checkpoint 2

☐ Lower your cost of credit by consolidating your debt through a second mortgage or a home equity line of credit.
☐ Consider carefully before taking out a home equity loan.

Checkpoint 3

Financial Security

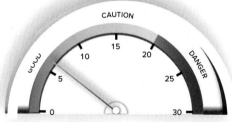

DEBT PAYMENTS-TO-INCOME RATIO

your personal finance dashboard

Debt Payments-to-Income Ratio

A key indicator of your creditworthiness is your capacity to handle a certain level of debt. Lenders will review your current debt payments-to-income ratio. Based upon this, they will determine how much credit they will extend and at what interest rate. Lenders will be more reluctant to lend to individuals who are near the top of the acceptable range of 20 percent.

YOUR SITUATION: Are you able to pay your credit cards off each month when the bill is due? If you carry a balance, is it steadily increasing? Are there debts that you can eliminate to reduce the amount of your overall debt payments?

195

LO5.1 Consumer credit is the use of credit by individuals and families for personal needs. Among the advantages of using credit are the ability to purchase goods when needed and pay for them gradually, the ability to meet financial emergencies, convenience in shopping, and establishment of a credit rating. Disadvantages are that credit costs money, encourages overspending, and ties up future income.

LO5.2 Closed-end and open-end credit are two types of consumer credit. With closed-end credit, the borrower pays back a one-time loan in a stated period of time and with a specified number of payments. With open-end credit, the borrower is permitted to take loans on a continuous basis and is billed for partial payments periodically.

The major sources of consumer credit are commercial banks, savings and loan associations, credit unions, finance companies, life insurance companies, and family and friends. Each of these sources has unique advantages and disadvantages.

Parents or family members are often the source of the least expensive loans. They may charge you only the interest they would have earned had they not made the loan. Such loans, however, can complicate family relationships.

LO5.3 Two general rules for measuring credit capacity are the debt payments-to-income ratio and the debt-to-equity ratio. In reviewing your creditworthiness, a creditor seeks information from one of the three national credit bureaus or a regional credit bureau.

Creditors determine creditworthiness on the basis of the five Cs: character, capacity, capital, collateral, and conditions.

LO5.4 Compare the finance charge and the annual percentage rate (APR) as you shop for credit. Under the Truth in Lending Act, creditors are required to state the cost of borrowing so that you can compare credit costs and shop for credit.

LO5.5 If a billing error occurs on your account, notify the creditor in writing within 60 days. If the dispute is not settled in your favor, you can place your version of it in your credit file. You may also withhold payment on any defective goods or services you have purchased with a credit card as long as you have attempted to resolve the problem with the merchant.

If you have a complaint about credit, first try to deal directly with the creditor. If that fails, you can turn to the appropriate consumer credit law. These laws include the Truth in Lending Act, the Consumer Leasing Act, the Equal Credit Opportunity Act, the Fair Credit Billing Act, the Fair Credit Reporting Act, the Consumer Credit Reporting Reform Act, and the Electronic Fund Transfer Act.

If you cannot meet your obligations, contact your creditors immediately. Also, contact your local Consumer Credit Counseling Service or other debt counseling organizations.

A debtor's last resort is to declare bankruptcy, permitted by the U.S. Bankruptcy Act of 1978. Consider the financial and other costs of bankruptcy before taking this extreme step. A debtor can declare Chapter 7 (straight) bankruptcy or Chapter 13 (wage earner plan) bankruptcy.

annual percentage rate (APR) 181

capacity 173

capital 173

character 173

closed-end credit 164

collateral 173

conditions 173

consumer credit 161

credit 161

Fair Credit Billing Act (FCBA) 186

finance charge 165

interest 165

line of credit 164

mobile commerce 168

open-end credit 164

revolving check credit 165

simple interest 184

Page	Topic	Formula
183	Calculating annual percentage rate (APR)	$APR = \dfrac{2 \times \text{Number of payment periods in one year} \times \text{Dollar cost of credit}}{\text{Loan amount (Total number of payments to pay off the loan} + 1)}$ $= 2 \times n \times I/P(N+1)$
184	Calculating simple interest	Interest (in dollars) = Principal borrowed × Interest rate × Length of loan in years $I = P \times r \times T$
172	Calculating debt payments-to-income ratio	Monthly debt payments (excluding mortgage payments) divided by net monthly income
172	Calculating debt-to-equity ratio	Total liabilities (excluding mortgage) divided by net worth

1. Suppose that your monthly net income is $3,000. Your monthly debt payments include your student loan payment and a gas credit card, and they total $400. What is your debt payments-to-income ratio?
2. Suppose you borrow $2,000 at 6 percent and will repay it in one payment at the end of one year. Use the simple interest formula to determine the amount of interest you will pay.

Solutions

1. Use the debt payments-to-income ratio formula: Monthly debt payments/Monthly net income.

$$\text{Debt payments-to-income ratio} = \frac{\$400}{\$3,000} = 0.13, \text{ or } 13\%$$

2. Using the simple interest formula (Interest = Principal × Rate of interest × Time), the interest is $120 computed as follows:
$120 = $2,000 × 0.06 × 1 (year)

1. A few years ago, Simon Powell purchased a home for $220,000. Today, the home is worth $300,000. His remaining mortgage balance is $100,000. Assuming that Simon can borrow up to 80 percent of the market value, what is the maximum amount he can borrow? (LO5.2)
2. Louise McIntyre's monthly gross income is $4,000. Her employer withholds $800 in federal, state, and local income taxes and $320 in Social Security taxes per month. Louise contributes $160 each month to her IRA. Her monthly credit payments for Visa and MasterCard are $70 and $60, respectively. Her monthly payment on an automobile loan is $570. What is Louise's debt payments-to-income ratio? Is Louise living within her means? (LO5.3)
3. Robert Sampson owns a $140,000 townhouse and still has an unpaid mortgage of $110,000. In addition to his mortgage, he has the following liabilities:

Visa	$565
MasterCard	480
Discover card	395
Education loan	920
Personal bank loan	800
Auto loan	4,250
Total	$7,410

Robert's net worth (not including his home) is about $21,000. This equity is in mutual funds, an automobile, a coin collection, furniture, and other personal property. What is Robert's debt-to-equity ratio? Has he reached the upper limit of debt obligations? Explain. (LO5.3)

4. Madeline Rollins is trying to decide whether she can afford a loan she needs in order to go to chiropractic school. Right now, Madeline is living at home and works in a shoe store, earning a gross income of $820 per month. Her employer deducts a total of $145 for taxes from her monthly pay. Madeline also pays $95 on several credit card debts each month. The loan she needs for chiropractic school will cost an additional $120 per month. Help Madeline make her decision by calculating her debt payments-to-income ratio with and without the college loan. (Remember the 20 percent rule.) (LO5.3)

5. Joshua borrowed $1,000 for one year and paid $100 in interest. The bank charged him a $10 service charge. What is the finance charge on this loan? (LO5.4)

6. In Problem 5, Joshua borrowed $1,000 on January 1, 2021, and paid it all back at once on December 31, 2021. What was the APR? (LO5.4)

7. If Joshua paid the $1,000 in 12 equal monthly payments in problem 5, what is the APR? (LO5.4)

8. Sidney took a $200 cash advance by using checks linked to her credit card account. The bank charges a 2 percent cash advance fee on the amount borrowed and offers no grace period on cash advances. Sidney paid the balance in full when the bill arrived. What was the cash advance fee? What was the interest for one month at an 18 percent APR? What was the total amount she paid? What if she had made the purchase with her credit card and paid off her bill in full promptly? (LO5.4)

9. Brooke lacks cash to pay for a $600 washing machine. She could buy it from the store on credit by making 12 monthly payments of $52.74 each. The total cost would then be $632.88. Instead, Brooke decides to deposit $50 a month in the bank until she has saved enough money to pay cash for the washing machine. One year later, she has saved $642—$600 in deposits plus interest. When she goes back to the store, she finds that the washing machine now costs $660. Its price has gone up 10 percent—the current rate of inflation. Was postponing her purchase a good trade-off for Brooke? (LO5.4)

10. What are the interest cost and the total amount due on a six-month loan of $1,500 at 13.2 percent simple annual interest? (LO5.4)

11. After visiting several automobile dealerships, Richard selects the car he wants. He likes its $10,000 price, but financing through the dealer is no bargain. He has $2,000 cash for a down payment, so he needs an $8,000 loan. In shopping at several banks for an installment loan, he learns that interest on most automobile loans is quoted at add-on rates. That is, during the life of the loan, interest is paid on the full amount borrowed even though a portion of the principal has been paid back. Richard borrows $8,000 for a period of four years at an add-on interest rate of 11 percent. (LO5.4)

   a. What is the total interest on Richard's loan?
   b. What is the total cost of the car?
   c. What is the monthly payment?
   d. What is the annual percentage rate (APR)?

 **To reinforce the content in this chapter, more problems are provided at connect.mheducation.com.**

RESEARCHING LOANS

Competency

Research and compare alternative credit sources.

Action Research

Based on this chapter and online research, complete the *Your Personal Financial Plan Sheet 17* for an auto loan or some other type of purchase on credit. (An Excel file for this sheet is available on Connect.)

Outcome

Report the findings and conclusion of the loan research with the use of an audio file, video, PowerPoint presentation, storyboard, or other visual format.

REAL LIFE PERSONAL FINANCE

FINANCING SUE'S HONDA CIVIC

After shopping around, Sue Wallace decided on the car of her choice, a used Honda Civic. The dealer quoted her a total price of $10,000. Sue decided to use $2,000 of her savings as a down payment and borrow $8,000. The salesperson wrote this information on a sales contract that Sue took with her when she set out to find financing.

When Sue applied for a loan, she discussed loan terms with the bank lending officer. The officer told her that the bank's policy was to lend only 80 percent of the total price of a used car. Sue showed the officer her copy of the sales contract, indicating that she had agreed to make a $2,000, or 20 percent, down payment on the $10,000 car, so this requirement caused her no problem. Although the bank was willing to make 48-month loans at an annual percentage rate of 9 percent on used cars, Sue chose a 36-month repayment schedule. She believed she could afford the higher payments, and she knew she would not have to pay as much interest if she paid off the loan at a faster rate. The bank lending officer provided Sue with a copy of the Truth-in-Lending Disclosure Statement shown here:

TRUTH-IN-LENDING DISCLOSURE STATEMENT (LOANS)

Annual Percentage Rate	Finance Charge	Amount Financed	Total of 36 Payments
The cost of your credit as a yearly rate. 9%	The dollar amount the credit will cost you. $1,158.32	The amount of credit provided to you or on your behalf. $8,000.00	The amount you will have paid after you have made all payments as scheduled. $9,158.32

You have the right to receive at this time an itemization of the Amount Financed.

☐ I want an itemization.   ☐ I do not want an itemization.

Your payment schedule will be:

Number of Payments	Amount of Payments	When Payments Are Due
36	$254.40	1st of each month

Sue decided to compare the APR she had been offered with the APR offered by another bank, but the 11 percent APR of the second bank (Bank B) was more expensive than the 9 percent APR of the first bank (Bank A). Here is her comparison of the two loans:

	Bank A 9% APR	Bank B 11% APR
Amount financed	$8,000	$8,000
Finance charge	1,158.32	1,428.75
Total of payments	9,158.32	9,428.75
Monthly payments	254.40	261.91

The 2 percent difference in the APRs of the two banks meant Sue would have to pay $7.51 extra every month if she got her loan from the second bank. Of course, she got the loan from the first bank.

Questions

1. What is perhaps the most important item shown on the disclosure statement? Why?
2. What is included in the finance charge?
3. What amount will Sue receive from the bank?
4. Should Sue borrow from Bank A or Bank B? Why?

CONTINUING CASE

CONSUMER CREDIT: ADVANTAGES, DISADVANTAGES, SOURCE, AND COSTS

Jamie Lee Jackson, age 27, full-time student and part-time bakery employee, has just moved into a bungalow-style, unfurnished home of her own. The house has only one bedroom, but the rent is manageable and it has plenty of room for Jamie Lee. She decided to give notice to her roommate that she would be leaving the apartment and the shared expenses after the incident with the stolen checkbook and credit cards a few weeks back. Jamie Lee had to dip into her emergency savings account to help cover the deposit and moving expenses because she had not planned to move out of the apartment and be on her own this soon.

Jamie Lee is in need of a few appliances, as there is a small laundry room but no washer or dryer, nor is there a refrigerator in the kitchen. She will also need a living room set and a television because she had only a bedroom set to move in with. Jamie is so excited to finally have the say in how she will furnish her home, and she began shopping for it as soon as the lease was signed.

The home appliance store was the first stop, where Jamie Lee chose a stacking washer and dryer set that would fit comfortably in the laundry space provided. A stainless steel refrigerator with a built-in television screen was her next choice, and the salesperson quickly began to write up the order. She informed Jamie Lee that if she opened up a credit card through the appliance store, she would receive a discount of 10 percent off her total purchase. As she waited for her credit to be approved, Jamie Lee decided to continue shopping for her other needed items.

Living room furniture was next on the list. Jamie Lee went to a local retailer who offered seemingly endless choices of complete sofa sets that included the coffee and end tables as well as matching lamps. She chose a contemporary-style set and again was offered the tempting deal of opening a credit card through the store in exchange for a percentage off her purchase and free delivery.

Jamie Lee's last stop was the local big box retailer, where she chose a 52-inch 1080p LED HDTV. For the third time, a percentage off her first purchase at the big box retailer was all that was needed to get Jamie Lee to sign on the dotted line of the credit card application.

She was daydreaming of how wonderful her new home would look when a call from the appliance store came through asking her to return to the store.

Jamie Lee received the unfortunate news that her credit application at the appliance store had been denied. She left the store only to be greeted at the next two stores where she had chosen the living room set and television with the same bad news: credit application denied! She was informed that her credit score was too low for approval. "How could this be?" Jamie Lee wondered and immediately contacted the credit bureau for further explanation.

Current Financial Situation

Assets:

Checking account, $1,800

Savings account, $7,200

Emergency fund savings account, $2,700

IRA balance, $410

Car, $2,800

Liabilities:

Student loan balance, $10,800 (Jamie Lee is still a full-time student, so no payments are required on the loan until after graduation.)

Credit card balance, $4,250 (total of three store credit cards)

Income:

Gross monthly salary from the bakery, $2,750 (net income, $2,175)

Monthly Expenses:

Rent, $350

Utilities, $70

Food, $125

Gas/Maintenance, $130

Credit card payment, $0

Questions

1. What steps should Jamie Lee take to discover the reason for the denial of her credit applications?
2. Jamie Lee discovers that she has become the victim of identity theft, as her credit report indicates that two credit cards have been opened in her name without her authorization! The police had already been notified the evening of the theft incident in the apartment, but what other measures should Jamie Lee take now that she has become aware of the identity theft?
3. Fortunately for Jamie Lee, she was able to show proof of the theft to the credit bureau, and her credit applications for her home furnishings were approved. The purchase total for the appliances, living room furniture, and television amounted to $4,250. The minimum payments among the three accounts total $325 a month. What is Jamie Lee's debt payments-to-income ratio?
4. Oh, no! The television was finally delivered today but was left on the porch by the delivery company. When Jamie Lee was finally able to attach all the wires and cables according to the owner's manual, it played for half an hour and then shut off. Jamie Lee was unable to get the television to turn back on, although she read the trouble-shooting guide in the manual and contacted the manufacturer's tech support.

Jamie Lee lugged the television back to the store, but they would not accept a return on electronics. What should Jamie Lee do now?

5. Jamie Lee now has to juggle the three monthly credit card bills for each of the retailers where she purchased her home furnishings. She is interested in getting one loan to consolidate the three store consumer credit cards so she may make a single payment on the goods per month. Using *Your Personal Financial Plan Sheet 17*, compare the consumer loan options that Jamie Lee may consider. What are your recommendations for her to consolidate her monthly consumer charge bills?

"I ADMIRE PEOPLE WHO ARE ABLE TO PAY OFF THEIR CREDIT CARDS EACH MONTH."

Directions Your ability to monitor spending and credit use is a fundamental skill for wise money management and long-term financial security. Use the Daily Spending Diary sheets to record all of your spending in the categories provided. Be sure to indicate the use of a credit card with (CR). The Daily Spending Diary sheets are available at the end of Chapter 1 and in Connect Finance.

Questions

1. Describe any aspects of your spending habits that might indicate an overuse of credit.
2. How might your Daily Spending Diary provide information for wise credit use?

Consumer Credit Usage Patterns

Purpose: To create a record of current consumer debt balances.

Financial Planning Activities: Record account names, numbers, and payments for current consumer debts. This sheet is also available in an Excel spreadsheet format in Connect Finance.

Suggested Websites: www.ftc.gov, www.creditcards.com

Automobile, Education, Personal, and Installment Loans

Financial institution	Account number	Current balance	Monthly payment
_____	_____	_____	_____
_____	_____	_____	_____
_____	_____	_____	_____
_____	_____	_____	_____
_____	_____	_____	_____

Charge Accounts and Credit Cards

_____	_____	_____	_____
_____	_____	_____	_____
_____	_____	_____	_____
_____	_____	_____	_____
_____	_____	_____	_____

Other Loans (overdraft protection, home equity, life insurance loan)

_____	_____	_____	_____
_____	_____	_____	_____
_____	_____	_____	_____

Totals   _____   _____

$$\text{Debt payments-to-income ratio} = \frac{\text{Total monthly payments}}{\text{Net (after-tax) income}}$$

What's Next for Your Personal Financial Plan?

- Survey three or four individuals to determine their uses of credit.
- Talk to several people to determine how they first established credit.

Suggested App:
- Lemon Wallet

McGraw Hill

Name: _____ Date: _____

Credit Card/Charge Account Comparison

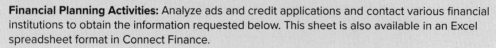

Purpose: To compare the benefits and costs associated with different credit cards and charge accounts.

Financial Planning Activities: Analyze ads and credit applications and contact various financial institutions to obtain the information requested below. This sheet is also available in an Excel spreadsheet format in Connect Finance.

Suggested Websites: www.bankrate.com, www.creditcards.com, www.consumerfinance.gov

Type of credit/charge account			
Name of company/account			
Address/phone			
Website			
Type of purchases that can be made			
Annual fee (if any)			
Annual percentage rate (APR) (interest calculation information)			
Credit limit for new customers			
Minimum monthly payment			
Other costs: • credit report • late fee • other _____			
Restrictions (age, minimum annual income)			
Other information for consumers to consider			
Frequent flyer or other bonus points			

What's Next for Your Personal Financial Plan?

- Make a list of the pros and cons of using credit or debit cards.
- Contact a local credit bureau to obtain information on the services provided and the fees charged.

Name: _____ Date: _____

Consumer Loan Comparison

Purpose: To compare the costs associated with different sources of loans.

Financial Planning Activities: Contact or visit a bank, credit union, and consumer finance company to obtain information on a loan for a specific purpose. This sheet is also available in an Excel spreadsheet format in Connect Finance.

Suggested Websites: www.eloan.com, www.wellsfargo.com, www.ftc.gov

Type of financial institution			
Name			
Address			
Phone			
Website			
What collateral is required?			
Amount of down payment			
Length of loan (months)			
Amount of monthly payment			
Total amount to be repaid (monthly amount × number of months + down payment)			
Total finance charge/ cost of credit			
Annual percentage rate (APR)			
Other costs • credit life insurance • credit report • other _____			
Is a cosigner required?			
Other information			

What's Next for Your Personal Financial Plan?
- Ask several individuals how they would compare loans at different financial institutions.
- Survey several friends and relatives to determine if they ever cosigned for a loan. If yes, what were the consequences of cosigning?

Chapter 5 Appendix:
Education Financing, Loans, and Scholarships

The desire to pursue higher education has grown steadily since the 1940s. According to the U.S. Census Bureau, in 1940 approximately 5 percent of the population held a bachelor's degree. Today, that percentage has grown to greater than 30 percent. The increase in demand for education has created an expansion in many areas, including the number of higher education institutions, the development of different types of degree programs, and specialization in occupations. All of these have contributed to the overall higher cost of a college education.

What is driving the increase in demand for education? Some of the main drivers appear to be higher projected salaries with additional education and reduced potential for unemployment. Numerous studies have shown a correlation between additional education and higher salaries. In addition, lower unemployment rates are correlated with higher education levels (see Exhibit 5-A). However, along with additional education come the opportunity costs associated with it: lost wages while in school and the associated tuition and living costs. Paying for these educational pursuits is the primary focus of this appendix.

Exhibit **5-A** **Education Pays**

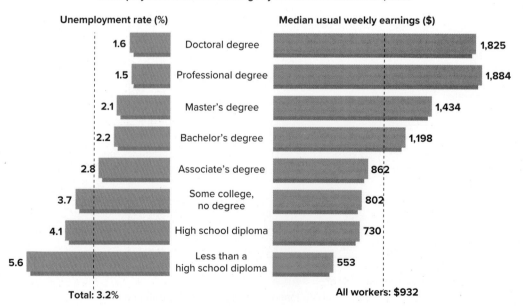

Unemployment rates and earnings by educational attainment, 2018

Unemployment rate (%)		Median usual weekly earnings ($)
1.6	Doctoral degree	1,825
1.5	Professional degree	1,884
2.1	Master's degree	1,434
2.2	Bachelor's degree	1,198
2.8	Associate's degree	862
3.7	Some college, no degree	802
4.1	High school diploma	730
5.6	Less than a high school diploma	553

Total: 3.2%   **All workers: $932**

NOTE: Data are for persons age 25 and over. Earnings are for full-time wage and salary workers.
SOURCE: U.S. Department of Labor, U.S. Bureau of Labor Statistics, accessed March 1, 2020.

Return on Investment

For years, the business community has used the concept of return on investment (ROI). ROI is simply a profitability measure. While there are a few ways to calculate ROI, remember that what you are trying to measure is "bang for your buck." Students who are faced with increasing tuition amounts and large loan balances upon graduation are now able to review schools based upon their ROI. This will help give a general idea about how much income to expect compared to tuition costs and potential loan amounts. One website that provides this information is **www.payscale.com/college-roi**.

Increasing Costs of Education

As college enrollments have swelled, increases in tuition, especially over the last decade, have been significant. Not only are there major increases in the numbers of traditional students coming straight from high school, but the number of those who are returning to school to "retool" and change careers has risen greatly as well. A common issue for many of these students is finding ways to pay for tuition, books, school fees, and living expenses while they pursue an education.

money minute focus

Total student loans have tripled! Student loan balances in 2019 are $1.51 trillion, up from $0.51 trillion, in 2007.

Source: Federal Reserve Bank of New York, *Quarterly Report on Household Debt and Credit,* Q4, 2019, accessed March 1, 2020.

For some students, being accepted into their "dream college" can be a euphoric experience. The more earthbound question is how do you pay for the education? This question should clearly be asked before students apply to schools, but school endowments and additional assistance available frequently add to the challenge of determining the full costs until the college applications are accepted and the financial aid process begins.

The majority of students fund their education through a combination of loans, scholarships, grants, savings, and current earnings. Loans have specific repayment terms, but scholarships and grants do not need to be repaid and thus are sometimes referred to as "free money." Yet nothing in life is free, as the saying goes, and although there are no repayment requirements, you will have to put in some time and effort to find these scholarships. Information about scholarships will be provided later in this appendix.

Free Application for Federal Student Aid

The very first step to funding your education, whether with loans, scholarships, or certain grants, is completing and submitting the Free Application for Federal Student Aid (FAFSA) form. Most state and institutional aid programs require this form to be filed before they consider providing any type of funding. After the FAFSA has been processed, you will receive notification of your expected family contribution (EFC). For dependent students being claimed on their parents' tax return, the amount of parental income, assets, and college savings accounts will be important factors in determining the amount of the EFC. For an independent student, individual assets will also be carefully considered in determining eligibility for aid.

The schools that the student designates on the FAFSA will receive notification that the FAFSA has been processed. Once the admission application is accepted, the schools will take the FAFSA information and prepare a financial aid package. The goal is to evaluate each student's situation and provide the best possible selection of aid. In many cases, the aid package will not cover the full cost of attendance. In addition, the federal student aid may be reduced based on other aid that has been awarded (scholarships, state aid, etc.).

The financial aid package received from the school will often include a combination of grants, loans, and work-study options. The student will be sent an award letter with each portion designated (see Exhibit 5-B). The family should carefully consider their ability to

Exhibit **5-B**

Sample Financial Aid Award Package

Cost of Attendance		
Tuition and fees	$ 22,000	
Room and meals	10,000	
Books and personal	3,500	
Travel	700	
Total Cost of Attendance (1)	**$36,200**	
Expected Family Contribution		
Student	$ 2,000	
Parent	6,000	
Total Family Contribution (2)	**$ 8,000**	
Calculated Financial Need (1 - 2)	$ 28,200	
	Fall 20XX	**Spring 20XX**
Your college merit grant	$ 3,500	$ 3,500
Federal Unsubsidized Stafford Loan	$ 6,000	$ 6,000
Parent PLUS Loan Option	$ 4,600	$ 4,600
Total	**$14,100**	**$14,100**

fund the expected family contribution and repay the loans offered in the aid package. These aid types will now be reviewed with the goal of understanding the repayment requirements and the terms of acceptance of each.

Scholarships

Scholarships do not have to be repaid. Scholarships awarded from organizations outside the school have to be reported on the FAFSA or to the financial aid office, if awarded later. Big-name scholarships (e.g., Coca-Cola and Prudential) receive an extraordinary number of applicants, but there are many other places to consider. Examples include Rotary clubs, churches, professional associations, and local or regional businesses. Although the reward amounts may be smaller, they might add up to big dollars, and some may have the benefit of being renewed in subsequent years. Special attention should be spent on knowing the deadlines for each scholarship. Carefully research the type of candidate they are interested in helping and tailor your information to show how you qualify, much like you would do with a résumé.

Grants

Grants also do not need to be repaid. They can be used to pay for education, training, books, tuition, or any school-related expenses. Students who have demonstrated financial need may receive grants. The most common type is the Federal Pell Grant, which offers a maximum of $6,345 for the 2020–21 academic year. The maximum amount can change each year and has increased significantly in the past few years. For the most up-to-date numbers, visit **studentaid.ed.gov**. The Pell Grant will only be disbursed for a maximum of 12 semesters. Another grant that is available is the Federal Supplemental Educational Opportunity Grant (FSEOG). It can be worth up to $4,000 annually. You must receive a Pell Grant to be eligible for the FSEOG. This grant is typically provided to students who have demonstrated exceptional financial need.

The Teacher Education Assistance for College and Higher Education (TEACH) Grant may also be available depending upon the types of courses taken and the student's future career. This grant provides up to $4,000 annually and requires a signed TEACH Grant agreement that the student will fulfill his or her teaching requirement within eight years of graduation or leaving school. Failure to complete the teaching obligation will convert the amounts due to a direct unsubsidized loan.

Another relatively new grant is the Iraq and Afghanistan Service Grant. These are available to students whose parents have died as a result of military service in Iraq or Afghanistan after September 11, 2011. The grant offers a maximum of $6,195 for the 2019–20 academic year.

In addition to these federal grants, many states offer institutional grants that are distributed through the schools' financial aid offices. Certain colleges and schools also provide grants to women and minority groups and for certain degree programs, to encourage enrollment.

Loans

Education loans are often a substantial part of the financial aid package. These types of loans have also become a significant part of outstanding consumer debt. The Federal Reserve Bank of New York and the U.S. Department of Education reported that the total amount of student loans distributed annually in recent years was $100 billion. Additionally, they have reported that total student loan balances outstanding are more than $1.51 trillion, an amount that is almost double the total amount owed on consumer credit cards.[1]

Federal education loans available today originate from the Direct Loan Program. Each college's financial aid office disburses the funds provided by the U.S. Department of Education. The interest rates and fees can change annually and are adjusted by the federal government. The current (2019–2020) range for interest rates for federal loans is between 4.53 percent and 7.08 percent.[2] Interest rates are expected to rise in the future. The rates are adjusted annually on July 1 for the coming academic year.

1. Stafford Loans

   a. Stafford Loans were initially called the Fede ral Guaranteed Student Loan Program. In 1988, the loans were renamed to honor U.S. Senator Robert Stafford, based on his work with higher education.

   b. Stafford Loans are the most frequently disbursed loan. They are typically disbursed directly from the financial aid office directly to the student. (*NOTE:* The Stafford Loan can also be disbursed through a private lender, which will be discussed later.)

   c. One key element of the Stafford Loan is how the interest accrues while the student is in school. In cases of extreme financial need, the federal government will pay the interest payments during the time that the student is in school and for certain grace periods. This type of loan is commonly referred to as a *subsidized loan.* Subsidized loans are no longer available for graduate or professional education programs.

   d. The more common Stafford Loan makes paying the interest the responsibility of the borrower while in school and during the grace period. This type of loan is commonly referred to as an *unsubsidized loan.* Two options exist for paying the interest: Pay the interest while still enrolled in school or have the interest added to the balance of the loan. The borrower must carefully calculate the cost of allowing this interest to be added to the loan. This process is commonly called *negative amortization* and occurs when the amount of the loan exceeds the original amount borrowed. This not only adds to the amount of the loan but can also extend the time for repayment.

   e. The maximum amounts allowed for Stafford Loans vary considerably based on many factors, including the student's current year in school, type of schooling, cumulative amount of subsidized and unsubsidized loans, and dependency status. The federal government website with the most up-to-date information is **studentaid.ed.gov**.

---

[1] Federal Reserve Bank of New York, Quarterly Report on Household Debt and Credit, 2019 Q4 (**www.new yorkfed.org**), accessed March 1, 2020.

[2] **http://studentaid.ed.gov/types/loans/interest-rates.**

2. Perkins Loans

    a. Perkins Loans are named after Carl D. Perkins, a former member of the U.S. House of Representatives from Kentucky. Perkins was an advocate for higher education, as well as a strong supporter of education for underprivileged students.

    b. The Perkins Loan is typically provided to students who have demonstrated exceptional financial need. This program is administered by individual schools, which serve as the lender using money provided by the federal government. This type of loan is provided only in a subsidized form; it offers a very low interest rate, a long repayment schedule of 10 years, and a slightly longer grace period to begin repayment.

    c. Although each school's financial aid office will determine the amount each student receives, there are still annual and cumulative limits for this loan. Currently, the maximum Perkins Loan allowed for undergraduate students is $5,500 per academic year, with a cumulative maximum of $27,500. For graduate students, the annual maximum is $8,000, with a cumulative maximum of $60,000.

3. Parent loans (PLUS loans), formerly known as the Parent Loan for Undergraduate Students

    a. There are times when parents of dependent children want to contribute financially to help with educational expenses. If they do not currently have funds to contribute, they may apply for a loan. After July 1, 2010, all new PLUS loans are provided by the government and can only be obtained by contacting the financial aid office of the school, not a private lender. Currently, there is no maximum amount; however, the parent may only borrow amounts not covered by the student's current financial aid package, up to the total cost of attending the school.

    b. For PLUS loans, the parent is responsible for repaying the loan. The parent's creditworthiness is a factor in determining whether the loan will be granted. If the parent does not qualify, the student may have the option of taking out additional unsubsidized Stafford Loans.

    c. One variant of the PLUS loan program is the Grad PLUS loan that allows graduate students to borrow for educational expenses.

    d. PLUS loans and Grad PLUS loans have higher interest rates than Stafford and Perkins Loans, so they should be considered very carefully.

4. Private student loans (also called alternative student loans)

    a. Private student loans should also be considered very carefully. They tend to have higher interest rates than those through the government programs. In addition, the interest rates are commonly variable, which can make the payments more challenging to manage.

    b. The three most common reasons that borrowers choose private student loans are:

        I. To fund additional education expenses above the limits that the other programs provide.

        II. There is no requirement for a FAFSA form to be completed. The loan is based upon the creditworthiness of the borrower.

        III. To provide additional flexibility to the borrower in terms of repayment or deferral while the student is in school.

In addition to traditional student loans, a new form of nontraditional lending has also begun to be used to fund education expenses. It is known as *social lending* or *peer-to-peer lending*. This newest form of student loan comes from the private sector. The basic premise is that borrowers can post relevant information and stories regarding why they need money, and prospective lenders or individuals can view the information and choose to fund these aspirations. A large majority of social lending has been in the form of short-term lending, covering periods of six months to three years. Student lending has been slow to catch on, primarily due to the time frame for repayment. Now, however, a few websites have started to offer longer repayment periods. Examples of social lending sites are **www.prosper.com**, **www.lendingclub.com**, **www.sofi.com** and **www.zopa.com**.

Repaying Your Loans

Acquiring the funds to attend school is only the beginning of the financial aid process. The more lengthy part of the process is the repayment. Many of the different types of loans have differing *grace periods* before the first payment is due.

- Stafford Loans require repayment to begin six months after the student no longer attends school or has dropped below half-time enrollment.
- Perkins Loans require repayment to begin nine months after the student no longer attends school or has dropped below half-time enrollment.
- Federal PLUS loans, which are typically taken out by parents or graduate students, require repayment to begin 60 days after the loan is disbursed. The repayment can sometimes be deferred while the student is in school, but the interest will still accrue, much like an unsubsidized Stafford Loan.

Once repayment begins, federal borrowers have numerous options to consider regarding repaying the loan. The most common plans are as follows:

1. *Standard Repayment.* This is one of the most common repayment plans. A fixed monthly amount is paid for a repayment term not to exceed 10 years, or up to 30 years for consolidated loans.
2. *Extended Repayment.* Students elect this option to lower the monthly payment amounts. The length of the repayment term is up to 25 years. One point to consider is the increase in the amount of total interest that will be paid over this time period.
3. *Graduated Repayment.* This repayment plan allows newly graduated students to make lower payments as they start their careers and then slowly increase the amount of the monthly payment over the life of the loan. The payments usually increase every two years.
4. *Income-Contingent Repayment (ICR).* This repayment plan is designed to provide the borrower with some leniency in terms of the amount to be repaid. The monthly payments are recalculated annually, based on the most recent reported income as well as the total debt amount. The length of the repayment is up to 25 years. If the borrower follows through with the entire repayment plan, any remaining balance will be forgiven.
5. *Income-Sensitive Repayment.* This repayment plan is similar to the income-contingent repayment plan. The income-sensitive plan allows the borrower the option to set the monthly payment amount based upon a percentage of gross monthly income. The length of this repayment is limited to 15 years.
6. *Income-Based Repayment (IBR).* This repayment plan is calculated as 10 or 15 percent of discretionary income. To calculate discretionary income, take your adjusted gross income (see Chapter 3) and subtract 150 percent of the poverty line for your state and family size. The plan provides a reduction to the previously discussed income-contingent and Income-Sensitive Repayment Plans. This program provides forgiveness beyond a 20- or 25-year time period, if all prior payments were timely, depending on when the loan was first distributed.
7. *Pay As You Earn Repayment (PAYE).* This repayment amount is capped at 10 percent of discretionary income (see IBR plan above to calculate). This program

provides forgiveness beyond a 20-year time period, if all prior payments were timely. The plan does require proof of a partial financial hardship to qualify for the more favorable terms compared to the IBR plan. This program was phased out in 2011 by the Revised Pay as You Earn Repayment Plan.

8. *Revised Pay As You Earn Repayment (REPAYE).* This is the newest repayment option. This repayment plan is open to all borrowers regardless of when disbursements were made. Loan types include Stafford Loans and PLUS loans (excluding parent loans). This program provides forgiveness beyond a 20-year time period for undergraduate students and a 25-year time period for graduate students, if all prior payments were timely.

Most of the eight plans are available for student loans, but only the first three plans are available for PLUS loans to parents. In addition, one thing to keep in mind is that any forgiven amount may be considered taxable income to the borrower.

CAUTION!

Repayment plans based upon income will typically result in:
1. Paying more interest than with a standard repayment plan.
2. Providing income documentation each year to reassess your payments for the coming year.
3. Taxable income for any amount forgiven at the end of the repayment period.

Consolidation Loan

Another attractive repayment option for borrowers is the option to combine their student loans into one loan and thus have one convenient monthly payment. Just like the Extended Repayment Plan, this method will lower the total monthly payment amount and increase the length of the loan up to 30 years. Remember to carefully consider the increase in the amount of total interest that will be paid over this time period. Unless you are struggling to make the individual loan payment amounts, typically there is no advantage to consolidating loans other than ease of administration (i.e., one payment).

Private loans may have the option of refinancing to obtain a lower interest rate based on an improved credit situation for the borrower. However, in most cases, a federal consolidated loan does not offer this option.

Student Loan Default Statistics

The ease of obtaining money and the ever-increasing student loan balances that new graduates must begin to repay have created many challenges. These issues, combined with a significant number of graduates who are all vying for a smaller pool of available jobs, have created some very unfortunate side effects relating to students' abilities to repay loans. The percentage of student borrowers who are more than 90 days late on their student loan payments has increased significantly in the last decade (see Exhibit 5-C).

Default rates on student loans have increased dramatically for students who have attended all types of higher education: public, private, and for-profit schools. Student loans will not typically be included in bankruptcy. There are no limitations on the number of years that the lender can seek repayment. For federal student loans, the government can garnish wages, take tax refunds, or take other federal benefits for which you might be eligible. Careful consideration should be given to the costs associated with repaying loans.

Loan Deferment

Loan deferments allow you to temporarily stop making payments on existing student loans. In many cases, the deferment will not increase the amount owed because the deferment will be interest free for most types of federal loans. The most common reasons for the deferments are re-enrollment in school, demonstrated financial hardship, unemployment, and military deployment.

Exhibit **5-C** **Percentage of Balances 90+ Days Delinquent**

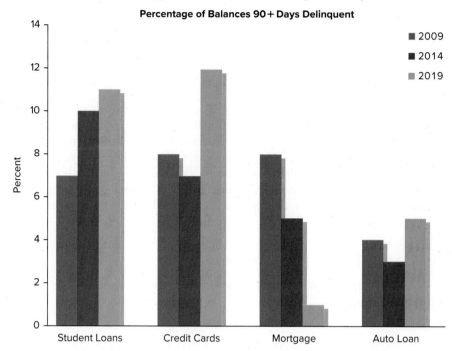

Sources: Federal Reserve Bank of New York Consumer Credit Panel, Equifax. Accessed March 1, 2020.

The Department of Education Appropriations Act of 2019 will now allow deferment on student loans for individuals diagnosed with cancer while they undergo treatment.

Loan Forbearance

Loan forbearance also allows you to temporarily stop making payments on existing student loans. However, this should only be considered as a temporary solution if you are unable to make your monthly payment because a loan in forbearance will continue to accrue interest the entire time. If you are at least able to make payments to cover the interest owed, this would help with the overall balance over a long period of time.

Loan Forgiveness

Loan forgiveness is the option to have all or a portion of your student loan forgiven (paid off on your behalf). The most common forgiveness options are for volunteer work and public or military service.

The Public Service Loan Forgiveness Program was established by the College Cost Reduction and Access Act of 2007. Under this program, full-time qualifying public service employees who make 120 qualifying loan payments on eligible federal Direct Loans will have the balance of their federal Direct Loans forgiven. Eligibility for the public service provision includes working for the government or for an organized nonprofit organization, service in the Peace Corps or AmeriCorps, or even working for a private organization that provides public service.

Many of these organizations also have specific programs to allow a portion of the loan to be canceled even sooner. For example:

- The Peace Corps provides partial cancellation of Perkins Loans (15 percent for each year of service, up to 70 percent in total).

- AmeriCorps Volunteers in Service to America (VISTA) participants who serve for 12 months can receive $5,775 to be used toward cancellation of their loan.
- Military service also offers a cancellation program. Students who enlist in the Army National Guard may be eligible for up to $10,000 of cancellation of student loans.
- Many corporate employers, such as Fidelity and Price Waterhouse Coopers, have incentive programs to pay off loans based upon years of service.
- In addition, there are a variety of other programs for teachers who serve in low-income areas, work with students with disabilities, or work in high-need schools. Law students can find loan forgiveness programs for serving with nonprofit or public interest organizations. Medical students may be eligible for loan forgiveness for performing certain medical research or working in low-income or remote areas. It is strongly advised that you review each program's requirements for eligibility, conditions of employment, and repayment to ensure that you are a good candidate for the program.

Loan Cancellation (Discharge)

In very special circumstances, student loans may be permanently canceled. The most common situations include:

- Death.
- Total and permanent disability.
- School closure (while you were enrolled).
- Fraud by the school (e.g., in the event of forged promissory notes, the school owes the lender a refund).
- Bankruptcy (very rare because the bankruptcy court would need to establish that repayment would create a significant hardship).

Work-Study Programs

Aside from loans, there are other ways to earn money to pay for educational expenses. The Federal Work-Study Program is available at many schools. It is commonly included as part of the financial aid package. Students who decline this option are expected to fund the amount from another source. Some students like the options that the program offers; they can work on campus without needing additional transportation, apply to a variety of positions that interest them, and get to know faculty and staff that they may want to work with on teaching or research assignments. Some students decline the option in favor of higher-paying jobs off-campus. You should consider very carefully the opportunity costs with this decision (fuel costs, commuting time, flexibility, wardrobe needs, etc.).

Your Future and Financial Aid

Navigating the process of financing an education can be very daunting and time-consuming, but the rewards are very high. Finding the money for school and repaying the loans in a manner that works best for your personal situation can lead to long-term success, improved credit scores, higher salaries, lower potential for future unemployment, and higher rates of home ownership (See Exhibit 5-D). One excellent source for choosing a school and the financial aid package for your needs is the College Affordability and Transparency Center (**collegecost.ed.gov**). This is a one-stop website where you can evaluate a college based on net price, average student debt, state funding, graduation rates, and much more. It is very important for your financial future that you find the most affordable education that fits your budget, future career, and long-term financial goals.

Exhibit **5-D** **Home Ownership and Education**

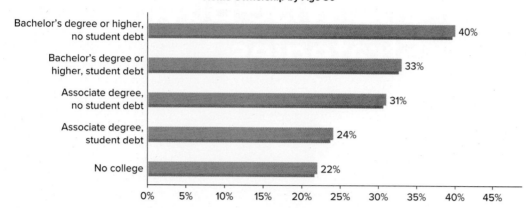

Source: New York Fed Consumer Credit Panel/Equifax and National Student Clearinghouse. Accessed June 21, 2018.

6 Consumer Purchasing and Wise Buying Strategies

3 Steps to Financial Literacy . . . Avoiding Unplanned Spending

1 Research products, shopping locations, brands, and prices for purchases that meet your needs.
App: PriceGrabber

2 Develop a specific shopping list to guide your daily purchasing decisions.
App: AnyList

3 Make a commitment to buy only items on your list of identified needs.
Website: www.thesimpledollar.com

Avoiding impulse buying can help to reduce overuse of credit and improve your personal financial situation. At the end of the chapter, *Your Personal Finance Road Map and Dashboard* will provide additional information on unplanned spending.

CHAPTER 6 LEARNING OBJECTIVES

In this chapter, you will learn to:

LO6.1 Identify strategies for effective consumer buying.

LO6.2 Implement a process for making consumer purchases.

LO6.3 Describe steps to take to resolve consumer problems.

LO6.4 Evaluate legal alternatives available to consumers.

YOUR PERSONAL FINANCIAL PLAN SHEETS

18. Consumer Purchase Comparison
19. Used-Car Purchase Comparison
20. Buying versus Leasing a Vehicle
21. Legal Services Cost Comparison

Consumer Buying Activities

Buy now: cash or credit? Or save and buy later? Which path is for you? Daily buying decisions involve a trade-off between current spending and saving for the future. Economic, social, and personal factors affect your daily buying habits. These factors are the basis for spending, saving, investing, and achieving financial goals. In very simple terms, the only way you can have long-term financial security is to not spend all of your current income. In addition, overspending leads to misuse of credit and financial difficulties.

Practical Purchasing Strategies

Comparison shopping is the process of considering alternative stores, brands, and prices. In contrast, *impulse buying* involves unplanned purchasing, which can result in financial problems. Several buying techniques are commonly suggested for wise buying.

TIMING PURCHASES Certain items go on sale the same time each year. You can obtain bargains by buying winter clothing in mid- or late winter, or summer clothing in mid- or late summer. Many people save by buying holiday items and other products at reduced prices in late December and early January.

PURCHASE LOCATION Your decision to use a particular retailer is probably influenced by location, price, product selection, and services available. Competition and technology have changed retailing with superstores, specialty shops, and online buying. This expanded shopping environment provides consumers with greater choice, potentially

LO6.1

Identify strategies for effective consumer buying.

ACTION ITEM

I stay informed on wise buying strategies.

☐ Agree ☐ Disagree

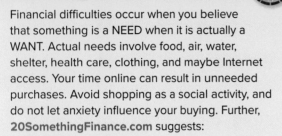

money minute focus

Financial difficulties occur when you believe that something is a NEED when it is actually a WANT. Actual needs involve food, air, water, shelter, health care, clothing, and maybe Internet access. Your time online can result in unneeded purchases. Avoid shopping as a social activity, and do not let anxiety influence your buying. Further, **20SomethingFinance.com** suggests:

- Don't buy an item right away. Delay a purchase to consider the value.
- Review delayed purchases in a month to determine if the urge still exists, and if money is available.
- Return items, as allowed, when an item does not meet expectations.
- Put a reminder note in your wallet: "Do you REALLY need this?"

lower prices, and the need to carefully consider buying alternatives. The availability of online shopping can easily result in overspending and financial difficulties.

BRAND COMPARISON Food and other products come in various brands. *National-brand* products are highly advertised items available in many stores. *Store-brand* and *private-label* products, sold by one chain of stores, are low-cost alternatives to famous-name products. Since store-brand products are frequently manufactured by the same companies that produce brand-name items, these lower-cost alternatives can result in extensive savings. The use of a product comparison app or website can assist you when comparing brands.

LABEL INFORMATION Certain label information is helpful; other information is nothing more than advertising. Federal law requires that food labels contain certain information. Product labeling for appliances includes information about operating costs to assist you in selecting the most energy-efficient models. *Open dating* describes the freshness or shelf life of a perishable product. Phrases such as "Use before May 25, 2022" or "Not to be sold after October 8" appear on most food products. However, these labels can be confusing. Most expiration dates relate to quality, not safety. Items used after the "sell by" date are likely to still be safe for consumption. Canned and packaged food items, if not opened, will usually be safe beyond the expiration date.

PRICE COMPARISON *Unit pricing* uses a standard unit of measurement to compare the prices of packages of different sizes. To calculate the unit price, divide the price of the item by the number of units of measurement, such as ounces, pounds, gallons, or number of sheets (for items such as paper towels and facial tissues). Then compare the unit prices for various sizes, brands, and stores. Apps for bar code scanning may be used to quickly compare prices.

EXAMPLE: Unit Pricing

To calculate the unit price of an item, divide the cost by the number of units. For example, a 64-ounce product costing $8.32 would be calculated in this manner:

$$\text{Unit price} = \$8.32 \div 64$$
$$= \$0.13, \text{ or 13 cents an ounce}$$

Coupons and rebates also provide better pricing for wise consumers. A family saving about $8 a week on their groceries by using coupons will save $416 over a year and $2,080 over five years (not counting interest). A *rebate*, a partial refund of the price of a product, can also save you money. Many websites and apps are available with money-saving coupons and rebates. When searching for ones you might use, be sure to read reviews to avoid possible scams and deceptive promotions.

When comparing prices, remember that:

- More store convenience (location, hours, sales staff) usually means higher prices.
- Ready-to-use products have higher prices.
- Large packages are usually the best buy, but compare using unit pricing.

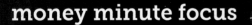

money minute focus

Minimalists and frugal people buy store brands; avoid shopping for pleasure; avoid waste; plan ahead; shop for used items first; take advantage of free and low-cost leisure activities; buy based on utility and reliability; and attempt to repair broken items.

- "Sale" may not always mean saving money.
- The use of online sources and shopping apps can save time and money.

Exhibit 6–1 summarizes techniques that can assist you in your online buying decisions.

Exhibit **6–1** Wise Online Buying Activities

1. Conduct online research.
- Compare brands and features
- Use label and warranty information
- Use product testing reports to assess quality, safety, nutrition

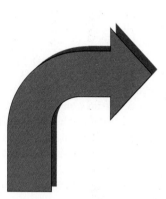

4. Plan for future purchases.
- Keep receipts, other documents
- Know return, complaint process
- Watch e-mails for special offers
- Evaluate time, effort involved

2. Compare stores.
- Consider both stores and online
- Evaluate price, service, product quality, warranties, shipping cost and time, return policy
- Determine reputation, location

3. Make purchase.
- Use secure buying website
- Seek discounts, coupons
- Select payment method based on security, fees, other factors

(1) **Consumersearch.com**; (2) **PriceGrabber.com**, Inc.; (3) Paypal; (4) Groupon, Inc.

Warranties

warranty A written guarantee from the manufacturer or distributor of a product that specifies the conditions under which the product can be returned, replaced, or repaired.

Most products come with some guarantee of quality. A **warranty** is a written guarantee from the manufacturer or distributor that gives the conditions under which the product can be returned, replaced, or repaired. An *express warranty,* usually in written form, is created by the seller or manufacturer and has two forms: the full warranty and the limited warranty. A *full warranty* states that a defective product can be fixed or replaced during a reasonable amount of time.

A *limited warranty* covers only certain aspects of the product, such as parts, or requires the buyer to incur part of the costs for shipping or repairs. An *implied warranty* covers a product's intended use or other basic understandings that are not in writing. For example, an implied *warranty of title* indicates that the seller has the right to sell the product. An implied *warranty of merchantability* guarantees that the product is fit for the ordinary uses for which it is intended: A toaster must toast bread, and an MP3 player must play music or other recorded files. Implied warranties vary from state to state.

FinTech for Financial Literacy

Retailing technology trends include:

- AmazonGo stores allow shoppers to pay with an app using *just walk out* technology.
- Shopping personalization uses an app to suggest a store movement pattern based on frequently purchased items.
- V-commerce (using virtual reality) allows trying on products or using an item in a cyber setting.
- The Internet of Things (IoT) connects a smart refrigerator to order needed groceries.
- *Omnichannel* marketing integrates online, social media, in-store, data access, catalog, and delivery for the information search, purchase, and after-sale phases of shopping.

USED-CAR WARRANTIES The Federal Trade Commission (FTC) requires used car dealers to use a buyer's guide sticker telling if a vehicle comes with a warranty and, if so, what protection is included. If no warranty is offered, the car is sold "as is," and the seller assumes no responsibility for any repairs, regardless of any oral claims. FTC used-car regulations do not apply to vehicles purchased from private owners.

While a used car may not have an express warranty, most states have implied warranties to protect used-car buyers. An implied warranty of merchantability means the product is guaranteed to do what it is supposed to do. The used car is guaranteed to run—at least for a while!

NEW-CAR WARRANTIES New-car warranties provide buyers with an assurance of quality. These warranties vary in the time, mileage, and parts they cover. The main conditions of a new-car warranty are (1) coverage of basic parts against defects; (2) power train coverage for the engine, transmission, and drive train; and (3) the corrosion warranty, which usually applies only to holes due to rust, not to surface rust. Other important conditions of a warranty are a statement regarding whether the warranty is transferable to other owners of the car and details about the charges, if any, for major repairs in the form of a *deductible,* an amount paid by the car owner.

service contract An agreement between a business and a consumer to cover the repair costs of a product.

SERVICE CONTRACTS A **service contract** is an agreement between a business and a consumer to cover the repair costs of a product. Frequently called *extended warranties,* they are not warranties. For a fee, these agreements insure the buyer for the cost of certain repairs and other issues. Beware of service contracts that offer coverage for three years but really only cover two since the item may have a manufacturer's one-year warranty.

Automotive service contracts can cover repairs not included in the manufacturer's warranty. Service contracts range from $400 to more than $1,000 but do not always include everything you might expect. These contracts usually cover engine cooling system failure but might exclude coverage if the failure is caused by overheating.

Because of costs and exclusions, service contracts may not be a wise financial decision. Minimize concerns about expensive repairs with a special emergency fund. Then, if you need repairs, the money will be available.

Research-Based Buying

Major buying decisions should be based on a planned decision-making process, which may be viewed in four phases.

PHASE 1: PRESHOPPING ACTIVITIES

Start the buying process with actions that include:

- Problem identification to set a goal and focus your purchasing activities.
- Information gathering to benefit from the buying experiences of others.

PHASE 2: EVALUATING ALTERNATIVES

With every decision, consider various options:

- Attribute assessment with a comparison of product features.
- Price analysis including consideration of the costs at various buying locations.
- Comparison shopping activities to evaluate shopping locations.

PHASE 3: SELECTION AND PURCHASE

When making your final choice, actions may include:

- Negotiation activities to obtain lower price or added quality.
- Payment alternatives including use of cash and various credit plans.
- Assessment of acquisition and installation that might be encountered.

PHASE 4: POSTPURCHASE ACTIVITIES

After making a purchase, several actions are encouraged:

- Proper maintenance and operation.
- Identification and comparison of after-sale service alternatives.
- Resolution of any purchase concerns that may occur.

PRACTICE QUIZ 6–1

Sheet 18 Consumer Purchase Comparison

1. What types of brands are commonly available to consumers?

2. In what situations can comparing prices help in purchasing decisions?

3. How does a service contract differ from a warranty?

4. Match the following descriptions with the warranties listed here. Write your answers in the spaces provided.

express warranty   limited warranty

full warranty   service contract

implied warranty

a. _____ Covers only aspects of the item purchased.
b. _____ Is commonly referred to as an extended warranty.
c. _____ Usually is in a written form.
d. _____ Covers a product's intended use; it may not be in writing.
e. _____ Covers fixing or replacement of a product for a set time period.

Major Consumer Purchases: Buying Motor Vehicles

LO6.2

Implement a process for making consumer purchases.

To make wise decisions in purchasing a vehicle, the steps in Exhibit 6–2 are recommended.

Exhibit 6–2 A Research-Based Approach for Purchasing a Motor Vehicle

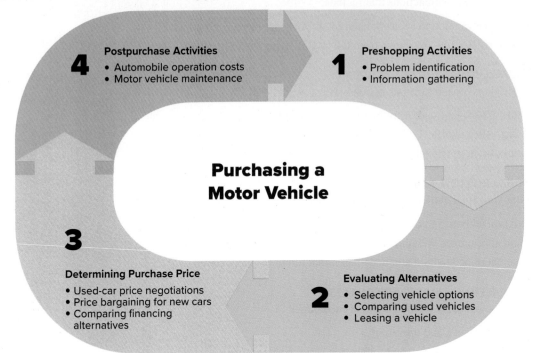

4 Postpurchase Activities
- Automobile operation costs
- Motor vehicle maintenance

1 Preshopping Activities
- Problem identification
- Information gathering

Purchasing a Motor Vehicle

3 Determining Purchase Price
- Used-car price negotiations
- Price bargaining for new cars
- Comparing financing alternatives

2 Evaluating Alternatives
- Selecting vehicle options
- Comparing used vehicles
- Leasing a vehicle

ACTION ITEM

I carefully plan major purchases with research and comparison shopping.

☐ Agree   ☐ Disagree

Phase 1: Preshopping Activities

First, define your needs and obtain relevant product information. These activities are the foundation for buying decisions to help you achieve your goals.

PROBLEM IDENTIFICATION Effective decision making should start with an open mind. Some people always buy the same brand when another brand at a lower price would also serve their needs or when another brand at the same price may provide better quality. A narrow view of the problem is a weakness in problem identification. You may think the problem is "I need to have a car" when the real problem is "I need transportation."

INFORMATION GATHERING Information is power. The better informed you are, the more effective you will be in making good decisions. Some people spend very little time gathering and evaluating information. At the other extreme are people who spend much time obtaining consumer information. While information is necessary for wise purchasing, too much information can create confusion and frustration. The most useful information sources include:

1. *Personal contacts* allow you to learn about product performance, brand quality, and prices from others.
2. *Business organizations* offer advertising, product labels, and packaging that provide information about price, quality, and availability.
3. *Media information* (websites, apps, television, magazines) can provide valuable information with purchasing advice.
4. *Independent testing organizations,* such as Consumers Union in its monthly *Consumer Reports,* provide information about the quality of products and services.
5. *Government agencies,* local, state, and federal, provide publications, toll-free telephone numbers, websites, and community programs.
6. *Online reviews* can provide buying guidance and shopping suggestions. Be cautious since some may be fictitious postings.

Basic information about car buying may be obtained at **www. edmunds.com**, **www.caranddriver.com**, **www.safercar.gov**, **www.autotrader.com**, and **autos.msn.com**. Consumers Union (**www.consumerreports.org**) offers a computerized car cost data service. Car-buying services, such as **www.acscorp.com** and **www.autobytel.com**, allow you to order your vehicle online.

Phase 2: Evaluating Alternatives

Every purchasing situation will likely have several acceptable alternatives. Ask yourself: Is it possible to delay the purchase or to do without the item? Should I pay for the item with cash or buy it on credit? Which brands should I consider? How do the price, quality, and service compare at different stores? Is it possible to rent the item instead of buying it? Considering such alternatives will result in more effective purchasing decisions.

Research shows that prices can vary for all types of products. For a phone, prices may range from under $100 to well over $500. The price for 100 tablets of 325 mg aspirin may range from less than $1 to over $3. While differences in quality and attributes may exist among the phones, the aspirin tablets are equivalent in quantity and quality.

Many people view comparison shopping as a waste of time. Although this may be true in some situations, comparison shopping can be beneficial when (1) buying expensive or complex items; (2) buying items that you purchase often; (3) shopping can be done easily, such as with ads, catalogs, or online; (4) different sellers offer different prices and services; and (5) product quality or prices vary greatly.

SELECTING VEHICLE OPTIONS Optional equipment for cars may be viewed in three categories: (1) mechanical devices to improve performance, such as power steering, power brakes, and cruise control; (2) convenience options, including power seats, air conditioning, audio systems, power locks, rear window defoggers, and tinted glass; and (3) aesthetic features that add to the vehicle's visual appeal, such as metallic paint, special trim, and upholstery.

High-tech safety features help to avoid crashes. Forward-collision warning (FCW) systems alert drivers of a potential crash. Automatic emergency braking (AEB) senses a collision and begins braking. Blind-spot warning (BSW) reminds drivers of vehicles not in their vision line. Adaptive cruise control (ACC) adjusts speed based on traffic. Lane-keeping assist (LKA) and lane-departure warning (LDW) offer warnings when drifting. Vehicle features for older drivers and others include larger mirrors, swivel-seat cushions, pedal extenders, and left-foot accelerators. The *Figure It Out!* feature covers the net present value of buying a hybrid car.

COMPARING USED VEHICLES The average used car costs about $10,000 less than the average new car. Common sources of used cars include:

- New-car dealers offer late-model vehicles and may include a warranty. Prices will be higher than at other sources.
- Used-car dealers usually have older vehicles. Warranties, if offered, will be limited. Prices are usually lower than at new-car dealers.
- Individuals selling their own cars can create a bargain purchase opportunity if the vehicle was well-maintained. Since few regulations apply to private-party sales, caution is suggested.

Figure It Out!

Net Present Value of a Consumer Purchase: Is a Hybrid Car Worth the Cost?

The time value of money (explained in Chapter 1) may be used to evaluate the financial benefits of a consumer purchase. For example, when deciding to buy a hybrid car, the money saved on gas would be considered a cash *inflow* (since money not going out is like money coming in). The cost difference between a hybrid and a fuel-version vehicle would be the current *cash outflow*. If the car has an expected life of eight years, the *net present value* calculations might be as shown here:

Step 1: Estimate the annual savings on gas (for example, 8,000 miles at $3 a gallon), with a vehicle getting 50 miles per gallon rather than 25 miles per gallon.

Step 2: Calculate the present value (PV) of a series using either the time value of money tables (Chapter 1 Appendix) or a financial calculator. Assume a 2 percent interest rate, eight years.

Step 3: Subtract the difference in cost of hybrid car compared with a gasoline-powered car.

| Annual gas savings $960 | PV of annual savings $7,032 | − | Vehicle cost difference $6,000 |

The result: $1,032 is a positive (favorable) net present value of the savings from a hybrid car compared to a gasoline-powered car. A negative net present value would indicate that the financial aspects of the purchase are not desirable.

This analysis for buying a hybrid car (or electric vehicle) will vary based on other factors, such as vehicle maintenance costs, miles driven per year, and gas prices. Hybrid car cost calculators are also available online. Remember that this decision will also be influenced by personal attitudes and social factors. This calculation format may be used to assess the financial benefits of other consumer purchases by comparing the present value of the cost savings over time with the price of the item.

- Auctions and dealers sell automobiles previously owned by businesses, auto rental companies, and government agencies.
- Banks, credit unions, and other financing organizations have repossessed vehicles for sale.
- Used-car superstores, such as CarMax, offer a large inventory of previously owned vehicles, often with the convenience of online sales.

Certified preowned (CPO) vehicles are nearly new cars that come with the original manufacturer's guarantee of quality. The rigorous inspection and repair process means a higher price than for other used vehicles, usually an extra $1,500 to $2,500. CPO programs were originally created to generate demand for the many low-mileage vehicles returned at the end of a lease.

WHAT WOULD YOU DO? You are considering the purchase of one of these vehicles: Vehicle 1: A three-year-old car with 45,000 miles, costing $16,700 and requiring $1,385 of immediate repairs. Vehicle 2: A five-year-old car with 62,000 miles, costing $14,500 and requiring $1,760 of immediate repairs. Based on financial and opportunity costs, which of the following do you believe would be the wiser purchase?

The appearance of a used car can be deceptive. A well-maintained engine may be inside a body with rust; a clean, shiny exterior may conceal major operational problems. Therefore, conduct a used-car inspection as outlined in Exhibit 6–3. Have a trained and trusted mechanic of *your* choice check the car to estimate the costs of potential repairs. This service will help you avoid surprises.

LEASING A MOTOR VEHICLE *Leasing* is a contractual agreement with monthly payments for the use of an automobile over a set time period, typically three, four, or five years. At the end of the lease term, the vehicle is usually returned to the leasing company.

Leasing offers several advantages: (1) Only a small cash outflow may be required for the security deposit, whereas buying can require a large down payment; (2) monthly lease payments are usually lower than monthly financing payments; (3) the lease agreement provides detailed records for business purposes; and (4) you are usually able to obtain a more expensive vehicle.

Leasing also has drawbacks: (1) You have no ownership interest in the vehicle; (2) you must meet requirements similar to qualifying for credit; and (3) additional costs may be incurred for extra mileage, certain repairs, turning the car in early, or even moving to another state.

Exhibit **6–3**
Checking Out a Used Car

Issarawat Tattong/Getty Images

Checking Out a Used Car

Outside the Car
- Look for major dents and signs of accidents.
- Inspect the trunk and spare tire.
- Check tire tread wear.
- Observe smoothness of springs and shocks when pushing down on car.
- Check operation of doors and windows.
- Look for leaking fluids under vehicle.

Inside the Car
- Look for wear on pedals and steering column.
- Check for operation of dash lights and accessories.
- Check instrument panel for operation of gauges.
- Start engine and check operation of power accessories such as radio, wipers, and heater.

The Engine
- Check for leakage of fluids and overheating.
- Check oil level and for signs of leaks.
- Check radiator cap, radiator for cracks and repairs, and for oil in coolant.
- Check battery and cables.
- Expect a smooth, clean start.

The Road Test
- Let vehicle warm up.
- Test-drive car on a road with which you are familiar.
- Listen for smoothness of acceleration and transmission (forward and reverse).
- Check brakes at different speeds.
- Check ease of steering and vehicle control.

Figure It Out!

Buying versus Leasing a Motor Vehicle

To compare the costs of purchasing and leasing a vehicle, use the following framework.

Purchase Costs	Example	Your Figures
Total vehicle cost, including tax, title, license ($20,000)		
Down payment (or full amount if paying cash)	$ 2,000	$_____
Monthly loan payment: $385 × 48-month length of financing (this item is zero if vehicle is not financed)	18,480	
Opportunity cost of down payment (or total cost of the vehicle if it is bought for cash): $2,000 × 4 years of financing/ownership × 3 percent	240	_____
Less: Estimated value of vehicle at end of loan term/ownership period	−6,000	_____
Total cost to buy	$14,720	$_____

Leasing Costs	Example	Your Figures
Security deposit ($300)		
Monthly lease payments: $295 × 48-month length of lease	$14,160	$_____
Opportunity cost of security deposit: $300 security deposit × 4 years × 3 percent	36	_____
End-of-lease charges* (if applicable)	800	_____
Total cost to lease	$14,996	$_____

*Such as charges for extra mileage.

Avoiding Lease Traps

When considering a lease agreement for a motor vehicle, beware of these common pitfalls:

- Not knowing the total cost of the agreement, including the cost of the vehicle, not just the monthly payment.
- Making a larger up-front payment than is required or paying unnecessary add-on costs.
- Negotiating the monthly payment rather than the capitalized cost of the vehicle.
- Not having the value of any trade-in vehicle reflected in the lease.
- Signing a contract you don't understand.

Compare monthly payments and other terms among several leasing companies. People have been known to pay over $24,000 to lease a vehicle worth only $20,000 at the start of the lease agreement. Comparison of leasing terms is available at websites such as **www.leasesource.com**, **www.leaseguide.com**, and **www.carinfo.com**.

When leasing, you arrange for the dealer to sell the vehicle through a financing company. As a result, be sure you know the true cost, including:

1. The *capitalized cost,* which is the price of the vehicle. The average car buyer pays about 92 percent of the list price for a vehicle; the average leasing arrangement has a capitalized cost of 96 percent of the list price.
2. The *money factor,* which is the interest rate being paid on the capitalized cost.
3. The *payment schedule,* which is the amount paid monthly and the number of payments.
4. The *residual value,* or the expected value of the vehicle at the end of the lease.

After the final payment, you may return, keep, or sell the vehicle. If the current market value is greater than the residual value, you may be able to sell it for a profit. However, if the residual value is more than the market value (which is the typical case), returning the vehicle to the leasing company is usually the best decision. The *Figure It Out!* feature provides an example comparing buying and leasing a motor vehicle

Phase 3: Determining Purchase Price

Once you've done your research and evaluations, other activities and decisions may be appropriate. Products such as real estate or automobiles may be purchased using price negotiation. Negotiation may also be used in other buying situations to obtain a lower price or additional features. Two vital factors in negotiation are (1) having all the necessary information about the product and the buying situation, and (2) dealing with a person who has the authority to give you a lower price or additional features, such as the owner or store manager.

USED-CAR PRICE NEGOTIATION Begin to determine a fair price by checking ads in newspapers and online for the prices of comparable vehicles. Other sources of current used-car prices are *Edmund's Used Car Prices* and the *Kelley Blue Book.*

Various factors influence the price of a used car, such as the number of miles it has been driven along with features and options. A low-mileage car will have a higher price than a comparable car with high mileage. The condition of the vehicle and the demand for the model also affect price.

PRICE BARGAINING FOR NEW CARS An important new-car price information source is the *sticker price* label, printed on the vehicle with the suggested retail price. This label presents the base price of the car with costs of added features. The dealer's cost, or *invoice price,* is an amount less than the sticker price. The difference between the sticker price and the dealer's cost is the range available for negotiation. This range is larger for more expensive vehicles; less expensive cars usually do not have a wide negotiation range. Information about dealer's cost is available from sources such as *Edmund's New Car Prices* and *Consumer Reports.*

Set-price dealers use no-haggling car selling with the prices presented to be accepted or rejected as stated. *Car-buying services* are businesses that help buyers obtain a specific new car at a reasonable price. Also referred to as *auto brokers,* these businesses offer desired models with options for prices ranging between $50 and $200 over the dealer's cost. First, the auto broker charges a small fee for price information on desired models. Then, if you decide to buy a car, the auto broker arranges the purchase with a dealer near your home.

To prevent confusion in determining the true price of the new car, do not mention a trade-in vehicle until the cost of the new car has been settled. Then ask how much the dealer is willing to pay for your old car. If the offer price is not acceptable, sell the old car on your own. A typical negotiating conversation might go like this:

1. *Customer:* "I'm willing to give you $25,600 for the car. That's my top offer."
2. *Auto salesperson:* "Let me check with my manager." After returning, "My manager says $26,200 is the best we can do."
3. *Customer* (who should be willing to walk out at this point): "I can go to $25,650."
4. *Auto salesperson:* "We have the car you want, ready to go. How about $25,700?"

If the customer agrees, the dealer receives $100 more than the customer's "top offer."

Other sales techniques you should avoid include:

- *Lowballing,* quoted a low price that increases when add-on costs are included.
- *Highballing,* offered a high amount for a trade-in vehicle; the extra amount is made up by increasing the new-car price.

money minute focus

Electric vehicles (EVs) are increasing in popularity as a result of being environmentally beneficial, nearly silent engine sound, potential tax credits, lower maintenance costs, and smartphone apps to program charging times and to heat or cool the cabin in advance of driving. Concerns associated with EVs include the higher initial cost, short driving ranges for some models, slow charging time, charging station availability, and loss of cargo space for the battery pack. The two main EV types are battery electric vehicles (BEVs) only running on electricity, and plug-in hybrid electric vehicles (PHEVs) that use electricity for a limited distance before switching to a gas-electric hybrid mode. Some models have an onboard generator for greater driving distances.

CR Consumer Reports

Since 1936, Consumers Union, a nonprofit organization, has published *Consumer Reports* to provide information and advice on product safety, food, health care, and financial services. Before each monthly issue is published, more than 100 experts work in over 40 labs to test, analyze, evaluate, and rate the performance, safety, reliability, and value of products. Consumers Union does not accept product samples or advertising, and will not allow its name to be used to promote products it has evaluated.

Appliances and other products for testing are purchased by staff shoppers or anonymous "secret shoppers." Over $27 million is spent each year buying the items to be tested and rated. When testing food, Consumers Union staff make use of very sensitive instruments, such as a liquid chromatograph to measure the caffeine in coffee. Food tasting is done by a panel trained by experts in food science, nutrition, statistics, and psychology.

The Consumer Reports Auto Test Center covers more than 300 acres in rural Connecticut. Each year, about 50 cars and trucks are pushed to their limits, being driven hundreds of thousands of miles. To maintain independence, every vehicle tested is purchased from a dealer with the style and options most often bought by consumers. Subscribers to the magazine also provide reliability and satisfaction survey data.

More than 50 items are assessed on the auto test track, including acceleration, braking, emergency handling, emissions, fuel economy, headlights, ride comfort, safety features, trunk and cargo space, and off-road capability for vehicles designed for that type of driving. In addition to testing cars, nearly 600 child safety seats are crash-tested. And, each year, more than 50 tire models are tested and evaluated for 14 safety and performance factors.

ACTION STEPS FOR. . .

. . .Information Literacy

Locate an article related to testing of appliances, food, or another product at **consumerreports.org**. Explain the process to another person, and have them comment on how the testing procedures might be improved.

. . .Financial Literacy

Select a product you use regularly. Search **consumerreports.org** for information about that item. Describe how your findings might change your buying behavior for that product.

. . .Digital Literacy

Based on an article related to the testing of appliances, food, or another product at **consumerreports.org**, create a visual (photo, poster) or brief video to report the testing procedures.

- The question "How much can you afford per month?" Be sure to also ask how many months.
- An offer to hold the vehicle for a small deposit only. Never leave a deposit unless you are ready to buy a vehicle or are willing to lose your deposit.
- Unrealistic statements, such as "Your price is only $100 above our cost." Usually, hidden costs have been added in to get the dealer's cost.
- Sales agreements with preprinted amounts. Cross out numbers you believe are not appropriate for your purchase.
- Attempts to upsell vehicle features and services, such as clear coating, fabric treatment, window tinting, audio-video upgrades, and service agreements.
- Efforts to inflate the loan interest rate or lengthen the term of the loan.
- Not informing you of dealer rebates or price-matching offers.

COMPARING FINANCING ALTERNATIVES While you may pay cash, many people buy cars on credit. Auto loans are available from banks, credit unions, consumer finance companies, and other financial institutions. Many lenders will *preapprove* you for a certain loan amount, which separates financing from negotiating the car price. Until the new-car price is set, you should not indicate that you intend to use the dealer's credit plan.

The lowest interest rate or the lowest payment does not necessarily mean the best credit plan. Also consider the loan length. Otherwise, after two or three years, the value of your car may be less than the amount you still owe; this situation is referred to as *upside-down* or *negative equity.* If you default on your loan or sell the car at this time, you will have to pay the difference.

EXAMPLE: Upside Down

A $26,000 vehicle is purchased with an initial loan of $18,000. After a period of time, the vehicle may only be worth $12,000 while you still owe $15,000. To avoid this situation, make a large down payment, have a short loan term (less than five years), and pay off the loan faster than the value of the vehicle declines.

Automobile manufacturers frequently present opportunities for low-interest financing. They may offer rebates at the same time, giving buyers a choice between a rebate and a low-interest loan. Carefully compare low-interest financing and the rebate. Special rebates are sometimes offered to students, teachers, credit union members, real estate agents, and other groups.

Phase 4: Postpurchase Activities

Start by submitting the manufacturer registration by mail or online, if appropriate. Next, consider maintenance and ownership costs associated with major purchases. Proper operation will usually result in improved performance and fewer repairs. When you need repairs not covered by a warranty, follow a pattern similar to that used when making the original purchase. Investigate, evaluate, and negotiate various service options.

In the past, when major problems occurred with a new car and the warranty didn't solve the difficulty, many consumers lacked a course of action. As a result, all 50 states and the District of Columbia enacted *lemon laws* that require a refund for the vehicle after the owner has made repeated attempts to obtain servicing. These laws apply when four attempts are made to get the same problem corrected or when the vehicle has been out of service for more than 30 days within 12 months of purchase or the first 12,000 miles. The terms of the state laws vary. You can find additional information about "lemon laws" online.

AUTOMOBILE OPERATION COSTS Over a lifetime, most people will spend more than $200,000 on automobile-related expenses. Driving costs will vary based on two main factors: the size of your automobile and the number of miles you drive. These costs involve two categories:

1. Fixed Ownership Costs	2. Variable Operating Costs
Depreciation	Gasoline and oil
Interest on auto loan	Tires
Insurance	Maintenance and repairs
License, registration, taxes, and fees	Parking and tolls

The largest fixed expense associated with a new automobile is *depreciation,* the loss in the vehicle's value due to time and use. Since money is not paid out for depreciation, many people do not consider it an expense. However, this decreased value is a cost that owners incur. Well-maintained vehicles and certain high-quality, expensive models, such as BMW and Lexus, depreciate at a slower rate.

Costs for gasoline, oil, maintenance, and tires rise with increased driving, unexpected trips, and vehicle age. For determining vehicle ownership costs, search online for the "Edmunds True Cost to Own" calculator.

Exhibit **6–4**

Extending Vehicle Life with Proper Maintenance

- Get regular oil changes.

- Check fluids (brake, power steering, transmission).

- Inspect hoses and belts for wear.

- Get a tune-up (new spark plugs, fuel filter, air filter) every 25,000–30,000 miles.

- Check and clean battery cables and terminals.

- Check spark plug wires after 50,000 miles.

- Flush radiator and service transmission every 25,000–30,000 miles.

- Keep lights, turn signals, and horn in good working condition.

- Check muffler and exhaust pipes.

- Check tires for wear; rotate tires at regular intervals.

- Check condition of brakes.

(NOTE: Service times will vary based on type and age of vehicle as well as driving habits.)

MOTOR VEHICLE MAINTENANCE People who sell, repair, or drive automobiles for a living stress the importance of regular vehicle care. While owner's manuals and articles suggest mileage or time intervals for certain servicing, more frequent oil changes or tune-ups can minimize major repairs and maximize vehicle life. Exhibit 6–4 suggests maintenance areas to consider.

AUTOMOBILE SERVICING SOURCES The following businesses offer automobile maintenance and repair service:

- Car dealers have service departments with a wide range of car care services. Service charges at a car dealer may be higher than those of other repair businesses.
- Service stations and independent auto repair shops can service your vehicle at fairly competitive prices. Since the quality of these repair shops varies, talk with previous customers.
- Retailers, such as Walmart, may emphasize sale of tires and batteries as well as brakes, oil changes, and tune-ups.
- Specialty shops offer brakes, tires, automatic transmissions, and oil changes at a reasonable price with fast service.

To avoid unnecessary expenses, be aware of common repair frauds (Exhibit 6–5). Remember to work with reputable auto service businesses. Be sure to get a written, detailed estimate in advance and a detailed, paid receipt when the service is complete. Auto repairs are consistently reported as one of the top consumer complaints. Some people avoid problems and minimize costs by working on their own vehicles.

Exhibit **6–5**

Common Automobile Repair Frauds

Most automobile servicing sources are fair and honest. Sometimes, consumers waste dollars when they fall prey to unethical actions such as:

- When checking the oil, the attendant puts the dipstick only partway down and then shows you that you need oil.

- An attendant cuts a fan belt or punctures a hose. Watch carefully when someone checks under your hood.

- A garage employee puts some liquid on your battery and then tries to convince you that it is leaking and you need a new battery.

- Removing air from a tire instead of adding air to it can make an unwary driver open to buying a new tire or paying for an unneeded patch on a tire that is in perfect condition.

- The attendant puts grease near a shock absorber or on the ground and then tells you your present shocks are dangerous and you need new ones.

- You are charged for two gallons of antifreeze with a radiator flush when only one gallon was put in.

Dealing with reputable businesses and a basic motor vehicle knowledge are the best ways to avoid deceptive repair practices.

Sheet 19 Used-Car Purchase Comparison
Sheet 20 Buying versus Leasing a Vehicle

PRACTICE QUIZ 6–2

1. What are the major sources of consumer information?

2. What actions are appropriate when buying a used car?

3. When might leasing a motor vehicle be appropriate?

4. What maintenance activities could increase the life of your vehicle?

Resolving Consumer Complaints

Most customer complaints result from defective products, low quality or short product lives, unexpected costs, deceptive pricing, and poor repairs. Federal consumer agencies estimate annual consumer losses from fraudulent business activities at $10 billion to $40 billion for telemarketing and mail order, $3 billion for credit card fraud and credit "repair" scams, and $10 billion for investment swindles.

While you may not anticipate problems with purchases, you should be prepared for them. To minimize consumer problems before making a purchase: (1) obtain recommendations from friends, family members, and online reviews; (2) verify company affiliations, certifications, and licenses; and (3) understand the sale terms, return policies, and warranty provisions. If you encounter a consumer problem, consider the process for resolving complaints shown in Exhibit 6–6.

Before starting this process, know your rights and the laws that apply to your situation. Information on consumer rights is available online and through apps. For example, several apps are available that allow airline passengers to monitor the status of their flights. Information on delays, cancellations, and other situations can be submitted to keep airlines accountable.

To help ensure success when you make a complaint, keep a file of receipts, names of people you talked to, dates of attempted repairs, copies of letters and e-mails, and costs incurred. These documents can help resolve a problem in your favor. An automobile owner kept detailed records and receipts for all gasoline purchases, oil changes, and repairs. When

LO6.3

Describe steps to take to resolve consumer problems.

ACTION ITEM

I am well informed on how to take action on a consumer complaint.

☐ Agree ☐ Disagree

STEP 1. Initial Communication
- Return to place of purchase or contact online retailer.
- Provide a detailed explanation and the action you desire.
- Be pleasant yet persistent in your efforts to obtain a resolution.

STEP 2. Communicate with the Company
- Send an e-mail with the details of the situation (Exhibit 6–7).
- Post your concerns on the company's online social media sites.
- Comment on a blog or a consumer review website.

STEP 3. Consumer Agency Assistance
- Seek guidance from a local, state, or federal consumer agency.
- Determine if any laws have been violated in the situation.
- Consider the use of mediation or arbitration.

STEP 4. Legal Action
- Consider bringing your case to small claims court.
- Determine if a class-action suit is appropriate.
- Seek assistance from a lawyer or legal aid organization.

Exhibit **6–6**
Resolving Consumer Complaints

money minute focus

Common consumer complaints and fraud involve (1) debt collectors and fake checks; (2) impostor scams, a person pretending to be from a government agency; (3) identity theft; (4) telephone and mobile services; (5) banks and lending organizations; (6) prizes, contests, and sweepstakes; (7) online scams; (8) text message or e-mail link for a fake package, requesting personal or bank information; (9) home and auto repairs; (10) work at home, starting your own business, phony training courses, employment scams; (11) diets, health claims, such as COVID-19 scams; (12) phony charities; (13) high-return investments, multilevel marketing. Beware of websites not ending in .com, .gov. or .org.

a warranty dispute occurred, the owner was able to prove proper maintenance and received a refund for the defective vehicle. Perseverance is vital since companies might ignore your request or delay their response.

Step 1: Initial Communication

Most consumer complaints are resolved at the original sales location. As you talk with the salesperson, customer service person, or store manager, avoid talking loudly, threatening a lawsuit, or demanding unreasonable action. A calm, rational, yet persistent approach is usually most effective. For online purchases, call or contact the retailer by e-mail.

Step 2: Communicate with the Company

If a problem is not resolved at the local level, express your concern to customer service at the corporate level. Call or use a letter or e-mail such as the one in Exhibit 6–7. You can obtain contact information for companies through an online search or at **www.usa.gov**. This information is also commonly included on product packages.

Step 3: Consumer Agency Assistance

If you do not receive a satisfactory result for your complaint from the company, organizations are available to assist with automobiles, appliances, health care, and other concerns. **Mediation** involves the use of a third party to settle grievances. An impartial person—the

mediation The attempt by an impartial third party to resolve a difference between two parties through discussion and negotiation.

Exhibit **6–7**
Sample Complaint E-mail

NOTE: Keep copies of your e-mail, letters, and related documents.
Source: *Consumer Action Handbook* (**www.usa.gov/handbook**).

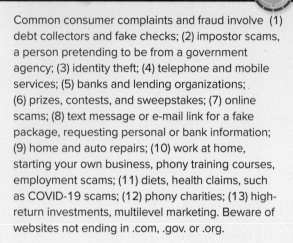

Name of Contact Person (if available)
Title (if available)
Company Name
Consumer Complaint Division (if you have no specific contact)

Dear (Contact Person or Organization Name):

Re: (account or transaction number, if applicable)

Describe your purchase.

On (date), I (purchased, leased, rented, or had repaired) a (name of the product, with serial or model number, or service performed) at (location and other important details of the transaction).

Name product, serial or model number, or service.

Indicate date, location of purchase, other details.

State problem.

Unfortunately, your product (or service) has not performed well (or the service was inadequate) because (state the problem). I am disappointed because (explain the problem: for example, the product does not work properly, the service was not performed correctly, I was billed the wrong amount, something was not disclosed clearly or was misrepresented, etc.).

Give history of problem.

To resolve the problem, I would appreciate your (state the specific action you want—money back, charge card credit, repair, exchange, etc.) Attached are copies (do not send originals) of my records (include receipts, guarantees, warranties, canceled checks, contracts, model and serial numbers, and any other documents).

Ask for specific action.

Attach copies of documents.

State reasonable time for action.

I look forward to your reply and a resolution to this situation, and will wait until (set a time limit) before seeking help from a consumer protection agency. Please contact me by e-mail or by phone.

Sincerely,

Your Name
Phone
E-mail

mediator—tries to resolve a conflict between a customer and a business through discussion and negotiation. Mediation is a nonbinding process. This action can save time and money compared to other dispute settlement methods.

Arbitration is the settlement of a difference by a third party—the *arbitrator*—whose decision is legally binding. After both sides agree to arbitration, each party presents its case. Arbitrators are selected from volunteers trained for this purpose. Most major automobile manufacturers and many industry organizations have arbitration programs to resolve consumer complaints.

A network of government agencies is available. Problems with local restaurants or food stores may be handled by a city or county health department. Every state has agencies to handle problems involving deceptive advertising, fraudulent business practices, banking, insurance companies, and utility rates. Federal agencies are available to help with consumer concerns (see Chapter 6 Appendix). When uncertain about which agency to contact, conduct an online search to guide you.

CAUTION!

The Federal Trade Commission warns students of these scholarship and financial aid scams: "The scholarship is guaranteed," "You can't get this information anywhere else," "I just need your credit card or bank account number to hold this scholarship," "We'll do all the work. You just pay a processing fee," "You've been selected" by a "national foundation" to receive a scholarship—or "You're a finalist" in a contest you never entered. Also beware of offers for student loan forgiveness and requests for your username and password to help repay loans. For guidance on financing your education, see the Chapter 5 Appendix.

WHAT WOULD YOU DO? Each day, hundreds of people are victims of scams and frauds. What actions do you take to avoid losing money to deceptive business activities? If you had a friend who was a victim of fraud, what steps would you recommend to that person?

arbitration The settlement of a difference by a third party whose decision is legally binding.

Step 4: Legal Action

The Legal Options for Consumers section considers various legal alternatives available to resolve consumer problems.

small claims court A court that settles legal differences involving amounts below a set limit and employs a process in which the litigants usually do not use a lawyer.

PRACTICE QUIZ 6–3

1. What are common causes of consumer problems and complaints?

2. How can most consumer complaints be resolved?

3. How does arbitration differ from mediation?

Legal Options for Consumers

If the actions discussed previously fail to resolve your complaint, what would you do next? One of the following options may be appropriate.

LO6.4

Evaluate legal alternatives available to consumers.

Small Claims Court

In **small claims court**, a person may file a claim involving amounts below a set dollar limit. The maximum varies from state to state, ranging from $500 to $25,000; most states have a limit of between $2,500 and $10,000. The process usually takes place without a lawyer, although in many states attorneys are allowed in small claims court. To effectively use small claims court, experts suggest that you:

- Become familiar with court procedures and filing fees (usually from $5 to $50).
- Observe other cases to learn about the process.

ACTION ITEM

I know the legal actions to take for consumer problems.

☐ Agree   ☐ Disagree

- Present your case in a polite, calm, and concise manner.
- Submit evidence such as photographs, contracts, receipts, and other documents.
- Use witnesses who can testify on your behalf.

For additional details about small claims court, see the *Financial Literacy in Practice* feature.

Class-Action Suits

class-action suit A legal action taken by a few individuals on behalf of all the people who have suffered the same alleged injustice.

Occasionally, a number of people have the same complaint. A **class-action suit** is a legal action taken by a few individuals on behalf of all the people who have suffered the same alleged injustice. These people are represented by one or more lawyers. Once a situation qualifies as a class-action suit, all affected parties are notified. At this point, a person must decide whether to opt in or opt out. Nonrespondents will not be part of the complaint. If a plaintiff chooses not to participate in the class-action suit, the person may select to file an individual lawsuit.

If the court ruling is favorable to the class, the funds awarded may be divided among the class members, used to reduce future rates, assigned for government use, or donated to charity. Past examples of class-action suits include auto owners who were sold unneeded replacement parts, investors who sued a brokerage company for unauthorized transactions resulting in high commission charges, and consumers who were charged unfair fees by an online ticket seller.

CAUTION

Buying fake and counterfeit products can be dangerous. A fake purse or watch may not cost much money, but other products can cost lives. Counterfeit prescription medications may not be effective, or a knockoff airbag used as a replacement part in a vehicle after an accident may not deploy properly. Carefully investigate purchases for your personal safety.

Using a Lawyer

In some situations, you may seek the services of an attorney. Common sources of lawyers are referrals from friends, online research, and the local division of the American Bar Association.

Straightforward legal situations such as appearing in small claims court, renting an apartment, or defending yourself on a minor traffic violation will usually not need legal counsel. More complicated matters such as writing a will, settling a real estate purchase, or suing for injury damages will likely require the services of an attorney. Websites such as LegalZoom, Nolo, and Rocket Lawyer are available to assist with basic legal documents.

When selecting a lawyer, consider several questions: Is the lawyer experienced in your type of case? Will you be charged on a flat-fee basis, at an hourly rate, or on a contingency basis? Is there a fee for the initial consultation? How and when will you be required to make payment for services?

WHAT WOULD YOU DO? While using a hair dryer you recently purchased, you receive a burn on your hand. What actions might be taken related to this situation? How would you determine if legal action is appropriate? What steps would you take if you needed to hire a lawyer?

Other Legal Alternatives

legal aid society One of a network of publicly supported community law offices that provide legal assistance to consumers who cannot afford their own attorney.

Legal services can be expensive. A **legal aid society** is one of a network of community law offices that provide legal assistance to people who cannot afford their own attorney. These community agencies provide this assistance at a minimal or no cost.

Prepaid legal services provide unlimited or reduced-fee legal assistance for a set fee. Some programs provide basic services, such as telephone consultation and preparation of a simple will, for an annual fee. Prepaid legal programs are designed to prevent minor troubles from becoming complicated legal problems.

Financial Literacy in Practice

How to File a Suit in Small Claims Court

In every state, small claims courts are available to handle legal disputes involving minor amounts. While specific procedures vary from state to state, these actions are usually involved:

Step 1. Notify the defendant to request a payment for damages with a deadline, such as within 30 days. Note in your letter that you will initiate legal action after that point in time.

Step 2. Determine the appropriate location for filing the case. Also, decide if your type of case is allowed in small claims court in your state and if the amount is within the state limit. (Information on state limits is available at www.nolo.com/legal-encyclopedia/article-30031.html.)

Step 3. Obtain and complete the required filing documents. These forms can be obtained at the courthouse or may be available online. The petition will include the plaintiff's name (you), the defendant (person or organization being sued), the amount being requested, a detailed and clear description of the claim with dates of various actions, and copies of any pertinent documents (contracts, receipts).

Step 4. File the documents and pay the required fee. The petition will be served to the defendant notifying that person of the suit. After being served, the defendant is usually required to file a written response, denying or not contesting the claim. If the defendant does not respond, a default judgment will most likely be entered.

Step 5. Next, a hearing date will be set. Prepare evidence with a clear and concise presentation of (*a*) the details of what happened and when; (*b*) evidence, such as contracts, leases, receipts, canceled checks, credit card statements, or photographs; and (*c*) the testimony of people who witnessed aspects of the dispute or who are knowledgeable about the type of situation. If both parties decide to settle before the hearing, be sure that you receive payment before the case is dismissed.

Step 6. At the hearing, be as clear and concise as possible, and bring supporting documentation with you. A subpoena may be needed requiring witnesses whom you wish present at the hearing to appear in court.

Step 7. Once you receive a favorable judgment, you still have to collect the funds. While the court does not collect the money for you, the party may pay when the judgment is rendered. If not, a letter from you or an attorney may result in payment. Or more formal debt collection actions might be necessary.

Every state has different procedures and regulations related to small claims court. Conduct a web search to obtain information for your specific location. Careful and detailed preparation of your case is the key to a successful small claims court case.

Personal Consumer Protection

While many laws, agencies, legal tools, and online sources are available to protect your rights, none will be of value unless you use them. Consumer protection experts suggest that to prevent being taken by deceptive business practices, you should:

1. Do business only with reputable companies with a record of satisfying customers.
2. Avoid signing contracts and other documents you do not understand.
3. Be cautious of deals that seem too good to be true—they probably are!
4. Compare the cost of buying on credit with the cost of paying cash; also, compare the interest rates the seller offers with those offered by a bank or a credit union.
5. Avoid rushing to get a good deal; successful con artists depend on impulse buying.

Sheet 21 Legal Services Cost Comparison

PRACTICE QUIZ 6–4

1. In what types of situations would small claims court and class-action suits be helpful?

2. Describe situations in which you might use the services of a lawyer.

3. For the following situations, identify the legal action that would be most appropriate to take.

   a. A low-income person wants to obtain the services of a lawyer to file a product-liability suit.
   b. A person is attempting to obtain a $150 catering deposit that was never returned.
   c. A consumer wants to settle a dispute out of court with the use of a third party whose decision will be legally binding.
   d. A group of telephone customers were overcharged by $1.10 a month over the past 22 months.

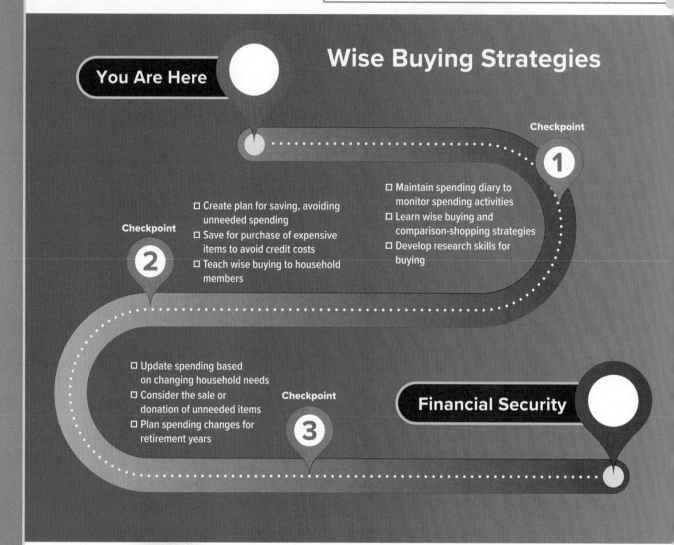

Wise Buying Strategies

You Are Here

Checkpoint 1
- ☐ Maintain spending diary to monitor spending activities
- ☐ Learn wise buying and comparison-shopping strategies
- ☐ Develop research skills for buying

Checkpoint 2
- ☐ Create plan for saving, avoiding unneeded spending
- ☐ Save for purchase of expensive items to avoid credit costs
- ☐ Teach wise buying to household members

Checkpoint 3
- ☐ Update spending based on changing household needs
- ☐ Consider the sale or donation of unneeded items
- ☐ Plan spending changes for retirement years

Financial Security

UNPLANNED SPENDING PERCENT

your personal finance dashboard

Unplanned Spending Percent

Unplanned spending, called impulse buying, prevents good financial planning. While people may spend to feel good about themselves, that often results in budget problems, high debt levels, and greater financial stress. Controlling unplanned spending contributes to financial progress. Careful spending results in lower debt, more savings, and achieving financial goals.

YOUR SITUATION: Are you able to minimize your unplanned purchases? Are there areas of spending you might reduce? A low unplanned spending ratio can result in improved financial security.

LO6.1 Timing purchases, comparing stores and brands, using label information, computing unit prices, and evaluating warranties are common strategies for effective purchasing.

LO6.2 A research-based approach to consumer buying involves (1) preshopping activities, such as problem identification and information gathering; (2) evaluating alternatives; (3) determining the purchase price; and (4) postpurchase activities, such as proper operation and maintenance.

LO6.3 Most consumer problems can be resolved by following these steps: (1) return to the place of purchase; (2) contact the company's main office; (3) obtain assistance from a consumer agency; and (4) take legal action.

LO6.4 Small claims court, class-action suits, the services of a lawyer, legal aid societies, and prepaid legal services are legal means for handling consumer problems that cannot be resolved through communication with the company involved or with help from a consumer protection agency.

arbitration 233

class-action suit 234

legal aid society 234

mediation 232

service contract 220

small claims court 233

warranty 220

1. An item bought on credit with a $60 down payment and monthly payments of $70 for 36 months. What would be the total cost of the item?
2. A food package with 32 ounces costs $1.76. What is the unit cost of the package?

Solutions

1. 36 × $70 = $2,520 plus the $60 down payment for a total of $2,580.
2. $1.76 ÷ 32 = 5.5 cents an ounce.

1. An online buying club offers a membership for $300, for which you will receive a 10 percent discount on all brand-name items you purchase. How much would you have to buy to cover the cost of the membership? (LO6.1)
2. John Walters is comparing the cost of credit to the cash price of an item. If John makes an $80 down payment and pays $35 a month for 24 months, how much more will that amount be than the cash price of $685? (LO6.1)
3. Calculate the unit price of each of the following items: (LO6.1)
   a. Motor oil—2.5 quarts for $1.95   *cents/quart*
   b. Cereal—15 ounces for $2.17   *cents/ounce*
   c. Canned fruit—13 ounces for 89 cents   *cents/ounce*
   d. Facial tissue—300 tissues for $2.25   *cents/100 tissues*
4. A service contract for a video projection system costs $80 a year. You expect to use the system for six years. Instead of buying the service contract, what would be the future value of these annual amounts after six years if you earn 3 percent on your savings? (LO6.1)
5. A work-at-home opportunity is available in which you will receive 3 percent of the sales to customers you refer to the company. The cost of your "franchise fee" is $600. How much would your customers have to buy to cover the cost of this fee? (LO6.1)
6. What would be the net present value of a microwave oven that costs $159 and will save you $68 a year in time and food away from home? Assume an average return on your savings of 4 percent for five years. (*Hint:* Calculate the present value of the annual savings, then subtract the cost of the microwave.) (LO6.1)

7. If a person saves $62 a month by using coupons and doing comparison shopping, (a) what is the amount for a year? (b) What would be the future value of this annual amount over 10 years, assuming an interest rate of 4 percent?   (LO6.1)

8. Based on the following data, prepare a financial comparison of buying and leasing a motor vehicle with a $24,000 cash price:

Down payment (to finance vehicle), $4,000   Down payment for lease, $1,200
Monthly loan payment, $560   Monthly lease payment, $440
Length of loan, 48 months   Length of lease, 48 months
Value of vehicle at end of loan, $7,200   End-of-lease charges, $600

What other factors should a person consider when choosing between buying and leasing?   (LO6.2)

9. Based on the data provided here, calculate the items requested: (LO6.2)

Annual depreciation, $2,500   Annual mileage, 13,200
Current year's loan interest, $650   Miles per gallon, 24
Insurance, $680   License and registration fees, $65
Average gasoline price, $3.50 per gallon   Oil changes/repairs, $370
Parking/tolls, $420

a. The total annual operating cost of the motor vehicle.
b. The operating cost per mile.

10. Based on the following, calculate the costs of buying versus leasing a motor vehicle: (LO6.2)

Purchase Costs   *Leasing Costs*
    Down payment, $1,500   Security deposit, $500
    Loan payment, $450 for 48 months   Lease payment, $450 for 48 months
    Estimated value at end of loan, $4,000   End-of-lease charges, $600
    Opportunity cost interest rate, 4 percent

11. A class-action suit against a utility company resulted in a settlement of $1.4 million for 62,000 customers. If the legal fees, which must be paid from the settlement, are $300,000, what amount will each plaintiff receive? (LO6.4)

 To reinforce the content in this chapter, more problems are provided at connect.mheducation.com.

FINANCIAL LITERACY PORTFOLIO. . .
PLANNING A CONSUMER PURCHASE

Competency. . .

(1) Researching a consumer purchase; (2) Avoiding unwise spending and consumer fraud.

Action Research. . .

(1) Based on Chapter 6, online research, and store or car dealer visits, complete *Your Personal Financial Plan Sheet 18* or *19* for a major consumer purchase or used car purchase. (Excel files for these two sheets are available on Connect.) (2) Based on Chapter 6 and online research, select a recent scam or unwise spending action.

Outcome. . .

(1) Report the findings and conclusion of the comparison shopping research with the use of an audio file, video, PowerPoint presentation, storyboard, or other visual format. (2) Create a warning to inform and educate others regarding this fraud or poor spending habits using one or more of these formats: print advertisement, audio file/podcast, video, smartphone app, storyboard, or photo essay.

REAL LIFE PERSONAL FINANCE

ONLINE CAR BUYING

With a click of the mouse, Mackenzie enters the auto "showroom." In the past few months, she had realized that the repair costs for her 11-year-old car were accelerating. She thought it was time to start shopping for a new car online and decided to start her search for a vehicle by looking at small and mid-sized SUVs.

Her friends suggested that Mackenzie research more than one type of vehicle. They reminded her that comparable models were available from various auto manufacturers.

In her online car-buying process, Mackenzie next did a price comparison.

She obtained more than one price quote by using various online sources. She then prepared an overview of her online car-buying experiences.

Mackenzie's next step was to make her final decision. After selecting what she planned to buy, she finalized the purchase online and decided to take delivery at a local dealer.

While the number of motor vehicles being sold online is increasing, car-buying experts strongly recommend that you make a personal examination of the vehicle before taking delivery.

Online Car-Buying Action	Online Activities	Websites Consulted
Information gathering	• Review available vehicle models and options. • Evaluate operating costs and safety features.	autos.msn.com www.consumerreports.org www.caranddriver.com www.motortrend.com
Comparing prices	• Identify specific make, model, and features desired. • Locate availability and specific price in your geographic area.	www.autobytel.com www.edmunds.com www.kbb.com www.nadaguides.com
Finalizing purchase	• Make payment or financing arrangements. • Conduct in-person inspection. • Arrange for delivery.	www.autobytel.com www.autonation.com www.safercar.gov www.carsdirect.com

Questions

1. Based on Mackenzie's experience, what benefits and drawbacks are associated with online car buying?

2. What additional actions might Mackenzie consider before buying a motor vehicle?

3. What do you consider to be the benefits and drawbacks of shopping online for motor vehicles and other items?

4. What actions might a car buyer take if a *lemon* is purchased?

CONSUMER PURCHASING STRATEGIES AND WISE BUYING OF MOTOR VEHICLES

It sputtered and squeaked, and with a small hesitation followed by an exaggerated shudder, it was finally over. Ol' Reliable, the car Jamie Lee had driven since she first earned her driver's license at the age of 17, completed its last mile. Thirteen years and 140,000 miles later, it was time for a new vehicle.

After skimming the Sunday newspaper and browsing the online advertisements, Jamie Lee was ready to visit car dealers to see what vehicles would interest her. She was unsure if she would purchase a new car or used and how she would pay for the car. "No money down and only $219 a month," Jamie Lee read, "with approved credit." It sounded like an offer she would be interested in. Jamie Lee knew she had a good credit rating, as she made sure she paid all of her bills on time each month and had kept a close eye on her credit score ever since she was the victim of identity theft several years ago. The more she thought about the brand-new car, the more excited she became. That new car fit her personality perfectly!

As Jamie Lee inquired about the advertised vehicle with the salesperson, her excitement quickly turned to dismay. The automobile advertised was available for $219 a month with no money down, based on approved credit, but Jamie Lee unexpectedly found that there were further qualifications in order to get the advertised price. The salesman explained that the information in the fine print of the newspaper advertisement stated that the price was based on all of the following criteria: being active in the military, a college graduate within the last three months, a current lessee of the automobile company, and having a top-tier credit score, which, he noted, was above 800. If Jamie Lee did not meet all of the qualifications, she would not receive the price advertised in the promotion. He could get her in that vehicle, but it would cost her an additional $110 per month. Jamie budgeted a maximum of $275 for her monthly car payment. She could not afford the vehicle.

Jamie Lee had to start over from scratch. She decided that she must fully research the vehicle purchase process before browsing at another dealership. She felt she was getting caught up in the moment and vowed to do her research before speaking with another salesperson.

Questions

1. Jamie Lee is considering a used vehicle but cannot decide where to begin her search. Using *Your Personal Financial Plan Sheet 19*, name the sources available to Jamie Lee for a used-car purchase. What are the advantages and disadvantages of each?
2. Jamie Lee is attracted to the low monthly payment advertised for a vehicle lease. She may well be able to afford a more expensive car than she originally thought. Jamie Lee really needs to think this through. What are the advantages and disadvantages to leasing a vehicle?
3. Jamie Lee sat down with a salesperson to discuss a new vehicle and its $24,000 purchase price. Jamie Lee has heard that "no one really pays the vehicle sticker price." What guidelines may be suggested for negotiating the purchase price of a vehicle?
4. Jamie Lee has decided to purchase a certified preowned vehicle. What might she expect as far as reliability and a warranty on the used car?

"USING THE DAILY SPENDING DIARY HAS HELPED ME CONTROL IMPULSE BUYING. WHEN I HAVE TO WRITE DOWN EVERY AMOUNT, I'M MORE CAREFUL WITH MY SPENDING. I CAN NOW PUT MORE IN SAVINGS."

Directions Start (or continue) your Daily Spending Diary or use your own format to record and monitor spending in various categories. Most people who have participated in this activity have found it beneficial for monitoring and controlling their spending habits. The Daily Spending Diary sheets are located at the end of Chapter 1 and in Connect Finance.

Questions

1. What daily spending items are amounts that might be reduced or eliminated to allow for higher savings amounts?
2. How might a Daily Spending Diary result in wiser consumer buying and more saving for the future?

Name: _____   Date: _____

Consumer Purchase Comparison

Purpose: To research and evaluate brands and store services for a major consumer purchase.

Financial Planning Activities: When considering the purchase of a major consumer item, use ads, catalogs, an online search, store visits, and other sources to obtain the information below. This sheet is also available in an Excel spreadsheet format in Connect Finance.

Suggested Websites: www.consumerreports.org, www.consumerworld.org, www.clarkhoward.com

Product

Exact description (size, model, features, etc.)

_____

Research the item in consumer periodicals and online for information regarding your product.

Article/Periodical _____   **Website** _____

Date/Pages _____   **Date** _____

What buying suggestions are presented in the articles?

_____

Which brands are recommended in these articles? Why?

_____

Contact or visit two or three stores that sell the product to obtain the following information:

	Store 1	Store 2	Store 3
Company			
Address			
Phone/website			
Brand name/cost			
Variation from the description above (if any)			
Warranty (describe)			
Which brand and at which store would you buy this product? Why?			

What's Next for Your Personal Financial Plan?

- Which consumer information sources are most valuable for your future buying decisions?
- List guidelines to use in the future when making major purchases.

Name: _____ **Date:** _____

Used-Car Purchase Comparison

Purpose: To research and evaluate different types and sources of used vehicles.

Financial Planning Activities: When considering a used-car purchase, use advertisements, online sources, and visits to new- and used-car dealers to obtain the information below. This sheet is also available in an Excel spreadsheet format in Connect Finance.

Suggested Websites: www.carbuyingtips.com, www.kbb.com, www.safercar.gov

Automobile (year, make, model)			
Name/source			
Address			
Phone			
Website (if applicable)			
Cost			
Mileage			
Condition of auto			
Condition of tires			
Radio			
Air conditioning			
Other options			
Warranty (describe)			
Items in need of repair			
Inspection items: • Rust, major dents?			
• Oil or fluid leaks?			
• Condition of brakes?			
• Proper operation of heater, wipers, other accessories?			
Other information			

Suggested App:
• KBB

McGraw Hill

What's Next for Your Personal Financial Plan?

- Maintain a record of automobile operating costs.
- Prepare a plan for regular maintenance of your vehicle.

Name: _____   **Date:** _____

Buying versus Leasing a Vehicle

Purpose: To compare costs of buying or leasing an automobile or other vehicle.

Financial Planning Activities: Obtain costs related to leasing and buying a vehicle. This sheet is also available in an Excel spreadsheet format in Connect Finance.

Suggested Websites: www.leasesource.com, www.moneyunder30.com/buy-vs-lease-calculator

Purchase Costs

Total vehicle cost, including sales tax ($ _____)

Down payment (or full amount if paying cash) $ _____

Monthly loan payment: $ _____ times _____ month loan $ _____
(This item is zero if vehicle is not financed.)

Opportunity cost of down payment (or total cost of the vehicle if bought for cash):

$ _____ times number of years of financing/ownership times _____
percent (interest rate that funds could earn) $ _____

Less: estimated value of vehicle at end of loan term/ownership $ _____

Total cost to buy . . . . $

Leasing Costs

Security deposit $ _____

Monthly lease payments: $ _____ times _____ months $ _____

Opportunity cost of security deposit: $ _____ times years
times _____ percent $ _____

End-of-lease charges (if applicable)* $ _____

Total cost to lease . . . . $

*WITH A CLOSED-END LEASE, CHARGES FOR EXTRA MILEAGE OR EXCESSIVE WEAR AND TEAR; WITH AN OPEN-END LEASE, END-OF-LEASE PAYMENT IF APPRAISED VALUE IS LESS THAN ESTIMATED ENDING VALUE.

What's Next for Your Personal Financial Plan?

- Prepare a list of future actions to use when buying, financing, and leasing a car.
- Maintain a record of operating costs and maintenance actions for your vehicle.

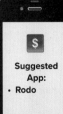

Suggested App:
- Rodo

McGraw Hill

Legal Services Cost Comparison

Purpose: To compare cost of services from various legal assistance sources.

Financial Planning Activities: Contact various legal services (lawyer, prepaid legal service, legal aid society) and online sources to compare costs and available services. This sheet is also available in an Excel spreadsheet format in Connect Finance.

Suggested Websites: www.nolo.com, www.americanbar.org

Type of legal service			
Organization name			
Address			
Phone			
Website			
Contact person			
Recommended by			
Areas of specialization			
Maximum initial deposit			
Cost of initial consultation			
Cost of simple will			
Cost of real estate closing			
Cost method for other services—flat fee, hourly rate, or contingency basis			
Other information			

What's Next for Your Personal Financial Plan?

- Determine the best alternative for your future legal needs.
- Maintain a file of legal documents and other financial records.

Suggested App:
- Ask a Lawyer

McGraw Hill

YOUR PERSONAL FINANCIAL PLAN

Chapter 6 Appendix:
Consumer Agencies and Organizations

Government agencies and other organizations are available to assist when you want to:

- Research a financial or consumer topic.
- Obtain information for planning a purchase decision.
- Seek assistance to resolve a consumer problem.

Section 1 of this appendix provides an overview of federal, state, and local agencies and other organizations you may contact related to financial planning and consumer topics. Section 2 covers state consumer protection offices that can assist you in local matters.

Section 1

Most federal agencies may be contacted online; websites are noted below. In addition, consumer information from several federal government agencies may be accessed at **www.usa.gov/consumer**.

Information on additional government agencies and private organizations available to assist you may be obtained in the *Consumer Action Handbook*, available at no charge at **www.usa.gov/handbook**.

Exhibit **6–A** Federal, State, and Local Agencies and Other Organizations

Topic Area	Federal Agency	State, Local Agency; Other Organizations
Advertising False advertising Product labeling Deceptive sales practices Warranties	Federal Trade Commission 1-877-FTC-HELP (www.ftc.gov)	State Consumer Protection Office c/o State Attorney General or Governor's Office (see Section 2) National Fraud Information Center (www.fraud.org)
Air Travel Air safety Airport regulation Airline routes	Federal Aviation Administration 1-800-FAA-SURE (www.faa.gov)	International Airline Passengers Association 1-800-527-5888 (www.iapa.com)
Appliances/Product Safety Potentially dangerous products Complaints against retailers, manufacturers	Consumer Product Safety Commission 1-800-638-CPSC (www.cpsc.gov)	Council of Better Business Bureaus 1-800-955-5100 (www.bbb.org)

Topic Area	Federal Agency	State, Local Agency; Other Organizations
Automobiles New cars Used cars Automobile repairs Auto safety	Federal Trade Commission 1-877-FTC-HELP (www.ftc.gov) National Highway Traffic Safety Administration 1-800-424-9393 (www.nhtsa.gov; www.safercar.gov)	National Automobile Dealers Association 1-800-252-6232 (www.nada.org) Center for Auto Safety (202) 328-7700 (www.autosafety.org)
Banking and Financial Institutions Checking accounts Savings accounts Deposit insurance Financial services	Federal Deposit Insurance Corporation 1-877-275-3342 (www.fdic.gov) Comptroller of the Currency (202) 447-1600 (www.occ.treas.gov) Federal Reserve Board (202) 452-3693 (www.federalreserve.gov) National Credit Union Administration (703) 518-6300 (www.ncua.gov)	Credit Union National Association (608) 232-8256 (www.cuna.org) American Bankers Association (202) 663-5000 (www.aba.com) Treasury Direct U.S. Savings Bonds 1-800-US-BONDS (www.savingsbonds.gov)
Career Planning Job training Employment information	Coordinator of Consumer Affairs Department of Labor (202) 219-6060 (www.dol.gov)	State Department of Labor or State Employment Service
Consumer Credit Credit cards Deceptive credit advertising Truth-in-Lending Act Credit rights of women, minorities	Consumer Financial Protection Bureau (855) 411-2372 (www.consumerfinance.gov) Federal Trade Commission 1-877-FTC-HELP (www.ftc.gov)	Clearpoint Credit Counseling 1-800-251-2227 (www.clearpoint.org) National Foundation for Credit Counseling (301) 589-5600 (www.nfcc.org)
Environment Air, water pollution Toxic substances	Environmental Protection Agency 1-800-438-4318 (indoor air quality) 1-800-426-4791 (drinking water safety) (www.epa.gov)	Clean Water Action (202) 895-0420 (www.cleanwater.org)
Food Food grades Food additives Nutritional information	U.S. Department of Agriculture 1-800-424-9121 (www.usda.gov) Food and Drug Administration 1-888-463-6332 (www.fda.gov)	Center for Science in the Public Interest (202) 332-9110 (www.cspinet.org)
Funerals Cost disclosure Deceptive business practices	Federal Trade Commission 1-877-FTC-HELP (www.ftc.gov)	National Funeral Directors Association 1-800-228-6332 (www.nfda.org)

Exhibit **6–A** *(continued)*

Topic Area	Federal Agency	State, Local Agency; Other Organizations
Housing and Real Estate Fair housing practices Mortgages Community development	Department of Housing and Urban Development (HUD) 1-800-669-9777 (www.hud.gov) HUD - Tenant's Rights (**https://www.hud.gov/topics/ rental_assistance/tenantrights**)	National Association of Realtors 1-800-874-6500 (**www.realtor.com**) (**www.move.com**) Tenant Advocacy Project (**www.lcbh.org/programs/ tenant-advocacy**)
Insurance Policy conditions Premiums Types of coverage Consumer complaints	Federal Trade Commission 1-877-FTC-HELP (**www.ftc.gov**) National Flood Insurance Program 1-888-CALL-FLOOD (**www.floodsmart.gov**)	State insurance regulator (see Section 2) American Council of Life Insurance (**www.acli.com**) Insurance Information Institute 1-800-331-9146 (**www.iii.org**)
Investments Stocks, bonds Mutual funds Commodities Investment brokers	Securities and Exchange Commission (202) 551-6551 (**www.sec.gov**) Commodity Futures Trading Commission (202) 418-5000 (**www.cftc.gov**)	Investment Company Institute (202) 293-7700 (**www.ici.org**) Financial Industry Regulatory Authority (301) 590-6500 (**www.finra.org**) National Futures Association 1-800-621-3570 (**www.nfa.futures.org**) Securities Investor Protection Corporation (202) 371-8300 (**www.sipc.org**)
Legal Matters Consumer complaints Arbitration	Department of Justice Office of Consumer Litigation (202) 514-2401 (**www.justice.gov/civil/ consumerprotection-branch**)	American Arbitration Association (212) 484-4000 (**www.adr.org**) American Bar Association 1-800-285-2221 (**www.americanbar.org**)
Internet/Mail Order Damaged products Deceptive business practices Illegal use of U.S. mail	Internet Crime Complaint Center (**www.ic3.gov**) U.S. Postal Service 1-800-ASK-USPS (**www.usps.com**)	Direct Marketing Association (212) 768-7277 (**thedma.org**)
Medical Concerns Prescription medications Over-the-counter medications Medical devices Health care	Food and Drug Administration 1-888-463-6332 (**www.fda.gov**) Public Health Service 1-800-621-8335 (**www.usphs.gov**)	American Medical Association 1-800-336-4797 (**www.ama-assn.org**) Public Citizen Health Research Group (202) 588-1000 (**www.citizen.org**)

Topic Area	Federal Agency	State, Local Agency; Other Organizations
Retirement Old-age benefits Pension information Medicare	Social Security Administration 1-800-772-1213 (www.ssa.gov)	AARP (202) 434-2277 (www.aarp.org)
Taxes Tax information Audit procedures	Internal Revenue Service 1-800-829-1040 1-800-TAX-FORM (www.irs.gov)	State revenue department (see Section 2) The Tax Foundation (202) 464-6200 (www.taxfoundation.org) National Association of Enrolled Agents 1-800-424-4339 (www.naea.org)
Telemarketing Deceptive phone calls Robocalls	Federal Communications Commission 1-888-225-5322 (www.fcc.gov) Federal Trade Commission 1-877-FTC-HELP (www.ftc.gov)	National Consumers League (202) 835-3323 (www.nclnet.org)
Utilities Cable television Utility rates	Federal Communications Commission 1-988-225-5322 (www.fcc.gov)	State utility commission (in your state's capital city)

Section 2

State, county, and local consumer protection offices provide consumers with publications, online information, and assistance for complaint handling. In addition, agencies regulating banking, insurance, securities, and utilities are available in each state; these may be located with an online search.

Consumer Action Handbook	www.usa.gov/handbook
State consumer offices	National Association of Attorneys General (www.naag.org) or search "(*state*) consumer protection agency"
State departments of insurance	www.naic.org/state_web_map.htm
State tax departments	www.taxadmin.org/state-tax-agencies www.aicpa.org/research/externallinks/taxesstatesdepartmentsofrevenue.html

    To save time, call or e-mail the office before sending in a complaint. Determine if the office handles the type of complaint you have or if online complaint forms are available.

7 Selecting and Financing Housing

3 Steps to Financial Literacy . . .
Building Home Equity

1 Save for a down payment by reducing unnecessary spending for various monthly budget items.
Website: www.americasaves.org

2 Make monthly payments on time to avoid late penalties and to maintain your credit rating.
App: Bills Reminder

3 Pay an additional principal amount each month, which will result in saving thousands of dollars on interest.
Website: www.bankrate.com

What are the financial benefits of increased home equity?

You will have the financial security of less debt and will be able to borrow against the equity if needed. At the end of the chapter, *Your Personal Finance Road Map and Dashboard* will provide additional information for measuring the progress of your home equity amount along with suggested actions for wise housing decisions.

HOME FOR SALE

CHAPTER 7 LEARNING OBJECTIVES

In this chapter, you will learn to:

LO7.1 Assess costs and benefits of renting.

LO7.2 Implement the home-buying process.

LO7.3 Determine costs associated with purchasing a home.

LO7.4 Develop a strategy for selling a home.

YOUR PERSONAL FINANCIAL PLAN SHEETS

22. Renting versus Buying Housing
23. Apartment Rental Comparison
24. Housing Affordability and Mortgage Qualification
25. Mortgage Company Comparison

Evaluating Renting and Buying

LO7.1

Assess costs and benefits of renting.

As you walk around a neighborhood, you are likely to see a variety of housing types. When assessing housing alternatives, start by identifying factors that will influence your choice.

Your Lifestyle and Your Choice of Housing

Although the concept of *lifestyle*—how you spend your time and money—may seem intangible, it materializes in the consumer purchases you make. Every buying decision is a statement about your lifestyle. Personal preferences are the foundation of a housing decision, but financial factors will modify your final choice.

Traditional financial guidelines suggest that "you should spend no more than 25 or 30 percent of your take-home pay on housing" or "your home should cost about 2½ times your annual income." Changes in economic and social conditions have resulted in revised guidelines. Your budgeting activities and financial records provide information to determine an appropriate amount for housing expenses.

ACTION ITEM

The most important attribute when selecting a place to live is:

☐ **proximity to work or school.**

☐ **cost.**

☐ **flexibility for future moves.**

Renting versus Buying Housing

The choice between renting and buying your residence should be analyzed based on lifestyle and financial factors. Mobility is a primary motivator of renters, whereas buyers usually want stability of location (see Exhibit 7–1). As you can see in the nearby *Figure It Out!* feature, the choice between renting and buying may not be well defined. In general, renting is less costly in the short run, but home ownership often has long-term financial advantages.

Exhibit **7–1**
Comparing Renting and Buying Housing

Advantages	Disadvantages
RENTING	
• Easy to move • Fewer responsibilities for maintenance • Minimal financial commitment	• No tax benefits • Limitations regarding remodeling • Restrictions regarding pets, other activities
BUYING	
• Pride of ownership • Financial benefits • Lifestyle flexibility	• Financial commitment • Higher living expenses than renting • Limited mobility

Rental Activities

In the past, apartment rental ads presented information like this: "2-bd.garden apt, a/c, crptg, mod bath, lndry, sec $850." Translated, this means a two-bedroom garden apartment (at or below ground level) with air conditioning, carpeting, a modern bath, and laundry facilities. An $850 security deposit is required. Today, most information is presented clearly.

At some point in your life, you are likely to rent. As a tenant, you pay for the right to live in a residence owned by someone else. Exhibit 7–2 presents the activities for finding and living in a rental unit.

Exhibit **7–2** Housing Rental Activities

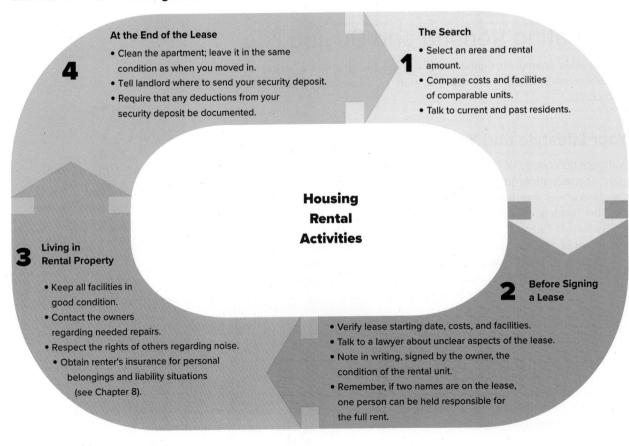

At the End of the Lease

4
- Clean the apartment; leave it in the same condition as when you moved in.
- Tell landlord where to send your security deposit.
- Require that any deductions from your security deposit be documented.

The Search

1
- Select an area and rental amount.
- Compare costs and facilities of comparable units.
- Talk to current and past residents.

Living in Rental Property

3
- Keep all facilities in good condition.
- Contact the owners regarding needed repairs.
- Respect the rights of others regarding noise.
- Obtain renter's insurance for personal belongings and liability situations (see Chapter 8).

Housing Rental Activities

Before Signing a Lease

2
- Verify lease starting date, costs, and facilities.
- Talk to a lawyer about unclear aspects of the lease.
- Note in writing, signed by the owner, the condition of the rental unit.
- Remember, if two names are on the lease, one person can be held responsible for the full rent.

Figure It Out!

Renting versus Buying Your Place of Residence

Comparing the costs of renting and buying involves a variety of factors. The following items and example provide a framework for assessing these two housing alternatives. The apartment in the example has a monthly rent of $1,250, and the home costs $200,000. A 28 percent tax rate is assumed.

Although the estimated numbers in this example favor buying, remember that in any financial decision, calculations provide only part of the answer. Also consider your needs and values, and assess the opportunity costs associated with renting and buying.

	Example	Your Figures
Rental Costs		
Annual rent payments	$ 15,000	$ _____
Renter's insurance	210	_____
Interest lost on security deposit (amount of security deposit times after-tax savings account interest rate)	36	_____
Total annual cost of renting	$ 15,246	_____
Buying Costs		
Annual mortgage payments	$15,168	_____
Property taxes (annual costs)	4,800	_____
Homeowner's insurance (annual premium)	600	_____
Estimated maintenance and repairs (1%)	2,000	_____
After-tax interest lost on down payment and closing costs	750	_____
Less (financial benefits of home ownership):		
Growth in equity	−1,120	−_____
Tax savings for mortgage interest (annual mortgage interest times tax rate)	−3,048	−_____
Tax savings for property taxes (annual property taxes times tax rate)	−1,344	−_____
Estimated annual appreciation (1.5%)*	−3,000	−_____
Total annual cost of buying	$ 14,806	_____

*This is a nationwide average; actual appreciation of property will vary by geographic area and economic conditions

SELECTING A RENTAL UNIT An apartment is the most common type of rental housing. Apartments range from modern, luxury units with extensive recreational facilities to simple one- and two-bedroom units in quiet neighborhoods. If you need more room, consider renting a house. If less space is needed, rent a room in a private house. The main information sources for rental units are online ads, real estate and rental offices, and people you know. When comparing rental units, consider the factors in Exhibit 7–3.

ADVANTAGES OF RENTING Renting offers mobility when a person needs to move to a different geographic location. Renters have fewer responsibilities than homeowners since they usually do not have to be concerned with maintenance and repairs. The costs to take possession of a rental unit are usually less than buying a home.

Exhibit **7–3**
Selecting an Apartment

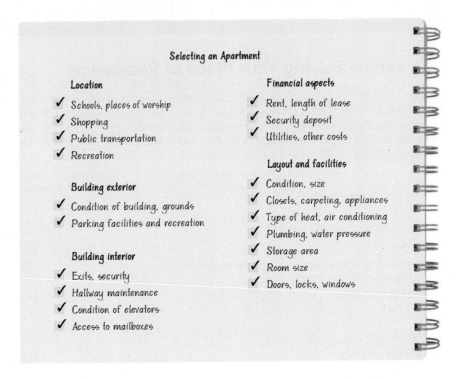

Selecting an Apartment

Location
- ✔ Schools, places of worship
- ✔ Shopping
- ✔ Public transportation
- ✔ Recreation

Building exterior
- ✔ Condition of building, grounds
- ✔ Parking facilities and recreation

Building interior
- ✔ Exits, security
- ✔ Hallway maintenance
- ✔ Condition of elevators
- ✔ Access to mailboxes

Financial aspects
- ✔ Rent, length of lease
- ✔ Security deposit
- ✔ Utilities, other costs

Layout and facilities
- ✔ Condition, size
- ✔ Closets, carpeting, appliances
- ✔ Type of heat, air conditioning
- ✔ Plumbing, water pressure
- ✔ Storage area
- ✔ Room size
- ✔ Doors, locks, windows

DISADVANTAGES OF RENTING Renters do not have the financial advantages of homeowners. Tenants cannot take tax deductions for mortgage interest and property taxes, or benefit from increased real estate values. Renters are generally limited in the types of activities they can pursue in their place of residence. Loud music or parties may be monitored closely. Tenants are often subject to restrictions regarding pets and decorating.

lease A legal document that defines the conditions of a rental agreement.

LEGAL DETAILS Most tenants sign a **lease**, a legal document that defines the conditions of a rental agreement. This document presents:

- A description of the property, including the address.
- The name and address of the owner/landlord (the *lessor*).
- The name of the tenant (the *lessee*).
- The effective date of the lease and the length of the *lease.*
- The amount of the security deposit and the amount and due date of the monthly rent.
- The date and amount due of charges for late rent payments.
- A list of the utilities, appliances, furniture, or other facilities that are included in the rental amount.
- Restrictions regarding certain activities (pets, remodeling); tenant's right to sublet.
- Charges for damages or for moving out of the rental unit later (or earlier) than the lease expiration date.
- The conditions under which the landlord may enter the apartment.

Standard lease forms include conditions you may not want to accept. Just because a lease is preprinted does not mean you must accept every clause. If you have a high credit score, you may be able to negotiate a lower rent or a reduced security deposit. Also, discuss with the landlord any lease terms you consider unacceptable.

Some leases give you the right to *sublet* the rental unit. Subletting may be necessary if you must vacate the premises before the lease expires. Subletting allows you to have another person take over rent payments and live in the rental unit.

While most leases are written, oral leases can be valid. In those situations, one party must give a 30-day written notice to the other party before terminating the lease or imposing a rent increase. A lease provides protection to both landlord and tenant. The tenant is protected from rent increases unless the lease contains a provision allowing an increase. The lease gives the landlord the right to take legal action against a tenant for nonpayment of rent or destruction of property.

> **WHAT WOULD YOU DO?** When renting, you may encounter various move-in expenses. These can include first month's rent, security deposit for rent and pets, security deposit for utilities, moving truck, other moving expenses, household items (dishes, towels, bedding), furniture and appliances (as required), renter's insurance, refreshments for friends who helped you move, and other items. What amount do you estimate might be needed for you to move into an apartment? What actions can you take to reduce these move-in costs?

COSTS OF RENTING A *security deposit,* usually required when you sign a lease, is often one month's rent. This money is held by the landlord to cover the cost of any damages. Some state and local laws require landlords to pay interest on a security deposit if a building has a certain number of rental units. After you vacate the rental unit, your security deposit must be refunded within a reasonable time. If money is deducted, you have the right to an itemized list of repair costs. In some situations, a pet or move-in fee may be charged.

As a renter, you will incur other expenses. For many apartments, water is covered by the rent; however, other utilities may not be included. If you rent a house, you will probably pay for heat, electricity, water, and Internet. When you rent, be sure to obtain insurance coverage on your personal property.

FinTech for Financial Literacy

Technology to research, build, buy, sell, and manage real estate is *PropTech* (property technology). These digital innovations connect buyers, sellers, brokers, lenders, and landlords through artificial intelligence, virtual reality, 3D printing, drones, and crowdfunding for added competition in the real estate industry. PropTech involves three main areas: (1) *smart home* using digital platforms and apps for smart thermostats, smoke detectors, security cameras, ceiling fans, and lighting; (2) *sharing real estate* facilitates leasing and renting of land, offices, storage, and apartments, including coworking and house swapping; (3) *real estate FinTech* with blockchain technology reducing paperwork for selling and buying property. Commercial real estate (CRETech) as well as construction (ConTech) are creating new business models based on technological innovations.

CAUTION!

Renter's insurance is often overlooked by people living in an apartment. Damage or theft of personal property (clothing, furniture, stereo equipment, jewelry) is usually not covered by the landlord's insurance policy.

Sheet 22 Renting versus Buying Housing
Sheet 23 Apartment Rental Comparison

PRACTICE QUIZ 7–1

1. What are the main benefits and drawbacks of renting a place of residence?

2. Which components of a lease are likely to be most negotiable?

3. For the following situations, would you recommend that the person rent or buy housing? (Circle your answer.)

    a. A person who desires to reduce income taxes paid   rent   buy

    b. A person who expects to be transferred for work soon   rent   buy

    c. A person with few assets for housing expenses   rent   buy

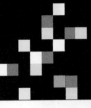

Money

Where do you plan to live during the next three to five years? If you're not sure, you should probably rent. If you plan to be in the same area for several years, you might buy a home. This is one of many personal financial decisions with which **Money.com** can help guide you.

An action to determine if you qualify for a mortgage is to estimate monthly housing costs—including mortgage payment, insurance, property taxes, and maintenance. Compare this amount to your current rent, then set aside the difference for a few months. If you are able to regularly cover those costs, buying may be an option for you. That additional money you set aside can go toward a down payment.

Consider other aspects of home ownership, such as increased *home equity,* which is the difference between a home's value and the mortgage amount owed. However, do not view your home purchase as an investment since housing prices can fluctuate greatly in a geographic area due to changing economic conditions. Owning a home also has the benefits of location stability and freedom to decorate and remodel.

Recent tax laws changed the financial benefits of home ownership for many Americans. A higher standard deduction along with limits on deducting property taxes and mortgage interest reduced the tax advantages. As a result, renting may be financially more attractive for some.

When evaluating and selecting rental units, compare costs in a location with the average rents to avoid overpaying. Consider the cost of utilities, convenience of public transportation, and the walkability of the city to save on travel expenses. Apartment selection might also be influenced by the availability of a dishwasher, washer and dryer, pool, fitness center, parking garage, and if pets are allowed.

ACTION STEPS FOR. . .

. . .Information Literacy

At **money.com**, locate a rent-versus-buy calculator and a mortgage payment calculator. Describe how these tools might be used when deciding on a place to live.

. . .Financial Literacy

Select a "home buying" article at **money.com**. Prepare a visual (photo, poster) or brief video that reflects one or more actions you might take from the article.

. . .Digital Literacy

Based on an article you select from **money.com** and comments from friends and relatives, prepare a summary of the information obtained that might be posted as a blog entry to help others.

LO7.2

Implement the home-buying process.

Home-Buying Activities

Many people desire a place of residence they can call their own. Home ownership is a common financial goal. Exhibit 7–4 presents the process for achieving this goal.

Step 1: Determine Home Ownership Needs

As a starting point, consider the benefits and drawbacks of this major financial commitment. Also, evaluate the types of housing units and determine the amount you can afford.

ACTION ITEM

The best housing purchase for me would be:

☐ a house.

☐ a condo or townhouse.

☐ a mobile home.

EVALUATE HOME OWNERSHIP Stability of residence and a personalized living location are important motives of many home buyers. A major financial benefit of home buying is that mortgage interest and real estate may be deducted on your federal income taxes.

A disadvantage of home ownership is financial uncertainty. Obtaining money for a down payment and securing mortgage financing may be a concern. Changing property values can affect your financial investment. Home ownership does not provide the ease of changing living location that renting does. If changes in your situation necessitate selling your home, doing so may take time.

Owning your place of residence can be expensive. The homeowner is responsible for maintenance and costs of repainting, repairs, and home improvements. Real estate taxes

Exhibit **7–4** The Home-Buying Process

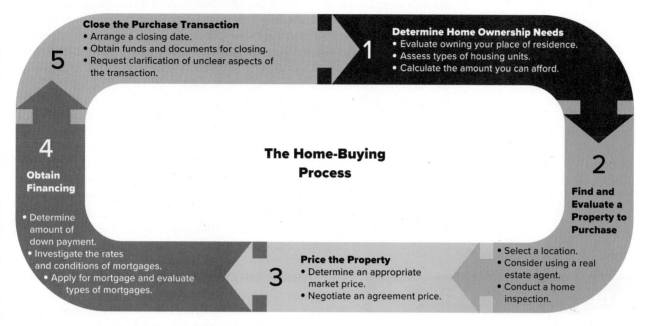

Close the Purchase Transaction
5
- Arrange a closing date.
- Obtain funds and documents for closing.
- Request clarification of unclear aspects of the transaction.

Determine Home Ownership Needs
1
- Evaluate owning your place of residence.
- Assess types of housing units.
- Calculate the amount you can afford.

4
Obtain Financing
- Determine amount of down payment.
- Investigate the rates and conditions of mortgages.
- Apply for mortgage and evaluate types of mortgages.

The Home-Buying Process

2
Find and Evaluate a Property to Purchase

Price the Property
3
- Determine an appropriate market price.
- Negotiate an agreement price.

- Select a location.
- Consider using a real estate agent.
- Conduct a home inspection.

are a major expense of homeowners. Higher property values and increased tax rates mean higher real estate taxes.

TYPES OF HOUSING AVAILABLE Home buyers generally choose from these options:

1. *Single-family dwellings* include previously owned houses, new houses, and custom-built houses. Older houses may be preferred by people who want a certain style and quality of housing. Modern homes offer a more contemporary style and features. A *townhouse* is a single family home, often in rows of similar style, sharing one or more walls with other units. A homeowners association manages and maintains the common areas of the community.

2. *Multiunit dwellings* are dwellings with more than one living unit. A *duplex* is a building with two separate housing units. A multiunit dwelling might also include a two- or three-unit building with the owner living in one unit and renting out the others.

3. **Condominiums** are individually owned housing units in a building. Ownership does not include *common areas,* such as hallways, outside grounds, and recreational facilities. These areas are owned by the condominium association, run by the owners of housing units. The condominium association oversees the management and operation of the housing complex. Condominium owners are charged a monthly fee to cover the maintenance, repairs, improvements, and insurance for the building and common areas. A condominium is a legal form of home ownership.

    condominium An individually owned housing unit in a building with several such units.

4. **Cooperative housing** is a form of housing in which the units in a building are owned by a nonprofit organization. The shareholders purchase stock to obtain the right to live in a housing unit. While the residents do not own the units, they have the legal right to occupy a unit for as long as they own stock in the cooperative association. The title for the property belongs to the co-op. This ownership arrangement is different from condominiums, in which residents own their individual living units.

    cooperative housing A form of housing in which a building containing a number of housing units is owned by a nonprofit organization whose members rent the units.

5. *Factory-built houses* are living units that are fully or partially assembled in a factory and then moved to the living site. A *prefabricated home,* with components built in a factory, is then assembled at the housing site, which can keep building costs lower. A *modular home* has completed pieces transported and set on a concrete foundation. *Mobile homes,* legally referred to as *manufactured homes,* are not often moved from their original sites. These housing units, which are typically less than 1,000 square feet, can offer features of a conventional house, such as fully equipped kitchens, fireplaces, cathedral ceilings, and whirlpool baths. The site for a manufactured home may be either purchased or leased. Due to their tendency to quickly depreciate in value, obtaining financing for manufactured homes may be difficult.

6. *Building a home* is for people who want certain specifications. Before starting such a project, be sure you possess the necessary knowledge, money, and perseverance. When choosing a contractor to coordinate the project, consider (*a*) the contractor's experience and reputation; (*b*) the contractor's relationship with the architect, materials suppliers, electricians, plumbers, carpenters, and other personnel; and (*c*) payment arrangements during construction. Your written contract should include a time schedule, cost estimates, a description of the work, and a payment schedule.

money minute focus

When buying a home, plan for additional costs. Create a budget and consult with others. Determine amounts for closing costs, moving expenses, property taxes, insurance, utilities, and repairs. These actions can result in purchasing the home that best fits your budget and lifestyle. Once approved for a mortgage, do not make any significant financial transactions before closing. Obtaining a car loan or making a major credit card purchase can affect your loan qualification.

DETERMINE WHAT YOU CAN AFFORD The amount you spend on housing is affected by funds available for a down payment, your income, and your current living expenses. Other factors you should consider are current mortgage rates, the potential future value of the property, and your ability to make monthly payments. To determine how much of a house you can afford, contact a mortgage company or other financial institution to *prequalify* you. This service is provided without charge.

You may not get all the features you want in your first home, but financial advisors suggest getting into the housing market by purchasing what you can afford. As you move up in the housing market, your second or third home can include more features.

While the home you buy should be in good condition, you may decide to buy a *fixer-upper*—a home that needs work and with a lower price. You will then need to put more money into the house for repairs and improvements, perhaps doing some of the work yourself.

WHAT WOULD YOU DO? Some people consider buying a home that may require major repairs or other improvements. Before going in that direction, how would you research the situation and estimate costs? Identify online sources and apps that might be of assistance when assessing a home that requires repairs and improvements.

Step 2: Find and Evaluate a Home

Next, select a location, consider using the services of a real estate agent, and conduct a home inspection.

SELECT A LOCATION Location is considered the most important factor when buying a home. You may prefer an urban, a suburban, or a rural setting. Or perhaps you want to live in a small town or in a resort area. Be aware of **zoning laws**, restrictions on how the property in an area can be used. The location of businesses and future construction projects may influence your decision. A homeowners association may also have restrictions.

If you have a family, assess the school system. Educators recommend that schools be evaluated based on program quality, student achievement level, percentage of students who

zoning laws Restrictions on how the property in an area can be used.

go to college, dedication of the teachers, facilities, school funding, and parent involvement. Homeowners without children also benefit from strong schools, since the educational quality in a community helps maintain property values.

SERVICES OF REAL ESTATE AGENTS Real estate agents have information about housing in locations of interest to you. Their main services include (1) showing you homes based on your needs and your pre-approved mortgage amount; (2) presenting your offer to the seller based on a market analysis; (3) negotiating a purchase price; (4) assisting you in obtaining financing; and (5) representing you at the closing. A real estate agent may also recommend lawyers, insurance agents, home inspectors, and mortgage companies.

Since the home seller usually pays the commission, a buyer may not incur a direct cost. However, this expense is reflected in the price paid for the home. In some states, the agent could be working for the seller. In others, the agent may be working for the buyer, the seller, or as a *dual agent,* working for both the buyer and the seller. When dual agency exists, some states require that buyers sign a disclosure acknowledging that they are aware the agent is working for both buyer and seller. This agreement can limit the information provided to each party. Many states have *buyer agents* who represent the buyer's interests and are paid by either the seller or the buyer.

THE HOME INSPECTION An evaluation by a trained home inspector can minimize future problems. Being cautious will save you headaches and unplanned expenses. Exhibit 7–5 presents a guideline for inspecting a home. Some states, cities, and lenders require inspection documents for pests, radon, or mold. The mortgage company will

Exhibit **7–5** **Conducting a Home Inspection**

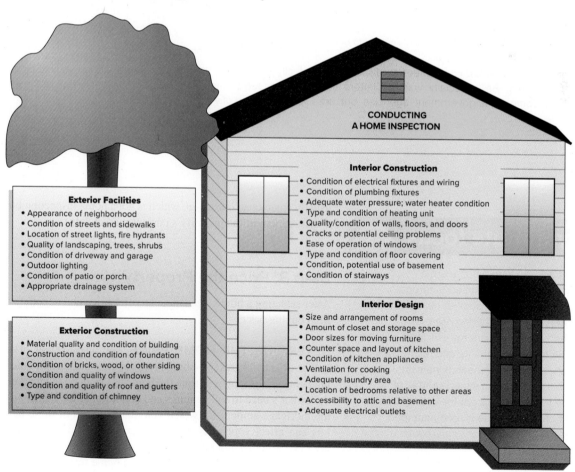

CONDUCTING A HOME INSPECTION

Exterior Facilities
- Appearance of neighborhood
- Condition of streets and sidewalks
- Location of street lights, fire hydrants
- Quality of landscaping, trees, shrubs
- Condition of driveway and garage
- Outdoor lighting
- Condition of patio or porch
- Appropriate drainage system

Exterior Construction
- Material quality and condition of building
- Construction and condition of foundation
- Condition of bricks, wood, or other siding
- Condition and quality of windows
- Condition and quality of roof and gutters
- Type and condition of chimney

Interior Construction
- Condition of electrical fixtures and wiring
- Condition of plumbing fixtures
- Adequate water pressure; water heater condition
- Type and condition of heating unit
- Quality/condition of walls, floors, and doors
- Cracks or potential ceiling problems
- Ease of operation of windows
- Type and condition of floor covering
- Condition, potential use of basement
- Condition of stairways

Interior Design
- Size and arrangement of rooms
- Amount of closet and storage space
- Door sizes for moving furniture
- Counter space and layout of kitchen
- Condition of kitchen appliances
- Ventilation for cooking
- Adequate laundry area
- Location of bedrooms relative to other areas
- Accessibility to attic and basement
- Adequate electrical outlets

Lowering Your Property Taxes

Property taxes vary from area to area and usually range from 2 to 4 percent of the market value of the home. Taxes are based on the *assessed value,* the amount that your local government determines your property to be worth for tax purposes. Assessed values normally are lower than the market value, often by about half. A home with a market value of $180,000 may be assessed at $90,000. If the tax rate is $60 per $1,000 of assessed value, this would result in annual taxes of $5,400 ($90,000 divided by $1,000 times $60). This rate is 6 percent of the assessed value but only 3 percent of the market value.

Although higher home values are desirable, this increase means higher property assessments. Quickly increasing property taxes are frustrating, but there are actions you can take:

Suggested Action	Your Action
Step 1: Know the appeal deadline. Call the local assessor's office. You will usually have between 14 and 60 days to initiate your appeal. Late requests are usually not accepted. Submit your appeal online or by certified mail to have proof that you met the deadline; keep copies of all documents.	
Step 2: Check for mistakes. The assessment office may have incorrect information. Obvious mistakes may include incorrect square footage, or an assessment may report a home with four bedrooms when there are only three.	
Step 3: Determine the issues to emphasize. A property tax appeal can be based on a mistake in the assessment or a higher assessment than comparable homes. Note items that negatively affect the value of your home. For example, a bridge is no longer in operation near your home, making your house much less accessible—and less valuable. Or if a garage has been taken down to increase garden space, the home's value likely would be lower. Compare your assessment with homes of the same size, age, and general location. Obtain comparisons for 5 to 10 homes.	
Step 4: Prepare for the hearing. Gather your evidence and prepare an organized presentation, which may be in person or online. Use photos of comparable properties. A spreadsheet can make it easy for the hearing officials to view your evidence. Suggest a specific corrected assessment, and give your reasons. Observe the hearing of another person's appeal to become familiar with the process.	

Beware of companies that charge fees to dispute your property assessment. Be especially wary of letters that look like they come from government agencies but are really from private companies. Avoid offers that require an up-front fee to challenge your assessment or that request a certified copy of your property deed.

money minute focus

Upgrades that add value to a home are a second-story addition, a remodeled bathroom with directional and "rainfall" shower heads, an updated kitchen, an outdoor living area, hardwood floors, a finished basement, energy-efficient appliances, windows and lighting, and technology-enhanced features. Recent research indicates that most rooms painted with varied shades of blue add value to a home, except the dining room, for which light brown or beige is recommended. Red, white, yellow, and pink walls can reduce a home's value.

usually conduct an *appraisal,* which is not a home inspection but an assessment of the property's current market value.

Step 3: Price the Property

After selecting a home, determine an offer price and negotiate a final buying price.

DETERMINE THE HOME PRICE The amount you offer will be affected by recent selling prices in the area, current housing demand, the length of time the home has been on the market, the owner's need to sell, features and condition of the home, and the mortgage amount for which you qualify. Each of these factors can affect your offer price. For example, you will probably offer a higher price in times of low interest rates and high demand for homes. On the other hand, a home that has been on the market for over a year could mean offering a lower price. Your bid will be in the form of a *purchase agreement,* or contract, which is your legal offer to purchase the home.

NEGOTIATE THE PURCHASE PRICE If your initial offer is accepted and signed, you have a valid contract. If your offer is rejected, you have several options. A *counteroffer* from the owner indicates a willingness to negotiate a price. If the counteroffer is only slightly lower than the asking price, you are expected to move closer to that price with your next offer. If the counteroffer is well below the asking price, you are closer to arriving at the purchase price. If no counteroffer is forthcoming, make another offer to see whether the seller is willing to negotiate. Negotiations may involve things other than price, such as closing date or inclusion of existing items, such as appliances.

As part of the offer, the buyer will often present **earnest money**, a portion of the purchase price deposited as evidence of good faith. At the closing of the home purchase, the earnest money is applied toward the down payment. This money is returned if the sale cannot be completed due to circumstances beyond the buyer's control.

Home purchase agreements may contain a *contingency clause,* stating the agreement is binding only if a certain event occurs. For example, the contract may be valid only if the buyer obtains financing for the home purchase within a certain time period, or it may make the purchase of a home contingent on the sale of the buyer's current home.

As a homeowner, you will be responsible for paying property taxes. The *Financial Literacy in Practice* feature offers guidance on actions to take if your property taxes rise to a level you believe to be inappropriate.

> **earnest money** A portion of the price of a home that the buyer deposits as evidence of good faith to indicate a serious purchase offer.

PRACTICE QUIZ 7–2

1. What are the advantages and disadvantages of owning a home?

2. What guidelines can be used to determine the amount to spend for a home purchase?

3. How can the quality of a school system benefit even homeowners in a community who do not have school-age children?

The Finances of Home Buying

When looking for a place to buy, also consider your financing options. Most home buyers will meet with a banker or mortgage broker early in the process to determine the home they can afford. Financing a home purchase requires obtaining a mortgage, having an awareness of types of mortgages, and settling the real estate transaction.

Step 4: Obtain Financing

THE DOWN PAYMENT The amount available for a down payment affects the size of the mortgage you can afford. If you make a large down payment, such as 20 percent or more, you will probably obtain a mortgage fairly easily. Personal savings, sales of investments or other assets, and assistance from relatives are common down payment sources. Parents can help children purchase a home. When accepting funds, be sure to assess the current and future financial impact for all family members, and evaluate the tax situation and costs. Consider other sources and possibilities, such as making it a loan rather than a gift; also investigate government or private programs available to lower-income or first-time home buyers.

LO7.3

Determine costs associated with purchasing a home.

ACTION ITEM

The type of mortgage I would likely use is:

☐ fixed-rate mortgage.

☐ interest-only mortgage.

☐ FHA or VA mortgage.

CAUTION!

A real estate "short sale" occurs when the new selling price is less than the amount owed on the previous mortgage. This alternative to foreclosure can result in a "bargain" for a home buyer. However, beware that it may take a long time before the lender accepts the offer, if the offer is accepted at all. Also, the home is usually sold "as is," which means some items expected to be in the home may be missing or damaged. When doing a short sale, be sure to use a lawyer and a negotiator, and obtain a release from any deficiencies for previous loan amounts.

mortgage A long-term loan on a specific piece of property such as a home or other real estate.

Private mortgage insurance (PMI) is usually required if the down payment is less than 20 percent. This coverage protects the lender from financial loss due to default. After building up 20 percent equity in a home, a home buyer should contact the lender to cancel PMI. The Homeowners Protection Act requires that a PMI policy be terminated automatically when the equity reaches 22 percent of the property value at the time the mortgage was executed. Homeowners can request termination earlier if they can prove the equity in the home is at least 22 percent of the current market value. FHA and VA mortgage loans, discussed later, have special provisions for mortgage insurance.

THE MORTGAGE   A **mortgage** is a long-term loan on a specific piece of property such as a home or other real estate. Payments on a mortgage are usually made over a time period ranging from 10 to 30 years. Applying for a mortgage involves these steps:

1. Complete the mortgage application and meet with the lender to present evidence of employment, income, ownership of assets, and existing debt amounts. Self-employed applicants should provide detailed evidence of income amounts, along with proof of savings to show financial stability.
2. The lender obtains a credit report, and verifies your application and financial status.
3. The mortgage is either approved or denied, with the decision based on your financial history and an evaluation of the home you want to buy.

With a credit score of at least 620, a person will usually be able to obtain home financing. The higher the credit score, the lower the mortgage rate with the same loan amount and down payment. To ensure your creditworthiness for a home loan, pay down your credit cards, make payments on time to existing loans, and obtain funds for a down payment. These actions will increase your ability to qualify for a mortgage.

The Ability-to-Repay (ATR)/Qualified Mortgage (QM) rule requires lenders to carefully consider a borrower's financial situation before granting a mortgage. ATR expects lenders to make a "reasonable and good faith determination" of repayment ability based on income, assets, employment status, liabilities, credit history, and debt-to-income (DTI) ratio. QM limits points and fees, prohibits or restricts certain mortgage features, and imposes a maximum on a borrower's DTI ratio. A concern with ATR/QM is balancing protection of borrowers from exploitive lending practices with maintaining access to mortgage credit for those who desire a home loan.

WHAT WOULD YOU DO?   As you apply for your first mortgage, you encounter an initial rejection due to your limited credit record. What actions might be appropriate for you to take to receive an approval for your mortgage?

As shown in Exhibit 7–6, the major factors that affect mortgage affordability are your income, other debts, the down payment amount, loan length, and current mortgage rates. The results of this calculation are (*a*) the monthly mortgage payment you can afford, (*b*) the mortgage amount you can afford, and (*c*) the home purchase price you can afford.

These sample calculations are typical of many financial institutions. The actual qualifications for a mortgage will vary by lender and type of mortgage. The *loan commitment* is the financial institution's decision to provide the funds needed to purchase a specific home. An approved mortgage application usually locks in an interest rate for 30 to 90 days.

Exhibit **7–6** **Housing Affordability and Mortgage Qualification Amount**

	Example A	Example B
Step 1: Determine your monthly gross income (annual income divided by 12).	$48,000 ÷ 12	$48,000 ÷ 12
Step 2: With a down payment of at least 5 percent, lenders use 33 percent of monthly gross income as a guideline for PITI (principal, interest, taxes, and insurance) and 38 percent of monthly gross income as a guideline for PITI plus other debt payments.	$ 4,000 × 0.38 $ 1,520	$ 4,000 × 0.33 $ 1,320
Step 3: Subtract other debt payments (e.g., payments on an auto loan) and an estimate of the monthly costs of property taxes and homeowner's insurance.	−380 −300	— −300
(a) Affordable monthly mortgage payment	$ 840	$ 1,020
Step 4: Divide this amount by the monthly mortgage payment per $1,000 based on current mortgage rates—an 5 percent, 30-year loan, for example (see Exhibit 7–7)—and multiply by $1,000.	÷ $ 5.37 × $ 1,000	÷ $ 5.37 × $ 1,000
(b) Affordable mortgage amount	$156,425	$189,944
Step 5: Divide your affordable mortgage amount by 1 minus the fractional portion of your down payment (e.g., 1 − 0.1 with a 10 percent down payment).	÷ 0.9	÷ 0.9
(c) Affordable home purchase price	$173,805	$211,049

NOTE: The two ratios lending institutions use (step 2) and other loan requirements may vary based on a variety of factors, including the type of mortgage, the amount of the down payment, your income level, credit score, and current interest rates. For example, with a down payment of 10 percent or more and a credit score exceeding 720, the ratios might increase to 40/45 percent in this exhibit.

The mortgage loan amount for which you qualify is larger when interest rates are low than when rates are high. For example, a person who can afford a monthly mortgage payment of $700 will qualify for a 30-year loan of:

$165,877 at 3 percent $116,667 at 6 percent
$146,750 at 4 percent $105,263 at 7 percent
$130,354 at 5 percent $95,368 at 8 percent

As interest rates rise, fewer people are able to afford the cost of an average-priced home.

EXAMPLE: Calculate Mortgage Payment

To determine the amount of your monthly mortgage payment, multiply the factor from Exhibit 7–7 by the number of thousands of the loan amount. For a 30-year, 5.5 percent, $223,000 mortgage:

Monthly payment amount = 223 × $5.68
                       = $1,266.64

In addition to a calculation using the mortgage payment factors from Exhibit 7–7, the monthly payment may be determined using a formula, a financial calculator, Excel spreadsheet, website, or app. Based the previous example, loan payment amounts may be determined using these methods:

Exhibit 7–7

Mortgage Payment Factors (principal and interest factors per $1,000 of loan amount)

Term Rate	30 Years	25 Years	20 Years	15 Years
3.0%	$4.22	$4.74	$5.55	$6.91
3.5	4.49	5.01	5.80	7.15
4.0	4.77	5.28	6.06	7.40
4.5	5.07	5.56	6.33	7.65
5.0	5.37	5.85	6.60	7.91
5.5	5.68	6.14	6.88	8.17
6.0	6.00	6.44	7.16	8.44
6.5	6.32	6.75	7.46	8.71
7.0	6.65	7.07	7.75	8.99
7.5	6.99	7.39	8.06	9.27
8.0	7.34	7.72	8.36	9.56

Formula	Financial Calculator	Excel
$M = P[i(1 + i)n]/[(1 + i)n - 1]$	(payments per year) 12 P/YR	= PMT(rate/12,30*12,loan amount)
M = mortgage payment (monthly)	(total loan payments) 360 N	= denotes a formula
P = principal of the loan (loan amount)	(interest rate) 5.5 I/YR	rate/12 provides monthly rate (.055/12)
i = interest rate divided by 12	(loan amount) 223,000 PV	total number of payments, such as 12 per year for 30 years
n = number of months of the loan	(calculate monthly payment) PMT	loan amount (beginning mortgage balance – $223,000)
223000[.055(1 + 0.55)360]/[(1 + .055)360 – 1] = $1,266.17 Monthly loan payment is $1,266.17	Monthly loan payment is $1,266.17	Monthly loan payment is $1,266.17

points Prepaid interest charged by the lender.

When comparing mortgage companies, consider other factors than just the interest rate. The down payment and the points charged will affect the interest rate. **Points** are prepaid interest charged by the lender. Each *discount point* is equal to 1 percent of the loan amount and is a premium paid for obtaining a lower mortgage rate. In deciding whether to take a lower rate with more points or a higher rate with fewer points, consider the following guidelines:

- If you plan to live in the home for a period of time (over five years, for example), the lower mortgage rate is probably the best action.
- If you plan to sell the home in the next few years, the higher mortgage rate with fewer discount points may be better.

Online research may be used to compare current mortgage rates, and most lending institutions allow you to apply for a mortgage online. The three main types of mortgage lenders are: (1) retail banks; (2) correspondent lenders, also called independent mortgage banks, include recent start-ups such as LoanDepot and SoFi; and (3) mortgage wholesalers and brokers.

FIXED-RATE, FIXED-PAYMENT MORTGAGES As Exhibit 7–8 shows, fixed-rate, fixed-payment mortgages are a major type of mortgage. This *conventional mortgage* usually has equal payments over 15, 20, or 30 years based on a fixed interest rate. Mortgage

Loan Type	Benefits	Drawbacks
1. Conventional 30-year mortgage	• Fixed monthly payments for 30 years provide certainty of principal and interest payments.	• Higher initial rates than adjustables.
2. Conventional 15- or 20-year mortgage	• Lower rate than 30-year fixed; faster equity buildup and quicker payoff of loan.	• Higher monthly payments.
3. FHA/VA fixed-rate mortgage (30-year and 15-year)	• Low down payment requirements and may be assumable with no prepayment penalties.	• May require additional processing time.
4. Adjustable-rate mortgage (ARM)—payment changes on 1-, 3-, 5-, 7-, or 10-year schedules	• Lower initial rates than fixed-rate loans, particularly on the 1-year adjustable. Offers possibility of future rate and payment decreases. Loans with rate "caps" may protect borrowers against increases in rates.	• Shifts far greater interest rate risk onto borrowers than fixed-rate loans. May push up monthly payments in future years.
5. Interest-only mortgage	• Lower payments; more easily affordable.	• No decrease in amount owed; no building equity unless home value increases; usually must convert to a higher fixed-rate mortgage after 10 years.

Exhibit **7–8**

Types of Mortgages

payments are set to allow **amortization** of the loan; that is, the balance owed is reduced with each payment. Since the amount borrowed is large, the payments made during the early years of the mortgage are applied mainly to interest, with only small reductions in the loan principal. As the amount owed declines, the monthly payments have an increasing impact on the loan balance. Near the end of the mortgage term, almost all of each payment is applied to the balance.

amortization The reduction of a loan balance through payments made over a period of time.

For example, a $125,000, 30-year, 6 percent mortgage would have monthly payments of $749.44. The payments would be divided as follows:

	Interest		Principal	Remaining Balance	
For the first month	$625.00	($125,000 × 0.06 × 1/12)	$124.44	$124,875.56	($125,000 – $124.44)
For the second month	624.72	($124,875.56 × 0.10 × 1/12)	125.06	$124,750.50	($124,875.56 – $125.06)
For the 360th month	3.73		745.71	-0-	

In the past, many conventional mortgages were *assumable*. This feature allowed a new home buyer to continue with the seller's original lending agreement. Today, assumable mortgages are seldom available.

GOVERNMENT-GUARANTEED FINANCING PROGRAMS These include loans insured by the Federal Housing Authority (FHA) and loans guaranteed by the Veterans Administration (VA). These government agencies do not provide the mortgage money; rather, they help home buyers obtain low-interest, low-down-payment loans.

To qualify for an FHA-insured loan, a person must meet certain conditions related to the down payment and fees. Most low- and middle-income people can qualify for the FHA loan program. The VA-guaranteed loan program assists eligible armed services veterans with home purchases. As with the FHA program, the funds for VA loans come from a financial

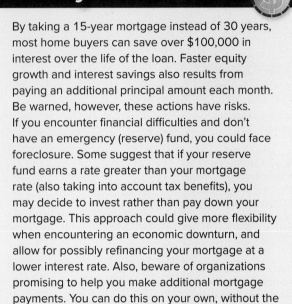

money minute focus

By taking a 15-year mortgage instead of 30 years, most home buyers can save over $100,000 in interest over the life of the loan. Faster equity growth and interest savings also results from paying an additional principal amount each month. Be warned, however, these actions have risks. If you encounter financial difficulties and don't have an emergency (reserve) fund, you could face foreclosure. Some suggest that if your reserve fund earns a rate greater than your mortgage rate (also taking into account tax benefits), you may decide to invest rather than pay down your mortgage. This approach could give more flexibility when encountering an economic downturn, and allow for possibly refinancing your mortgage at a lower interest rate. Also, beware of organizations promising to help you make additional mortgage payments. You can do this on your own, without the fee they will likely charge.

CAUTION!

Each year, billions of dollars are lost by home buyers due to e-mail hacking, identity theft, and wire transfer fraud related to home buying. Sensitive data is hacked, and the scammer assumes the identity of a representative of the mortgage or title company. Down payment funds are diverted to a fraudulent account. Con artists disguise their phone numbers to resemble those of legitimate businesses. To avoid this scam, verify that your real estate agent and lender have fraud-resistant procedures. Mobile connections, unsecured websites, call centers, and bank employees are some potential points of compromise.

institution or a mortgage company, with the risk reduced by government participation. A VA loan can be obtained without a down payment.

The U.S. Department of Agriculture (USDA) finances housing and community facilities in rural areas. USDA loan, grants, and loan guarantees are for single- and multifamily housing, and to buy and improve land.

ADJUSTABLE-RATE, VARIABLE-PAYMENT MORTGAGES

The **adjustable-rate mortgage (ARM)**, also referred to as a *flexible-rate mortgage* or a *variable-rate mortgage,* has an interest rate that increases or decreases during the life of the loan. ARMs usually have a lower initial interest rate than fixed-rate mortgages; however, the borrower, not the lender, bears the risk of future interest rate increases.

A *rate cap* restricts the amount by which the interest rate can increase or decrease during the ARM term. This limit prevents the borrower from having to pay an interest rate significantly higher than the original one. A *payment cap* keeps the payments on an adjustable-rate mortgage at a set level or limits the amount payments can rise. When mortgage payments do not rise but interest rates do, the amount owed can increase in months when the mortgage payment is less than the interest for that month. This increased loan balance, called *negative amortization,* means the amount of the home equity is decreasing instead of increasing.

Consider several factors when evaluating adjustable-rate mortgages: (1) determine the frequency of and restrictions on allowed interest rate changes; (2) consider the frequency of and restrictions on monthly payment changes; (3) investigate if the loan will be extended due to negative amortization, and determine the limit on the negative amortization amount; and (4) know the index used to set the mortgage interest rate.

INTEREST-ONLY MORTGAGE An *interest-only mortgage* allows a home buyer to have lower payments for the first few years of the loan. During that time, none of the mortgage payment goes toward the loan amount. Once the initial period ends, the mortgage adjusts to be interest-only at the new payment rate. Or a borrower may obtain a different type of mortgage to start building equity.

Remember, with an interest-only mortgage, higher payments will occur later in the loan. The new payment will be based on the amount of the original loan since no principal has been paid. Interest-only mortgages can be financially dangerous if the value of the property declines.

OTHER FINANCING METHODS A *buy-down* is an interest rate subsidy from a home builder, a real estate developer, or the borrower that reduces the mortgage payments during the first few years of the loan. This assistance is intended to stimulate sales among home buyers who cannot afford conventional financing. After the buy-down period, the mortgage payments increase to the level that would have existed without the financial assistance.

A *second mortgage,* more commonly called a *home equity loan,* allows a homeowner to borrow on the paid-up value of the property. Lending institutions offer a variety of home equity loans, including a line of credit program that allows the borrower to obtain additional funds. You need to be careful when using a home equity line of credit. This revolving credit plan can keep you continually in debt as you request new cash advances. The interest on a home equity loan may be tax deductible on your federal income tax return. A home equity loan creates the risk of losing the home if required payments on both the first and second mortgages are not made. To help prevent financial difficulties, home equity loans for more than 70 percent of your equity are not allowed in many states.

Reverse mortgages (also called *home equity conversion mortgages*) provide homeowners who are 62 or older with tax-free income in the form of a loan that is paid back (with interest) when the home is sold or the homeowner dies.

During the term of your mortgage, you may want to *refinance* your home, that is, obtain a new mortgage on your current home at a lower interest rate. Before taking this action, consider the refinancing costs in relation to the savings gained with a lower monthly payment.

money minute focus

Obtaining funds for a home purchase from parents can increase the amount of home you can afford. With *shared-equity financing,* parents or other relatives who provide part of the down payment share in the appreciation of the property. A contract among the parties should detail (a) who makes the mortgage payments and gets the tax deduction, (b) how much each person will pay of the real estate taxes, and (c) how and when the equity will be shared.

Step 5: Close the Purchase Transaction

Before you finalize the transaction, a *walk-through* allows you to inspect the condition of the home. Take photos or a video to collect evidence for any last-minute items you may need to negotiate.

The *closing* is a meeting of the buyer, seller, and lender of funds, or representatives of each party, to complete the transaction. Documents are signed, last-minute details are settled, and appropriate amounts are paid. Several expenses are incurred at the closing. The **closing costs,** also referred to as *settlement costs,* are the fees and charges paid when a real estate transaction is completed. Exhibit 7–9 presents the costs commonly associated with a closing. These expenses will vary based on the price of the house and your location, as other fees may be imposed by local regulations.

Title insurance has two phases. First, the title company conducts a survey to define the boundaries of the property and conducts a search to determine whether the property is free of claims, such as unpaid real estate taxes. Second, during the mortgage term, the title company protects the owner and lender against financial loss resulting from future defects in the title and from unforeseen property claims not excluded by the policy.

Also due at closing time is the deed recording fee. The **deed** is the document that transfers ownership of property from one party to another. With a *warranty deed,* the seller guarantees the title is good. This document certifies that the seller is the true owner of the property, there are no claims against the title, and the seller has the right to sell the property.

The Real Estate Settlement Procedures Act (RESPA) helps home buyers understand the closing process and settlement costs. This legislation requires that loan applicants be given an estimate of the closing costs three days before the closing. For information on RESPA and the "know before you owe" rule (with the technical label TRID) go to **www.consumerfinance.gov.**

At the closing and when you make your monthly payments, you will probably deposit money for home expenses. For example, the lender will require that you have property insurance. An **escrow account** is money, usually deposited with the lending institution, for the payment of property taxes and home insurance.

closing costs Fees and charges paid when a real estate transaction is completed; also called *settlement costs.*

title insurance Insurance that, during the mortgage term, protects the owner or the lender against financial loss resulting from future defects in the title and from other unforeseen property claims not excluded by the policy.

deed A document that transfers ownership of property from one party to another.

escrow account Money, usually deposited with the lending financial institution, for the payment of property taxes and homeowner's insurance.

Exhibit **7–9**

Common Closing Costs

At the transaction settlement of a real estate purchase and sale, the buyer and seller will encounter a variety of expenses that are commonly referred to as *closing costs*.

	COST RANGE ENCOUNTERED	
	By the Buyer	**By the Seller**
Title search fee	$150–$375	–
Title insurance(lender/owner policies)	$800–$1,800	$2000+
Attorney's fee	$400–$700	$50–$700
Property survey	–	$400–$500
Appraisal fee (or nonrefundable application fee)	$250–$300	–
Recording fees; transfer taxes	$95–$130	$15–$30
Settlement fee	$500–$1,000+	–
Wire transfer fee	$25–$100	
Lender's origination fee	1–3% of loan amount	–
Reserves for home insurance and property taxes	Varies	–
Interest paid in advance (from the closing date to the end of the month) and "points"	Varies	–
Real estate broker's commission	–	4–7% of purchase price

NOTE: The amounts paid by the buyer are in addition to the down payment.

As a new home buyer, you might also consider purchasing an agreement that gives you protection against defects in the home. *Implied warranties* created by state laws may cover some problem areas; other repair costs can occur. Home builders and real estate sales companies offer warranties to buyers. Coverage offered usually provides protection against structural, wiring, plumbing, heating, and other mechanical defects. Most home warranty programs have various limitations. Service contracts are also available to cover appliances, plumbing, air-conditioning and heating systems and other items. As with any service contract, decide whether the coverage provided and the chances of repair expenses justify the cost.

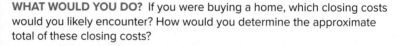

WHAT WOULD YOU DO? If you were buying a home, which closing costs would you likely encounter? How would you determine the approximate total of these closing costs?

Home Buying: A Summary

In recent years, the home buying process has become digital. Online mortgage prequalification, apps to compare mortgage rates, and completing a web-based mortgage application are common. Price negotiation involves e-mail and texts, and the online closing is conducted with the mortgage company sending the settlement documents electronically. Documents are "signed" on a formatted screen.

For most people, buying a home is the most expensive decision they will undertake. As a reminder, the *Financial Literacy in Practice* feature provides an overview of the major elements to consider when making this critical financial decision.

Financial Literacy in Practice

What Additional Home-Buying Information Do You Need?

For the following main aspects of home buying, list questions, additional information, or actions you might need to take. Locate websites or apps that provide information for these areas.

- **Location.** Consider the community and geographic region. In one area, $250,000 may be an average house, whereas elsewhere that may be expensive. Housing demand is largely affected by economic conditions and availability of jobs.

_____

- **Down payment.** A large down payment reduces mortgage payments. However, funds are also needed for closing costs, moving expenses, repairs, and furniture.

_____

- **Mortgage application.**
  You will likely be asked for recent tax returns, pay stubs, W–2 forms, a residence and employment history, bank account and investment balances, debt amounts, and evidence of auto and any real estate ownership.

_____

- **Points.**
  Compare a higher interest rate with no discount points with a lower rate requiring points paid at closing.

_____

- **Closing costs.**
  Settlement costs range from 2 to 6 percent of the loan. For a $100,000 mortgage, this could be $6,000; this amount is in addition to your down payment.

_____

- **PITI.**
  Your monthly payment for principal, interest, taxes, and insurance is a vital budget item. Beware of buying "too much house" and not having enough for other living expenses.

_____

- **Maintenance costs.**
  Owning a home can be expensive. Set aside funds for repairs and remodeling.

_____

Websites to consult:

_____

_____

Sheet 24 Housing Affordability and Mortgage Qualification

Sheet 25 Mortgage Company Comparison

PRACTICE QUIZ 7–3

1. What are the main sources of money for a down payment?

2. What factors affect a person's ability to qualify for a mortgage?

3. How do changing interest rates affect the amount of mortgage a person can afford?

4. Under what conditions might an adjustable-rate mortgage be appropriate?

5. For the following situations, select the type of home financing action that would be most appropriate:
   a. A mortgage for a person who desires to finance a home purchase at current interest rates for the entire term of the loan.
   b. A home buyer who wants to reduce the amount of monthly payments since interest rates have declined over the past year.
   c. A homeowner who wants to access funds that could be used to remodel the home.
   d. A person who served in the military and does not have money for a down payment.
   e. A retired person who wants to obtain income from the value of her home.

A Home-Selling Strategy

Studies reveal that early in the year, homes sell for 5 to 6 percent less than at other times since market prices are typically lowest in late December and January. The worst month to buy is June, but for sellers, that's the best time to be on the market. Most people who buy a home will eventually be on the other side. Selling your home requires preparing for sale, setting a price, and deciding whether to sell it yourself or use a real estate agent.

Preparing Your Home for Selling

The effective presentation of your home can result in a fast and financially favorable sale. Real estate salespeople recommend needed repairs and painting worn exterior and interior areas. Clear items from the garage and exterior areas, and keep the lawn cut and leaves raked. Maintain a clean kitchen and bathroom. Remove excess furniture, and dispose of unneeded items to make the house, closets, and storage areas look larger. When showing your home, open drapes and turn on lights. Use energy-saving light bulbs and water-saving faucets. These efforts give a positive image and make your home attractive to potential buyers.

ACTION ITEM

When selling a home, I would:

☐ **use a real estate agent.**

☐ **use an online service.**

☐ **sell by owner.**

Determining the Selling Price

appraisal An estimate of the current value of a property.

Putting a price on your home can be difficult. Too high of a price, and you risk not selling it quickly; or, you may not get a fair amount if the price is too low. An **appraisal**, an estimate of the current value of the property, can provide a good indication of the price you should set. An appraisal is likely to cost between $300 and $500. Also obtain a *market analysis* from a real estate agent to get a realistic property value. An asking price is influenced by recent selling prices of comparable homes in your area, demand in the housing market, and current mortgage rates.

Home improvements may or may not increase the selling price. A hot tub or exercise room may have no value for some potential buyers. Among the most desirable improvements are energy-efficient features, a remodeled kitchen, an additional or remodeled bathroom, added rooms and storage space, a finished basement, a fireplace, and an outdoor deck or patio. Daily maintenance, timely repairs, and home improvements will increase the future sales price of a home.

money minute focus

Tech-oriented companies called iBuyers will buy your home, usually in a few days. These quick sales usually come with a price lower than if you used a real estate agent. Also, a 7 to 9 percent service fee is likely. An iBuyer may require certain repairs before the sale is final. While iBuyers account for a very minor portion of home sales, the industry is growing with new companies entering the market.

Sale by Owner

Each year, about 10 percent of home sales are made by owners. If you sell your home without using a real estate agent, advertise in local newspapers and online, and create a detailed information sheet. Distribute the sheet at stores, in public areas, online, and by e-mail. When selling your home on your own, obtain information about the availability of financing and financing requirements. This information will help potential buyers determine whether they can afford the property. Use the services of a lawyer or title company to assist you with the contract, the closing, and other legal matters.

Require potential buyers to provide names, addresses, telephone numbers, and background information. Show your home only by appointment and only when two or more adults are home. Selling your own home can save several thousand dollars, but an investment of time and effort is required. Avoid selling at too low of a price by knowing the value and features of comparable homes.

WHAT WOULD YOU DO? You have been attempting to sell your home for several months without a serious offer to buy the property. What are some factors that might be limiting the market appeal of the home? How might you determine additional actions that could result in the sale of the home?

Listing with a Real Estate Agent

If you sell using a real estate agent, consider the person's knowledge of the community and the agent's efforts to market your home. A real estate agent will provide you with services that include a suggested listing price based on a market analysis, providing advice on features to highlight, hosting open houses, and coordinating showings to potential buyers. The agent will also help negotiate a selling price and guide you through the closing.

An agent's marketing materials include promotional materials such as brochures, flyers, and for-sale signs along with digital activities such as e-mail blasts and social media content. They also have contacts with real estate attorneys, repair companies, and other services that might be needed.

A real estate agent will screen potential buyers to determine whether they qualify for a mortgage. Discount real estate brokers are available to assist sellers who are willing to take on certain duties and want to reduce selling costs.

PRACTICE QUIZ 7–4

1. What actions are recommended when planning to sell your home?

2. What factors affect the selling price of a home?

3. What should you consider when deciding whether to sell your home on your own or use the services of a real estate agent?

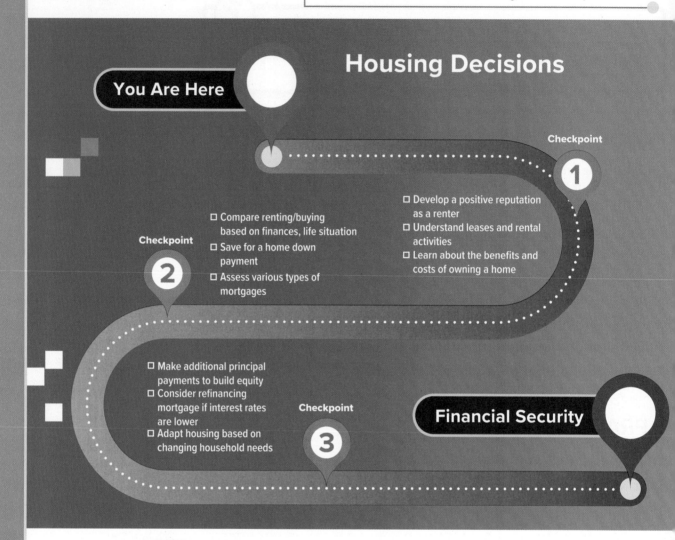

Housing Decisions

You Are Here

Checkpoint 1
- ☐ Develop a positive reputation as a renter
- ☐ Understand leases and rental activities
- ☐ Learn about the benefits and costs of owning a home

Checkpoint 2
- ☐ Compare renting/buying based on finances, life situation
- ☐ Save for a home down payment
- ☐ Assess various types of mortgages

Checkpoint 3
- ☐ Make additional principal payments to build equity
- ☐ Consider refinancing mortgage if interest rates are lower
- ☐ Adapt housing based on changing household needs

Financial Security

MORTGAGE EQUITY PERCENTAGE

your personal finance dashboard

Mortgage Equity Percentage

Home equity, the amount of your ownership, can be an indicator of financial progress. Equity is the current market value less the mortgage amount owed. A home worth $200,000 with an $80,000 mortgage would have equity of $120,000, or 60 percent of the home's value. Build equity through shorter mortgages and additional principal payments.

YOUR SITUATION: Do you make additional payments toward the loan principal to build equity? What budget items might be reduced to pay down your mortgage? Are there improvements you might make to increase the market value of your home?

LO7.1 Assess renting and buying alternatives in terms of their financial and opportunity costs. The main advantages of renting are mobility, fewer responsibilities, and lower initial costs. The main disadvantages of renting are few financial benefits, a restricted lifestyle, and legal concerns.

LO7.2 Home buying involves five major stages: (1) determining home ownership needs, (2) finding and evaluating a property to purchase, (3) pricing the property, (4) financing the purchase, and (5) closing the real estate transaction.

LO7.3 The costs associated with purchasing a home include the down payment; mortgage origination costs; closing costs such as a deed fee, prepaid interest, attorney's fees, payment for title insurance, and a property survey; and an escrow account for homeowner's insurance and property taxes.

LO7.4 When selling a home, you must decide whether to make certain repairs and improvements, determine a selling price, and choose between selling the home yourself and using the services of a real estate agent.

Chapter Summary

Key Terms

adjustable-rate mortgage (ARM) 265

amortization 265

appraisal 270

closing costs 267

condominium 257

cooperative housing 257

deed 267

earnest money 261

escrow account 267

lease 254

mortgage 262

points 264

title insurance 267

zoning laws 258

Self-Test Problems

1. What would be the monthly payment for a $180,000, 20-year mortgage at 6 percent?
2. What is the total amount of a 30-year mortgage with monthly payments of $850?

Solutions

1. Using Exhibit 7–7, multiply 180 times $7.16 to determine the monthly payment of $1,289.58.
2. 360 payments (30 years × 12 months) are multiplied by $850 for a total of $306,000.

Financial Planning Problems

1. Based on the following data, would you recommend buying or renting? (LO7.1)

Rental Costs	Buying Costs
Annual rent, $7,380	Annual mortgage payments, $9,800 ($9,575 is interest)
Insurance, $145	Property taxes, $1,780
Security deposit, $650	Down payment/closing costs, $4,500
	Growth in equity, $225
	Insurance/maintenance, $1,050
	Estimated annual appreciation, $1,700

Assume an after-tax savings interest rate of 6 percent and a tax rate of 28 percent. Assume this individual has other tax deductions that exceed the standard deduction amount.

2. Many locations require that renters be paid interest on their security deposits. If you have a security deposit of $1,800, how much interest would you expect to earn per year at 2 percent? (LO7.1)

3. Condominiums usually require a monthly fee for various services. At $235 a month, how much would a homeowner pay over a period of 10 years for living in this housing facility? (LO7.2)

4. Ben and Carla Covington plan to buy a condominium. They will obtain a $220,000, 30-year mortgage at 5 percent. Their annual property taxes are expected to be $1,800. Property insurance is $480 a year, and the condo association fee is $220 a month. Based on these items, determine the total monthly housing payment for the Covingtons. (LO7.2)

5. Estimate the affordable monthly mortgage payment, the affordable mortgage amount, and the affordable home purchase price for the following situation (see Exhibit 7–6). (LO7.3)

Monthly gross income, $2,950
Other debt (monthly payment), $160
30-year loan at 6 percent

Down payment to be made—15 percent of purchase price
Monthly estimate for property taxes and insurance, $210

6. Based on Exhibit 7–7, or use of a financial calculator, what would be the monthly mortgage payments for each of the following situations? (LO7.3)
   a. A $160,000,15-year loan at 4.5 percent.
   b. A $215,000, 30-year loan at 5 percent.
   c. A $190,000, 20-year loan at 6 percent.

7. Which mortgage would result in higher total payments? (LO7.3)
   Mortgage A: $985 a month for 30 years.
   Mortgage B: $780 a month for 5 years and $1,056 a month for 25 years.

8. If an adjustable-rate 30-year mortgage for $120,000 starts at 4.0 percent and increases to 5.5 percent, what is the increase in the monthly payment amount? (Use Exhibit 7–7.) (LO7.3)

9. Kelly and Tim Jarowski plan to refinance their mortgage to obtain a lower interest rate. They will reduce their mortgage payments by $56 a month. Their closing costs for refinancing will be $1,670. How long will it take them to cover the cost of refinancing? (LO7.3)

10. In an attempt to have funds for a down payment in five years, James Dupont plans to save $3,800 a year for the next five years. With an interest rate of 4 percent, what amount will James have available for a down payment after the five years? (LO7.3)

11. You estimate that you can save $3,450 by selling your home yourself rather than using a real estate agent. What would be the future value of that amount if invested for five years at 3 percent? (LO7.4)

 To reinforce the content in this chapter, more problems are provided at connect.mheducation.com.

FINANCIAL LITERACY PORTFOLIO

SELECTING A PLACE TO LIVE

Competency. . .

Comparing housing alternatives.

Action Research. . .

Using Figure It Out: Buying versus Renting Your Place of Residence in this chapter, *Your Personal Finance Plan Sheet 22,* online research, and visits to available housing, analyze an actual or hypothetical situation you might use when deciding if you would rent or buy a place to live.

Outcome. . .

Create a visual (PowerPoint presentation, video, storyboard, or other visual format) that reports the process you used, your findings, and your conclusion.

HOUSING DECISIONS

When Mark and Valerie Bowman first saw the house, they didn't like it. However, it was a dark, rainy day. They viewed the house more favorably on their second visit, which they thought would be a waste of time. Despite cracked ceilings, the need for new paint, and a kitchen built in the 1990s, the Bowmans saw a potential to create a place they could call their own.

Beth Young purchased her condominium several years ago. She obtained a mortgage rate of 6.5 percent, a very good rate then. Recently, when interest rates dropped, Beth was considering refinancing her mortgage at a lower rate.

Matt and Peggy Zoran had been married for five years and were still living in an apartment. Several of their friends had purchased homes recently. However, Matt and Peggy were not sure they wanted to follow this example. Although they liked their friends' homes and had viewed online videos of homes on the market, they also liked the freedom from maintenance responsibility they enjoyed as renters.

In today's economic and social environment, fewer young people (ages 22–37) are buying homes due to marrying at an older age, having children later in life, and high levels of student debt. Obstacles encountered by these home buyers include high home prices, limited money for a down payment, a poor credit history, and not having a stable income. Home features that younger home shoppers are willing to give up to live in their ideal neighborhood include a garage, an updated kitchen, storage space, a yard, and an updated bathroom.

Questions

1. How could the Bowmans benefit from buying a home that needs improvements?
2. How might Beth Young have found out when mortgage rates were at a level that would make refinancing her condominium more affordable?
3. Although the Zorans had good reasons for continuing to rent, what factors might make it desirable to buy a home?
4. Based on websites, apps, and other sources, what advice would you give young consumers (ages 22–37) about home buying?

SELECTING AND FINANCING HOUSING

Five years have passed and Jamie Lee, now 34, is considering taking the plunge: Not only is she engaged to be married, but she is also deciding whether to purchase a new home.

Jamie Lee's cupcake café is a success! It has been open over a year now and has earned rave reviews in the local press and from its regular customers, who just cannot get enough of her delicious cupcakes. One such customer, who stopped by on a whim in the café's first week of business, is Ross. After a whirlwind courtship, Ross, a self-employed web page designer, proposed and Jamie Lee accepted.

The bungalow that Jamie Lee has been renting for the past five years is too small for the soon-to-be newlyweds, so Jamie Lee and Ross are trying to decide if they should move to another rental or purchase a home of their own. They agreed to visit their local banker to get an idea of how much home they can afford with their combined incomes.

Current Financial Situation

Assets (Jamie Lee and Ross combined):
Checking account, $4,300
Savings account, $55,200

Emergency fund savings account, $19,100
IRA balance, $24,000

Cars, $12,000 (Jamie Lee) and $20,000 (Ross)

Liabilities *(Jamie Lee and Ross combined):*

Student loan balance, $0

Credit card balance, $0

Car loans, $8,000

Income:

Jamie Lee, $45,000 gross income ($31,500 net income after taxes)

Ross, $70,000 gross income ($59,000 net income after taxes)

Monthly Expenses *(Jamie Lee and Ross combined):*

Utilities, $160

Food, $325

Gas/Maintenance, $275

Credit card payment, $0

Car loan payment, $289

Entertainment, $300

Questions

1. Using *Your Personal Financial Plan Sheet 22,* compare the advantages and the disadvantages of renting a home or apartment to those of purchasing a home.
2. Jamie Lee and Ross are estimating that they will be putting $40,000 from their savings account toward a down payment on their home purchase. Using the traditional financial guideline suggestion of "two and a half times your salary plus your down payment," calculate approximately how much Jamie Lee and Ross can spend on a house.
3. Using *Your Personal Financial Plan Sheet 24,* calculate the affordable mortgage amount that would be suggested by a lending institution based on Jamie Lee and Ross's income. How does this amount compare with the traditional financial guideline found in question 2? Use the following amounts for Jamie Lee and Ross's calculations:
   - 10 percent down payment.
   - 28 percent for TIPI
   - $500.00 per month for estimated combined property taxes and insurance.
   - 5 percent interest rate for 30 years (see Exhibit 7–7).
4. Jamie Lee and Ross found a brand-new three-bedroom, 2½-bath home for sale in a quiet neighborhood. The listing price is $275,000. They placed a bid of $270,000 on the home. The seller's counteroffer was $273,000. What should Jamie Lee and Ross do next to demonstrate to the owner that they are serious buyers?
5. Jamie Lee and Ross accepted the seller's counteroffer of $273,000. The seller also agreed to pay two points toward Jamie Lee and Ross's mortgage. Calculate the benefit of having points paid toward the mortgage if Jamie Lee and Ross are putting a $40,000 down payment on the home.
6. Calculate Jamie Lee and Ross's mortgage payment, using the 5 percent rate for 30 years on the mortgage balance of $233,000.

Spending Diary

"AFTER I PAY MY RENT, UTILITIES, AND RENTER'S INSURANCE, I HAVE VERY LITTLE FOR OTHER EXPENSES."

Directions Your Daily Spending Diary will help you manage your housing expenses to create a better overall spending plan. As you record daily spending, your comments should reflect what you have learned about your spending patterns and help you consider possible changes you might want to make. The Daily Spending Diary sheets are located at the end of Chapter 1 and in Connect Finance.

Questions

1. What portion of your daily spending involves expenses associated with housing?
2. What types of housing expenses might be reduced with more careful spending habits?

Renting versus Buying Housing

Purpose: To compare the cost of renting or buying your place of residence.

Financial Planning Activities: Obtain estimates for comparable housing units for the data requested below. This sheet is also available in an Excel spreadsheet format in Connect Finance.

Suggested Websites: www.homefair.com, smartasset.com/mortgage/rent-vs-buy, www.nerdwallet.com/mortgages/rent-vs-buy-calculator

Rental Costs

Annual rent payments (monthly rent $_____ × 12) $_____

Renter's insurance $_____

Interest lost on security deposit (deposit times after-tax savings account interest rate) $_____

Total annual cost of renting $

Buying Costs

Annual mortgage payments $_____

Property taxes (annual costs) $_____

Homeowner's insurance (annual premium) $_____

Estimated maintenance and repairs $_____

After-tax interest lost because of down payment/closing costs $_____

Less: financial benefits of home ownership

Growth in equity $ –_____

Tax savings for mortgage interest (annual mortgage interest times tax rate) $ –_____

Tax savings for property taxes (annual property taxes times tax rate) $ –_____

Estimated annual appreciation $ –_____

Total annual cost of buying $

Suggested App:
• Realtor

McGraw Hill

What's Next for Your Personal Financial Plan?

• Determine if renting or buying is most appropriate at the current time.
• List some circumstances or actions that might change your housing needs.

YOUR PERSONAL FINANCIAL PLAN

Name: _____ Date: _____

Apartment Rental Comparison

Purpose: To evaluate and compare rental housing alternatives.

Financial Planning Activities: Obtain the information requested below to compare costs and facilities of three apartments. This sheet is also available in an Excel spreadsheet format in Connect Finance.

Suggested Websites: www.apartments.com, www.apartmentguide.com, www.thespruce.com/apartment-living-4127933

Name of rental company or person			
Address			
Phone/E-mail			
Monthly rent			
Amount of security deposit			
Length of lease			
Utilities included in rent			
Parking facilities			
Storage area in building			
Laundry facilities			
Distance to schools			
Distance to public transportation			
Distance to shopping			
Pool, recreation area, other facilities			
Estimated utility costs: • Electric • Cable/Internet • Gas • Water			
Other costs			
Other information			

$

Suggested App:
• PadMapper

McGraw Hill

What's Next for Your Personal Financial Plan?

• Which of these rental units would best serve your current housing needs?

• What additional information should be considered when renting an apartment?

Housing Affordability and Mortgage Qualification

Purpose: To estimate the amount of affordable mortgage payment, mortgage amount, and home purchase price.

Financial Planning Activities: Enter the amounts requested to estimate the amount of affordable mortgage payment, mortgage amount, and home purchase price. This sheet is also available in an Excel spreadsheet format in Connect Finance.

Suggested Websites: www.realestate.com, www.mba.org, mtgprofessor.com

Step 1

Determine your monthly gross income (annual income divided by 12). $ _____

Step 2

With a down payment of at least 10 percent, lenders use 28 percent of monthly gross income as a guideline for TIPI (taxes, insurance, principal, and interest), 36 percent of monthly gross income as a guideline for TIPI plus other debt payments (enter 0.28 or 0.36).   × _____

Step 3

Subtract other debt payments (such as payments on an auto loan), if applicable.   − _____

Subtract estimated monthly costs of property taxes and homeowner's insurance.   − _____

Affordable monthly mortgage payment . . . . $ _____

Step 4

Divide this amount by the monthly mortgage payment per $1,000 based on current mortgage rates (see Exhibit 7–7). For example, for an 8 percent, 30-year loan, the number would be $7.34.   ÷ _____

Multiply by $1,000.   × _____ $1,000 _____

Affordable mortgage amount . . . . $ _____

Step 5

Divide your affordable mortgage amount by 1 minus the fractional portion of your down payment (for example, 0.9 for a 10 percent down payment).   ÷ _____

Affordable home purchase price. . . . . $ _____

Note: The two ratios used by lending institutions (Step 2) and other loan requirements are likely to vary based on a variety of factors, including the type of mortgage, the amount of the down payment, your income level, your credit score, and current interest rates. If you have other debts, lenders will calculate both ratios and then use the one that allows you greater flexibility in borrowing.

Suggested App:
• Mortgage Calculator

McGraw Hill

What's Next for Your Personal Financial Plan?

* Identify actions you might need to take to qualify for a mortgage.
* Discuss your mortgage qualifications with a mortgage broker or other lender.

YOUR PERSONAL FINANCIAL PLAN

Mortgage Company Comparison

Purpose: To compare the services and costs for different home mortgage alternatives.

Financial Planning Activities: Using online research and other sources, obtain the information requested below to compare the services and costs for different home mortgage companies. This sheet is also available in an Excel spreadsheet format in Connect Finance.

Suggested Websites: www.hsh.com, www.eloan.com, www.bankrate.com, mtgprofessor.com

Amount of mortgage: $_____	Down payment: $_____	Years: _____
Company		
Address		
Phone		
Website		
Contact person/E-mail		
Application, credit report, and property appraisal fees		
Loan origination fee		
Other fees, charges (commitment, title, tax transfer)		
Fixed-rate mortgage		
Monthly payment		
Discount points		
Adjustable-rate mortgage		
• Time until first rate charge • Frequency of rate charge		
Monthly payment		
Discount points		
Payment cap		
Interest rate cap		
Rate index used		
Commitment period		
Other information		

Suggested App:
• Bankrate Mortgages

McGraw Hill

What's Next for Your Personal Financial Plan?

- What additional information should be considered when selecting a mortgage?
- Which of these mortgage companies would best serve your current and future needs?

8 Home and Automobile Insurance

3 Steps to Financial Literacy . . .
Percent of Personal Property Coverage

1 Prepare a household inventory with a description and the value of belongings, furniture, clothing, electronics, and other personal property.
App: III Inventory

2 Compare various insurance companies and levels of coverage to obtain home or renter's insurance for your life situation.
Website: www.iii.org

3 Determine if additional personal property coverage is needed based on the value of your household inventory.
Website: www.allstate.com

Each year homeowners and renters in the United States lose billions of dollars from more than 3.7 million burglaries, 1.5 million fires, and 250,000 cases of damage from other perils. A major portion of these claims is due to losses for personal property. At the end of the chapter, *Your Personal Finance Road Map and Dashboard* will provide guidelines for measuring the level of your personal property coverage.

Stefan Witas/E+/Getty Images

CHAPTER 8 LEARNING OBJECTIVES

In this chapter, you will learn to:

LO8.1 Identify types of risks and risk management methods, and develop a risk management plan.

LO8.2 Assess the insurance coverage and policy types available to homeowners and renters.

LO8.3 Analyze the factors that influence the amount of coverage and cost of home insurance.

LO8.4 Identify the important types of automobile insurance coverage.

LO8.5 Evaluate factors that affect the cost of automobile insurance.

YOUR PERSONAL FINANCIAL PLAN SHEETS

26. Current Insurance Policies and Needs
27. Home Inventory
28. Determining Needed Property Insurance
29. Apartment/Home Insurance Comparison
30. Automobile Insurance Cost Comparison

Insurance and Risk Management

In today's world of the "strange but true," you can get insurance for just about anything. You might purchase a policy to protect yourself in the event that you're abducted by aliens. Some insurance companies will offer you protection if you think that you have a risk of turning into a werewolf. If you're a fast runner, you might be able to get a discount on a life insurance policy. Some people buy wedding disaster insurance just in case something goes wrong on the big day. You may never need these types of insurance, but you'll certainly need insurance on your home, your vehicle, and your personal property. The more you know about insurance, the better able you will be to make decisions about buying it.

What Is Insurance?

Insurance is protection against possible financial loss. You can't predict the future. However, insurance allows you to be prepared for the worst. It provides protection against many risks, such as unexpected property loss, illness, and injury. Many kinds of insurance exist, and they all share some common characteristics. They give you peace of mind, and they protect you from financial loss when trouble strikes.

An **insurance company**, or **insurer**, is a risk-sharing business that agrees to pay for losses that may happen to someone it insures. A person joins the risk-sharing group by purchasing a contract known as a **policy**. The purchaser of the policy is called a **policyholder**. Under the policy, the insurance company agrees to take on the risk. In return, the policyholder pays the company a **premium**, or fee. The protection provided by the terms of

LO8.1

Identify types of risks and risk management methods and develop a risk management plan.

ACTION ITEM
Can you list several risk management methods?

☐ Yes ☐ No

insurance Protection against possible financial loss.

insurance company A risk-sharing firm that assumes financial responsibility for losses that may result from an insured risk.

insurer An insurance company.

policy A written contract for insurance.

policyholder A person who owns an insurance policy.

premium The amount of money a policyholder is charged for an insurance policy.

coverage The protection provided by the terms of an insurance policy.

insured A person covered by an insurance policy.

risk Chance or uncertainty of loss; also used to mean "the insured."

peril The cause of a possible loss.

hazard A factor that increases the likelihood of loss through some peril.

negligence Failure to take ordinary or reasonable care in a situation.

an insurance policy is known as **coverage**, and the people protected by the policy are known as the **insured**.

Types of Risk

You face risks every day. You can't cross the street without some danger that a motor vehicle might hit you. You can't own property without running the risk that it will be lost, stolen, damaged, or destroyed.

Risk, peril, and *hazard* are important terms in insurance. In everyday use, these terms have almost the same meanings. In the insurance business, however, each has a distinct meaning.

Risk is the chance of loss or injury. In insurance, it refers to the fact that no one can predict trouble. This means that an insurance company is taking a chance every time it issues a policy. Insurance companies frequently refer to the insured person or property as the risk.

Peril is anything that may possibly cause a loss. It's the reason someone takes out insurance. People buy policies for protection against a wide range of perils, including fire, windstorms, explosions, robbery, and accidents.

Hazard is anything that increases the likelihood of loss through some peril. For example, defective house wiring is a hazard that increases the chance that a fire will start.

The most common risks are personal risks, property risks, and liability risks. *Personal risks* involve loss of income or life due to illness, disability, old age, or unemployment. *Property risks* include losses to property caused by perils, such as fire or theft, and hazards. *Liability risks* involve losses caused by negligence that leads to injury or property damage. **Negligence** is the failure to take ordinary or reasonable care to prevent accidents from happening. If a homeowner doesn't clear the ice from the front steps of her house, for example, she creates a liability risk because visitors could fall on the ice.

Personal risks, property risks, and liability risks are types of *pure,* or *insurable, risk.* The insurance company will have to pay only if some event that the insurance covers actually happens. Pure risks are accidental and unintentional. Although no one can predict whether a pure risk will occur, it's possible to predict the costs that will accrue if one does.

A *speculative risk* is a risk that carries a chance of either loss or gain. Starting a small business that may or may not succeed is an example of speculative risk. Speculative risks are not insurable.

Risk Management Methods

Risk management is an organized plan for protecting yourself, your family, and your property. It helps reduce financial losses caused by destructive events. Risk management is a long-range planning process. Your risk management needs will change at various points in your life. If you understand how to manage risks, you can provide better protection for yourself and your family. Most people think of risk management as buying insurance. However, insurance is not the only way of dealing with risk. Four general risk management techniques are commonly used.

RISK AVOIDANCE You can avoid the risk of a traffic accident by not driving to work. A car manufacturer can avoid the risk of product failure by not introducing new cars. These are both examples of risk avoidance. They are ways to avoid risks, but they require serious trade-offs. You might have to give up your job if you can't get there. The car manufacturer might lose business to competitors who take the risk of producing exciting new cars.

In some cases, though, risk avoidance is practical. By taking precautions in high-crime areas, you might avoid the risk that you will be robbed.

RISK REDUCTION You can't avoid risks completely. However, you can decrease the likelihood that they will cause you harm. For example, you can reduce the risk of injury in an automobile accident by wearing a seat belt. You can reduce the risk of developing lung cancer by not smoking. By installing fire extinguishers in your home, you reduce the potential damage that could be caused by a fire. Your risk of illness might be lower if you eat properly and exercise regularly.

RISK ASSUMPTION Risk assumption means taking on responsibility for the negative results of a risk. It makes sense to assume a risk if you know that the possible loss will be small. It also makes sense when you've taken all the precautions you can to avoid or reduce the risk.

When insurance coverage for a particular item is expensive, that item may not be worth insuring. For instance, you might decide not to purchase collision insurance on an older car. If an accident happens, the car may be wrecked, but it wasn't worth much anyway. *Self-insurance* is setting up a special fund, perhaps from savings, to cover the cost of a loss. Self-insurance does not eliminate risks, but it does provide a way of covering losses as an alternative to an insurance policy. Some people self-insure because they can't obtain insurance from an insurance company.

RISK SHIFTING The most common method of dealing with risk is to shift it, which means to transfer it to an insurance company. In exchange for the fee you pay, the insurance company agrees to pay for your losses.

Most insurance policies include deductibles. Deductibles are a combination of risk assumption and risk shifting. A **deductible** is the set amount that the policyholder must pay per loss on an insurance policy. For example, if a falling tree damages your car, you may have to pay $200 toward the repairs. Your insurance company will pay the rest.

Exhibit 8–1 summarizes various risks and effective ways of managing them.

deductible The set amount that the policyholder must pay per loss on an insurance policy.

Exhibit 8–1 Examples of Risks and Risk Management Strategies

RISKS		STRATEGIES FOR REDUCING FINANCIAL IMPACT		
Personal Events	Financial Impact	Personal Resources	Private Sector	Public Sector
Disability	Loss of one's income Increased expenses	Savings, investments	Disability insurance	Disability insurance
Illness	Loss of one's income Catastrophic hospital expenses	Health-enhancing behavior	Health insurance Health maintenance organizations	Military health care Medicare, Medicaid
Death	Final expenses	Estate planning Risk reduction	Life insurance	Veteran's life insurance Social Security survivor's benefits
Retirement	Decreased income Unplanned living expenses	Savings Investments Hobbies, skills	Retirement and/or pensions	Social Security Pension plan for government employees
Property loss	Catastrophic storm damage to property Repair or replacement cost of theft	Property repair and upkeep Security plans	Automobile insurance Homeowner's insurance Flood insurance (joint program with government)	Flood insurance (joint program with business)
Liability	Claims and settlement costs Lawsuits and legal expenses Loss of personal assets and income	Observing safety precautions Maintaining property	Homeowner's insurance Automobile insurance Malpractice insurance	

Planning an Insurance Program

Your personal insurance program should change along with your needs and goals. Dave and Ellen are a young couple. How will they plan their insurance program to meet their needs and goals?

Exhibit 8–2 outlines the steps in developing a personal insurance program.

STEP 1: SET INSURANCE GOALS Dave and Ellen's main goal should be to minimize personal, property, and liability risks. They also need to decide how they will cover costs resulting from a potential loss. Income, age, family size, lifestyle, experience, and responsibilities will be important factors in the goals they set. The insurance they buy must reflect those goals. Dave and Ellen should try to come up with a basic risk management plan that achieves the following:

- Reduces possible loss of income caused by premature death, illness, accident, or unemployment.
- Reduces possible loss of property caused by perils, such as fire or theft, or hazards.
- Reduces possible loss of income, savings, and property because of personal negligence.

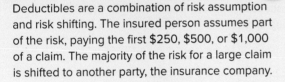

money minute focus

Deductibles are a combination of risk assumption and risk shifting. The insured person assumes part of the risk, paying the first $250, $500, or $1,000 of a claim. The majority of the risk for a large claim is shifted to another party, the insurance company.

STEP 2: DEVELOP A PLAN TO REACH YOUR GOALS
Planning is a way of taking control of life instead of just letting life happen to you. Dave and Ellen need to determine what risks they face and what risks they can afford to take. They also have to determine what resources can help them reduce the damage that could be caused by serious risks.

Furthermore, they need to know what kind of insurance is available. The cost of different kinds of insurance and the way the costs vary among companies will be the key factors in their plan. Finally, this couple needs to research the reliability record of different insurance companies.

Dave and Ellen must ask four questions as they develop their risk management plan:

- What do they need to insure?
- How much should they insure it for?
- What kind of insurance should they buy?
- Whom should they buy insurance from?

STEP 3: PUT YOUR PLAN INTO ACTION Once they've developed their plan, Dave and Ellen need to follow through by putting it into action. During this process, they might discover that they don't have enough insurance protection. If that's the case, they could

Exhibit **8–2**

Creating a Personal Insurance Program

4 Check Your Results   **1** Set Insurance Goals

Your Insurance Plan

3 Put Your Plan into Action   **2** Develop a Plan to Reach Your Goals

How Can You Plan an Insurance Program?

Did you:	Yes	No
• Seek advice from a competent and reliable insurance advisor?	☐	☐
• Determine what insurance you need to provide your family with sufficient protection if you die?	☐	☐
• Consider what portion of the family protection is met by Social Security and what portion by group insurance?	☐	☐
• Decide what other needs insurance must meet (funeral expenses, savings, retirement annuities, etc.)?	☐	☐
• Decide what types of insurance best meet your needs?	☐	☐
• Plan an insurance program and implement it, including the scheduling of periodic reviews of changing needs and changing conditions?	☐	☐
• Avoid buying more insurance than you need or can afford?	☐	☐
• Consider dropping one policy for another that provides the same coverage for less money?	☐	☐

NOTE: **Yes** answers reflect wise actions for insurance planning.

purchase additional coverage or change the kind of coverage they have. Another alternative would be to adjust their budget to cover the cost of additional insurance. Finally, Dave and Ellen might expand their savings or investment programs and use those funds in the case of an emergency.

The best risk management plans will be flexible enough to allow Dave and Ellen to respond to changing life situations. Their goal should be to create an insurance program that can grow or shrink as their protection needs change.

STEP 4: CHECK YOUR RESULTS Dave and Ellen should take the time to review their plan every two or three years, or whenever their family circumstances change.

Until recently, Dave and Ellen were satisfied with the coverage provided by their insurance policies. However, when the couple bought a house six months ago, the time had come for them to review their insurance plan. With the new house the risks became much greater. After all, what would happen if a fire destroyed part of their home?

The needs of a couple renting an apartment differ from those of a couple who own a house. Both couples face similar risks, but their financial responsibility differs greatly. When you're developing or reviewing a risk management plan, ask yourself if you're providing the financial resources you'll need to protect yourself, your family, and your property. The nearby *Financial Literacy in Practice* feature suggests several guidelines to follow in planning your insurance programs.

Property and Liability Insurance in Your Financial Plan

Major natural disasters have caused catastrophic amounts of property loss in the United States and other parts of the world. In the 2017 hurricane season, Harvey, Irma, Jose, and Maria caused over $100 billion in property damage, according to some estimates. Then, in 2019, tropical storm Nestor and Hurricane Dorian caused economic losses of over $22 billion.

Most people invest large amounts of money in their homes and motor vehicles. Therefore, protecting these items from loss is extremely important. Each year, homeowners and renters in the United States lose billions of dollars from more than 3.7 million burglaries, 1.5 million fires, and 250,000 cases of damage from other perils. The cost of injuries and property damage caused by vehicles is also enormous.

Think of the price you pay for home and motor vehicle insurance as an investment in protecting your most valuable possessions. The cost of such insurance may seem high. However, the financial losses from which it protects you are much higher.

Two main types of risk are related to your home and your car or other vehicle. One is the risk of damage to or loss of your property. The second type involves your responsibility for injuries to other people or damage to their property.

POTENTIAL PROPERTY LOSSES People spend a great deal of money on their houses, vehicles, furniture, clothing, and other personal property. Property owners face two basic types of risk. The first is physical damage caused by perils such as fire, wind, water, and smoke. These perils can damage or destroy property. For example, a windstorm might cause a large tree branch to smash the windshield of your car. You would have to find another way to get around while it was being repaired. The second type of risk is loss or damage caused by criminal behavior such as robbery, burglary, vandalism, and arson.

liability Legal responsibility for the financial cost of another person's losses or injuries.

LIABILITY PROTECTION You also need to protect yourself from liability. **Liability** is legal responsibility for the financial cost of another person's losses or injuries. You can be held legally responsible even if the injury or damage was not your fault. For example, suppose that Terry falls and gets hurt while playing in her friend Lisa's yard. Terry's family may be able to sue Lisa's parents, even though Lisa's parents did nothing wrong. Similarly, suppose that Sanjay accidentally damages a valuable painting while helping Ed move some furniture. Ed may take legal action against Sanjay to pay the cost of the painting.

Usually, if you're found liable, or legally responsible in a situation, it's because negligence on your part caused the mishap. Examples of such negligence include letting young children swim in a pool without supervision or cluttering a staircase with things that could cause someone to slip and fall.

Sheet 26 Current Insurance Policies and Needs

PRACTICE QUIZ 8–1

1. What are the three types of risk? Give an example for each.

2. What are the four methods of managing risks? Give an example for each.

3. List the four steps in planning for your insurance program.

4. Give an example of each kind of risk: personal, property, and liability.

LO8.2

Assess the insurance coverage and policy types available to home owners and renters.

homeowner's insurance
Coverage for a place of residence and its associated financial risks.

Home and Property Insurance

Your home and personal belongings are probably a major portion of your assets. Whether you rent or own a home, property insurance is vital. **Homeowner's insurance** is coverage for your place of residence and its associated financial risks, such as damage to personal property and injuries to others (see Exhibit 8–3).

Renter's Insurance

For people who rent, home insurance coverage includes personal property protection, additional living expenses coverage, and personal liability and related coverage. Renter's insurance does not provide coverage on the building or other structures.

Exhibit **8–3** Home Insurance Coverage

Building and other structures

Personal property

Loss of use/additional living expenses while home is uninhabitable

Personal liability and related coverages

There are two standard renter's insurance policies. The *broad form* covers your personal property against perils specified in the policy, such as fires and thefts, and the *comprehensive form* protects your personal property against all perils not specifically excluded in the policy. When shopping for renter's insurance, be aware that these policies:

- Normally pay only the actual cash value of your losses. Replacement cost coverage is available for an extra premium.
- Fully cover your personal property only at home. When traveling, your luggage and other personal items are protected up to a certain percentage of the policy's total amount of coverage.
- Automatically provide liability coverage if someone is injured on your premises.
- May duplicate other coverage. For instance, if you are still a dependent, your personal property may be covered by your parents' homeowner's policy. This coverage is limited, however, to an amount equal to a certain percentage of the total personal property coverage provided by the policy.

The most important part of renter's insurance is the protection it provides for your personal property. Many renters believe that they are covered under the landlord's insurance. In fact, that's the case only when the landlord is proved liable for some damage. For example, if bad wiring causes a fire and damages a tenant's property, the tenant may be able to collect money from the landlord. Renter's insurance is relatively inexpensive and provides many of the same kinds of protection as a homeowner's policy.

ACTION ITEM

Do you have enough home and property insurance?

☐ Yes   ☐ No

money minute focus

While more than 9 out of 10 homeowners have property insurance, only about 4 out of 10 renters are covered.

WHAT WOULD YOU DO? You are about to rent your first apartment. You have approximately $10,000 worth of personal belongings. Your landlord advised you to purchase your own renter's insurance. What type of renter's insurance policy would you choose and why?

Homeowner's Insurance Coverages

A homeowner's insurance policy provides coverage for the following:

- The building in which you live and any other structures on the property.
- Additional living expenses.
- Personal property.
- Personal liability and related coverage.
- Specialized coverage.

BUILDING AND OTHER STRUCTURES The main purpose of homeowner's insurance is to protect you against financial loss in case your home is damaged or destroyed. Detached structures on your property, such as a garage or toolshed, are also covered. Homeowner's coverage even includes trees, shrubs, and plants.

ADDITIONAL LIVING EXPENSES If a fire or other event damages your home, additional living expense coverage pays for you to stay somewhere else. For example, you may need to stay in a motel or rent an apartment while your home is being repaired. These extra living expenses will be paid by your insurance. Some policies limit additional living expense coverage to 10 to 20 percent of the home's coverage amount. They may also limit payments to a maximum of six to nine months. Other policies may pay additional living expenses for up to a year.

PERSONAL PROPERTY Homeowner's insurance covers your household belongings, such as furniture, appliances, and clothing, up to a portion of the insured value of the home. That portion is usually 55, 70, or 75 percent. For example, a home insured for $300,000 might have $210,000 (70 percent) worth of coverage for household belongings.

Personal property coverage typically limits the payout for the theft of certain items, such as $10,000 for jewelry. It provides protection against the loss or damage of articles that you take with you when you are away from home. For example, items you take on vacation or use at college are usually covered up to the policy limit. Personal property coverage even extends to property that you rent, such as a rug cleaner, while it's in your possession.

Most homeowner's policies include optional coverage for personal computers, including stored data, up to a certain limit. Your insurance agent can determine whether the equipment is covered against data loss and damage from spilled drinks or power surges.

If something does happen to your personal property, you must prove how much it was worth and that it belonged to you. To make the process easier, you can create a household inventory. A **household inventory** is a list or other documentation of personal belongings, with purchase dates and cost information. You can get a form for such an inventory from an insurance agent. Exhibit 8–4 provides a list of items you might include if you decide to compile your own inventory. For items of special value, you should have receipts, serial numbers, brand names, and proof of value.

Your household inventory can include a video recording or photographs of your home and its contents. Make sure that the closet and storage area doors are photographed open. On the back of the photographs, indicate the date and the value of the objects. Update your inventory, photos, and related documents on a regular basis. Keep a copy of each document in a secure location, such as a safe deposit box.

If you own valuable items, such as expensive musical instruments, or need added protection for computers and related equipment, you can purchase a personal property floater. A **personal property floater** is additional property insurance that covers the damage or loss of a specific item of high value. The insurance company will require a detailed description of the item and its worth. You'll also need to have the item appraised, or evaluated by an expert, from time to time to make sure that its value hasn't changed.

PERSONAL LIABILITY AND RELATED COVERAGE Every day people face the risk of financial loss due to injuries to other people or their property. The following are examples of this risk:

- A guest falls on a patch of ice on the steps to your home and breaks his arm.
- A spark from the barbecue in your backyard starts a fire that damages a neighbor's roof.
- Your son or daughter accidentally breaks an antique lamp while playing at a neighbor's house.

In each of these situations, you could be held responsible for paying for the damage. The personal liability portion of a homeowner's policy protects you and members of your

household inventory A list or other documentation of personal belongings, with purchase dates and cost information.

personal property floater Additional property insurance to cover the damage or loss of a specific item of high value.

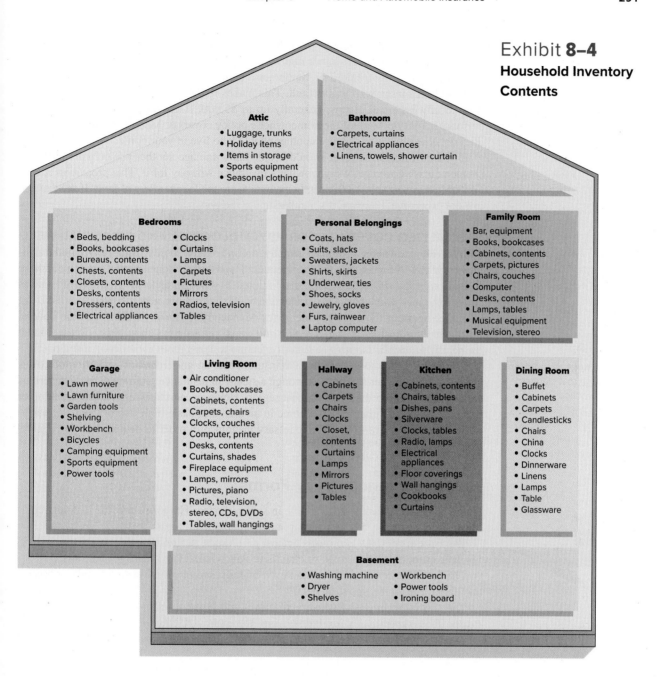

Exhibit **8–4**
Household Inventory Contents

Attic
- Luggage, trunks
- Holiday items
- Items in storage
- Sports equipment
- Seasonal clothing

Bathroom
- Carpets, curtains
- Electrical appliances
- Linens, towels, shower curtain

Bedrooms
- Beds, bedding
- Books, bookcases
- Bureaus, contents
- Chests, contents
- Closets, contents
- Desks, contents
- Dressers, contents
- Electrical appliances
- Clocks
- Curtains
- Lamps
- Carpets
- Pictures
- Mirrors
- Radios, television
- Tables

Personal Belongings
- Coats, hats
- Suits, slacks
- Sweaters, jackets
- Shirts, skirts
- Underwear, ties
- Shoes, socks
- Jewelry, gloves
- Furs, rainwear
- Laptop computer

Family Room
- Bar, equipment
- Books, bookcases
- Cabinets, contents
- Carpets, pictures
- Chairs, couches
- Computer
- Desks, contents
- Lamps, tables
- Musical equipment
- Television, stereo

Garage
- Lawn mower
- Lawn furniture
- Garden tools
- Shelving
- Workbench
- Bicycles
- Camping equipment
- Sports equipment
- Power tools

Living Room
- Air conditioner
- Books, bookcases
- Cabinets, contents
- Carpets, chairs
- Clocks, couches
- Computer, printer
- Desks, contents
- Curtains, shades
- Fireplace equipment
- Lamps, mirrors
- Pictures, piano
- Radio, television, stereo, CDs, DVDs
- Tables, wall hangings

Hallway
- Cabinets
- Carpets
- Chairs
- Clocks
- Closet, contents
- Curtains
- Lamps
- Mirrors
- Pictures
- Tables

Kitchen
- Cabinets, contents
- Chairs, tables
- Dishes, pans
- Silverware
- Clocks, tables
- Radio, lamps
- Electrical appliances
- Floor coverings
- Wall hangings
- Cookbooks
- Curtains

Dining Room
- Buffet
- Cabinets
- Carpets
- Candlesticks
- Chairs
- China
- Clocks
- Dinnerware
- Linens
- Lamps
- Table
- Glassware

Basement
- Washing machine
- Dryer
- Shelves
- Workbench
- Power tools
- Ironing board

family if others sue you for injuries they suffer or damage to their property. This coverage includes the cost of legal defense.

Not all individuals who come to your property are covered by your liability insurance. Friends, guests, and babysitters are probably covered. However, if you have regular employees, such as a housekeeper, a cook, or a gardener, you may need to obtain worker's compensation coverage for them.

Most homeowner's policies provide basic personal liability coverage of $100,000, but often that's not enough. An **umbrella policy**, also called a *personal catastrophe policy*, supplements your basic personal liability coverage. This added protection covers you for all kinds of personal injury claims. For instance, an umbrella policy will cover you if someone sues you for saying or writing something negative or untrue or for damaging his or her reputation. Extended liability policies are sold in amounts of $1 million or more and are useful for wealthy people. If you are a business owner, you may need other types of liability coverage as well.

umbrella policy
Supplementary personal liability coverage; also called a *personal catastrophe policy*.

medical payments coverage Automobile insurance that covers medical expenses for people injured in one's car.

Medical payments coverage pays the cost of minor accidental injuries to visitors on your property. It also covers minor injuries caused by you, members of your family, or even your pets while away from home. Settlements under medical payments coverage are made without determining who was at fault. This makes it fast and easy for the insurance company to process small claims, generally up to $5,000. If the injury is more serious, the personal liability portion of the homeowner's policy covers it. Medical payments coverage does not cover injury to you or the other people who live in your home.

If you or a family member should accidentally damage another person's property, the supplementary coverage of homeowner's insurance will pay for it. This protection is usually limited to $500 or $1,000. Again, payments are made regardless of fault. If the damage is more expensive, however, it's handled under the personal liability coverage.

SPECIALIZED COVERAGE FOR PSYCHOLOGICAL AND FINANCIAL WELL-BEING Homeowner's insurance usually doesn't cover losses from floods and earthquakes. If you live in an area that has frequent floods or earthquakes, you need to purchase special coverage. In some places, the National Flood Insurance Program (NFIP) makes flood insurance available. This protection is separate from a homeowner's policy. An insurance agent or the Federal Emergency Management Agency (FEMA) of the Federal Insurance Administration can give you additional information about this coverage. Read the nearby *Financial Literacy in Practice* feature to learn more about flood insurance.

endorsement An addition of coverage to a standard insurance policy.

You may be able to get earthquake insurance as an **endorsement**—addition of coverage—to a homeowner's policy or through a state-run insurance program. The most serious earthquakes occur in the Pacific Coast region. However, earthquakes can happen in other regions, too. If you plan to buy a home in an area that has a high risk of floods or earthquakes, you may have to buy the necessary insurance in order to be approved for a mortgage loan.

Home Insurance Policy Forms

Home insurance policies are available in several forms. The forms provide different combinations of coverage. Some forms are not available in all areas.

The basic form (HO-1) protects against perils such as fire, lightning, windstorms, hail, volcanic eruptions, explosions, smoke, theft, vandalism, glass breakage, and riots.

The broad form (HO-2) covers an even wider range of perils, including falling objects and damage from ice, snow, or sleet.

The special form (HO-3) covers all basic- and broad-form risks, plus any other risks except those specifically excluded from the policy. Common exclusions are flood, earthquake, war, and nuclear accidents. Personal property is covered for the risks listed in the policy.

CAUTION!

Computers and other equipment used in a home-based business are not usually covered by a home insurance policy. Contact your insurance agent to obtain needed coverage.

The tenant's form (HO-4) protects the personal property of renters against the risks listed in the policy. It does not include coverage on the building or other structures.

The comprehensive form (HO-5) expands the coverage of the HO-3. The HO-5 includes endorsements for items such as replacement cost coverage on contents and guaranteed replacement cost coverage on buildings.

Condominium owner's insurance (HO-6) protects personal property and any additions or improvements made to the living unit. These might include bookshelves, electrical fixtures, wallpaper, or carpeting. The condominium association purchases insurance on the building and other structures.

Manufactured housing units and mobile homes usually qualify for insurance coverage with conventional policies. However, some mobile homes may need special policies with higher rates because the way they are built increases their risk of fire and wind damage. The cost of mobile home insurance coverage depends on the home's location and the way

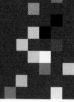

Financial Literacy in Practice

I Don't Have Flood Insurance—Why Do I Need It?

- **FACT:** Floods are the nation's most common and costly natural disaster and cause millions of dollars in damage every year. According to a recent report, floods cost Americans, on average, $8.2 billion each year. Recovering from just one inch of water inside your building can cost about $27,000.
- **FACT:** Homeowner's and renter's insurance do not typically cover flood damage.
- **FACT:** Floods can happen anywhere. More than 20 percent of flood claims are from properties outside the high-risk flood zone.
- **FACT:** Flood insurance can pay regardless of whether or not there is a presidential disaster declaration.
- **FACT:** Most federal disaster assistance is in the form of low-interest disaster loans from the U.S. Small Business Administration (SBA), and you have to pay them back. FEMA offers disaster grants that don't need to be paid back, but this amount is often much less than what is needed to recover. A claim against your flood insurance policy could, and often does, provide more funds for recovery than those you could qualify for from FEMA or the SBA—and you don't have to pay the money back.
- **FACT:** You may be required to have flood insurance. Congress has mandated federally regulated or insured lenders to require flood insurance on mortgaged properties that are located in areas at high risk of flooding. But even if your property is not in a high-risk flood area, your mortgage lender may still require you to have flood insurance.

How Can I Buy Flood Insurance?

You can only purchase flood insurance through an insurance agent or an insurer participating in the NFIP. You cannot buy it directly from the NFIP. If your insurance agent does not sell flood insurance, you can contact the NFIP Referral Call Center at **1-800-427-4661** to request an agent referral.

What Questions Should I Ask My Agent to Help Me Get the Coverage I Need?

Talk to your insurance agent about flood insurance. Here are helpful questions to ask your agent:

- Does my community participate in the National Flood Insurance Program? Flood insurance from the NFIP is only available in participating communities, but most communities do participate. Your agent can tell you if your state and community participate, or you can look it up online on FEMA's website in the Community Status Book.
- What flood zone do I live in?
- Is flood insurance mandatory for my property? Will the lender require it?
- Do I qualify for a preferred risk policy?
- Does my community participate in the NFIP Community Rating System (CRS)? If so, does my home qualify for a CRS rating discount?
- What will and won't be covered if a flood occurs?
- Will the federal government back my flood insurance policy?
- How much coverage should I get for my building and for my belongings?
- How can I reduce the cost of my flood insurance?
- Are there additional expenses or agency fees?
- Will my policy provide replacement cost value or actual cash value—and what's the difference between the two?
- Who should I call if I have a flood claim?
- How do I renew my policy?

Source: www.fema.gov/national-flood-insurance-program/How-Buy-Flood-Insurance, accessed February 28, 2020.

it's attached to the ground. Mobile home insurance is quite expensive: A $60,000 mobile home can cost as much to insure as a $180,000 house.

In addition to the risks previously discussed, home insurance policies include coverage for:

- Credit card fraud, check forgery, and counterfeit money.
- The cost of removing damaged property.
- Emergency removal of property to protect it from damage.
- Temporary repairs after a loss to prevent further damage.
- Fire department charges in areas with such fees.

As **Exhibit 8-5** shows, not everything is covered by home insurance.

Exhibit **8–5** Not Everything Is Covered

CERTAIN PERSONAL PROPERTY IS NOT COVERED BY HOMEOWNER'S INSURANCE:

- Items insured separately, such as jewelry, furs, boats, or expensive electronic equipment.
- Animals, birds, or fish.
- Motorized vehicles not licensed for road use, except those used for home maintenance.
- Sound devices used in motor vehicles, such as radios and CD players.

- Aircraft and parts.
- Property belonging to tenants.
- Property contained in a rental apartment.
- Property rented by the homeowner to other people.
- Business property.

Separate coverage may be available for personal property that is not covered by a homeowner's insurance policy.

Sheet 27 Home Inventory

PRACTICE QUIZ 8–2

1. Define the following terms:
   a. Homeowner's insurance
   b. Household inventory
   c. Personal property floater
   d. Renter's insurance

2. Identify the choice that best completes the statement or answers the question:
   a. The personal liability portion of a homeowner's insurance policy protects the insured against financial loss when his or her: (i) house floods, (ii) jewelry is stolen, (iii) guests injure themselves, (iv) reputation is damaged.
   b. Renter's insurance includes coverage for all of the following, except: (i) the building, (ii) personal property, (iii) additional living expenses, (iv) personal liability.
   c. The basic home insurance policy form protects against several perils, including: (i) sleet, (ii) lightning, (iii) flood, (iv) earthquake.

3. Define the following terms:
   a. Umbrella policy
   b. Medical payments coverage
   c. Endorsement

4. List at least four personal property items that are not covered by a homeowner's insurance policy.

LO8.3

Analyze the factors that influence the amount of coverage and cost of home insurance.

ACTION ITEM
Do you have enough insurance coverage for your home?

☐ Yes ☐ No

Home Insurance Cost Factors

How Much Coverage Do You Need?

You can get the best insurance value by choosing the right coverage amount and knowing the factors that affect insurance costs (see Exhibit 8–6). Your insurance should be based on the amount of money you would need to rebuild or repair your house, not the amount you paid for it. As construction costs rise, you should increase the amount of coverage. In fact, today most insurance policies automatically increase coverage as construction costs rise.

In the past, many homeowner's policies insured the building for only 80 percent of the replacement value. If the building were destroyed, the homeowner would have to pay for part of the cost of replacing it, which could be expensive. Today, most companies recommend full coverage.

Exhibit **8–6** Determining the Amount of Home Insurance You Need

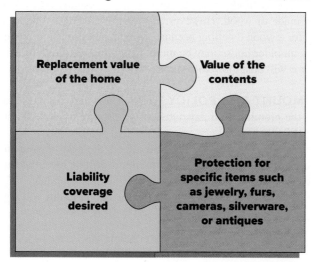

If you are borrowing money to buy a home, the lender will require that you have property insurance. Remember, too, that the amount of insurance on your home determines the coverage on your personal belongings. Coverage for personal belongings is usually from 55 to 75 percent of the insurance amount on your home.

Insurance companies base claim settlements on one of two methods. Under the **actual cash value (ACV)** method, the payment you receive is based on the replacement cost of an item minus depreciation. Depreciation is the loss of value of an item as it gets older. This means you would receive less for a five-year-old bicycle than you originally paid for it.

Under the **replacement value** method for settling claims, you receive the full cost of repairing or replacing an item. Depreciation is not considered. Many companies limit the replacement cost to 400 percent of the item's actual cash value. Replacement value coverage is more expensive than actual cash value coverage.

actual cash value (ACV) A claim settlement method in which the insured receives payment based on the current replacement cost of a damaged or lost item, less depreciation.

replacement value A claim settlement method in which the insured receives the full cost of repairing or replacing a damaged or lost item.

EXAMPLE: Replacement Cost and Time Value of Money

To save on future home insurance costs, you need a new roof and a burglar alarm system that will cost $10,000 five years from now. You can earn 3 percent on your savings. How much should you deposit now to obtain $10,000 five years from today?

PV = $10,000 × 0.863 = $8,630 (from Exhibit 1–C, Chapter 1 Appendix)

Factors That Affect Home Insurance Costs

The cost of your home insurance will depend on several factors, such as the location of the building and the type of building and construction materials. The amount of coverage and type of policy you choose will also affect the cost of home insurance. Furthermore, different insurance companies offer different rates.

LOCATION OF HOME The location of your home affects your insurance rates. Insurance companies offer lower rates to people whose homes are close to a water supply or fire hydrant or located in an area that has a good fire department. On the other hand, rates are higher in areas where crime is common. People living in regions that experience severe weather, such as tornadoes and hurricanes, may also pay more for insurance.

TYPE OF STRUCTURE The type of home and its construction influence the price of insurance coverage. A brick house, for example, will usually cost less to insure than a similar structure made of wood. However, earthquake coverage is more expensive for a brick house than for a wood dwelling because a wooden house is more likely to survive an earthquake. Also, an older house may be more difficult to restore to its original condition, which means that it will cost more to insure.

COVERAGE AMOUNT AND POLICY TYPE The policy and the amount of coverage you select affect the premium you pay. Obviously, insuring a $300,000 home costs more than insuring a $100,000 home.

The deductible amount in your policy also affects the cost of your insurance. If you increase the amount of your deductible, your premium will be lower because the company will pay out less in claims. The most common deductible amount is $250. Raising the deductible from $250 to $500 or $1,000 can reduce the premium you pay by 15 percent or more.

EXAMPLE: Increase a Deductible to Reduce the Premium

Suppose your annual home insurance policy premium is $800 with a $250 deductible. If you increase the amount of your deductible to $500, you reduce the premium by 10 percent, or $80.

---

money minute focus

In some areas, a home can be automatically rejected for insurance coverage if it has had two or three claims of any sort in the past three years. Homes that have had water damage, storm damage, and burglaries are most vulnerable to rejection.

HOME INSURANCE DISCOUNTS Most companies offer discounts if you take action to reduce risks to your home. Your premium may be lower if you have smoke detectors or a fire extinguisher. If your home has dead-bolt locks and alarm systems, which make breaking in harder for thieves, insurance costs may be lower. Some companies offer discounts to people who don't file any claims for a certain number of years.

COMPANY DIFFERENCES You can save more than 30 percent on homeowner's insurance by comparing rates from several companies. Some insurance agents work for only one company. Others are independent agents who represent several different companies. Talk to both types of agent. You'll get the information you need to compare rates.

Don't select a company on the basis of price alone; also consider service and coverage. Not all companies settle claims in the same way. Suppose that all homes on Evergreen Terrace are dented on one side by large hail. They all have the same kind of siding. Unfortunately, the homeowners discover that this type of siding is no longer available, so all the siding on all of the houses will need to be replaced. Some insurance companies will pay to replace all the siding. Others will pay only to replace the damaged parts.

State insurance commissions and consumer organizations can give you information about different insurance companies. *Consumer Reports* rates insurance companies on a regular basis.

Remember, insurance companies are just like any other businesses. Do your own research to obtain the best option at the best cost. Read the nearby *Financial Literacy in Practice* feature to learn how you can lower the cost of homeowner's and renter's insurance.

How to Lower the Cost of Insurance

How can you lower your cost of homeowner's and renter's insurance? Shop around and compare the cost. Here are a few tips that can save you hundreds of dollars annually.

1. ***Consider a higher deductible.*** Increasing your deductible by just a few hundred dollars can make a big difference in your premium.

2. ***Ask your insurance agent about discounts.*** You may be able to secure a lower premium if your home has safety features such as dead-bolt locks, smoke detectors, an alarm system, storm shutters, or fire-retardant roofing material. Persons over 55 years of age or long-term customers may also be offered discounts.

3. ***Insure your house, NOT the land under it.*** After a disaster, the land is still there. If you don't subtract the value of the land when deciding how much homeowner's insurance to buy, you will pay more than you should.

4. ***Make certain you purchase enough coverage to replace what is insured.*** "Replacement" coverage gives you the money to rebuild your home and replace its contents. An actual cash value policy is cheaper but pays only what your property is worth at the time of the loss—your cost minus depreciation.

5. ***Ask about special coverage you might need.*** You may have to pay extra for computers, cameras, jewelry, art, antiques, musical instruments, stamp collections, and other items.

6. ***Remember that flood and earthquake damage is not covered by a standard homeowner's policy.*** The cost of a separate earthquake policy will depend on the likelihood of earthquakes in your area. Homeowners who live in areas prone to flooding should take advantage of the National Flood Insurance Program. Call 1-888-CALLFLOOD or visit **www.fema.gov/national-flood-insurance-program**.

7. ***If you are a renter, do NOT assume your landlord carries insurance on your personal belongings.*** Purchase a special policy for renters.

Sheet 28 Determining Needed Property Insurance

Sheet 29 Apartment/Home Insurance Comparison

PRACTICE QUIZ 8–3

1. In the space provided, write "T" if you believe the statement is true or "F" if the statement is false.
   a. Today, most insurance policies automatically increase coverage as construction costs rise. _____
   b. In the past, many homeowner's policies insured the building for only 50 percent of the replacement value. _____
   c. Most mortgage lenders do not require that you buy home insurance. _____
   d. Coverage for personal belongings is usually from 55 to 75 percent of the insurance amount on your home. _____

2. What are the two methods insurance companies use in settling claims?

3. List the five factors that affect home insurance costs.

Automobile Insurance Coverages

According to National Highway Traffic Safety Administration, motor vehicle crashes cause more than 38,000 deaths and cost over $871 billion in lost wages and medical bills every year. Traffic accidents can destroy people's lives physically, financially, and emotionally. Buying insurance can't eliminate the pain and suffering that vehicle accidents cause. It can, however, reduce the financial impact.

Every state in the United States has a **financial responsibility law**, a law that requires drivers to prove that they can pay for damage or injury caused by an automobile accident.

LO8.4

Identify the important types of automobile insurance coverage.

financial responsibility law State legislation that requires drivers to prove their ability to cover the cost of damage or injury caused by an automobile accident.

ACTION ITEM
Do you have an adequate amount of automobile insurance?

☐ Yes ☐ No

All states have laws requiring people to carry motor vehicle insurance. These laws impose heavy fines, suspension of a driver's license, community service, and even imprisonment if you don't carry motor vehicle insurance. Indeed, opportunity costs of driving without insurance can be very high. Very few people have the money they would need to meet financial responsibility requirements on their own.

The coverage provided by motor vehicle insurance falls into two categories. One is protection for bodily injury. The other is protection for property damage (see Exhibit 8–7).

Exhibit 8–7 Two Major Categories of Automobile Insurance

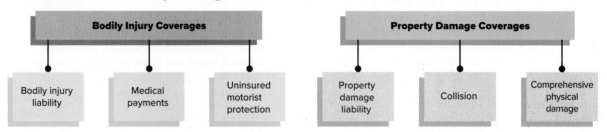

Buying bodily injury and property damage coverage can reduce the financial impact of an accident. *What type of expenses would be paid for by bodily injury liability coverage?*

Motor Vehicle Bodily Injury Coverages

Most of the money that motor vehicle insurance companies pay out in claims goes for legal expenses, medical expenses, and other costs that arise when someone is injured. The main types of bodily injury coverage are bodily injury liability, medical payments, and uninsured motorist protection.

bodily injury liability
Coverage for the risk of financial loss due to legal expenses, medical costs, lost wages, and other expenses associated with injuries caused by an automobile accident for which the insured was responsible.

BODILY INJURY LIABILITY Bodily injury liability is insurance that covers physical injuries caused by a vehicle accident for which you were responsible. If pedestrians, people in other vehicles, or passengers in your vehicle are injured or killed, bodily injury liability coverage pays for expenses related to the crash.

Liability coverage is usually expressed by three numbers, such as 100/300/50. These amounts represent thousands of dollars of coverage. The first two numbers refer to bodily injury coverage. In this example, $100,000 is the maximum amount that the insurance company will pay for the injuries of any one person in any one accident. The second number, $300,000, is the maximum amount the company will pay all injured parties (two or more) in any one accident. The third number, $50,000, indicates the limit for payment for damage to the property of others (see Exhibit 8–8).

Exhibit 8–8 Automobile Liability Insurance Coverage

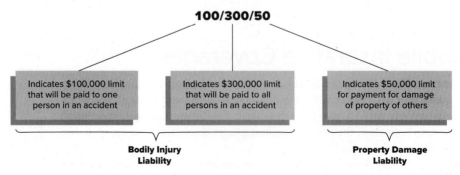

The three numbers used to describe liability coverage refer to the limits on different types of payments. *Why do you think the middle number is the highest?*

MEDICAL PAYMENTS COVERAGE Medical payments coverage is insurance that applies to the medical expenses of anyone who is injured in your vehicle, including you. This type of coverage also provides additional medical benefits for you and members of your family; it pays medical expenses if you or your family members are injured while riding in another person's vehicle or if any of you are hit by a vehicle.

medical payments coverage Automobile insurance that covers medical expenses for people injured in one's car.

UNINSURED MOTORIST PROTECTION Unfortunately, you cannot assume that everyone who is behind the wheel is carrying insurance. How can you guard yourself and your passengers against the risk of getting into an accident with someone who has no insurance? The answer is uninsured motorist protection.

Uninsured motorist protection is insurance that covers you and your family members if you are involved in an accident with an uninsured or hit-and-run driver. In most states, it does not cover damage to the vehicle itself. Penalties for driving uninsured vary by state, but they generally include stiff fines and suspension of driving privileges.

Underinsured motorist coverage protects you when another driver has some insurance but not enough to pay for the injuries he or she has caused.

money minute focus

Buckle up. One of the safest choices you can make while in a motor vehicle is to buckle up. In 2019, 90.7 percent of drivers used seat belts, thus saving more than 16,000 lives.

Motor Vehicle Property Damage Coverage

One afternoon, during a summer storm, Carrie was driving home from her job as a hostess at a pancake house. The rain was coming down in buckets, and she couldn't see very well. As a result, she didn't realize that the car in front of her had stopped to make a left turn, and she hit the car. The crash totaled Carrie's new car. Fortunately, she had purchased property damage coverage. Property damage coverage protects you from financial loss if you damage someone else's property or if your vehicle is damaged. It includes property damage liability, collision, and comprehensive physical damage. (See the nearby *Financial Literacy in Practice* feature, "Are You Covered?")

uninsured motorist protection Automobile insurance coverage for the cost of injuries to a person and members of his or her family caused by a driver with inadequate insurance or by a hit-and-run driver.

PROPERTY DAMAGE LIABILITY Property damage liability is motor vehicle insurance that applies when you damage the property of others. In addition, it protects you when you're driving another person's vehicle with the owner's permission. Although the damaged property is usually another vehicle, the coverage also extends to buildings and to equipment such as street signs and telephone poles.

property damage liability Motor vehicle insurance coverage that protects a person against financial loss when that person damages the property of others.

COLLISION Collision insurance covers damage to your vehicle when it is involved in an accident. It allows you to collect money no matter who was at fault. However, the amount you can collect is limited to the actual cash value of your vehicle at the time of the accident. If your vehicle has many extra features, make sure that you have a record of its condition and value.

collision Motor vehicle insurance that pays for damage to the insured's vehicle when it is involved in an accident.

COMPREHENSIVE PHYSICAL DAMAGE Comprehensive physical damage coverage protects you if your vehicle is damaged in a nonaccident situation. It covers your vehicle against risks such as fire, theft, falling objects, vandalism, hail, floods, tornadoes, earthquakes, and avalanches.

No-Fault Insurance

To reduce the time and cost of settling vehicle injury cases, various states are trying a number of alternatives. Under the **no-fault system**, drivers who are involved in accidents collect money from their own insurance companies. It doesn't matter who caused the accident.

no-fault system A motor vehicle insurance program in which drivers involved in accidents collect medical expenses, lost wages, and related injury costs from their own insurance companies.

Are You Covered?

Often people believe their insurance will cover various financial losses. For each of the following situations, name the type of home or automobile insurance that would protect you:

1. While you are on vacation, clothing and other personal belongings are stolen. _____

2. Your home is damaged by fire, and you have to live in a hotel for several weeks. _____

3. You and members of your family suffer injuries in an automobile accident caused by a hit-and-run driver. _____

4. A delivery person is injured on your property and takes legal action against you. _____

5. Your automobile is accidentally damaged by some people playing baseball. _____

6. A person takes legal action against you for injuries you caused in an automobile accident. _____

7. Water from a local lake rises and damages your furniture and carpeting. _____

8. Your automobile needs repairs because you hit a tree. _____

9. You damaged a valuable tree when your automobile hit it, and you want to pay for the damage. _____

10. While riding with you in your automobile, your nephew is injured in an accident and incurs various medical expenses. _____

ANSWERS (1) Personal property coverage of home insurance; (2) Additional living expenses from home insurance; (3) Uninsured motorist protection; (4) Personal liability coverage of home insurance; (5) Comprehensive physical damage; (6) Bodily injury liability; (7) Flood insurance—requires coverage separate from home insurance; (8) Collision; (9) Property damage liability of automobile insurance; (10) Medical payments.

FinTech for Financial Literacy

InsurTech, a subset of FinTech, refers to technology innovations to improve customer service, simplify policy management, and offer new products in the insurance industry. These start-ups are funded by existing insurance companies, as well as venture capitalists. InsurTech includes:

- Apps providing travel insurance customers with information on potential travel restrictions and the location of emergency medical services.
- Artificial intelligence (AI) that creates chatbots to communicate with policyholders, complete applications, and process claims.
- The Internet of Things (IoT) that collects data to provide discounts, improve safety, and analyze accidents.
- Drones that inspect property in hazardous places, such as rooftops and disaster areas, for settling claims.

Each company pays the insured up to the limits of his or her coverage. Because no-fault systems vary by state, you should investigate the coverage of no-fault insurance in your state.

Other Automobile Insurance Coverages

Several other kinds of motor vehicle insurance are available to you. *Wage loss insurance* pays for any salary or income you might have lost because of being injured in a vehicle accident. Wage loss insurance is usually required in states with a no-fault insurance system. In other states, it's available by choice.

Towing and emergency road service coverage pays for mechanical assistance in the event that your vehicle breaks down. This can be helpful on long trips or during bad weather. If necessary, you can get your vehicle towed to a service station. However, once your vehicle arrives at the repair shop, you are responsible for paying the bill. If you belong to an automobile club, your membership may include towing coverage. If that's the case, paying for emergency road service coverage could be a waste of money. *Rental reimbursement coverage* pays for a rental car if your vehicle is stolen or being repaired.

PRACTICE QUIZ 8–4

1. List the three main types of bodily injury coverage.

2. In the space provided, write "T" if the statement is true or "F" if it is false.

   a. Financial responsibility law requires drivers to prove that they can pay for damage or injury caused by a motor vehicle accident. _____

   b. Insurance that covers physical injuries caused by a vehicle accident for which you were responsible is called uninsured motorist protection. _____

   c. Motor vehicle liability coverage is usually expressed by three numbers, 100/300/50. _____

   d. The first two numbers in 100/300/50 refer to the limit for payment for damage to the property of others. _____

   e. Uninsured motorist protection is insurance that covers you and your family members if you are involved in an accident with an uninsured motorist or hit-and-run driver. _____

   f. Collision insurance covers damage to your vehicle when it is involved in an accident. _____

3. What is no-fault insurance? What is its purpose?

4. List at least three kinds of motor vehicle insurance that are available to you.

Automobile Insurance Costs

Motor vehicle insurance is not cheap. The average household spends more than $1,200 for motor vehicle insurance yearly. The premiums are related to the amount of claims insurance companies pay out each year. Your automobile insurance cost is directly related to coverage amounts and factors such as the vehicle, your place of residence, and your driving record.

Amount of Coverage

The amount you will pay for insurance depends on the amount of coverage you require. You need enough coverage to protect yourself legally and financially.

LEGAL CONCERNS As discussed earlier, most people who are involved in motor vehicle accidents cannot afford to pay an expensive court settlement with their own money. For this reason, most drivers buy liability insurance.

   In the past, bodily injury liability coverage of 10/20 was usually enough. However, some people have been awarded millions of dollars in recent cases, so coverage of 100/300 is usually recommended.

PROPERTY VALUES Just as medical expenses and legal settlements have increased, so has the cost of vehicles. Therefore, you should consider a policy with a limit of $50,000 or even $100,000 for property damage liability.

Motor Vehicle Insurance Premium Factors

Vehicle type, rating territory, and driver classification are three other factors that influence insurance costs.

LO8.5

Evaluate factors that affect the cost of automobile insurance.

ACTION ITEM
Do you know what factors determine your motor vehicle insurance premium?

☐ **Yes** ☐ **No**

money minute focus

Foods and drinks that were reported as the most common distractions in motor vehicle accidents include: coffee, hot soup, tacos, chili-covered foods, hamburgers, chicken, jelly- or cream-filled doughnuts, and soft drinks.

VEHICLE TYPE The year, make, and model of a vehicle will affect insurance costs. Vehicles that have expensive replacement parts and complicated repairs will cost more to insure. Also, premiums will probably be higher for vehicle makes and models that are frequently stolen.

WHAT WOULD YOU DO? You have recently purchased a fully restored 1957 Chevy, something you have always dreamed of owning and driving on special occasions. The car cost $30,000, but you thought it was worth the expense. After shopping around for insurance, you discovered that the cost of insuring such a vehicle is quite significant. The best price you can find on the coverage you need is $3,500 per year. You can cut corners on the insurance coverage to save money; however, you will be taking a risk. Is it worth the insurance expense to protect your prized vehicle, or is it too much to spend to insure what is, after all, just a car?

FinTech for Financial Literacy

Global positioning systems and other technologies are being used to encourage safer driving and reduce auto insurance costs. In Britain, one insurance company adjusts premiums each month based on a driver's braking and acceleration habits. The Car Chip (www.carchipconnect.com) allows parents to monitor the speed and braking actions of young drivers.

assigned risk pool
Consists of people who are unable to obtain motor vehicle insurance due to poor driving or accident records and must obtain coverage at high rates through a state program that requires insurance companies to accept some of them.

An automobile insurance company once paid $3,600 for damages to a car in an accident caused by a mouse. The critter apparently got into the car while it was parked and then crawled up the driver's pant leg while the car was on an interstate highway. The driver lost control of the vehicle and crashed into a roadside barrier. Another claim resulted when a barbecued steak fell off a 17th-floor balcony and dented a car.

RATING TERRITORY In most states, your rating territory is the place of residence used to determine your vehicle insurance premium. Different locations have different costs. For example, rural areas usually have fewer accidents and less frequent occurrences of theft. Your insurance would probably cost less there than if you lived in a large city.

DRIVER CLASSIFICATION Driver classification is based on age, sex, marital status, driving record, and driving habits. In general, young drivers (under 25) and elderly drivers (over 70) have more frequent and more serious accidents. As a result, these groups pay higher premiums. Your driving record will also influence your insurance premiums. If you have accidents or receive tickets for traffic violations, your rates will increase.

The cost and number of claims that you file with your insurance company will also affect your premium. If you file expensive claims, your rates will increase. If you have too many claims, your insurance company may cancel your policy. You will then have more difficulty getting coverage from another company. To deal with this problem, every state has an assigned risk pool. An **assigned risk pool** includes all the people who can't get motor vehicle insurance. Some of these people are assigned to each insurance company operating in the state. These policyholders pay several times the normal rates, but they do get coverage. Once they establish a good driving record, they can reapply for insurance at regular rates.

Insurance companies may also consider your credit score when deciding whether to sell, renew, or cancel a policy and what premium to charge. However, an insurer cannot refuse to issue you a home or auto insurance policy solely based on your credit report. Read the nearby *Digital Financial Literacy* feature to understand how insurance companies share your information to decide whether to issue you a new or to renew your existing policy .

REDUCING VEHICLE INSURANCE PREMIUMS Two ways in which you can reduce your vehicle insurance costs are by comparing companies and taking advantage of discounts.

COMPARING COMPANIES Rates and services vary among motor vehicle insurance companies. Even among companies in the same area, premiums can vary by as much as 100 percent. You should compare the service and rates of local insurance agents.

Digital Financial Literacy with. . .

Insurance Companies Sharing Your Information

 **cfpb** Consumer Financial Protection Bureau

Do auto and homeowners insurance companies share your information about claims and policies? The answer is: YES.

Specialty consumer reporting agencies collect information about the insurance claims you have made on your property and casualty insurance policies, such as your homeowners and auto policies. They may also collect your driving records. Insurance companies use information in these reports to choose the types of policies they offer you and the premiums you pay.

As with the big three consumer reporting agencies – Experian, Equifax, and TransUnion – you can get free copies of your reports every 12 months from many of the specialty consumer reporting agencies. Other specialty consumer reporting agencies may charge you up to $12.50 (in 2020) fee for your report. Requesting copies of your own consumer reports does not hurt your credit scores.

Be aware that not every agency has information on everyone. You have to request the reports individually from each reporting agency. The Consumer Financial Protection Bureau has compiled a list of some of these specialty consumer reporting agencies, along with information about how you can obtain copies of your reports.

Suppose an insurance company turns you down for a homeowners or an auto insurance policy based on a consumer report. This is an example of an "adverse action." The insurance company must provide you with an "adverse action" notice that includes the name and contact information of the consumer reporting agency from which the insurance company got the consumer report. A consumer reporting agency, including a specialty agency, must also give you a free copy of your consumer report upon request if you have received an "adverse action" notice.

Review the report to see what information the consumer reporting agency has on file about your insurance history. You can then ask for corrections of any errors in the report. Check your reports before you shop for home or auto insurance or if you have been denied coverage or offered coverage with higher premiums in the past. You should check your reports to make sure they do not contain mistakes. If they do, you can ask for corrections of any errors in the report.

Source: https://www.consumerfinance.gov/ask-cfpb/do-auto-and-home-owners-insurance-companies-share-my-information-about-claims-and-policies-en-1821/

ACTION STEPS FOR. . .

. . .Information Literacy

Based on this article, or your personal life situation, create a list of your own questions that might be used to decide if you should look for another insurance company

. . .Financial Literacy

Search several home/auto insurance websites and various digital sources—apps, podcasts, social media, blogs, and tweets—to understand reasons why insurance companies use your credit scores in deciding whether to issue you a policy.

. . .Digital Literacy

Based on this article, other sources, and information from friends and relatives, write a summary of the information received from these sources. Describe how this information might be communicated to others with an online video or app.

Most states publish this type of information. Furthermore, you can check a company's reputation with sources such as *Consumer Reports* or your state insurance department.

PREMIUM DISCOUNTS The penalties of poor driving behavior can be severe. For example, recently car insurance premiums increased 18 percent if you had only one moving violation; for two moving violations, the average premium increased 34 percent compared to drivers with no violations. Annual premiums jumped 53 percent if you had three violations.

The best way for you to keep your rates down is to maintain a good driving record by avoiding accidents and traffic tickets. In addition, most insurance companies offer various discounts. If you are under 25, you can qualify for reduced rates by taking a driver training program or maintaining good grades in college.

CAUTION!

Your insurance company may charge an extra fee if you are involved in an accident or cited for a serious traffic violation. Worse, the insurer may not renew your insurance policy.

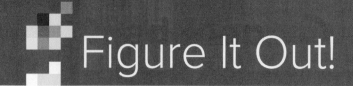

Motor Vehicle Insurance—How Much Will It Cost?

Before Mario bought the car he wanted, he needed to be sure he could afford the insurance for it. In this example, he chose low liability, uninsured motorist coverage, and high deductibles to keep his insurance payments as low as possible. Clearly, insurer B offered a lower price for the same coverage.

Investigating Insurance Companies		
	Insurer A	**Insurer B**
Bodily injury coverage:		
• Bodily injury liability $50,000 each person; $100,000 each accident	$472	$358
• Uninsured motorist protection	208	84
• Medical payments coverage $2,000 each person	48	46
Property damage coverage:		
• Property damage liability $50,000 each accident	182	178
• Collision with $500 deductible	562	372
• Comprehensive physical damage with $500 deductible	263	202
Car rental	40	32
Discounts: good driver, air bags, garage parking	−165	
Annual total	$1,610	$1,272

RESEARCH

Identify a make, model, and year of a vehicle you might like to own. Research two insurance companies and get prices using this example. You can get their rates by telephone. Many also have websites. Using your workbook or on a separate sheet of paper, record your findings. How do they compare? Which company would you choose and why?

Furthermore, installing security devices will decrease the chance of theft and lower your insurance costs. Being a nonsmoker can qualify you for lower motor vehicle insurance premiums as well. Discounts are also offered for insuring two or more vehicles with the same company.

Increasing the amounts of deductibles will also lead to a lower premium. If you have an old car that's not worth much, you may decide not to pay for collision and comprehensive coverage. However, before you make this move, you should compare the value of your car with the cost of these coverages.

Choose your car carefully. Some makes and models are more costly to insure than others. Contact your insurance agent before purchasing your car. And finally, maintain a good credit history. Many insurers are now examining your credit reports.

The nearby *Figure It Out!* feature presents motor vehicle insurance cost comparison.

EXAMPLE: Time Value of Money—Insuring Two Vehicles with the Same Insurer

Suppose you insure your cars with two separate companies, paying $600 and $800 a year. If you insure both cars with the same company, you may save 10 percent on the annual premiums, or $140 a year. What is the future value of the annual savings over 10 years based on an annual interest rate of 3 percent?

The total premium $600 plus $800 = $1,400

Ten percent of 1,400 = $1,400 × 0.10 = $140

Future value of $140 over 10 years at 3 percent:

$140 × 11.464 = $1,604.96 (from Exhibit 1–B)

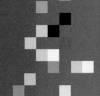

Financial Literacy in Practice

Filing a Homeowner/Automobile Insurance Claim

Consider the value of a claim

Insurance companies generally consider your claims history when deciding to continue covering you or adjusting your premiums. If you have a claims-free record for several years, filing a claim might be appropriate. However, several claims in a short time period may increase your rates or make it difficult to obtain future coverage.

So make sure the claim is worthwhile. For example, if your deductible is $1,000 and you have $1,200 of damage, not reporting the claim might be appropriate. Consider not turning in a claim and just pay for the repairs yourself.

How to file a claim

- Contact your agent or company as soon as possible. Review your policy with them and ask what's covered.
- Ask what information the company needs to process your claim. Provide that information, including contact information if you cannot live in the home.
- Do not make permanent repairs until the insurance company reviews the damages.
- Be ready to provide receipts, photos or videos of the damage and so forth to prove your loss.
- Keep copies of all documents.

What to expect after you file a claim

Stop any further damage to your home or automobile. Take photos or videos to document the damage, and keep track of your expenses—your insurer may reimburse you.

What to expect from your insurer

Your insurance company will send an adjuster to determine the damage.

Then the discussion on who you'd like to do the repairs starts. Obtain repair estimates from trusted local contractors. In general, your insurer must complete its investigation of your claim within 15 to 30 days from the date you file the claim.

What do you need to do?

- Stay involved.
- Don't expect your adjuster to be your general contractor.
- Stay in contact with both your adjuster and contractor.
- If something doesn't make sense, ask questions.
- Know your claim responsibilities and rights.

Sources: Office of the Insurance Commissioner, Washington State (www.insurance.wa.gov) and Oklahoma Insurance Department (www.oid.ok.gov), accessed March 1, 2020.

Finally, the nearby *Financial Literacy in Practice* feature provides suggestions on how to file an insurance claim for home or automobile.

Sheet 30 Automobile Insurance Cost Comparison

PRACTICE QUIZ 8–5

1. In the space provided, write "A" if you agree with the statement, or "D" if you disagree.

   a. Motor vehicle insurance is not cheap. _____
   b. The average household spends less than $500 for motor vehicle insurance yearly. _____
   c. Most people who are involved in a motor vehicle accident can afford to pay an expensive court settlement with their own money. _____
   d. Liability coverage of 100/300 is usually recommended. _____
   e. You should consider a policy with a limit of $50,000 or even $100,000 for property damage liability. _____
   f. The year, make, and model of a vehicle does not affect insurance costs. _____
   g. Your automobile insurance would probably cost more in rural areas than if you lived in a large city. _____

2. List the five factors that determine driver classification.

3. What are the two ways by which you can reduce your vehicle insurance costs?

Road Map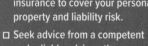

to financial literacy

You Are Here

Personal Property Coverage

Checkpoint 1

- ☐ Determine how you can lower the cost of homeowner's and renter's insurance.
- ☐ Determine additional home property and motor vehicle insurance coverage based on your current life situation.
- ☐ If you live in a flood-prone area, visit the Federal Emergency Management Agency's website at www.floodsmart.gov.

- ☐ If you rent, consider renter's insurance to cover your personal property and liability risk.
- ☐ Seek advice from a competent and reliable adviser; then decide what types of insurance best meet your needs.
- ☐ Review home insurance policies to determine possible coverage changes and discounts.

Checkpoint 2

- ☐ Assess motor vehicle insurance coverage based on changes in household and vehicle situation.
- ☐ Determine potential changes in driving habits that might affect vehicle insurance costs.

Checkpoint 3

Financial Security

PERCENT OF PERSONAL PROPERTY COVERAGE

your personal finance dashboard

Your household belongings, such as furniture, appliances, and clothing, are covered by the personal property portion of a homeowner's insurance policy up to a portion of the insured value of the home. That portion may range from 55 to 75 percent.

YOUR SITUATION: Have you established a specific and measurable portion of coverage for your household belongings? Do you have adequate additional living expense coverage if a fire or other event damages your home? Some policies limit additional living expense coverage to 10 to 20 percent of a home's total coverage amount. Have you considered a personal property floater for additional property insurance that covers the damage or loss of a specific item of high value?

LO8.1 The main types of risk are personal risk, property risk, and liability risk. Risk management methods include avoidance, reduction, assumption, and shifting.

Planning an insurance program is a way to manage risks.

Property and liability insurance protect your homes and motor vehicles against financial loss.

LO8.2 Renter's insurance provides many of the same kinds of protection as homeowner's policies. A homeowner's policy provides coverage for buildings and other structures, additional living expenses, personal property, personal liability and related coverages, and specialized coverages.

LO8.3 The factors that affect home insurance coverage and costs include the location, the type of structure, the coverage amount and policy type, the discounts, and the choice of insurance company.

LO8.4 Motor vehicle bodily injury coverages include bodily injury liability, medical payments coverage, and uninsured motorist protection.

Motor vehicle property damage coverages include property damage liability, collision, and comprehensive physical damage.

LO8.5 Motor vehicle insurance costs depend on the amount of coverage you need as well as vehicle type, rating territory, and driver classification.

actual cash value (ACV) 295

assigned risk pool 302

bodily injury liability 298

collision 299

coverage 284

deductible 285

endorsement 292

financial responsibility law 297

hazard 284

homeowner's insurance 288

household inventory 290

insurance 283

insurance company 283

insured 284

insurer 284

liability 288

medical payments coverage 292, 299

negligence 284

no-fault system 299

peril 284

personal property floater 290

policy 284

policyholder 284

premium 284

property damage liability 299

replacement value 295

risk 284

umbrella policy 291

uninsured motorist protection 299

1. Eric and Susan Fowler just purchased their first home, which cost $130,000. They purchased a homeowner's policy to insure the home for $120,000 and personal property for $75,000. They declined any coverage for additional living expenses. The deductible for the policy is $500.

   Soon after Eric and Susan moved into their new home, a strong windstorm caused damage to their roof. They reported the roof damage to be $17,000. While the roof was under repair, the couple had to live in a nearby hotel for three days. The hotel bill amounted to $320. Assuming the insurance company settles claims using the replacement value method, what amount will the insurance company pay for the damages to the roof?

2. Eric's Ford Mustang and Susan's Toyota Prius are insured with the same insurance agent. They have 50/100/15 vehicle insurance coverage and no deductibles. The very week of the windstorm, Susan had an accident. She lost control of her car, hit a parked car, and damaged a storefront. The damage to the parked car was $4,300 and the damage to the store was $15,400. What amount will the insurance company pay for Susan's car accident?

Solutions

1. Home damages:
   Home value: $130,000
   Insured amount: $120,000
   Damage amount reported: $17,000
   Additional living expenses incurred: $320
   Total expenses incurred from windstorm: $17,320
   Deductible on the policy: $500
   Insurance company covered amount ($17,000 – $500 deductible): $16,500
   Eric and Susan's costs ($500 + $320 hotel bill): $820

2. Car accident:
   Store damage amount: $15,400
   Parked car damage amount: $4,300
   Total damages: $19,700
   Insurance company covered amount (50/100/15): $15,000
   Eric and Susan's costs ($19,700 – $15,000): $4,700

Financial Planning Problems

1. Most home insurance policies cover jewelry for $2,000 and silverware for $5,000 unless items are covered with additional insurance. If $9,000 worth of jewelry and $12,000 worth of silverware were stolen from a family without additional insurance, what amount of the claim would not be covered by insurance? (LO8.2)

2. What amount would a person with actual cash value coverage receive for two-year-old furniture destroyed by a fire? The furniture would cost $2,000 to replace today and had an estimated life of five years. (LO8.2)

3. What would it cost an insurance company to replace a family's personal property that originally cost $40,000? The replacement costs for the items have increased 15 percent. (LO8.2)

4. If Carissa Dalton has a $260,000 home insured for $200,000, based on the 80 percent coinsurance provision, how much would the insurance company pay on a claim of $10,000? Assume there is no deductible. (LO8.2)

5. For each of the following situations, what amount would the insurance company pay? (LO8.2)
   a. Wind damage of $1,835; the insured has a deductible of $500.
   b. Theft of a stereo system worth $4,000; the insured has a deductible of $500.
   c. Vandalism that does $425 of damage to a home; the insured has a deductible of $500.

6. Becky Fenton has 25/50/10 automobile insurance coverage. If two other people are awarded $35,000 each for injuries in an auto accident in which Becky was judged at fault, how much of this judgment would the insurance cover? (LO8.4)

7. Kurt Simmons has 50/100/15 auto insurance coverage. One evening, he lost control of his vehicle, hitting a parked car and damaging a storefront along the street. Damage to the parked car was $5,400, and damage to the store was $12,650. What amount will the insurance company pay for the damages? What amount will Kurt have to pay? (LO8.4)

8. Karen and Mike currently insure their cars with separate companies, paying $700 and $900 a year. If they insured both cars with the same company, they would save 10 percent on the annual premiums. What would be the future value of the annual savings over 10 years based on an annual interest rate of 4 percent? (LO8.5)

9. When Carolina's house burned down, she lost household items worth a total of $50,000. Her house was insured for $160,000, and her homeowner's policy provided

coverage for personal belongings up to 55 percent of the insured value of the house. Calculate how much insurance coverage Carolina's policy provides for her personal possessions and whether she will receive payment for all of the items destroyed in the fire. (LO8.2)

10. Dave and Ellen are newly married and living in their first house. The yearly premium on their homeowner's insurance policy is $450 for the coverage they need. Their insurance company offers a discount of 5 percent if they install dead-bolt locks on all exterior doors. The couple can also receive a discount of 2 percent if they install smoke detectors on each floor. They have contacted a locksmith, who will provide and install dead-bolt locks on the two exterior doors for $60 each. At the local hardware store, smoke detectors cost $8 each, and the new house has two floors. Dave and Ellen can install the smoke detectors themselves. What discount will Dave and Ellen receive if they install the dead-bolt locks? If they install smoke detectors? (LO8.2)

11. In the preceding example, assuming their insurance rates remain the same, how many years will it take Dave and Ellen to earn back in discounts the cost of the dead-bolts? The cost of the smoke detectors? Would you recommend Dave and Ellen invest in the safety items if they plan to stay in the house for about five years? Why or why not? (LO8.2)

12. Shaan and Anita currently insure their cars with separate companies, paying $650 and $575 a year. If they insure both cars with the same company, they would save 10 percent on their annual premiums. What would be the future value of the annual savings over 10 years based on an annual interest rate of 6 percent? (LO8.5)

 **To reinforce the content in this chapter, more problems are provided at connect.mheducation.com.**

FINANCIAL LITERACY PORTFOLIO

HOME/AUTO INSURANCE COVERAGE

Competency

Research and select renter's/homeowner's and auto insurance coverage.

Action Research

(1) Based on this chapter, *Your Personal Financial Plan Sheet 28* and *Sheet 29*, and online research, identify needed renter's/homeowner's insurance now or in the future along with the source and cost of the coverage.

(2) Based on this chapter and *Your Personal Financial Plan Sheet 30*, identify needed motor vehicle insurance now or in the future along with the source and cost of the coverage.

Outcome

Prepare a visual summary of the actions you are currently taking or might take in the future related to: (1) home/property insurance; and (2) automobile insurance. For each type of insurance, in addition to action steps, include the types and amounts of coverage needed as well as the source and cost of the insurance.

REAL LIFE PERSONAL FINANCE

WE RENT, SO WHY DO WE NEED INSURANCE?

"Have you been down in the basement?" Nathan asked his wife, Erin, as he entered their apartment.

"No, what's up?" responded Erin.

"It's flooded because of all that rain we got last weekend!" he exclaimed.

"Oh no! We have the extra furniture my mom gave us stored down there. Is everything ruined?" Erin asked.

"The couch and coffee table are in a foot of water; the love seat was the only thing that looked OK. Boy, I didn't realize the basement of this building wasn't waterproof. I'm going to call our landlady to complain."

As Erin thought about the situation, she remembered that when they moved in last fall, Kathy, their landlady, had informed them that her insurance policy covered the building but not the property belonging to each tenant. Because of this, they had purchased renter's insurance. "Nathan, I think our renter's insurance will cover the damage. Let me give our agent a call."

When Erin and Nathan purchased their insurance, they had to decide whether they wanted to be insured for cash value or for replacement costs. Replacement was more expensive, but it meant they would collect enough to go out and buy new household items at today's prices. If they had opted for cash value, the couch for which Erin's mother had paid $1,000 five years ago would be worth less than $500 today.

Erin made the call and found out their insurance did cover the furniture in the basement and at replacement value after they paid the deductible. The $300 they had invested in renter's insurance last year was well worth it!

Not every renter has as much foresight as Erin and Nathan. About 4 in 10 renters have renter's insurance. Some aren't even aware they need it. They may assume they are covered by the landlord's insurance, but they aren't. This mistake can be costly.

Think about how much you have invested in your possessions and how much it would cost to replace them. Start with your stereo equipment or the flat screen television and DVD player that you bought last year. Experts suggest that people who rent start thinking about these things as soon as they move into their first apartment. Your policy should cover your personal belongings and provide funds for living expenses if you are dispossessed by a fire or other disaster.

Questions

1. Why is it important for people who rent to have insurance?
2. Does the building owner's property insurance ever cover the tenant's personal property?
3. What is the difference between cash value and replacement value?
4. When shopping for renter's insurance, what coverage features should you look for?

CONTINUING CASE

HOME AND AUTOMOBILE INSURANCE

Jamie Lee and Ross have had several milestones in the past year. They got married, recently purchased their first home, and now have twins on the way!

Jamie Lee and Ross have to seriously consider their insurance needs and develop a risk management plan to help them should an unexpected event arise.

Current Financial Situation

Assets *(Jamie Lee and Ross combined):*

Checking account, $4,300

Savings account, $22,200

Emergency fund savings account, $20,500

IRA balance, $26,000

Cars, $10,000 *(Jamie Lee)* and $18,000 *(Ross)*

Liabilities *(Jamie Lee and Ross combined):*

Student loan balance, $0

Credit card balance, $2,000

Car loans, $6,000

Income:

Jamie Lee, $50,000 gross income ($37,500 net income after taxes)

Ross, $75,000 gross income ($64,000 net income after taxes)

Monthly Expenses *(Jamie Lee and Ross combined):*

Mortgage, $1,252

Property taxes and insurance, $500

Utilities, $195

Food, $400

Gas/Maintenance, $275

Credit card payment, $250

Car loan payment, $289

Entertainment, $300

Questions

1. Based on their current life status, what are some of the goals Jamie Lee and Ross should set when developing their insurance plan?
2. What four questions should Jamie Lee and Ross ask themselves as they develop the risk management plan?
3. Once Jamie Lee and Ross put their insurance plan into action, what should they do to maintain their plan?
4. Jamie and Ross decided to conduct a checkup on their homeowner's insurance policy. They noticed that they had omitted covering Jamie Lee's diamond wedding band set in their policy. What if it got lost or stolen? It was a major purchase, and besides the emotional value, the cost to replace the diamond jewelry would be very high. What type of policy should Jamie Lee and Ross consider to cover the wedding rings?
5. Mr. Ferrell, Jamie Lee and Ross's insurance agent, suggested a flood insurance policy in addition to their regular homeowner's policy. Jamie Lee and Ross looked quizzically at the agent, as they do not live within 2 miles of a body of water. What is the basis for Mr. Ferrell's claim for the necessity of the flood policy?
6. Using *Your Personal Financial Plan Sheet 27*, create a home inventory for Jamie Lee and Ross. Consider items of value that may be located in each of the rooms of the house and determine a dollar amount for each item. What is the total cost of the items?
7. Considering the value of Jamie Lee and Ross's automobiles, what type of automobile insurance coverage would you suggest for them?
8. What financial strategy would you suggest to Jamie Lee and Ross to enable them to save money on their insurance premiums?

"MY SPENDING TAKES MOST OF MY MONEY, SO AFTER PAYING FOR CAR INSURANCE, MY BUDGET IS REALLY TIGHT."

Directions As you continue (or start) using your Daily Spending Diary sheets, you should be able to make better choices for your spending priorities. The financial data you develop will help you better understand your spending patterns and help you plan for achieving financial goals. The Daily Spending Diary sheets are located at the end of Chapter 1 and in Connect Finance.

Questions

1. What information from your Daily Spending Diary might encourage you to use your money differently?
2. How can your spending habits be altered to ensure that you will be able to afford appropriate home and motor vehicle insurance coverage?

Name: _____ Date: _____

Current Insurance Policies and Needs

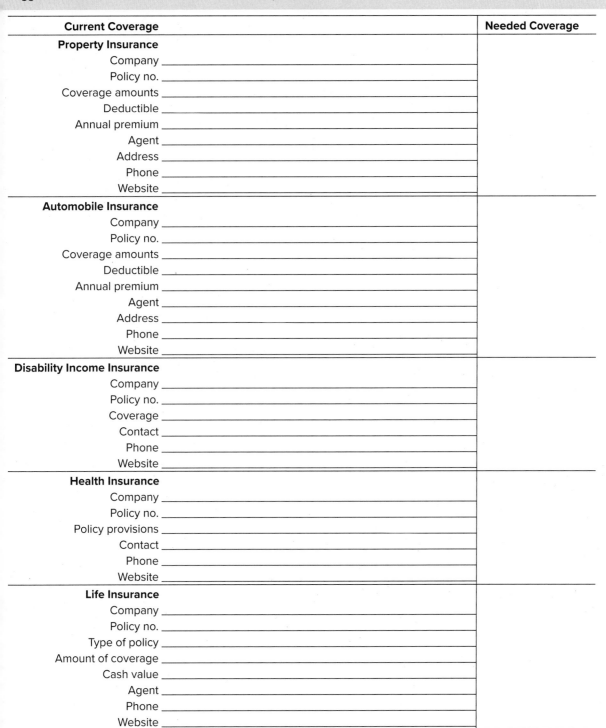

Purpose: To establish a record of current and needed insurance coverage.

Financial Planning Activities: List current insurance policies and areas where new or additional coverage is needed. This sheet is also available in an Excel spreadsheet format in Connect Finance.

Suggested Websites: www.insure.com, www.accuquote.com

Current Coverage	Needed Coverage
Property Insurance	
Company _____	
Policy no. _____	
Coverage amounts _____	
Deductible _____	
Annual premium _____	
Agent _____	
Address _____	
Phone _____	
Website _____	
Automobile Insurance	
Company _____	
Policy no. _____	
Coverage amounts _____	
Deductible _____	
Annual premium _____	
Agent _____	
Address _____	
Phone _____	
Website _____	
Disability Income Insurance	
Company _____	
Policy no. _____	
Coverage _____	
Contact _____	
Phone _____	
Website _____	
Health Insurance	
Company _____	
Policy no. _____	
Policy provisions _____	
Contact _____	
Phone _____	
Website _____	
Life Insurance	
Company _____	
Policy no. _____	
Type of policy _____	
Amount of coverage _____	
Cash value _____	
Agent _____	
Phone _____	
Website _____	

What's Next for Your Personal Financial Plan?

- Talk with friends and relatives to determine the types of insurance coverage they have.
- Conduct a web search for various types of insurance for which you need additional information.

Name: _____ **Date:** _____

Home Inventory

Purpose: To create a record of personal belongings for use when settling home insurance claims.

Financial Planning Activities: For each area of the home, list your possessions, including a description (model, serial number), cost, and date of acquisition. Also consider taking photographs and videos of your possessions. This sheet is also available in an Excel spreadsheet format in Connect Finance.

Suggested Websites: www.money.com, www.ambest.com

Item, Description	Cost	Date Acquired
Attic		
Bathroom		
Bedrooms		
Family room		
Living room		
Hallways		
Kitchen		
Dining room		
Basement		
Garage		
Other items		

Suggested App: Home Inventory

McGraw Hill

What's Next for Your Personal Financial Plan?

1. Determine common items that may be overlooked when preparing a home inventory.
2. Talk to a local insurance agent to determine the areas of protection that many people tend to overlook.

Determining Needed Property Insurance

Purpose: To determine property insurance needed for a home or apartment.

Financial Planning Activities: Estimate the value and your needs for the categories below. This sheet is also available in an Excel spreadsheet format in Connect Finance.

Suggested Websites: www.iii.org, www.quicken.com, www.naic.org

Real Property (this section not applicable to renters)

Current replacement value of home $ _____

Personal Property

Estimated value of appliances, furniture, clothing, and other household $ _____
items (conduct an inventory)

Type of coverage for personal property (check one)

Actual cash value   ☐

Replacement value   ☐

Additional coverage for items with limits on standard personal property coverage such as jewelry, firearms, silverware, and photographic, electronic, and computer equipment

Item	Amount
_____	_____
_____	_____
_____	_____

Personal Liability

Amount of additional personal liability coverage desired for possible personal $ _____
injury claims

Specialized Coverages

If appropriate, investigate flood or earthquake coverage excluded from $ _____
home insurance policies

NOTE: Use *Your Personal Financial Plan Sheet 29* to compare companies, coverages, and costs for apartment or
home insurance.

What's Next for Your Personal Financial Plan?

- Outline the steps involved in planning an insurance program.
- Outline special types of property and liability insurance such as personal computer insurance, trip cancellation
  insurance, and liability insurance.

Name: _____ Date: _____

Apartment/Home Insurance Comparison

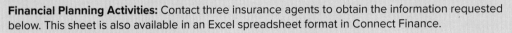

Purpose: To research and compare companies, coverages, and costs for apartment or home insurance.

Financial Planning Activities: Contact three insurance agents to obtain the information requested below. This sheet is also available in an Excel spreadsheet format in Connect Finance.

Suggested Websites: www.freeinsurancequotes.com, www.insure.com, www.insureuonline.org

Type of building   ☐ apartment   ☐ home   ☐ condominium

Location _____

Type of construction _____ Age of building _____

Company name			
Agent's name, address, and phone			
Coverage:	**Premium**	**Premium**	**Premium**
Dwelling $			
Other structure $ (does not apply to apartment/condo coverage)			
Personal property $			
Additional living expenses $			
Personal liability Bodily injury $ Property damage $			
Medical payments Per person $ Per accident $			
Deductible amount			
Other coverage $			
Service charges or fees			
Total Premium			

What's Next for Your Personal Financial Plan?

- List the reasons most commonly given by renters for not having renter's insurance.
- Determine cost differences for home insurance among various local agents and online providers.

Automobile Insurance Cost Comparison

Purpose: To research and compare companies, coverages, and costs for auto insurance.

Financial Planning Activities: Contact three insurance agents to obtain the information requested below. This sheet is also available in an Excel spreadsheet format in Connect Finance.

Suggested Websites: www.autoinsuranceindepth.com, www.progressive.com, www.standardandpoors.com

Vehicle (year, make, model, engine size) _____

Total miles driven in a year _____

Full- or part-time driver? _____

Driver's education completed? _____

Accidents or violations within the past three years? _____

Company name			
Agent's name, address, and phone			
E-mail, website			
Policy length (6 months, 1 year)			
Coverage:	Premium	Premium	Premium
Bodily injury liability Per person $ Per accident $			
Property damage liability per accident $			
Collision deductible $			
Comprehensive deductible $			
Medical payments per person $			
Uninsured motorist liability Per person $ Per accident $			
Other coverage			
Service charges			
Total Premium			

Suggested App:
• Pact I Car Insurance

McGraw Hill

What's Next for Your Personal Financial Plan?

• Research actions that you might take to reduce motor vehicle insurance costs.

• Talk to friends, relatives, and insurance agents to determine methods of reducing the cost of motor vehicle insurance.

9 Health and Disability Income Insurance

3 Steps to Financial Literacy . . .
Income Percent Covered by Disability

1 Calculate the amount of income that you would need if you are unable to work due to a non-work-related accident or illness. *App:* Mint

2 Determine if you have disability income insurance coverage through your employer. *Website:* www.ssa.gov

3 Decide if you need additional disability income insurance to protect you against loss of income. *Website:* www.usa.gov/ disability-benefits-insurance

A commonly overlooked element of financial planning is disability income insurance. Many financial experts point out that people between the ages of 40 and 65 have a greater chance of missing at least three months of work due to an accident or illness than they do of dying. At the end of the chapter, *Your Personal Finance Road Map and Dashboard* will provide guidelines for determining the appropriate coverage for disability income insurance for your life situation.

CHAPTER 9 LEARNING OBJECTIVES

In this chapter, you will learn to:

LO9.1 Recognize the importance of health insurance in financial planning.

LO9.2 Analyze the costs and benefits of various types of health insurance coverage as well as major provisions in health insurance policies.

LO9.3 Assess the trade-offs of different health insurance plans.

LO9.4 Evaluate the differences among health care plans offered by private companies and by the government.

LO9.5 Explain the importance of disability income insurance in financial planning and identify its sources.

LO9.6 Explain why the costs of health insurance and health care have been increasing.

YOUR PERSONAL FINANCIAL PLAN SHEETS

31. Assessing Current and Needed Health Care Insurance
32. Disability Income Insurance Needs

Health Insurance and Financial Planning

What Is Health Insurance?

Health insurance is a form of protection that eases the financial burden people may experience as a result of illness or injury. You pay a *premium,* or fee, to the insurer. In return, the company pays most of your medical costs. Although plans vary in what they cover, they may reimburse you for hospital stays, doctors' visits, medications, and sometimes vision and dental care.

Health insurance includes both medical expense insurance, as discussed above, and disability income insurance. *Medical expense insurance* typically pays only the actual medical costs. *Disability income insurance* provides payments to make up for some of the income of a person who cannot work as a result of injury or illness. In this chapter, the term *health insurance* refers to medical expense insurance.

Health insurance plans can be purchased in several different ways: group health insurance, individual health insurance, and a federal law known as COBRA.

GROUP HEALTH INSURANCE Most people who have health insurance are covered under group plans. Typically, these plans are employer sponsored. This means that the employer offers the plans and usually pays some or all of the premiums. However, not all employers provide health insurance to their employees. The Affordable Care Act of 2010 (ACA), discussed in the "Private Health Care Plans and Government Health Care Programs" section of this chapter, requires large employers to provide health insurance coverage for all employees. The ACA protections related to employment-based group health plans include extending dependent coverage until age 26, prohibiting preexisting condition exclusions, banning annual and life-time limits on coverage for essential health benefits, and requiring group health plans and insurers to provide an easy-to-understand summary of a health plan's benefits and coverage. Other organizations, such as labor unions and professional associations, also offer group plans. Group insurance plans cover you and your immediate family. The Health Insurance Portability and Accountability Act of 1996 (HIPAA) set federal

LO9.1

Recognize the importance of health insurance in financial planning.

ACTION ITEM

I am aware of several different ways of purchasing health insurance.

☐ Yes ☐ No

Financial Literacy in Practice

Starting a New Job? Make Your Health Benefits Work for You

The U.S. Department of Labor's Employee Benefits Security Administration administers several important health benefit laws covering employer-based health plans. These laws govern your basic rights to information about how your health plan works, how to qualify for benefits, and how to make claims for benefits. In addition, there are specific laws protecting your right to health benefits when you lose coverage or change jobs.

- **Realize that your options are important.** There are many different types of health benefit plans. Find out which one your employer offers, and then check out the plan, or plans, offered. Your employer's human resource office, the health plan administrator, or your union can provide information to help you match your needs and preferences with the available plans. If your employer offers a high-deductible health plan, look into setting up a health savings account to save money for future medical expenses on a tax-free basis. The more information you have, the better your health care decisions will be.

- **Review the benefits available.** Do the plans cover preventive care, well-baby care, vision or dental care? Are there deductibles? Answers to these questions can help determine the out-of-pocket expenses you may face. Matching your needs and those of your family members will result in the best possible benefits. Cheapest may not always be best. Your goal is to obtain high-quality health benefits.

- **Read your plan's summary plan description (SPD).** Provided by your health plan administrator, the SPD outlines your benefits and your legal rights under the Employee Retirement Income Security Act, the federal law that protects your health benefits. It should contain information about the coverage of dependents, what services will require a copay, and the circumstances under which your employer can change or terminate a health benefits plan. Save the SPD and all other health plan brochures and documents, along with memos or correspondence from your employer relating to health benefits.

- **Assess your benefit coverage as your family status changes.** Marriage, divorce, childbirth or adoption, or the death of a spouse are life events that may require changes in your health benefits. You, your spouse, and dependent children may be eligible for a special enrollment period under provisions of the Health Insurance Portability and Accountability Act. Even without life-changing events, the information provided by your employer should tell you how you can change benefits or switch plans, if more than one plan is offered.

- **Know that changing jobs and other life events can affect your health benefits.** Under COBRA, you, your covered spouse, and your dependent children may be eligible to purchase extended health coverage under your employer's plan if you lose your job, change employers, get divorced, or upon occurrence of certain other events.

- **Look for wellness programs.** More and more employers are establishing wellness programs that encourage employees to exercise, stop smoking, and generally adopt healthier lifestyles.

- **Plan for retirement.** Before you retire, find out what health benefits, if any, extend to you and your spouse during your retirement years. Consult with your employer's human resources office, your union, and the plan administrator, and check your SPD.

- **Know how to file an appeal if your health benefits claim is denied.** Understand how your plan handles grievances and where to make appeals of the plan's decisions. Keep records and copies of correspondence. Check your health benefits package and your SPD to determine who is responsible for handling problems with benefit claims.

Source: U.S. Department of Labor, *Top 10 Ways to Make Your Health Benefits Work for You*, https://www.dol.gov/sites/dolgov/files/EBSA/about-ebsa/our-activities/resource-center/publications/top-10-ways-to-make-your-health-benefits-work-for-you.pdf, accessed March 4, 2020.

standards to ensure that workers would not lose their health insurance if they changed jobs. As a result, a parent with a sick child, for example, can move from one group health plan to another without a lapse in coverage. Moreover, the parent will not have to pay more for coverage than other employees do. HIPAA also protects against discrimination in health coverage based on certain health factors such as prior medical conditions, previous claims experience, and genetic information.

Are you starting a new job? Read the nearby *Financial Literacy in Practice* feature to learn how to make your group health benefits work for you.

The cost of group insurance is relatively low because many people are insured under the same *policy*—a contract with a risk-sharing group, or insurance company. However, group insurance plans vary in the amount of protection that they provide.

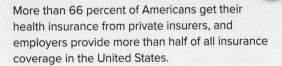

money minute focus

More than 66 percent of Americans get their health insurance from private insurers, and employers provide more than half of all insurance coverage in the United States.

For example, some plans limit the amount that they will pay for hospital stays and surgical procedures. If your plan does not cover all of your health insurance needs, you have several choices.

If you are married, you may be able to take advantage of a coordination of benefits provision, which is included in most group insurance plans. This provision allows you to combine the benefits from more than one insurance plan. The benefits received from all the plans are limited to 100 percent of all allowable medical expenses. For example, a couple could use benefits from one spouse's group plan and from the other spouse's plan up to 100 percent.

If this type of provision is not available to you, or if you are single, you can buy individual health insurance for added protection.

money minute focus

The Family and Medical Leave Act of 1993 provides eligible employees with up to 12 weeks of unpaid job-protected leave per year. It also requires that their group health benefits be maintained during the leave.

INDIVIDUAL HEALTH INSURANCE Some people do not have access to an employer-sponsored group insurance plan because they are self-employed or work for an employer that doesn't offer it. Others are simply dissatisfied with the coverage that their group plan provides. In these cases, individual health insurance may be the answer. You can buy individual health insurance directly from the company of your choice. Plans usually cover you as an individual or you and your family. Individual plans can be adapted to meet your own needs. You should comparison shop, however, because rates vary.

THE CONSOLIDATED OMNIBUS BUDGET RECONCILIATION ACT OF 1986 (COBRA). If you are covered under your employer's health plan and you lose your job, have your hours reduced, or get laid off and your employer's health plan continues to exist, you and your dependents may qualify to purchase temporary extended health coverage under COBRA at group rates under the employer's plan. Divorce, legal separation, loss of dependent child status, the covered employee's death, or entitlement to Medicare may also give your covered spouse and dependent children the right to elect continued coverage under COBRA. Your plan must be notified of these events. Generally, COBRA covers group health plans maintained by employers with 20 or more employees. The group health plan is required to provide you with a written notice indicating your eligibility for COBRA coverage. If you are eligible, you will have 60 days from the date the notice is sent or from the date your coverage ends—whichever is later—to elect COBRA. If the employer is too small to be subject to COBRA, state law may require the plan's insurer to provide some continuation coverage. Caution: Not everyone qualifies for COBRA, and the coverage may be quite expensive. You have to work for a private company or state or local government to benefit.

What are your options if you are unemployed or cannot afford health insurance? You may be able to get an affordable health insurance plan through the Health Insurance Marketplace (discussed in the "Health Insurance and Financial Planning" section in this chapter). You may also qualify for free or low-cost coverage through Medicaid or the Children's Health Insurance Program (CHIP). CHIP provides coverage for children and, in some states, pregnant women if you cannot afford private insurance. Each state offers CHIP coverage and works closely with its state Medicaid program. For more information, call HealthCare.gov at 1-800-318-2596.

PRACTICE QUIZ 9–1

1. What is health insurance?

2. What are the three ways of purchasing health insurance?

3. For the following statements, circle "T" for true or "F" for false.

    a. Health insurance is available only as a benefit from an employer.   T   F

    b. You can continue your health insurance even if you leave a job.   T   F

basic health insurance coverage Hospital expense insurance, surgical expense insurance, and physician expense insurance.

hospital expense insurance Pays part or all of hospital bills for room, board, and other charges.

surgical expense insurance Pays part or all of the surgeon's fees for an operation.

physician expense insurance Provides benefits for doctors' fees for nonsurgical care, X rays, and lab tests.

coinsurance A provision under which both the insured and the insurer share the covered losses.

stop-loss A provision under which the policyholder pays a certain amount, after which the insurance company pays 100 percent of the remaining covered expenses.

Health Insurance Coverage

Several types of health insurance coverage are available, either through a group plan or through individual purchase. Some benefits are included in nearly every health insurance plan; other benefits are seldom offered.

Types of Health Insurance Coverage

BASIC HEALTH INSURANCE COVERAGE Basic health insurance coverage includes hospital expense coverage, surgical expense coverage, and physician expense coverage.

HOSPITAL EXPENSE Hospital expense coverage pays for some or all of the daily costs of room and board during a hospital stay. Routine nursing care, minor medical supplies, and the use of other hospital facilities are covered as well. For example, covered expenses would include anesthesia, laboratory fees, dressings, X rays, local ambulance service, and the use of an operating room.

Be aware, though, that most policies set a maximum amount they will pay for each day you are in the hospital. They may also limit the number of days they will cover. Recall from Chapter 8 that many policies require a deductible.

SURGICAL EXPENSE Surgical expense insurance pays all or part of the surgeon's fees for an operation, whether it is done in a hospital or in the doctor's office. Policies often have a list of the services that they cover, which specifies the maximum payment for each type of operation. For example, a policy might allow $500 for an appendectomy. If the entire surgeon's bill is not covered, the policyholder has to pay the difference. People often buy surgical expense coverage in combination with hospital expense coverage.

PHYSICIAN EXPENSE Physician expense insurance meets some or all the costs of physician care that do not involve surgery. This form of health insurance covers treatment in a hospital, a doctor's office, or even a patient's home. Plans may cover routine doctor visits, X rays, and lab tests. Like surgical expense coverage, physician expense coverage specifies maximum benefits for each service. Physician expense coverage is usually combined with surgical and hospital coverage in a package called basic health insurance.

MAJOR MEDICAL EXPENSE INSURANCE COVERAGE Most people find that basic health insurance meets their usual needs. The cost of a serious illness or accident, however, can quickly go beyond the amounts that basic health insurance will pay. For example, Chen had emergency surgery, which meant an operation, a two-week hospital stay, a number of lab tests, and several follow-up visits. He was shocked to discover that his basic health insurance paid less than half of the total bill, leaving him with debts of more than $25,000.

Chen would have been better protected if he had had major medical expense insurance. This coverage pays the large costs involved in long hospital stays and multiple surgeries. In other words, it takes up where basic health insurance coverage leaves off. Almost every type of care and treatment prescribed by a physician, in and out of a hospital, is covered. Maximum benefits can range from $10,000 to more than $1 million per illness per year.

Of course, this type of coverage isn't cheap. To control premiums, most major medical plans require a deductible. Some plans also include a coinsurance provision. **Coinsurance** is the percentage of the medical expenses the policyholder must pay in addition to the deductible amount. Many policies require policyholders to pay more than 25 percent of expenses after they have paid the deductible.

Some major medical policies contain a stop-loss provision. **Stop-loss** is a provision that requires the policyholder to pay all costs up to a certain amount, after which the insurance

> **EXAMPLE: Deductibles and Coinsurance**
>
> Ariana's policy includes an $800 deductible and a coinsurance provision requiring her to pay 20 percent of all bills. If her bill total is $3,800, for instance, the company will first exclude $800 from coverage, which is Ariana's deductible. It will then pay 80 percent of the remaining $3,000, or $2,400. Therefore, Ariana's total costs are $1,400 ($800 for the deductible and $600 for the coinsurance).

company pays 100 percent of the remaining expenses, as long as they are covered in the policy. Typically, the policyholder will pay between $5,000 and $8,000 in out-of-pocket expenses before the coverage begins.

Major medical expense insurance may be offered as a single policy with basic health insurance coverage, or it can be bought separately. Comprehensive major medical insurance is a type of complete insurance that helps pay hospital, surgical, medical, and other bills. It has a low deductible, usually $500 to $1,000. Many major medical policies set limits on the benefits they will pay for certain expenses, such as surgery and hospital room and board.

HOSPITAL INDEMNITY POLICIES A hospital indemnity policy pays benefits when you're hospitalized. Unlike most of the other plans mentioned, however, these policies don't directly cover medical costs. Instead, you are paid in cash, which you can spend on medical or nonmedical expenses as you choose. Hospital indemnity policies are used as a supplement to—and not a replacement for—basic health or major medical policies. The average person who buys such a policy, however, usually pays much more in premiums than he or she receives in payments.

money minute focus

The Coalition Against Insurance Fraud provides "scam alerts" on phony health coverage, including a list of 10 warning signs. Visit **www.insurancefraud.org**.

DENTAL EXPENSE INSURANCE Dental expense insurance provides reimbursement for the expenses of dental services and supplies. It encourages preventive dental care. The coverage normally provides for oral examinations (including X rays and cleanings), fillings, extractions, oral surgery, dentures, and braces. As with other insurance plans, dental insurance may have a deductible and a coinsurance provision, stating that the policyholder pays from 20 to 50 percent after the deductible. The Affordable Care Act requires dental and vision care insurance for children under age 19.

VISION CARE INSURANCE An increasing number of insurance companies are including vision care insurance as part of group plans. Vision care insurance may cover eye examinations, glasses, contact lenses, eye surgery, and the treatment of eye diseases.

DREAD DISEASE INSURANCE Dread disease, travel insurance, death insurance, and cancer policies are usually sold through the mail, in newspapers and magazines, or by door-to-door salespeople. These kinds of policies play upon unrealistic fears, and they are illegal in many states. They cover only specific conditions, which are already fully covered if you are insured under a major medical plan.

LONG-TERM CARE INSURANCE Long-term care insurance (LTC) provides coverage for the expense of daily help that you may need if you become seriously ill or disabled and are unable to care for yourself. It is useful whether you require a lengthy stay in a nursing home or just need help at home with daily activities such as dressing, bathing, and household chores. Annual premiums range from less than $2,000 to over $19,000, depending on your age and extent of the coverage. The older you are when you enroll, the higher your

long-term care insurance (LTC) Provides day-in, day-out care for long-term illness or disability.

annual premium. Typically, individual insurance plans are sold to the 50- to 80-year age group, pay benefits for a maximum of two to six years, and carry a dollar limit on the total benefits they will pay.

According to experts, long-term care protection makes sense for people with a net worth of $100,000 to $2 million. If your net worth is less than $100,000, you will exhaust your assets and qualify for Medicaid; if your assets are more than $2 million, you can fund your own long-term care. If you purchase a policy, consider at least a three-year term with a daily benefit that would cover the nursing-facility cost in your area. Recently, the national daily average cost of a nursing home facility was $275, or more than $100,375 per year.

Explore services available in your community to help meet long-term care needs. Care given by family members can be supplemented by visiting nurses, home health aides, friendly visitor programs, home-delivered meals, chore services, adult day care centers, and respite services for caregivers who need a break from daily responsibilities.

These services are becoming more widely available. Some or all of them may be found in your community. Your local area Agency on Aging or Office on Aging can help you locate the services you need. Call the Eldercare Locator at 1-800-677-1116 to locate your local office.

Major Provisions in a Health Insurance Policy

All health insurance policies have certain provisions in common. You have to be sure that you understand what your policy covers. What are the benefits? What are the limits? The following are details of provisions that are usually found in health insurance policies:

- *Eligibility:* The people covered by the policy must meet specified eligibility requirements, such as family relationship and, for children, a certain age.

- *Assigned benefits:* You are reimbursed for payments when you turn in your bills and claim forms. When you assign benefits, you let your insurer make direct payments to your doctor or hospital.

- *Internal limits:* A policy with internal limits sets specific levels of repayment for certain services. Even if your hospital room costs $1,000 a day, you won't be able to get more than $250 if an internal limit specifies that maximum.

copayment A provision under which the insured pays a flat dollar amount each time a covered medical service is received after the deductible has been met.

- *Copayment:* A **copayment** is a flat fee that you pay every time you receive a covered service. The fee is usually between $20 and $40, and the insurer pays the balance of the cost of the service. This is different from coinsurance, which is the percentage of your medical costs for which you are responsible after paying your deductible

- *Service benefits:* Policies with this provision list coverage in terms of services, not dollar amounts: You're entitled to X rays, for instance, not $100 worth of X rays per visit. Service benefits provisions are always preferable to dollar amount coverage because the insurer will pay all the costs.

- *Benefit limits:* This provision defines a maximum benefit, either in terms of a dollar amount or in terms of number of days spent in the hospital.

- *Exclusions and limitations:* This provision specifies services that the policy does not cover. It may include preexisting conditions (a condition you were diagnosed with before your insurance plan took effect), cosmetic surgery, or more.

- *Guaranteed renewable:* This provision means that the insurer can't cancel the policy unless you fail to pay the premiums. It also forbids insurers from raising premiums unless they raise all premiums for all members of your group.

- *Cancellation and termination:* This provision explains the circumstances under which the insurer can cancel your coverage. It also explains how you can convert your group contract into an individual contract.

PRACTICE QUIZ 9–2

1. What three types of coverage are included in the basic health insurance?

2. What benefits are provided by:
  a. Hospital expense coverage?
  b. Surgical expense coverage?
  c. Physician expense coverage?

3. Match the following terms with an appropriate statement.

coinsurance   *a.* Requires the policyholder to pay all costs up to a certain amount _____

stop-loss   *b.* The percentage of the medical expenses you must pay _____

hospital indemnity   *c.* A policy used as a supplement to basic health or major medical policies _____
policy

exclusions and   *d.* Defines who is covered by the policy _____
limitations

copayment   *e.* Specifies services that the policy does not cover _____

eligibility   *f.* A flat fee that you pay every time you receive a covered service _____

Health Insurance Trade-Offs

Different health insurance policies may offer very different benefits. As you decide which insurance plan to buy, consider the following trade-offs.

Coverage Trade-Offs

REIMBURSEMENT VERSUS INDEMNITY A reimbursement policy pays you back for actual expenses. An indemnity policy provides you with specific amounts, regardless of how much the actual expenses may be.

> **EXAMPLE: Reimbursement versus Indemnity**
>
> Katie and Seth are both charged $200 for an office visit to the same specialist. Katie's reimbursement policy has a deductible of $300. Once she has met the deductible, the policy will cover the full cost of such a visit. Seth's indemnity policy will pay him $125, which is what his plan provides for a visit to any specialist.

INTERNAL LIMITS VERSUS AGGREGATE LIMITS A policy with internal limits will cover only a fixed amount for an expense, such as the daily cost of room and board during a hospital stay. A policy with aggregate limits will limit only the total amount of coverage (the maximum dollar amount paid for all benefits in a year), such as $1 million in major expense benefits, or it may have no limits.

LO9.3

Assess the trade-offs of different health insurance plans.

ACTION ITEM

In choosing health insurance coverage, I should get a basic plan and a major medical supplement policy.

☐ Yes ☐ No

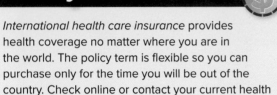

DEDUCTIBLES AND COINSURANCE The cost of a health insurance policy can be greatly affected by the size of the deductible (the set amount that the policyholder must pay toward medical expenses before the insurance company pays benefits). It can also be affected by the terms of the *coinsurance provision* (which states what percentage of the medical expenses the policyholder must pay in addition to the deductible amount).

OUT-OF-POCKET LIMITS Some policies limit the amount of money you must pay for the deductible and coinsurance. After you have reached that limit, the insurance company covers 100 percent of any additional costs. The out-of-pocket limit does not include your monthly premiums, out-of-network care and services, and anything for services your plan does not cover. The out-of-pocket limits for Health Insurance Marketplace plans vary but cannot go over a set amount each year. For example, in 2020, the limit was $8,150 for an individual and $16,300 for a family. Out-of-pocket limits help you lower your financial risk, but they also increase your premiums.

BENEFITS BASED ON REASONABLE AND CUSTOMARY CHARGES Some policies consider the average fee for a service in a particular geographical area. They then use the amount to set a limit on payments to policyholders. If the standard cost of a certain procedure is $1,500 in your part of the country, then your policy won't pay more than that amount.

Which Coverage Should You Choose?

Now that you are familiar with the available types of health insurance and some of their major provisions, how do you choose one? The type of coverage you choose will depend on the amount you can afford to spend on the premiums and the level of benefits that you feel you want and need. It may also depend on the kind of coverage your employer offers, if you are covered through your employer.

You can buy basic health coverage, major medical coverage, or both basic and major medical coverage. Any of these three choices will take care of at least some of your medical expenses. Ideally, you should get a basic plan and a major medical supplement. Another option is to purchase a comprehensive major medical policy that combines the value of both plans in a single policy. Exhibit 9–1 describes the most basic features you should look for.

Exhibit **9–1**

Health Insurance Must-Haves

A health insurance plan should:

- Offer basic coverage for hospital and doctor bills.

- Provide at least 120 days' hospital room and board paid in full.

- Pay at least 80 percent of out-of-hospital expenses after a yearly deductible of $1,000 per person or $2,000 per family.

- Impose no unreasonable exclusions.

- Limit your out-of-pocket expenses to no more than $8,000 to $9,000 a year, excluding dental, vision care, and prescription costs.

Although health insurance plans vary greatly, all plans should have the same basic features. Would you add anything to this list of must-haves?

WHAT WOULD YOU DO?   You are 35, single, and in reasonably good health. You have the choice of three health insurance plans offered by your employer. The first, with a $40 monthly premium, has a lifetime benefit of $1 million for all covered expenses, an annual deductible of $500, and a 15 percent coinsurance provision up to the first $2,000 in covered charges. The second requires a monthly premium of $50 and sets a $500,000 lifetime limit on benefits, no annual deductible, and a $25 copayment per office visit. The third, carries a $60 monthly premium, has an annual deductible of $250 and a 25 percent coinsurance provision up to the first $1,500 in covered charges, with a lifetime limit of benefits of $700,000. Which of these three plans makes the most sense for you?

Sheet 31 Assessing Current and Needed Health Care Insurance

PRACTICE QUIZ 9–3

1. As you decide which health insurance plan to buy, what trade-offs would you consider?

2. Match the following terms with an appropriate statement.

reimbursement	a. A policy that will cover only a fixed amount of an expense _____
indemnity	b. A policy that pays you back for actual expenses _____
internal limits	c. A policy that provides you with specific amounts, regardless of how much the actual expenses may be _____
deductible	d. After you have reached a certain limit, the insurance company covers 100 percent of any additional cost. _____
out-of-pocket limit	e. The set amount that you must pay toward medical expenses before the insurance company pays benefits _____

3. What basic features should be included in your health insurance plan?

Private Health Care Plans and Government Health Care Programs

Private Health Care Plans

Most health insurance in the United States is provided by private organizations rather than by the government. Private health care plans may be offered by a number of sources: private insurance companies; hospital and medical service plans; health maintenance organizations; preferred provider organizations; home health care agencies; and employer self-funded health plans.

PRIVATE INSURANCE COMPANIES Several hundred private insurance companies are in the health insurance business. They provide mostly group health plans to employers, which in turn offer them to their employees as a benefit. Premiums may be fully or partially paid by the employer, with the employee paying any remainder. These policies typically pay you for medical costs you incur, or they send the payment directly to the doctor, hospital, or lab that provides the services.

LO9.4

Evaluate the differences among health care plans offered by private companies and by the government.

ACTION ITEM

I am aware of health care plans offered by private companies and by the government.

☐ Yes ☐ No

Blue Cross An independent membership corporation that provides protection against the cost of hospital care.

HOSPITAL AND MEDICAL SERVICE PLANS Blue Cross and Blue Shield are statewide organizations similar to private health insurance companies. Each state has its own Blue Cross and Blue Shield. The "Blues" provide health insurance to millions of Americans. **Blue Cross** provides hospital care benefits. **Blue Shield** provides benefits for surgical and medical services performed by physicians.

FinTech for Financial Literacy

CROWDFUNDING You may use crowdfunding websites to raise money to pay for medical expenses, education, or emergencies. If you create a crowdfunding campaign, the money you collect may be taxed by the IRS. You could also lose your eligibility for Medicaid, Social Security income, or food vouchers. Contact your local Medicaid, Social Security, or SNAP benefits offices to learn how crowdfunding affects your eligibility for benefits.

HEALTH MAINTENANCE ORGANIZATIONS Rising health care costs have led to an increase in managed care plans. According to a recent industry survey, 23 percent of employed Americans are enrolled in some form of managed care. **Managed care** refers to prepaid health plans that provide comprehensive health care to their members. Managed care is designed to control the cost of health care services by controlling how they are used. Managed care is offered by health maintenance organizations (HMOs), exclusive provider organizations (EPOs), preferred provider organizations (PPOs), and point-of-service plans (POSs).

Health maintenance organizations are an alternative to basic health insurance and major medical expense insurance. A **health maintenance organization (HMO)** is a health insurance plan that directly employs or contracts

Blue Shield An independent membership corporation that provides protection against the cost of surgical and medical care.

managed care Prepaid health plans that provide comprehensive health care to members.

health maintenance organization (HMO) A health insurance plan that provides a wide range of health care services for a fixed, prepaid monthly premium.

with selected physicians and other medical professionals to provide health care services in exchange for a fixed, prepaid monthly premium.

HMOs are based on the idea that preventive services will minimize future medical problems. Therefore, these plans typically cover routine immunizations and checkups, screening programs, and diagnostic tests. They also provide customers with coverage for surgery, hospitalization, and emergency care. If you have an HMO, you will usually pay a small copayment for each covered service. Supplemental services may include vision care and prescription services, which are typically available for an additional fee.

When you first enroll in an HMO, you must choose a plan physician from a list of doctors provided by the HMO. The physician provides or arranges for all of your health care services. You must receive care through your plan physician; if you don't, you are responsible for the cost of the service. The only exception to this rule is in the case of a medical emergency. If you experience a sudden illness or injury that would threaten your life or health if not treated immediately, you may go to the emergency room of the nearest hospital. All other care must be provided by hospitals and doctors under contract with the HMO.

HMOs are not for everyone. Many HMO customers complain that their HMO denies them necessary care. Others feel restricted by the limited choice of doctors and the use of only the in-network physicians. Because HMOs require you to use only certain doctors, you should make sure that these doctors are near your home or office. You should also be able to change doctors easily if you don't like your first choice. Similarly, second opinions should always be available at the HMO's expense, and you should be able to appeal any case in which the HMO denies care. Finally, look at the costs and benefits: Will you incur out-of-pocket expenses or copayments? What services will the plan provide?

Exclusive Provider Plans (EPO) A hybrid health insurance plan in which services are covered only if the plan's network providers are used (except in an emergency).

EXCLUSIVE PROVIDER ORGANIZATIONS With **Exclusive provider plans (EPOs),** as with HMO plans, you are required to use providers in the network. If you don't use in-network providers, you have to pay the full cost of your care. However, there are exceptions for emergencies and if you need care that is not available in the network. EPO plans usually don't require you to have a primary care physician. You also don't need a referral to go to a specialist.

preferred provider organization (PPO) A group of doctors and hospitals that agree to provide health care at rates approved by the insurer.

PREFERRED PROVIDER ORGANIZATIONS A variation on the HMO is a **preferred provider organization (PPO)**, a group of doctors and hospitals that agree to provide specified medical services to members at prearranged fees. PPOs offer these discounted services to employers either directly or indirectly through an insurance company. The premiums for PPOs are slightly higher than the premiums for HMOs.

PPO plan members often pay no deductibles and may make minimal copayments. Whereas HMOs require members to receive care from HMO providers only, PPOs allow members greater flexibility. Members can either visit a preferred provider (a physician whom you select from a list, as in an HMO) or go to their own physicians. Patients who decide to use their own doctors do not lose coverage as they would with an HMO. Instead, they must pay deductibles and larger copayments.

Increasingly, the difference between PPOs and HMOs is becoming less clear. A **point-of-service (POS) plan** combines features of both HMOs and PPOs. POSs use a network of participating physicians and medical professionals who have contracted to provide services for certain fees. As with your HMO, you choose a plan physician who manages your care and controls referrals to specialists. As long as you receive care from a plan provider, you pay little or nothing, just as you would with an HMO. However, you're allowed to seek care outside the network at a higher charge, as with a PPO. Exhibit 9-2 compares the major features of HMOs, EPOs, PPOs, and POS plans.

point-of-service (POS) plan A network of selected, contracted, participating providers; also called an *HMO-PPO hybrid* or *open-ended HMO.*

HOME HEALTH CARE AGENCIES Rising hospital costs, new medical technology, and the increasing number of elderly people have helped make home care one of the fastest-growing areas of the health care industry. Home health care consists of home health agencies; home care aide organizations; and hospices, facilities that care for the terminally ill. These providers offer medical care in a home setting in agreement with a medical order, often at a fraction of the cost hospitals would charge for a similar service.

EMPLOYER SELF-FUNDED HEALTH PLANS Some companies choose to self-insure. The company runs its own insurance plan, collecting premiums from employees and paying medical benefits as needed. However, these companies must cover any costs that exceed the income from premiums. Unfortunately, not all corporations have the financial assets necessary to cover these situations, which can mean a financial disaster for the company and its employees.

HEALTH SAVINGS ACCOUNTS Health savings accounts (HSAs), which Congress authorized in 2003, are the newest addition to the alphabet soup of health insurance available to American workers. Now you and your employer must sort through HSAs, health reimbursement accounts (HRAs), and flexible spending accounts (FSAs). Each has its own rules about how money is spent, how it can be spent, and how it is taxed.

Exhibit 9–2 How Managed Care Health Plans Compare

	HMO	EPO	PPO	Point-of-service
What's the cost?	Generally lowest of all plans	Usually lower than PPO	Generally highest of all plans	Usually lower than PPO
Do I have to use providers in the network?	Yes (except for emergencies and for care that isn't available in network)	Yes (except for emergencies and for care that isn't available in network)	No (but you'll have to pay more if you go out of network)	No (but you'll have to pay more if you go out of network)
Do I have to choose a primary care physician?	Yes	No	No	Usually
Do I need a referral to a specialist?	Yes	No	No	Usually

Source: Texas Department of Insurance, **www.tdi.texas.gov/pubs/consumer/cb005.pdf**, accessed March 6, 2020.

Financial Literacy in Practice

HSAs: How They Work in 2020

High-deductible plans with HSAs are now available outside of your employer via Marketplace plans.

An HSA is a savings account that allows you to contribute money to a tax-free account that can be used for out-of-pocket health care expenses if you buy high-deductible insurance.

1. Your company offers a health insurance policy with an annual deductible of at least $1,400 for an individual or $2,800 for a family.

2. You can put pretax dollars into an HSA each year, up to the amount of the deductible—but no more than $7,100 for family coverage or $3,550 for individual coverage, plus a $1,000 catch-up contribution for those who are over 55.

3. You withdraw the money from your HSA tax-free, but it can be used only for your family's medical expenses.

After the deductible and copays are met, insurance still typically covers 80 percent of health costs.

4. HSA plans are required to have maximum out-of-pocket spending limits: $6,900 for individuals and $13,800 for families. That's when your company's insurance kicks in again at 100 percent coverage.

5. Your company can match part or all of your HSA contributions if it wishes, just as it does with 401(k)s.

6. You can invest your HSA in stocks, bonds, or mutual funds. Unused money remains in your account at the end of the year and grows tax-free.

7. You can also take your HSA with you if you change jobs or retire.

Source: U.S. Department of the Treasury, www.irs.gov/pub/irs-pdf/p969.pdf, accessed April 29, 2020.

How do FSAs, HRAs, and HSAs differ? FSAs allow you to contribute pretax dollars to an account managed by your employer. You use the money for health care spending but forfeit anything left over at the end of the year.

HRAs are tied to high-deductible policies. They are funded *solely* by your employer and give you a pot of money to spend on health care. You can carry over unspent money from year to year, but you lose the balance if you switch jobs. Premiums tend to be lower than for traditional insurance but higher than for HSAs. You can invest the funds in stocks, bonds, and mutual funds. The money grows tax-free but can be spent only on health care.

HSAs allow you to contribute money to a tax-free account that can be used for out-of-pocket health care expenses if you buy high-deductible health insurance policies to cover catastrophic expenses. Exhibit 9–3 summarizes the important features of HSAs, FSAs, and HRAs. Also, read the nearby *Financial Literacy in Practice* feature to learn how HSAs work in 2020.

In addition to the private sources of health insurance and health care discussed in this section, government health care programs cover over 50 million people. The next section discusses these programs.

Exhibit 9–3 Comparison of HSAs, FSAs, and HRAs

Health Savings Accounts (HSAs)	Flexible-Spending Accounts (Arrangements) (FSAs)	Health Reimbursement Accounts (HRAs)
• Set-aside tax-free dollars you can use to pay for medical expenses that are not covered by insurance • Tied to a high-deductible policy • Unspent money can be carried over and accumulate year to year • Can invest the funds in stocks, bonds, and mutual funds • The money grows tax-free but can be spent only on health care • You own the funds; you take any unspent funds with you if you leave the employer	• Employer-sponsored • Set-aside tax-free dollars you can use to pay for medical expenses that are not covered by insurance • Not tied to a high-deductible policy • Money left over can't be carried over; if you don't use it, you lose it to your employer	• Employer-sponsored • Funded solely by your employer to spend on your health care • Reimbursement of claims is tax-deductible for employers • Tied to high-deductible policies • The maximum annual contribution is determined by your employer's plan document • Can carry over unspent money from year to year, but you lose the balance if you change jobs • Premiums tend to be lower than for traditional insurance but higher than for HSAs

Financial Literacy in Practice

A Brief Look at Medicare

Medicare is health insurance for people age 65 or older, under age 65 with certain disabilities, and any age with end-stage renal disease (permanent kidney failure requiring dialysis or a kidney transplant).

Most people get their Medicare health care coverage in one of two ways. Your costs vary depending on your plan, coverage, and the services you use.

ORIGINAL MEDICARE PLAN	
Part A (Hospital)	**Part B** (Medical)
Medicare provides this coverage. Part B is optional. You have your choice of doctors. Your costs may be higher than in Medicare Advantage Plans.	

+

Part D (Prescription Drug Coverage)
You can choose this coverage. Private companies approved by Medicare run these plans. Plans cover different drugs. Medically necessary drugs must be covered.

+

Medigap (Medicare Supplement Insurance) Policy
You can choose to buy this private coverage (or an employer or union may offer similar coverage) to fill in gaps in Part A and Part B coverage. Costs vary by policy and company.

or

MEDICARE ADVANTAGE PLANS SUCH AS HMOs AND PPOs
This "Part C" option combines your Part A (Hospital) and Part B (Medical).
Private insurance companies approved by Medicare provide this coverage. Generally, you must see doctors in the plan. Your costs may be lower than in the original Medicare plan, and you may get extra benefits.

+

Part D (Prescription Drug Coverage)
Most Part C plans cover prescription drugs. If they don't, you may be able to choose this coverage. Plans cover different drugs. Medically necessary drugs must be covered.

For information about Medicare, visit **www.medicare.gov** or call 1-800-MEDICARE (1-800-633-4227).

Source: Centers for Medicare and Medicaid Services, *Medicare & You*, 2020.

Government Health Care Programs

The health insurance coverage discussed thus far is normally purchased through private companies. Some consumers, however, are eligible for health insurance coverage under programs offered by federal and state governments.

MEDICARE Perhaps the best-known government health program is *Medicare*. Medicare is a federally funded health insurance program available mainly to people over 65 and to people with disabilities. Medicare has four parts: hospital insurance (Part A), medical insurance (Part B), Medicare Advantage Plan (Part C), and prescription drug coverage (Part D). Medicare hospital insurance is funded by part of the Social Security payroll tax. Part A (hospital insurance) helps pay for inpatient hospital care, inpatient care in a skilled nursing facility, home health care, and hospice care. Program participants pay a single annual deductible.

Part B (medical insurance) helps pay for doctors' services and a variety of other medical services and supplies not covered or not fully covered by Part A. Part B has a deductible and a 20 percent coinsurance provision. Medicare medical insurance is a supplemental program paid for by individuals who feel that they need it. A regular monthly premium is charged. The federal government matches this amount. For a brief summary of Medicare Parts A, B, C, and D, see the nearby *Financial Literacy in Practice* feature.

> ## CAUTION!
>
> You cannot contribute to your HSA once your Medicare coverage begins. However, you may use money that is already in your HSA after you enroll in Medicare to help pay for deductibles, premiums, copayments, or coinsurance. If you or your employer contribute to your HSA after your Medicare coverage starts, you may have to pay a tax penalty. If you would like to continue contributing to your employer-sponsored HSA without penalty after you turn 65, you should not apply for Medicare, Social Security, or Railroad Retirement Board benefits.
>
> Source: Centers for Medicare and Medicaid Services, *Medicare & You*, 2020, p. 19.

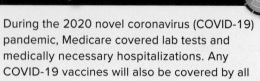

money minute focus

During the 2020 novel coronavirus (COVID-19) pandemic, Medicare covered lab tests and medically necessary hospitalizations. Any COVID-19 vaccines will also be covered by all Part D plans.

Medicare is constantly in financial trouble. Health care costs continue to grow, and the proportion of senior citizens in society is rising. This situation puts Medicare in danger of running out of funds. According to recent projections, the program will be bankrupt by the year 2035 if no changes are made.

The Balanced Budget Act of 1997 created the new Medicare Choice program. This program allows many Medicare members to choose a managed care plan in addition to their Medicare coverage. For some additional costs, members can receive greater benefits. Exhibit 9–4 compares features of different Medicare options.

See the nearby *Digital Financial Literacy with . . .* feature to learn about the newest Medicare's Blue Button information.

Exhibit 9–4 A Comparison of Various Medicare Plans

	Current Options	New Options (Medicare and Choice)	Plan Description
Original Medicare	✓	✓	• You choose your health care providers • Medicare pays your providers for covered services • Most beneficiaries choose Medicare supplemental insurance to cover deductible and copayment
Medicare health maintenance organization	✓	✓	• You must live in the plan's service area • You agree to use the plan network of doctors, hospitals, and other health providers, except in an emergency • Medicare pays the HMO to provide all medical services
Preferred provider organization		✓	• Works like an HMO, except you have the choice to see a health provider out of the network • If you do see an out-of-network provider, you will pay a high
Provider-sponsored organization		✓	• Works like a Medicare HMO, except the networks are managed by health care providers (doctors and hospitals) rather than an insurance company
Private fee for service		✓	• Medicare pays a lump sum to a private insurance health plan • Providers can bill more than what the plan pays; you are responsible for paying the balance • The plan may offer more benefits than original Medicare
Medical savings account (MSA)		✓	• Medicare MSAs are a special type of savings account that can be used to pay medical bills • The Centers for Medicare and Medicaid Services will make an annual lump-sum deposit into enrollee's account (only Medicare can deposit funds into this account) • MSAs work with a special private insurance company and carry a very high deductible

Source: Centers for Medicare and Medicaid Services, *Medicare & You,* 2020.

What's the Medicare Blue Button?

MyMedicare.gov's Blue Button makes it easy for you to download your personal health information to a file. Having access to your information can help you make more informed decisions about your health care. Blue Button is safe, secure, reliable, and easy to use. By getting your information through Blue Button, you can:

- Download and save a file of your personal health information on your computer or other device, including your Part A, Part B, and Part D claims.
- Print or e-mail the information to share with others after you've saved the file.
- Import your saved file into other computer-based personal health management tools.

What's Blue Button 2.0?

Medicare has released a new data service that makes it easy for you to share your Part A, Part B, and Part D claim information with a growing list of authorized applications, services, and research programs. You authorize each application individually, and you can return to **MyMedicare.gov** at anytime to change how an application uses your information.

Once you authorize sharing of your information with an application (by using your **MyMedicare.gov** account information), you can use that application to view your past and current Medicare claims.

For Medicare Advantage Plans, only Part D information is available through this service. If you have a Medicare Advantage Plan, check with your plan to see if it offers a similar service to Blue Button 2.0. Medicare keeps a list of authorized applications.

How do I download and share my health information?

- Log into **MyMedicare.gov**.
- Click your username in the top right corner.
- Select "Get a Report of My Data" from the drop-down menu that appears.
- Select the information you want to download, and select "Create Report."
- Save the file to your computer as either a PDF or a TXT file.

*My*Medicare.gov

Why should I download and share my health information?

By using Medicare's Blue Button and Blue Button 2.0 to download and share your personal health information, you:

- Get control over your health information.
- Make it easy to share your health information with doctors, caregivers, or anyone you choose.
- Get help managing and improving your health through a wide range of apps and other computer-based services.

How do I protect my information?

Since you control access to your health information, it's your responsibility to take steps to keep it safe. Treat your personal and health information the same way you'd treat your banking or other confidential information. Here are some important things to remember:

- Keep your log-in information private and secure.
- You may want to download your information to a CD, flash drive or mobile app. Medicare recommends you use encrypted and password-protected flash drives, CDs, and mobile apps.
- If you want to send your information by e-mail, encrypt the message.
- Keep paper copies in a safe and secure place that you can control.
- Blue Button and Blue Button 2.0 are optional services. You decide whether you want to share your personal information with others.
- Medicare reviews all of the organizations that want to connect to Blue Button 2.0, but it's up to you to choose the apps or other services you want to use.

Call Medicare at 1-800-MEDICARE (1-800-633-4227) if:

- You think your information may have been downloaded by someone else.
- You want to remove an app's or service's access to your information

Source: U.S. Department of Health and Human Services, Centers for Medicare and Medicaid Services, **www.medicare.gov/manage-your-health/medicares-blue-button-blue-button-20, accessed March 2, 2020**.

ACTION STEPS FOR. . .

. . .Information Literacy

Go to **Medicare.gov** website and click on "Medicare's Blue Button." Find an app based on what you would like to do with your Medicare health information. For example, Achievement app is a reward platform for healthy activities that is backed by the top investors in Silicon Valley and driven by a social mission to help drive scientific research forward and make America healthier.

. . .Financial Literacy

To learn how to make shopping for Medicare plans easier by using your previous doctors, pharmacies, and Medicare prescription history, etc., click on Allwell-Absolute Total Care app. Based on information, prepare a summary of your findings.

. . .Diginal Literacy

Go to **Medicare.gov** website and click "Find apps to use with Medicare Blue Button." You can browse an alphabetical list of all Medicare apps, or you can find apps based on what you would like to do with your Medicare health information.

WHAT IS NOT COVERED BY MEDICARE? Although Medicare is very helpful for meeting medical costs, it does not cover everything. In addition to the deductibles and coinsurance payments, Medicare will not cover some medical expenses at all. Some expenses not covered include certain types of skilled or long-term nursing care, out-of-hospital prescription drugs, routine checkups, dental care, and most immunizations. (Medicare does cover the annual wellness visit). Medicare also limits the amount it will pay for covered services. If your doctor does not accept Medicare's approved amount as payment in full, you're responsible for the difference.

You can find general Medicare information online. Just visit Medicare.gov to:

- Get information about the Medicare health and prescription drug plans in your area, including what they cost and what services they provide.
- Find Medicare-participating doctors or other health care providers and suppliers.
- See what Medicare covers, including preventive services (such as screenings, vaccines, and yearly "wellness" visits).
- Get Medicare appeals information and forms.
- Get information about the quality of care provided by plans, nursing homes, hospitals, doctors, home health agencies, dialysis facilities, hospices, inpatient rehabilitation facilities, and long-term care hospitals.

Medigap (MedSup) insurance Supplements Medicare by filling the gap between Medicare payments and medical costs not covered by Medicare.

MEDIGAP Those eligible for Medicare who would like more coverage may buy **Medigap (MedSup) insurance**. You must have Medicare Part A and Medicare Part B to buy Medigap insurance. Medigap insurance supplements Medicare by filling the gap between Medicare payments and medical costs not covered by Medicare. It is offered by private companies. Insurance companies generally can't sell you a Medigap policy if you have coverage through Medicaid or Medicare Advantage Plan. Generally, Medigap policies don't cover long-term care, vision or dental care, hearing aids, eye glasses, or private-duty nursing. For more information about Medicare supplement insurance, visit **www.medicare.gov/ publications**, or call 1-800-Medicare and request the booklet "Choosing a Medigap Policy: A Guide to Health Insurance for People with Medicare." You may also visit **http://www .medicare.gov/supplement-other-insurance/medigap/whats-medigap.html** or call your state insurance department.

MEDICAID The other well-known government health program is *Medicaid,* a medical assistance program offered to certain low-income individuals and families. Medicaid is administered by states, but it is financed by a combination of state and federal funds. Unlike Medicare, Medicaid coverage is so comprehensive that people with Medicaid do not need supplemental insurance. Typical Medicaid benefits include physicians' services, inpatient and outpatient hospital services, lab services, skilled nursing and home health services, prescription drugs, eyeglasses, and preventive care for people under the age of 21.

OTHER SOURCES You can get help from your state to pay for your Medicare premiums. In some cases, Medicare savings programs may also pay Medicare Part A and Part B deductibles, coinsurance, and copayments if you meet certain conditions. Programs of All-Inclusive Care for the Elderly (PACE) organizations provide care and services in the home, the community and the PACE center. PACE is only available in states that offer PACE under Medicaid.

Health Insurance and the Patient Protection and Affordable Care Act of 2010

Americans had been debating for years whether the nation needs health care reform to ensure that we get high-quality, affordable health care. The Patient Protection and Affordable Care Act of 2010 (ACA) set aside $635 billion over the next 10 years to help finance this reform. Here are the key provisions of the act that will take effect now and in the years to come. The act:

- Offers tax credits for small businesses to make employee coverage more affordable.
- Prohibits denying coverage to children with preexisting medical conditions.
- Provides access to affordable insurance for those who are uninsured because of a preexisting condition through a temporary subsidized high-risk pool.
- Bans insurance companies from dropping people from coverage when they get sick.
- Eliminates copayments for preventive services and exempts preventive services from deductibles under the Medicare program.
- Requires new health plans to allow young people up to their twenty-sixth birthday to remain on their parents' insurance policy.
- Prohibits health insurance companies from placing lifetime caps on coverage.
- Restricts the use of annual limits to ensure access to needed care in all plans.
- Requires new private plans to cover preventive services with no copayment and with preventive services being exempt from deductibles.
- Ensures that consumers in new plans have access to an effective internal and external appeals process to appeal decisions by their health insurance plans.
- Provides aid to states in establishing offices of health insurance consumer assistance to help individuals with filing complaints and appeals.
- Provides new investments to increase the number of primary care practitioners, including doctors, nurses, nurse practitioners, and physician assistants.
- Requires health insurance companies to submit justification for all requested premium increases.
- Creates state-based health insurance marketplaces (also called *insurance exchanges*) through which individuals can purchase coverage, with subsidies available to lower-income individuals.
- Expands the Medicaid program for the nation's poorest individuals.
- Requires employers with more than 20 employees to provide health insurance to their employees or pay penalties.[1]

The law is expansive and is being implemented over several years, but all major provisions took effect in January 2014. On June 28, 2012, the Supreme Court, in a 5-to-4 vote, upheld the majority of the landmark Affordable Care Act.

SUBSIDIZED COVERAGE The Affordable Care Act provides numerous rights and protections along with subsidies through premium tax credits and cost-savings reductions. Examples of subsidized coverage include Medicaid and the Children's Health Insurance Program. Thus health care coverage is available at reduced or no cost for people with incomes below certain limits.

THE HEALTH INSURANCE MARKETPLACE The Affordable Care Act also created the Health Insurance Marketplace, sometimes known as the health insurance "exchange" or "Obamacare exchange." The Health Insurance Marketplace makes buying health care coverage easier and more affordable. Starting in 2014, the Marketplace allowed you to compare health plans, get answers to questions, find out if you are eligible for tax credits for private insurance, and enroll in a health plan that meets your needs.

---

[1]HealthCare.gov, **www.healthcare.gov**, accessed March 20, 2013.

GOVERNMENT CONSUMER HEALTH INFORMATION WEBSITES The Department of Health and Human Services operates more than 60 websites with a wealth of reliable information related to health and medicine. For example:

- *Healthfinder:* Healthfinder includes links to more than 1,000 websites operated by government and nonprofit organizations. It lists topics according to subject (**www.hhs.gov**).
- *MedlinePlus:* MedlinePlus is the world's largest collection of published medical information. It was originally designed for health professionals and researchers, but it's also valuable for students and others who are interested in health care and medical issues (**www.nlm.nih.gov/medlineplus**).
- *NIH Health Information Page:* The National Institutes of Health (NIH) operates a website called the NIH Health Information Page, which can direct you to the consumer health information in NIH publications and on the Internet (**www.nih.gov**).
- *Food and Drug Administration:* This consumer protection agency's site provides information about the safety of various foods, drugs, cosmetics, and medical devices (**www.fda.gov**).

PRACTICE QUIZ 9–4

1. What are the seven sources of private health plans?

2. Match the following terms with the appropriate statement.

Blue Cross	a. A medical assistance program offered to certain low-income individuals and families _____
Blue Shield	b. A health insurance plan that combines features of both HMOs and PPOs _____
HMOs	c. A statewide organization that provides hospital care benefits _____
PPOs	d. A federally funded health insurance program available mainly to people over 65 and to people with disabilities _____
point-of-service (POS)	e. Health insurance plans that directly employ or contract with selected physicians to provide health services in exchange for a fixed, prepaid monthly premium _____
Medicare	f. A statewide organization that provides benefits for surgical and medical services performed by physicians _____
Medicaid	g. Groups of doctors and hospitals that agree to provide specified medical services to members at prearranged fees _____

3. What health care services are not covered by Medicare?

LO9.5

Explain the importance of disability income insurance in financial planning and identify its sources.

Disability Income Insurance

The Need for Disability Income

Before disability insurance existed, people who were ill lost more money from missed paychecks than from medical bills. Disability income insurance was set up to protect against such loss of income. This kind of coverage is very common today, and several hundred insurance companies offer it.

Disability income insurance provides regular cash income when you're unable to work because of a pregnancy, a non-work-related accident, or an illness. It protects your earning power, your most valuable resource.

The exact definition of a disability varies from insurer to insurer. Some insurers will pay you when you are unable to work at your regular job. Others will pay only if you are so ill or badly hurt that you can't work at any job. A violinist with a hand injury, for instance, might have trouble doing his or her regular work but might be able to perform a range of other jobs. A good disability income insurance plan pays you if you can't work at your regular job. A good plan will also pay partial benefits if you are able to work only part-time.

Many people make the mistake of ignoring disability insurance, not realizing that it's very important insurance to have. Disability can cause even greater financial problems than death. Disabled persons lose their earning power but still have to meet their living expenses. In addition, they often face huge costs for their medical treatment and special care that their disabilities require.

ACTION ITEM

Since I am a healthy adult, I don't need to worry about disability income insurance.

☐ Yes ☐ No

disability income insurance Provides payments to replace income when an insured person is unable to work.

Sources of Disability Income

Before you buy disability income insurance from a private insurance company, remember that you may already have some form of insurance of this kind. This coverage may be available through worker's compensation if you're injured on the job. Disability benefits may also be available through your employer or through Social Security in case of a long-term disability.

WORKER'S COMPENSATION If your disability is a result of an accident or illness that occurred on the job, you may be eligible to receive worker's compensation benefits in your state. Benefits will depend on your salary and your work history.

EMPLOYER PLANS Many employers provide disability income insurance through group insurance plans. In most cases, your employer will pay part or all of the cost of such insurance. Some policies may provide continued wages for several months only, whereas others will give you long-term protection.

SOCIAL SECURITY Social Security may be best known as a source of retirement income, but it also provides disability benefits. If you're a worker who pays into the Social Security system, you're eligible for Social Security funds if you become disabled. How much you get depends on your salary and the number of years you've been paying into Social Security. Your dependents also qualify for certain benefits. However, Social Security has very strict rules. Workers are considered disabled if they have a physical or mental condition that prevents them from working and that is expected to last for at least 12 months or to result in death. Benefits start at the sixth full month the person is disabled. They stay in effect as long as the disability lasts.

money minute focus

Nearly one in five Americans will become disabled for one year or more before the age of 65, according to the Life Foundation, a nonprofit organization dedicated to helping consumers make smart financial decisions. The number of workers who become disabled has risen by 35 percent since 2000, according to the Social Security Administration.

PRIVATE INCOME INSURANCE PROGRAMS Privately owned insurance companies offer many policies to protect people from loss of income resulting from illness or disability. Disability income insurance gives weekly or monthly cash payments to people who cannot work because of illness or accident. The amount paid is usually 40 to 60 percent of a person's normal income. Some plans, however, pay as much as 75 percent.

Disability Income Insurance Trade-Offs

As with the purchase of health insurance, you must make certain trade-offs when you decide among different private disability insurance policies. Keep the following in mind as you look for a plan that is right for you.

WAITING OR ELIMINATION PERIOD Benefits won't begin the day you become disabled. You'll have to wait anywhere between one and six months before you can begin collecting. The span of time is called an elimination period. Usually a policy with a longer elimination period charges lower premiums.

DURATION OF BENEFITS Every policy names a specified period during which benefits will be paid. Some policies are valid for only a few years. Others are automatically canceled when you turn 65. Still others continue to make payments for life. You should look for a policy that pays benefits for life. If your policy stops payments when you turn 65, then permanent disability could be a major financial as well as physical loss.

AMOUNT OF BENEFITS You should aim for a benefit amount that, when added to other sources of income, will equal 70 to 80 percent of your take-home pay. Of course, the greater the benefit, the greater the cost, or premium.

ACCIDENT AND SICKNESS COVERAGE Some disability policies pay only for accidents. Coverage for sickness is important, though. Accidents are not the only cause of disability.

GUARANTEED RENEWABILITY If your health becomes poor, your disability insurer may try to cancel your coverage. Look for a plan that guarantees coverage as long as you continue to pay your premiums. The cost may be higher, but it's worth the extra security and peace of mind. You may even be able to find a plan that will stop charging the premiums if you become disabled, which is an added benefit.

Your Disability Income Needs

Once you have found out what your benefits from the numerous public and private sources would be, you should determine whether those benefits would meet your disability income needs. Ideally, you'll want to replace all the income you otherwise would have earned. This should enable you to pay your day-to-day expenses while you're recovering. You won't have work-related expenses and your taxes will be lower during the time you are disabled. In some cases, you may not have to pay certain taxes at all. Use Exhibit 9–5 to determine how much income you will have available if you become disabled.

Exhibit **9–5** Calculating Disability Income

How much income will you have available if you become disabled?

	Monthly Amount:	After Waiting:	For a Period of:
Sick leave or short-term disability	_____	_____	_____
Group long-term disability	_____	_____	_____
Social Security	_____	_____	_____
Other government programs	_____	_____	_____
Individual disability insurance	_____	_____	_____
Credit disability insurance	_____	_____	_____
Other income:	_____	_____	_____
Savings	_____	_____	_____
Spouse's income	_____	_____	_____
Total monthly income while disabled:	$_____		

PRACTICE QUIZ 9–5

1. What is the purpose of disability income insurance?

2. What are the four sources of disability income?

3. Match the following terms with an appropriate statement.

waiting or elimination period	*a.* A specified period during which benefits are paid _____
duration of benefits	*b.* A plan that guarantees coverage as long as you continue to pay your premiums _____
guaranteed renewability	*c.* A period of one to six months that must elapse before benefits can be collected _____

High Medical Costs

Affordable health care has become one of the most important social issues of our time. News broadcasts abound with special reports on "America's health care crisis" or politicians demanding "universal health insurance."

What do an aging and overweight population, the cost of prescription drugs, the growing number of uninsured, and advancements in medical technology have in common? These and other factors all add up to rising health costs. The United States has the highest per capita medical expenditures of any country in the world. We spend twice as much on health care as the average for the 24 industrialized countries in Europe and North America.

Health care costs were estimated at $4.26 trillion in 2021 (see Exhibit 9-6). In 2020, health care spending as a percentage of gross domestic product was 17.8 percent. The latest projections from the Centers for Medicare and Medicaid Services show that improving economic conditions, the provisions of the Affordable Care Act, and the aging population will continue to increase health care spending in 2020 and beyond. By 2027, health spending financed by federal, state, and local governments is projected to account for 47 percent of national health spending.

HIGH ADMINISTRATIVE COSTS In the United States, administrative costs consume nearly 26 percent of health care dollars, compared to 1 percent under Canada's socialized system. These costs include activities such as enrolling beneficiaries in a health plan, paying health insurance premiums, checking eligibility, obtaining authorizations for specialist referrals, and filing reimbursement claims. More than 1,100 different insurance forms are now in use in the United States.

LO9.6

Explain why the costs of health insurance and health care have been increasing.

ACTION ITEM

To avoid high medical costs, I eat a balanced diet and keep my weight under control.

☐ Yes ☐ No

FinTech for Financial Literacy

Health information technology (health IT) allows health care providers to better manage patient care through secure use and sharing of health information. It includes the use of electronic health records (EHRs) instead of paper medical records to maintain your health information. Health IT promises to expand access to affordable care and to make our health care system more efficient and reduce paperwork for patients and doctors. For more information, visit the U.S. Department of Health and Human Services website at **HealthIT.gov**.

Exhibit 9–6 U.S. National Health Expenditures, 1960–2027

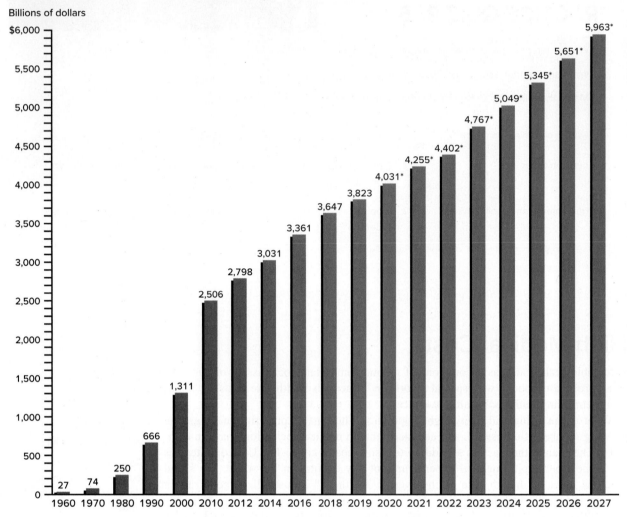

Billions of dollars

* Projected.

Source: U.S. Department of Health and Human Services, Centers for Medicare and Medicaid Services, **www.cms.gov/Research-Statistics-Data-and-Systems/Statistics-Trends-and-Reports/NationalHealthExpendData/NationalHealthAccountsProjected**, accessed March 3. 2020.

Why Does Health Care Cost So Much?

The high and rising costs of health care are attributable to many factors, including:

- The use of sophisticated, expensive technologies.
- Duplication of tests and sometimes duplication of technologies that yield similar results.
- Increases in the variety and frequency of treatments, including allegedly unnecessary tests.
- The increasing number and longevity of elderly people.
- Regulations that result in cost shifting rather than cost reduction.
- The increasing number of accidents and crimes that require emergency medical services.
- Limited competition and restrictive work rules in the health care delivery system.

- Labor intensiveness and rapid average earnings growth for health care professionals and executives.
- Using more expensive medical care than necessary, such as going to an emergency room with a bad cold.
- Built-in inflation in the health care delivery system.
- Aging baby boomers' use of more health care services, whether they're going to the doctor more often or snapping up pricier drugs, from Celebrex to Viagra.
- Other major factors that cost billions of dollars each year, including fraud, administrative waste, malpractice insurance, excessive surgical procedures, a wide range of prices for similar services, and double health coverage.

Because third parties—private health insurers and government—pay such a large part of the nation's health care bill, hospitals, doctors, and patients often lack the incentive to make the most economical use of health care services.

What Is Being Done about the High Costs of Health Care?

In the private sector, concerned groups such as employers, labor unions, health insurers, health care professionals, and consumers have undertaken a wide range of innovative activities to contain the costs of health care. These activities include:

- Programs to carefully review health care fees and charges and the use of health care services.
- The establishment of incentives to encourage preventive care and provide more services out of hospitals, where this is medically acceptable.
- Involvement in community health planning to help achieve a better balance between health needs and health care resources.
- The encouragement of prepaid group practices and other alternatives to fee-for-service arrangements.
- Community health education programs that motivate people to take better care of themselves.
- Physicians encouraging patients to pay cash for routine medical care and lab tests.

What Can You Do to Reduce Personal Health Care Costs?

As health care costs continue to rise, there are a few steps that you can take to reduce your own medical costs:

- Consider participating in a flexible spending account if your employer offers it.
- Consider a high-deductible health plan that provides medical insurance coverage and a tax-free opportunity to save for future medical needs.
- Ask your physician and pharmacist if a less expensive generic drug is available.
- Consider using a mail-order or legitimate online pharmacy, especially if you will take a drug for a long period.
- Most states offer free or low-cost coverage for children under 19 who do not have health insurance. Visit **www.insurekidsnow.gov** or call 1-877-KIDS-NOW for more information.
- Many states offer state pharmacy assistance programs that help pay for prescription drugs based on financial need, age, or medical condition.

- If your doctor wants you to return for a follow-up visit, ask if it is really necessary or can you follow up by phone.
- If your doctor suggests a nonurgent procedure, ask for information and some time to think about it. Research the suggested treatment on WebMD (**www.webmd.com**) and compare costs on Health Care Blue Book (**www.healthcarebluebook.com**) or New Choice Health (**www.newchoicehealth.com**).
- Review billing statements from medical providers for billing errors.
- Appeal unfair decisions by your health plan.
- Practice preventive care and stay well.

In addition, know your care options and costs. For example, if you wake up with a sore throat but can't get an appointment with your doctor, don't run to the nearest emergency room. You have several options to get the care you need—and avoid a big bill later. These options might include:

- **Nurse line.** Does your doctor's office have a nurse line or online chat feature? Many of these services are available at all hours, and generally there is no charge to use them.
- **Virtual visit.** There are several online services that allow you to connect to a doctor from your phone, tablet, or computer. Virtual visits are usually available at all hours and on weekends and holidays. Copays may be lower than for an office visit or even free.
- **Retail clinics.** These clinics located in many pharmacies and large retailers can treat minor conditions and provide vaccinations and screening exams. They accept most insurance plans. Copays are often the same as a visit to your doctor, and some plans have lower copays for these clinics.
- **Urgent care.** These centers have a doctor on staff and can treat injuries and illnesses that are not an emergency but do need quick action, such as a sprain or cut. Copays vary by insurance plan, and you may be responsible for a deductible. Ask whether the facility is in your plan's network.

Save emergency room visits for real medical emergencies, such as an illness, injury, symptom, or condition that is so serious that a reasonable person would seek care immediately to avoid severe harm.

The best way to avoid the high cost of illness is to stay well. The prescription is the same as it has always been:

- Eat a balanced diet, and keep your weight under control.
- Avoid smoking, and don't drink to excess.
- Get sufficient rest, relaxation, and exercise.
- Drive carefully, and watch out for accident and fire hazards in the home.
- Protect yourself from medical ID theft.

Sheet 32 Disability Income Insurance Needs

PRACTICE QUIZ 9-6

1. What are the reasons for rising health care expenditures?

2. What are various groups doing to curb the high costs of health care?

3. What can individuals do to reduce health care costs

Disability Insurance

You Are Here

Checkpoint 1

- ☐ Review your disability income policy and explanation of benefits
- ☐ Check if your employer provides disability income through group insurance plans

- ☐ Contact the Social Security Administration. If you pay into the Social Security system, you are eligible for Social Security funds if you become disabled.
- ☐ After you find out what your benefits would be from public and private sources, you should determine whether those benefits would meet your disability income needs.

Checkpoint 2

Checkpoint 3

- ☐ For more information on disability insurance, visit www.iii.org and www.ahip.org.
- ☐ Take meaningful actions to insure your own good health

Financial Security

your personal finance dashboard

Income Percent Covered by Disability

Disability can be disastrous financially. If you are disabled, you lose your earning power, but you still have living expenses and often huge expenses for medical care.

YOUR SITUATION: Do you know how disability is defined? When do your benefits begin? How long do your benefits last? What is the amount of your benefits? Can benefits be reduced by Social Security disability and worker's compensation payments? Are the benefits adjusted for inflation? You should aim for benefit amounts that, when added to your other income, equal 70 or 80 percent of your gross pay.

LO9.1 Health insurance is protection that provides payments of benefits for a covered sickness or injury. Health insurance should be a part of your overall insurance program to safeguard your economic security. Health insurance plans can be purchased through group health insurance, individual health insurance, and COBRA.

LO9.2 Four basic types of health insurance are available under group and individual policies: hospital expense insurance, surgical expense insurance, physician expense insurance, and major medical expense insurance.

Major provisions of a health insurance policy include eligibility requirements, assigned benefits, internal limits, copayment, service benefits, benefit limits, exclusions and limitations, guaranteed renewability, and cancellation and termination.

LO9.3 Health insurance policy trade-offs include reimbursement versus indemnity, internal limits versus aggregate limits, deductibles and coinsurance, out-of-pocket limits, and benefits based on reasonable and customary charges.

LO9.4 Health insurance and health care are available from private insurance companies, hospital and medical service plans such as Blue Cross/Blue Shield, health maintenance organizations (HMOs), preferred provider organizations (PPOs),

point-of-service plans (POSs), home health care agencies, and employer self-funded health plans

The federal and state governments offer health coverage in accordance with laws that define the premiums and benefits. Two well-known government health programs are Medicare and Medicaid.

LO9.5 Disability income insurance provides regular cash income lost by employees as the result of an accident, illness, or pregnancy. Sources of disability income insurance include the employer, Social Security, worker's compensation, and private insurance companies.

LO9.6 Health care costs, except during 1994–1996, have gone up faster than the rate of inflation. Among the reasons for high and rising health care costs are the use of expensive technologies, duplication of tests and sometimes technologies, increases in the variety and frequency of treatments, unnecessary tests, the increasing number and longevity of elderly people, regulations that shift rather than reduce costs, the increasing number of accidents and crimes requiring emergency services, limited competition and restrictive work rules in the health care delivery system, rapid earnings growth among health care professionals, and built-in inflation in the health care delivery system.

Key Terms

basic health insurance coverage 322

Blue Cross 328

Blue Shield 328

coinsurance 322

copayment 324

disability income insurance 337

exclusive provider organization (EPO) 328

health maintenance organization (HMO) 328

hospital expense insurance 322

long-term care insurance (LTC) 323

managed care 328

Medigap (MedSup) insurance 334

physician expense insurance 322

point-of-service (POS) plan 329

preferred provider organization (PPO) 328

stop-loss 322

surgical expense insurance 322

1. The MacDonald family of five has health insurance coverage that pays 75 percent of out-of-hospital expenses after a $600 deductible per person. Mrs. MacDonald incurred doctor and prescription medication expenses of $1,380. She had not yet met her deductible. What amount would the insurance company pay?
2. Under Rose's PPO, emergency room care at a network hospital is 80 percent covered after the member has met a $300 annual deductible. Assume that Rose went to a hospital within her PPO network and that she had not met her annual deductible yet. Her total emergency room bill was $850. What amount did Rose have to pay? What amount did the PPO cover?
3. Gene, an assembly line worker at an automobile manufacturing plant, has take-home pay of $900 a week. He is injured in an accident that keeps him off work for 18 weeks. His disability insurance coverage replaces 65 percent of his earnings after a six-week waiting period. What amount would he receive in disability benefits?

Solutions

1. Total expenses = $ 1,380
Deductible = − 600
$ 780

Insurance company will pay 75 percent of $780 or $780 × 0.75 = $585.

2. Total bill = $ 850
Deductible = − 300
$ 550

Rose pays $550 × 0.20 = $110 + $300 = $410.
PPO covers $440 ($850–$410).

3. Insurance will replace 65 percent of $900, or $900 × 0.65 = $585 per week. Insurance will pay for 18 minus 6 weeks, or 12 weeks, or $585 × 12 = $7,020.

1. The Tucker family has health insurance coverage that pays 80 percent of out-of-hospital expenses after a deductible of $1,000 per person. If one family member has doctor and prescription medication expenses of $2,200, what amount would the insurance company pay? (LO9.2)
2. A health insurance policy pays 65 percent of physical therapy costs after a deductible of $200. In contrast, an HMO charges $15 per visit for physical therapy. How much would a person save with the HMO if he or she had 10 physical therapy sessions costing $50 each? (LO9.2)
3. Becky's comprehensive major medical health insurance plan at work has a deductible of $750. The policy pays 85 percent of any amount above the deductible. While on a hiking trip, Becky contracted a rare bacterial disease. Her medical costs for treatment, including medicines, tests, and a six-day hospital stay, totaled $8,893. A friend told her that she would have paid less if she had a policy with a stop-loss feature that capped her out-of-pocket expenses at $3,000. Was her friend correct? Show your computations. Then determine which policy would have cost Becky less and by how much. (LO9.2)

4. Georgia, a widow, has take-home pay of $1,200 a week. Her disability insurance coverage replaces 70 percent of her earnings after a four-week waiting period. What amount would she receive in disability benefits if an illness kept Georgia from work for 16 weeks? (LO9.5)

5. Stephanie was injured in a car accident and was rushed to the emergency room. She received stitches for a facial wound and treatment for a broken finger. Under Stephanie's PPO plan, emergency room care at a network hospital is 80 percent covered after the member has met an annual deductible of $300. Assume that Stephanie went to a hospital within her PPO network. Her total emergency room bill was $850. What amount did Stephanie have to pay? What amount did the PPO cover? (LO9.2)

Questions 6, 7, and 8 are based on the following scenario:

Ronald Roth started his new job as controller with Aerosystems today. Carole, the employee benefits clerk, gave Ronald a packet that contains information on the company's health insurance options. Aerosystems offers its employees the choice between a private insurance company plan (Blue Cross/Blue Shield), an HMO, and a PPO. Ronald needs to review the packet and make a decision on which health care program fits his needs. The following is an overview of that information.

  a. The monthly premium cost to Ronald for the Blue Cross/Blue Shield plan will be $42.32. For all doctor office visits, prescriptions, and major medical charges, Ronald will be responsible for 20 percent, and the insurance company will cover 80 percent of covered charges. The annual deductible is $500.

  b. The HMO is provided to employees free of charge. The copayment for doctors' office visits and major medical charges is $10. Prescription copayments are $5. The HMO pays 100 percent after Ronald's copayment. There is no annual deductible.

  c. The POS requires that the employee pay $24.44 per month to supplement the cost of the program with the company's payment. If Ron uses health care providers within the plan, he pays the copayments as described above for the HMO with no annual deductible. He can also choose to use a health care provider out of the network and pay 20 percent of all charges after he pays a $500 deductible. The POS will pay for 80 percent of those covered visits.

Ronald decided to review his medical bills from the previous year to see what costs he had incurred and to help him evaluate his choices. He visited his general physician four times during the year at a cost of $125 for each visit. He also spent $65 and $89 on two prescriptions during the year. Using these costs as an example, what would Ron pay for each of the plans described above? (For the purposes of the POS computation, assume that Ron visited a physician outside of the network plan but had his prescriptions filled at a network-approved pharmacy.)

6. What annual medical costs will Ronald pay using the sample medical expenses provided if he enrolls in the Blue Cross/Blue Shield plan? (LO9.2)

7. What total costs will Ronald pay if he enrolls in the HMO plan? (LO9.2)

8. If Ronald selects the POS plan, what will his annual medical costs be? (LO9.2)

9. In 2007, Joelle spent $5,000 on her health care. If this amount increased by 6 percent per year, what would be the amount Joelle spent in 2017 for the same health care? (*Hint:* Use the time value of money table in Chapter 1 Appendix, Exhibit 1–A.) (LO9.6)

10. In 2012, per capita spending on health care in the United States was about $9,000. If this amount increased by 7 percent a year, what would be the amount of per capita spending for health care in eight years? (*Hint:* Use the time value of money table in Chapter 1 Appendix, Exhibit 1–A.) (LO9.6)

 **To reinforce the content in this chapter, more problems are provided at** connect.mheducation.com.

Competency. . .

Research and select health and disability insurance.

Action Research. . .

Based on this chapter, *Your Personal Financial Plan Sheet 31* and *Sheet 32*, online research, and conversations with others, identify various health and disability insurance coverages that you currently have and that you might consider in the future.

Outcome. . .

Create an audio file, video, PowerPoint presentation, or other visual to report a summary of the actions you are currently taking or might take in the future related to health and disability insurance. Describe insurance coverage that you currently have and/or potentially will need in the future

REAL LIFE PERSONAL FINANCE

BUYING ADEQUATE HEALTH INSURANCE COVERAGE

Kathy Jones was a junior at Glenbard High School. She had two younger brothers. Her father, the assistant manager of a local supermarket, had take-home pay of $4,000 a month. He had a group health insurance policy and a $40,000 life insurance policy. He said that he could not afford to buy additional insurance. All of his monthly salary was used to meet current expenses, including car and house payments, food, clothing, transportation, children's allowances, recreation and entertainment, and vacation trips.

One evening, Kathy was talking with her father about insurance, which she was studying in an economics course. She asked what kind of insurance program her father had for their family. The question started Mr. Jones thinking about how well he was planning for his wife and children. Since the family had always been in good health, Mr. Jones felt that additional health and life insurance was not essential. Maybe after he received a raise in his salary and after his daughter was out of high school, he could afford to buy more insurance.

Questions

1. Do you think Kathy's father was planning wisely for the welfare of his family? Can you suggest ways in which this family could have cut monthly expenses and thus set aside some money for more insurance?

2. Although Mr. Jones's salary was not big enough to buy insurance for all possible risks, what protection do you think he should have had at this time?

3. Suppose Mr. Jones had been seriously injured and unable to work for at least one year. What would his family have done? How might this situation have affected his children?

HEALTH AND DISABILITY INCOME INSURANCE

Jamie Lee and Ross, happy newlyweds with a new home and twins on the way, are anxiously awaiting their new bundles of joy. Ross was understandably nervous as he wondered if everything would go smoothly with Jamie's pregnancy. Fortunately, they coordinated benefits from the medical insurance group plan offered by Ross's employment at the graphics agency and Jamie Lee's own plan, although Ross's plan would be their primary. His employer offers a health care savings plan, but Ross had not previously realized the benefit of participating.

Jamie Lee has had maternity care that she has been comfortable with so far, but Ross needed to review their health insurance policies with the potential of extensive medical expenses just on the horizon. He wondered if his salary would be enough to pay for the expenses that were not covered for out-of-network doctors.

Current Medical Insurance Plan Provisions

Jamie Lee and Ross have a preferred provider organization (PPO) plan.

In-Network Medical Care:

Jamie Lee and Ross currently have a $15 copayment for regular preventive care doctor visits and a $30 copayment for specialists that are preferred providers or participating members from the PPO plan's list.

Out-of-Network Medical Care:

Jamie Lee and Ross have the choice of seeking medical care from the professional of their choice outside the PPO member list, but they will incur a deductible of $500 per person or $1,000 per family per year.

After the deductible is met, there is a coinsurance of 80 percent/20 percent. The insurance company will cover 80 percent of the allowable medical fees, and the policyholder will be responsible for the other 20 percent of the allowable medical fees.

Medical fees that are not allowed under the medical plan provisions would be 100 percent of the policyholder's responsibility.

Out-of-Pocket Limits:

Their health insurance plan provides an out-of-pocket limit of $7,500 per year.

Questions

1. Using the information on the ACA and health planning from the *Financial Literacy in Practice* feature in this chapter, what are some of the strategies that Ross can use to better prepare financially for the arrival of the twins?
2. How could Jamie Lee and Ross prepare for the birth of the twins with their existing PPO plan?
3. Jamie Lee and Ross learned that the hospital that they plan to use for the delivery is not a participating hospital. What will their financial responsibility be for the nonparticipating hospital expenses?
4. The doctor's office has estimated the hospital expense for Jamie Lee and the babies' delivery, without complications, to be approximately $18,000. Based on their health insurance policy, how much would Jamie Lee and Ross owe for this out-of-network hospital stay?
5. Surprise! The babies arrived five weeks early, and Jamie Lee and Ross are the proud parents of *triplets:* two boys and a girl! Since the babies were preterm, they will need to spend a few extra days in the hospital for observation. How will Ross and Jamie Lee make provisions for adding the babies to their health insurance policy now that they have arrived?

"SOME OF MY EATING HABITS NOT ONLY WASTE MONEY BUT ARE ALSO NOT BEST FOR MY HEALTH."

Directions Continue your Daily Spending Diary to record and monitor spending in various categories. Your comments should reflect what you have learned about your spending patterns and help you consider possible changes you might want to make in your spending habits. The Daily Spending Diary sheets are located at the end of Chapter 1 and in Connect Finance.

Questions

1. What spending actions might directly or indirectly affect your health and physical well-being?
2. What amounts (if any) are currently required from your spending for the cost of health and disability insurance?

Name: _____ Date: _____

Assessing Current and Needed Health Care Insurance

Purpose: To assess current and needed medical and health care insurance.

Financial Planning Activities: Assess current and needed medical and health care insurance. Investigate your existing medical and health insurance, and determine the need for additional coverages. This sheet is also available in an Excel spreadsheet format in Connect Finance.

Suggested Websites: www.insure.com, www.lifehappens.org, www.insurekidsnow.gov

Insurance company

Address

Type of coverage
- ☐ Individual health policy
- ☐ Group health policy
- ☐ HMO
- ☐ PPO
- ☐ Other

Premium amount (monthly/quarterly/semiannually/annually)

Main coverages

Amount of coverage for

- Hospital costs

- Surgery costs

- Physicians' fees

- Lab tests

- Outpatient expenses

- Maternity

- Major medical

Other items covered/amounts

Policy restrictions (deductible, coinsurance, maximum limits)

Items not covered by this insurance

Of items not covered, would supplemental coverage be appropriate for your personal situation?

What actions related to your current (or proposed additional) coverage are necessary?

Suggested App:
- **Healthcare Bluebook**

McGraw Hill

What's Next for Your Personal Financial Plan?

- Talk to others about the impact of their health insurance on other financial decisions.
- Contact an insurance agent to obtain cost information for an individual health insurance plan.

Disability Income Insurance Needs

Purpose: To determine financial needs and insurance coverage related to employment disability situations.

Financial Planning Activities: Use the categories below to determine your potential income needs and disability insurance coverage. This sheet is also available in an Excel spreadsheet format in Connect Finance.

Suggested Websites: www.ssa.gov, www.usa.gov/disability-benefits-insurance, www.dol.gov

Monthly Expenses

	Current	When Disabled
Mortgage (or rent)	$ _____	$ _____
Utilities	$ _____	$ _____
Food	$ _____	$ _____
Clothing	$ _____	$ _____
Insurance payments	$ _____	$ _____
Debt payments	$ _____	$ _____
Auto/transportation	$ _____	$ _____
Medical/dental care	$ _____	$ _____
Education	$ _____	$ _____
Personal allowances	$ _____	$ _____
Recreation/entertainment	$ _____	$ _____
Contributions, donations	$ _____	$ _____
Total current monthly expenses	$ _____	
Total monthly expenses when disabled		$ _____

Substitute Income

Monthly Benefit*

Group disability insurance	$ _____
Social Security	$ _____
State disability insurance	$ _____
Worker's compensation	$ _____
Credit disability insurance (in some auto loan or home mortgages)	$ _____
Other income (investments, etc.)	$ _____
Total projected income when disabled	$ _____

If projected income when disabled is less than expenses, additional disability income insurance should be considered.

*Most disability insurance programs have a waiting period before benefits start, and they may have a limit on how long benefits are received.

What's Next for Your Personal Financial Plan?

- Survey several people to determine if they have disability insurance.
- Talk to an insurance agent to compare the costs of disability income insurance available from several insurance companies.

Suggested App:
- myCigna

McGraw Hill

10 Financial Planning with Life Insurance

3 Steps to Financial Literacy . . .
Determining Your Life Insurance Coverage

1 Calculate the current and future financial needs of your dependents and household members.
App: Life Happens Needs Calculator

2 Determine the amount of life insurance based on the financial needs from Step 1.
Website: **www.bankrate.com**

3 Compare types of life insurance policies and costs among various companies and sources of life insurance.
App: Life Insurance Quotes

Why is life insurance important?
Providing for the financial needs of family members and other dependents is the primary purpose of life insurance. At the end of the chapter, *Your Personal Finance Road Map and Dashboard* will provide additional information on planning for an appropriate amount of life insurance.

CHAPTER 10 LEARNING OBJECTIVES

In this chapter, you will learn to:

LO10.1 Define life insurance and determine your life insurance needs.

LO10.2 Distinguish between the types of life insurance companies and analyze various life insurance policies these companies issue.

LO10.3 Select important provisions in life insurance contracts and create a plan to buy life insurance.

LO10.4 Recognize how annuities provide financial security.

YOUR PERSONAL FINANCIAL PLAN SHEETS

33. Determining Life Insurance Needs
34. Life Insurance Policy Comparison

What Is Life Insurance?

Even though putting a price on your life is impossible, you probably own some life insurance—through a group plan where you work, as a veteran, or through a policy you bought. Life insurance is one of the most important and expensive purchases you may ever make; therefore, it is important that you budget for this need. Deciding whether you need it and choosing the right policy from dozens of options take time, research, and careful thought. This chapter will help you make decisions about life insurance. It describes what life insurance is and how it works, the major types of life insurance coverage, and how you can use life insurance to protect your family.

When you buy life insurance, you're making a contract with the company issuing the policy. You agree to pay a certain amount of money—the premium—periodically. In return the company agrees to pay a death benefit, or a stated sum of money upon your death, to your beneficiary. A **beneficiary** is a person named to receive the benefits from an insurance policy.

The Purpose of Life Insurance

Most people buy life insurance to protect the people who depend on them from financial losses caused by their death. Those people could include a spouse, children, an aging parent, or a business partner or corporation. Life insurance benefits may be used to:

- Pay off a home mortgage or other debts at the time of death.
- Provide lump-sum payments through an endowment for children when they reach a specified age.
- Provide an education or income for children.
- Make charitable donations after death.
- Provide a retirement income.
- Accumulate savings.
- Establish a regular income for survivors.
- Set up an estate plan.
- Pay estate and gift taxes.

LO10.1

Define life insurance and determine your life insurance needs.

ACTION ITEM
I need life insurance because someone depends on me for financial support.

☐ Yes ☐ No

beneficiary A person designated to receive something, such as life insurance proceeds, from the insured.

The Principle and Psychology of Life Insurance

No one can say with any certainty how long a particular person will live. Still, insurance companies are able to make some educated guesses. Over the years, they've compiled tables that show about how long people live. Using these tables, the company will make a rough guess about a person's life span and charge him or her accordingly. The sooner a person is likely to die, the higher the premiums he or she will pay.

How Long Will You Live?

If history is a guide, you'll live longer than your ancestors did. In 1900, an American male could be expected to live 46.3 years. By 2017, in contrast, life expectancy had risen to 76.1 years for men and 81.1 for women. Exhibit 10–1 shows about how many years a person can be expected to live today. For instance, a 30-year-old woman can be expected to live another 52.1 years. That doesn't mean that she has a high probability of dying at age 82.1. This just means that 52.1 is the average number of additional years a 30-year-old woman may expect to live.

Do You Need Life Insurance?

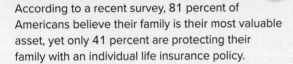

money minute focus

According to a recent survey, 81 percent of Americans believe their family is their most valuable asset, yet only 41 percent are protecting their family with an individual life insurance policy.

Not everyone needs life insurance. Before you buy life insurance, you'll have to decide whether you need it at all. Generally, if your death would cause financial hardship for somebody, then life insurance is a wise purchase. Households with children usually have the greatest need for life insurance. Single people who live alone or with their parents, however, usually have little or no need for life insurance unless they have a great deal of debt or want to provide for their parents, a friend, a relative, or a charity.

Exhibit 10–1 Life Expectancy Tables, All Races, 2017

This table helps insurance companies determine insurance premiums. Use the table to find the average number of additional years a 20-year-old male and female are expected to live.

EXPECTATION OF LIFE IN YEARS			EXPECTATION OF LIFE IN YEARS		
Age	Male	Female	Age	Male	Female
0	76.1	81.1	50	29.8	33.4
1	75.6	80.5	55	25.6	28.9
5	71.7	76.6	60	21.7	24.7
10	66.7	71.6	65	18.0	20.6
15	61.8	66.7	70	14.5	16.7
20	57.0	61.8	75	11.3	13.0
25	52.4	56.9	80	8.4	9.8
30	47.8	52.1	85	5.9	7.0
35	43.2	47.3	90	4.1	4.8
40	38.7	42.6	95	2.8	3.2
45	34.2	37.9	100	2.0	2.2

Source: Centers for Disease Control and Prevention, National Vital Statistics Report, https://www.cdc.gov/nchs/data/nvsr/nvsr68/nvsr68_07-508.pdf, accessed March 11, 2020.

Estimating Your Life Insurance Requirements

In estimating your life insurance requirements, consider the insurance coverage that your employer offers you as a fringe benefit. Many employers provide employees with life insurance coverage equal to their yearly salary. For example, if you earn $75,000 per year, you may receive $75,000 of insurance coverage. Some employers offer insurance of two or more times the salary with increased contributions from employees. The premiums are usually lower than premiums for individual life insurance policies, and you don't have to pass a physical exam.

There are four general methods for determining the amount of insurance you may need: the easy method, the DINK method, the "nonworking" spouse method, and the "family need" method.

THE EASY METHOD Simple as this method is, it is remarkably useful. It is based on the insurance agent's rule of thumb that a "typical family" will need approximately 70 percent of your salary for seven years before they adjust to the financial consequences of your death. In other words, for a simple estimate of your life insurance needs, just multiply your current gross income by 7 (7 years) and 0.70 (70 percent).

EXAMPLE: The Easy Method

$65,000 current income × 7 = $455,000 ×0.70 = $318,500

Example from Your Life

$ _____ current income × 7 = $ _____ × 0.70 = $ _____

This method assumes your family is "typical." You may need more insurance if you have four or more children, if you have above-average family debt, if any member of your family suffers from poor health, or if your spouse has poor employment potential. On the other hand, you may need less insurance if your family is smaller.

THE DINK (DUAL INCOME, NO KIDS) METHOD If you have no dependents and your spouse earns as much or more than you do, you have very simple insurance needs. Basically, all you need to do is ensure that your spouse will not be unduly burdened by debts should you die. Here is an example of the DINK method:

EXAMPLE: The DINK Method

	Example	Your Figures
Funeral expenses	$ 10,000	$_____
One-half of mortgage	60,000	_____
One-half of auto loan	7,000	_____
One-half of credit card balance	1,500	_____
One-half of personal debt	1,500	_____
Other debts	1,000	_____
Total insurance needs	$ 81,000	$_____

This method assumes your spouse will continue to work after your death. If your spouse suffers poor health or is employed in an occupation with an uncertain future, you should consider adding an insurance cushion to see him or her through hard times.

THE "NONWORKING" SPOUSE METHOD Insurance experts have estimated that extra costs of up to $20,000 a year may be required to replace the services of a homemaker in a family with small children. These extra costs may include the cost of a housekeeper, child care, more meals out, additional carfare, laundry services, and so on. They do not

A Worksheet to Calculate Your Life Insurance Need

1. Five times your personal yearly income   _____ (1)

2. Total approximate expenses above and beyond your daily living costs for you and your dependents   _____ (2)
   (e.g., tuition, care for a disabled child or parent) amount to

3. Your emergency fund (3 to 6 months of living expenses) amounts to   _____ (3)

4. Estimated amount for your funeral expenses (U.S. average is $8,700)   + _____ (4)

5. Total estimate of your family's financial needs (add lines 1 through 4)   = _____ (5)

6. Your total liquid assets (e.g., savings accounts, CDs, money market funds, existing life insurance   − _____ (6)
   both individual and group, pension plan death benefits, and Social Security benefits)

7. Subtract line 6 from line 5 and enter the difference here   = _____ (7)

The net result (Line 7) is an estimate of the shortfall your family would face upon your death. Remember, these are just rules of thumb. For a complete analysis of your needs, consult a professional.

Sources: Metropolitan Life Insurance Company, *About Life Insurance,* February 1997, p. 3; Teachers Insurance and Annuity Association, *The TIAA Guide to Life Insurance Planning for People in Education,* January 1997, p. 3. Updated March 18, 2020.

include the lost potential earnings of the surviving spouse, who often must take time away from the job to care for the family.

To estimate how much life insurance a homemaker should carry, simply multiply the number of years before the youngest child reaches age 18 by $20,000:

EXAMPLE: The "Nonworking" Spouse Method

Youngest child's age = 8 years
10 years × $20,000 = $200,000

Example from Your Life

_____ years × $20,000 = $_____

If there are teenage children, the $20,000 figure can be reduced. If there are more than two children under age 13 or if anyone in the family suffers poor health or has special needs, the $20,000 figure should be adjusted upward.

THE "FAMILY NEED" METHOD The first three methods assume you and your family are "typical" and ignore important factors such as Social Security and your liquid assets. The nearby *Figure It Out!* feature provides a detailed worksheet for making a thorough estimate of your life insurance needs.

Although this method is quite thorough, if you believe it does not address all of your special needs, you should obtain further advice from an insurance expert or a financial planner.

As you determine your life insurance needs, don't forget to consider the life insurance you may already have. You may have ample coverage through your employer and through any mortgage and credit life insurance you have purchased.

Before you consider types of life insurance policies, you must decide what you want your life insurance to do for you and your dependents. First, how much money do you want to leave to your dependents should you die today? Will you require more or less insurance protection to meet their needs as time goes on? Second, when would you like to be able to retire? What amount of income do you believe you and your spouse would need then? Third, how much will you be able to pay for your insurance program? Are the demands on your family budget for other living expenses likely to be greater or lower as time goes on?

When you have considered these questions and developed some approximate answers, you are ready to select the types and amounts of life insurance policies that will help you accomplish your objectives.

WHAT WOULD YOU DO? You and your wife just became proud parents of a baby girl, Sophia. Your combined annual income is $85,000, and you recently purchased a home and have a mortgage of $150,000. You have not started to save for retirement or college for Sophia. Now that you have a child who is financially dependent on you and your wife, you have decided to buy life insurance. There are many different types of insurance available to you: whole life, term life, universal life, and endowment life. What type of insurance would you choose and why?

Sheet 33 Determining Life Insurance Needs

PRACTICE QUIZ 10–1

1. What is life insurance? What is its purpose?

2. For each of the following statements, indicate your response by writing "T" or "F."

   a. Life insurance is one of the least important and least expensive purchases. _____
   b. A beneficiary is a person named to receive the benefits from an insurance policy. _____
   c. Life insurance benefits may be used to pay off a home mortgage or other debts at the time of death. _____
   d. The sooner a person is likely to die, the higher the premiums he or she will pay. _____
   e. All people need to purchase a life insurance policy. _____

3. What are the four methods of determining life insurance needs?

Types of Life Insurance Companies and Policies

Types of Life Insurance Companies

You can purchase the new or extra life insurance you need from two types of life insurance companies: stock life insurance companies, owned by shareholders, and mutual life insurance companies, owned by policyholders. Of the 841 life insurance companies in the United States, about 75 percent are stock companies, and about 25 percent are mutual.

Stock companies generally sell **nonparticipating policies**, or *nonpar policies,* whereas mutual companies specialize in the sale of **participating policies**, or *par policies.* A participating policy has a somewhat higher premium than a nonparticipating policy, but a part of the premium is refunded to the policyholder annually. This refund is called the *policy dividend.*

A long debate about whether stock companies or mutual companies offer less expensive life insurance has been inconclusive. You should check with both stock and mutual companies to determine which type offers the best policy for your particular needs at the lowest price.

If you wish to pay exactly the same premium each year, you should choose a nonparticipating policy with its guaranteed premiums. However, you may prefer life insurance whose annual price reflects the company's experience with its investments, the health of its policyholders, and its general operating costs, that is, a participating policy.

LO10.2

Distinguish between the types of life insurance companies and analyze various life insurance policies these companies issue.

ACTION ITEM
I am aware of different types of life insurance companies and policies they offer.

☐ Yes ☐ No

nonparticipating policy
Life insurance that does not provide policy dividends; also called a *nonpar policy.*

participating policy Life insurance that provides policy dividends; also called a *par policy.*

Nevertheless, as with other forms of insurance, price should not be your only consideration in choosing a life insurance policy. You should consider the financial stability of and service provided by the insurance company.

FinTech for Financial Literacy

How insurers can turn vision into reality

Today insurers win by offering a product. Tomorrow, insurers will win by providing access to prevention and assistance services—and by offering the right product to the right customer at the right time.

(McKinsey & Company)

Types of Life Insurance Policies

Both mutual insurance companies and stock insurance companies sell two basic types of life insurance: temporary and permanent insurance. Temporary insurance can be term, renewable term, convertible term, or decreasing term insurance. Permanent insurance is known by different names, including whole life, straight life, ordinary life, and cash-value life insurance. As you will learn in the next section, permanent insurance can be limited payment, variable, adjustable, or universal life insurance. Other types of insurance policies—group life and credit life insurance—are generally temporary forms of insurance. Exhibit 10–2 lists major types and subtypes of life insurance.

term insurance Life insurance protection for a specified period of time; sometimes called *temporary life insurance.*

TERM LIFE INSURANCE **Term insurance**, sometimes called *temporary life insurance,* provides protection against loss of life for only a specified term, or period of time. A term insurance policy pays a benefit only if you die during the period it covers, which may be 1, 5, 10, or 20 years, or up to age 70. If you stop paying the premiums, your coverage stops. Term insurance is often the best value for customers. You need insurance coverage most while you are raising children. As your children become independent and your assets increase, you can reduce your coverage. Term insurance comes in many different forms. Here are some examples:

RENEWABLE TERM The coverage of term insurance ends at the conclusion of the term, but you can continue it for another term—five years, for example—if you have a renewable option. However, the premium will increase because you will be older. It also usually has an age limit; you cannot renew after you reach a certain age.

MULTIYEAR LEVEL TERM The most popular, a multiyear level term, or *straight term,* policy guarantees that you will pay the same premium for the duration of your policy.

CONVERSION TERM This type of policy allows you to change from term to permanent coverage. This will have a higher premium.

DECREASING TERM Term insurance is also available in a form that pays less to the beneficiary as time passes. The insurance period you select might depend on your age or on how long you decide that the coverage will be needed. For example, if you have a mortgage on a house, you might buy a 25-year decreasing term policy as a way to make sure

Exhibit **10–2**

Major Types and Subtypes of Life Insurance

Term (temporary)	Whole, Straight, or Ordinary Life	Other Types
• Renewable term	• Limited payment	• Group life
• Multiyear level term	• Variable life	• Credit life
• Convertible term	• Adjustable life	• Endowment life
• Decreasing term	• Universal life	
• Return of premium		

that the debt could be paid if you died. The coverage would decrease as the balance on the loan decreased.

RETURN-OF-PREMIUM TERM   A few years ago, insurance companies began to sell return-of-premium term life policies. These policies return all the premiums if you survive to the end of the policy term. Premiums are higher than for the regular term policy, but you do get all your money back if you live through the term.

WHOLE LIFE INSURANCE   The other major type of life insurance is known as whole life insurance (also called a *straight life policy,* a *cash-value policy,* or an *ordinary life policy*). **Whole life insurance** is a permanent policy for which you pay a specified premium each year for the rest of your life. In return, the insurance company pays your beneficiary a stated sum when you die. The amount of your premium depends mostly on the age at which you purchase the insurance.

Whole life insurance may also serve as an investment. Part of each premium you pay is set aside in a savings account. When and if you cancel the policy, you are entitled to the accumulated savings, which is known as the **cash value**. Whole life policies are popular because they provide both a death benefit and a savings component. You can borrow from your cash value if necessary, although you must pay interest on the loan. Cash-value policies may make sense for people who intend to keep the policies for the long term or who want a more structured way to save. However, the Consumer Federation of America Insurance Group suggests that you explore other savings and investment strategies before investing your money in a permanent policy.

Remember, the primary purpose of buying life insurance is not for investment; it is to protect loved ones who depend on you for financial support upon your death. Furthermore, buying life insurance later in life can be expensive, and you may not qualify because of poor health or chronic diseases.

The premium of a term insurance policy will increase each time you renew your insurance. In contrast, whole life policies have a higher annual premium at first, but the rate remains the same for the rest of your life. Several types of whole life policies have been developed to meet the needs of different customers. These include the limited payment policy, the variable life policy, the adjustable life policy, and universal life insurance.

LIMITED PAYMENT POLICY   Limited payment policies charge premiums for only a certain length of time, usually 20 or 30 years or until the insured reaches a certain age. At the end of this time, the policy is "paid up," and the policyholder remains insured for life. When the policyholder dies, the beneficiary receives the full death benefit. The annual premiums are higher for limited payment policies because the premiums have to be paid within a shorter period of time.

VARIABLE LIFE POLICY   With a variable life policy, your premium payments are fixed. As with a cash-value policy, part of your premium is placed in a separate account; this money is invested in a stock, bond, or money market fund. The death benefit is guaranteed, but the cash value of the benefit can vary considerably according to the ups and downs of the stock market. Your death benefit can also increase, depending on the earnings of that separate fund.

ADJUSTABLE LIFE POLICY   An adjustable life policy allows you to change your coverage as your needs change. For example, if you want to increase or decrease your death benefit, you can change either the premium payments or the period of coverage.

UNIVERSAL LIFE   **Universal life insurance** is essentially a term policy with a cash value. Part of your premium goes into an investment account that grows and earns interest. You are able to borrow or withdraw your cash value. Unlike a traditional whole life policy, a universal life policy allows you to change your premium without changing your coverage.

whole life insurance An insurance plan in which the policyholder pays a specified premium each year for as long as he or she lives; also called a *straight life policy,* a *cash-value life policy,* or an *ordinary life policy.*

cash value The amount received after giving up a life insurance policy.

universal life insurance A whole life policy that combines term insurance and investment elements.

Exhibit **10–3** Comparing the Major Types of Life Insurance

	Term Life	Whole Life	Universal Life
Premium	Lower initially, increasing with each renewal	Higher initially than term; normally doesn't increase	Flexible premiums
Protects for	A specified period	Entire life if you keep the policy	A flexible time period
Policy benefits	Death benefits only	Death benefits and eventually a cash and loan value	Flexible death benefits and eventually a cash and loan value
Advantages	Low outlay Initially, you can purchase a larger amount of coverage for a lower premium	Helps you with financial discipline Generally fixed premium amount Cash value accumulation You can take loan against policy	More flexibility Takes advantages of current interest rates Offers the possibility of improved mortality rates (increased life expectancy because of advancements in medicine, which may lower policy costs)
Disadvantages	Premium increases with age No cash value	Costly if you surrender early Usually no cash value for at least three to five years May not meet short-term needs	Same as whole life Greater risks due to program flexibility Low interest rates can affect cash value and premiums
Options	May be renewable or convertible to a whole life policy	May pay dividends May provide a reduced paid-up policy Partial cash surrenders permitted	May pay dividends Minimum death benefit Partial cash surrenders permitted

Exhibit 10–3 compares the important features of term life, whole life, and universal life insurance.

OTHER TYPES OF LIFE INSURANCE POLICIES Other types of life insurance policies include group life insurance, credit life insurance, and endowment life insurance.

GROUP LIFE INSURANCE Group life insurance is basically a variation of term insurance. It covers a large number of people under a single policy. The people included in the group do not need medical examinations to get the coverage. Group insurance is usually offered through employers, who pay part or all of the costs for their employees, or through professional organizations, which allow members to sign up for the coverage. Group plans are easy to enroll in, but they can be much more expensive than similar term policies. If you leave your employer, some states require that you be allowed to convert the policy to a whole life policy with the same insurance company.

CREDIT LIFE INSURANCE Credit life insurance is used to pay off certain debts, such as auto loans or mortgages, in the event that you die before they are paid in full. These types of policies are not the best buy for the protection that they offer. Decreasing term insurance is a better option.

ENDOWMENT LIFE INSURANCE Endowment life insurance provides coverage for a specific period of time and pays an agreed-upon sum of money to the policyholder if he or she is still living at the end of the endowment period. If the policyholder dies before that time, the beneficiary receives the money.

> **WHAT WOULD YOU DO?** Your friend Jake is asking for your advice. He is a 27-year-old single man with no children. He has a younger sister who has a developmental disability. Both of his parents are living, though neither is in good health. Jake has an auto loan, a $50,000 mortgage on his condominium, and no other consumer debt. Is Jake a good candidate for life insurance? If so, what kind and how much insurance should he buy? What would you do?

PRACTICE QUIZ 10–2

1. What are the two types of life insurance companies?

2. For each of the following statements, indicate your response by writing "T" or "F."

    a. Stock life insurance companies generally sell participating (or par) policies. _____
    b. Mutual life insurance companies specialize in the sale of nonparticipating (nonpar) policies. _____
    c. If you wish to pay exactly the same premium each year, you should choose a nonpar policy. _____
    d. Permanent insurance is known as whole life, straight life, ordinary life, and cash-value life insurance. _____
    e. Term life insurance is the most expensive type of policy. _____

3. What are the five forms of term insurance?

4. What are the four forms of whole life insurance?

5. Define the following types of life insurance policies:

    a. Group life insurance.
    b. Credit life insurance.
    c. Endowment life insurance.

Selecting Provisions and Buying Life Insurance

Key Provisions in a Life Insurance Policy

LO10.3
Select important provisions in life insurance contracts and create a plan to buy life insurance.

Study the provisions in your policy carefully. The following are some of the most common features.

NAMING YOUR BENEFICIARY You decide who receives the benefits of your life insurance policy: your spouse, your child, or your business partner, for example. You can also name contingent beneficiaries, those who will receive the money if your primary beneficiary dies before or at the same time as you do. Update your list of beneficiaries as your needs change.

INCONTESTABILITY CLAUSE The incontestability clause says that the insurer can't cancel the policy if it's been in force for a specified period, usually two years. After that time, the policy is considered valid during the lifetime of the insured. This is true even if the policy was gained through fraud. The incontestability clause protects the beneficiaries from financial loss in the event that the insurance company refuses to meet the terms of the policy.

THE GRACE PERIOD When you buy a life insurance policy, the insurance company agrees to pay a certain sum of money under specified circumstances, and you agree to pay

ACTION ITEM
I have started budgeting for my life insurance premiums while I am still young and healthy.

☐ Yes ☐ No

a certain premium regularly. The *grace period* allows 28 to 31 days to elapse, during which time you may pay the premium without penalty. After that time, the policy lapses if you have not paid the premium.

POLICY REINSTATEMENT A lapsed policy can be put back in force, or reinstated, if it has not been turned in for cash. To reinstate the policy, you must again qualify as an acceptable risk, and you must pay overdue premiums with interest. There is a time limit on reinstatement, usually one or two years.

nonforfeiture clause
A provision that allows the insured not to forfeit all accrued benefits.

NONFORFEITURE CLAUSE One important feature of the whole life policy is the **nonforfeiture clause**. This provision prevents the forfeiture of accrued benefits if you choose to drop the policy. For example, if you decide not to continue paying premiums, you can exercise specified options with your cash value.

MISSTATEMENT OF AGE PROVISION The misstatement of age provision says that if the company finds out that your age was incorrectly stated, it will pay the benefits your premiums would have bought if your age had been correctly stated. The provision sets forth a simple procedure to resolve what could otherwise be a complicated legal matter.

POLICY LOAN PROVISION A loan from the insurance company is available on a whole life policy after the policy has been in force for one, two, or three years, as stated in the policy. This feature, known as the *policy loan provision,* permits you to borrow any amount up to the cash value of the policy. However, a policy loan reduces the death benefit by the amount of the loan plus interest if the loan is not repaid.

SUICIDE CLAUSE In the first two years of coverage, beneficiaries of someone who dies by suicide receive only the amount of the premiums paid. After two years, beneficiaries receive the full value of death benefits.

rider A document attached to a policy that modifies its coverage.

RIDERS TO LIFE INSURANCE POLICIES An insurance company can change the conditions of a policy by adding a rider to it. A **rider** is a document attached to a policy that changes its terms by adding or excluding specified conditions or altering its benefits.

WAIVER OF PREMIUM DISABILITY BENEFIT One common rider is a waiver of premium disability benefit. This clause allows you to stop paying premiums if you're totally and permanently disabled before you reach a certain age, usually 60. The company continues to pay the premiums at its own expense.

double indemnity
A benefit under which the company pays twice the face value of the policy if the insured's death results from an accident.

ACCIDENTAL DEATH BENEFIT Another common rider to life insurance is an accidental death benefit, sometimes called **double indemnity**. Double indemnity pays twice the value of the policy if you are killed in an accident. Again, the accident must occur before a certain age, generally 60 to 65. Experts counsel against adding this rider to your coverage. The benefit is very expensive, and your chances of dying in an accident are slim.

GUARANTEED INSURABILITY OPTION A third important rider is known as a guaranteed insurability option. This rider allows you to buy a specified additional amount of life insurance at certain intervals without undergoing medical exams. This is a good option for people who anticipate needing more life insurance in the future.

COST-OF-LIVING PROTECTION This special rider is designed to help prevent inflation from eroding the purchasing power of the protection your policy provides. A *loss, reduction,* or *erosion of purchasing power* refers to the impact inflation has on a fixed amount of money. As inflation increases the cost of goods and services, that fixed amount will not buy as much in the future as it does today. Exhibit 10–4 shows the effects of inflation on a $100,000 life insurance policy. However, your insurance needs are likely to be smaller in later years.

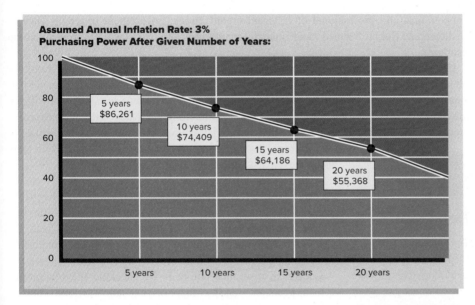

Assumed Annual Inflation Rate: 3%
Purchasing Power After Given Number of Years:

5 years
$86,261

10 years
$74,409

15 years
$64,186

20 years
$55,368

Exhibit **10–4**

Effects of Inflation on a $100,000 Life Insurance Policy

Source: Teachers Insurance and Annuity Association, *The TIAA Guide to Life Insurance Planning for People in Education* (January 1997), p. 8.

ACCELERATED BENEFITS *Accelerated benefits,* also known as *living benefits,* are life insurance policy proceeds paid to the policyholder who is terminally ill before he or she dies. The benefits may be provided for directly in the policies, but more often they are added by riders or attachments to new or existing policies. For more information, check with your insurance agent or your state department of insurance.

CAUTION!

Each insurance rating agency uses its own criteria to determine financial ratings. Even though all use an "A," "B," or "C" grading system, what is "A" for one might be "AA+" or "Aa1" for another.

SECOND-TO-DIE OPTION A *second-to-die life insurance policy,* also called *survivorship life,* insures two lives, usually husband and wife. The death benefit is paid when the second spouse dies. Usually, a second-to-die policy is intended to pay estate taxes when both spouses die. However, some attorneys claim that with the right legal advice, you can minimize or avoid estate taxes completely.

Now that you know the various types of life insurance policies and the major provisions of and riders to such policies, you are ready to make your buying decisions.

Buying Life Insurance

You should consider a number of factors before buying life insurance. As discussed earlier in this chapter, these factors include your present and future sources of income, other savings and income protection, group life insurance, group annuities (or other pension benefits), Social Security, and, of course, the financial strength of the company underwriting the policy.

money minute focus

If you have misplaced a life insurance policy, your state's insurance commissioner may be able to help you locate it. Or you can search for it at **www.mib.com**.

FROM WHOM TO BUY? Look for insurance coverage from financially strong companies with professionally qualified representatives. It is not unusual for a relationship with an insurance company to extend over a period of 20, 30, or even 50 years. For that reason alone, you should choose carefully when deciding on an insurance company or an insurance agent. Fortunately, you have a choice of sources.

SOURCES Protection is available from a wide range of private and public sources, including insurance companies and their representatives; private groups such as employers, labor unions, and professional or fraternal organizations; government programs such as Medicare and Social Security; and financial institutions and manufacturers offering credit insurance.

If you shop for insurance on the Internet, make sure that the website is secure. Look for the lock icon in the address bar or a URL that begins with "https:", and never provide personal data if you don't trust the site. It is not easy to find an insurance company that will sell you a commission-free policy even if you type "no-load life insurance" into Internet search engines. For more information on life insurance, visit www.accuquote.com, www.acli.com, www.iii.org, www.naic.org, www.insure.com, and your state insurance department.

RATING INSURANCE COMPANIES Some of the strongest, most reputable insurance companies in the nation provide excellent insurance coverage at reasonable costs. In fact, the financial strength of an insurance company may be a major factor in holding down premium costs for consumers.

Locate an insurance company by checking the reputations of local agencies. Ask members of your family, friends, or colleagues about the insurers they prefer. Exhibit 10–5 presents the rating systems used by A. M. Best and the other major rating agencies.

FinTech for Financial Literacy

According to the 2019 Insurance Barometer Study, almost half of Americans are more likely to buy life insurance using simplified underwriting, which generally means getting coverage more quickly and without a medical exam, versus traditional underwriting approaches.

Exhibit 10–5
Rating Systems of Major Rating Agencies

You should deal with companies rated as superior or excellent.

	A. M. Best	Standard & Poor's, Duff & Phelps	Moody's	Weiss Research
Superior	A++	AAA	Aaa	A+
	A+			
Excellent	A	AA+	Aa1	A
	A−	AA	Aa2	A−
		AA−	Aa3	B+
Good	B++	A+	A1	B
	B+	A	A2	B−
		A−	A3	C+
Adequate	B	BBB+	Baa1	C
	B−	BBB	Baa2	C−
		BBB−	Baa3	D+
Below average	C+	BB+	Ba1	D
	C+	BB	Ba2	D−
		BB−	Ba3	E+
Weak	C	B+	B1	E
	C−	B	B2	E−
	D	B−	B3	
Nonviable	E	CCC	Caa	F
	F	CC	Ca	
		C,D	C	

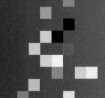

Financial Literacy in Practice

Checklist for Choosing an Insurance Agent

	Yes	No
1. Is your agent available when needed? Clients sometimes have problems that need immediate answers.	☐	☐
2. Does your agent advise you to have a financial plan? Each part of the plan should be necessary to your overall financial protection.	☐	☐
3. Does your agent pressure you? You should be free to make your own decisions about insurance coverage.	☐	☐
4. Does your agent keep up with changes in the insurance field? Agents often attend special classes or study on their own so that they can serve their clients better.	☐	☐
5. Is your agent happy to answer questions? Does he or she want you to know exactly what you are paying for an insurance policy?	☐	☐

CHOOSING YOUR INSURANCE AGENT An insurance agent handles the technical side of insurance. However, that's only the beginning. The really important part of the agent's job is to apply his or her knowledge of insurance to help you select the proper kind of protection within your financial boundaries.

Is it ethical for an attorney who is also a licensed insurance agent to sell life insurance to clients? Yes, according to experts, if terms are fair and reasonable to you and you consent in writing to the terms of the transactions and to the conflict of interest.

Choosing a good agent is among the most important steps in building your insurance program. How do you find an agent? One of the best ways to begin is by asking your parents, friends, neighbors, and others for their recommendations. The nearby *Financial Literacy in Practice* feature offers guidelines for choosing an insurance agent.

COMPARING POLICY COSTS Each life insurance company designs the policies it sells to make them attractive and useful to many policyholders. One policy may have features another policy doesn't; one company may be more selective than another company; one company may get a better return on its investments than another company. These and other factors affect the prices of life insurance policies.

In brief, five factors affect the price a company charges for a life insurance policy: the company's cost of doing business, the return on its investments, the mortality rate it expects among its policyholders, the features the policy contains, and competition among companies with comparable policies.

Consider the time value of money in comparing policy costs. Ask your agent to give you interest-adjusted indexes. An **interest-adjusted index** is a method of evaluating the cost of life insurance by taking into account the time value of money. Highly complex mathematical calculations and formulas combine premium payments, dividends, cash-value buildup, and present value analysis into an index number that makes possible a fairly accurate cost comparison among insurance companies. The lower the index number, the lower the cost of the policy. The nearby *Figure It Out!* feature shows how to use an interest-adjusted index to compare the costs of insurance.

interest-adjusted index
A method of evaluating the cost of life insurance by taking into account the time value of money.

OBTAINING AND EXAMINING A POLICY A life insurance policy is issued after you submit an application for insurance and the insurance company accepts the application. The company determines your insurability by means of the information in your application, the results of a medical examination, and the inspection report. When you receive a

Figure It Out!

Determining the Cost of Insurance: The Time Value of Money

In determining the cost of insurance, don't overlook the time value of money. You must include as part of that cost the interest (opportunity cost) you would earn on money if you did not use it to pay insurance premiums. For many years, insurers did not assign a time value to money in making their sales presentations. Only recently has the insurance industry widely adopted interest-adjusted cost estimates.

If you fail to consider the time value of money, you may get the false impression that the insurance company is giving you something for nothing. Here is an example. Suppose you are 35 and have a $10,000 face amount, 20-year, limited-payment, participating policy. Your annual premium is $210, or $4,200 over the 20-year period. Your dividends over the 20-year payment period total $1,700, so your total net premium is $2,500 ($4,200 − $1,700). Yet the cash value of your policy at the end of 20 years is $4,600. If you disregard the interest your premiums could otherwise have earned, you might get the impression that the insurance company is giving you $2,100 more than you paid ($4,600 − $2,500). But if you consider the time value of money (or its opportunity cost), the insurance company is

not giving you $2,100. What if you had invested the annual premiums in a conservative stock mutual fund? At an 8 percent annual yield, your account would have accumulated to $9,610 in 20 years. (See Exhibit 1–B.) Therefore, instead of having received $2,100 from the insurance company, you have paid the company $5,010 for 20 years of insurance protection:

Premiums you paid over 20 years	$4,200	
Time value of money	5,410	($9,610 − $4,200)
Total cost	9,610	
Cash value	4,600	
Net cost of insurance	5,010	($9,610 − $4,600)

Be sure to request interest-adjusted indexes from your agent; if he or she doesn't give them to you, look for another agent. As you have seen in the example, you can compare the costs among insurance companies by combining premium payments, dividends, cash-value buildup, and present value analysis into an index number.

life insurance policy, read every word of the contract, and, if necessary, ask your agent for a point-by-point explanation of the language. Many insurance companies have rewritten their contracts to make them more understandable. These are legal documents, and you should be familiar with what they promise, even though they use technical terms.

After you buy new life insurance, you have a 10-day "free-look" period during which you can change your mind. If you do so, the company will return your premium without penalty.

CHOOSING SETTLEMENT OPTIONS Selecting the appropriate settlement option is an important part of designing a life insurance program. The most common settlement options are lump-sum payment, limited installment payment, life income option, and proceeds left with the company.

CAUTION!

Never buy coverage you don't understand. It is the agent's responsibility to explain your coverage in terms you can understand.

LUMP-SUM PAYMENT The insurance company pays the face amount of the policy in one installment to the beneficiary or to the estate of the insured. This form of settlement is the most widely used option. However, it may be a wrong option if you wish to financially protect your spouse for the rest of his or her life or until your children finish their education.

LIMITED INSTALLMENT PAYMENT This option provides for payment of the life insurance proceeds in equal periodic installments for a specified number of years after your death.

LIFE INCOME OPTION Under the life income option, payments are made to the beneficiary for as long as she or he lives. The amount of each payment is based primarily on

10 Golden Rules of Buying Life Insurance

Remember that your need for life insurance coverage will change over time. Your income may go up or down, or your family size might change. Therefore, it is wise to review your coverage periodically to ensure that it keeps up with your changing needs.

Follow these rules when buying life insurance:	Done
1. Understand and know what your life insurance needs are before you make any purchase, and make sure the company you choose can meet those needs.	☐
2. Buy your life insurance from a company that is licensed in your state.	☐
3. Select an agent who is competent, knowledgeable, and trustworthy.	☐
4. Shop around and compare costs.	☐
5. Buy only the amount of life insurance you need and can afford.	☐
6. Ask about lower premium rates for nonsmokers.	☐
7. Read your policy and make sure you understand it.	☐
8. Inform your beneficiaries about the kinds and amount of life insurance you own.	☐
9. Keep your policy in a safe place at home, and keep your insurance company's name and your policy number in a safe deposit box.	☐
10. Check your coverage periodically or whenever your situation changes to ensure that it meets your current needs.	☐

Source: American Council of Life Insurance

the sex and attained age of the beneficiary at the time of the insured's death. It is probably the best option if you wish to provide sufficient income for your spouse for the rest of his or her life.

PROCEEDS LEFT WITH THE COMPANY The life insurance proceeds are left with the insurance company at a specified rate of interest. The company acts as trustee and pays the interest to the beneficiary. The guaranteed minimum interest rate paid on the proceeds varies among companies.

SWITCHING POLICIES Think twice if your agent suggests that you replace the whole life or universal life insurance you already own. Before you give up this protection, make sure you are still insurable (check medical and any other qualification requirements). Ask your agent or company for an opinion about the new proposal to get both sides of the argument. The nearby *Financial Literacy in Practice* feature presents 10 important guidelines for purchasing life insurance. And to learn how to shop for life insurance, read the nearby *Digital Financial Literacy* feature.

WHAT WOULD YOU DO? You realize that choosing the right type of life insurance policy is complicated. You have many options available, and it is somewhat difficult to sort out the details to decide what is best. Another complicating factor is that con artists may try to defraud you. What would you do to choose the right policy?

How to shop for life insurance

You may be able to estimate how much you need online, but that's just the start of your search.

No one needs to tell you why you should have life insurance: If you die and your family or anyone who depends on you for support could no longer count on your income, life insurance would replace that income—assuming you choose a policy with the amount of coverage that is right for you.

In addition to deciding on the coverage amount, you have a few more hoops to jump through—namely, whether to buy a whole life or term life policy.

Whole life (often called cash-value or permanent life insurance) provides coverage for life and has an investing component that allows you to take a loan against the policy. The downside: Compared with term coverage, it's expensive, especially in the early years of the policy. *Term life* provides coverage for a defined period of time—typically 5, 10, or 20 years—without the investment and loan bells and whistles. What you see is what you get. Another advantage: Term life policies typically cost far less than whole life.

For most people, term insurance makes the most sense and, dollar for dollar, gives you the most protection for your money. An insurance agent you trust may be able to make a compelling case for buying some version of cash-value insurance. To counteract the argument that with cash-value insurance you reap generous rewards after you've held a policy for a number of years, term proponents urge consumers to buy term and invest the difference in premiums.

How much do you need? Rules of thumb—such as buying coverage equal to 7 to 10 times your annual pretax income—and calculators provided by the insurance industry are a handy starting point. But these shortcuts gloss over specifics that shape how much coverage you'll need. A recent analysis by online insurance broker Policygenius found that 77 percent of term life insurance shoppers were lowballing the amount of coverage they applied for. "Half a million dollars seems like a large lump sum, but over 20 to 30 years, it could leave you at the poverty line if there aren't other sources of income," says Nicholas Mancuso, a senior operations manager at Policygenius.

If an insurance company quotes a steep rate because of your risk profile, shopping around can help.

A more reliable approach to determining the right coverage is to add up the income your family would need to cover ongoing expenses as long as they need it (say, the number of years until your youngest child graduates college); the estimated cost of sending your kids to college; your debts; and final expenses at death. Then subtract savings, college funds, and other life insurance policies. Finally, adjust the amount to reflect your situation. For example, you may want to increase coverage if a stay-at-home parent provides child care.

According to the Insurance Information Institute, similar policies often have annual premiums that differ by hundreds of dollars a year. You can get preliminary quotes from multiple insurers using websites such as **AccuQuote.com**, **LifeQuotes.com**, and **Policygenius.com**. How much you'll actually pay for a policy depends on your age, gender, health, and family history. Insurers generally ask about your height, weight, blood pressure, cholesterol levels, and any medical issues, and they will often require a medical exam. Some will also factor in your driving record, credit history, and any risky hobbies, such as scuba diving.

If an insurance company quotes a steep rate because of your risk profile, shopping around can help. Some insurers charge much more than others for similar health conditions.

You may already get life insurance as a benefit from your job, and you may be able to buy extra coverage through your employer without a medical exam. That could be a good deal if you have health issues, but if you're in good health, you can usually buy a policy elsewhere for less.

ACTION STEPS FOR. . .

. . .Information Literacy

Choose a recent life insurance article from **kiplinger.com** or **iii.org**. What aspects of the articles do you believe are most pertinent for your life insurance needs?

. . .Financial Literacy

Select an article from **iii.org**, **naic.org**, or **kiplinger.com**. Develop an outline of four key ideas from it that might be the basis for creating a podcast.

. . .Diginal Literacy

Ask a classmate or a friend to select a life insurance article from **kiplinger.com**. Prepare a summary of why the article was selected and how the information might be used for their own life insurance needs.

Sheet 34 Life Insurance Policy Comparison

PRACTICE QUIZ 10–3

1. What are the key provisions in a life insurance policy?

2. What is a rider?

3. What are the various riders in a life insurance policy?

4. What factors do you consider in choosing an insurance agent?

5. What are the four most common settlement options?

6. Match the following terms with the appropriate definition:

endowment   *a.* Person named to receive the benefits from an insurance policy _____

beneficiary   *b.* Provides coverage for a specific period of time and pays an agreed-upon sum of money to the policyholder if he or she is still living at the end of the period _____

whole life insurance   *c.* A permanent policy for which the policyholder pays a specified premium for the rest of his or her life _____

double indemnity   *d.* A rider to a life insurance policy that pays twice the value of the policy if the policyholder is killed in an accident _____

Financial Planning with Annuities

As you have seen so far, life insurance provides a set sum of money at your death. However, if you want to enjoy benefits while you are still alive, you might consider annuities. An annuity protects you against the risk of outliving your assets.

An **annuity** is a financial contract written by an insurance company that provides you with regular income. Generally, you receive the income monthly, often with payments arranged to continue for as long as you live. Annuities may be fixed, providing a specific income for life, or variable, with payouts above a guaranteed minimum level dependent on investment return. The payments may begin at once (*immediate annuity*) or at some future date (*deferred annuity*).

IMMEDIATE ANNUITIES People approaching retirement age can purchase immediate annuities. These annuities provide income payments at once. They are usually purchased with a lump-sum payment. When you are 65, you may no longer need all of your life insurance coverage—especially if you have grown children. You may decide to convert the cash value of your insurance policy into a lump-sum payment for an immediate annuity.

DEFERRED ANNUITIES With deferred annuities, income payments start at some future date. Meanwhile, interest accumulates on the money you deposit. Younger people often buy such annuities to save money toward retirement. A deferred annuity purchased with a lump-sum payment is known as a *single-premium deferred annuity*. A premium is the payment you make. These annuities are popular because of the greater potential for tax-free growth. If you are buying a deferred annuity on an installment basis, you may want one that allows flexible premiums, or payments. That means that your contributions can vary from year to year.

As with the life insurance principle discussed earlier, the predictable mortality experience of a large group of individuals is fundamental to the annuity principle. By determining the average number of years most people in a given age group will live, the insurance company can calculate the annual amounts to pay to each person in the group over his or her entire life.

Because the annual payouts per premium amount are determined by average mortality experience, annuity contracts are more attractive for people whose present health, living

LO10.4

Recognize how annuities provide financial security.

ACTION ITEM
An annuity protects me against the risk of outliving my assets.

☐ Yes ☐ No

annuity A contract that provides a regular income for as long as the person lives.

habits, and family mortality experience suggest that they are likely to live longer than average. As a general rule, annuities are not advisable for people in poor health, although exceptions to this rule exist.

INDEX ANNUITIES A type of fixed annuity, an index annuity, has earnings that accumulate at a rate based on a formula linked to one or more equity-based indexes, such as the S&P 500. These annuities are very complex so it is important that you understand their features before purchasing an index annuity. Index annuities may offer death benefit protection.

Why Buy Annuities?

A primary reason for buying an annuity is to give you retirement income for the rest of your life. You should fully fund your IRAs, Keoghs, and 401(k)s before considering annuities. We discuss retirement income in Chapter 14.

> **CAUTION!**
>
> An annuity is a long-term financial contract. You should enter into an annuity arrangement only after a thorough review of your personal finances and retirement goals.

Although people have been buying annuities for many years, the appeal of variable annuities increased during the mid-1990s due to a rising stock market. A *fixed annuity* states that the annuitant (the person who is to receive the annuity) will receive a fixed amount of income over a certain period or for life. With a *variable annuity,* the monthly payments vary because they are based on the income received from stocks or other investments.

Today, variable annuities are part of the retirement and investment plans of many Americans. Before buying any variable annuity, however, request a prospectus from the insurance company or from your insurance agent and read it carefully. The prospectus contains important information about the annuity contract, including fees and charges, investment options, death benefits, and annuity payout options. Compare the benefits and costs of the annuity to other variable annuities and to other types of investments, such as mutual funds, discussed in Chapter 13. Annuities are complicated; consult a professional before purchasing an annuity.

Some of the growth in the use of annuities can be attributed to the passage of the Employee Retirement Income Security Act (ERISA) of 1974. Annuities are often purchased for individual retirement accounts (IRAs), which ERISA made possible. They may also be used in Keogh-type plans for self-employed people. As you will see in Chapter 14, contributions to both IRA and Keogh plans are tax-deductible up to specified limits.

Costs of Annuities

You will pay several charges when you purchase a variable annuity. Be sure you understand all the costs before you invest. These costs will reduce the value of your account and the return on your investment. The most common costs are:

- *Surrender charges.* The insurance company will assess a "surrender" charge if you withdraw money within a certain period, usually within six to eight years. Generally, the surrender charge declines gradually over a period of seven to 10 years.

> **EXAMPLE: Surrender Charge**
>
> You purchase a variable annuity contract with a $10,000 purchase payment. The contract has a schedule of surrender charges, beginning with a 7 percent charge in the first year and declining by 1 percent each year. In addition, you are allowed to withdraw 10 percent of your contract value each year free of surrender charges. In the first year, you decide to withdraw $5,000, or one-half of your contract value of $10,000 (assuming that your contract value has not increased or decreased because of investment performance). In this case, you could withdraw $1,000 (10 percent of contract value) free of surrender charges, but you would pay a surrender charge of 7 percent, or $280, on the other $4,000 withdrawn.

- *Mortality and expense risk charge.* This charge is equal to a certain percentage of your account value, usually 1.25 percent per year. The charge compensates the insurance company for insurance risks it assumes under the annuity contract. Profit from the mortality and expense risk charge is sometimes used to pay the insurer's costs of selling the variable annuity, such as a commission paid to your financial professional for selling the variable annuity to you.

EXAMPLE: Mortality and Expense Risk Charge

Your variable annuity has a mortality and expense risk charge at an annual rate of 1.25 percent of account value. Your average account value during the year is $20,000, so you will pay $250 in mortality and expense risk charges that year.

- *Administrative fees.* Your insurance company may deduct fees to cover recordkeeping and other administrative expenses. The fee may be charged as a flat account maintenance fee (perhaps $25 or $30 per year) or as a percentage of your account value (usually 0.15 percent per year).

EXAMPLE: Administrative Fees

Your variable annuity charges administrative fees at an annual rate of 0.15 percent of account value. Your average account value during the year is $50,000. You will pay $75 in administrative fees.

- *Fund expenses.* You will also indirectly pay the fees and expenses imposed by the mutual funds that are the underlying investment options for your variable annuity.

Tax Considerations

When you buy an annuity, the interest on the principal, as well as the interest compounded on that interest, builds up free of current income tax. The Tax Reform Act of 1986 preserves the tax advantage of annuities (and insurance) but curtails deductions for IRAs. With an annuity, there is no maximum annual contribution. Also, if you die during the accumulation period, your beneficiary is guaranteed no less than the amount invested.

As with any other financial product, the advantages of annuities are tempered by drawbacks. In the case of variable annuities, these drawbacks include reduced flexibility and fees that lower investment return.

PRACTICE QUIZ 10–4

1. What is an annuity?
2. What is the difference between an immediate and a deferred annuity?
3. As a general rule, are annuities advisable for people in poor health? Why or why not?
4. What are fixed and variable annuities?

Road Map

to financial literacy

Life Insurance

You Are Here

Checkpoint 1

☐ Choose a reputable life insurance company; then obtain and compare premiums for $100,000 term, whole life, and universal life insurance.

☐ As children arrive, you will need more life insurance.

☐ If you are providing financial support for aging parents or siblings, keep adequate life insurance coverage.

Checkpoint 2

☐ Check if your employer provides life insurance through group insurance plans.

☐ Buy term insurance if you have debts or dependents who need financial support from you.

Checkpoint 3

☐ Examine your life insurance policy and note its contractual provisions.

☐ As children grow and leave home, reevaluate your need for life insurance.

Financial Security

your personal finance dashboard

Life Insurance Coverage

Your need for life insurance will change with changes in your life. For example, if you are single or live with your parents, you may not need life insurance unless you have a debt or want to provide for your parents, a friend, a relative, or charity. However, as children are born, your need for life insurance will increase. As children grow older and leave the nest, you will probably need less insurance.

YOUR SITUATION: Do you know if you need life insurance? Have you taken time to consider why you need life insurance and to find a sales agent who is knowledgeable and trustworthy?

LO10.1 Life insurance protects the people who depend on you from financial losses caused by your death. You can use the easy method, the DINK method, the "nonworking" spouse method, or the "family need" method to determine your life insurance needs.

LO10.2 Two types of insurance companies—stock and mutual—sell nonparticipating and participating policies. Both sell two basic types of insurance: term life and whole life. Many variations and combinations of these types are available.

LO10.3 Most life insurance policies have standard features. An insurance company can change the conditions of a policy by adding a rider to it.

Before buying life insurance, consider all your present and future sources of income; then compare the costs and choose appropriate settlement options.

LO10.4 An annuity pays while you live, whereas life insurance pays when you die. With a fixed annuity, you receive a fixed amount of income over a certain period or for life. With a variable annuity, the monthly payments vary because they are based on the income received from stocks or other investments.

annuity 369

beneficiary 353

cash value 359

double indemnity 362

interest-adjusted
  index 365

nonforfeiture clause 362

nonparticipating
  policy 357

participating policy 358

rider 362

term insurance 358

universal life
  insurance 359

whole life insurance 359

1. Suppose that yours is a typical family. Your annual income is $60,000. Use the easy method to determine your need for life insurance.
2. Using the "nonworking" spouse method, what should be the life insurance needs for a family whose youngest child is 2 years old?
3. Suppose your annual premium for a $20,000, 20-year limited-payment policy is $420 over the 20-year period. The cash value of your policy at the end of 20 years is $9,200. Assume that you could have invested the annual premium in a mutual fund yielding 7 percent annually. What is the net cost of your insurance for the 20-year period?

Solutions

1. Current gross income   = $60,000
   Multiply gross income by 7 years   = $420,000
   Take 70 percent of $420,000   = $420,000 × 0.70
   Approximate insurance needed   = $294,000

2. Youngest child's age   = 2 years
   Years before the child is 18 years old   = 16 years
   Insurance needed   = 16 × $20,000 = $320,000

3. Premiums paid over 20 years   = $420 × 20 = $8,400
   Time value of 20-year annual payments of $420 at 7 percent yield
   (See Exhibit 1–B; use a factor of 40.995)   = 40.995 × $420 = $17,218
   Cash value   = $9,200
   Net cost of insurance   = $17,218 − 9,200 = $8,018

1. You are the wage earner in a "typical family" with a $58,000 gross annual income. Use the easy method to determine how much insurance you should carry. (LO10.1)

2. You and your spouse are in good health and have reasonably secure careers. Each of you makes about $55,000 annually. You own a home with a mortgage of $120,000, and you owe $15,000 on car loans, $5,000 in personal debts, and $4,000 on credit card loans. You have no other debts. You have no plans to increase the size of your family in the near future. Assume funeral expenses of $10,000. Estimate your total insurance needs using the DINK method. (LO10.1)

3. Shaan and Anita are married and have two children, ages 4 and 7. Anita is a "nonworking" spouse who devotes all of her time to household activities. Estimate how much life insurance Shaan and Anita should carry. (LO10.1)

4. Use the *Figure It Out!* feature in this chapter to calculate your own life insurance needs. (LO10.1)

5. Use Exhibit 10–1 to find the average number of additional years a male and female, age 25, are expected to live based on the statistics gathered by the U.S. government as of 2017. (LO10.1)

6. Mark and Parveen are the parents of three young children. Mark is a store manager in a local supermarket. His gross salary is $75,000 per year. Parveen is a full-time stay-at-home mom. Use the easy method to estimate the family's life insurance needs. (LO10.1)

7. You are a dual-income, no-kids family. You and your spouse have the following debts (total): mortgage, $200,000; auto loan, $10,000; credit card balance, $4,000; other debts, $10,000. Further, you estimate that your funeral will cost $8,000. Your spouse expects to continue to work after your death. Using the DINK method, what should be your need for life insurance? (LO10.1)

8. Using the "nonworking" spouse method, what should be the life insurance needs for a family whose youngest child is 10 years old? (LO10.1)

9. Using the "nonworking" spouse method, what should be the life insurance needs for a family whose youngest child is 5 years old? (LO10.1)

10. Your variable annuity charges administrative fees at an annual rate of 0.15 percent of account value. Your average account value during the year is $200,000. What is the administrative fee for the year? (LO10.4)

11. Sophia purchased a variable annuity contract with a purchase payment of $25,000. Surrender charges begin with 7 percent in the first year and decline by 1 percent each year. In addition, Sophia can withdraw 10 percent of her contract value each year without paying surrender charges. In the first year, Sophia needed to withdraw $6,000. Assume that the contract value had not increased or decreased because of investment performance. What was the surrender charge Sophia had to pay? (LO10.4)

12. Shelly's variable annuity has a mortality and expense risk charge at an annual rate of 1.25 percent of account value. Her account value during the year is $50,000. What was Shelly's mortality and expense risk charge for the year? (LO10.4)

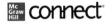 **To reinforce the content in this chapter, more problems are provided at connect.mheducation.com.**

LIFE INSURANCE COVERAGE

Competency

Determine the type and amount of life insurance coverage.

Action Research

Based on this chapter, *Your Personal Financial Plan Sheets 33* and *34*, online research, and conversations with others, create a proposal for your current or future life insurance needs. Identify sources and costs for various types and amounts of coverage.

Outcome

Create an audio file, video, storyboard, or other visual that communicates your current and future life insurance needs. Also report your findings related to various types, sources, and costs for various amounts of coverage.

REAL LIFE PERSONAL FINANCE

LIFE INSURANCE FOR THE YOUNG MARRIED

Jeff and Ann are both 28 years old. They have been married for three years, and they have a son who is almost 2. They expect their second child in a few months.

Jeff is a teller in a local bank. He has just received a $30-a-week raise. His income is $960 a week, which, after taxes, leaves him with $3,296 a month. His company provides $70,000 of life insurance, a medical/hospital/surgical plan, and a major medical plan. All of these group plans protect him as long as he stays with the bank.

When Jeff received his raise, he decided that part of it should be used to add to his family's protection. Jeff and Ann talked to their insurance agent who reviewed the insurance Jeff obtained through his job. Under Social Security, they also have some basic protection against the loss of Jeff's income if he becomes totally disabled or if he dies before the children were 18.

Most of this protection was only basic, a kind of floor for Jeff and Ann to build on. For example, monthly Social Security payments to Ann would be approximately $2,000 if Jeff died leaving two children under age 18. Although the family's expenses would be lowered if Jeff died, their expenses would soon amount to $250 more than Social Security would provide, given the upcoming addition of their second child.

1. What type of policy would you suggest for Jeff and Ann? Why?
2. In your opinion, do Jeff and Ann need additional insurance? Why or why not?

FINANCIAL PLANNING WITH LIFE INSURANCE

Surprise! Jamie Lee and Ross were stunned to find that their family of two has grown to a family of five. They were expecting twins until they found out the day the children were born that they were actually the parents of triplets!

Ross immediately had worries of being able to provide for the growing family: diapers, formula, college expenses times three. What if something happened to him or Jamie Lee? How would the surviving parent be able to provide for such a large family?

Current Financial Situation

Assets (Jamie Lee and Ross combined):

Checking account, $2,500

Savings account, $16,000

Emergency fund savings account, $19,100

IRA balance, $25,000

Cars, $11,500 (Jamie Lee) and $19,000 (Ross)

Liabilities (Jamie Lee and Ross combined):

Student loan balance, $0

Credit card balance, $3,500

Car loans, $7,000

Income:

Jamie Lee, $45,000 gross income ($31,500 net income after taxes)

Ross, $73,000 gross income ($60,800 net income after taxes)

Monthly Expenses

Mortgage, $1,225

Property taxes, $400

Homeowner's insurance, $200

Utilities, $160

Food, $500

Gas/Vehicle maintenance, $275

Credit card payment, $275

Car loan payment, $289

Entertainment, $125

Questions

1. Within days of the triplets' arrival, Jamie Lee and Ross began researching and comparing various agencies for the purchase of a life insurance policy. What characteristics should Jamie Lee and Ross look for when choosing a life insurance agency? What sources could they reference for help when choosing a life insurance agency?

2. Jamie Lee and Ross need to ensure that the surviving spouse and the children will not have financial hardship in the event of a loss. Using the easy method and considering Ross's salary in the calculation, how much life insurance will they need?

3. With so many policy variations to choose from, Ross and Jamie Lee are unsure which company is offering the most competitive rates. How will they be able to compare the rates between the various companies?

4. Jamie Lee and Ross have a limited budget for the life insurance necessity now that they have the additional present-day expenses of the triplets to consider. What type of life insurance would you recommend for the family at this life stage, and what are its associated advantages and disadvantages?

Spending Diary

"I'M NOT SURE SPENDING FOR LIFE INSURANCE IS NECESSARY FOR MY LIFE SITUATION."

Directions As you continue to record and monitor spending in various categories, be sure to consider how various decisions will affect your long-term financial security. Various comments you record might remind you to consider possible changes you might want to make in your spending habits. The Daily Spending Diary sheets are located at the end of Chapter 1 and in Connect Finance.

Questions

1. Are there any spending amounts or items that you might consider reducing or eliminating?
2. What actions might you consider now or in the future regarding spending on life insurance?

Name: _____ Date: _____

Determining Life Insurance Needs

Purpose: To estimate life insurance coverage needed to cover expected expenses and future family living costs.

Financial Planning Activities: Estimate the amounts for the categories listed below. This sheet is also available in an Excel spreadsheet format in Connect Finance.

Suggested Websites: www.insure.com, www.bankrate.com/calculators/insurance/life-insurance-calculator.aspx

Household expenses to be covered

Final expenses (funeral, estate taxes, etc.)	1 $ _____
Payment of consumer debt amounts	2 $ _____
Emergency fund	3 $ _____
College fund	4 $ _____

Expected living expenses:

Average living expense	$ _____
Spouse's income after taxes	$ – _____
Annual Social Security benefits	$ – _____
Net annual living expenses	$ _____
Years until spouse is 90	$ _____
Investment rate factor (see below)	$ _____

Total living expenses	$ _____
Total monetary needs (1 + 2 + 3 + 4 + 5)	$ _____
Less: Total current investments	$ _____
Life insurance needs	$ _____

Investment rate factors

Years until spouse is 90	25	30	35	40	45	50	55	60
Conservative investment	20	22	25	27	30	31	33	35
Aggressive investment	16	17	19	20	21	21	22	23

Note: Use *Your Personal Financial Plan* sheet 34 to compare life insurance policies.

What's Next for Your Personal Financial Plan?

- Survey several people to determine their reasons for buying life insurance.
- Talk to an insurance agent to compare the rates charged by different companies and for different age categories.

Name: _____ Date: _____

Life Insurance Policy Comparison

Purpose: To research and compare companies, coverages, and costs for different insurance policies.

Financial Planning Activities: Analyze ads and contact life insurance agents to obtain the information requested below. This sheet is also available in an Excel spreadsheet format in Connect Finance.

Suggested Websites: www.insure.com, www.accuquote.com

Your Age:			
Company			
Agent's name, address, and phone			
Type of insurance (term, straight/whole, limited payment, endowment, universal)			
Type of policy (individual, group)			
Amount of coverage			
Frequency of payment (monthly, quarterly, semiannually, annually)			
Premium amount			
Other costs: • Service charges • Medical exam			
Rate of return (annual percentage increase in cash value; not applicable for term policies)			
Benefits of insurance as stated in ad or by agent			
Potential problems or disadvantages of this coverage			

What's Next for Your Personal Financial Plan?

- Talk to a life insurance agent to obtain information on the methods he or she suggests for determining the amount of life insurance a person should have.

- Research the differences in premium costs between a mutual and a stock insurance company.

Suggested App:
• Ladder

McGraw Hill

11 Investing Basics and Evaluating Bonds

3 Steps to Financial Literacy . . .
Starting an Investment Program

1 Establish investment goals and perform a financial checkup.
Website: https://www.thebalance.com/top-financial-goals-to-achieve-in-a-life-time-4179050

2 Save the money needed to open a brokerage account.
Website: https://www.investopedia.com/articles/younginvestors/08/eight-tips.asp

3 Evaluate all investments before investing your money.
Website: finance.yahoo.com

Why invest?

While many people dream of being the world's next millionaire, dreaming doesn't make it happen. You must learn how to evaluate different investments to become a smart investor. At the end of the chapter, *Your Personal Finance Road Map and Dashboard* will help you take the next steps to improve your investing skills.

In this chapter, you will learn to:

LO11.1 Explain why you should establish an investment program.

LO11.2 Describe how safety, risk, income, growth, and liquidity affect your investment program.

LO11.3 Identify the factors that can reduce investment risk.

LO11.4 Understand why investors purchase government bonds.

LO11.5 Recognize why investors purchase corporate bonds.

LO11.6 Evaluate bonds when making an investment.

YOUR PERSONAL FINANCIAL PLAN SHEETS

35. Establishing Investment Goals
36. Assessing Risk for Investments
37. Evaluating Corporate Bonds

Preparing for an Investment Program

Many people ask the question: Why begin an investment program now? Answer: The sooner you start an investment program, the more time your investments have to work for you. For example, if you save $1,500 each year for 20 years, your total investment totals $30,000. If your investments earn 6 percent each year and all your investments earnings are added to your contributions, the value of your annual contributions and investment earnings will total $55,178. This example is "for real," and you'll learn more about the value of a long-term investment program and how the time value of money can help you obtain your financial goals later in this section. But first, you have to get your financial affairs in order before you can begin investing.

Establishing Investment Goals

The *specific* goals you want to accomplish must be the driving force behind your investment plan. Some financial planners suggest that investment goals be stated in terms of money: "By December 31, 2030, I will have total assets of $120,000." Other financial planners believe investors are more motivated to work toward goals that are stated in terms of the particular things they desire: "By January 1, 2032, I will have accumulated enough money to purchase a second home in the mountains." Regardless of how they are stated, investment goals must be specific and measurable. The following questions will help you establish valid investment goals:

1. How much money do you need to satisfy your investment goals?
2. How much risk are you willing to assume in your investment program?
3. What possible economic or personal conditions could alter your investment goals?

LO11.1

Explain why you should establish an investment program.

ACTION ITEM

My investment goals are written down, and I have completed my financial checkup.

☐ Yes ☐ No

4. Considering your economic circumstances and how long your investments can work for you, are your investment goals reasonable?

5. Are you willing to make the sacrifices necessary to ensure that you meet your investment goals?

Your investment goals are always oriented toward the future. For example, you may establish a short-term goal of accumulating $3,000 in a savings account over the next 12 months. You may then use the $3,000 to purchase stocks or mutual funds to help you obtain your intermediate or long-term investment goals.

Performing a Financial Checkup

In this section, we examine several factors you should consider before making your first investment.

ETHICAL CONCERNS: PAYING YOUR BILLS ON TIME While there are many reasons why people can't pay their bills on time, the problem often starts with people wanting (and then purchasing) more than they can afford. From both a legal *and* ethical standpoint, you have an obligation to pay for credit purchases.

If you don't pay for products or services purchased on credit, there are serious repercussions. For example:

- Merchandise can be repossessed.
- A business can sue to recover the cost of the product or service.
- Your credit score can be lowered to reflect late or missed payments.
- The cost of additional credit, if available, may be higher because of lower credit scores or late or missed payments.

Some consumers believe the only way out of their financial problems is to declare personal bankruptcy, but think about the long-term consequences. First, filing bankruptcy is not cheap, and most lawyers expect to be paid (usually in cash) before they file the necessary legal documents and represent you in court. Second, remember that bankruptcy will affect your ability to obtain future credit for a home, automobile, or other consumer purchases.

WORK TO BALANCE YOUR BUDGET Many individuals regularly spend more than they make. They purchase items on credit and then must make monthly installment payments and pay finance charges ranging between 12 and 21 percent or higher. In addition, there may be fees for late payments or if your purchases push your balance over your credit limit. With this situation, investing in certificates of deposit, bonds, stocks, mutual funds, or other investments that might earn 1 to 10 percent makes no sense until credit card and installment purchases, along with the accompanying finance charges, are reduced or eliminated. A good rule of thumb is to limit monthly payments for all types of consumer credit to 20 percent of your net (after-tax) income.

EXAMPLE: Calculating Recommended Maximum Consumer Credit Purchase Amounts

If your net (after-tax) monthly income is $3,000, the maximum amount of consumer credit payments is $600, as illustrated below.

Maximum Credit Payment = Net (after tax income) × 20 percent

= $3,000 × 20 percent

$600 = $3,000 × 0.20

Example from Your Life

$ _____ Net income x 20 percent = $ _____

Purchasing a home is one of the most important decisions people make during their lifetime. It's so important that most people do their homework. They walk through different homes that are for sale, evaluate financing options, and determine if they can afford the home of their dreams. Then after all their research, they make a decision that can change their life. Another decision that is just as important is the decision to start investing. In fact, a long-term investment program with a portfolio of quality investments can be worth far more than the value of the average home. And yet, people often wait or never begin investing.

So why don't people invest? For many people, the answers center around three factors: (1) they don't know anything about investing; (2) they are afraid they will lose their money; and, (3) they don't have the money to start investing. While there are many websites that will help would-be investors learn about managing their finances and investing, the Motley Fool site deserves special attention. Started by David and Tom Gardner, the goal of the Motley Fool site (**https://www.fool.com**) is to help average people

The Motley Fool.
To Educate, Amuse & Enrich™

make the best decisions about every dollar they spend, save, and invest. The Motley Fool is an excellent choice for "beginning" investors as well as more experienced investors.

Visit the Motley Fool website to learn how to:

- manage your money and learn about different investments.
- start investing with as little as $100 a month.
- plan for retirement if you are in your 20s, 30s, 40s, or 50s.

The information on the Motley Fool website is good stuff. Why not take a look and see how it can help you obtain your financial goals?

ACTION STEPS FOR. . .

. . .Information Literacy

Select a topic in the Trending section of the Motley Fool website. Based on the information in the article, prepare a list of actions you could take to help you achieve your personal finance goals.

. . .Financial Literacy

Click on the retirement tab on the Motley Fool website. Then click the link for "How Much Do I Need to Retire". Prepare a list of suggestions to help you begin saving and investing for retirement.

. . .Diginal Literacy

Look through the list of industry sectors that are described in the Stocks tab on the Motley Fool website. Then choose one of the sectors that interests you. Create a video or audio summary of important factors to evaluate if you were going to invest in a stock issued by a company in this sector.

For help balancing your budget and monitoring your spending, you can use the Daily Spending Diary sheets located in Chapter 1. You can also visit one of the following websites: Quicken at **www.quicken.com**; MoneyStrands at **www.moneystrands.com**; or Mint at **https://www.mint.com/how-mint-works/budgets**.

MANAGE YOUR CREDIT CARD DEBT While all cardholders have reasons for using their credit cards, it is *very* easy to get in trouble. Watch for the following five warning signs:

1. Experts suggest that you pay your credit card balance in full each month. One of the first warning signs is the inability to pay your entire balance each month.
2. Don't use your credit cards to pay for many small purchases during the month. Often this leads to a "real surprise" when you open your credit card statement and realize how much you spent during the month.

3. Don't use the cash advance provision that accompanies most credit cards. The reason is simple: The annual percentage rate is usually higher for cash advances.

4. Think about the number of cards you really need. Most experts recommend that an individual have one or two cards and use those cards for emergencies.

5. Get help if you think you are in trouble. You may want to review the discussion on organizations that help people manage their finances presented in Chapter 5.

emergency fund An amount of money you can obtain quickly in case of immediate need.

START AN EMERGENCY FUND An **emergency fund** is an amount of money you can obtain quickly in case of immediate need. This money should be deposited in a savings account or in a money market mutual fund that provides immediate access to cash, if needed.

Most financial planners agree that an amount equal to at least three months' living expenses is reasonable. And while any emergency fund is better than no fund, there are times when you may want to increase the amount. For example, if you think you are about to lose your job, you may want to increase the amount in your emergency fund.

EXAMPLE: Calculating an Amount for Emergencies

If your monthly expenses total $1,800, you should save at least $5,400 before you begin investing.

$$\text{Minimum emergency fund} = \text{Monthly expenses} \times 3 \text{ months}$$
$$= \$1,800 \times 3 \text{ months}$$
$$= \$5,400$$

Example from Your Life

$ _____ \times 3 \text{ months} = \$ _____
    monthly expenses

---

line of credit A short-term loan that is approved before the money is actually needed.

To meet unexpected emergencies, you may also want to establish a line of credit at a bank, savings and loan association, or credit union. A **line of credit** is a short-term loan that is approved before you actually need the money. The cash advance provision offered by major credit card companies can also be used in an emergency. However, both lines of credit and credit cards have a ceiling, or maximum dollar amount, that limits the amount of available credit. If you have already exhausted both of these sources of credit on everyday expenses, they will not be available in an emergency.

Getting the Money Needed to Start an Investment Program

How badly do you want to achieve your investment goals? Are you willing to sacrifice some immediate purchases to provide financing for your investments? The answers to both questions are extremely important. Take Rita Johnson, a 32-year-old nurse in a large St. Louis hospital. As part of a divorce settlement in 2013, she received a cash payment of almost $65,000. At first, she was tempted to spend this money on a new BMW and new furniture. But after some careful planning, she decided to save $25,000 in a certificate of deposit and invest the remainder in a conservative mutual fund. On May 31, 2020, these investments were valued at $89,000.

Important Question! What is important to you? Your answer to this question will affect your savings and investment goals. At one extreme are people who save or invest as much of each paycheck as they can. At the other extreme are people who spend everything they earn and run out of money before their next

money minute focus

If you're serious about managing your spending, you might consider using the 50/20/30 rule. In a nutshell, this rule helps you allocate income into three categories: living expenses or necessities (50 percent), savings and investing (20 percent), and stuff you want but don't necessary need (30 percent). To learn more, go to https://www.discover.com/online-banking/banking-topics/budgeting-with-the-50-20-30-rule/.

Suggestion	Comments
1. Pay your bills, then pay yourself.	Many financial experts recommend that you (1) pay your monthly bills, (2) save or invest a reasonable amount of money, and (3) use the money left over for personal expenses and entertainment.
2. Take advantage of employer-sponsored retirement programs.	Some employers will match part or all of the contributions you make to a company-sponsored retirement program.
3. Participate in an elective savings program.	You can elect to have money withheld from your paycheck each payday and automatically deposited in a savings or investment account.
4. Make a special savings effort one or two months each year.	By cutting back to the basics, you can obtain money for investment purposes.
5. Take advantage of gifts, inheritances, and windfalls.	Use money from unexpected sources to fund an investment program.

Exhibit 11–1

Five Suggestions to Help You Accumulate the Money Needed to Fund Your Investments

paycheck. Most people find either extreme unacceptable and take a more middle-of-the-road approach. These people often save enough to fund an investment program and spend some money on the items that make their lives more enjoyable. Suggestions to help you obtain the money you need to fund an investment program are listed in Exhibit 11–1.

For many people, the easiest way to begin an investment program is to participate in an employer-sponsored retirement account—often referred to as a 401(k) or a 403(b) account. Many employers will match part or all of your contributions to retirement accounts. For example, an employer may contribute $0.50 for every $1.00 the employee contributes up to a certain percentage of their annual salary. More information on different types of retirement accounts is provided in Chapter 14.

CAUTION!

When interviewing for a new job or before accepting a job offer, be sure to ask about health care and retirement benefits. Today many employers only pay for a portion of employee health care costs and have reduced or eliminated the matching provisions in their employee retirement plans.

How the Time Value of Money Affects Your Investments

Mary and Peter Miller began their investment program by investing $1,000 *each year* when they were in their 20s. Now 20 years later, their investment portfolio is worth over $42,000. How did they do it?

To answer that question, let's review the time value of money that was discussed in Chapter 1. The *time value of money* involves increases in an amount of money that you save or invest because your savings or investments earn interest or dividends or increase in value. The Millers took advantage of the time value of money. Simply put: If you save money over a long period of time and make quality investments that appreciate in value and/or pay dividends or interest, you can achieve the same type of result. For example, assume you invest $2,400 each year for 25 years. Also, assume that the investment earns 7 percent each year. If you want to know how much your investment is worth at the end of 25 years, read the material in the nearby *Figure It Out!* feature.

In this sample problem, your investments total $60,000 ($2,400 × 25 years = × $60,000). To determine your investment earnings during the 25-year period, subtract the total of all investments from the total dollar return at the end of 25 years ($151,798 – $60,000 = $91,798).

Notice the value of your investments increases each year because of two factors. First, it is assumed you will invest another $2,400 each year. Second, all investment earnings you earn each year are allowed to accumulate and are added to your yearly deposits.

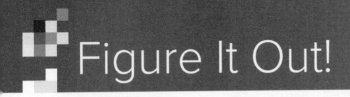

Figure It Out!

Using the Time Value of Money to Calculate Investment Returns

How much is $2,400 invested each year at 7 percent for 25 years worth at the end of 25 years?

ANSWER: While this problem can be solved using a future value formula or a future value table—both illustrated in the Chapter 1 Appendix—today many people use a future value calculator that can be found on many websites. To work this problem, follow these steps:

1. Use an Internet search engine such as Google or Yahoo! and enter the term *future value calculator*. (To see how easy it is to work the above problem, go to **keisan.casio.com** and enter future value of periodic payments in the search box.)

2. Enter the interest rate, number of years, annual payment frequency made at the end of each year, and payment amount.

3. For most Internet calculators, once all the information has been entered, you simply click on "execute" or "calculate."

4. The answer for the sample problem is $151,798.

NOW IT'S YOUR TURN.

Using an Internet future value calculator, determine the future value of a $2,400 annual investment that earns 10 percent a year for 25 years.

Tryout problem answer: $236,033

Also, notice that if investments earn a higher rate of return each year, *total* dollar returns increase dramatically. In the tryout problem in the *Figure It Out!* feature, the amount of annual payment ($2,400) and the time period (25 years) are the same. The only difference is the investment in the tryout problem earns 10 percent instead of 7 percent. In this case, an investment that earned 10 percent was worth $236,033 compared to the investment that earned 7 percent that was worth $151,798 at the end of 25 years. The search for higher returns is one reason many investors choose stocks, mutual funds, and other investments that offer higher potential returns compared to certificates of deposit or government or corporate bonds. The length of time your money is invested also makes a difference. The longer your money can work for you and earn interest or dividends and/or appreciate in value, the more your investments will be worth. That's why many personal finance experts always say it's better to begin savings and investing sooner than later.

PRACTICE QUIZ 11–1

Sheet 35 Establishing Investment Goals

1. What factors should you consider when performing a financial checkup?

2. How can you obtain the money needed to begin investing?

3. In your own words, describe the time value of money concept and how it could affect your investment program.

LO11.2

Describe how safety, risk, income, growth, and liquidity affect your investment program.

Factors Affecting the Choice of Investments

Although each investor may have specific, individual goals for investing, all investors must consider a number of factors before choosing an investment alternative.

Safety and Risk

The safety and risk factors are two sides of the same coin. *Safety* in an investment means minimal risk or loss. On the other hand, *risk* in an investment means a measure of uncertainty about the outcome. Investments range from very safe to very risky. Very safe investments include savings accounts, certificates of deposit, government bonds, and certain corporate bonds, stocks, and mutual funds. Real estate may also be a very safe investment. Investors pick investments that have less risk because they know there is very little chance such investments will become worthless.

Investors sometimes purchase certain investments because they want a predictable source of income. The most conservative and safe investments—passbook savings accounts, certificates of deposit, and securities issued by the U.S. government—are also the most predictable sources of income. You can also choose municipal bonds, corporate bonds, selected common stock issues, some mutual funds, or real estate that provide income.

At the other end of the investment spectrum are speculative investments. A **speculative investment** is a high-risk investment made in the hope of earning a relatively large profit in a short time. Such investments offer the possibility of a larger dollar return, but if they are unsuccessful, you may lose most or all of your original investment.

Investors often choose more speculative stocks because of greater growth potential. *Growth* means their stock investments will increase in value. For example, companies with earnings potential, sales revenues that are increasing, and managers who can solve the problems associated with rapid expansion are often considered to be growth companies. These same companies generally pay little or no dividends. The money the companies keep can provide at least part of the financing they need for future growth and expansion and can help control the cost of borrowing money. Growth financed by profits reinvested in the company normally increases the dollar value of a share of stock for the investor.

Other investments that may offer growth potential include mutual funds that invest in stocks, real estate, high-risk bonds, commodities, options, precious metals, and precious stones. For example, many mutual funds are referred to as growth funds or aggressive growth funds because of the growth potential of the individual securities included in the fund.

ACTION ITEM

I understand how the factors of safety and risk may affect my investment decisions.

☐ Yes ☐ No

speculative investment A high-risk investment made in the hope of earning a relatively large profit in a short time.

WHAT WOULD YOU DO? Assume you are the investor in each of the following situations. Then choose either income or growth investments and justify your choice.

Life Situation	Income or Growth	Justification
A 26-year-old single investor with a full-time job that pays $42,000 a year		
A retired couple with $720,000 in retirement savings and investments		

From an investor's standpoint, one basic rule sums up the relationship between the factors of safety and risk: *Your potential return on any investment should be directly related to the risk you assume.* There is some risk associated with all investments. In fact, you may experience two types of risks with many investments:

- First, with the exception of savings accounts, certificates of deposit, and securities issued by the U.S. Treasury, the income provided by other investments is not guaranteed. For example, The Coca-Cola company has a long history of paying dividends since 1893, but if the soft drink company—or any corporation— experiences financial difficulties, it may reduce or omit dividend payments to stockholders.

- A second type of risk associated with many investments is that an investment will decrease in value. For example, the value of a share of Facebook stock dropped 19 percent on July 26, 2018. The stock dropped in value because of investor concerns about lower quarterly earnings than expected.[1]

  Even the price of bonds can fluctuate when investors purchase corporate or government bonds and then begin to worry about the issuer's ability to pay interest or repay the bondholders when the bonds mature. For example, the price of bonds issued by J. C. Penney dropped when the retailer reported poor sales and store closings in 2020.

Often beginning investors are afraid of the risk associated with many investments. But remember that without the risk, obtaining the larger returns that really make an investment program grow is impossible. To help you determine how much risk you are willing to assume, take the test for risk tolerance presented in Exhibit 11–2.

Exhibit 11-3 lists a number of factors related to safety and risk that can also affect your choice of investments.

Components of the Risk Factor

When choosing an investment, you must carefully evaluate changes in the risk factor. In fact, the overall risk factor can be broken down into four components.

INFLATION RISK As defined in Chapter 1, inflation is a rise in the general level of prices. During periods of high inflation, there is a risk that the financial return on an investment will not keep pace with the inflation rate. To see how inflation reduces your buying power, let's assume you have deposited $10,000 in a certificate of deposit at 1 percent interest. At the end of one year, your money will have earned $100 in interest ($10,000 × 1% = $100). Assuming an inflation rate of 3 percent, it will cost you an additional $300 ($10,000 × 3% = $300), or a total of $10,300, to purchase the same amount of goods you could have purchased for $10,000 a year earlier. Thus, even though you earned $100, you lost $200 in purchasing power. And after paying taxes on the $100 interest, your loss of purchasing power is even greater.

INTEREST RATE RISK The interest rate risk associated with preferred stocks or government or corporate bonds is the result of changes in the interest rates in the economy. The value of these investments decreases when overall interest rates increase. In contrast, the value of these same investments increases when overall interest rates decrease. Assume you purchase an Amazon corporate bond that pays 3.15 percent interest and hold it for three years before deciding to sell it. The value of your bond will decrease if interest rates for new comparable bonds increase during the three-year period. On the other hand, the value of your Amazon bond will increase if interest rates for new comparable bonds decrease during the three-year period.

BUSINESS FAILURE RISK The risk of business failure is associated with investments in stock and corporate bonds or mutual funds that invest in stocks or bonds. With each of these investments, you face the possibility that bad management, unsuccessful products, competition, or a host of other factors will cause the business to be less profitable than originally anticipated or experience a loss. The business may even fail and be forced to file for bankruptcy, in which case your investment may become totally worthless. Consider what happened when Payless Shoe Source closed all of it 2,100 stores in the United States and Puerto Rico. The retailer's investors and creditors lost money, and the firm's employees lost their jobs.

MARKET RISK Economic growth is not as systematic and predictable as most investors might believe. Generally, a period of rapid expansion is followed by a period of recession. For instance, since 1990, periods of economic expansion for the U.S. economy have lasted an average of almost eight years. Periods of contractions—recessions or depressions—when the overall economy is in decline have lasted an average of 11 months.[2]

---

[1] Fred Imbert and Gina Francolla, "Facebook's $100 Billion-Plus Rout Is the Biggest Loss in Stock Market History," CNBC, **https://www.cnbc.com/2018/07/26/facebook-on-pace-for-biggest-one-day-loss-in-value-for-any-company-sin.html,** accessed July 26, 2018.

[2] Investopedia, **https://www.investopedia.com/terms/b/businesscycle.asp,** accessed March 27, 2017.

Exhibit **11–2** A Quick Test to Determine Your Risk Tolerance

With investing, there's always a risk of losing some or even all of your money if the investment doesn't perform well. In general, the greater the risk of a loss on an investment, the greater the potential return. The lower the risk of loss, the lower the potential return. It's important that you feel comfortable with the way your money is invested. Assess your risk tolerance with this quick, five question quiz.

Risk Tolerance Survey
1. With which types of savings or investments are you most comfortable?
    a. Money market accounts.
    b. Government savings bonds.
    c. Corporate bonds or bond funds.
    d. Stocks or stock funds.

2. After you make a savings or investment decision, you feel:
    a. Worried.
    b. Satisfied.
    c. Hopeful.
    d. Invigorated.

3. Say you invest $20,000. Each of the following answers shows the range of dollar values that your investment may experience after just one year. Which investment would you be most comfortable holding?
    a. $21,000 – $19,000.
    b. $23,000 – $17,000.
    c. $27,000 – $13,000.
    d. $30,000 – $10,000.

4. For the last five years, your investment has returned an average 10 percent per year—in line with other similar investments. However, it loses 20 percent over the next year. What do you do?
    a. Sell all of the investment.
    b. Sell a portion of the investment.
    c. Nothing.
    d. Buy more of the same investment.

5. Which phrase best describes your take on life?
    a. Proceed with caution—take no unnecessary risks.
    b. Take small, measurable risks and patiently pursue your dreams.
    c. Prepare well, but follow your goals without fear.
    d. No hesitation—go for it!

Understand Your Investor Type

If you selected mostly (a)s:
You are highly risk-averse. You're also a strong candidate to learn as much as you can about investing because the more you know about risk and reward potential, the better you can manage your portfolio to take advantage of growth opportunities.

If you selected mostly (b)s:
You are somewhat risk-averse, but you understand the importance of investing and do so with a measure of caution and calculated risk. You would probably benefit from a diversified portfolio. It's important to remember to build in some component of growth in your portfolio in order to mitigate the impact of taxes and inflation.

If you selected mostly (c)s:
You understand the concept of risk and are prepared to deal with the consequences in an effort to attain greater growth opportunities. You seem comfortable with your investment selections, which generally are the product of research and a balanced strategy that combines conservative-, medium-, and high-growth oriented investments.

If you selected mostly (d)s:
You like taking risks and probably have an aggressive growth-oriented portfolio. If you are quite young (in your 20s or 30s) with sufficient income so that you're not dependent on your investments, taking the high-risk road may reward you over time. However, make sure that your equity holdings are diversified and always maintain a long-term perspective.

The information contained herein is being provided as-is and without representation or warranty. The enclosed information is not intended as legal, tax, or financial planning advice. Any discussion of tax or accounting matters herein (including any attachments) should not and may not be relied on by any recipient or reader. The recipient/reader should consult his/her tax adviser, legal consultant and/or accountant for a statement of tax and accounting rules applicable to his/her particular situation and for all other tax and accounting advice.

Source: Adapted from "Determine Your Risk Tolerance," Hands on Banking, **https://handsonbanking.org/articles/determine-your-risk-tolerance/**, accessed January 20, 2020.

Exhibit 11–3
Factors That Can Affect Your Tolerance for Risk and Your Investment Choices

Investments with Lower Risks	Investments with Higher Risk
People with no financial training or investment background	Investors with financial training and investment background
Older investors	Younger investors
Lower-income investors	Higher-income investors
Families with children	Single individuals or married couples with no children
Employees worried about job loss	Employees with secure employment positions

The prices of stocks, bonds, mutual funds that invest in stocks or bonds, and other investments may also fluctuate because of the behavior of investors in the marketplace and may have nothing to do with the fundamental changes in the financial health of the corporations that issue these investments. Such fluctuations may be caused by political or social conditions or many other factors that affect the stability of a nation or countries around the globe. For example, the coronavirus COVID-19 became a major concern as more and more cases were reported not only in China, but throughout the world. People were worried about both the increasing number of cases and the increasing number of deaths. The fear of a worldwide pandemic also caused many countries to require people to "shelter in place." Businesses that were not considered essential were told to shut down brick-and-mortar stores, which led to lower sales, decreased profits or losses, and, in some cases, bankruptcy. As a result, investors experienced huge losses because the "financial" health of both small businesses and large corporations was affected by COVID-19. Many investors who experienced large gains in 2019 saw those gains wiped out in a two-to-three-week period in early 2020. Fluctuations like these underscore the need for a personal financial plan that will provide money for emergencies or market downturns without having to sell investments at depressed prices.

CAUTION!

To avoid investment scams, the experts suggest:

- Verify the credentials of all salespeople.
- Be skeptical of "your profit is guaranteed" claims.
- Ignore the story that "everyone is doing it."
- Refuse to be rushed to make a decision.
- Never feel obligated to invest.
- Arm yourself with information.

Above all, take your time and check out any investment before you invest.

Source: "How to Spot an Investment Scam in 6 Steps," Financial Industry Regulatory Authority, **https://www.finra.org/investors/red-flags-fraud**, accessed January 20, 2020.

Investment Liquidity

liquidity The ability to buy or sell an investment quickly without substantially affecting the investment's value.

Liquidity is the ability to buy or sell an investment quickly without substantially affecting the investment's value. Investments range from near-cash investments to frozen investments from which it is virtually impossible to get your money. Interest-bearing checking and savings accounts are very liquid because they can be quickly converted to cash. Certificates of deposit impose penalties for withdrawing money before the maturity date. With other investments, you may be able to sell quickly, but market conditions, economic conditions, political uncertainty, or many other factors may prevent you from regaining the amount you originally invested.

Sheet 36 Assessing Risk for Investments

PRACTICE QUIZ 11–2

1. Why are safety and risk two sides of the same coin?

2. How do income, growth, and liquidity affect the choice of an investment?

3. In your own words, describe each of the four components of the risk factor.

Factors That Reduce Investment Risk

Consider the following: The stock market—as measured by the Standard and Poor 500 stock index—increased almost 32 percent in 2019.[3] While returns like this are "great" for investors, you should know that this return is not the norm. There are many factors that can cause investments (or the financial markets) to decrease in value. As mentioned earlier in this chapter, those huge gains that many investors experienced in 2019 were wiped out in a two-to-three-week period as the coronavirus spread across the globe. With such large losses in the first part of 2020, many investors were wondering whether the market will continue to decline. What will happen to the stock market in the next few years? Will the market continue to provide above average returns? Will investors experience lower returns or lose money? All good questions.

Reality check: For almost 100 years, stocks have returned an average return of a little less than 10 percent a year. Of course, this return is not guaranteed, and there were some years in which the market experienced losses. Still the long-term average return for the stock market is well ahead of inflation and the return on bonds, real estate, and savings accounts or certificates of deposit. These facts suggest that everyone should invest in stocks because they offer the largest returns. In reality, stocks may have a place in your investment portfolio, but establishing an investment program is more than just picking a bunch of stocks or mutual funds that invest in stocks. Before making the decision to purchase stocks, consider how asset allocation can help you create a balanced portfolio and may help reduce risk in your investment program.

Asset Allocation and Diversification

Earlier in this chapter, we examined how the factors of safety, risk, income, growth, and liquidity affect your investment choices. Now let's compare the factors that affect the choice of investments with some typical investment alternatives. Exhibit 11–4 ranks each alternative in terms of safety, risk, income, growth, and liquidity. More detailed information on each investment alternative is provided later in this chapter and in Chapters 12 and 13.

ASSET ALLOCATION Asset allocation is the process of spreading your assets among several different types of investments to lessen risk. The term *asset allocation* is a fancy way of saying you need to diversify and avoid the pitfall of putting all your eggs in one basket. Asset allocation is often expressed in percentages. For example, what percentage of my assets do I want to put in stocks and mutual funds? What percentage do I want to put in bonds or certificates of deposit? The diversification provided by investing in *different* investments provides a measure of safety and reduces risk because a loss in one type of investment may be offset by gains from other types of investments. Typical investments include:

- Stocks issued by large corporations (large cap).
- Stocks issued by medium-size corporations (midcap).

	FACTORS TO BE EVALUATED				
Type of Investment	**Safety**	**Risk**	**Income**	**Growth**	**Liquidity**
Corporate stock	Average	Average	Average	High	Average
Corporate bonds	Average	Average	High	Low	Average
Government bonds	High	Low	Low	Low	High
Mutual funds	Average	Average	Average	Average	Average
Real estate	Average	Average	Average	Average	Low

[3] Ben Carlson, "Comparing the Stock Market in 2018 vs. 2019 Gives Us Clues about What to Expect in 2020," Fortune, **https://fortune.com/2020/01/07/stock-market-2020-2018-2019-what-to-expect-investing/**, accessed January 7, 2020.

LO11.3

Identify the factors that can reduce investment risk.

ACTION ITEM

I undersand how asset allocation can minimize risk.

☐ Agree   ☐ Disagree

asset allocation The process of spreading your assets among several different types of investments to lessen risk.

Exhibit **11–4**

Factors Used to Evaluate Traditional Investment Alternatives

- Stocks issued by small, rapidly growing companies (small cap).
- Foreign stocks.
- Bonds.
- Cash.

Note: Mutual funds can also be included as an investment, but the typical mutual fund will invest in the securities just listed or a combination of these securities.

The percentage of your investments that should be invested in each asset class is determined by:

- Your age;
- Your investment objectives;
- How much you can save and invest each year;
- The dollar value of your current investments;
- The economic outlook for the economy; and
- Other factors.

FinTech for Financial Literacy

Today a growing number of investors use asset allocation calculators to create a well-balanced portfolio. One calculator is provided by **Bankrate. com.** It's easy to use. All you have to do is enter your information and click on the execute tab. Try it out at **https://www.bankrate.com/calculators/ retirement/asset-allocation.aspx.**

Today, many personal finance websites provide asset allocation calculators to help you determine the right types of investments for your investment program. For example, an asset allocation calculator considers your age, tolerance for risk, how much you can save or invest each year, and some of the other factors mentioned above to determine the appropriate types of investments for your situation. To find an asset allocation calculator, you can use a search engine such as Google or Yahoo! To learn more, take a look at the nearby FinTech for Financial Literacy feature.

To help you decide how much risk is appropriate for your investment program, many financial planners suggest that you think of your investment program as a pyramid consisting of four levels ranging from low risk to high risk, as illustrated in Exhibit 11–5. *Be warned:* Many investors may decide the investments in Level 4 are too speculative for their investment program. Regardless of which type of investment you choose for your investment program and the percentage you invest in each type, it may be necessary to adjust your asset allocation from time to time. Often, the main reasons for making changes are the amount of time that your investments have to work for you and your age.

THE TIME FACTOR The amount of time that your investments have to work for you is another important factor when managing your investment portfolio. Recall the investment

Exhibit 11–5

Typical Investments for Financial Security, Safety and Income, Growth, and Speculation

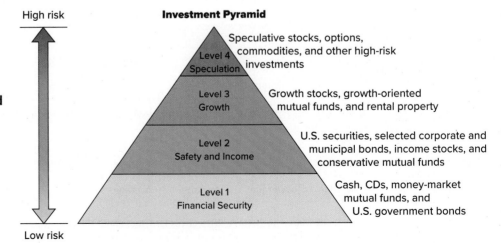

returns presented earlier in this section. For almost 100 years, stocks have returned an average return of a little less than 10 percent a year and have returned more than other investment alternatives. And yet, during the same time period, there were years when stocks decreased in value. The point is that if you invested at the wrong time and then couldn't wait for the investment to recover before selling your investment, you lost money.

The amount of time you have before you need your investment money is crucial. If you can leave your long-term investments alone and let them work for 5 to 10 years or more, then you can invest in stocks and mutual funds. On the other hand, if you need your investment money in two years or less, you should probably invest in certificates of deposit, short-term government bonds, or highly rated corporate bonds. By taking a more conservative approach for short-term investments, you reduce the possibility of having to sell your investments at a loss because of depressed market value or a staggering economy.

YOUR AGE   A final factor to consider when choosing an investment is your age. Younger investors tend to invest a large percentage of their nest egg in growth-oriented investments. If their investments take a nosedive, they have time to recover. On the other hand, older investors tend to be more conservative and invest in government bonds, high-quality corporate bonds, and very safe corporate stocks or mutual funds. As a result, a smaller percentage of their nest egg is placed in growth-oriented investments.

Financial experts suggest that you subtract your age from 100, and the difference is the percentage of your assets that should be invested in growth investments. For example, if you are 30 years old, subtract 30 from 100, which gives you 70. Therefore, 70 percent of your assets should be invested in growth-oriented investments while the remaining 30 percent should be kept in safer, conservative investments.

Your Role in the Investment Process

What makes one investor successful? Why do some investors lose money? Both good questions. The information in this section can help answer those questions. This same information can help you increase investment profits and reduce losses.

EVALUATE POTENTIAL INVESTMENTS   Let's assume you have $25,000 to invest. Also assume your investment will earn a 10 percent return the first year. At the end of one year, you will have earned $2,500, and your investment will be worth $27,500. Now ask yourself: How long would it take to earn $2,500 if I had to work for this amount of money at a job? For some people, it might take a month; for others, it might take longer. The point is that if you want this type of return, you should be willing to work for it, but the work takes a different form than a job. When choosing an investment, the work is the time required to research different investments so that you can make an informed decision. More information on evaluating different investment alternatives is presented at the end of this chapter and in Chapters 12 (stocks) and 13 (mutual funds). For additional help when choosing investments and conquering your fear of investing, read the nearby *Financial Literacy in Practice* feature.

WHAT WOULD YOU DO? Seven years ago, you were hired as an associate marketing manager for a computer software company. The salary was extraordinary, and you have managed to purchase a home, a nice used automobile, and save and invest over $95,000. Now, there are rumors that the company is going to be acquired by a larger company and a lot of people will be let go. While you've been a good employee, you're not sure if you will have a job if your company is bought out. What should you do? *Note:* Answer this question, and then see how your answer compares to the information in the section "Monitor the Value of Your Investments and Your Financial Health."

Psychology 101: Conquering the Fear of Investing

Just the thought of losing hard-earned cash on a "bad" investment often keeps would-be investors from making their first investment. Still, if you want to become financially secure and enjoy the peace of mind that establishing a well-planned investment program can provide, you must overcome the fear of investing. According to the experts, the five steps below can reduce fear and at the same time help you become a "smart" investor.

Take This Step	Why This Step Is Important
1. Don't start investing before you create an emergency fund.	By creating an emergency fund equal to at least three months of living expenses, you reduce the possibility of having to sell investments at a loss because of depressed market value.
2. Do your homework before investing any money.	Learn to be a good investor. Begin by looking at investment websites such as Yahoo! Finance (http://finance.yahoo.com), The Street (https://www.thestreet.com/topic/47481/how-to-invest.html), and the Motley Fool (www.fool.com).
3. Begin investing with small amounts of money.	After learning all you can about different investment alternatives, begin by investing small amounts of money you can afford to lose. Once successful, you can add to existing investments or purchase additional investments.
4. After the purchase, monitor the value of all investments.	Monitor the value of your investments to determine if you should hold, sell, or increase your stake in a specific investment.
5. Continue to learn about investing.	Once you begin investing, it is important to continue to learn. Begin by determining the type of investments that interest you. Then develop a plan to organize information about specific investment alternatives.

MONITOR THE VALUE OF YOUR INVESTMENTS AND YOUR FINANCIAL HEALTH Monitoring the value of your investments can help you spot opportunities to maximize profits or reduce dollar losses when you sell your investments. Monitoring the value of your investments can also help you decide whether you want to invest additional funds in a particular investment. To monitor the value of their investments, many investors use a simple chart. To construct a chart, place the original purchase price of your investment in the middle on the side of the chart. Then use price increments of a logical amount to show increases and decreases in dollar value. Place individual dates along the bottom of the chart. For stocks, bonds, mutual funds, and similar investments, you may want to graph every two weeks and chart current values on, say, a Friday. For longer-term investments such as real estate, you can chart current values every six months. *A word of caution:* If an investment is beginning to have a large increase or decrease in value, you may want to check dollar values more frequently—in some cases, daily.

Computer software or investment portfolio management tools are available on many investment websites to help you track the value of your investments. Consider using the software provided by Fidelity (https://www.fidelity.com), Schwab (https://www.schwab.com/public/schwab/client_home), Merrill Edge (https://www.merrilledge.com), and most brokerage firms to chart your investments in stocks, bonds, and mutual funds.

Monitoring the value of your investments will also help if you experience a personal financial crisis, become unemployed, or the nation experiences an economic crisis. Unfortunately, many people are caught off guard and must scramble to find the money to pay their monthly bills when they experience a crisis. In some cases, individuals are forced to sell some or all of their investments at depressed prices just to buy food for the family and pay everyday necessities. Here are six steps you can take to safeguard against a crisis:

1. *Establish a larger emergency fund.* Under normal circumstances, an emergency fund of three months' living expenses is considered adequate, but you may want to increase your fund in anticipation of a crisis.

2. *Know what you owe.* Make a list of all your debts and the amount of the required monthly payments; then identify the debts that *must* be paid. Typically, these include the mortgage or rent, medicine, utilities, food, and transportation costs.

3. *Reduce spending.* Cut back to the basics and reduce the amount of money spent on entertainment, dining at restaurants, and vacations. The money saved from reduced spending can be used to increase your emergency fund or pay for everyday necessities.

4. *Notify credit card companies and lenders if you are unable to make payments.* Although not all lenders are willing to help, many will work with you and lower your interest rate, reduce your monthly payment, or extend the time for repayment.

5. *Monitor the value of your investment and retirement accounts.* Tracking the value of your stock, mutual fund, and retirement accounts, for example, will help you decide which investments to sell if you need cash for emergencies.

6. *Consider converting investments to cash to preserve value.* According to personal finance experts, most investors accumulate more money when they use a buy-and-hold approach over a long period of time. Still, there may be times when you could sell some of your investments and place the cash in a savings account to weather a crisis.

Above all, don't panic. While financial problems are stressful, staying calm and considering all the options may help reduce the stress.

KEEP ACCURATE RECORDS   Accurate recordkeeping will help you decide to hold an investment, buy more, or sell. At the very least, you should keep purchase records for each of your investments that include the actual dollar cost of the investment, plus any commissions or fees you paid. It is also useful to keep a list of the sources of information (website addresses, business periodicals, research publications, etc.), along with copies of the material you used to evaluate each investment. Then, when it is time to reevaluate an existing investment, you will know where to begin your search for current information.

Accurate recordkeeping is also necessary for tax purposes. Whether you are making your own decisions or have professional help, you must also consider the tax consequences of selling your investments. Taxes were covered in Chapter 3, and it is not our intention to cover them again. You are responsible for determining how taxes affect your investment decisions. To find more information about how investments are taxed, visit the Internal Revenue Service website at **www.irs.gov**.

OTHER FACTORS THAT IMPROVE INVESTMENT DECISIONS   To achieve their financial goals, many people seek professional help. In many cases, they turn to stockbrokers, lawyers, accountants, bankers, or insurance agents. However, these professionals are specialists in one specific field and may not be qualified to provide the type of advice required to develop a thorough financial plan. *Be warned:* Some of these professionals earn commissions on the investments they recommend. The fact they are receiving commissions may influence which investments they recommend. Another source of investment help is a financial planner who has had training in securities, insurance, taxes, real estate, and estate planning. While financial planners can receive commissions for the investment products they recommend, many charge consulting fees instead.

PRACTICE QUIZ 11–3

1. Assume you must choose an investment that will help you obtain your investment goals. Rank the following investments from 1 (low) to 5 (high), and then justify your choice for your investment portfolio. (See Exhibit 11–4 and Exhibit 11–5 for help evaluating each investment.)

Investment	Rank (1 = low; 5 = high)	Justification
Corporate stocks		
Corporate bonds		
Government bonds		
Mutual funds		
Real estate		

2. Why should investors be concerned with asset allocation, their age, and the time their investments have to work for them?

3. Why should you monitor the value of your investments?

LO11.4

Understand why investors purchase government bonds.

Conservative Investment Options: Government Bonds

Provide feedback on the following statements to see if bond investments may be right for you:

ACTION ITEM

I know why some people invest in government bonds.

☐ Agree ☐ Disagree

Statement	Yes	No
1. Stocks seem to be overpriced and will probably go down in the next 12 to 24 months.	_____	_____
2. I need to convert my investments to cash in a short period of time.	_____	_____
3. I'm afraid I will lose the money invested in more speculative investments.	_____	_____

   If you answered yes to any of these questions, you may want to consider the more conservative investments described in the next two sections.

The Psychology of Investing in Bonds

Bonds are a conservative investment option that may offer more income or growth potential than savings accounts or certificates of deposit. They also are a safer investment when compared to stocks, mutual funds, or other investments and are often considered a "safe harbor" in troubled economic times. And, investors may purchase bonds as a way to use asset allocation to diversify their investment portfolio. For example, Mary and David Samuelson, a couple in their late 30s decided it was time diversify their investments. At the time, their goal was to choose investments that were more conservative but still offered larger returns than certificates of deposit. To obtain their asset allocation goal, they decided to invest 25 percent of their $210,000 investment portfolio in government and corporate bonds.

If diversification is your goal, you may also purchase bond funds. Bond funds are an indirect way of owning bonds issued by the U.S. Treasury, state and local governments, and corporations. Many financial experts recommend bond funds for investors with small amounts of money because they offer diversification *and* professional management. The advantages and disadvantages of bond funds are discussed in more detail in Chapter 13.

Government Bonds and Debt Securities

The U.S. government and state and local governments issue bonds to obtain financing. A **government bond** is a written pledge of a government or a municipality to repay a specified sum of money, along with interest. In this section, we discuss bonds issued by each level of government and look at why investors purchase these bonds.

government bond The written pledge of a government or a municipality to repay a specified sum of money, along with interest.

U.S. TREASURY BILLS, NOTES, AND BONDS Investors choose U.S. government securities because they are backed by the full faith and credit of the U.S. government and have always carried a decreased risk of default. Even with concerns about the nation's national debt, economic stability, and political turmoil, investors from around the world still regard U.S. government securities as a very conservative and safe investment.

In this section, we discuss four principal types of securities issued by the U.S. Treasury: Treasury bills, Treasury notes, Treasury bonds, and Treasury Inflation-Protected Securities (TIPS). Just about everything you want to know about these securities can be found at Treasury Direct (**www.treasurydirect .gov**). In addition to purchasing Treasury securities online there, you can access research information, financial calculators, and other tools to fine-tune your investment program.

Treasury Direct conducts auctions to sell Treasury securities, and buyers interested in purchasing these securities at such auctions may bid competitively or noncompetitively. If they bid competitively, they must specify the rate or interest yield they are willing to accept. If they bid noncompetitively, they are willing to accept the interest rate determined at auction. Treasury securities may also be purchased through banks or brokers, which charge a commission. For U.S. Treasury bills, notes, bonds, and Treasury Inflation-Protected Securities, the minimum purchase is $100 with additional increments of $100 above the minimum.

money minute focus

Yields for investors who invest in 10-year Treasury notes:

Source: **Investing.com, https://www.investing.com/rates-bonds/u.s.-10-year-bond-yield-historical-data**, accessed January 28, 2020.

U.S. government securities can be held until maturity or sold before maturity. Interest paid on U.S. government securities (and growth in principal for TIPS) is taxable for federal income tax purposes but is exempt from state and local taxation. More information about U.S. government securities is provided in Exhibit 11–6.

WHAT WOULD YOU DO? You've worked hard since graduating from college. You've saved and invested a portion of your salary every payday. You've also signed up for your employer's 401(k) retirement account. While everything seems to be on track for a 35-year-old person with a great job, excellent benefits, and an investment portfolio worth $215,000, you are afraid the U.S. economy is headed for recession. One of your older friends suggests that you sell some of your stocks and mutual funds and purchase U.S. Treasury securities. Does this seem like a good way to safeguard your investments? What factors should you consider before making a decision to sell some or all of the stocks and mutual funds and invest in more conservative Treasury securities?

Exhibit 11–6

Information about Treasury Bills, Treasury Notes, Treasury Bonds, and Treasury Inflation-Protected Securities

Type of Security	Maturity	Interest	Notes
Treasury bills (T-bills)	4, 8, 13, 26, or 52 weeks	Discounted securities because the actual purchase price is less than the maturity value.	At maturity, the government repays the face value of T-bills. The difference between the purchase price and the face value is interest.
Treasury notes (T-notes)	2, 3, 5, 7, and 10 years	Interest is paid every six months until maturity.	Interest rate is slightly higher than that for T-bills because of the longer maturity.
Treasury bonds	20 or 30 years	Interest is paid every six months until maturity.	Interest rate is slightly higher than that for T-bills and T-notes because of the longer maturity.
Treasury Inflation-Protected Securities (TIPS)	5, 10, or 30 years. At maturity, you are paid the adjusted principal or original principal, whichever is greater.	Interest is paid every six months until maturity at a fixed rate applied to the adjusted principal.	TIPS principal increases with inflation and decreases with deflation.

municipal bond A debt security issued by a state or local government.

general obligation bond A bond backed by the full faith, credit, and taxing power of the government that issued it.

revenue bond A bond that is repaid from the income generated by the project it is designed to finance.

CAUTION!

Whether or not the interest on municipal bonds is tax exempt often depends on how the funds obtained from their sale are used. You are responsible, as an investor, for determining whether or not interest on municipal bonds is taxable.

STATE AND LOCAL GOVERNMENT SECURITIES A **municipal bond** is a debt security issued by a state or local government. Such securities are used to finance the ongoing activities of state and local governments and major projects such as airports, schools, toll roads, and toll bridges. They may be purchased directly from the government entity that issued them or through account executives.

State and local securities are classified as either general obligation bonds or revenue bonds. A **general obligation bond** is backed by the full faith, credit, and taxing power of the government that issued it. A **revenue bond** is repaid from the income generated by the project it is designed to finance.

Although both general obligation and revenue bonds are relatively safe, defaults have occurred in recent years. If the risk of default worries you, you can purchase insured municipal bonds. A number of private insurers, after evaluation of a municipal bond issue, will guarantee payments on selected securities. Even if a municipal bond issue is insured, however, financial experts worry about the insurer's ability to pay off in the event of default on a large bond issue. Most experts advise investors to determine the underlying quality of a bond whether or not it is insured.

One of the most important features of municipal bonds is that the interest on them may be exempt from federal taxes. Municipal bonds exempt from federal taxation are generally exempt from state and local taxes only in the state where they are issued. Although the *interest* on municipal bonds may be exempt from taxation, a *capital gain* that results when you sell a municipal bond before maturity *and* at a profit may be taxable just as capital gains on other investments sold at a profit are.

Because of their tax-exempt status, the interest rates on municipal bonds are lower than those on taxable bonds. By using the following formula, you can calculate the *taxable equivalent yield* for a municipal security:

$$\text{Taxable equivalent yield} = \frac{\text{Tax-exempt yield}}{1.0 - \text{Your tax rate}}$$

> **EXAMPLE:** Determining Taxable Equivalent Yield
>
> The taxable equivalent yield on a 3 percent, tax-exempt municipal bond for a person in the 32 percent tax bracket is 4.41 percent, as follows:
>
> $$\text{Taxable equivalent yield} = \frac{0.03}{1.0 - 0.32}$$
>
> $$= 0.0441, \text{or } 4.41 \text{percent}$$

Once you have calculated the taxable equivalent yield, you can compare the return on tax-exempt securities with the return on taxable investments.

corporate bond A corporation's written pledge to repay a specified amount of money with interest.

PRACTICE QUIZ 11-4

1. What is the difference between a Treasury bill, a Treasury note, a Treasury bond, and TIPS?

2. Explain the difference between a general obligation bond and a revenue bond.

3. Using the formula presented in this section, calculate the taxable equivalent yield for a tax-free bond that pays 3.5 percent for a taxpayer in a 35 percent tax bracket.

Conservative Investment Options: Corporate Bonds

A **corporate bond** is a corporation's written pledge to repay a specified amount of money with interest. The **face value** is the dollar amount the bondholder will receive at the bond's maturity. The usual face value of a corporate bond is $1,000. Between the time of purchase and the maturity date, the corporation pays interest to the bondholder.

The **maturity date** of a corporate bond is the date on which the corporation is to repay the borrowed money. Maturity dates for bonds generally range from 1 to 30 years after the date of issue.

The actual legal conditions for a corporate bond are described in a bond indenture. A **bond indenture** is a legal document that details all of the conditions relating to a bond issue. Since corporate bond indentures are very difficult for the average person to read and understand, a corporation issuing bonds appoints a trustee. The **trustee** is a financially independent firm that acts as the bondholders' representative. Usually, the trustee is a commercial bank or some other financial institution. If the corporation fails to live up to all the provisions in the indenture agreement, the trustee may bring legal action to protect the bondholders' interests.

Why Corporations Sell Corporate Bonds

Bonds are often referred to as the workhorse of corporate finance. Bonds can be used to finance a corporation's ongoing business activities or when it is difficult to sell stock. The sale of bonds can also improve a corporation's financial leverage—the use of borrowed funds to increase the corporation's return on investment. Finally, the interest paid to bond owners is a tax-deductible expense and thus can be used to reduce the taxes the corporation must pay to federal and state governments.

Corporate bonds are a form of *debt financing*. Bond owners must be repaid at a future date, and interest payments on bonds are required. In the event of bankruptcy, bondholders have a claim to the assets of the corporation prior to that of stockholders.

LO11.5

Recognize why investors purchase corporate bonds.

ACTION ITEM

I appreciate why investors purchase corporate bonds.

☐ Agree ☐ Disagree

face value The dollar amount the bondholder will receive at the bond's maturity.

maturity date For a corporate bond, the date on which the corporation is to repay the borrowed money.

bond indenture A legal document that details all of the conditions relating to a bond issue.

trustee A financially independent firm that acts as the bondholders' representative.

debenture A bond that is backed only by the reputation of the issuing corporation.

mortgage bond A corporate bond secured by various assets of the issuing firm.

convertible bond A bond that can be exchanged, at the owner's option, for a specified number of shares of the corporation's common stock.

CAUTION! ⚠

You should not invest in high-yield bonds unless you fully understand all of the risks associated with this type of investment.

high-yield bond A corporate bond that pays higher interest but also has a higher risk of default.

call feature A feature that allows the corporation to call in, or buy, outstanding bonds from current bondholders before the maturity date.

sinking fund A fund to which annual or semiannual deposits are made for the purpose of redeeming a bond issue.

serial bonds Bonds of a single issue that mature on different dates.

TYPES OF BONDS Most corporate bonds are debentures. A **debenture** is a bond that is backed only by the reputation of the issuing corporation. If the corporation fails to make either interest payments or repayment at maturity, debenture bondholders become unsecured creditors, much like the firm's suppliers.

To make a bond issue more appealing to conservative investors, a corporation may issue a mortgage bond. A **mortgage bond** (sometimes referred to as a *secured bond*) is a corporate bond secured by various assets of the issuing firm. Because of this added security, interest rates on mortgage bonds are usually lower than interest rates on unsecured debentures.

A **convertible bond** can be exchanged, at the owner's option, for a specified number of shares of the corporation's common stock. This conversion feature allows investors to enjoy the lower risk of a corporate bond but also take advantage of the speculative nature of common stock. For example, assume you purchase a $1,000 convertible bond that is issued by Square, a company that specializes in new online payment technology. Each convertible bond can be converted to 12.8456 shares of the company's common stock. This means you could convert the bond to common stock whenever the price of the company's common stock is $77.85 ($1,000 ÷ 12.8456 = $77.85) or higher. Generally, the interest rate on a convertible bond is 1 to 2 percent lower than that on traditional bonds because of the conversion factor.

A **high-yield bond** is a corporate bond that pays higher interest but also has a higher risk of default. Before investing in high-yield bonds, keep in mind these investments are often referred to as "junk bonds" in the financial world. High-yield (junk) bonds are sold by companies with a poor earnings history, companies with a questionable credit record, and newer companies with the unproven ability to increase sales and earn profits. They are also frequently used in connection with leveraged buyouts—a situation in which investors acquire a company and sell high-yield bonds to raise money to pay for the company. So why do investors purchase high-yield bonds? The answer is simple: Corporations issuing high-yield bonds must offer investors interest rates that are often 3 to 4 percentage points higher than safer bond issues.

PROVISIONS FOR REPAYMENT Today most corporate bonds are callable. A **call feature** allows the corporation to call in, or buy, outstanding bonds from current bondholders before the maturity date. In many cases, corporations issuing callable bonds agree not to call them for the first 5 to 10 years after the bonds have been issued. The money needed to call a bond may come from the firm's profits, the sale of additional stock, or the sale of a new bond issue that has a lower interest rate.

A corporation may use one of two methods to ensure that it has sufficient funds available to redeem a bond issue at maturity. First, the corporation may establish a sinking fund. A **sinking fund** is a fund to which annual or semiannual deposits are made for the purpose of redeeming a bond issue. For a bond issue that matures in 2030, Union Pacific Corporation agreed to make annual deposits to a sinking fund to accumulate the money to pay bondholders when the bonds mature.

Second, a corporation may issue serial bonds. **Serial bonds** are bonds of a single issue that mature on different dates. For example, Seaside Productions used a 20-year, $100 million bond issue to finance its expansion. None of the bonds matures during the first 10 years. Thereafter, 10 percent of the bonds mature each year until all the bonds are retired at the end of the 20-year period.

Why Investors Purchase Corporate Bonds

Basically, investors purchase corporate bonds for three reasons: (1) interest income, (2) possible increase in value, and (3) repayment at maturity.

1. INTEREST INCOME Bondholders normally receive interest payments every six months until the bond's maturity. The formula to calculate the amount of interest is:

Amount of annual interest = Face value × Interest rate

EXAMPLE: Interest Calculation (H. J. Heinz)

Assume you purchase a $1,000 bond issued by H. J. Heinz, the company that makes ketchup, mustard, mayonnaise, and other consumer food products. The bond pays 5.2 percent interest each year. Using the following formula, you can calculate the annual interest amount.

$$\text{Amount of annual interest} = \text{Face value} \times \text{Interest rate}$$
$$= \$1,000 \times 5.2 \text{ percent}$$
$$= \$1,000 \times 0.052$$
$$= \$52$$

Note: Yearly interest of $52 will be paid in two installments of $26 at the end of each six-month period.

The method used to pay bondholders their interest depends on whether they own registered bonds or registered coupon bonds. A **registered bond** is registered in the owner's name by the issuing company. Most registered bonds are now tracked electronically, using computers to record the owners' information. Interest checks for registered bonds are mailed directly to the bondholder of record. A variation of a registered bond is the registered coupon bond. A **registered coupon bond** is registered for principal only, not for interest. While only the registered owner can collect the principal at maturity, interest payments can be paid to anyone who presents one of the detachable coupons to the issuing corporation or the paying agent. Coupon bonds are increasingly rare since the advent of electronic tracking and payment technology.

registered bond A bond that is registered in the owner's name by the issuing company.

registered coupon bond A bond that is registered for principal only, not for interest.

2. DOLLAR APPRECIATION OF BOND VALUE The price of a corporate bond may fluctuate until the maturity date. Changes in overall interest rates in the economy are the primary cause of most bond price fluctuations and are an example of interest rate risk discussed earlier in this chapter. When H. J. Heinz issued the bond mentioned earlier, the 5.2 percent interest rate was competitive with the interest rates offered by other corporations issuing comparable bonds at that time. If overall interest rates fall, the price of your Heinz bond will increase due to its higher 5.2 percent fixed interest rate. Because your Heinz bond has increased in value, you may want to sell your bond at the current higher price. Or, if you prefer, you can hold your bond until maturity and receive interest payments until maturity and the bond's face value at maturity. *Note:* While the interest rate for corporate bonds is fixed, the price for your Heinz bond is not and can fluctuate until maturity.

On the other hand, if overall interest rates for comparable bonds rise, the price of your Heinz bond will decrease due to its fixed 5.2 percent stated interest rate. Keep in mind, you can always sell your bond, but if the price has decreased below the price you paid, you will incur a loss. In this situation, many investors choose to hold the bond until maturity and collect the face value.

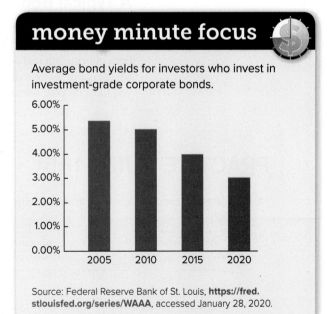

money minute focus

Average bond yields for investors who invest in investment-grade corporate bonds.

Source: Federal Reserve Bank of St. Louis, **https://fred. stlouisfed.org/series/WAAA**, accessed January 28, 2020.

When interest rates are increasing or decreasing, it is possible to approximate a bond's current market value using the following formula:

$$\text{Approximate market value} = \frac{\text{Dollar amount of annual interest}}{\text{Comparable interest rate}}$$

EXAMPLE: Calculating Approximate Market Value

Assume you purchase a $1,000 Heinz bond that pays 5.2 percent, or annual interest of $52 each year. Also assume new corporate bond issues of comparable quality are currently paying 4.75 percent. The approximate market value is $1,094.74 as follows:

$$\text{Approximate market value} = \frac{\text{Dollar amount of annual interest}}{\text{Comparable interest rate}} = \frac{\$52}{4.75\%}$$

$$= \$1,094.74$$

In the above example, the Heinz bond increased in value because interest rates for comparable bonds were lower than the 5.2 percent rate for the Heinz bond. The price of a bond may also be affected by the financial condition of the corporation or government entity issuing the bond, the factors of supply and demand, an upturn or downturn in the economy, political uncertainty, and the proximity of the bond's maturity date.

3. BOND REPAYMENT AT MATURITY Corporate bonds are repaid at maturity. After you purchase a bond, you have two options: You may keep the bond until maturity and then redeem it, or you may sell the bond to another investor. In either case, the value of your bond is closely tied to the corporation's ability to pay interest until maturity and repay its bond indebtedness at maturity. For example, the value of bonds issued by Pacific Gas and Electric—the largest utility company in the nation—dropped in value when it experienced large dollar losses and lawsuits related to wildlfires in California. In fact, Pacific Gas and Electric filed for bankruptcy protection in 2019 after it failed to make interest payments on some bonds.

A Typical Bond Transaction

Most bonds are sold through full-service brokerage firms, discount brokerage firms, or the Internet. If you use a full-service brokerage firm, your account executive should provide both information and advice about bond investments. As with other investments, the chief advantage of using a discount brokerage firm or trading online is lower commissions, but you must do your own research.

PRACTICE QUIZ 11-5

1. Calculate the annual interest and the semiannual interest payment for corporate bond issues with a face value of $1,000.

Annual Interest Rate	Annual Interest	Semiannual Interest Payment
4%		
5.5%		
3.75%		

2. In your own words, describe why corporations issue corporate bonds.

3. List the three reasons investors purchase corporate bonds.

While brokerage firms charge commissions (sometimes referred to as transaction costs) to buy and sell bonds, the actual amount you pay is often hard to determine. Unlike stocks, where commissions are stated in plain language, commissions on bonds may be a combination of a stated dollar amount for each bond you buy or sell plus an additional charge (often called a markup when buying and a markdown when selling). If you want to know the exact dollar amount a brokerage firm is charging you to buy or sell a bond, the best advice is to ask the brokerage firm or your account executive.

The Decision to Buy or Sell Bonds

LO11.6

Evaluate bonds when making an investment.

One basic principle we have stressed throughout this chapter is the need to evaluate any potential investment. As you will see in this section, a number of sources of information can be used to evaluate bond investments.

The Internet

By accessing a corporation's web page and locating the topics "investor relations," "annual report," or "financial information," you can find many of the answers to the questions asked in *Your Personal Financial Plan Sheet 37.*

When investing in bonds, you can use the Internet in three other ways. First, you can obtain price information on specific bond issues to track the value of your investments. Second, you can trade bonds online and pay lower commissions than you would pay a full-service brokerage firm. Third, you can get research about a corporation or government entity and its bond issues by accessing specific bond websites. The following are popular websites for corporate and government bond investors:

ACTION ITEM

I know how to evaluate bond investments.

☐ Yes ☐ No

- http://finra-markets.morningstar.com/BondCenter/Results.jsp
- https://markets.businessinsider.com/bonds/finder?borrower
- https://bondevalue.com/
- https://finance.yahoo.com/bonds/
- www.treasurydirect.gov
- www.fmsbonds.com
- https://www.municipalbonds.com/screener/

Be warned: Bond websites are not as numerous as websites that provide information on stocks, mutual funds, or other investment alternatives, and many of the better bond websites require that you register and provide personal information and/or charge a fee for their research and recommendations.

Financial Coverage for Bond Transactions

In bond quotations, prices are given as a percentage of the face value, which is usually $1,000. Thus, to find the actual current price for a bond, you must multiply the face value (usually $1,000) by the bond quotation.

EXAMPLE: Determining Bond Prices

At the time of publication, the quote for a 4 percent Walmart bond that matures in April 2043 is 117. To calculate the current price for the Walmart bond, multiply the face value—usually $1,000—by the bond price quotation. If the bond price quotation is 117, the current price is $1,170, as shown below.

$$\text{Current price} = \text{Face Value} \times \text{Bond Price Quotation}$$
$$= \$1,000 \times 117 \text{ percent}$$
$$= \$1,000 \times 1.17$$
$$= \$1,170$$

In this case, the Walmart bond is priced above its $1,000 face value because Walmart is paying bondholders 4 percent at a time when comparable bonds are paying less interest. *Remember,* when interest rates in the economy go down, a bond with a fixed interest rate will increase in value.

While some information about bonds may be available in *The Wall Street Journal* or larger metropolitan newspapers, today most bond investors use the Internet to obtain detailed information on bond issues. Detailed information obtained from the Financial Industry Regulatory Authority website for a $1,000 Visa corporate bond, which pays 2.75 percent interest and matures in 2027, is provided in Exhibit 11–7.

Bond Ratings

Detailed information about the quality and risk for a bond issue, bond rating, provisions for repayment, maturity date, interest rate, call provisions, trustee, and details about security (if any) is provided by:

- Moody's, **www.moodys.com.**
- Standard & Poor's, **www.standardandpoors.com.**
- Fitch Ratings, **www.fitchratings.com.**

Exhibit 11–7

Bond Information Available by Accessing the Financial Investment Regulatory Authority (FINRA) Website

Visa Corporate Bond	
Overview	
1. Price:	105
2. Coupon (%):	2.75
3. Maturity date:	09/15/2027
4. Lookup symbol:	V4539215
5. Yield (%):	2.62
6. Standard & Poor's rating:	AA-
7. Coupon payment frequency:	Semiannual
8. First coupon date:	03/15/2018
9. Type:	Corporate debenture
10. Callable:	Yes

1. Price quoted as a percentage of the face value: $1,000 × 105% = $1,050
2. Coupon (%) is the rate of interest: 2.75%.
3. Maturity date is the date when bondholders will receive repayment of the face value: September 15, 2027.
4. Lookup Symbol is the information you can use to determine the current price and other information about this bond issue on Internet sites: V4539215.
5. Yield (%) is determined by dividing the dollar amount of annual interest by the current price of the bond: $27.50 ÷ $1,050 = 0.0262, or 2.62%.
6. Standard & Poor's rating is issued by Standard & Poor's and is used to assess the risk associated with this bond: AA-. An AA- rating represents a bond classified as an "investment grade" bond.
7. Coupon payment frequency tells bondholders how often they will receive interest payments: semiannually, or every six months.
8. First coupon date was March 15, 2018.
9. Type indicates this is a corporate debenture bond.
10. Callable tells the bondholder if the bond is callable: Yes.

SOURCES: Financial Industry Regulatory Authority, **http://finra-markets.morningstar.com/BondCenter/BondDetail. jsp?ticker=C709073&symbol=V4539215**, accessed January 23, 2020.

As Exhibit 11–8 illustrates, bond ratings range from Aaa (the highest) to C (the lowest) for Moody's and AAA (the highest) to D (the lowest) for Standard & Poor's. Fitch ratings are similar to the bond ratings provided by Moody's and Standard & Poor's. For both Moody's and Standard & Poor's, the first four categories (high grade and medium grade) represent investment-grade securities. Investment-grade securities are suitable for conservative investors who want a safe investment that provides a predictable source of income. Bonds in the next two categories (speculative) are considered higher risk and vulnerable to potential financial problems. Finally, the C and D categories are used to rank bonds for which there are poor prospects of repayment or even continued payment of interest. Bonds in these categories may be in default. Generally, the ratings for government securities securities are similar to those of corporate bonds.

Exhibit **11–8** Description of Bond Ratings Provided by Moody's Investors Service and Standard & Poor's Corporation

Quality	Moody's	Standard & Poor's	Description
High grade	Aaa	AAA	Bonds that are judged to be of the highest rating by Moody's and Standard and Poor's
	Aa	AA	Bonds that are judged to be of high quality by all standards. Together with the first group, they comprise what are generally known as high-grade bonds.
Medium grade	A	A	Bonds that possess many favorable investment attributes and are considered upper-medium-grade obligations
	Baa	BBB	Bonds that are considered medium-grade obligations, but adverse economic conditions could lead to a weakened capacity to meet fiinancial obligations
Speculative	Ba	BB	Bonds that are judged to have more speculative elements than higher-rated bond issues; their future may be determined by economic or adverse business conditions
	B	B	Bonds that are speculative and generally lack characteristics of a desirable investment and subject to high risk of nonpayment of interest and principal
Poor prospects or Default	Caa	CCC	Bonds that are of poor standing and very high risk and are dependent on favorable business conditions
	Ca		Bonds that represent obligations that are highly speculative and are likely in, or very near, default
	C		Bonds that are in default with little prospect for recovery of principal and interest
		CC	Bonds that are very close to default and Standard & Poor's expects default to be a virtual certainty
		C	Standard & Poor's rating given to bonds that are highly vulnerable to nonpayment and have lower prospects of eventual recovery of principal or interest
		D	Bond issues in default

Source: "Long-Term Corporate Obligation Ratings," Moody's, **https://www.moodys.com/researchdocumentcontentpage.aspx?docid=PBC_79004**, accessed January 23, 2020, and "Standard & Poor's Ratings Definitions," Standard & Poor's Corporation, **https://www.spratings.com/documents/20184/86966/ Standard+%26+Poor%27s+Ratings+Definitions/fd2a2a96-be56-47b8-9ad2-390f3878d6c6**, accessed January 23, 2020.

WHAT WOULD YOU DO? Five years ago, you purchased a corporate bond for $1,080. The bond pays 4 percent interest, matures in 2026, and is rated AAA by Standard & Poor's. Today the bond was downgraded by Standard & Poor's to BB. To make matters worse, the bond's current price has dropped to $889 because comparable bonds are paying 4.5 percent. Now you must decide if you should sell your bond at the current price or hold the bond until maturity. What would you do?

Yield Calculations

current yield Determined by dividing the annual interest amount by the bond's current price.

The yield is the rate of return earned by an investor who holds an investment for a stated period of time—usually a 12-month period. Changes in the yield for a bond are caused by an increase or a decreased in the current price of a bond. The **current yield** is determined by dividing the annual interest amount by the bond's current price. The following formula will help you complete this calculation:

$$\text{Current yield} = \frac{\text{Annual interest amount}}{\text{Current price}}$$

EXAMPLE: Calculating Current Yield (McDonald's)

Assume you own a McDonald's corporate bond that pays 3.25 percent interest on an annual basis. The face value for your bond is $1,000. This means that each year, you will receive $32.50 ($1,000 × 3.25 percent = $32.50). Also assume the current price of the McDonald's bond is $1,058. The current yield is 3.07 percent, as follows:

$$\text{Current yield} = \frac{\$32.50}{\$1,058}$$
$$= 0.0307, \text{ or } 3.07 \text{ percent}$$

Whereas the interest rate for a corporate bond is fixed, the price of a bond and the current yield is not. In the above example, the current price of $1,058 for the McDonald's was more than the bond's $1,000 face value. As a result, the current yield decreased to 3.07 percent. Keep in mind that a bond's price can also decrease below its face value. When this happens, the current yield will increase and be higher than the fixed interest rate.

This calculation allows you to compare the yield on a bond investment with the yields of other investment alternatives, which include savings accounts, certificates of deposit, common stock, preferred stock, and mutual funds. Naturally, the higher the current yield, the better! A current yield of 4 percent is better than a current yield of 3.07 percent.

Other Sources of Information

Investors can use two additional sources of information to evaluate potential bond investments. First, business and personal finance magazines often provide information about the economy, interest rates, and investment information about a corporation or government entity that issues bonds.

Second, a number of federal agencies provide information that may be useful to bond investors in either printed form or on the internet. You can obtain information that corporations have reported to the Securities and Exchange Commission (SEC) by accessing the SEC website at **www.sec.gov**. Reports and research published by the Federal Reserve System, the U.S. Treasury, the Bureau of Economic Analysis, and the U.S. Department of Commerce may also be used to assess the nation's economy. Finally, state and local governments will provide information about specific municipal bond issues.

Sheet 37 Evaluating Corporate Bonds

PRACTICE QUIZ 11–6

1. What type of information about bonds is available on the Internet?

2. Calculate the current price for the following bonds:

Face Value	Bond Quotation	Current Price
$1,000	103	
$1,000	77.5	

3. Explain what the following bond ratings mean for investors:

   a. Aaa
   b. BBB
   c. CC

4. What is the current yield for a $1,000 bond that pays 4.25 percent interest and has a current price of $920?

Road Map to financial literacy

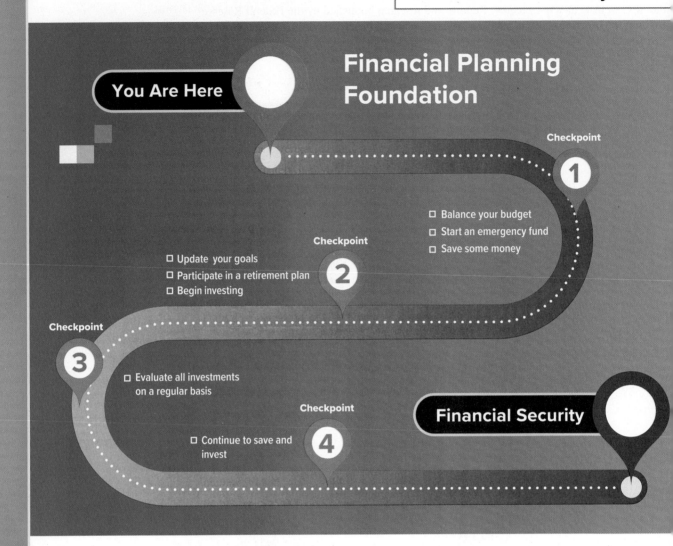

Financial Planning Foundation

You Are Here

Checkpoint 1
- ☐ Balance your budget
- ☐ Start an emergency fund
- ☐ Save some money

Checkpoint 2
- ☐ Update your goals
- ☐ Participate in a retirement plan
- ☐ Begin investing

Checkpoint 3
- ☐ Evaluate all investments on a regular basis

Checkpoint 4
- ☐ Continue to save and invest

Financial Security

NO PROGRESS · SOME PROGRESS · READY TO INVEST

0% 10% 20% 30% 40% 50% 60% 70% 80% 90% 100%

MY FINANCIAL CHECKUP IS COMPLETE AND I'M READY TO INVEST

your personal finance dashboard

Preparing for an Investment Program

What have you done to prepare for an investment program? Have you established specific goals and objectives? Have you saved money for emergencies? Do you have any money to invest?

YOUR SITUATION: Once you have established your investment goals, completed your financial checkup, and saved some money to invest, the next step is to evaluate different investment alternatives. Once you identify a quality investment, then it's time to invest.

LO11.1 In addition to developing investment goals, you must make sure your personal financial affairs are in order. The next step is the accumulation of an emergency fund equal to at least three months' living expenses. Then, it's time to save the money needed to establish an investment program. The time value of money concept can help you achieve your goals—especially if you start sooner rather than later.

LO11.2 All investors must consider the factors of safety, risk, income, growth, and liquidity. Especially important is the relationship between safety and risk. Basically, this relationship can be summarized as follows: Your potential return for any investment should be directly related to the risk you assume. In addition to safety and risk, investors choose investments that provide income, growth, or liquidity.

LO11.3 Asset allocation is the process of spreading your assets among several different types of investments to lessen risk. In addition to asset allocation, the amount of time before you need your money is a critical component in the types of investments you choose. Finally, your age is a factor that influences investment choices. You can also improve your investment returns by evaluating all potential investments, monitoring the value of your investments, developing a plan if you experience a personal or an economic crisis, and keeping accurate and current records. Professional help and your tax situation may also affect your investment decisions.

LO11.4 Generally, U.S. government securities—Treasury bills, notes, bonds, and Treasury Inflation-Protected Securities—are chosen because most investors consider them to be a safe harbor in troubled economic times. While securities issued by the U.S. Treasury are taxable for federal income tax purposes, they are exempt from state and local taxation. Municipal bonds are also conservative investments and may provide tax-exempt income.

LO11.5 Bonds are issued by corporations to raise capital. Corporate bonds may be debentures, mortgage bonds, convertible bonds, or high-yield bonds. Investors purchase corporate bonds for three reasons: (1) interest income, (2) possible increase in value, and (3) repayment at maturity. The method used to pay bondholders interest depends on whether they own registered bonds or registered coupon bonds. Most corporate bonds are bought and sold through full-service brokerage firms, discount brokerage firms, or the Internet. Investors pay brokers when bonds are bought and sold.

LO11.6 Today it is possible to obtain information on the Internet that can be used to evaluate both government and corporate bonds. It is also possible to trade bonds online. To determine the quality of a bond issue, most investors study the ratings provided by Moody's, Standard & Poor's, and Fitch Ratings. Investors can also calculate a current yield to evaluate a decision to buy or sell bond issues. Finally, newspapers, business magazines, and government sources can be used to evaluate both government and corporate bonds and the economy.

asset allocation 391

bond indenture 399

call feature 400

convertible bond 400

corporate bond 399

current yield 406

debenture 400

emergency fund 384

face value 399

general obligation
 bond 398

government bond 397

high-yield bond 400

line of credit 384

liquidity 390

maturity date 399

mortgage bond 400

municipal bond 398

registered bond 401

registered coupon
 bond 401

revenue bond 398

serial bonds 400

sinking fund 400

speculative
 investment 387

trustee 399

Page	Topic	Formula
382	Credit Purchase Amounts	Maximum Credit Payment = Net (after-tax income) × 20 percent
384	Emergency fund	Minimum emergency fund = Monthly expenses × 3 months
398	Taxable equivalent yield	$\text{Taxable equivalent yield} = \dfrac{\text{Tax-exempt yield}}{1.0 - \text{Your tax rate}}$
401	Interest calculation for a bond	Amount of annual interest = Face value × Interest rate
402	Approximate market value	$\text{Approximate market value} = \dfrac{\text{Dollar amount of annual interest}}{\text{Comparable interest rate}}$
403	Current price for a bond	Current price = Face Value × Bond Price Quotation
406	Current yield for a bond	$\text{Current yield} = \dfrac{\text{Annual interest amount}}{\text{Current price}}$

Self-Test Problems

1. For Ned Masterson, the last few years have been a financial nightmare. It all started when he lost his job. Because he had no job and no income, he began using his credit cards to obtain the cash needed to pay everyday living expenses. Finally, after an exhaustive job search, he has a new job that pays $42,000 a year. While his take-home pay is $2,450 a month, he must now establish an emergency fund, pay off his $6,200 credit card debt, and start saving the money needed to begin an investment program.
   a. If monthly expenses are $1,750, how much money should Ned save for an emergency fund?
   b. Ned has decided that he will save $2,500 a year for the next five years in order to establish a long-term investment program. If his savings and investments earn 2 percent each year, how much money will he have at the end of five years? (Use the information in this chapter's *Figure It Out!* feature to answer this question.)

2. Betty Forrester is 55 years old, wants to diversify her investment portfolio, and must decide if she should invest in tax-free municipal bonds or corporate bonds. The tax-free bonds are highly rated and pay 4.25 percent. The corporate bonds are more speculative and pay 6.1 percent.
   a. If Betty is in the 32 percent tax bracket, what is the taxable equivalent yield for the municipal bond?
   b. If you were Betty, would you choose the municipal bonds or corporate bonds? Justify your answer.

3. Mary Glover purchased 10 $1,000 corporate bonds issued by American Express. The annual interest rate for the bonds is 4.05 percent.
   a. What is the annual interest amount for each American Express bond?
   b. If the bonds have a current bond price quotation of 121, what is the current price of the bond?
   c. Given the above information, what is the current yield for an American Express bond?

Solutions

1. *a.* The minimum emergency fund is $5,250.

$$\text{Minimum emergency fund} = \text{Monthly expenses} \times 3 \text{ months}$$
$$= \$1,750 \times 3$$
$$\$5,250$$

b. Ned will have invested $12,500 at the end of five years. If his savings and investments earn 2 percent, he will have $13,010.10 at the end of five years that can be used to fund additional investments. To solve this problem, you can use a future value calculator available on the Internet such as the one at **keisan.casio.com**. You can also solve the problem using the future value formula for a series of deposits over a specified time or a future value table such as the one in the Chapter 1 Appendix.

2. *a.* The taxable equivalent yield for the municipal bond is:

$$\text{Taxable equivalent yield} = \frac{\text{Tax-exempt yield}}{1.0 - \text{Your tax rate}}$$
$$= \frac{0.0425}{1.0 - 0.32}$$
$$= 0.0625, \text{ or } 6.25\%$$

b. The taxable equivalent yield for the municipal bonds is 6.25 percent; the yield for the corporate bonds is 6.1 percent. Also, it should be noted that the corporate bonds are more speculative, and the interest income on the corporate bonds is taxable. In this case, Betty should choose the tax-free municipal bonds because the yield is higher and they are more conservative.

3. *a.* The annual interest for each American Express bond is $40.50.

$$\text{Amount of annual interest} = \text{Face value} \times \text{Interest rate}$$
$$= \$1,000 \times 0.0405$$
$$= \$40.50$$

b. The current price is $1,210.

$$\text{Current price} = \text{Face Vaue} \times \text{Bond Price Quotation}$$
$$= \$1,000 \times 121\%$$
$$= \$1,000 \times 1.21$$
$$= \$1,210$$

c. The current yield is:

$$\text{Current yield} = \frac{\text{Annual interest amount}}{\text{Current price}}$$
$$= \frac{\$40.50}{\$1,210}$$
$$= 0.033 = 3.3\%$$

Financial Planning Problems

1. Jane and Bill Collins have total take-home pay of $5,400 a month. Their monthly expenses total $4,250. Calculate the minimum amount this couple needs to establish an emergency fund. (LO11.1)

2. Use the information in the *Figure It Out!* box earlier in the chapter to complete the following table. (LO11.1)

Annual Deposit	Rate of Return	Number of Years	Investment Value at the End of Time Period	Total Amount of Investment	Total Amount of Earnings
$3,000	2%	10			
$3,000	8%	10			
$3,000	3%	30			
$3,000	9%	30			

3. Assume you are in the 24 percent tax bracket and purchase a municipal bond with a yield of 2.90 percent. Use the formula presented in this chapter to calculate the taxable equivalent yield for this investment. (LO11.4)

4. Assume you are in the 35 percent tax bracket and purchase a municipal bond with a yield of 3.20 percent. Use the formula presented in this chapter to calculate the taxable equivalent yield for this investment. (LO11.4)

5. Three years ago, you purchased a corporate bond that pays 4.30 percent. The purchase price was $1,000. What is the annual dollar amount of interest that you receive from your bond investment? (LO11.5)

6. Five years ago, you purchased seven corporate bonds that each pay 3.84 percent annual interest. Each bond has a face value of $1,000. How much interest do you earn on the seven bonds each year? (LO11.5)

7. Assume that you purchased a $1,000 convertible corporate bond. Also assume the bond can be converted to 18.5 shares of the firm's stock. What is the dollar value that the stock must reach before investors would consider converting to common stock? (LO11.5)

8. Five years ago, you purchased a $1,000 par value corporate bond with an interest rate of 3.6 percent. Today comparable bonds are paying 4.2 percent. (LO11.5)
   a. What is the approximate dollar price for which you could sell your bond?
   b. In your own words, describe why your bond decreased in value.

9. In 2009, you purchased a $1,000 par value corporate bond with an interest rate of 4 percent. Today, comparable bonds are paying 3.30 percent. (LO11.5)
   a. What is the approximate dollar price for which you could sell your bond?
   b. In your own words, describe why your bond increased in value.

10. Determine the current yield on a corporate bond investment that has a face value of $1,000, pays 4.45 percent, and has a current price of $920. (LO11.6)

11. Assume you own a corporate bond that has a face value of $1,000 and pays 4.60 percent. What is the current yield if the bond is currently selling for $1,080? (LO11.6)

 **connect** To reinforce the content in this chapter, more problems are provided at connect.mheducation.com.

FINANCIAL LITERACY PORTFOLIO

INVESTMENT START-UP PLAN

Competency

Create an investment start-up plan.

Action Research

Based on the information in this chapter, *Your Personal Financial Plan Sheets 35* and *36*, online research, and conversations with friends and family, create four to six specific actions you would take to design and implement a personal investment plan.

Outcome

Create a visual presentation (PowerPoint presentation, video, smartphone app prototype, storyboard, or other format) to communicate the steps in your proposed investment plan. Describe your personal progress for each step.

REAL LIFE PERSONAL FINANCE

THREE DIFFERENT INVESTMENTS. . . WHICH ONE IS RIGHT FOR YOU?

Assume that one year ago, you purchased a certificate of deposit (CD) for $50,000. At the time, the annual interest rate was 2.50 percent. Twelve months later, your CD has matured, and you must decide where to invest your money. You talked to your banker, and she told you that one-year CDs are now paying 1.60 percent. Disappointed, you start thinking about other alternatives but quickly realize there are important differences that you should consider before investing your money.

Savings accounts and certificates of deposit are safe because they are insured by the Federal Deposit Insurance Corporation (FDIC). The interest paid on both a savings account and a CD can be left on deposit to grow your nest egg, or the interest can provide you with a predictable source of income. And yet, the 1.60 interest rate currently offered on certificates of deposit is low.

Maggie Anderson, an older friend with substantively more money and investment experience than you have, suggests that you consider corporate bonds as a conservative alternative. She points out that they are safer than most common stock or mutual funds but offer larger returns than savings accounts and CDs. Still, corporate bonds are not guaranteed. Factors to consider include:

- if the corporation will continue paying interest until maturity.
- if the corporation will be able to repay bondholders at maturity.
- the financial outlook for the corporation that issued the bond.

Maggie tells you to begin your search for a corporate bond by looking at the bond ratings provided by Standard & Poor's. Standard & Poor's ratings range from AAA (the highest) to D (the lowest). She points out that most investors consider a bond rated BBB or better as an investment-grade security with smaller risks than more speculative bond issues. A bond rated BB or lower is considered speculative and has a higher risk of default at maturity. Even interest payments can be omitted if a corporation experiences financial problems. Bonds rated C or D may be in default because the corporation is behind on interest payments to bondholders or unable to repay bondholders at maturity.

After researching bonds on the Internet and in the library, you are considering two different bonds. Now you must decide if you are willing to accept the additional risk that accompany corporate bonds or should just purchase a CD that pays 1.60. To help you decide, consider the following options:

1. A one-year certificate of deposit that pays 1.60 percent and is guaranteed by the FDIC.
2. Corporate bonds issued by Microsoft that pay 2.70 percent and are rated AAA by Standard & Poor's. Each bond has a face value of $1,000. The bonds in this issue mature on February 12, 2025.
3. Corporate bonds issued by Dollar Tree that pay 4.0 percent and are rated BBB by Standard & Poor's. Each bond has a face value of $1,000. Bonds in this issue mature on May 15, 2025.

Questions

1. To help evaluate the CD and the two bonds, complete the table below.

Investment Alternative	Annual Interest Rate	Annual Dollars of Interest
Certificate of Deposit		
Microsoft Corporate Bond		
Dollar Tree Corporate Bond		

2. While both bonds are considered investment grade bonds, the Microsoft bond is rated higher than the Dollar Tree bond. What does the AAA rating for the Microsoft bond mean? What does the BBB rating for Dollar Tree bond mean?

3. What other information would you need to evaluate these two bonds? Where would you get this information?

4. Based on your research, which investment would you choose? Why? (*Note:* To help evaluate the bonds, begin by answering the questions on *Your Personal Financial Plan Sheet 37.* One information source you might use is the Financial Industry Regulatory Authority website at **http://finra-markets.morningstar.com/BondCenter/Results.jsp**.

CONTINUING CASE

INVESTING BASICS AND EVALUATING BONDS

The triplets are now three-and-a-half years old, and Jamie Lee and Ross, both 38, are finally beginning to settle down into a regular routine. The first three years were a blur of diapers, feedings, baths, mounds of laundry, and crying babies!

Recently, Jamie Lee and Ross went out for dinner, while Ross's parents watched the triplets. They had a conversation about their future and the future of the kids. They guessed that college expenses would be $150,000, and their eventual retirement is a major worry for both of them. They have dreamed of owning a beach house when they retire. That could be another $350,000, 30 years from now. They wondered how could they possibly afford all of this.

They agreed that it was time to talk to a financial planner, but they wanted to organize all of their financial information and discuss their family's financial goals before setting up the appointment.

Current Financial Situation

Assets (Jamie Lee and Ross combined):

Checking account, $4,500

Savings account, $20,000

Emergency fund savings account, $21,000

IRA balance, $32,000

Cars, $8,500 (*Jamie Lee*) and $14,000 (*Ross*)

Liabilities (Jamie Lee and Ross combined):

Student loan balance, $0

Credit card balance, $4,000

Car loans, $2,000

Income:

Jamie Lee, $45,000 gross income ($31,500 net income after taxes)

Ross, $80,000 gross income ($64,500 net income after taxes)

Monthly Expenses:

Mortgage, $1,225

Property taxes, $400

Homeowner's insurance, $200

IRA contribution, $300

Utilities, $250

Food, $600

Baby essentials (diapers, clothing, toys, etc.), $200

Gas/Vehicle maintenance, $275

Credit card payment, $400

Car loan payment, $289

Entertainment, $125

Questions

1. Describe the stage in the adult life cycle (Chapter 1, Exhibit 1-1) that Jamie Lee and Ross are experiencing right now. What are some of the financial activities that they should be participating in at this stage?
2. After reviewing Jamie Lee and Ross's current financial situation, suggest specific and measurable short-term and long-term investment goals that can be implemented at this stage.
3. Using the investment goal guidelines listed below, assess the validity of Jamie Lee and Ross's short- and long-term goals (college education for the kids, retirement, and a second home).

Financial Question	Short-Term Goals	Long-Term Goals
1. How much money do they need to satisfy their investment goals?		
2. How much risk are they willing to assume in an investment program?		
3. What possible economic or personal conditions could alter their investment goals?		
4. Considering their economic conditions, are their investment goals reasonable?		
5. Are they willing to make the sacrifices necessary to ensure that they meet their investment goals?		

4. Using the formula to determine the percentage of growth investments discussed in this chapter, determine how much of Jamie Lee and Ross's investments should be growth investments. How should the remaining investments be distributed, and what is the associated risk of each type of investment?
5. Jamie Lee and Ross need to evaluate their emergency fund of $21,000. Will their present emergency fund be sufficient to cover them should one of them lose their job?
6. Jamie Lee and Ross agree that by accomplishing their short-term goals, they can budget $7,000 a year toward their long-term investment goals. They are estimating that

with the allocations recommended by their financial adviser, they will see an average return of 7 percent on their investments. The triplets will begin college in 15 years and will need $150,000 for tuition.

Using the time value of money information found in the *Figure It Out!* feature in this chapter, decide if Jamie Lee and Ross will be on track to reach their long-term financial goals of having enough money from their investments to pay the triplets' college tuition.

Spending Diary

"WHILE I HAVE A FAIRLY LARGE AMOUNT IN A SAVINGS ACCOUNT, I SHOULD THINK ABOUT INVESTING SOME OF THIS MONEY IN OTHER WAYS."

Directions The use of your Daily Spending Diary can provide an important foundation for monitoring and controlling spending. This will enable you to make better purchasing and investing decisions both now and in the future. The Daily Spending Diary sheets are located at the end of Chapter 1 and in Connect Finance.

Questions

1. Explain how the use of a Daily Spending Diary could help you start an investment program.
2. Based on your Daily Spending Diary, describe actions that you might take to identify and achieve various financial and investment goals.

Establishing Investment Goals

Purpose: To determine specific goals for an investment program

Financial Planning Activities: Based on short- and long-term goals for your investment program, enter the items requested below. This sheet is also available in an Excel spreadsheet format in Connect Finance.

Suggested Websites: www.moneymanagement.org, https://www.thebalance.com/setting-investment-goals-for-financial-independence-4120968

Description of Investment Goal	Dollar Amount	Date Needed	Possible Investments to Achieve This Goal	Level of Risk (high, medium, low)

Suggested App:
• The Motley Fool

McGraw Hill

What's Next for Your Personal Financial Plan?

- Use the suggestions listed in this chapter to perform a financial checkup.
- Discuss the importance of investment goals and financial planning with other household members.

Name: _____ Date: _____

Assessing Risk for Investments

Purpose: To assess the risk of various investments in relation to your personal risk tolerance and financial goals

Financial Planning Activities: List various investments you are considering based on the type and level of risk associated with each. This sheet is also available in an Excel spreadsheet format in Connect Finance.

Suggested Websites: www.fool.com, https://investor.vanguard.com/investing/how-to-invest/investment-risk

Type of Investment	Loss of Market Value (market risk)	Type of Risk		
		Inflation Risk	Interest Rate Risk	Business Failure Risk
High risk				
Moderate risk				
Low risk				

What's Next for Your Personal Financial Plan?

- Identify current economic trends that might increase or decrease the risk associated with your choice of investments.
- Based on the risk associated with the investments you chose, which investment would you choose to attain your investment goals?

Evaluating Corporate Bonds

Purpose: To determine if a specific corporate bond can help you attain your financial goals

Financial Planning Activities: No checklist can serve as a foolproof guide for choosing a corporate bond. However, the following questions will help you evaluate a potential bond investment. This sheet is also available in an Excel spreadsheet format in Connect Finance.

Suggested Websites: www.morningstar.com, http://finra-markets.morningstar.com/BondCenter/Default.jsp

1. What is the corporation's name, website address, and phone number?
2. What type of products or services does this firm provide?
3. Briefly describe the prospects for this company (include significant factors such as product development, plans for expansion, plans for mergers, etc.).

Category A: Bond Basics

4. What type of bond is this?
5. What is the face value for this bond?
6. What is the interest rate for this bond?
7. What is the dollar amount of annual interest for this bond?
8. What is the current price for this bond?
9. What is the current yield for this bond?
10. When are interest payments made to the bondholders?
11. Is the corporation currently paying interest as scheduled? ☐ Yes ☐ No
12. What is the maturity date for this bond?
13. What is Moody's rating for this bond?
14. What is Standard & Poor's rating for this bond?

15. What do these ratings mean?
16. Is the bond secured with collateral? ☐ Yes ☐ No If so, what?
17. Is the bond callable? If so, when?

Category B: Financial Performance

18. What are the firm's earnings per share for the last year?
19. Have the firm's earnings increased over the past five years?
20. What are the firm's projected earnings for the next year?
21. Do the analysts indicate that this is a good time to invest in this company? Why or why not?
22. Briefly describe any other information that you obtained from Moody's, Standard & Poor's, or other sources of information.

A Word of Caution

The above checklist is not a cure-all, but it does provide some very sound questions that you should answer before making a decision to invest in bonds. If you need other information, *you* are responsible for obtaining it and for determining how it affects your potential investment.

What's Next for Your Personal Financial Plan?

- Talk with various people who have invested in government, municipal, or corporate bonds.
- Discuss with other household members why bonds might be a logical choice for your investment program.

Suggested App:
- Yahoo! Finance

McGraw Hill

12 Investing in Stocks

3 Steps to Financial Literacy . . .
Begin Investing in Stocks

1 Save the money needed to purchase your first stock.
Website: daveramsey.com/article/the-secret-to-saving-money

2 Evaluate different stocks that match your personal investment goals.
Website: https://www.incharge.org/financial-literacy/budgeting-saving/how-to-set-financial-goals/

3 Research the services and fees offered by different brokerage firms.
Website: https://www.fool.com/the-ascent/buying-stocks/best-online-stock-brokers-beginners/

Often people don't invest in stocks because it seems too complicated. In reality, it may be easier than you think. As an incentive, keep in mind that for almost 100 years, stocks have returned an average return of a little less than 10 percent a year. As you read this chapter, you'll learn how to determine if stocks are the right investment for you and how to evaluate stocks. At the end of the chapter, *Your Personal Finance Road Map and Dashboard* will provide additional suggestions to help you establish a long-term investment program.

CHAPTER 12 LEARNING OBJECTIVES

In this chapter, you will learn to:

LO12.1 Identify the most important features of common and preferred stock.

LO12.2 Explain how you can evaluate stock investments.

LO12.3 Analyze the numerical measures that cause a stock to increase or decrease in value.

LO12.4 Describe how stocks are bought and sold.

LO12.5 Explain the trading techniques used by long-term investors and short-term speculators.

YOUR PERSONAL FINANCIAL PLAN SHEETS

38. Evaluating Corporate Stocks
39. Investment Broker Comparison

Common and Preferred Stock

Many investors face two concerns when they begin an investment program. First, they don't know where to get the information they need to evaluate potential investments. In reality, more information is available than most investors can read. Yet, as crazy as it sounds, some investors invest in stocks without doing any research at all. As you begin this chapter, you should know that *there is no substitute for researching a potential stock investment.*

Second, beginning investors sometimes worry that they won't know what the information means when they do find it. Yet common sense goes a long way when evaluating potential investments. For example, consider the following questions:

1. Is an increase in sales revenues a healthy sign for a corporation? (*Answer: yes*)
2. Should a firm's profits increase or decrease over time? (*Answer: increase*)

Although the answers to these two questions are obvious, you will find more detailed answers to these and other questions in this chapter.

The Psychology of Stock Investing

Why invest in stocks? To answer this question, consider the returns provided by stocks over a long period of time. For almost 100 years, stocks have returned an average return of a little less than 10 percent a year—well above the nation's inflation rate. In fact, stock returns were substantially higher than the returns provided by more conservative investments, including bonds, real estate, and other investment alternatives.[1] Simply put, investors who want larger returns choose stocks. And yet, you should remember three facts:

1. While the almost 10 percent average annual return on stock investments described above is enticing, keep in mind that the value of stocks can also decrease. The nation's economy, high inflation, changes in interest rates, and a host of other factors can cause

LO12.1

Identify the most important features of common and preferred stock.

ACTION ITEM

I understand how investors can profit from stock investments.

☐ Yes ☐ No

---

[1] "Money 101 Lesson 4: Basics of Investing," CNN/Money, **https://money.cnn.com/pf/money-essentials-stocks/index.html,** accessed February 6, 2020.

stocks to decrease in value. For example, many investors, fearing that the coronavirus would turn into a world pandemic, sold stocks at depressed prices in early 2020. These investors (and the financial markets) experienced huge losses—all over a two- to three-month period. Certainly, lower sales and lower profits or no profits can cause the stock for a specific company to decrease.

2. There is risk when you invest in stocks. Stock investments are not guaranteed. In fact, stock investments are a practical example of the risk-return ratio discussed in Chapter 11. Simply put: *Your potential return on any investment should be directly related to the risk you assume.*

3. The key to success with any investment program is often allowing your investments to work for you over a long period of time, and stocks are no exception. While some investors do make money in a short period of time, these speculators often lose money over time. A better approach is to invest for the long-term. A long-term investment program allows you to ride through the rough times and enjoy the good times.

Before you decide to purchase stocks, read this chapter. We want you to learn how to evaluate a stock and to make money from your investment decisions.

Why Corporations Issue Common Stock

common stock The most basic form of corporate ownership.

Common stock is the most basic form of ownership for a corporation. Corporations issue common stock to finance their business start-up costs and help pay for expansion and their ongoing business activities. Corporate managers prefer selling common stock as a method of financing for several reasons.

equity financing Money received from the owners or from the sale of shares of ownership in a business.

A FORM OF EQUITY *Important point:* Stock is equity financing. **Equity financing** is money received from the owners or from the sale of shares of ownership in a business. One reason corporations prefer selling stock is because the money obtained from equity financing doesn't have to be repaid and the company doesn't have to buy back shares from the stockholders. On the other hand, a stockholder who buys common stock may sell his or her stock to another individual.

dividend A distribution of money, stock, or other property that a corporation pays to stockholders.

DIVIDENDS NOT MANDATORY *Important point:* Dividends are paid out of profits, and dividend payments must be approved by the corporation's board of directors. A **dividend** is a distribution of money, stock, or other property that a corporation pays to stockholders. However, the last type of dividend is extremely unusual. Dividend policies vary among corporations, but most firms distribute between 30 and 70 percent of their earnings to stockholders. On the other hand, some corporations follow a policy of smaller or no dividend distributions to stockholders. In general, these are rapidly growing firms, such as Amazon (online sales), Alphabet, the parent company of Google (online websites), or Facebook (social networking), that retain a large share of their earnings for research and development, expansion, or major projects. On the other hand, utility companies, such as Duke Energy, Consolidated Edison, and American Electric Power, and other financially secure corporations may distribute 70 to 90 percent of their earnings.

proxy A legal form that lists the issues to be decided at a stockholders' meeting and requests that stockholders transfer their voting rights to some individual or individuals.

VOTING RIGHTS AND CONTROL OF THE COMPANY In return for the financing provided by selling common stock, management must make concessions to stockholders that may restrict corporate policies. For example, corporations are required to have an annual meeting at which stockholders have a right to vote, usually casting one vote per share of stock. Stockholders may vote in person or by proxy. A **proxy** is a legal form that lists the issues to be decided at a stockholders' meeting and requests that stockholders transfer their voting rights to some individual or individuals. Also, the common stockholders elect the corporation's board of directors and must approve major changes in corporate policies.

Why Investors Purchase Common Stock

Let's begin with two basic assumptions. First, no one invests in stocks in order to lose money. Second, every investor wants to earn a better-than-average return on stock investments. How do you make money by buying common stock? Basically, there are two ways: income from dividends and dollar appreciation of stock value,

record date The date on which a stockholder must be registered on the corporation's books in order to receive dividend payments.

INCOME FROM DIVIDENDS While the corporation's board members are under no legal obligation to pay dividends, most board members like to keep stockholders happy (and prosperous). Therefore, board members usually declare dividends if the corporation's profits are sufficient for them to do so. Since dividends are a distribution of profits, investors must be concerned about future profits.

If the board of directors declares a cash dividend, each common stockholder receives an equal amount per share. Although dividend policies vary, most corporations pay dividends on a quarterly basis. Notice in Exhibit 12–1 that Microsoft declared a quarterly dividend of $0.51 per share to stockholders who owned the stock on the record date of February 20, 2020. The **record date** is the date on which a stockholder must be registered on the corporation's books in order to receive dividend payments. When a stock is traded around the record date, the company must determine whether the buyer or the seller is entitled to the dividend. To solve this problem, this rule is followed: *Dividends remain with the stock until one business day before the record date.* On the business day before the record date, the stock begins selling *ex-dividend.* Investors who purchase an ex-dividend stock are not entitled to receive dividends for that quarter, and the dividend is paid to the previous owner of the stock.

For example, Microsoft declared a quarterly dividend of $0.51 per share to stockholders who owned its stock on February 20, 2020. The stock went ex-dividend on February 19, 2020, *one business day* before the February 20, 2020 date. A stockholder who purchased the stock on February 19, or after

FinTech for Financial Literacy

Tracking Dividends and Stock Prices

Question 1: What is the amount of dividends American Express paid stockholders over the last three years?

Questions 2: Has the price for a share of Facebook stock increased over the last five years?

Answer: Many investing websites, including Morningstar (**www.morningstar.com**), Yahoo! Finance (**finance.yahoo.com**), and Value Line (**valueline.com**) provide historical data for both dividends and stock prices that you can access with a simple click of your mouse. All you have to do is go to one of the above websites, enter the stock symbol for a specific corporation, and then locate the information for dividends or stock prices. Often, the information will be displayed in a table or interactive chart. It's that easy.

Information about Microsoft's dividend is available by using the Internet to access a corporation's website. The numbers above each of the columns correspond to the numbered entries in the list of explanations that appear at the bottom of the exhibit.

Exhibit **12–1**
Dividend Information

1	2	3	4	5
Company	**Amount of Dividend**	**Record Date**	**Ex-Dividend Date**	**Payable Date**
Microsoft	$0.51	February 20, 2020	February 19, 2020	March 12, 2020

1. The name of the company paying the dividend is Microsoft.

2. The dollar amount of the quarterly dividend is $0.51.

3. The record date is February 20, 2020. Stockholders must be registered on the corporate books by the record date in order to receive this quarterly dividend payment.

4. The ex-dividend date is February 19, 2020—one business day before the record date. Investors who purchase a stock on the ex-dividend date or after are not entitled to this quarterly dividend.

5. The dividend will be paid on March 12, 2020, to stockholders who own the stock on the record date.

Source: Microsoft Corporation, www.microsoft.com, accessed February 6, 2020.

was not entitled to this quarterly dividend payment. The actual dividend payment was paid on March 12, 2020, to stockholders who owned the stock on the record date. Investors are generally very conscious of the date on which a stock goes ex-dividend, and the dollar value of the stock may go down by the value of the dividend.

DOLLAR APPRECIATION OF STOCK VALUE The price for a share of stock is determined by how much a buyer is willing to pay for the stock. The price may change if potential investors or current stockholders receive information about the firm or its future prospects. For example, information about future sales revenues or expected earnings can increase *or* decrease the price for the firm's stock. In most cases, you purchase stock and then hold on to that stock for a period of time. If the price of the stock increases, you must decide whether to sell the stock at the higher price or continue to hold it. If you decide to sell the stock, the dollar amount of difference between the purchase price and the selling price represents your profit.

Let's assume that on January 31, 2018, you purchased 100 shares of Nike common stock at a cost of $67 a share. Your cost for the stock was $6,700 plus $25 in commission charges, for a total investment of $6,725. (*Note:* Commissions, a topic covered in "Commission Charges" in this chapter, are charged when you purchase stock *and* when you sell stock.) Let's also assume you held your 100 shares until January 31,2020, and then sold them for $98 a share. During the two-year period you owned Nike shares, the company paid dividends totaling $1.73 per share. Exhibit 12–2 shows your return on the investment. In this case, you made money because of dividend payments and because the stock increased in value from $67 to $98 per share. As Exhibit 12–2 shows, your total return is $3,223. Of course, if the stock's value should decrease or if the firm's board of directors reduces or votes to omit dividends, your return may be less than the original investment.

stock split A procedure in which the shares of stock owned by existing stockholders are divided into a larger number of shares.

WHAT HAPPENS WHEN A CORPORATION SPLITS ITS STOCK A **stock split** is a procedure in which the shares of stock owned by existing stockholders are divided into a larger number of shares. In late 2019, for example, the board of directors of Middlefield Banc Corporation, a financial company that provides various commercial banking services to businesses, professionals, small business owners, and retail customers in northeastern and central Ohio, declared a 2-for-1 stock split. After the stock split, a stockholder who had previously owned 100 shares now owned 200 shares. The most common stock splits are 2-for-1, 3-for-1, or 4-for-1.

Exhibit 12–2
Sample Stock Transaction for Nike

Assumptions			
100 shares of common stock purchased January 31, 2018, sold January 31, 2020; dividends of $1.73 per share for the two-year investment period.			
Costs When Purchased		**Return When Sold**	
100 shares @ $67 =	$6,700	100 shares @ $98 =	$9,800
Plus commission	+25	Minus commission	−25
Total investment	$6,725	Total return	$9,775
Transaction Summary			
Stock return			$ 9,775
Minus total investment			− 6,725
Profit from stock sale			$ 3,050
Plus dividends			+173
Total return for the transaction			$ 3,223

NOTE: The percentage of return for each year was 16% ($3,223 Total Return ÷ $6,725 Original Investment ÷ 2 years = 0.24, or 24 percent).

Why do corporations split their stock? In many cases, a firm's management has a theoretical ideal price range for the firm's stock. If the price per share of stock rises above the ideal range, a stock split brings the price per share back in line. In the case of Middlefield Banc Corporation, the 2-for-1 stock split reduced the price per share to one-half of the stock's value on the day prior to the split. The lower price per share was the result of dividing the dollar value of the company by a larger number of shares of common stock. Also, a decision to split a company's stock and the resulting lower price per share may make the stock more attractive to the investing public. This attraction is based on the belief that most corporations split their stock only when their financial future is improving and on the upswing.

Be warned: There are no guarantees that a stock's price per share will go up after a split. This is important to understand because investors often think that a stock split leads to immediate profits. Nothing could be farther from the truth. Here's why: The total market capitalization—the value of the company's stock and other securities—does not change because a corporation splits its stock. A company that has a market capitalization of $100 million before a 2-for-1 stock split is still worth $100 million after the split. Simply put, there are twice as many shares, but each share is worth half of its previous value before the stock split occurred. *If a stock's value does increase after a stock split, it increases because of the firm's financial performance after the split and not just because there are more shares of stock.*

Preferred Stock

In addition to or instead of purchasing common stock, you may purchase preferred stock. **Preferred stock** is a type of stock that gives the owner the advantage of receiving cash dividends before common stockholders are paid any dividends. This is the most important priority an investor in preferred stock enjoys. Unlike the amount of the dividend on common stock, the dollar amount of the dividend on preferred stock is known before the stock is purchased.

Preferred stocks are often referred to as "middle" investments because they represent an investment midway between common stock and corporate bonds. When compared to corporate bonds, the yield on preferred stocks is often higher than the yield on bonds to compensate for more risk. And yet, because it is a type of equity (ownership) financing, preferred stock is less secure than bonds (debt) issued by the same company. When compared to common stocks, preferred stocks are safer investments that offer more secure dividends. They are often purchased by individuals who need a predictable source of income greater than that offered by common stock investments. *For all other investors, preferred stocks lack the growth potential that common stocks offer and the safety of many corporate bond issues.*

When compared to the sale of common stock by corporations, the issuance of preferred stock is used less often and by only a few corporations. Keep in mind that dividends on preferred stock, as on common stock, may be omitted by action of the board of directors. While preferred stock does not represent a legal debt that must be repaid, if the firm is dissolved or declares bankruptcy, preferred stockholders do have first claim to the corporation's assets after creditors and bondholders. In reality, preferred stockholders don't receive anything if a corporation goes through bankruptcy because creditors must be paid before preferred stockholders.

preferred stock A type of stock that gives the owner the advantage of receiving cash dividends before common stockholders are paid any dividends.

PRACTICE QUIZ 12–1

1. Why do corporations sell stock? Why do investors purchase stock?

2. Why do corporations split their stock? Is a stock split good or bad for investors?

3. From an investor's viewpoint, what is the difference between common stock and preferred stock?

Evaluating a Stock Issue

Many people purchase investments without doing *any* research. They wouldn't buy a car without a test drive or purchase a home without comparing different houses, but for some unknown reason, they invest without doing their homework. The truth is that there is no substitute for a few hours of detective work when choosing an investment. In reality, it is important to evaluate not only the corporation that issues the individual stock you are interested in purchasing but also the industry in which the corporation operates. For example, if the automobile industry experiences lower sales and lower profits because of the number of people unemployed and higher interest rates for auto loans, most companies in the industry will find it difficult to increase sales and profits. Also, keep in mind that the nation's and even the world's economy—the big picture—may impact the way a corporation operates and cause a corporate stock to increase or decrease in value.

Another factor to consider when evaluating stocks is the amount of risk you are comfortable with. Some people are more willing to take risks than others. As mentioned in Chapter 11, younger investors choose more risk-oriented investments because they have more time to recover if their investments decrease in value. On the other hand, older investors tend to be more conservative and choose investments with less risk. Also, keep in mind that there are two different types of market risk you should consider when evaluating stock investments. *Systematic risk* occurs because of overall risks in the market and the economy. Factors such as an economic crisis, increasing interest rates, changes in consumer purchasing power, political activity, and wars all represent sources of systematic risk. Because this type of risk affects the entire market, it is not possible to eliminate the risk through diversification. *Unsystematic risk* affects a specific company or a specific industry. Because this type of risk affects one company or one industry, unsystematic risk can be reduced by diversifying an investment portfolio. For example, an investor who owns 20 different stocks in different industries can reduce unsystematic risk because she or he is well diversified. Anything that happens to one company in the investor's portfolio is not likely to wipe out the value of the entire portfolio.

A wealth of information is available to stock investors, and a logical place to start the evaluation process for stocks is with the classification of different types of stock investments described in Exhibit 12–3. Once you have identified stocks that may help you obtain your investment goals, you may want to use the Internet and other sources of information to evaluate a potential investment.

WHAT WOULD YOU DO? Assume you have $5,000 to invest and are trying to decide between two different companies. One company is a tobacco company that has increased sales, profits, and dividends over the last five years. The second company manufactures high-tech "green" products. The second company has only been in existence for three years, has seen a slow increase in sales and profits, and pays no dividends. You like the second company because it is a green company that could help to sustain the planet, but you like the financials of the tobacco company. Which company would you choose?

The Internet

In this section, we examine some websites that are logical starting points when evaluating a stock investment, but there are many more than those described.

Today most corporations have a website, and the information such sites provide is especially useful. First, it is easily accessible. All you have to do is type in the corporation's URL or use a search engine to locate the corporation's home page. Second, the information on the website may be more up-to-date and thorough than printed material obtained from

Type of Stock	Characteristics of This Type of Investment
Blue chip	A stock that is issued by large, stable corporations that often have a history of paying dividends and that generally attracts conservative investors.
Cyclical	A stock that follows the business cycle of advances and declines in the economy.
Defensive	A stock that remains stable during declines in the economy.
Growth	A stock issued by a corporation that has the potential of increasing sales revenues and earning profits above the average of all firms in the economy.
Income	An investment that pays regular and often higher-than-average dividends.
Large-cap	A stock that is issued by a corporation that has a large amount of capitalization in excess of $10 billion.
Micro-cap	A stock that is issued by a company that has a capitalization of between $50 million and $300 million.
Mid-cap	A stock that is issued by a corporation that has a capitalization of between $2 billion and $10 billion.
Penny	A stock that typically trades for less than $5 per share (or in some cases, less than $1 per share) and has a small amount of capitalization.
Small-cap	A stock that is issued by a company that has a capitalization of between $300 million and $2 billion.

Exhibit **12–3**

Classification of Stock Investments

When evaluating a stock investment, investors often classify stocks into these 10 categories.

the corporation or outside sources. Once at the corporation's home page, look for a link to "investor relations." Just by clicking on a button, you can access information on the firm's sales, earnings, and other financial factors that could affect the value of the company's stock. Keep in mind that the information on a company's website is provided by the company and in some cases is created to showcase the company. Read between the lines, and verify any information or financial information that looks too good to be true.

You can also use Google, Yahoo!, and other search engines to obtain information about stock investments. Take a look at Exhibit 12–4, which illustrates a portion of the summary page taken from Yahoo! Finance for Walmart, the world's largest retailer. In addition to the current price, the Yahoo! Finance website provides even more specific information if you click on the buttons for Chart, Conversations, Statistics, Historical Data, Profile, Financials, and Analysis that are part of the screen for each corporation. How about picking a company like The Gap (symbol GPS), Coca-Cola (symbol KO), or Amazon (symbol AMZN) and going exploring on the Internet? To begin, enter the web address for Yahoo! Finance (**finance.yahoo.com**) in your computer's browser. Then enter the symbol for one of the above corporations in the Quote Lookup box and click the tab with the magnifying glass on the right. You'll be surprised at the amount of information you can obtain with a click of your mouse.

In addition to company websites and Internet search engines, you can access personal finance websites such as the Motley Fool (**fool.com**), Kiplinger (**www.kiplinger.com**), and The Balance (**thebalance.com/**). In addititon, the following four websites can also help you monitor financial news that could affect your investments: The Street (**thestreet. com**), Market Watch (**marketwatch.com**), MSN Money (**money.msn.com**), and CNN Business (**cnn.com/business**).

Stock Advisory Services

Many serious investors use information provided by stock advisory services. The information ranges from simple alphabetical listings to detailed financial reports. While some

Exhibit 12–4 A Portion of the Opening Page from the Yahoo! Finance Website for Walmart

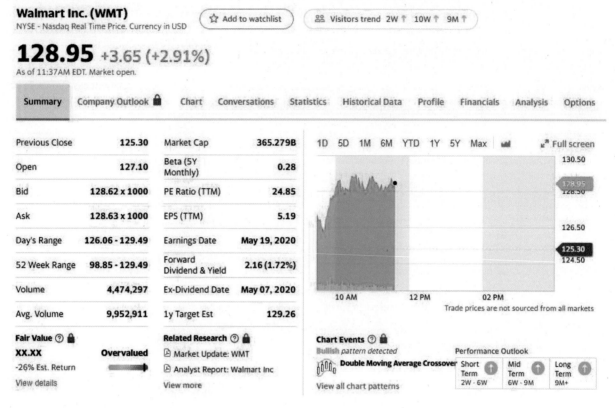

Yahoo! Finance, https://finance.yahoo.com/quote/WMT?p=WMT&. tsrc=fin-srch, accessed April 14, 2020.

of the information provided by these services is free, often there is a charge for the more detailed online information you may need to evaluate a stock investment.

Value Line (**valueline.com**), Morningstar (**morningstar.com**), and Zacks (**zacks.com**) are three widely used advisory services that provide detailed research for stock investors. Here we will examine a detailed report for Microsoft, one of the world's leading software companies, that is published in *The Value Line Investment Survey* (see Exhibit 12–5).

Because there is a lot of information about Microsoft in Exhibit 12–5, it helps to break down the entire Value Line report into different sections. For example:

- Overall ratings for timeliness, safety, and technical, along with price information, projections for the price of a share of stock, and total return are included at the top of the report.

- Detailed information about revenues per share, earnings per share, dividends, total revenues, net profit, capital structure, and other important financial information is included in the middle and along the left side of the report.

- Information about the type of business and prospects for the future is provided toward the bottom and in the lower right-hand corner.

While other stock advisory services provide basically the same types of information as that in Exhibit 12–5, it is the investor's job to interpret such information and decide whether the company's stock is a good investment.

Newspaper Coverage and Corporate News

Although some newspapers have eliminated or reduced the amount of financial coverage they offer, *The Wall Street Journal* and most metropolitan newspapers still contain some

Exhibit **12–5** **Value Line Report for Microsoft Corporation**

MICROSOFT NDQ-MSFT	RECENT PRICE 165.46	P/E RATIO 29.3 (Trailing: 33.2 / Median: 16.0)	RELATIVE P/E RATIO 1.58	DIV'D YLD 1.2%	VALUE LINE

TIMELINESS **1** Raised 8/16/19	High:	36.0	31.5	31.6	29.5	32.9	39.0	50.0	56.8	64.1	87.5	116.2	159.5	Target Price Range 2022 2023 2024
SAFETY **1** Raised 5/26/06	Low:	17.5	14.9	22.7	23.7	26.3	26.3	34.6	39.7	48.0	61.9	83.8	97.2	
TECHNICAL **3** Raised 1/3/20														
BETA 1.10 (1.00 = Market)														

LEGENDS
— 19.0 x "Cash Flow" p sh
.... Relative Price Strength
Options: Yes
Shaded area indicates recession

18-Month Target Price Range
Low-High   Midpoint (% to Mid)
$129-$222 $176 (5%)

2022-24 PROJECTIONS
	Price	Gain	Ann'l Total Return
High	205	(+25%)	7%
Low	170	(+5%)	2%

Institutional Decisions
	1Q2019	2Q2019	3Q2019
to Buy	1449	1307	1347
to Sell	1465	1579	1548
Hld's(000)	5539998	5600565	5567498

Percent shares traded: 21 14 7

% TOT. RETURN 12/19
	THIS STOCK	VL ARITH.* INDEX
1 yr.	57.6	23.6
3 yr.	167.8	26.5
5 yr.	278.2	42.2

2003	2004	2005	2006	2007	2008	2009	2010	2011	2012	2013	2014	2015	2016	2017	2018	2019	2020	© VALUE LINE PUB. LLC	22-24
3.00	3.39	3.72	4.40	5.45	6.60	6.56	7.21	8.35	8.80	9.34	10.54	11.66	11.78	12.54	14.38	16.47	18.80	Revenues per sh A	26.50
1.12	1.15	1.27	1.34	1.65	2.16	1.92	2.47	3.09	3.12	3.15	3.31	3.47	3.71	4.26	5.28	6.35	7.40	"Cash Flow" per sh	10.50
.97	1.04	1.16	1.20	1.42	1.87	1.62	2.10	2.69	2.72	2.65	2.63	2.65	2.79	3.08	3.88	4.75	5.65	Earnings per sh B	8.00
.08	.16	.32	.34	.40	.44	.52	.52	.64	.80	.89	1.12	1.24	1.44	1.56	1.68	1.80	1.99	Div'ds Decl'd per sh E■	3.00
.08	.10	.08	.16	.24	.35	.35	.23	.28	.28	.51	.67	.74	1.07	1.15	1.52	1.82	2.00	Cap'l Spending per sh	2.00
5.69	6.89	4.49	3.99	3.32	3.97	4.44	5.33	6.82	7.92	9.48	10.90	9.98	9.22	9.39	10.77	13.39	15.85	Book Value per sh D	22.25
10718	10862	10710	10062	9380.0	9151.0	8908.0	8668.0	8376.0	8381.0	8328.0	8239.0	8027.0	7808.0	7708.0	7677.0	7643.0	7575.0	Common Shs Outst'g C	7425.0
26.1	25.8	22.9	21.7	19.9	16.3	13.4	13.1	9.6	10.4	11.2	14.0	17.0	18.1	20.2	22.1	23.7		Avg Ann'l P/E Ratio	25.0
1.49	1.36	1.22	1.17	1.06	.98	.89	.83	.60	.66	.63	.74	.86	.95	1.02	1.19	1.34		Relative P/E Ratio	1.40
.3%	.6%	1.2%	1.3%	1.4%	1.4%	2.4%	1.9%	2.5%	2.8%	3.0%	3.0%	2.7%	2.9%	2.5%	2.0%	1.6%		Avg Ann'l Div'd Yield	1.5%

CAPITAL STRUCTURE as of 12/31/19
Total Debt $69608 mill. Due in 5 Yrs $19720 mill.
LT Debt $63361 mill.   LT Interest $2175 mill.
(37% of Cap'l)

Leases, Uncapitalized $1678 mill.

No Defined Benefit Pension Plan
Pfd Stock None

Common Stock 7,606,047,010 shs.
as of 1/24/20
MARKET CAP: $1263 billion (Large Cap)

	58437	62484	69943	73723	77811	86833	93580	91964	96657	110360	125843	142500	Revenues ($mill) A	197500
	39.2%	42.9%	42.8%	41.9%	40.3%	38.0%	36.5%	37.6%	39.4%	41.1%	43.4%	45.0%	Operating Margin	45.5%
	2562.0	2673.0	2766.0	2967.0	3755.0	5212.0	5957.0	6622.0	8778.0	10261	11682	12500	Depreciation ($mill)	17000
	14569	18760	23150	23171	22453	22074	21885	22329	24084	30267	36830	43460	Net Profit ($mill)	61000
	26.5%	25.0%	17.5%	18.6%	19.6%	20.7%	23.3%	18.8%	20.2%	17.0%	15.7%	17.0%	Income Tax Rate	17.0%
	24.9%	30.0%	33.1%	31.4%	28.9%	25.4%	23.4%	24.3%	24.9%	27.4%	29.3%	30.5%	Net Profit Margin	30.9%
	22246	29529	46144	52396	64049	68621	74854	80303	95324	111174	106132	100000	Working Cap'l ($mill)	125000
	3746.0	4939.0	11921	10713	12601	20645	27808	40783	76073	72242	66662	68000	Long-Term Debt ($mill)	80000
	39558	46175	57083	66363	78944	89784	80083	71997	72394	82718	102330	120000	Shr. Equity ($mill) D	165000
	33.6%	36.8%	33.8%	30.3%	24.7%	20.3%	20.6%	20.3%	17.0%	20.4%	22.6%	23.5%	Return on Total Cap'l	25.5%
	36.8%	40.6%	40.6%	34.9%	28.4%	24.6%	27.3%	31.0%	33.3%	36.6%	36.0%	36.0%	Return on Shr. Equity	37.0%
	25.5%	30.7%	31.5%	25.3%	19.0%	14.7%	15.0%	15.7%	16.9%	21.2%	22.5%	23.5%	Retained to Com Eq	23.5%
	31%	24%	22%	28%	33%	40%	45%	49%	49%	42%	37%	35%	All Div'ds to Net Prof	37%

CURRENT POSITION
($MILL.)	2018	2019	12/31/19
Cash Assets	133768	133819	134253
Receivables	26481	29524	23525
Inventory (Avg Cst)	2662	2063	1823
Other	6751	10146	7473
Current Assets	169662	175552	167074
Accts Payable	8617	9382	8811
Debt Due	3998	5516	6247
Unearned Revenue	28905	32676	27343
Other	16968	21846	17239
Current Liab.	58488	69420	59640

ANNUAL RATES
of change (per sh)	Past 10 Yrs.	Past 5 Yrs.	Est'd '17-'19 to '22-'24
Revenues	9.0%	8.5%	12.0%
"Cash Flow"	10.5%	10.5%	13.0%
Earnings	9.0%	8.0%	14.0%
Dividends	14.0%	12.5%	11.5%
Book Value	11.0%	3.5%	12.5%

QUARTERLY REVENUES ($ mill.) A
Fiscal Year Ends	Sep.30	Dec.31	Mar.31	Jun.30	Full Fiscal Year
2016	21660	25506	22156	22642	91964
2017	22334	26066	23557	24700	96657
2018	24538	28918	26819	30085	110360
2019	29084	32471	30571	33717	125843
2020	33055	36906	37939		142500

EARNINGS PER SHARE AB
Fiscal Year Ends	Sep.30	Dec.31	Mar.31	Jun.30	Full Fiscal Year
2016	.70	.77	.63	.69	2.79
2017	.76	.83	.73	.75	3.08
2018	.84	.96	.95	1.13	3.88
2019	1.14	1.10	1.14	1.37	4.75
2020	1.38	1.51	1.32	1.44	5.65

QUARTERLY DIVIDENDS PAID E■
Cal-endar	Mar.31	Jun.30	Sep.30	Dec.31	Full Year
2016	.36	.36	.39	.39	1.50
2017	.39	.39	.42	.42	1.62
2018	.42	.42	.42	.46	1.72
2019	.46	.46	.46	.51	1.89
2020					

BUSINESS: Microsoft Corp. is the largest independent maker of software. It develops and sells software products for a wide range of computing environments in consumer and enterprise markets. Hardware products include the *Xbox* video game console and *Surface* laptops. Revenue sources in fiscal 2019: Productivity & Business Processes, 33%; Intelligent Cloud, 31%; More Personal Com-puting, 36%. R&D, 13.4% of 2019 revenues. Employed 144,000 at 6/30/19. Stock owners: William H. Gates, 1.34%;, other offs. & dirs., 0.05%; The Vanguard Group, 7.8%; BlackRock, Inc., 6.6%; (10/19 proxy). Chrmn: John W. Thompson. CEO: Satya Nadella. Inc.: Washington. Addr.: One Microsoft Way, Redmond, Washington 98052-6399. Tel.: 425-882-8080. Internet: www.microsoft.com.

Microsoft's revenue and earnings should continue moving forward nicely. The company's published key perform-ance metrics are generally trending in the positive direction, particularly in its Com-mercial business where commercial book-ings, cloud revenue, and cloud gross mar-gin are each advancing nicely. Meanwhile, our sense is *Office 365* will remain an im-portant factor in Microsoft's fortunes, both in the commercial and consumer arenas. We look for seat growth in commercial and subscriber growth in consumer to remain favorable. In addition, the company's col-laborative offering, *Teams*, which appears to be well received given the rapid adop-tion, should work to expand *Office 365* in commercial markets.
Server products and cloud services are progressing at a good pace. Micro-soft *Azure* is continuing to advance at a high rate, and the platform's gross margin is expanding with increasing scale and the offering of higher-valued services. Tradi-tional server products should remain a sweet spot, as well, as large corporations balance their needs with respect to the pri-vate/public clouds. That said, the cloud platform business is very competitive, with Amazon Web Services (AWS) and Google Cloud staking claims. At this juncture, AWS seems to have the lead, but *Azure* is getting a lot of attention, particularly given Microsoft's long-term relationships with its commercial customers. We would also not discount Google's efforts with its cloud platform, which seems to be getting better traction in the market.
These high-quality shares have been stellar performers. We envision average annual revenue growth of 11%-12% over the next few years, with earnings (and net income) progressing at a 12%-13% rate. Dividends may advance at a somewhat faster pace, say 14%. In this regard, the dividend payout should range between 35% and 37%, as shares outstanding con-tinue to trend lower. That said, at a price/earnings ratio of nearly 30, there is the question whether the stock's current valuation is on the rich side, despite the company's prospects. Indeed, one may posit that earnings may need some time to catch up to the stock's current price, making new commitments less interesting.
Charles Clark   *February 7, 2020*

(A) Fiscal year ends June 30th.
(B) Diluted earnings. Quarters may not add to total. Excl. nonrec. items: '03, d5¢; '04, d29¢; '05, d4¢; '12, d72¢; '13, d7¢; '15, d$1.17;
'16, d70¢; '17, d37¢; '18, d$1.75; '19, d33¢.
(C) In mill.
(D) Includes intangibles. In 2019: $42.0 billion, $5.50 a share.
(E) Dividends historically paid in March, June, Sept., and Dec. ■Dividend reinvestment plan available. Special dividend of $3.00 a share paid December 2, 2004.

Company's Financial Strength	A++
Stock's Price Stability	80
Price Growth Persistence	90
Earnings Predictability	85

To subscribe call 1-800-VALUELINE

Next earnings report late April.

Digital Financial Literacy with. . .

One of the missions of the U.S. Securities and Exchange Commission (SEC) is to protect investors. To fulfill this mission, the SEC provides investors with top-notch online information they can use to become better investors. One site sponsored by the SEC is Investor.gov (**investor.gov**). This easy-to-use site provides information written in accessible language that is easy to understand. Some of the topics on the home page of the **Investor.gov** site will immediately catch your attention and make you want to dig deeper and see what's behind the tabs. Tabs at the top of the home page include:

- **Introduction to Investing**—discusses how to establish financial goals, how to save and invest, and how the stock market works.
- **Financial Tools and Calculators**—explains how to use the SEC's database to checkout an investment professional's background and calculators to help you plan for retirement.

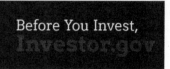

Before You Invest,

- **Protect Your Investment**—describes information about different investment scams and how to avoid the bad guys.
- **Additional Resources**—provides an easy-to-use compound interest calculator to help you determine what your investments will be worth in the future.

The Investor.gov site (**investor.gov**) also provides additional links to other topics that you may want to examine to fine-tune your investment program. Conclusion: Take a look and see why investors—especially beginning investors—think this site's a winner!

ACTION STEPS FOR. . .

. . .Information Literacy

Click on the "Protect Your Investment" tab at the top of the **Investor.gov** site. Then click on "Types of Fraud." Choose one type of fraud listed and prepare a one-page summary of how the fraud works and tips on how you could avoid becoming a victim.

. . .Financial Literacy

Companies are required to report information to the SEC in a form 10-K report. To learn how to read a 10-K, go to the **Investor.gov** site and click on "Introduction to Investing." Next, click on the link "Researching Investments." Then choose the link "How to Read a 10-K." Based on the information, prepare a video or audio presentation describing the information contained in a 10-K that an investor might use to evaluate a company's stock.

. . .Digital Literacy

Click on the "Introduction to Investing" tab on the **Investor. gov** site. Next click on "Investment Products." Then choose the link for "Stocks." After considering the information for stocks, prepare a report that describes (1) what are stocks, (2) why investors purchase stocks, and (3) what are the benefits and risks of investing in stocks.

information about stocks. Although not all newspapers print exactly the same information, they usually provide the basic information. Stocks are listed alphabetically, so your first task is to move down the table to find the stock you're interested in. Then, to read the stock quotation, you simply read across the table. Typical information provided by newspapers includes the name of the company, stock symbol, current price information, and net change from one day to the next.

The federal government requires corporations selling new issues of securities to disclose information about corporate earnings, assets and liabilities, products or services, and the qualifications of top management in a prospectus. In addition, all publicly owned corporations provide an annual report to stockholders and investors that contains detailed financial data and information about the corporation. For most corporations, all it takes to obtain this information is a visit to the corporation's website, a call to a toll-free phone number, or a written request to the corporation's headquarters.

In addition to corporate publications, you can access the Securities and Exchange Commission website (www.sec.gov) to obtain financial and other important information that a corporation has reported to the federal government.

Finally, many periodicals, including *Bloomberg Businessweek, Fortune, Forbes, Money, Kiplinger's Personal Finance,* and similar publications, contain information about stock investing in both print and online versions.

PRACTICE QUIZ 12–2

1. Describe how each of the following sources of investment information could help you evaluate a stock investment.

Source of Information	Type of Information	How Could This Help
The Internet		
Stock advisory services		
A newspaper		
Securities and Exchange Commission website		
Business periodicals		

2. What is the difference between a prospectus and an annual report?

3. Using the Value Line report in Exhibit 12–5, pick three financial measures and describe how they could help you evaluate a corporate stock.

Numerical Measures That Influence Investment Decisions

How do you determine whether the time is right to buy or sell a particular stock? Good question! Unfortunately, there is no simple answer. In addition to the material discussed in the section "**Evaluating a Stock Issue**," many investors rely on numerical measures to decide when to buy or sell a stock. We begin this section by examining the relationship between a stock's price and a corporation's earnings.

Why Corporate Earnings Are Important

Many financial experts believe that a corporation's ability or inability to generate earnings in the future may be one of the most significant factors that account for an increase or decrease in the value of a stock. Simply put, higher earnings generally equate to higher stock prices. Unfortunately, the reverse is also true. If a corporation's earnings decline,

money minute focus

The Dow Jones Industrial Average measures 30 different stocks that are considered leaders in the economy. (Closing values as of end of December for 2010, 2012, 2014, 2016, 2018, and February 7, 2020.)

Year	Value
2010	11,578
2012	12,938
2014	17,983
2016	19,763
2018	23,062
2020	29,103

Source: Yahoo! Finance, https://finance.yahoo.com/quote/%5EDJI/ history?period1=1482624000&period2=1483142400&interval= 1d&filter=history&frequency=1d, accessed February 7, 2020.

LO12.3

Analyze the numerical measures that cause a stock to increase or decrease in value.

ACTION ITEM

I understand how financial calculations can help me pick a stock that will be profitable.

☐ Agree ☐ Disagree

earnings per share A corporation's earnings divided by the number of outstanding shares of a firm's common stock.

price-earnings (PE) ratio The price of a share of stock divided by the corporation's earnings per share of stock.

generally the stock's price will also decline. Corporate earnings are reported in the investor relations section on a corporation's website and in the firm's annual report. You can also obtain information about a corporation's current earnings by using a professional advisory service or accessing the Yahoo! Finance website or one of the other websites described in the "**Evaluating a Stock Issue**" section.

EARNINGS PER SHARE Many investors calculate earnings per share to evaluate the financial health of a corporation. **Earnings per share** are a corporation's earnings divided by the number of outstanding shares of a firm's common stock. Given the information in the following example, global food manufacturer General Mills earns $2.90 per share.

EXAMPLE: Earnings per Share (General Mills)

General Mills's earnings are $1,753 million. Also assume that General Mills has 605 million shares of common stock. Earnings per share are $2.90 as illustrated below.

$$\text{Earnings per share} = \frac{\text{Earnings}}{\text{Number of shares outstanding}}$$

$$= \frac{\$1,753 \text{ million}}{605 \text{ million}} = \$2.90$$

Most stockholders consider the amount of earnings per share important because it is a measure of the company's profitability. No meaningful average for this measure exists, mainly because the number of shares of a firm's stock is subject to change via stock splits and stock dividends. *As a general rule, however, an increase in earnings per share is a healthy sign for any corporation and its stockholders.*

PRICE-EARNINGS RATIO Another calculation, the price-earnings ratio, can be used to evaluate a potential stock investment. The **price-earnings (PE) ratio** is the price of a share of stock divided by the corporation's earnings per share of stock. Given the information in the following example, the PE ratio for ULTA Beauty—the retailer famous for cosmetics, fragrances, skin care, and hair care products—is 27.

EXAMPLE: Price-Earnings (PE) Ratio (ULTA BEAUTY)

ULTA Beauty's common stock is selling for $296 a share. ULTA Beauty's earnings per share are $11. The corporation's price-earnings ratio is 27, as illustrated below.

$$\text{Price-earnings (PE) ratio} = \frac{\text{Price per share}}{\text{Earnings per share}}$$

$$= \frac{\$296}{\$11} = 27$$

Generally, a price-earnings ratio gives investors an idea of how much they are paying for a company's earning power. The higher the price-earnings ratio, the more investors are paying for earnings. For example, an investor might say that ULTA Beauty stock is selling for 27 times its current earnings. Historically, the average PE ratio for the stock market is usually between 15 and 25 for any specific year. Based on the Standard & Poor's 500 stock index, the PE ratio for the market was 24 at the beginning of 2020. Stocks with high price-earnings ratios (those above the average PE ratio for the market) often indicate investor optimism because of the expectation of higher earnings in the future. If future earnings do increase, the stock usually becomes more valuable in the future. On the other hand, having a low price-earnings ratio (below the average for the market) indicates that investors have lower earnings expectations for a company's stock. If future earnings decrease or don't maintain the same level of growth, the stock will become less valuable in the future. Stocks with low price-earnings ratios tend to be issued by established, large corporations or corporations in mature industries.

When researching a stock, comparing the PE ratio of one company to other companies in the same industry is usually the most helpful. It is also possible to compare a company's PE ratio against the company's own historical PE ratios or the market in general.

PROJECTED EARNINGS Both earnings per share and the price-earnings ratio are based on historical numbers—in other words, what the company has done in the past. With this fact in mind, many investors will also look at earnings estimates for a corporation. The MarketWatch website or similar financial websites provide earnings estimates for major corporations. At the time of publication, for example, MarketWatch provided the following earnings per share estimates for Starbucks, the company that offers coffee, espresso beverages, and complementary food products.[2]

Starbucks	This Year	Next Year
Yearly earnings per share estimates	$2.82 per share	$3.44 per share

From an investor's standpoint, a projected increase in earnings from $2.82 per share to $3.44 per share is a good sign. By using the same projected earnings amount, it is possible to calculate a projected price-earnings ratio or a projected price per share of stock. Of course, you should remember that these are estimates and are not "etched in stone." Changes that affect the economy, industry, or company's sales and profit amounts could cause analysts to revise these estimates.

Dividend Yield and Total Return

One of the calculations investors use most frequently to monitor the value of their investments is the dividend yield. The **dividend yield** is the annual dividend amount divided by the stock's current price per share. The dividend yield for Walmart—-the world's largest retailer—is 1.72 percent, as calculated below.

dividend yield The annual dividend amount divided by the stock's current price per share.

EXAMPLE: Dividend Yield (Walmart)

A share of Walmart stock pays an annual dividend of $2.16 and is currently selling for $125.30 a share. The current dividend yield is 1.72 percent.

$$\text{Dividend yield} = \frac{\text{Annual dividend amount}}{\text{Current price per share}}$$

$$= \frac{\$2.16}{\$125.30} = 0.0172, \text{ or } 1.72 \text{ percent}$$

An increase in dividend yield is a healthy sign for any stock investment. A dividend yield of 3 percent is better than a 1.72 percent dividend yield.

Although the dividend yield calculation is useful, you should also consider whether the stock's price per share is increasing or decreasing in dollar value.

Total return is a calculation that includes not only the yearly dividend amount but also any increase or decrease in the original purchase price of the investment. In the example below, the total return for Pepsico—the parent company of Pepsi—is $3,380.

total return A calculation that includes the yearly dividend amount as well as any increase or decrease in the original purchase price of the investment.

---

[2] MarketWatch, **http://www.marketwatch.com/investing/stock/sbux/analystestimates,** accessed February 8, 2020.

EXAMPLE: Total Return (Pepsico)

Assume you own 100 shares of Pepsico stock that you purchased for $113 a share and hold your stock for one year before selling it for $143 a share. The increase in value is $3,000. Dividend income totaled $380. Your total return is $3,380.

$$\text{Total return} = \text{Dividends} + \text{Capital gain}$$
$$= \$380 + \$3,000 = \$3,380$$

The dividend of $380 results from the payment of dividends for one year ($3.80 per-share dividend × 100 shares). The capital gain of $3,000 results from the increase in the stock price from $113 a share to $143 a share ($30 per-share increase × 100 shares). Of course, commissions to buy and sell your stock, a topic covered in the next section, would reduce your total return.

WHAT WOULD YOU DO? You are trying to decide which of the two companies described below would be the best investment. Based on the information below, which would you choose? To help you make your decision, you may want to use the earnings per share, price-earnings (PE) ratio, and dividend yield calculations illustrated in this section and work the tryout problems in the nearby *Figure It Out!* feature.

Company	Price per share	Annual dividend	Current earnings	Projected earnings next year	Number of shares outstanding
Jackson Utility Construction	$22	$0.30	$34 million	$39 million	20 million shares
West Coast Homes	$46	$0.52	$182 million	$142 million	130 million shares

---

Beta, Book Value, and Other Factors That Affect the Price of a Stock

beta A measure reported in many financial publications that compares the volatility associated with a specific stock issue with the volatility of the stock market or an index such as the Standard & Poor's 500 stock index.

The **beta** is a measure reported in many financial publications that compares the volatility associated with a corporation stock issue with the volatility of the stock market or an index such as the Standard & Poor's 500 Index. The beta for the market is 1.0. The majority of stocks have betas between 0.5 and 2.0. Generally, conservative stocks have low betas, whereas more speculative stocks have betas greater than one. In the example below, the expectation is that Sony stock with a beta of 1.40 will increase by 14 percent if the market increases by 10 percent.

EXAMPLE: Beta Calculation (Sony)

Assume that the overall stock market increases by 10 percent and that Sony has a beta of 1.40. Based on the calculation below, Sony stock will increase 14 percent when the market increases 10 percent.

$$\text{Volatility for a stock} = \text{Increase in overall market} \times \text{Beta for a specific stock}$$
$$= 10 \text{ percent} \times 1.40$$
$$= 0.14, \text{ or } 14 \text{ percent}$$

Figure It Out!

Calculations Can Improve Investment Decisions!

Numbers, numbers, numbers! The truth is that if you are going to be a good investor, you must learn the numbers game. As mentioned in the text, many calculations can help you gauge the value of a potential stock investment. These same calculations can help you decide if the time is right to buy, hold, or sell a stock investment.

Now it's your turn. Use the formulas in this section and the following financial information for Bozo Oil Company to calculate the earnings per share, price-earnings (PE) ratio, and dividend yield:

After-tax income	$7,500,000
Dividend amount	$1.20
Price per share	$60
Number of shares outstanding	2,500,000

Because individual stocks generally move in the same direction as the stock market, most betas are positive, but it is possible for a stock to have a negative beta. A negative beta occurs when a corporation's stock moves in the opposite direction compared to the stock market as a whole.

The **book value** for a share of stock is determined by deducting all liabilities from the corporation's assets and dividing the remainder by the number of outstanding shares of common stock. Although little correlation may exist between the price of a stock and its book value, book value is widely reported in financial publications. Therefore, it deserves mention. For Southwest Airlines—a major passenger airline in the United States—book value is $17.20 per share, as illustrated below.

book value Determined by deducting all liabilities from the corporation's assets and dividing the remainder by the number of outstanding shares of common stock.

EXAMPLE: Book Value (Southwest Airlines)

Assume Southwest Airlines has assets of $26,243 million and liabilities of $16,390 million. The company has also issued 573 million shares of stock.

$$\text{Book value} = \frac{\text{Assets} - \text{Liabilities}}{\text{Number of shares outstanding}}$$

$$= \frac{\$26,243 \text{ million} - \$16,390 \text{ million}}{573 \text{ million}} = \$17.20 \text{ per share}$$

Some investors believe they have found a bargain when a stock's current price per share is about the same as or lower than its book value. *Be warned:* Book value calculations may be misleading because the dollar amount of assets used in the above formula may be understated or overstated on the firm's financial statements. From a practical standpoint, most financial experts suggest that book value is just another piece of the puzzle, and you must consider other factors along with book value when evaluating a possible stock investment.

Two other factors can affect the price of a stock. First, predicting the future value for a share of stock is a practical example of the time value of money concepts presented in Chapter 1. The price that a successful investor is willing to pay for a share of stock is determined by:

- The amount of dividends you expect to receive in the future, or

- A potential increase in the price for a share of stock, and/or
- A combination of future dividends and a potential increase in the price of the stock.

Second, always remember that the price for a share of stock is determined by what another investor is willing to pay for it. While most successful investors use investment research and financial calculations to choose stock investments, there are times when investors may pay a high, inflated price for a share of stock. For example, the term **stock market bubble** is used to describe a situation in which stocks are trading at prices above their actual worth. Often the high stock prices are driven by investor optimism and irrational expectations. Unfortunately, the bubble for a specific stock can burst when a company lowers estimates for future earnings, reduces or omits dividend payments to stockholders, or experiences product failures, or when stockholders begin to sell the stock for any other reason. Stock market bubbles may also burst because of an economic slowdown, high unemployment rates, higher interest rates, and other factors that affect the economy.

stock market bubble A situation in which stocks are trading at prices above their actual worth.

Making a Decision to Buy, Hold, or Sell a Stock: A Summary

Many investors have trouble making the decision to buy, hold, or sell a stock. There is always a danger of overlooking important relevant information when you use a summary like the one below. Still, it does help to develop a plan using the following suggestions to evaluate individual stocks.

- Evaluate each investment. Too often, investors purchase or sell a stock without doing their homework. A much better approach is to become an expert and learn all you can about the company (and its stock). The information in the section "**Evaluating a Stock Issue**" and this section will help you play detective to find the right stock. Also, *Your Personal Financial Plan Sheet 38* will help you summarize important information.

- Access a professional advisory service such as Value Line, Morningstar, or Zacks. As mentioned in this chapter, you may have to register or pay for some of the detailed information you need to evaluate a potential stock. It may be possible to access some information from advisory services on the Internet or by visiting a library.

- Analyze the firm's finances. Look at the company's financial information, which is available in the firm's annual report or on many investment websites. Examine trends for sales, profits, dividends, and other important financial data.

- Track the firm's product line. If the firm's products or services become obsolete and the company fails to introduce new, state-of-the art products or services, its sales—and, ultimately, profits—may take a nosedive.

- Monitor economic developments. An economic recovery or an economic recession may cause the value of a stock investment to increase or decrease. Also, watch the unemployment rate, inflation rate, interest rates, productivity rates, and similar economic indicators.

- Be patient. For most people, stock investing is long-term and is not a method to get rich overnight. The secret to success in making money with stocks is often time. If you choose quality stocks based on quality research and are willing to wait, eventually your stock investments will provide average or even above-average returns. Remember: There are no guarantees when investing in stocks. Larger returns are always accompanied by increased risk when investing in stocks.

Sheet 38 Evaluating Corporate Stocks

PRACTICE QUIZ 12–3

1. Explain the relationship between corporate earnings and a stock's market value.

2. Write the formula for the following stock calculations, and then describe how this calculation could help you make a decision to buy or sell a stock.

Calculation	What Is the Formula?	Why Is This Calculation Useful?
Earnings per share		
Price-earnings (PE) ratio		
Dividend yield		
Total return		
Beta		
Book value		

Buying and Selling Stocks

To purchase common or preferred stock, you generally have to work through a brokerage firm. In turn, the brokerage firm buys the stock for you in either the primary or secondary market. In the **primary market**, you purchase financial securities, via an investment bank or other representative, from the issuer of those securities. An **investment bank** is a financial firm that assists corporations in raising funds, usually by helping to sell new security issues.

New security issues sold through an investment bank can be issued by corporations that have sold stocks and securities before and need to sell new issues to raise additional financing to expand, to increase the firm's cash balance, or for any valid business purpose. New securities can also be initial public offerings. An **initial public offering (IPO)** occurs when a corporation sells stock to the general public for the first time. In 2020, Casper Sleep—a firm that provides mattresses and other sleep products through its e-commerce website, its retail stores, and a network of retail partners—used an IPO to raise just over $100 million.[3] The money from the IPO can be used for expansion or any other activity to create a larger and more successful company.

Be warned: The promise of quick profits often lures investors to purchase IPOs. An IPO is generally classified as a high-risk investment—one made in the hope of earning a relatively large profit in a short time. Depending on the corporation selling the new security, IPOs are usually too speculative for most people.

Once stocks are sold in the primary market, they can be sold time and again in the secondary market. The **secondary market** is a market for existing financial securities that are currently traded among investors. A corporation does not receive money each time its stock is bought or sold in the secondary market. However, the ability to obtain cash by selling stock investments is one reason why investors purchase corporate stock. Without the secondary market, investors would not purchase stock in the primary market because there would be no way to sell shares to other investors.

Secondary Markets for Stocks

When you purchase stock in the secondary market, the transaction is completed on a securities exchange or through the over-the-counter market.

[3] Javier E. David, "Casper Ends First Day Up Nearly 13%, Jumping Over Lowered Bar of Expectations," Yahoo! Finance, **https://finance.yahoo.com/news/casper-prices-ipo-222615705.html,** accessed February 6, 2020.

LO12.4

Describe how stocks are bought and sold.

ACTION ITEM

I know how to buy and sell stocks.

☐ Yes ☐ No

primary market A market in which an investor purchases financial securities, via an investment bank or other representative, from the issuer of those securities.

investment bank A financial firm that assists corporations in raising funds, usually by helping to sell new security issues.

initial public offering (IPO) Occurs when a corporation sells stock to the general public for the first time.

secondary market A market for existing financial securities that are currently traded among investors.

securities exchange A marketplace where member brokers who represent investors meet to buy and sell securities.

SECURITIES EXCHANGES A **securities exchange** is a marketplace where member brokers who represent investors meet to buy and sell securities. Generally, the securities issued by nationwide corporations are traded at the New York Stock Exchange or regional exchanges in the United States. There are also foreign securities exchanges—in Tokyo, London, or Shanghai, for example.

The New York Stock Exchange (NYSE) is one of the largest securities exchanges in the world. Most of the NYSE members represent brokerage firms that often charge commissions on security trades made by their representatives for their customers. Other members are called *specialists* or *specialist firms.* A *specialist* buys or sells a particular stock in an effort to maintain a fair and orderly market.

Before a corporation's stock is approved for listing on the NYSE, the corporation must meet specific listing requirements. The various regional exchanges also have listing requirements, but typically these are less stringent than the NYSE requirements. The stock of corporations that cannot meet the NYSE requirements, find it too expensive to be listed on the NYSE, or choose not to be listed on the NYSE is often traded on one of the regional exchanges or through the over-the-counter market.

over-the-counter (OTC) market A network of dealers who buy and sell the stocks of corporations that are not listed on a securities exchange.

THE OVER-THE-COUNTER MARKET Not all securities are traded on organized exchanges. Stocks issued by several thousand companies are traded in the over-the-counter market. The **over-the-counter (OTC) market** is a network of dealers who buy and sell the stocks of corporations that are not listed on a securities exchange. Today these stocks are not really traded over the counter. The term was coined more than 100 years ago when securities were sold "over the counter" in stores and banks.

Most over-the-counter securities are traded through Nasdaq (pronounced "nazz-dack"). **Nasdaq** is an electronic marketplace for stocks.[4] In addition to providing price information, this electronic system allows investors to buy and sell shares of companies traded on Nasdaq. When you want to buy or sell shares of a company that trades on Nasdaq—say, Microsoft—your account executive sends your order into the Nasdaq computer system, where it shows up on the screen with all the other orders from people who want to buy or sell Microsoft. Then a Nasdaq dealer (sometimes referred to as a *market maker*) sitting at a computer terminal matches buy and sell orders for Microsoft to complete your transaction. Dealers may also complete buy or sell orders from their own inventory of shares that they maintain to meet the demands of investors.

money minute focus

"Wall Street" is a street name of historical significance. Back in the 17th century, Dutch settlers on the southern tip of Manhattan Island erected a wall to protect their colony. Even though the wall was never used for defensive purposes, it left its name to what is now recognized as one of the most famous streets in the financial world.

Nasdaq An electronic marketplace for stocks.

Brokerage Firms and Account Executives

account executive A licensed individual who works for a brokerage firm and buys or sells securities for clients; also called a *stockbroker.*

An **account executive,** or *stockbroker,* is a licensed individual who works for a brokerage firm and buys or sells investments for his or her clients. Before choosing an account executive, you should have already determined your financial objectives. Then you must be careful to communicate those objectives to the account executive so that he or she can do a good job of advising you. To help avoid a situation in which your account executive's recommendations are automatically implemented, you should be *actively* involved in the decisions related to your investment program, and you should never allow your account executive to use his or her discretion without your approval. Finally, keep in mind that account executives generally are not liable for client losses that result from their recommendations. In fact, most brokerage firms require clients to sign a statement in which they agree to submit any complaints to an arbitration board. This arbitration clause generally prevents a client from suing an account executive or a brokerage firm.

[4] Nasdaq, **https://www.nasdaq.com/**, accessed February 9, 2020.

Should You Use a Full-Service or a Discount Brokerage Firm?

Today a healthy competition exists between full-service and discount brokerage firms. While the most obvious difference between full-service and discount firms is the amount of the commissions they charge when you buy or sell stock and other securities, there are at least three other factors to consider. First, consider how much research information is available. Both types of brokerage firms offer excellent research materials, but you may have to pay for more detailed research information and access to professional advisory reports if you choose a discount brokerage firm.

Type of Brokerage Firm	Type of Investor
• Full-service	Beginning investors with little or no experience. Individuals who are uncomfortable making investment decisions. Individuals who are uncomfortable trading stocks online.
• Discount	People who understand how to research stocks and prefer to make their own decisions. Individuals who are comfortable trading stocks online.

Second, consider how much help you need when making an investment decision. Many full-service brokerage firms argue that you need a professional to help you make important investment decisions. On the other side, discount brokerage firms argue that you alone are responsible for making your investment decisions. They are quick to point out that the most successful investors are the ones involved in their investment programs. And they argue that they have both personnel and materials dedicated to helping you learn how to become a better investor. Although there are many exceptions, the information below may help you decide whether to use a full-service or discount brokerage firm.

Finally, consider how easy it is to buy and sell stock and other securities when using a full-service or discount brokerage firm. Questions to ask include:

market order A request to buy or sell a stock at the best available price.

1. Can I buy or sell stocks using the Internet or over the phone?
2. What is the typical commission for a stock transaction?
3. Is there a toll-free telephone number for customer use?
4. Is there a charge for statements, research reports, and other financial reports?
5. Are there any fees in addition to the commissions I pay when I buy or sell stocks?

See the nearby *Financial Literacy in Practice* feature to learn how to open a brokerage account.

CAUTION!

To find out if other investors have lodged complaints about an account executive or a brokerage firm, go to the Financial Industry Regulatory Authority at **www.finra.org** or the Securities and Exchange Commission at **www.sec.gov**.

Sample Stock Transactions

Once you have opened an account at a brokerage firm and evaluated a possible stock investment, it's time to execute an order to buy your stock. Let's begin by examining three types of orders used to trade stocks.

A **market order** is a request to buy or sell a stock at the best available price. Payment for stocks is generally required within two business days after the transaction. Today it is common practice for investors to leave stock certificates with a brokerage firm. Because the stock certificates are in the broker's care,

money minute focus

Before you begin investing your money, you may want to practice. Today, a number of investment websites provide simulations that allow you to practice stock investing for free. To find a stock investment simulation, enter the term *stock practice* or *virtual stock game* in an Internet search engine such as Google or Yahoo!

How to Open an Account with a Brokerage Firm

Want to purchase stocks? Want to choose the right brokerage firm to help you achieve your financial goals? Then take a look at the steps described below:

Take This Step	Suggested Action
1. Develop your investment goals.	Your goals should describe something that is important to you and that you are willing to work to achieve. The goals you develop should be specific, measurable, and tailored to your financial needs both now and in the future.
2. Establish an emergency fund.	Most financial experts suggest an amount equal to at least three month's living expenses.
3. Choose the type of broker-age account that meets your needs.	Before opening an account, research the following three types of accounts: • A taxable account with no immediate tax benefits. • A traditional IRA or retirement account with immediate tax benefits but that requires you to pay taxes when money is withdrawn. • A Roth IRA with no immediate tax benefits but on which you pay no taxes on qualified withdraw-als after age 59 ½.
4. Save some money.	Depending on the type of account and the brokerage firm, most brokerage firms require an initial deposit of $250 to $2,500 to open an account. Note: Some brokerage firms don't require you to deposit any money to open an account.
5. Research different broker-age firms.	All brokerage firms have a website where you can get information about commissions, fees, avail-able research, financial advice, and other important topics. Don't just choose the last company you saw advertised on TV. Do the research.
6. Do the paperwork.	Once you have made your choice, go online and follow the steps required to open an account. You can also talk to a representative of the firm and open an account by telephone or by going to a branch office.

transfers when the stock is sold are much easier. The phrase "left in the street name" is used to describe investor-owned securities held by a brokerage firm.

limit order A request to buy or sell a stock at a specified price.

A **limit order** is a request to buy or sell a stock at a specified price. When you purchase stock, a limit order ensures that you will buy at the limit price or lower. When you sell stock, a limit order ensures that you will sell at the limit price or higher. For example, if you place a limit order to buy JetBlue Airways stock for $15 a share, the stock will not be purchased until the price drops to $15 a share or lower. Likewise, if your limit order is to sell JetBlue for $15 a share, the stock will not be sold until the price rises to $15 a share or higher. *Be warned:* Limit orders are executed if and when the specified price or better is reached and *all* other previously received orders have been filled.

Many stockholders are certain they want to sell their stock if it reaches a specified price. A limit order does not guarantee this will be done. With a limit order, as mentioned above, orders by other investors may be placed ahead of your order. If you want to guarantee that your order will be executed, you place a special type of limit order known as a stop-loss order. A **stop-loss order** (sometimes called a *stop order*) is an order to sell a particular stock at the next available opportunity after its market price reaches a specified amount. This type of order is used to protect an investor against a sharp drop in price and thus stop the dollar loss on a stock investment. For example, assume you purchased Macy's stock at $16 a share. Two weeks after you made that investment, Macy's reports lower-than-expected sales and profits and announces it is closing a large number of stores. Fearing that the market value of your stock will decrease, you enter a stop-loss order to sell your Macy's stock at $10. This means that if the price of the stock decreases to $10 or

stop-loss order An order to sell a particular stock at the next available opportunity after its market price reaches a specified amount.

lower, the brokerage firm will sell it. While a stop-loss order does not guarantee that your stock will be sold at the price you specified, it does guarantee that it will be sold at the next available opportunity. Both limit and stop-loss orders may be good for one day, one week, one month, or until canceled (GTC).

Commission Charges

Many brokerage firms charge a minimum commission ranging from $5 to $25 for buying and selling stock. Additional commission charges may be based on the number of shares and the value of stock bought and sold. In addition to buying and selling stocks, you can also use the brokerage firm you choose to invest in mutual funds and exchange-traded funds. Commissions and fees for these investments are discussed in Chapter 13.

Exhibit 12–6 shows the minimum account balance, typical commissions charged, and other factors to consider for five popular brokerage firms. At the beginning of 2020, the minimum account balance for all of the firms in Exhibit 12–6 is $0. Also, the commission for Internet trades for all five firms is $0. The fact that both the minimum account balance and the commission for Internet trades are $0 illustrates how competitive the brokerage business is. Since cost is not a factor, you may want to examine the material in the fourth column on the right. The factors in the fourth column can make a difference—especially for beginning investors. Also, some brokerage firms offer free trades, but strings may be attached. For example, free trades may be an introductory offer, good for a limited time, or you may have to maintain a large balance in your investment account. Finally, don't forget annual fees, research fees, and other fees that you may have to pay. It pays to look at the fine print when choosing a brokerage firm.

Generally, full-service brokerage firms charge higher commissions than those charged by discount brokerage firms. As a rule of thumb, full-service brokers may charge approximately 1 percent of the transaction amount. In return for charging higher commissions, full-service brokers may spend more time with each client, help make investment decisions, and provide free research information. *Be warned:* Often account executives at full-service brokerage firms don't spend a lot of time with investors that have only small amounts to invest.

WHAT WOULD YOU DO? You have taken an accounting course and have almost completed a Personal Finance course. You enjoy working with numbers, find different investments interesting, and like the idea of helping people manage their finances. And yet, you are unsure if you would like working in the financial industry. How can you find out more information about what it takes to become a certified financial planner? What steps can you take to see if this the right career for you?

Exhibit 12–6

Typical Commission Charges for Stock Transactions

Brokerage Firm	Minimum Account Balance	Internet Trades	Factors to Consider
E*Trade	$0	$0	**Caters to active traders and long-term investors**
Charles Schwab	$0	$0	**Reduced fees and commissions and is now one of the least expensive brokerage firms**
Fidelity	$0	$0	**Top-notch research, outstanding customer service, and simple investing platform**
Merrill Edge	$0	$0	**Strong research and fantastic customer service**
TD Ameritrade	$0	$0	**One of the top all-around brokers and has great investing tools**

Source: Matt Frankel, "Best Online Stock Brokers for Beginners for February 2020," Motley Fool, **https://www.fool.com/the-ascent/buying-stocks/best-online-stock-brokers-beginners**, accessed January 15, 2020.

PRACTICE QUIZ 12–4

1. What is the difference between the primary market and the secondary market? What is an initial public offering (IPO)?

2. Assume you want to purchase stock. Would you use a full-service broker or a discount broker? Would you ever trade stocks online?

3. Explain the important characteristics of each of the following types of stock transaction orders:

   a. Market order.
   b. Limit order.
   c. Stop-loss order.

LO12.5

Explain the trading techniques used by long-term investors and short-term speculators.

ACTION ITEM

I know the difference between long-term and short-term investment techniques.

☐ Agree ☐ Disagree

Long-Term and Short-Term Investment Strategies

Once you purchase stock, the investment may be classified as either long-term or short-term. Generally, individuals who hold an investment for a year or longer are referred to as *investors*. Individuals who routinely buy and then sell stocks within a short period of time are called *speculators* or *traders*.

Long-Term Techniques

In this section, we discuss the long-term techniques of buy and hold, dollar cost averaging, direct investment programs, and dividend reinvestment programs.

BUY-AND-HOLD TECHNIQUE Many long-term investors purchase stock and hold on to it for a number of years. When they do this, their investment can increase in value in two ways. First, they are entitled to dividends if the board of directors approves dividend payments to stockholders. Second, the price of the stock may go up, or appreciate in value. To see how an investor using the buy-and-hold technique can earn profits from dividends and an increase in stock value, review the Nike investment illustrated in Exhibit 12–2. In addition to dividends and dollar appreciation of value, stock splits may increase the value of your stock investments. Just remember, there are *no guarantees* that a stock split will increase the value of a stock.

dollar cost averaging A long-term technique used by investors who purchase an equal dollar amount of the same stock at equal intervals.

DOLLAR COST AVERAGING Dollar cost averaging is a long-term technique used by investors who purchase an equal dollar amount of the same stock at equal intervals. Assume you invest $2,000 in Johnson & Johnson's common stock each year for a period of seven years. The results of your investment program are illustrated in Exhibit 12–7. Notice that when the price of the stock was higher, you purchased fewer shares. And when the price of the stock was lower, you purchased more shares. The average cost for a share of stock, determined by dividing the total investment ($14,000) by the total number of shares (117.9 shares), is $118.74 ($14,000 ÷ 117.9 = $118.74). Other applications of dollar cost averaging occur when employees purchase shares of their company's stock through a payroll deduction plan or as part of an employer-sponsored retirement plan over an extended period of time.

The two goals of dollar cost averaging are to minimize the average cost per share and to avoid the common pitfall of buying high and selling low. In the situation shown in Exhibit 12–7, you would lose money only if you sold your stock at less than the average

Year	Investment	Stock Price	Shares Purchased
2014	$ 2,000	$ 95	21.1
2015	2,000	102	19.6
2016	2,000	112	17.9
2017	2,000	135	14.8
2018	2,000	118	16.9
2019	2,000	138	14.5
2020	2,000	153	13.1
Total	$14,000		117.9

Average cost = Total investment ÷ Total shares

    = $14,000 ÷ 117.9

    = $118.74

Exhibit 12–7

Dollar Cost Averaging for Johnson & Johnson

direct investment plan A plan that allows stockholders to purchase stock directly from a corporation without having to use an account executive or a brokerage firm.

cost of $118.74. Thus, with dollar cost averaging, you can make money if the stock is sold at a price higher than the average cost for a share of stock.

DIRECT INVESTMENT AND DIVIDEND REINVESTMENT PLANS Today a large number of corporations offer direct investment plans. A **direct investment plan** allows you to purchase stock directly from a corporation without having to use an account executive or a brokerage firm. Similarly, a **dividend reinvestment plan** (often called a DRIP) allows you the option to reinvest your cash dividends to purchase stock of the corporation. For stockholders, the chief advantage of both types of plans is that these plans enable them to purchase stock without using a broker or paying a commission charge to a brokerage firm. The fees (if any), minimum investment amounts, rules, and features for both direct investment and dividend reinvestment vary from one corporation to the next. Also, with the direct investment and dividend reinvestment plans, you can take advantage of dollar cost averaging, discussed earlier in this section. For corporations, the chief advantage of both types of plans is that they provide an additional source of capital. As an added bonus, they provide a service to their stockholders. For more information about direct investment plans and dividend reinvestment plans, go to **https://www.sec.gov/fast-answers/answers-driphtm.html** or **www.dripinvesting.org**.

Short-Term Techniques

Investors sometimes use more speculative, short-term techniques. In this section, we discuss buying stock on margin, selling short, and trading in options. *Be warned:* The methods presented in this section are high-risk and speculative; do not use them unless you fully understand the underlying risks. Also, you should not use them until you have experienced success using the more traditional long-term techniques described in the "Long-Term Techniques" section.

CAUTION!

- It is important to keep track of the stock price each time you make an investment.
- This information will come into play when you sell stock and have to determine your cost basis for tax purposes.

dividend reinvestment plan A plan that allows current stockholders the option to reinvest or use their cash dividends to purchase stock of the corporation.

FinTech for Financial Literacy

TD Ameritrade's Mobile App

Ranked five stars by NerdWallet, the mobile investor app available at brokerage firm TD Ameritrade allows you to access all the essentials you need to manage your accounts wherever you are. You can track both the market and your personal portfolio with this simple, easy-to-use app on your phone, tablet, or Apple watch. You can also view real-time quotes; access news, research, and charts; and trade stocks wherever you go.

Source: Andrea Coombes, "10 Best Investment Apps of 2020," NerdWallet, **https://www.nerdwallet.com/best/investing/investment-apps**, accessed January 2, 2020.

margin A speculative technique whereby an investor borrows part of the money needed to buy a particular stock.

BUYING STOCK ON MARGIN When buying stock on **margin**, you borrow part of the money needed to buy a particular stock. The margin requirement is set by the Federal Reserve Board. The current margin requirement is 50 percent. This requirement means you may borrow up to half of the total stock purchase price. Although margin is regulated by the Federal Reserve, specific requirements and the interest charged on the loans used to fund margin transactions may vary among brokerage firms. Usually, the brokerage firm either lends the money or arranges the loan with another financial institution.

Investors buy on margin because the financial leverage created by borrowing money can increase the return on an investment. Because they can buy up to twice as much stock by buying on margin, they can earn larger returns. Suppose you expect the market price of a share of IBM to increase in the next three to four months. Let's say you have enough money to purchase 100 shares of the stock. However, if you buy on margin, you can purchase an additional 100 shares for a total of 200 shares.

EXAMPLE: Margin Transaction (IBM)

If the price of IBM's stock increases by $7 a share, your profit will be:

Without margin: $ 700 = $7 increase per share x 100 shares
With margin: $1,400 = $7 increase per share x 200 shares

In this example, buying more shares on margin enables you to earn more profit (less the interest you pay on the borrowed money and customary commission charges).

Keep in mind that the IBM stock in this margin transaction serves as collateral for the loan. If the value of a margined stock decreases past a certain point, you will receive a *margin call* from the brokerage firm. After the margin call, you must pledge additional cash or securities to serve as collateral for the loan. If you don't have cash or acceptable collateral, the margined stock is sold and the proceeds are used to repay the loan. The exact price at which the brokerage firm issues the margin call is determined by the amount of money you borrowed when you purchased the stock. Generally, the more money you borrow, the sooner you will receive a margin call if the value of the margined stock drops.

In addition to facing the possibility of larger dollar losses because you own more shares, you must pay interest on the money borrowed to purchase stock on margin. While the interest rates for a margin transactions vary, most brokerage firms charge 1 to 4 percent above the prime rate. Normally, economists define the prime rate as the interest rate that the best business customers must pay. Interest charges can absorb the potential profits if the value of margined stock does not increase rapidly enough and the margined stocks must be held for long periods of time.

WHAT WOULD YOU DO? You began an investment program about 10 years ago. Your returns have averaged 7.5 percent each year. Assuming the returns remain the same, you will be able to meet your long-term financial goals. And yet, like many investors, you would like larger returns and are now considering buying stock on margin. Is this a good decision or not? What are the risks involved in margin trading? What should you do?

SELLING SHORT Your ability to make money by buying and selling securities is related to how well you can predict whether a certain stock's price will increase or decrease. Normally, you buy stocks and assume they will increase in value, a procedure referred to as *buying long*. But not all stocks increase in value. In fact, the value of a stock may decrease for many reasons, including lower sales, lower profits, reduced dividends, product failures, increased competition, product liability lawsuits, and labor strikes. In addition, the health of a nation's economy can make a difference.

When stock prices are declining, you may use a procedure called *selling short* to make money. **Selling short** is selling stock that has been borrowed from a brokerage firm and must be replaced at a later date. When you sell short, you sell today, knowing you must buy or *cover* your short transaction at a later date. To make money in a short transaction, you must take these steps:

1. Arrange to *borrow a stock certificate* for a specific number of shares of a particular stock from a brokerage firm.
2. *Sell the borrowed stock,* assuming it will drop in value in a reasonably short period of time.
3. *Buy the stock at a lower price* than the price it sold for in Step 2.
4. Use the stock purchased in Step 3 to *replace the stock borrowed from the brokerage firm* in Step 1.

When selling short, your profit is the difference between the amount received when the stock is sold in Step 2 and the amount paid for the stock in Step 3. For example, assume that you think General Motors stock is overvalued at $35 a share. You also believe the stock will *decrease* in value over the next four to six months because of lower sales revenues and profits and a large number of potential product recalls. You call your broker and arrange to borrow 100 shares of General Motors stock (Step 1). The broker then sells your borrowed stock for you at the current market price of $35 a share (Step 2). Also assume that four months later, General Motors stock drops to $27 a share. You instruct your broker to purchase 100 shares of General Motors stock at the current lower price (Step 3). The newly purchased stock is given to the brokerage firm to repay the borrowed stock (Step 4).

> **selling short** Selling stock that has been borrowed from a brokerage firm and must be replaced at a later date.

EXAMPLE: Selling Short (General Motors)

Your profit from the General Motors short transaction was $800 because the price declined from $35 to $27.

$3,500 Selling price	= $35 price per share x 100 shares (step 2)
−$2,700 Purchase price	= $27 price per share x 100 shares (step 3)
$ 800 Profit from selling short	

With a short transaction, the brokerage firm receives its regular commission when the stock is bought and sold. In some situations, the brokerage firm may even charge interest and fees for the use of the borrowed stock. Before selling short, consider two factors. First, since the stock you borrow from your broker is actually owned by another investor, you must pay any dividends the stock earns before you replace the stock. Eventually, dividends can absorb the profits from your short transaction if the price of the stock does not decrease rapidly enough. Second, to make money selling short, you must be correct in predicting that a stock will decrease in value. If the value of the stock increases, you lose.

TRADING IN OPTIONS An **option** gives you the right—but not the obligation—to buy or sell a stock at a predetermined price during a specified period of time. If you think the market price of a stock will increase during a short period of time, you may decide to purchase a call option. A *call option* is sold by a stockholder and gives the purchaser the right to buy 100 shares of a stock at a guaranteed price before a specified expiration date. With a call option, the purchaser is betting that the price of the stock will increase in value before the expiration date. If the stock's price does increase, the purchaser will be able to purchase the stock for the lower price guaranteed by the call option and then sell it for a

> **option** The right—but not the obligation—to buy or sell a stock at a predetermined price during a specified period of time.

profit. In this example, the investor's profit is reduced by commission charges and the cost of the call option.

It is also possible to purchase a put option. A *put option* is the right to sell 100 shares of a stock at a guaranteed price before a specified expiration date. With a put option, the purchaser is betting that the price of the stock will decrease in value before the expiration date. If the stock's price does decrease, the purchaser will be able to purchase stock at the lower price and then sell the stock for a higher price that is guaranteed by the put option. Like call options, the investor's profit is reduced by commission charges and the cost of the put option.

Because of the increased risk involved in option trading, a more detailed discussion of how you profit or lose money with options is beyond the scope of this book. *Be warned:* Amateurs and beginning investors should stay away from options unless they fully understand all of the risks involved. For the rookie, the lure of large profits over a short period of time may be tempting, but the risks are real.

PRACTICE QUIZ 12–5

1. In your own words, describe the difference between an investor and a speculator.

2. Describe each of the following investment techniques:

   a. Buy and hold.
   b. Dollar cost averaging.
   c. Direct investment.
   d. Dividend reinvestment.
   e. Margin.
   f. Selling short.
   g. Options.

Road Map

to financial literacy

Investing in Stocks

You Are Here

Checkpoint 1

☐ Reconsider your responses to the "Action Items" for this chapter to determine if you are ready to begin investing in stock.

Checkpoint 2

☐ Save the money needed to begin investing
☐ Evaluate different stocks that match your goals

a brokerage account
ase quality stocks

Checkpoint 3

☐ Evaluate the existing stocks you own and monitor the value of those stocks
☐ Evaluate additional stocks that could help you obtain your goals Revise your goals as necessary to reflect changes in your life

Checkpoint 4

Financial Security

HAVE YOU SAVED ENOUGH MONEY TO OPEN A BROKERAGE ACCOUNT AND PURCHASE YOUR FIRST STOCK?

your personal finance dashboard

Money for Investing in Stocks

Beginning investors are often reluctant to begin investing because of three factors. First, they don't have the money to establish an investment program. Second, they don't know how to research different investment alternatives. Third, they must use the services of a brokerage firm in order to buy or sell stock.

YOUR SITUATION: First, you should determine if you have saved enough money to begin investing. Next, you should research any potential investment. Finally, you should open an account with a brokerage firm and purchase quality stocks and investments.

LO12.1   Corporations sell stock (a form of equity) to finance their business start-up costs and help pay for their ongoing business activities. In return for providing the money needed to finance the corporation, stockholders have the right to elect the board of directors. They must also approve major changes to corporate policies.

People invest in stock because they want the larger returns that stocks offer. Possible reasons for stock investments include dividend income, appreciation of value, and the *possibility* of gain through stock splits. In addition to common stock, a few corporations may issue preferred stock. The most important priority an investor in preferred stock enjoys is receiving cash dividends before any cash dividends are paid to common stockholders.

LO12.2   A wealth of information is available to stock investors. A logical place to start the evaluation process is with the classification of different types of stock investments that range from very conservative to very speculative; see Exhibit 12–3. Today, many investors use the information available on the Internet to evaluate individual stocks. Information is also available from stock advisory services such as Value Line, Morningstar, and Zacks. Newspapers, corporations that issue stocks, business and personal finance periodicals, and government publications and websites can also help you evaluate a stock investment.

LO12.3   Many analysts believe that a corporation's ability or inability to generate earnings in the future may be one of the most significant factors that account for an increase or decrease in a stock's price. Generally, higher earnings equate to higher stock prices, and lower earnings equate to lower stock prices. Investors can also calculate earnings per share and a price-earnings ratio to evaluate a stock investment. Whereas both earnings per share and the price-earnings ratio are historical numbers based on what a corporation has already done, investors can obtain earnings estimates for most corporations. Other calculations that help evaluate stock investments include dividend yield, total return, beta, and book value. Stock prices are also affected by what another investor will pay for a share of stock. A number of suggestions to help you evaluate a stock investment were included in this section.

LO12.4   A corporation may sell a new stock issue with the help of an investment banking firm in the primary market. Once the stock has been sold in the primary market, it can be sold time and again in the secondary market. In the secondary market, investors purchase stock listed on a securities exchange or traded in the over-the-counter market. Securities transactions are made through a full-service brokerage firm or a discount brokerage firm. Whether you trade online or use more traditional trading techniques, you must decide if you want to use a market, limit, or stop-loss order to buy or sell stock. Although some brokerage firms have eliminated commissions on stock transactions, other brokerage firms do charge a minimum commission. Additional commission charges are based on the number and value of the stock shares bought or sold. Generally, full-service brokerage firms charge higher commissions than those charged by discount brokerage firms.

LO12.5   Purchased stock may be classified as either a long-term investment or a speculative investment. Long-term investors typically hold their investments for at least a year or longer; speculators (sometimes referred to as *traders*) usually sell their investments within a shorter time period. Traditional trading techniques long-term investors use include the buy-and-hold technique, dollar cost averaging, direct investment plans, and dividend reinvestment plans. More speculative techniques include buying stock on margin, selling short, and trading in options.

account executive 438	direct investment plan 443	dividend yield 433
beta 434	dividend 422	dollar cost averaging 442
book value 435	dividend reinvestment	earnings per share 432
common stock 422	plan 443	equity financing 422

Key Formulas

Page	Topic	Formula
432	Earnings per share	$$\text{Earnings per share} = \frac{\text{Earnings}}{\text{Number of shares outstanding}}$$
432	Price-earnings (PE) ratio	$$\text{Price-earnings (PE) ratio} = \frac{\text{Price per share}}{\text{Earnings per share}}$$
433	Dividend yield	$$\text{Dividend yield} = \frac{\text{Annual dividend amount}}{\text{Current price per share}}$$
434	Total return	$$\text{Total return} = \text{Dividends} + \text{Capital gain}$$
434	Volatility for a stock	Increase in overall market $\times$ Beta for a specific stock
435	Book value	$$\text{Book value} = \frac{\text{Assets} - \text{Liabilities}}{\text{Number of shares outstanding}}$$

Self-Test Problems

1. Four years ago, Ken Guessford purchased 200 shares of Mountain View Manufacturing. At the time, each share of Mountain View was selling for $30. He also paid a $24 commission when the shares were purchased. Now, four years later, he has decided it's time to sell his investment. The Mountain View share price when sold was $32.50. In addition, he paid a $36 commission to sell his shares. He also received total dividends of $1.80 per share over the four-year investment period.
   a. What is the total amount of dividends Ken Guessford received over the four-year period?
   b. What was the total return for Guessford's investment?

2. Karen and William Newton are trying to decide if they should sell or hold their investment in Oakwood Electronics, and they ask for your help. Financial information for Oakdale Electronics is below.

Company	Price When Purchased	Current Price per Share	Annual Dividend	Earnings This Year	Projected Earnings Next Year	Number of Shares Outstanding
Oakdale Electronics	$32	$26	$0.30	$34 million	$25 million	20 million shares

   a. Based on the current price for a share of stock, calculate the dividend yield for this company.
   b. Calculate the earnings per share for this company.
   c. Calculate the current PE ratio for this company.
   d. Based on this information, would you recommend to sell or hold this company?

Solutions

1. *a.* Total dividends = $1.80 per share dividends × 200 shares = $360.
   b. Dividends = $1.80 per share dividends × 200 shares = $360.
      Purchase price = $30 per share × 200 shares + $24 commission = $6,024.
      Selling price = $32.50 per share × 200 shares – $36 commission = $6,464.
      Capital gain = $6,464 selling price – $6,024 purchase price = $440.
      Total return = $360 dividends + $440 capital gain = $800.

2. *a.* The dividend yield for this company is:

$$\text{Dividend yield} = \frac{\$0.30 \text{ annual dividend}}{\$26 \text{ current price}} = 0.012 = 1.2 \text{ percent}$$

   b. The earnings per share for this company is:

$$\text{Earnings per share} = \frac{\$34,000,000 \text{ earnings}}{20,000,000 \text{ shares}} = \$1.70$$

   c. Current PE ratio is:

$$\text{Current PE ratio} = \frac{\$26 \text{ current price}}{\$1.70 \text{ earnings per share}} = 15$$

   d. All of the calculations in this problem should be considered when making a decision to sell or hold this investment. While the company is paying a $0.30 a share dividend, the dividend yield is 1.2 percent and is comparable to current rates for certificates of deposit. For now, dividends appear to be secure because the company is earning $1.70 a share and should be able to continue to pay dividends—even with lower projected earnings next year. The PE ratio is 15, which may indicate that investors are not optimistic about future earnings growth. Also, consider two additional factors. First, the stock price has declined from $32 to $26 a share. Is there a reason why this company's stock should rebound at this point? Second, earnings are projected to decline next year. This may lead to a further decline in stock value from its present value. Based on this information, it may be time to sell this investment and look for another one that has more potential. What do you think?

Financial Planning Problems

1. Jamie and Peter Dawson own 180 shares of Duke Energy common stock. Duke Energy's quarterly dividend is $0.95 per share. What is the amount of the dividend check the Dawson couple will receive for this quarter? (LO12.1)

2. During the four quarters for 2020, the Browns received two quarterly dividend payments of $0.32, one quarterly payment of $0.40, and one quarterly payment of $0.52. If they owned 270 shares of stock, what was their total dividend income for 2020? (LO12.1)

3. Jim Johansen noticed that a corporation he is considering investing in is about to pay a quarterly dividend. The record date is Thursday, April 23, 2020. In order for Jim to receive this quarterly dividend, what is the last date that he could purchase stock in this corporation and receive this quarter's dividend payment? (LO12.1)

4. Sarah and James Hernandez purchased 160 shares of Macy's stock at $20 a share. One year later, they sold the stock for $24 a share. They paid a broker a commission of $8 when they purchased the stock and a commission of $12 when they sold the stock. During the 12-month period the couple owned the stock, Macy's paid dividends that totaled $1.51 a share. Calculate the Hernandezes' total return for this investment. (LO12.1)

5. Wanda Sotheby purchased 120 shares of Home Depot stock at $235 a share. One year later, she sold the stock for $218 a share. She paid her broker a commission of $34 when she purchased the stock and a commission of $39 when she sold it. During the 12 months she owned the stock, she received $653 in dividends. Calculate Wanda's total return on this investment.   (LO12.1)

6. In September, the board of directors of Chaparral Steel approved a stock split of 2-for-1. After the split, how many shares of Chaparral Steel stock will an investor have if he or she owned 230 shares before the split?   (LO12.1)

7. Michelle Townsend owns stock in National Computers. Based on information in its annual report, National Computers reported after-tax earnings of $9,700,000 and has issued 7,000,000 shares of common stock. The stock is currently selling for $32 a share.   (LO12.3)
   a. Calculate the earnings per share for National Computers.
   b. Calculate the price-earnings (PE) ratio for National Computers.

8. Analysts who follow JPMorgan Chase, one of the nation's largest providers of financial services, estimate that the corporation's earnings per share will increase from $10.87 in the current year to $11.55 next year.   (LO12.3)
   a. What is the amount of the increase?
   b. What effect, if any, should this increase have on the value of the corporation's stock?

9. Currently, 3M Company pays an annual dividend of $5.88. If the stock is selling for $160, what is the dividend yield?   (LO12.3)

10. General Motors has a beta of 1.34. If the overall stock market increases by 6 percent, based on this information, how much should investors assume that General Motors will increase?   (LO12.3)

11. Casper Energy Exploration reports that the corporation's assets are valued at $185,000,000, its liabilities are $80,000,000, and it has issued 6,000,000 shares of stock. What is the book value for a share of Casper stock?   (LO12.3)

12. For four years, Marty Campbell invested $4,000 each year in Harley-Davidson. The stock was selling for $55 in 2017, $47 in 2018, $36 in 2019, and $33 in 2020.   (LO12.5)
   a. What is Marty's total investment in Harley-Davidson?
   b. After four years, how many shares does Marty own?
   c. What is the average cost per share of Marty's investment?

13. Bob Orleans invested $3,000 and borrowed $3,000 to purchase shares in Verizon Communications. At the time of his investment, Verizon was selling for $60 a share.   (LO12.5)
   a. If Bob paid a commission of $20, how many shares could he buy if he used only his own money and did not use margin?
   b. If Bob paid a commission of $40, how many shares could he buy if he used his $3,000 and borrowed $3,000 on margin to buy Verizon stock?
   c. Assume Bob did use margin to buy his Verizon stock. Also, assume he paid another $40 to sell his stock and sold the stock for $64 a share. How much profit did he make on his Verizon stock investment?

14. After researching Valero Energy common stock, Sandra Pearson is convinced the stock is overpriced. She contacts her account executive and arranges to sell short 250 shares of Valero Energy. At the time of the sale, a share of common stock had a value of $85. Three months later, Valero Energy is selling for $76 a share, and Sandra instructs her broker to cover her short transaction. Total commissions to buy and sell the stock were $26. What is her profit for this short transaction?   (LO12.5)

 **To reinforce the content in this chapter, more problems are provided at connect.mheducation.com.**

FINANCIAL LITERACY PORTFOLIO

CORPORATE STOCK EVALUATION

Competency

Research potential stock investments.

Action Research

Based on current economic and business trends, select a company with potential growth over the next few years. Use the material in this chapter, online research, library resources, and *Your Personal Financial Plan Sheet 38* to conduct research for this company.

Outcome

Create an audio file or video presentation that communicates the research process used, your main findings about the stock, and your recommended actions related to investing in the stock.

REAL LIFE PERSONAL FINANCE

RESEARCH INFORMATION AVAILABLE FROM VALUE LINE

This chapter stressed the importance of evaluating potential investments. Now it's your turn to try your skill at evaluating a potential investment in the Microsoft Corporation. Assume you could invest $10,000 in the common stock of this company. To help you evaluate this potential investment, carefully examine Exhibit 12–5, which reproduces the research report about Microsoft from Value Line. The report was published on February 7, 2020.

Questions

1. Based on the research provided by Value Line, would you invest in Microsoft stock? Justify your answer.
2. What other investment information would you need to evaluate Microsoft

common stock? Where would you obtain this information?

3. On February 7, 2020, Microsoft stock was selling for $165.46 a share. Using the Internet or a newspaper, determine the current price for a share of Microsoft. Based on this information, would your Microsoft investment have been profitable? (*Hint:* Microsoft's stock symbol is MSFT.)

4. Assuming you purchased Microsoft stock on February 7, 2020, and based on your answer to Question 3, how would you decide if you want to buy more shares, hold your Microsoft shares, or sell your Microsoft stock? Explain your answer.

CONTINUING CASE

INVESTING IN STOCKS

The triplets are now entering high school, and Jamie Lee and Ross are comfortable with their financial and investment strategies. They budgeted throughout the years and are on track to reach their long-term investment goals of paying the triplets' college tuition and accumulating enough to purchase a beach house to enjoy when Jamie and Ross retire.

Recently, Ross inherited $50,000 from his uncle's estate. Ross would like to invest in stocks to supplement their retirement income goals.

Jamie Lee and Ross have been watching a technology company that has an upcoming initial public offering and several other stocks for well-established companies, but they are unsure which stocks to invest in and are also wondering if their choices will fit their moderate-risk investment strategies. They want to make the best decisions they can to maximize their investment returns.

Questions

1. What are the advantages and disadvantages of investing in a technology company's IPO? Will they be guaranteed a large return from this investment? At this life stage, would you recommend that Jamie Lee and Ross invest in an IPO? Why or why not?
2. Jamie Lee's father suggested that they purchase stock in a company that he has held shares in for decades. They want to take advantage of the stock tip, but Jamie Lee and Ross are trying to decide between purchasing the company's common stock and preferred stock. How would you describe the differences between common and preferred?
3. Currently, the economy is beginning to slow down, and there is talk that there may be a recession in the near future. Referring to Exhibit 12–3, what types of stock would you suggest for Jamie Lee and Ross to invest in considering their life stage and current moderate-risk investment strategies? What characteristics are associated with the types of investments you suggested?
4. Suppose Jamie Lee and Ross are evaluating corporate stocks to add to their investment portfolio. Using *Your Personal Financial Plan Sheet 38*, select a company from your own personal experience, such as an automobile or technology company, and research the information needed to complete the worksheet.
   a. Based on your research, should Jamie Lee and Ross invest in this company? Provide support for your evaluation based on the information you reported in *Your Personal Financial Plan Sheet 38*.
   b. If they should invest in the company you suggested, how much of their $50,000 inheritance should they allocate toward the purchase of shares in the company?
   c. Regardless of your position on whether they should invest in your chosen company, if Jamie Lee and Ross went ahead and purchased shares of stock in that company, how many shares could they purchase with the $50,000?
   d. What would be the total transaction cost if they purchased the shares online? (List the source for your answer.)

"INVESTING IN STOCK IS NOT POSSIBLE. I'M BARELY ABLE TO PAY MY VARIOUS LIVING EXPENSES."

Spending Diary

Directions Your Daily Spending Diary will help you manage your expenses to create a better overall spending plan. Once you know how much you spend and then try to reduce your spending where possible, you will be able to save the money needed to begin investing. The Daily Spending Diary sheets are located at the end of Chapter 1 and in Connect Finance.

Questions

1. What information from your daily spending records could help you achieve your financial goals?
2. Based on your observations of our society and the economy, what types of stocks might you consider for investing at this point in your life or in the near future?

Name: _____   Date: _____

Evaluating Corporate Stocks

Purpose: To identify a corporate stock that might help you attain your investment goals.

Financial Planning Activities: No checklist can serve as a foolproof guide for choosing a common or preferred stock. However, the following questions will help you evaluate a potential stock investment. Use stock websites on the Internet and/or library materials to answer these questions about a corporate stock that you believe could help you achieve your investment goals. This sheet is also available in an Excel spreadsheet format in Connect Finance.

Suggested Websites: valueline.com, finance.yahoo.com, morningstar.com

Category 1: The Basics

1. What is the corporation's name?

   _____

2. What are the corporation's website address and telephone number?

   _____

3. Have you read the latest annual report and quarterly report? ☐ Yes ☐ No

4. Have you looked at information about this company on the Securities and Exchange Commission website at **www.sec.gov**?

   _____

5. What information about the corporation is available on the Internet?

   _____

6. What types of products or services does this firm provide?

   _____

7. Briefly describe the prospects for this company. (Include significant factors such as product development, plans for expansion, plans for mergers, etc.)

   _____

Category 2: Dividend Income

8. Is the corporation currently paying dividends? If so, how much?

   _____

9. What is the dividend yield for this stock?

   _____

10. Have dividends increased or decreased over the past three years?

    _____

11. How does the dividend yield for this investment compare with other potential investments?

    _____

Category 3: Financial Performance

12. What are the firm's earnings per share for the last year?

    _____

13. Have the firm's earnings increased over the past three years?

    _____

14. What is the firm's current price-earnings ratio?

    _____

15. How does the firm's current price-earnings (PE) ratio compare with that of firms in the same industry?

    _____

16. Describe trends for the firm's price-earnings ratio over the past three years. Do these trends show improvement or decline in investment value?

    _____

17. What are the firm's projected earnings for the next year?

    _____

18. Have sales increased over the last five years?

    _____

19. What is the stock's current price?

    _____

20. What are the 52-week high and low prices for this stock?

    _____

21. Does your analysis indicate that this is a good stock to buy at this time?

    _____

22. Briefly describe any other information that you obtained from Value Line, Yahoo! Finance, Morningstar, or from other sources of information.

    _____

A Word of Caution

When you use a checklist, there is always a danger of overlooking important relevant information. Quite simply, it is a place to start. If you need more information, you are responsible for obtaining it and for determining how it affects your potential investment.

Suggested App:
• Yahoo! Finance

What's Next for Your Personal Financial Plan?

• Identify additional factors that may affect your decision to invest in this corporation's stock.

• Develop a plan for monitoring an investment's value once a stock is purchased.

Investment Broker Comparison

Purpose: To compare the benefits and costs of different investment brokers.

Financial Planning Activities: Compare the services of an investment broker based on the factors listed below. This sheet is also available in an Excel spreadsheet format in Connect Finance.

Suggested Websites: www.brokerage-review.com, www.stockbrokers.com, www.fool.com/the-ascent/buying-stocks/best-online-stock-brokers-beginners, finra.org

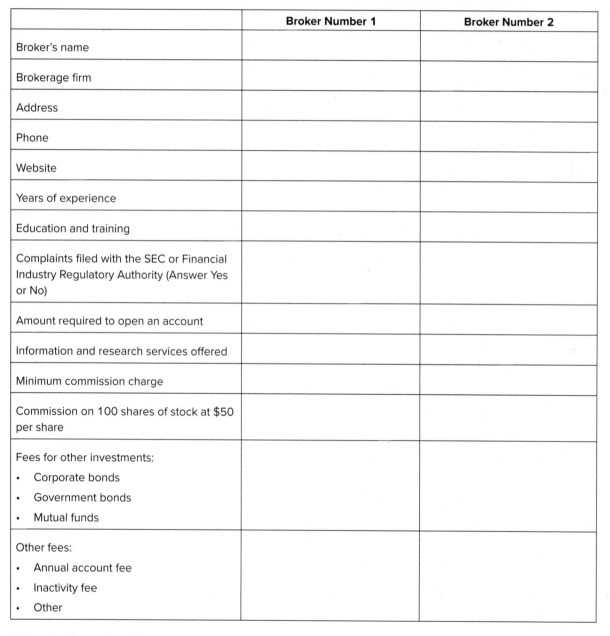

	Broker Number 1	Broker Number 2
Broker's name		
Brokerage firm		
Address		
Phone		
Website		
Years of experience		
Education and training		
Complaints filed with the SEC or Financial Industry Regulatory Authority (Answer Yes or No)		
Amount required to open an account		
Information and research services offered		
Minimum commission charge		
Commission on 100 shares of stock at $50 per share		
Fees for other investments: • Corporate bonds • Government bonds • Mutual funds		
Other fees: • Annual account fee • Inactivity fee • Other		

What's Next for Your Personal Financial Plan?

- Using the information you obtained, choose a brokerage firm that you feel will help you achieve your investment goals.
- Access the website for the brokerage firm you have chosen and answer the questions listed in the section *Should You Use a Full-Service or a Discount Brokerage Firm?* in this chapter.

13 Investing in Mutual Funds

3 Steps to Financial Literacy . . .
Begin Investing in Mutual Funds

1 Learn about different types of funds.
Website: imealliance.com

2 Find more information about fees and mutual fund investing.
Website: sec.gov/fast-answers/
answersmffeeshtm.html

3 Evaluate different funds that will help achieve your investment goals.
Website: https://www.investopedia.com/
investing/how-pick-best-mutual-fund/

For many investors, mutual funds have become the investment of choice. In fact, you can choose from more than 12,000 different funds. So how do you choose the right fund to help you attain your long-term investment goals? To help answer that question, read the material in this chapter. At the end of the chapter, *Your Personal Finance Road Map and Dashboard,* along with other end-of-chapter learning activities, will help you improve your ability to choose the right funds to build your investment portfolio and increase your financial security.

CHAPTER 13 LEARNING OBJECTIVES

In this chapter, you will learn to:

LO13.1 Explain the characteristics of mutual fund investments.

LO13.2 Classify mutual funds by investment objective.

LO13.3 Evaluate mutual funds.

LO13.4 Describe how and why mutual funds are bought and sold.

YOUR PERSONAL FINANCIAL PLAN SHEETS

40. Evaluating Mutual Fund Investment Information
41. Mutual Fund Evaluation

If you ever thought about buying stocks or bonds but decided not to, your reasons were probably like most other people's: You didn't know enough to make a good decision, and you lacked enough money to diversify your investments among several choices. These same two reasons explain why people invest in mutual funds. A **mutual fund** pools the money from many investors—its shareholders—to invest in securities such as stocks, bonds, money market instruments, and other assets.[1] For a fee, a professional fund manager or team of managers invests money from shareholders in a variety of investments that are appropriate to a fund's investment objective.

Mutual funds are an excellent choice for many individuals. In many cases, they can also be used for retirement accounts, including traditional individual retirement accounts, Roth IRAs, and 401(k) and 403(b) retirement accounts.

An investment in mutual funds is based on the concept of opportunity costs, which we have discussed throughout this text. Simply put, you have to be willing to take some risks if you want to get larger returns on your investments. The fact that fund investments can decrease in value underscores the need to understand the risk associated with all investments, including mutual funds.

mutual fund Pools the money of many investors—its shareholders—to invest in a variety of securities such as stocks, bonds, money market instruments, and other assets.

LO13.1

Explain the characteristics of mutual fund investments.

Why Investors Purchase Mutual Funds

For many investors, the notion of investing their money in a mutual fund may be a new idea, but mutual funds have been around for a long time. Fund investing began in Europe in the late 1700s and became popular in the United States before the Great Depression in 1929. After the Depression, government regulation increased, the number of funds grew, and the amount invested in funds continued to increase. New types of funds, including index funds, aggressive growth funds, life-cycle funds, and social responsibility (or green) funds, were created to meet the needs of a larger and more demanding group of investors.

ACTION ITEM

I understand the reasons investors invest in mutual funds.

☐ **Agree** ☐ **Disagree**

[1] Investopedia, https://www.investopedia.com/terms/m/mutualfund.asp, accessed February 15, 2020.

During this same time period, the cost of investing in funds decreased while the popularity of fund investing increased. Experts often say that one man, John Bogle, was the driving force behind attempts to make fund investing affordable for the average American. When he introduced the Vanguard 500 Index Fund in 1976, he gave investors a low-cost way to invest in funds while providing investment diversification. Today, the Vanguard Group is one of the largest fund companies that competes with other companies in the fund industry.

Despite the accusations of fraud and mutual fund scandals in the first part of the 21st century and poor fund performance and investor losses during the 2008 economic crisis and the 2020 pandemic, mutual funds are still the investment of choice for many investors. The following statistics illustrate how important mutual fund investments are to both individuals and the nation's economy:

1. Almost 99.5 million individuals own mutual funds in the United States.[2]
2. Fifty-six million households own mutual funds.[3]
3. With $17.7 trillion in total assets, the U.S. mutual fund industry is the largest in the world.[4]

No doubt about it, the mutual fund industry is big business. And yet you may be wondering why so many people invest in mutual funds.

The Psychology of Investing in Funds

The major reasons investors purchase mutual funds are *professional management* and *diversification.* Most investment companies do everything possible to convince you that they can do a better job of picking securities than you can. Sometimes these claims are true, and sometimes they are just so much hot air. Still, investment companies do have professional fund managers who try to pick just the "right" securities for their funds' portfolios. *Be warned:* Even the best portfolio managers make mistakes. So you must be careful and evaluate a fund before investing your money.

The diversification mutual funds offer spells safety because a loss incurred with one investment contained in a fund may be offset by gains from other investments in the fund. For example, consider the diversification provided in the portfolio of the Fidelity Balanced Fund, shown in Exhibit 13–1. An investment in the $35.9 billion Fidelity Balanced Fund represents ownership in over 10 different industry sectors and a wide selection of quality stocks and bonds. For beginning investors or investors without a great deal of money to invest, the diversification offered by funds is especially important because there is no other practical way to purchase the individual stocks and bonds issued by a large number of corporations. A fund such as the Fidelity Balanced Fund can provide a practical way for investors to obtain diversification because the fund can use the pooled money of a large number of investors to purchase securities issued by many different companies.

WHAT WOULD YOU DO? After college, you got a full-time job in marketing for a sporting goods retail chain. Now, five years later, you have saved $13,000, which is invested in certificates of deposit that are guaranteed by the Federal Deposit Insurance Corporation. The problem is that your CDs are paying only between 1 and 2 percent. A friend suggested that you should consider mutual funds, but you don't know much about funds. Do you think this is a better option than CDs? Explain your answer.

[2] Investment Company Institute, *2019 Investment Company Fact Book*, **www.ici.org,** accessed February 15, 2020.
[3] Ibid.
[4] Ibid.

Top 5 Industry Sectors	% of Total Assets
Information Technology	21.1
Health Care	14.5
Financials	13.2
Industrials	10.6
Communication Services	10.0
Asset Allocation	**% of Total Assets**
Domestic Stocks	64.0
Bonds	28.4
International Stocks	4.3
Cash and Other Assets	3.3
Top 4 Equity Holdings	**% of Total Assets**
Apple	2.9
Microsoft	2.5
Amazon	1.7
Alphabet (Google)	1.7

Exhibit 13–1

Types of Securities Included in the Portfolio of the Fidelity Balanced Fund

Source: Fidelity, **https://fundresearch.fidelity.com/mutual-funds/summary/316345206?type=o-NavBar,** accessed February 24, 2020, and Yahoo! Finance, **https://finance.yahoo.com/quote/FBALX/holdings?p=FBALX,** accessed February 24, 2020.

Characteristics of Funds

Today, funds may be classified as closed-end funds, exchange-traded funds, or open-end funds.

CLOSED-END, EXCHANGE-TRADED, OR OPEN-END MUTUAL FUNDS

Approximately 500, or about 4 percent, of all mutual funds are closed-end funds offered by investment companies.[5] A **closed-end fund** is a fund in which shares are issued by an investment company only when the fund is organized. As a result, only a certain number of shares are available to investors. After all the shares originally issued have been sold, an investor can purchase shares only from another investor who is willing to sell. Most closed-end funds are actively managed by professional fund managers and shares are traded on the floors of stock exchanges or in the over-the-counter market. Like the prices of stocks, the prices of shares for closed-end funds are determined by the factors of supply and demand, the value of stocks and other securities contained in the fund's portfolio, and investor expectations.

Most **exchange-traded funds (ETF)** are funds that invest in the stocks or other securities contained in a specific stock or securities index. While most investors think of an ETF as investing in the stocks contained in the Standard & Poor's 500 stock index, many different types of ETFs available today attempt to track all kinds of indexes, including:

- Mid-cap stocks.
- Small-cap stocks.
- Fixed-income securities.
- Stocks issued by companies in specific industries.
- Stocks issued by corporations in different countries.

closed-end fund A fund in which shares are issued by an investment company only when the fund is organized.

exchange-traded funds (ETF) A fund that invests in the stocks or other securities contained in a specific stock or securities index and has shares that are traded on a securities exchange or in the over-the-counter market.

[5] Ibid.

As in a closed-end fund, shares of an exchange-traded fund are traded on a securities exchange or in the over-the-counter market. With both types of funds, an investor can purchase as little as one share of a fund. Also as in a closed-end fund, prices for shares in an ETF are determined by supply and demand, the value of stocks and other investments contained in the fund's portfolio, and investor expectations.

Although exchange-traded funds are similar to closed-end funds, there is an important difference. Most closed-end funds are actively managed, with portfolio managers selecting the stocks and other securities contained in a closed-end fund. Almost all exchange-traded funds, on the other hand, invest in the securities included in a specific index. Exchange-traded funds tend to mirror the performance of the index, moving up or down as the individual securities contained in the index move up or down. Therefore, there is less need for a portfolio manager to make investment decisions. Because of passive management, fees associated with owning shares are generally lower than those of both closed-end and open-end funds. *Note:* A *few* ETFs are actively managed with a portfolio manager buying and selling stocks, bonds, and securities. In addition to lower fees, other advantages to investing in ETFs include:

- There is no minimum investment amount because shares are traded on an exchange and not purchased from an investment company.
- Shares can be bought or sold through a brokerage firm any time during regular market hours at the current price.
- You can use limit orders and the more speculative techniques of selling short and buying on margin—all discussed in Chapter 12—to buy and sell ETF shares.

Although increasing in popularity, approximately 2,000, or about 17 percent of all funds, are exchange-traded funds.[6]

Approximately 9,600, or about 79 percent of all mutual funds, are open-end funds.[7] An **open-end fund** is a mutual fund in which shares are issued and redeemed by the investment company at the request of investors. Investors are free to buy and sell shares at the net asset value. The **net asset value (NAV)** per share is equal to the market value of securities contained in the fund's portfolio minus the fund's liabilities divided by the number of shares outstanding.

open-end fund A mutual fund in which shares are issued and redeemed by the investment company at the request of investors.

net asset value (NAV) The market value of the securities contained in the fund's portfolio minus the fund's liabilities divided by the number of shares outstanding.

> **EXAMPLE: Net Asset Value (American Frontiers Mutual Fund)**
>
> The investments contained in the New American Frontiers Mutual Fund have a current market value of $980 million. The fund also has liabilities that total $10 million. If this mutual fund has 40 million shares, the net asset value per share is $24.25, as shown below.
>
> $$\text{Net asset value} = \frac{\text{Value of the fund's portfolio} - \text{Liabilities}}{\text{Number of shares outstanding}}$$
>
> $$= \frac{\$980 \text{ million} - \$10 \text{ million}}{40 \text{ million shares}} = \$24.25 \text{ NAV per share}$$

For open-end funds, the net asset value is calculated typically at the close of trading each day.

In addition to buying and selling shares on request, most open-end funds provide their investors with a wide variety of services, including payroll deduction programs, automatic reinvestment programs, automatic withdrawal programs, and the option to change shares in one fund to another fund within the same fund family—all topics discussed later in this chapter.

[6] Ibid.
[7] Ibid.

COSTS: LOAD FUNDS COMPARED TO NO-LOAD FUNDS With regard to cost, mutual funds are classified as load funds or no-load funds. A **load fund** (sometimes referred to as an *A fund*) is a mutual fund in which investors pay a commission every time they purchase shares. The commission, often referred to as the *sales charge,* may be as high as 8.5 percent of the purchase price for investments. Many exceptions exist, but the average load charge for mutual funds is between 3 and 5 percent. Notice in the example below, the J.P. Morgan Large Cap Growth Fund has a load charge of 5.25 percent. As illustrated below, this represents a sales charge of $525 on a $10,000 investment. After the $525 is paid, the remaining $9,475 can be used to purchase shares in the fund.

load fund A mutual fund in which investors pay a commission every time they purchase shares.

EXAMPLE: Sales Charge Calculation (J.P. Morgan Large Cap Growth Fund)

The J.P. Morgan Large Cap Growth Fund charges a sales load of 5.25 percent. If you invest $10,000, you must pay a $525 commission to purchase shares.

Load charge = Dollar amount of investment × Load stated as a percentage
= $10,000 × 5.25 percent = $525

Amount available for investment = Investment amount − Load charge
= $10,000 − $525 = $9,475

There are two specific exceptions that should be noted. First, investment companies offering front-end load funds often waive or lower fees for shares purchased for retirement accounts. Second, load fund fees are often lower for investors who make large purchases.[8]

The "stated" advantage of a load fund is that the fund's sales force (account executives, financial planners, or employees of brokerage divisions of banks and other financial institutions) will explain the mutual fund, help you determine which fund will help you achieve your financial goals, and offer advice as to when shares of the fund should be bought or sold.

A **no-load fund** is a mutual fund in which the individual investor pays no sales charge. No-load funds don't charge commissions when you buy shares because they have no salespeople. If you want to buy shares of a no-load fund, you must make your own decisions and deal directly with the investment company. The usual means of contact is by Internet, telephone, or mail. You can also purchase shares in a no-load fund from many brokers, including Charles Schwab, TD Ameritrade, Fidelity, and E*Trade.

no-load fund A mutual fund in which the individual investor pays no sales charge.

As an investor, you must decide whether to invest in a load fund or a no-load fund. Some investment salespeople have claimed that load funds outperform no-load funds. Most studies show that no-load funds outperform funds that charge commissions.[9] Since no-load funds don't have sales "loads," or charges, and offer the same investment opportunities as load funds, you should investigate them further before deciding which type of mutual fund is best for you.

Instead of charging investors a fee when they purchase shares in a mutual fund, some mutual funds charge a **contingent deferred sales load** (sometimes referred to as a *back-end load* or a *B fund*), a fee that shareholders pay when they sell shares in a mutual fund. Typically, these fees range from 1 to 5 percent, depending on how long you own the mutual fund before making a withdrawal. For example, you may pay a 5 percent contingent deferred sales load if you withdraw money the first year after your initial investment. In most cases, this fee declines every year until it disappears if you own shares in the fund for more than five years.

contingent deferred sales load A 1 to 5 percent charge that shareholders pay when they sell shares in a mutual fund.

---

[8] Ibid.

[9] Michael Weiss, "The Lowdown on No-Load Mutual Funds," Investopedia, **https://www.investopedia .com/articles/mutualfund/07/no-load.asp,** accessed June 25, 2019.

> ### EXAMPLE: Contingent Deferred Sales Load (Alger Mid Cap Growth Fund)
>
> Assume you withdraw $6,000 from B shares that you own in the Alger Mid Cap Growth Fund within a year of your purchase date. You must pay a 5 percent fee for any withdrawals during the first year. Your fee is $300. After deducting the fee, you will receive $5,700, as shown below.
>
> Contingent deferred sales load = Amount of withdrawal × Fee stated as a percentage
>
> $$= \$6{,}000 \times 5 \text{ percent} = \$300$$
>
> Amount you receive = Amount of withdrawal − Contingent deferred sales load
>
> $$= \$6{,}000 - \$300 = \$5{,}700$$

money minute focus

An App to Determine Fund Costs

The Fund Analyzer provided by the Financial Industry Regulatory Authority (FINRA) is easy to use and provides very useful information about the sales charges and different fees you will pay to invest in a specific fund. It also provides information for similar funds so you can compare fees. To use the app, go to **https://tools.finra.org/fund_analyzer.** Then enter the name of the fund or the fund's symbol, and click search. Why not give it a try?

Source: Financial Industry Regulatory Authority, **https://tools.finra.org/fund_analyzer,** accessed March 3, 2020.

12b-1 fee A fee that an investment company levies to defray the costs of advertising and marketing a mutual fund.

COSTS: MANAGEMENT FEES AND OTHER CHARGES Companies that sponsor funds charge management fees. This fee, which is disclosed in the fund's prospectus, is a fixed percentage of the fund's net asset value on a predetermined date. Today, annual management fees range between 0.25 and 1.5 percent of the fund's net asset value. While fees vary considerably, the average is 0.5 to 1 percent of the fund's net asset value.

The investment company may also levy a **12b-1 fee** (sometimes referred to as a *distribution fee*) to defray the costs of marketing a mutual fund, commissions paid to a broker who sold you shares in the fund, and shareholder service fees. Approved by the Securities and Exchange Commission, 12b-1 fees are taken out of the fund's assets and cannot exceed 1 percent of a fund's assets per year. *Note:* For a fund to be called a "no-load" fund, its 12b-1 fee and shareholder service fees must not exceed 0.25 percent of its assets.

Unlike the one-time sales load fees that mutual funds charge to purchase or sell shares, the 12b-1 fee is often an ongoing fee that is charged on an annual basis. Note that 12b-1 fees can cost you a lot of money over a period of years. Assuming there is no difference in performance offered by two different mutual funds, if one charges a 12b-1 fee while the other doesn't, choose the latter fund. The 12b-1 fee is so lucrative for investment companies that a number of them sell Class C shares that often charge a higher 12b-1 fee and no sales load or contingent deferred sales load to attract new investors. (*Note:* Some investment companies may charge a small contingent deferred sales load for Class C shares if withdrawals are made within a short time—usually one year.) When compared to Class A shares (commissions charged when shares are purchased) and Class B shares (commissions charged when withdrawals are made over the first five years), Class C shares, with their ongoing, higher 12b-1 fees, may be more expensive over a long period of time. On the other hand, Class C with no load charge or only a small charge, if any, for withdrawals may be a better choice for investors who are going to hold their fund shares for a short period of time.

To help you sort out all the research, statistics, and information about mutual funds and determine what to do first, read the suggestions in the nearby *Financial Literacy in Practice* feature.

HOW IMPORTANT ARE FEES? Mutual fund fees are important because they reduce your investment return and are a major factor to consider when choosing a fund. Although fees and expenses vary from fund to fund, a fund with high costs must perform better than a low-cost fund to generate the same returns to you, the investor.

Mutual Funds: Getting Started

Here are some suggestions for beginning a mutual fund investment program.

1. *Perform a financial checkup.* Before investing, you should make sure you have established your investment objectives, balanced your budget, and saved enough money for an emergency fund.

2. *Obtain the money you need to purchase mutual funds.* Although the amount will vary, $2,000 or less is usually required to open an account with a brokerage firm or an investment company. The amount you need may be lower if you open a retirement account.

3. *Find a fund with an objective that matches your objective.* Financial publications and personal finance magazines may help you match potential funds with your investment objectives.

4. *Evaluate, evaluate, and evaluate any fund before buying or selling.* Possible sources of information include the investment company sponsoring the fund, the Internet, professional advisory services, the fund's prospectus, the fund's annual report, financial publications, and newspapers—all sources described later in this chapter.

5. *Continue to evaluate your funds after your investment.* Evaluate your investments on a regular basis. If necessary, sell funds that no longer are helping you achieve your investment objectives or that you think will decrease in value.

Together, all the different management fees and fund operating costs are referred to as an **expense ratio**. Since it is important to keep fees and costs as low as possible, you should examine a fund's expense ratio as one more factor to consider when evaluating a mutual fund.

Make no mistake, fees can make a big difference. For example, assume you invested $10,000 in a fund that earned a 10 percent annual return and had an annual expense ratio of 1.5 percent. Also, assume you chose a second fund that earns 10 percent annual return but had an expense ratio of 0.5 percent. The value of both investments at the end of 20 years is illustrated below.

> ## CAUTION!
>
> Many financial planners recommend that you choose a mutual fund with an expense ratio of 1 percent or less.

expense ratio The amount that investors pay for all of a mutual fund's management fees and operating costs.

EXAMPLE: Expense Ratios Make a Difference in Return

Assume you invest in two different funds. Each fund returns 10 percent a year. One fund has an expense ratio of 1.5 percent; the other fund has an expense ratio of 0.5 percent.

Fund	Amount Invested	Annual Return	Expense Ratio	Value of the Investments at the End of 20 Years
Fund A	$10,000	10%	0.5%	$60,858
Fund B	$10,000	10%	1.5%	$49,725
			Difference in total return	$11,133

Source: Securities and Exchange Commission, "Mutual Fund Fees and Expenses," https://www.sec.gov/fast-answers/answersmffeeshtm.html, accessed February 25, 2020.

Although the two funds in the above example earned the same 10 percent return, the fund with the lower expense ratio earned over $11,000 more than the fund with the higher expense ratio. That's a lot of money that could be yours if you chose the fund with the lower expense ratio.

The investment company's prospectus must provide all details relating to management fees, sales fees, 12b-1 fees, and other expenses. Exhibit 13–2 reproduces the summary of expenses (sometimes called a *fee table*) taken from the Davis New York Venture Fund.

Notice that this fee table has two separate parts. The first part describes shareholder sales load charges. For this fund, the maximum sales charge is 4.75 percent. The second part describes the fund's annual operating expenses. For this fund, the expense ratio is 0.89 percent for Class A shares.

To reinforce the material on the costs of investing in funds, Exhibit 13–3 summarizes information for load charges, no-load charges, and contingent deferred sales loads, and reports typical management fees, 12b-1 charges, and expense ratios. It also summarizes the difference between Class A, Class B, and Class C shares.

By now, you are probably asking yourself, "How do I determine which fund can help me reach my financial goals?" As you will see in the next two sections, a number of sources of information can help you evaluate investment decisions.

Exhibit 13–2 Summary of Expenses Paid to Invest in the Davis New York Venture Fund

	Class A Shares	Class B Shares	Class C Shares
SHAREHOLDER FEES			
(fees paid directly from your investment)			
Maximum sales charge (load) imposed on purchases (as a percentage of offering price)	4.75%	None	None
Maximum deferred sales charge (load) imposed on redemptions (as a percentage of the lesser of the net asset value of the shares redeemed or the total cost of such shares). (*Only applies to Class A shares if you buy shares valued at $1 million or more without a sales charge and sell the shares within one year of purchase.)	0.50%*	4.00%	1.00%
Redemption fee (as a percentage of total redemption proceeds)	None	None	None
ANNUAL FUND OPERATING EXPENSES			
(expenses that you pay each year as a percentage of the value of your investment)			
Management fees	0.53%	0.53%	0.53%
Distribution and/or service (12b-1) fees	0.23%	1.00%	1.00%
Other expenses	0.13%	0.39%	0.15%
Total annual fund operating expenses	0.89%	1.92%	1.68%

Source: Davis Opportunity Fund Prospectus, **https://davisfunds.com/funds/nyventure_fund**, accessed February 15, 2020,

Exhibit 13–3 Typical Fees Associated with Mutual Fund Investments

Type of Fee or Charge	Customary Amount
Load fund	Up to 8.5 percent of the purchase.
No-load fund	No sales charge.
Contingent deferred sales load	1 to 5 percent fee for withdrawals, depending on how long you own shares in the fund before making a withdrawal.
Management fee	0.25 to 1.5 percent per year of the fund's assets.
12b-1 fee	Cannot exceed 1 percent of the fund's assets per year.
Expense ratio	The amount investors pay for all fees and operating costs. Financial experts recommend funds with an expense ratio of 1 percent or less.
Class A shares	Commission charge when shares are purchased.
Class B shares	Commission charge when money is withdrawn during the first five years. Generally, charges decline the longer you own the fund.
Class C shares	No commission to buy or sell shares. These shares may have a small fee for withdrawals and often have higher ongoing 12b-1 fees.

PRACTICE QUIZ 13–1

1. Closed-end, exchange-traded, and open-end funds are available today. Describe the differences between each type of fund.

2. What is the net asset value (NAV) for a mutual fund that has assets totaling $730 million, liabilities totaling $10 million, and 24 million shares outstanding?

3. In the table below, indicate the typical charges for a mutual fund.

Fee	Typical Charge
Load fund	
No-load fund	
Contingent deferred sales load	
Management fee	
12b-1 fee	

4. What is an expense ratio? Why is it important?

Classifications of Mutual Funds

LO13.2

Classify mutual funds by investment objective.

The managers of mutual funds tailor their investment portfolios to the investment objectives of their customers. Usually, a fund's objectives are plainly disclosed in its prospectus. For example, the objective and strategy for the Dodge and Cox Stock Fund is described as follows:

Objective: The fund seeks long-term growth of principal and income. A secondary objective is to achieve a reasonable current income.

Strategy: The Fund invests primarily in a diversified portfolio of equity securities. In selecting investments, the Fund typically invests in companies that, in Dodge & Cox's opinion, appear to be temporarily undervalued by the stock market but have a favorable outlook for long-term growth. The Fund focuses on the underlying financial condition and prospects of individual companies, including future earnings, cash flow, and dividends. Various other factors, including financial strength, economic condition, competitive advantage, quality of the business franchise, and the reputation, experience, and competence of a company's management, are weighed against valuation in selecting individual securities. [10]

ACTION ITEM

I can identify the types of mutual funds that will help me achieve my investment goals.

☐ Yes ☐ No

Although categorizing over 12,000 funds may be helpful, note that different sources of investment information may use different categories for the same fund. In most cases, the name of the category gives a pretty good clue to the types of investments included within the category. The *major* fund categories are stock funds, bond funds, and other funds.

Stock Funds

- *Aggressive growth funds* seek rapid growth by purchasing stocks for which prices are expected to increase dramatically in a short period of time. Turnover within an aggressive growth fund is high because managers are buying and selling stocks of small growth companies. Investors in these funds experience wide price swings because of the underlying speculative nature of the stocks in the fund's portfolio.

[10] Dodge and Cox, "The Dodge and Cox Growth Fund," https://www.dodgeandcox.com/stockfund.asp, accessed February 15, 2020.

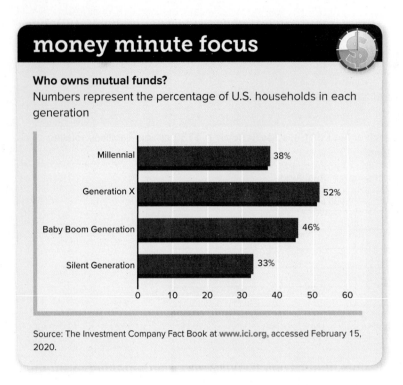

money minute focus

Who owns mutual funds?

Numbers represent the percentage of U.S. households in each generation

- Millennial — 38%
- Generation X — 52%
- Baby Boom Generation — 46%
- Silent Generation — 33%

(axis: 0, 10, 20, 30, 40, 50, 60)

Source: The Investment Company Fact Book at **www.ici.org**, accessed February 15, 2020.

- *Equity income funds* invest in stocks issued by companies with a long history of paying dividends. The major objective of these funds is to provide income to shareholders. These funds are attractive investment choices for conservative or retired investors.
- *Global stock funds* invest in stocks of companies throughout the world, including the United States.
- *Growth funds* invest in companies expecting higher-than-average revenue and earnings growth. While similar to aggressive growth funds, growth funds tend to invest in larger, well-established companies. As a result, the prices for shares in a growth fund are less volatile compared to those of aggressive growth funds.

- *Index funds* invest in the same companies included in an index such as the Standard & Poor's 500 stock index. Since fund managers pick the stocks issued by the companies included in the index, an index fund should provide approximately the same performance as the index. Also, since index funds are cheaper to manage, they often have lower management fees and expense ratios.
- *International funds* invest in foreign stocks sold throughout the world; thus, if the economy in one region or nation is in a slump, profits can still be earned in others. Unlike global funds, which invest in stocks issued by companies in both foreign nations and the United States, a true international fund invests outside the United States.
- *Large-cap funds* invest in companies with total capitalization of $10 billion or more. Large-capitalization stocks are generally stable, well-established companies and are likely to have minimal fluctuation in their value.
- *Mid-cap funds* invest in companies with total capitalization of $2 billion to $10 billion whose stocks offer more security than small-cap funds and more growth potential than funds that invest in large corporations.
- *Regional funds* seek to invest in stock traded within one specific region of the world, such as the European region, the Latin American region, or the Pacific region.
- *Sector funds* invest in companies within the same industry. Examples of sectors include health and biotechnology, science and technology, retailing, and natural resources.
- *Small-cap funds* invest in smaller, lesser-known companies with a total capitalization of between $300 million and $2 billion. Because these companies are small and innovative, these funds offer higher growth potential. They are more speculative than funds that invest in larger, more established companies.
- *Socially responsible funds* avoid investing in companies that may cause harm to people, animals, and the environment. Typically, these funds *do not* invest in companies that produce tobacco products, nuclear energy, or weapons, or in companies that have a history of discrimination. These funds invest in companies that have a history of making ethical decisions, establishing efforts to reduce pollution, and other socially responsible activities.

Bond Funds

- *High-yield (junk) bond funds* invest in high-yield, high-risk corporate bonds.
- *Intermediate corporate bond funds* invest in investment-grade corporate debt with maturities between 3 and 10 years.
- *Intermediate U.S. government bond funds* invest in U.S. Treasury securities with maturities between 3 and 10 years.
- *Long-term corporate bond funds* invest in investment-grade corporate bond issues with maturities in excess of 10 years.
- *Long-term (U.S.) government bond funds* invest in U.S. Treasury securities with maturities in excess of 10 years.
- *Municipal bond funds* invest in municipal bonds that provide investors with tax-free interest income.
- *Short-term corporate bond funds* invest in investment-grade corporate bond issues with maturities of less than three years.
- *Short-term (U.S.) government bond funds* invest in U.S. Treasury securities with maturities of less than three years.
- *World bond funds* invest in bonds and other debt securities offered by foreign companies and governments.

Other Funds

- *Asset allocation funds* invest in different types of investments, including stocks, bonds, fixed-income securities, and money market instruments. These funds seek high total return by maintaining precise amounts within each type of asset.
- *Balanced funds* invest in both stocks and bonds with the primary objectives of conserving principal, providing income, and providing long-term growth. Often the percentages of stocks, bonds, and other securities are stated in the fund's prospectus.
- *Fund of funds* invest in shares of other mutual funds. The main advantage of a fund of funds is increased diversification and asset allocation because this type of fund purchases shares in many different funds. Higher expenses and extra fees are common with this type of fund.
- *Lifecycle funds* (sometimes referred to as *lifestyle funds* or *target-date funds*) are popular with investors planning for retirement by a specific date. Typically, these funds initially invest in risk-oriented securities and become increasingly conservative and income-oriented as the specified retirement date gets closer.
- *Money market funds* invest in certificates of deposit, government securities, and other safe and highly liquid investments.
- *Total stock market funds* are designed to provide investors with exposure to most of the stocks traded in the United States, including small-cap, mid-cap, and large-cap stocks.

A **family of funds** exists when one investment company manages a group of mutual funds. Each fund within the family has a different financial objective. For instance, one fund may be a long-term government bond fund and another a growth stock fund. Most investment companies offer exchange privileges that enable shareholders to switch among the mutual funds in a fund family. For example, if you own shares in the Franklin Biotechnology Discovery Fund, you may, at your discretion, switch to the Franklin Income Fund. Generally, investors may give instructions to switch from one fund to another within the same family via the Internet, over the phone, or in writing. The family-of-funds concept allows shareholders to conveniently switch their investments among funds as different

family of funds A group of mutual funds managed by one investment company.

funds offer more potential, financial reward, or security. Charges for exchanges, if any, generally are small for each transaction. For funds that do charge, the fee may be as low as $1 to $5 per transaction.

WHAT WOULD YOU DO? After college, you started your own commercial landscaping business and the business is growing, but you are concerned because you have had to invest all of your profits back in the business to purchase more equipment. You are now at the point where business is good and money is left over after all the expenses are paid. You've never invested before, but a good friend has suggested mutual funds. After some Internet research, you know there are a lot of different kinds of funds. Which type of fund do you think can help you obtain your investment goals?

The Benefits of Portfolio Construction

While reading this section, keep in mind one important fact: As mentioned in the first part of this chapter, there are more than 12,000 funds to choose from. That's a lot of funds, and by now you realize that some funds will help you achieve your investment goals better than others. To decide which funds are right for you, first, you must decide what type of fund(s) you want. Choices include stock funds, bond funds, or the other funds that were described earlier. You can choose more than one type of fund and even other investment alternatives, including individual stocks, individual bonds, real estate, or more speculative investments, to construct a portfolio of investments that will help you obtain your investment goals. **Portfolio construction** is the process of choosing different types of stocks, bonds, funds, and other investment alternatives to obtain larger returns while reducing risk. Using the portfolio construction concept is a very personalized process, and the choice of investments is often determined by your goals, your tolerance for risk, your age, how much money you have to invest, how long before you retire, and other factors. In addition to personal factors, the nation's economy, world economy, unemployment rate, inflation rates, interest rates, and a host of other factors that could affect your investment portfolio must be considered. People who use portfolio construction are much more involved in their investment program and are willing to invest the time and effort to build a portfolio that is more suited to their particular needs—especially when they are planning for retirement.

portfolio construction The process of choosing different types of stocks, bonds, funds, and other investment alternatives to obtain larger returns while reducing risk.

Choosing the Right Fund for a Retirement Account

Assume you have just secured a new job and your employer offers you the opportunity to participate in the company's 401(k) or 403(b) retirement plan. In this situation, you must weigh at least three considerations that can affect your financial future.

1. *Do you want to participate in the retirement account?* The answer to this question is a definite yes for two reasons. The reasons are simple: Employer-sponsored retirement accounts—as explained in Chapter 14—provide a way to reduce the amount of current income tax that is withheld from your paycheck. So there are immediate tax savings. A second reason for participating in a retirement plan is because many employers will match your contributions. A common match would work like this: For every $1.00 the employee contributes, the employer contributes an additional $0.50. All monies—both the employer's and your contributions—are then invested in mutual funds that are selected by you. *Note:* Many employers that match place a limit on how much of the employee's salary can be matched each year.

2. *Which mutual funds do you want to invest in?*
Most retirement plans allow you to choose the
mutual funds for your plan from a number of
different fund options. When making your choices,
keep in mind your long-term goals and the time
value of money concept that was discussed in
Chapter 1. The time value of money concept is
especially important because the investments
in your plan will grow because you (and your
employer) continue to contribute money to your
retirement account *and* quality investments should
increase in value over a long period of time.

> ## CAUTION!
>
> Although some employers have reduced or
> eliminated matching provisions, many employers
> still match employee contributions. In fact, during
> a job interview, you may want to ask about the
> employer's matching provisions for a 401(k) or
> 403(b) retirement account.

3. *What is your stage in life?* The actual choice of investments for your retirement
account should be determined by your age, how long before you retire, and your
tolerance for risk. Typically, younger workers choose more risk-oriented funds that
have greater potential for growth over a long period of time. Older workers closer to
retirement tend to choose more conservative funds with less risk.

Regardless of the type of funds you choose for your retirement account, it is important
to evaluate each fund before making your choices. The information in the "How to Make a
Decision to Buy or Sell Mutual Funds" section will help you choose the right funds. Once
your investment choices are made, it is important to continue to monitor each of your funds
to determine if you are on the right track to achieve your financial objectives.

PRACTICE QUIZ 13–2

1. How important is the investment objective and strategy statement as presented in a mutual fund's prospectus?

2. Identify one mutual fund in each of the three categories (stocks, bonds, and other), and describe the
characteristics of the fund you select and the type of investor who would invest in that type of fund.

General Fund Type	Fund Name	Characteristics of Fund	Typical Investor
Stock			
Bond			
Other			

3. How can choosing the right fund help you save for retirement?

How to Make a Decision to Buy or Sell Mutual Funds

LO13.3

Evaluate mutual funds.

ACTION ITEM

I know what sources of
information to use to
evaluate a mutual fund.

☐ Yes ☐ No

Often the decision to buy or sell shares in mutual funds is "too easy" because investors
assume they do not need to evaluate these investments. Why question what the professional
portfolio managers decide to do? Yet professionals do make mistakes. And sometimes,
economic and financial conditions beyond the control of a fund manager cause a fund's
value to decrease. Because of these two factors, you should realize that the responsibility
for choosing the right mutual fund rests with *you.*

Fortunately, a lot of information is available to help you evaluate a specific mutual fund.
To begin the search for a fund that can help you achieve your financial goals, answer one
basic question: Do you want a managed fund or an index fund?

Managed Funds versus Index Funds

Most mutual funds are managed funds. In other words, there is a professional fund manager (or team of managers) who chooses the securities that are contained in the fund. The fund manager also decides when to buy and sell securities in the fund. To help evaluate a fund, you may want to determine how well a fund manager manages during both good and bad economic times. The benchmark for a good fund manager is the ability to increase share value when the economy is good and retain that value when the economy is bad. For example, most funds increased in value in 2019. Some funds even reported 20 to 30 percent or even higher gains for the year. Yet, the question remains whether these same funds can retain their value when there is another economic or world crisis. Consider what happened toward the end of February 2020—just two months after the end of a great year for investors. Many of those same funds lost value when the world became concerned with the threat of a coronavirus (COVID-19) pandemic. While people were worried about both an increasing number of cases and deaths worldwide, businesses were concerned about temporary factory and retail store closures, supply chain disruption, lower consumer spending, and a host of other problems caused by the COVID-19 virus. All of these factors led to record drops in stock and fund prices.

One important consideration is how long the present fund manager has been managing the fund. If a fund has performed well under its present manager over a 5-year, 10-year, or longer period, there is a strong likelihood that it will continue to perform well under that manager in the future. On the other hand, if the fund has a new manager, his or her decisions may affect the performance of the fund. Managed funds may be open-end funds or closed-end funds.

CAUTION!

Don't forget the role of the fund manager in determining a fund's success.

Instead of investing in a managed fund, some investors choose to invest in an index fund. Why? The answer to that question is simple: Over many years, the majority of managed funds fail to outperform the Standard & Poor's 500 stock index—a common benchmark of stock market performance often reported on financial news programs. Study after study shows disappointing results for actively managed funds. In fact, only a small percentage of actively managed funds ever do better than index funds.[11]

Because an index mutual fund is a mirror image of a specific index such as the S&P 500, the dollar value of a share in an index fund also increases when the index increases. Unfortunately, the reverse is also true. If the index goes down, the value of a share in an index fund goes down. Index funds, sometimes called "passive" funds, have managers, but they simply buy the stocks, bonds, or securities contained in the index.

A second and very important reason why investors choose index funds is the lower expense ratio charged by these passively managed funds. As mentioned earlier in this chapter, the total fees charged by a mutual fund are called the expense ratio. If a fund's expense ratio is 1.25 percent, then the fund has to earn at least that amount on its investment holdings just to break even each year. Typically the expense ratios for managed funds are approximately 1 percent or higher; expense ratios for index funds are approximately 0.50 percent or lower. And while lower fees may not sound significant, don't be fooled. Over a long period of time, even a small difference can become huge. Although expense ratios and the effect they have on investment returns was discussed in the "Characteristics of Funds" section of this chapter, a second example is presented in this section to reinforce this concept. Assume two different investors each invest $10,000. One investor chooses an index fund that has annual expenses of 0.20 percent; the other chooses a managed fund that has annual expenses of 1.22 percent. Both funds earn 10 percent a year. After 35 years, the index fund is worth $263,683, while the managed fund is worth $190,203.

---

[11] Pam Krueger, "Active vs. Passive Investing: What's the Difference," Investopedia, **https://www.investopedia.com/news/active-vs-passive-investing**, accessed February 29, 2020.

That's a difference of $73,480. Thus, even though the two funds earned the same 10 percent a year, the difference in annual expenses made a substantial difference in the amount of money each investor had at the end of 35 years.[12]

Should you choose a managed fund or an index fund? Good question. The answer depends on which managed fund you choose. If you pick a managed fund that has better performance than an index, then you made the right choice. If, on the other hand, the index (and the index fund) outperforms the managed fund—which happens most of the time—an index fund is a better choice. With both investments, the key is how well you can research a specific investment alternative using the sources of information described in the remainder of this section.

The Internet

Many investors have found a wealth of information about mutual fund investments on the Internet. Basically, you can access information three ways. First, you can obtain current market values for mutual funds by using a website such as Marketwatch (**www.marketwatch.com**), MSN Money (**https://www.msn.com/en-us/money**), or Yahoo! (**http://finance.yahoo.com/**). For example, the Yahoo! Finance page has a box in which you can enter the symbol of the mutual fund you want to research. If you don't know the symbol, you can enter in the name of the mutual fund in the "Quote Lookup" box. The Yahoo! Finance website will respond with the correct symbol. In addition to current market values, you can obtain a price history for a mutual fund, a profile including information about current holdings, performance, risk, sustainability, and purchasing shares.

Second, most investment companies that sponsor mutual funds have a web page. To obtain information, all you have to do is access an Internet search engine and type in the name of the fund or enter the investment company's Internet address (URL) in your browser. A sample of the information about the Fidelity Contrafund available from the Fidelity Investments website (**https://www.fidelity.com/**) is illustrated in Exhibit 13-4.

Exhibit **13–4** Information about the Fidelity Contrafund Available from the Fidelity Investment Website

"Fidelity Contrafund," Fidelity Investments Website, (https://fundresearch.fidelity.com/mutual-funds/summary/316071109?type=sq-NavBar), accessed February 29, 2020.

[12] Bankrate.com, "Index Funds vs. Actively Managed Funds," **http://www.bankrate.com/finance/retirement/index-funds-vs-actively-managed-funds.aspx**, accessed February 29, 2020.

Note that the information about this fund includes the Morningstar Snapshot describing the fund. Also included is information about the fund's average annual returns, investment holdings, risk, overall rating, fees and distributions, performance, and hypothetical growth of an investment.

Be warned: Investment companies want you to become a shareholder. As a result, the websites for *some* investment companies read like a sales pitch. Read between the glowing descriptions and look at the facts before investing your money.

Finally, more detailed information about funds is provided by the professional advisory services described in the next section. By using the Internet, you can obtain up-to-date information quickly without having to wait for research materials to be mailed or having to make a trip to the library.

Professional Advisory Services

As pointed out in the previous section, professional advisory services provide detailed information on mutual funds. Morningstar, Inc. (**https://www.morningstar.com/**), Value Line (**https://valueline.com/**), and Refinitiv Lipper (**https://www.refinitiv.com/en/ investment-management#products**) are three widely used sources of such information. Exhibit 13–5 illustrates the type of information provided by Morningstar for the T. Rowe Price Dividend Growth Fund. The Morningstar report provides a wealth of information designed to help you decide if this is the right fund for you.

Notice that the information is divided into various sections.

- At the top, there are tabs for Quote, Fund Analysis, Performance, Risk, Price, Portfolio, People, and Parent.
- A little farther down there are tabs for Morningstar Analysis, Summary, Full Analysis, and Report Archive. To view this information, you must register and pay a fee.
- Toward the bottom of the Exhibit, there is an interactive chart that illustrates the growth of a $10,000 investment, and statistics on the fund for a 10-year period.

Notice that this T. Rowe Price fund is rated five stars (the highest) and that it has an expense ratio of 0.64 percent. Also note this fund is a no-load fund and the minimum initial investment is $2,500.

In addition, various mutual fund newsletters provide financial information to fund investors. *Be warned:* While some information may be free, many professional advisory services require that you register and provide personal information and/or pay a fee for their research and recommendations. In some cases, some of this detailed fund research may be available in larger public libraries or in your college library.

WHAT WOULD YOU DO? You are participating in your employer's 401(k) retirement plan and have $165,000 invested in a conservative bond fund that has a year-to-date return of 1.8 percent. You also have $150,000 invested in a conservative large-cap fund that has a year-to-date return of 8.3 percent. You like the returns the large-cap fund has, but you like the safety of the bond fund. You also think that it may be time to pick at least one more fund to diversify your holdings or even start investing in stocks instead of funds. What should you do?

Exhibit **13–5** **Mutual Fund Research Information for the T. Rowe Price Dividend Growth Fund Provided by Morningstar.**

T. Rowe Price Dividend Growth PRDGX ★★★★★ ⊕ Morningstar Analyst Rating

Analyst rating as of Jul 8, 2019

Quote   Fund Analysis   Performance   Risk   Price   Portfolio   People   Parent

NAV / 1-Day Return	Total Assets	Adj. Expense Ratio ⓘ	Expense Ratio	Fee Level	Load
46.41 / -2.19%	13.6 Bil	0.640%	0.640%	Below Average	None

Category	Investment Style	Minimum Initial Investment	Status	SEC Yield	Turnover
US Fund Large Blend	▦ Large Blend	2,500	Open	1.36%	7%

USD | NAV as of Apr 20, 2020 | 1-Day Return as of Apr 20, 2020, 7:26 PM CDT

Morningstar's Analysis ⓘ

Performance Jul 8, 2019	Price Jul 8, 2019	Process Jul 8, 2019	People Jul 8, 2019	Parent Oct 1, 2018
⊡ PREMIUM	⊡ PREMIUM	⊡ PREMIUM	⊡ PREMIUM	⊡ PREMIUM

Stephen Welch
Analyst

Experience and consistency continue to pay dividends.

Summary | by Stephen Welch, CFA Jul 8, 2019

T. Rowe Price Dividend Growth's steadiness supports its Morningstar Analyst Rating of Silver.

⊡ **Read Full Analysis** ⌄

⊡ **View Report Archive** >

Growth of 10,000

— Fund
— Category
— Index
● Fund Flows

Manager Change
● Full
○ Partial

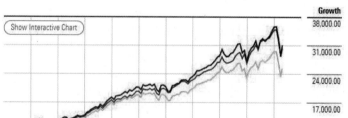

	Growth	As of Apr 20, 2020 | USD
	38,000.00	— **Index**
	31,000.00	**31,089**
	24,000.00	— **PRDGX**
		30,434
	17,000.00	— **Category**
	10,000.00	**25,382**
	3,000.00	

Fund Flows
636.33 Mil
0.00
-636.33 Mil

Total Return %	2010	2011	2012	2013	2014	2015	2016	2017	2018	2019	YTD
Fund	13.26	3.53	14.85	30.35	12.34	2.36	11.62	19.32	-1.06	31.02	-12.67
+/- Category	-0.75	4.81	-0.11	-1.15	1.38	3.43	1.25	-1.12	5.21	2.24	1.57
+/- Index	-2.84	2.03	-1.57	-2.76	-0.90	1.44	-0.44	-2.36	3.72	-0.41	0.02
Quartile Rank	▤	▤	▤	▤	▤	▤	▤	▤	▤	▤	▤
Percentile Rank	60	11	58	69	40	14	33	70	6	35	42
# of Funds in Cat.	2,010	1,786	1,686	1,559	1,568	1,606	1,409	1,396	1,402	1,387	1,416

The Morningstar (https://www.morningstar.com/funds/xnas/prdgx/quote), accessed April 20, 2020.

The Mutual Fund Prospectus and Annual Report

An investment company sponsoring a mutual fund must give potential investors a prospectus. You can also obtain a prospectus by accessing the investment company website, by calling a toll-free phone number, or by written request.

According to financial experts, the prospectus is usually the first piece of information investors receive, and they should read it completely before investing. Although it may look foreboding, a commonsense approach to reading a fund's prospectus can provide valuable insights. In addition to information about the fund's investment objective(s) and fees, the prospectus should provide the following:

- A statement describing the risk factor associated with the fund.
- A description of the fund's past performance.
- A statement describing the type of investments contained in the fund's portfolio.
- Information about dividends, distributions, and taxes.
- Information about the fund's management.
- Information on limitations or requirements, if any, the fund must honor when choosing investments.
- The process investors can use to open an account and to buy or sell shares in the fund.
- A description of services provided to investors and fees for services, if any.
- Information about how often the fund's investment portfolio changes (sometimes referred to as its *turnover ratio*).

If you are a prospective investor or have invested in a fund, you can read a fund's annual report by using the Internet to access an investment company's website. You can also request an annual report by calling a toll-free phone number or by writing the company. A fund's annual report contains a letter from the president of the investment company, from the fund manager, or both. The annual report also contains detailed financial information about the fund's assets and liabilities, performance, statement of operations, and statement of changes in net assets. Next, the annual report includes a schedule of investments. Finally, the fund's annual report should include a letter from the fund's independent auditors that provides an opinion as to the accuracy of the fund's financial statements.

Financial Publications and Newspapers

Business- and investment-oriented magazines such as *Bloomberg Businessweek, Forbes, Fortune, Kiplinger's Personal Finance,* and *Money* are excellent sources of information about mutual funds. Depending on the publication, coverage ranges from detailed articles that provide in-depth information to simple listings of which funds to buy or sell. And many investment-oriented magazines now provide information about mutual funds on the Internet. The material in Exhibit 13–6 was obtained from the Kiplinger website and is

Exhibit **13–6** Information about No-Load Funds Recommended by Kiplinger

Large-Company Stock Funds							*Data through April 30, 2020*
SYMBOL	**FUND NAME**	**1-YR RETURN**	**3-YR RETURN**	**5-YR RETURN**	**10-YR RETURN**	**20-YR RETURN**	**EXPENSE RATIO**
DODGX	Dodge & Cox Stock	−12.64%	1.72%	4.84%	9.39%	7.77%	0.52%
PRDGX	T. Rowe Price Dividend Growth	−0.22	8.92	9.14	11.26	7.28	0.62
MPGFX	Mairs & Power Growth	−0.28	6.78	7.84	10.59	9.09	0.65
TRBCX	T Rowe Price Blue Chip Growth	7.48	16.43	13.98	15.26	7.32	0.69
DFDMX	DF Dent Midcap Growth	6.93	16.80	12.58	–	–	0.98

Source: Kiplinger, "Kiplinger's 25 Favorite No-Load Mutual Funds," https://www.kiplinger.com/tool/investing/T041-S000-kiplingers-25-favorite-fund/index.php, accessed April 30, 2020.

WEALTH CREATION

INVESTING

RETIREMENT

TAXES

PERSONAL FINANCE

YOUR BUSINESS

The above six topics are what the Kiplinger website is all about. In fact, these six topics are one of the first things you see when you go to the Kiplinger website at **https://www.kiplinger.com/.** One of the premier sources of information about personal finance and investing, this site is also recognized for its information, research, and recommendations for funds and ETFs.

By clicking on one of the above tabs, you can access a great deal of information. For example, if you click on the investing tab, you can obtain:

- Real-time updates for the financial markets.

- Access articles that describe trends affecting funds and ETFs.

- Information about different brokerage firms.

The other tabs—Wealth Creation, Retirement, Taxes, Personal Finance, and Your Business—also contain information you can use to improve your financial planning and fine-tune your investment portfolio. By clicking on the links on the left side of the home page, you can access even more useful information, including articles e-newsletters, videos, podcasts, and more. There is a reason why many financial experts recommend the Kiplinger site for both beginning and experienced investors.

ACTION STEPS FOR. . .

. . .Information Literacy

Use the search button on the Kiplinger site (**https://www.kiplinger.com/**) to locate the article entitled "The 25 Best Mutual Funds of All Time." Read the article and then choose three funds included in the top-25 funds. Present your findings in an oral or written presentation that can be shared with your classmates or your instructor. Be sure to describe each fund's average performance since inception and what you think makes the three funds you chose outstanding.

. . .Financial Literacy

Click on the Investing button on the Kiplinger site (**https://www.kiplinger.com/**). Then read one of articles in the Mutual Fund section. Based on the information in the article, prepare a PowerPoint or video presentation that explains why you think the information in the article could help you become a better investor.

. . .Diginal Literacy

Use the search button on the Kiplinger site (**https://www.kiplinger.com/**) to locate the Kiplinger Net Worth Calculator. Then enter the dollar amounts of your assets and liabilities. Once you've completed entering your data, your current net worth will display at the bottom. Develop a plan of action that you can use to increase your net worth over the next 1-, 5-, and 10-year periods. Describe your plan in a journal that you can keep for future reference. Then use this calculator at least once a year to review your plan and make changes that will help increase your net worth.

a *partial* listing of 25 different funds that were recommended in the feature "Kiplinger's 25 Favorite No-Load Mutual Funds." Specific information is broken down by the type of stocks and securities in each category and includes:

- The fund name and symbol.
- The fund's 1-, 3-, 5-, 10-, and 20-year returns.
- The fund's expense ratio.

In addition to mutual fund information in business and investment publications, a number of mutual fund guidebooks are available at your local bookstore or public library.

Although many newspapers have reduced or eliminated mutual fund coverage, many large metropolitan newspapers and *The Wall Street Journal* often provide news and information about funds. In addition to feature articles about selected funds, typical information about prices and financial performance includes the name of the fund family and fund name, current net asset value for a share, net change, and year-to-date percentage of return. Much of this same information (along with more detailed information) is also available on the Internet.

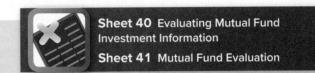

Sheet 40 Evaluating Mutual Fund Investment Information

Sheet 41 Mutual Fund Evaluation

PRACTICE QUIZ 13–3

1. In your own words, describe the difference between a managed fund and an index fund. Which one do you think could help you achieve your investment goals?

2. Describe how each of the following sources of investment information could help you evaluate a mutual fund investment.

Source of Information	Type of Information	How This Could Help
The Internet		
Professional advisory services		
Mutual fund prospectus		
Mutual fund annual report		
Financial publications		
Newspapers		

LO13.4

Describe how and why mutual funds are bought and sold.

ACTION ITEM

I am aware of the purchase and withdrawal options for a mutual fund.

☐ Yes ☐ No

The Mechanics of a Mutual Fund Transaction

For many investors, mutual funds have become the investment of choice. In fact, you probably either own shares or know someone who owns shares in a mutual fund—they're that popular! They may be part of a 401(k) or 403(b) retirement account, SEP IRA, Roth IRA, or traditional IRA retirement account, all topics discussed in Chapter 14. They can also be owned outright in a taxable account by purchasing shares through a registered sales representative who works for a bank or brokerage firm or an investment company that sponsors a mutual fund. Although there are exceptions, most individuals invest in mutual funds to achieve long-term financial objectives. When you invest your money, you are counting on the time value of money concept to help build your nest egg. Remember that in Chapter 1, *time value of money* was defined as the increases in an amount of money as a result of interest earned. For example, saving or investing $2,000 instead of spending it today results in a future amount greater than $2,000. If the $2,000 is used to purchase shares in a fund, your shares can increase in value, and you can receive income from your investment that can be reinvested to purchase more shares. As you will see later in this section, it's easy to purchase shares in a mutual fund. For $2,000 or less, you can open an account and begin investing. And there are other advantages that encourage investors to purchase shares in funds. Unfortunately, there are also disadvantages. Exhibit 13–7 summarizes the advantages and disadvantages of fund investments.

Exhibit **13–7** **Advantages and Disadvantages of Investing in Mutual Funds**

Advantages

- Diversification.

- Professional management.

- Ease of buying and selling shares.

- Multiple withdrawal options.

- Distribution or reinvestment of dividends and capital gain distributions.

- Switching privileges within the same fund family.

- Services that include toll-free telephone numbers, complete records of all transactions, and options for savings and checking.

Disadvantages

- Purchase/withdrawal costs.

- Ongoing management and 12b-1 fees.

- Poor performance that may not match that of the Standard & Poor's 500 stock index or some other index.

- Inability to control when capital gain distributions occur and complicated tax reporting issues.

- Potential market risk associated with all investments.

- Some sales personnel are aggressive and/or unethical.

One advantage of any investment is the opportunity to make money on the investment. In this section, we examine how you can make money by investing in funds. We also consider how taxes affect your fund investments. Then we look at the options used to purchase or sell shares in a fund.

Return on Investment

As with other investments, the purpose of investing in a closed-end fund, exchange-traded fund, or open-end fund is to earn a financial return. Shareholders in such funds can receive a return in one of three ways. First, all three types of funds pay income dividends. **Income dividends** are the earnings a fund pays to shareholders from its dividend and interest income. Second, investors may receive capital gain distributions. **Capital gain distributions** are the payments made to a fund's shareholders that result from the sale of securities in the fund's portfolio. Typically, most funds pay both income dividends and capital gain distributions once a year. *Note:* Many exchange-traded funds may pay monthly or quarterly income dividends, but exchange-traded funds don't usually pay end-of-the-year capital gain distributions. Third, as with stock and bond investments, you can buy shares in funds at a low price and then sell them after the price has increased. For example, assume you purchased shares in the Fidelity Stock Selector All Cap Fund at $42 per share and sold your shares two years later at $50 per share. In this case, you made $8 ($50 selling price minus $42 purchase price = $8) per share. When you sell shares in a fund, the profit that results from an increase in value is referred to as a *capital gain.*

FinTech for Financial Literacy

The Personal Capital App Tracks the Value of Your Investments

Today, many people use apps for all sorts of daily activities. So why not use an app to track the value of your investments? One popular app is Personal Capital. The app is free, and it's easy to create an account.

Once you've created an account, you can track the value of your investments with updated information throughout the trading day. It also provides information about asset allocation, tracks fees for the funds you own, and provides calculations to help you plan for retirement. You can even talk to an advisor or participate in a live chat. Take a look at **https://www.personalcapital.com/**.

Source: Rob Berger, "The Best Way to Track Your Investments Online (and It's Free)," DoughRoller, **https://www.doughroller.net/investing/the-best-way-to-track-your-investments-online-for-free/**, accessed March 3, 2020

income dividends The earnings a fund pays to shareholders from its dividend and interest income.

capital gain distributions The payments made to a fund's shareholders that result from the sale of securities in the fund's portfolio.

Figure It Out!

Calculating Total Return for Mutual Funds

In Chapter 12, we defined total return as a calculation that includes not only the yearly dollar amount of income but also any increase or decrease in market value. For funds, you can use the following calculation to determine the dollar amount of total return:

Income dividends + Capital gain distributions + Change in share price when sold = Dollar amount of total return

For example, assume you purchased 100 shares of the Majestic Growth Fund for $27 per share for a total investment of $2,700. During the next 12 months, you received income dividends of $0.40 a share and capital gain distributions of $0.55 a share. Also, assume you sold your investment at the end of 12 months for $31 a share. As illustrated below, the dollar amount of total return is $495:

Income dividends = 100 × $0.40 =	$ 40
Capital gain distributions = 100 × $0.55 =	+ 55
Change in share price = $31 − $27 = $ 4 × 100 =	+ 400
Dollar amount of total return	$ 495

To calculate the percentage of total return, divide the dollar amount of total return by the original cost of your mutual fund investment. The percentage of total return for the above example is 18.3 percent, as follows:

$$\text{Percent of total return} = \frac{\text{Dollar amount of total return}}{\text{Original cost of your investment}}$$

$$= \frac{\$495}{\$2,700}$$

$$= 0.183, \text{ or } 18.3 \text{ percent}$$

Now it's your turn. Use the following financial information for the Northeast Utility Fund to calculate the dollar amount of total return and percent of total return over a 12-month period.

Number of shares, 100
Purchase price, $14.00 a share
Income dividends, $0.30 a share
Capital gain distribution, $0.60 a share
Sale price, $15.25 a share

Calculation	Calculation Formula	Your Answer
Dollar amount of total return		
Percent of total return		

ANSWERS: The total return is $215, and the percent of total return is 15.4 percent.

Note the difference between a capital gain distribution and a capital gain. A *capital gain distribution* occurs when *the fund* distributes profits that result from *the fund* selling securities in the *fund's* portfolio at a profit. On the other hand, a *capital gain* is the profit that results when *you* sell your shares in your mutual fund for more than *you* paid for them. Of course, if the price of a fund's shares goes down between the time of your purchase and the time of sale, you incur a capital loss.

For any fund, it is possible to calculate total return and percentage of total return. To see how to calculate these amounts, read the information in the nearby *Figure It Out!* feature.

Taxes and Mutual Funds

Taxes on reinvested income dividends, capital gain distributions, and profits from the sale of shares can be *deferred* if fund investments are held in your retirement account. Assuming all qualifications are met, you can even *eliminate* taxes on reinvested income, capital gain distributions, and profits from the sale of shares for funds held in a Roth individual retirement account. For mutual funds held in taxable accounts, income dividends, capital gain distributions, and financial gains and losses from the sale of funds are subject to taxation. At the end of each year, investment companies are required to send each shareholder a statement specifying how much he or she received in income dividends and capital gain distributions. Investment companies report amounts for dividend income and capital gain distributions on IRS Form 1099 DIV. The same information may also be reported as part of their year-end statement. The following information provides general guidelines on how mutual fund transactions are taxed when held in a taxable account:

money minute focus

CHARACTERISTICS OF MUTUAL FUND OWNERS

63%	Purchased their first mutual fund through an employer- sponsored retirement plan.
93%	Are saving for retirement.
46%	Are saving for emergencies
45%	Own funds to reduce taxable income
24%	Are saving for education

Source: Investment Company Institute, **https://www.ici.org/pdf/2019_factbook.pdf**, accessed February 20, 2020.

- Income dividends are reported on your federal tax return and are taxed as income.
- Capital gain distributions that result from the fund selling securities in the fund's portfolio at a profit are reported on your federal tax return. Capital gain distributions are taxed as long-term capital gains, regardless of how long you own shares in the fund.[13]
- Capital gains or losses that result from your selling shares in a mutual fund are reported on your federal tax return. How long you hold the shares determines if your gains or losses are taxed as a short-term or long-term capital gain. (See Chapter 3 for more information on capital gains and capital losses, or visit the IRS website at **www.irs.gov.**)

Two specific problems develop with taxation of mutual funds. First, almost all investment companies allow you to reinvest income dividends and capital gain distributions from the fund to purchase additional shares instead of receiving cash. Even though you didn't receive cash because you chose to reinvest such dividends and distributions, they are still taxed in a taxable account and must be reported on your federal tax return as current income.

Second, when you purchase shares of stock, corporate bonds, or other securities, you decide when you sell. Thus, you can pick the tax year when you pay tax on capital gains or deduct capital losses. Mutual funds, on the other hand, buy and sell securities within the fund's portfolio on a regular basis during any 12-month period. At the end of the year, profits that result from the mutual fund's buying and selling activities are paid to shareholders in the form of capital gain distributions. Unlike the investments you manage, you have no control over when the mutual fund sells securities and when you will be taxed on capital gain distributions. Because capital gain distributions are taxable, one factor to consider when choosing a mutual fund is its turnover. For a mutual fund, the **turnover ratio** measures the percentage of a fund's holdings that have changed or "been replaced" during a 12-month period of time. Simply put, it is a measure of a fund's trading activity. *Caution:* A mutual fund with a high turnover ratio can result in higher income tax bills for the investor. A higher turnover ratio can also result in higher transaction costs and fund expenses.

turnover ratio A ratio that measures the percentage of a fund's holdings that have changed or "been replaced" during a 12-month period of time.

To ensure having all of the documentation you need for tax reporting purposes, it is essential that *you* keep accurate records. The same records will help you monitor the value of your fund investments and make more intelligent decisions with regard to buying, holding, or selling these investments.

---

[13] Internal Revenue Service, "Dividends and Other Distributions," **https://www.irs.gov/publications/p550/ch01.html#en_US_2016_publink100010089)**, accessed March 2, 2020.

Purchase Options

You can buy shares of a closed-end fund or exchange-traded fund through a stock exchange or in the over-the-counter market. You can purchase shares of an *open-end, no-load* fund by contacting the investment company that manages the fund. You can purchase shares of an *open-end load* fund through a salesperson who is authorized to sell them, through an account executive of a brokerage firm, or directly from the investment company that sponsors the fund.

You can also purchase both no-load and load funds from mutual fund supermarkets available through most brokerage firms. A mutual fund supermarket such as Fidelity, Charles Schwab, E*Trade, or TD Ameritrade offers at least two advantages. First, instead of dealing with numerous investment companies that sponsor funds, you can visit one website or make one toll-free phone call to obtain information, purchase shares, and sell shares in a large number of mutual funds. Second, you receive one statement from one brokerage firm instead of receiving a statement from each investment company or brokerage firm you deal with. One statement can be a real plus because it provides the information you need to monitor the value of your investments in one place and in the same format.

Because of the unique nature of open-end fund transactions, we will examine how investors buy and sell shares in this type of mutual fund. To purchase shares in an open-end mutual fund, you may use four options:

- Regular account transactions.
- Voluntary savings plans.
- Contractual savings plans.
- Reinvestment plans.

The most popular and least complicated method of purchasing shares in an open-end fund is through a regular account transaction. When you use a regular account transaction, you decide how much money you want to invest and when you want to invest, and then you simply buy as many shares as possible.

The chief advantage of the voluntary savings plans is that they often allow you to make smaller purchases than the minimum purchases required by the regular account method described above. At the time of the initial purchase, you declare an intent to make regular minimum purchases of the fund's shares. Although there is no penalty for not making purchases, most investors feel an "obligation" to make purchases on a regular basis, and, as pointed out throughout this text, small monthly investments are a great way to save for long-term objectives. For most voluntary savings plans, the minimum purchase ranges from $25 to $100 for each purchase after the initial investment. Funds try to make investing as easy as possible. Most offer payroll deduction plans, and many will deduct, upon proper shareholder authorization, a specified amount from a shareholder's bank account. Also, many investors can choose voluntary savings plans as a vehicle to invest money contributed to a 401(k), 403(b), or individual retirement account. When part of a retirement plan at work, the amount used to purchase shares is often a percentage of the employee's pay that is deducted each pay period.

Not as popular as they once were, contractual savings plans (sometimes referred to as *periodic payment plans*) require you to make regular purchases over a specified period of time, usually 10 to 15 years. These plans are sometimes referred to as *front-end load plans* because almost all of the commissions are paid in the first few years of the contract period. Also, you may incur penalties if you do not fulfill the purchase requirements. For example, if you drop out of a contractual savings plan before completing the purchase requirements, you may sacrifice some or all of the prepaid commissions. In some cases, contractual savings plans combine mutual fund shares and life insurance to make these plans more attractive. Many financial experts and government regulatory agencies are critical of contractual savings plans. As a result, the Securities and Exchange Commission and many states have imposed new rules on investment companies offering contractual savings plans.

You may also purchase shares in an open-end fund by using the fund's reinvestment plan. A **reinvestment plan** is a service provided by an investment company in which income dividends and capital gain distributions are automatically reinvested to purchase additional shares of the fund. Many reinvestment plans allow shareholders to use reinvested money to purchase shares without having to pay additional sales charges or commissions. *Reminder:* When your dividends or capital gain distributions are reinvested in a taxable account, you must still report these transactions as taxable income.

All four purchase options allow you to buy shares over a long period of time. As a result, you can use the principle of *dollar cost averaging,* which was explained in Chapter 12. With dollar cost averaging, you can make money if you sell your fund shares at a price higher than the *average* purchase price. This method helps you avoid the problem of buying high and selling low.

reinvestment plan
A service provided by an investment company in which income dividends and capital gain distributions are automatically reinvested to purchase additional shares of the fund.

Withdrawal Options

Because closed-end funds and exchange-traded funds are listed on stock exchanges or traded in the over-the-counter market, an investor may sell shares in such a fund to another investor. Shares in an open-end fund can be sold on any business day to the investment company that sponsors the fund or your brokerage firm. In this case, the shares are redeemed at their net asset value. All you have to do is give proper notification, and the investment company will send you a check. With some funds, you can even write checks to withdraw money from the fund.

In addition, most funds have provisions that allow investors with shares that have a minimum asset value (usually at least $5,000) to use four options to systematically withdraw money. First, you may withdraw a specified, fixed dollar amount each investment period until your fund has been exhausted. Normally, a systematic withdrawal plan allows investors to withdraw money from a fund investment on a monthly or quarterly basis.

A second option allows you to liquidate or "sell off" a certain number of shares each investment period. Since the net asset value of shares in a fund varies from one investment period to the next, the amount of money you receive will also vary.

A third option allows you to withdraw a fixed percentage of asset growth. If no asset growth occurs, no payment is made to you. Assuming you withdraw less than 100 percent of asset growth, your principal continues to grow.

EXAMPLE: Withdrawal Calculation

You arrange to receive 60 percent of the asset growth of your mutual fund investment. In one investment period, the asset growth amounts to $3,000. For that period, you will receive a check for $1,800, as shown below.

Amount you receive = Investment growth × Percentage of growth withdrawn
= $3,000 × 60 percent = $1,800

A final option allows you to withdraw all asset growth during an investment period. Under this option, your principal remains untouched.

PRACTICE QUIZ 13–4

1. In your own words, describe the advantages and disadvantages of mutual fund investments.

2. In the table below, indicate how each of the key terms affects a mutual fund investment and how each would be taxed.

Key Term	Type of Return on a Mutual Fund Investment	Type of Taxation
Income dividends		
Capital gain distributions		
Capital gains		

3. How would you purchase a closed-end fund? An exchange-traded fund?

4. What options can you use to purchase shares in or withdraw money from an open-end mutual fund?

Road Map

to financial literacy

Investing in Mutual Funds

You Are Here

Checkpoint 1

☐ Reexamine your goals and save the money needed to purchase mutual funds

☐ Open an account with a brokerage firm or investment company.

Checkpoint 2

☐ Use "Your Personal Financial Sheet 41 and the material in the section" How to Make a Decision to Buy or Sell Mutual Funds" to evaluate potential funds that could help you obtain your financial goals.

...er you have evaluated ...eral possible funds, ...hase the ones that you ...eve will help you achieve ... financial goals.

Checkpoint 3

☐ Evaluate the existing funds you own and monitor the value of those funds

☐ Continue to invest in funds and other investments that could help you obtain your goals

☐ Revise your goals as necessary to reflect changes in your life

Checkpoint 4

Financial Security

SOME MONEY AVAILABLE

HAVEN'T STARTED SAVING

READY TO INVEST

$1000

$500 $1500

$0 $2000

HAVE YOU SAVED ENOUGH MONEY TO INVEST IN MUTUAL FUNDS?

your personal finance dashboard

Money for Investing in Mutual Funds

Because of professional management and diversification, investors often choose mutual funds.

YOUR SITUATION: Are you ready to invest in mutual funds? The first step is to save the money you need to begin investing. Although the amount will vary, $2,000 or less is usually required to open an account with a brokerage firm or an investment company. The second step is to evaluate each fund alternative before investing your money.

Chapter Summary

LO13.1 The major reasons investors choose mutual funds are professional management and diversification. Mutual funds are also a convenient way to invest money—especially for retirement accounts. There are three types of funds: closed-end funds, exchange-traded funds, and open-end funds. A closed-end fund is a fund whose shares are issued only when the fund is organized. An exchange-traded fund (ETF) is a fund that usually invests in the stocks or other securities contained in a specific stock index or securities index. Both closed-end and exchange-traded funds are traded on a stock exchange or in the over-the-counter market. An open-end fund is a mutual fund whose shares are sold and redeemed by the investment company at the net asset value (NAV) at the request of investors.

Mutual funds can also be classified as A shares (commissions charged when shares are purchased), B shares (commissions charged when money is withdrawn during the first five years), and C shares (no commission to buy or sell shares but often higher, ongoing fees). C shares may charge a small fee to sell shares. You can also purchase no-load funds in which investors pay no sales charges. Other possible fees include management fees and 12b-1 fees. Together, all the different management fees and operating costs are referred to as an expense ratio. Since it is important to keep fees and costs as low as possible, you should examine a fund's expense ratio as one more consideration when evaluating a mutual fund.

LO13.2 The managers of funds tailor their investment portfolios to the investment objectives of their customers. The major fund categories are stock funds and bond funds. There are also funds that invest in a mix of different stocks, bonds, and other securities that include asset allocation funds, balanced funds, fund of funds, lifecycle funds, money market funds, and total market funds. Today, many investment companies use a family-of-funds concept, which allows shareholders to switch among funds as different funds offer more potential growth, financial reward, or security.

To reduce risk, investors often construct an investment portfolio. Portfolio construction is the process of choosing different types of stocks, bonds, funds, and other investment alternatives to obtain larger returns while reducing risk. Many investors also purchase different funds for their retirement plans in order to achieve their financial objectives.

LO13.3 The responsibility for choosing the "right" mutual fund rests with you, the investor. Often, the first question investors must answer is whether they want a managed fund or an index fund. With a managed fund, a professional fund manager (or team of managers) chooses the securities that are contained in the fund. Some investors choose to invest in an index fund because over many years, index funds have outperformed the majority of managed funds. To help evaluate different mutual funds, investors can use the information on the Internet, from professional advisory services, from the fund's prospectus and annual report, in financial publications, and in newspapers.

LO13.4 The advantages of mutual funds have made mutual funds the investment of choice for many investors. For $2,000 or less, you can open an account and begin investing. The shares of a closed-end fund or exchange-traded fund are bought and sold on organized stock exchanges or in the over-the-counter market. The shares of an open-end fund may be purchased through a salesperson who is authorized to sell them, through an account executive of a brokerage firm, from a mutual fund supermarket, or from the investment company that sponsors the fund. The shares in an open-end fund can be sold to the investment company that sponsors the fund. Shareholders in mutual funds can receive a return in one of three ways: income dividends, capital gain distributions when the fund buys and sells securities in the fund's portfolio at a profit, and capital gains when the shareholder sells shares in the mutual fund at a higher price than the price paid. To ensure you have all of the documentation you need for tax reporting purposes, it is essential that you keep accurate records. A number of purchase and withdrawal options are available for mutual fund investors.

capital gain distributions 477

closed-end fund 459

contingent deferred sales load 461

exchange-traded fund (ETF) 459

expense ratio 463

family of funds 467

income dividends 477

load fund 461

mutual fund 457

net asset value (NAV) 460

no-load fund 461

open-end fund 460

portfolio construction 468

reinvestment plan 481

turnover ratio 479

12b-1 fee 462

Page	Topic	Formula
460	Net asset value	$\text{Net asset value} = \dfrac{\text{Value of the fund's portfolio} - \text{Liabilities}}{\text{Number of shares outstanding}}$
461	Load charge	Load charge = Dollar amount of investment × Load stated as a percentage
461	Contingent deferred sales load	Contingent deferred sales load = Amount of withdrawal × Fee stated as a percentage Amount you receive = Amount of withdrawal − Contingent deferred sales load
478	Total return	Dollar amount of total return = Income dividends + Capital gain distributions + Change in share value if sold
478	Percent of total return	$\text{Percent of total return} = \dfrac{\text{Dollar amount of total return}}{\text{Original cost of your investment}}$
481	Withdrawal calculation	Amount you receive = Investment growth × Percentage of growth withdrawn

1. Three years ago, Mary Applegate's mutual fund portfolio was worth $410,000. Now, the total value of her investment portfolio has decreased to $296,000. Even though she has lost a significant amount of money, she has not changed her investment holdings, which consist of either aggressive growth funds or growth funds.
   a. How much money has Mary lost in the last three years?
   b. Given the above information, calculate the percentage of lost value.
   c. What actions would you take to get your investment back in shape if you were Mary?

2. Twelve months ago, Gene Peterson purchased 200 shares in the no-load Fidelity Select Software and IT Services Fund—a Morningstar five-star fund that seeks capital appreciation. His rationale for choosing this fund was that he wanted a fund that was highly rated. Each share in the fund cost $17.75. At the end of the year, he received dividends of $1.90 and did not receive a capital gain distribution. At the end of 12 months, the shares in the fund were selling for $21.
   a. How much did Gene invest in this fund?
   b. At the end of 12 months, what is the total return for this fund?
   c. What is the percentage of total return?

Solutions

1. *a.* Dollar loss = $410,000 Value three years ago − $296,000 Current value
= $114,000

b. Percent of dollar loss = $114,000 ÷ $410,000 Value three years ago
= 0.278, or 27.8%

c. While Mary has several options, any decision should be based on careful research and evaluation. First, she could do nothing. While she has lost a substantial portion of her investment portfolio ($114,000, or 27.8 percent), it may be time to hold on to her investments if she believes the value of her shares will increase in the future. Second, she could sell (or exchange) some or all of her shares in the aggressive growth or growth funds and move her money into more conservative money market or government bond funds or even certificates of deposit if she thinks the economy is headed for a recession. Finally, she could buy more shares of the funds she owns or different quality funds if she believes the economy will improve in the future. Deciding which option for her to take may depend on the economic conditions at the time you answer this question.

2. *a.* Total investment = Price per share × Number of shares
= $17.75 × 200 = $3,550

b. Income dividends = Dividend per share × Shares = $1.90 × 200 = $380
Capital Gain distribution = $0
Change in share value = Ending value − Begining value
= $21 − $17.75 = $3.25 a share gain
$3.25 × 200 shares = $650
Total increase in value = Income dividends + Capital gain distrubution
+ Gain = $380 + $0 + $650 = $1,030 change in share

c. Percent of dollar gain = $\dfrac{\$1,030 \text{ gain}}{\$3,550 \text{ investment}}$
= 0.29, or 29%

Financial Planning Problems

1. The Western Capital Growth mutual fund has:
Total assets, $836,000,000
Total liabilities, $6,000,000
Total number of shares, 40,000,000
What is the fund's net asset value (NAV)?   (LO13.1)

2. Jan Throng invested $61,000 in the Invesco Charter mutual fund. The fund charges a commission of 5.50 percent when shares are purchased. Calculate the amount of commission Jan must pay.   (LO13.1)

3. As Bart Brownlee approached retirement, he decided the time had come to invest some of his nest egg in a conservative fund. He chose the Franklin Utilities Fund. If he invests $25,000 and the fund charges a load of 3.75 percent when shares are purchased, what is the amount of commission Bart must pay?   (LO13.1)

4. Mary Canfield purchased shares in the New Dimensions Global Growth Fund. This fund doesn't charge a front-end load, but it does charge a contingent deferred sales load of 4 percent for any withdrawals during the first year. If Mary withdraws $6,000 during the first year, how much is the contingent deferred sales load?   (LO13.1)

5. The value of Mike Jackson's shares in the New Frontiers Technology Fund is $63,200. The management fee for this particular fund is 0.60 percent of the total asset value. Calculate the management fee Mike must pay this year.   (LO13.1)

6. Betty and James Holloway invested $71,000 in the Financial Vision Social Responsibility Fund. The management fee for this fund is 0.80 percent of the total asset value. Calculate the management fee the Holloways must pay.   (LO13.1)

7. As part of his 401(k) retirement plan at work, Ken Lowery invests 5 percent of his salary each month in the Capital Investments Lifecycle Fund. At the end of this year, Ken's 401(k) account has a dollar value of $330,700. If the fund charges a 12b-1 fee of 0.75 percent, what is the amount of the fee?   (LO13.1)

8. When Jill Thompson received a large settlement from an automobile accident, she chose to invest $140,000 in the Vanguard 500 Index Fund. This fund has an expense ratio of 0.14 percent. What is the amount of the fees that Jill will pay this year?   (LO13.1)

9. The Yamaha Aggressive Growth Fund has an expense ratio of 1.83 percent.   (LO13.1)
   a. If you invest $64,000 in this fund, what is the dollar amount of fees that you would pay this year?
   b. Based on the information in this chapter and your own research, is this a low, average, or high expense ratio?

10. Jason Mathews purchased 300 shares of the Hodge & Mattox Energy Fund. Each share cost $15.15. Fifteen months later, he decided to sell his shares when the share value reached $18.10.   (LO13.4)
   a. What was the amount of his total investment?
   b. What was the total amount Jason received when he sold his shares in the Hodge & Mattox fund?
   c. How much profit did he make on his investment?

11. Three years ago, James Matheson bought 200 shares of a mutual fund for $29 a share. During the three-year period, he received total income dividends of $1.90 per share. He also received total capital gain distributions of $2.80 per share during the three-year period. At the end of three years, he sold his shares for $34 a share. What was his total return for this investment?   (LO13.4)

12. Assume that one year ago, you bought 120 shares of a mutual fund for $31 a share, you received a capital gain distribution of $0.82 per share during the past 12 months, and the market value of the fund is now $36 a share.   (LO13.4)
   a. Calculate the total return for your $3,720 investment.
   b. Calculate the percentage of total return for your $3,720 investment.

13. Over a four-year period, LaKeisha Thompson purchased shares in the Oakmark Investor Class Fund. Using the information below, answer the questions that follow. You may want to review the concept of dollar cost averaging in Chapter 12 before completing this problem.   (LO13.4)

Year	Investment Amount	Price per Share	Number of Shares*
February 2017	$1,500	$61	
February 2018	$1,500	$72	
February 2019	$1,500	$78	
February 2020	$1,500	$71	
*Round answer to two decimal places.			

   a. At the end of four years, what is the total amount invested?
   b. At the end of four years, what is the total number of shares purchased?
   c. At the end of four years, what is the average cost for each share?

14. During one three-month period, Matt Roundtop's mutual fund grew by $4,000. If he withdraws 35 percent of the growth, how much will he receive?   (LO13.4)

 **To reinforce the content in this chapter, more problems are provided at connect.mheducation.com.**

FINANCIAL LITERACY PORTFOLIO

FINANCIAL LITERACY PORTFOLIO. . . INVESTMENT PORTFOLIO (CHAPTER 13)

Competency:

Construct an investment portfolio.

Action Research:

Based on Chapters 11, 12, and 13, the Your Personal Financial Plan sheets that accompany those chapters, and other research, construct an investment portfolio for long-term financial security. Determine the types of investments (stocks, bonds, mutual funds, and other securities) you would include and the proportion (percentage) of each type of investment when you are age 30 and when you are age 50.

Outcome:

Create a summary in an Excel file, PowerPoint presentation, video, or other visual format that reports the investments and proportion of each investment for your portfolios at age 30 and age 50. Include a discussion of your reasoning for the investments you chose for each portfolio.

REAL LIFE PERSONAL FINANCE

RESEARCH INFORMATION AVAILABLE FROM MORNINGSTAR

This chapter stressed the importance of evaluating potential investments. Now it is your turn to try your skill at evaluating a potential investment in the T. Rowe Price Dividend Growth Fund. Assume you could invest $10,000 in shares of this fund. To help you evaluate this potential investment, carefully examine Exhibit 13–5, which reproduces the Morningstar research report for the T. Rowe Price Dividend Growth Fund.

Questions

1. Based on the research provided by Morningstar, would you buy shares in the T. Rowe Price Dividend Growth Fund? Justify your answer.

2. What other investment information would you need to evaluate this fund? Where would you obtain this information?

3. On April 20, 2020, shares in the T. Rowe Price Dividend Growth Fund were selling for $46.41 per share. Using the Internet or a newspaper, determine the current price for a share of this fund. Based on this information, would your investment have been profitable? (*Hint:* The symbol for this fund is PRDGX.)

4. Assuming you purchased shares in the T. Rowe Price Dividend Growth Fund on April 20, 2020, and based on your answer to Question 3, how would you decide if you want to hold or sell your shares? Explain your answer.

CONTINUING CASE

INVESTING IN MUTUAL FUNDS

Jamie Lee and Ross did several weeks' worth of research trying to choose the right stock to invest in. After all, a $50,000 inheritance was a lot of money, and they wanted to make the most informed investment choices they could. They discovered, by doing their homework, the various companies' stocks that they were looking to invest in did not seem like they were going to have the promising future that Jamie Lee and Ross were hoping for. They were aware that they were taking a chance with any investment, but they were both nervous about "putting all of their eggs" in stocks and wanted to be more confident in making their investment choices. But how could they be more assured?

They decided to speak to their professional financial planner, who suggested that investing in mutual funds may be the way to lessen the risk by joining a pool of other investors in a variety of investments chosen by a professional mutual fund manager. This way, Jamie Lee and Ross could lessen the pressure of choosing the right company and minimize the chances of losing all of their investment money by diversifying their portfolio.

A mutual fund sounded like the sensible investment choice for them, but which mutual fund would best match their investment strategy? Jamie Lee and Ross are in their mid-40s and well on their way to reaching their long-term investment goals, as they committed to reaching their goals early in their marriage. They set their sights on having the triplets graduate from college debt-free and saving enough to purchase a beach house when they retire. They are looking for a mutual fund that will provide investment income while maintaining the moderate risk investment path that they are on, as they have some time to go before retirement.

Current Financial Situation

Assets (Jamie Lee and Ross combined):

Checking account, $7,500

Savings account, $83,000 (including the $50,000 inheritance)

Emergency fund savings account, $45,000

House, $410,000

IRA balance, $78,000

Life insurance cash value, $110,000

Investments (stocks, bonds), $230,000

Cars, $18,500 (*Jamie Lee*) and $24,000 (*Ross*)

Liabilities (Jamie Lee and Ross combined):

Mortgage balance, $73,000

Student loan balance, $0

Credit card balance, $0

Car loans, $0

Income:

Jamie Lee, $45,000 gross income ($31,500 net income after taxes)

Ross, $135,000 gross income ($97,200 net income after taxes)

Monthly Expenses

Mortgage, $1,225

Property taxes, $500

Homeowner's insurance, $300

IRA contribution, $300

Utilities, $250

Food, $600

Gas/Vehicle maintenance, $275

Entertainment, $300

Life insurance, $375

Questions

1. Jamie Lee and Ross's professional financial planner has suggested that they perform a financial checkup as the first step in investing in mutual funds, even though they are investing $50,000 that was inherited from Ross's late uncle's estate. Is it a good time to

invest the inheritance, or should Jamie Lee and Ross use the inheritance to pay down their home mortgage or increase the money they have in savings?

2. Jamie Lee and Ross have been reading quite a lot about stock funds. At Jamie Lee and Ross's stage in life, what different types of stock funds would you recommend for them to invest their $50,000 inheritance in? Why?

   a. The financial planner recommended looking into managed funds, which could help remove the burden of decision making about when to buy and sell for Jamie Lee and Ross. But Ross was considering index funds, which have lower management fees and expense ratios. Using your text as a guide, compare managed funds and index funds.

Managed Funds	Index Funds

   b. Which type of fund would you recommend for Ross and Jamie Lee? Why?

3. Jamie Lee and Ross are ready to evaluate a mutual fund more closely. Choose a specific mutual fund that has been mentioned in Chapter 13 or one that has been recommended by a friend or family member, and complete *Your Personal Financial Plan Sheet 41*. Based on this information, would you recommend this mutual fund for Jamie Lee and Ross? Why or why not?

Spending Diary

"I MUST CHOOSE BETWEEN SPENDING MONEY ON SOMETHING NOW OR INVESTING FOR THE FUTURE."

Directions Monitoring your daily spending will allow you to better consider financial planning alternatives. You will have better information and the potential for better control of your money if you use your spending information for making wiser choices. The Daily Spending Diary sheets are located at the end of Chapter 1 and in Connect Finance.

Questions

1. Are there any spending items that you might consider revising to allow you to increase the amount you invest?
2. Based on your investment goals and the amount available to invest, what types of mutual funds would you consider?

Name: _____ **Date:** _____

Evaluating Mutual Fund Investment Information

Purpose: To identify and assess the value of various mutual fund investment information sources.

Financial Planning Activities: Obtain samples of several items of information that you might consider to guide you in your investment decisions. This sheet is also available in an Excel spreadsheet format in Connect Finance.

Suggested Websites: **www.morningstar.com, www.kiplinger.com, imealliance.com**

Evaluation Criteria	Source 1	Source 2	Source 3
Information source			
Website			
Overview of information provided (main features)			
Cost, if any			
Ease of access			
Evaluation • Reliablility • Clarity • Value of information compared to cost			

What's Next for Your Personal Financial Plan?

- Talk with friends and relatives to determine what sources of information they use to evaluate mutual funds.

- Choose one source of information and describe how the information could help you achieve your investment goals.

Name: _____ **Date:** _____

Mutual Fund Evaluation

Purpose: No checklist can serve as a foolproof guide for choosing a mutual fund. However, the following questions will help you evaluate a potential investment in a specific fund.

Financial Planning Activities: Use mutual fund websites, investment company websites, professional advisory services, and/or library materials to answer these questions about a mutual fund that you believe could help you achieve your investment goals. This sheet is also available in an Excel spreadsheet format in Connect Finance.

Suggested Websites: www.morningstar.com, finance.yahoo.com, www.marketwatch.com

Category 1: Fund Characteristics

1. What is the fund's name? What is the fund's ticker symbol?

2. What is the fund's Morningstar rating?

3. What is the minimum investment?

4. Does this fund have a history of paying income dividends and capital gain distributions? ☐ Yes ☐ No

5. Is there a fee for exchanges? ☐ Yes ☐ No

Category 2: Costs

6. Is there a front-end load charge? If so, how much is it? _____

7. Is there a contingent deferred sales load? If so, how much is it?

8. How much is the annual management fee?

9. Is there a 12b-1 fee? If so, how much is it?

10. What is the fund's expense ratio?

Category 3: Diversification

11. What is the fund's objective?

12. What types of securities does the fund's portfolio include?

13. How many different securities does the fund's portfolio include?

14. How many types of industries does the fund's portfolio include?

15. What are the fund's five largest holdings?

Category 4: Fund Performance

16. How long has the fund manager been with the fund?

17. How would you describe the fund's performance over the past 12 months?

18. How would you describe the fund's performance over the past 5 years?

19. How would you describe the fund's performance over the past 10 years?

20. What is the current net asset value for this fund?

21. What is the high net asset value for this fund over the last 12 months?

22. What is the low net asset value for this fund over the last 12 months?

23. What do the experts say about this fund?

Category 5: Conclusion

24. Based on the above information, do you think an investment in this fund will help you achieve your investment goals? ☐ Yes ☐ No

25. Explain your answer to Question 24.

A Word of Caution

When you use a checklist, there is always a danger of overlooking important relevant information. This checklist is not a cure-all, but it does provide some very important questions that you should answer before making a fund investment decision. Quite simply, it is a place to start. If you need other information, *you* are responsible for obtaining it and for determining how it affects your potential investment.

Suggested App:
• Morningstar

What's Next for Your Personal Financial Plan?

• Identify additional factors that may affect your decision to invest in this fund.

• Develop a plan for monitoring an investment's value once a fund is purchased.

14 Starting Early: Retirement and Estate Planning

3 Steps to Financial Literacy . . .
Planning to Live Off of Preretirement Earnings

1 Conduct a financial analysis of your situation. Review assets, housing, life insurance, retirement funds, and other investments.
App: RetirePlan

2 Estimate the annual amount you will need to live comfortably during your retirement years.
App: Retirement Income Calculator

3 Develop a plan to create a retirement fund with a future amount based on your result in Step 2.
Website: money.cnn.com/retirement

For every 10 years you delay in starting to save for retirement, you will need to save three times as much each month to catch up. That's why, no matter how young you are, the sooner you begin saving for retirement, the better. Whether you are 18 or 58, take steps toward a more secure financial future. At the end of the chapter, *Your Personal Finance Road Map and Dashboard* will provide additional information on planning your retirement income.

In this chapter, you will learn to:

LO14.1 Analyze your current assets and liabilities for retirement and estimate your retirement living costs.

LO14.2 Determine your planned retirement income and develop a balanced budget based on your retirement income.

LO14.3 Analyze the personal and legal aspects of estate planning.

LO14.4 Distinguish among various types of wills and trusts.

YOUR PERSONAL FINANCIAL PLAN SHEETS

42. Retirement Plan Comparison
43. Forecasting Retirement Income
44. Estate Planning Activities
45. Will Planning
46. Trust Comparison

Planning for Retirement: Start Early

Why Is It Important Now?

Tomeeka recently learned that her grandparents had planned carefully for retirement during their working years. They watched as some of their friends spent money with little concern for the future. Tomeeka's grandparents, on the other hand, made sure that they saved enough money to have a comfortable retirement. Even though it seemed far in the future, Tomeeka decided to start planning early for her own retirement, just as her grandparents had done.

Your retirement years may seem a long way off right now. However, the fact is, it's never too early to start planning for retirement. Planning can help you cope with sudden changes that may occur in your life and give you a sense of control over your future.

A recent poll from Harris Interactive reported that 95 percent of people ages 55 to 64 years old plan to do at least some work after they retire. Another survey reported that future retirees expect to continue to learn and to pursue new hobbies and interests. Someday, when you retire, you too may desire an active life.

If you have not done any research on the subject of retirement, you may have some misconceptions about the "golden years." Here are some myths about retirement:

- You have plenty of time to start saving for retirement.
- Saving just a little bit won't help.
- You'll spend less money when you retire.

LO14.1

Analyze your current assets and liabilities for retirement and estimate your retirement living costs.

ACTION ITEM

I have plenty of time before I start saving for retirement.

☐ True ☐ False

- Your retirement will only last about 15 years.
- You can depend on Social Security and a company pension plan to pay your basic living expenses.
- Your pension benefits will increase to keep pace with inflation.
- Your employer's health insurance plan and Medicare will cover all your medical expenses when you retire.

Some of these statements were once true but are no longer true today. You may live for many years after you retire. If you want your retirement to be a happy and comfortable time of your life, you'll need enough money to suit your lifestyle. You can't count on others to provide for you. That's why you need to start planning and saving as early as possible. It's never too late to start saving for retirement, but the sooner you start, the better off you'll be. (See Exhibit 14–1.)

Saving Smart for Retirement: Even a Little Goes a Long Way

Long-term financial security starts with a savings plan. If you save on a regular basis, you will have money to pay your bills, make major purchases, meet your living expenses during your retirement, and cope with emergencies. Here are a few tips on how to start saving early.

- Start now. Don't wait. Time is critical.
- Start small, if necessary. Money may be tight, but even small amounts can make a big difference, given enough time, the right kind of investments, and tax-favored investments such as company retirement plans, IRAs, and SEPs (discussed later in this chapter).
- Use automatic deductions from your payroll or your checking account for deposit in mutual funds, IRAs, or other investments.
- Save regularly. Make saving for retirement a habit.
- Be realistic about investment returns. Never assume that a year or two of high market returns will continue indefinitely. The same goes for market declines.
- If you change jobs, keep your retirement account money in your former employer's plan or roll it over into your new employer's plan or an IRA.
- Don't dip into retirement savings unless it is absolutely necessary.

> **EXAMPLE: Starting Early**
>
> Consider this: If from age 25 to 65, you invest $300 per month and earn an average of 9 percent return a year, you'll have $1.4 million in your retirement fund by age 65. Waiting just 10 years until age 35 to begin your $300-a-month investing will yield about $549,000, whereas if you wait 20 years to begin this investment, you will have only about $200,000 at age 65. The chart in Exhibit 14–2 shows how even a $2,000 annual investment earning just 4 percent will grow.

Read the nearby *Financial Literacy in Practice* feature, for additional tips about the importance of saving now.

As you think about your retirement years, consider your long-range goals. What does retirement mean to you? Maybe it will simply be a time to stop working, sit back, and relax. Perhaps you imagine traveling the world, developing a hobby, or starting a second career. Where do you want to live after you retire? What type of lifestyle would you like to have? Once you've pondered these questions, your first step in retirement planning is to determine your current financial situation. That requires you to analyze your current assets and liabilities.

Exhibit **14–1** Tackling the Trade-Offs: Saving Now versus Saving Later—The Time Value of Money Get an early start on your plan for retirement.

SAVER ABE (THE EARLY SAVER)				SAVER BEN (THE LATE SAVER)			
Age	Years	Contributions	Year-End Value	Age	Years	Contributions	Year-End Value
25	1	$ 2,000	$ 2,188	25	1	$ 0	$ 0
26	2	2,000	4,580	26	2	0	0
27	3	2,000	7,198	27	3	0	0
28	4	2,000	10,061	28	4	0	0
29	5	2,000	13,192	29	5	0	0
30	6	2,000	16,617	30	6	0	0
31	7	2,000	20,363	31	7	0	0
32	8	2,000	24,461	32	8	0	0
33	9	2,000	28,944	33	9	0	0
34	10	2,000	33,846	34	10	0	0
35	11	0	37,021	35	11	2,000	2,188
36	12	0	40,494	36	12	2,000	4,580
37	13	0	44,293	37	13	2,000	7,198
38	14	0	48,448	38	14	2,000	10,061
39	15	0	52,992	39	15	2,000	13,192
40	16	0	57,963	40	16	2,000	16,617
41	17	0	63,401	41	17	2,000	20,363
42	18	0	69,348	42	18	2,000	24,461
43	19	0	75,854	43	19	2,000	28,944
44	20	0	82,969	44	20	2,000	33,846
45	21	0	90,752	45	21	2,000	39,209
46	22	0	99,265	46	22	2,000	45,075
47	23	0	108,577	47	23	2,000	51,490
48	24	0	118,763	48	24	2,000	58,508
49	25	0	129,903	49	25	2,000	66,184
50	26	0	142,089	50	26	2,000	74,580
51	27	0	155,418	51	27	2,000	83,764
52	28	0	169,997	52	28	2,000	93,809
53	29	0	185,944	53	29	2,000	104,797
54	30	0	203,387	54	30	2,000	116,815
55	31	0	222,466	55	31	2,000	129,961
56	32	0	243,335	56	32	2,000	144,340
57	33	0	266,162	57	33	2,000	160,068
58	34	0	291,129	58	34	2,000	177,271
59	35	0	318,439	59	35	2,000	196,088
60	36	0	348,311	60	36	2,000	216,670
61	37	0	380,985	61	37	2,000	239,182
62	38	0	416,724	62	38	2,000	263,807
63	39	0	455,816	63	39	2,000	290,741
64	40	0	498,574	64	40	2,000	320,202
65	41	0	545,344	65	41	2,000	352,427
		$20,000				$62,000	
Value at retirement*			$545,344	Value at retirement*			$352,427
Less total contributions			−20,000	Less total contributions			−62,000
Net earnings			$525,344	Net earnings			$290,427

*The table assumes a 9 percent fixed rate of return, compounded monthly, and no fluctuation of the principal. Distributions from an IRA are subject to ordinary income taxes when withdrawn and may be subject to other limitations under IRA rules.

Source: *The Franklin Investor* (San Mateo, CA: Franklin Distributors Inc., January 1989)

Financial Literacy in Practice

The Psychology of Planning for Retirement While You Are Still Young

Retirement probably seems vague and far off at this stage of your life. Besides, you have things to buy right now. Yet there are some crucial reasons to start preparing now for retirement.

- Due to cuts in Medicare benefits, the underfunding of Social Security, and the decline in defined-benefit plans (discussed later in the chapter), you'll have to pay for more of your own retirement than earlier generations did. The sooner you get started, the better.

- You have one huge ally—time. Let's say that you put $1,000 into an IRA at the beginning of each year from age 20 through age 30 (11 years) and then never put in another dime. The account earns 7 percent annually. When you retire at age 65, you'll have $168,515 in the account. A friend doesn't start until age 30 but saves the same amount annually for 35 years straight. Despite putting in three times as much money, your friend's account grows to only $138,237.

- You can start small and grow. Even setting aside a small portion of your paycheck each month will pay off in big dollars later.

- You can afford to invest more aggressively. You have years to overcome the inevitable ups and downs of the market.

- Developing the habit of saving for retirement is easier when you are young.

Source: U.S. Department of Labor, Employee Benefits Security Administration, *Savings Fitness: A Guide to Your Money and Your Financial Future,* (2015), p. 5.

Exhibit 14–2

It's Never Too Early to Start Planning for Retirement

Start young. A look at the performance of $2,000 per year of retirement plan investments over time, even at 4 percent, shows the value of starting early.

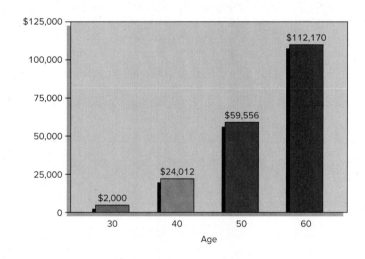

Conducting a Financial Analysis

As you learned in Chapter 2, an asset is any item of value that you own—cash, property, personal possessions, and investments—including cash in checking and savings accounts, a house, a car, a television, and so on. It also includes the current value of any stocks, bonds, and other investments that you may have as well as the current value of any life insurance and pension funds.

Your liabilities, on the other hand, are the debts you owe: the remaining balance on a mortgage or automobile loan, credit card balances, unpaid taxes, and so on. If you subtract your liabilities from your assets, you get your net worth. Ideally, your net worth should increase each year as you move closer to retirement.

It's a good idea to review your assets on a regular basis. You may need to make adjustments in your saving, spending, and investments in order to stay on track. Consider how the coronavirus (COVID-19) pandemic in early 2020 wiped out the investment gains of previous years in just a few weeks. As you review your assets, consider the following factors: housing, life insurance, and other investments. Each will have an important effect on your retirement income.

Your Retirement Housing

The place where you choose to live during retirement can have a significant impact on your financial needs. Use vacations in the years before you retire to explore areas you think you might enjoy. If you find a place you really like, go there at different times of the year. That way you'll know what the climate is like. Meet people who live in the area and learn about activities, transportation, and taxes.

ETHICAL AND PSYCHOLOGICAL ASPECTS OF MOVING

Consider the downside of moving to a new location. You may find yourself stuck in a place you really don't like after all. Moving can also be expensive and emotionally draining. You may miss your children, your grandchildren, and the friends and relatives you leave behind. Be realistic about what you'll have to give up as well as what you'll gain if you move after you retire.

AVOIDING RETIREMENT RELOCATION PITFALLS

Some retired people move to the location of their dreams and then discover that they've made a big mistake financially. Here are some tips from retirement specialists on how to uncover hidden taxes and other costs before you move to a new area:

- Contact the local chamber of commerce to get details on area property taxes and the local economy.

- Contact the state tax department to find out about income, sales, and inheritance taxes as well as special exemptions for retirees.

- Read the Sunday edition of the local newspaper of the city where you're thinking of moving. Relevant discussions about taxes, costs of living, or issues related to living in the area that may drive up costs may be covered.

- Check with local utility companies to get estimates on energy costs.

- Visit the area in different seasons, and talk to local residents about the various costs of living.

- Rent for a while instead of buying a home immediately.

What are your findings?

HOUSING A house will probably be your most valuable asset. However, if you buy a home with a large mortgage that prevents you from saving, you put your ability to meet your retirement goal at risk. In that case, you might consider buying a smaller, less expensive place to live. Remember that a smaller house is usually easier and cheaper to maintain. You can use the money you save to increase your retirement fund.

LIFE INSURANCE At some point in the future, you may buy life insurance to provide financial support for your spouse and children in case you die while they are still young. As you near retirement, though, your children will probably be self-sufficient. When that time comes, you might reduce your premium payments by decreasing your life insurance coverage. This would give you extra money to spend on living expenses or to invest for additional income.

FinTech for Financial Literacy

Kiplinger.com's retiree tax map (kiplinger.com/tools/retiree_map) is a state-by-state guide that can help determine the most tax-friendly states for you and your assets in retirement. You can sort the map by such categories as states that don't tax Social Security benefits and states that impose an estate tax.

OTHER INVESTMENTS When you review your assets, you'll also want to evaluate any other investments you have. When you originally chose these investments, you may have been more interested in making your money grow than in getting an early return from them. When you are ready to retire, however, you may want to use the income from those investments to help cover living expenses instead of reinvesting it.

Estimating Retirement Living Expenses

Next, you should estimate how much money you'll need to live comfortably during your retirement years. Where you live during retirement has significant impact on your financial needs. (See the nearby *Financial Literacy in Practice* feature, "Your Retirement Housing.") You can't predict exactly how much money you'll need when you retire. You can, however, estimate what your basic needs will be. To do this, you'll have to think about your spending patterns and how your living situation will change when you retire. For instance, you probably will spend more money on recreation, health insurance, and medical care in retirement than you do now. At the same time, you may spend less on transportation and clothing. Your federal income taxes may be lower. Also, some income from various retirement plans may be taxed at a lower rate or not at all. As you consider your retirement living expenses, remember to plan for emergencies. Look at Exhibit 14–3 for an example of retirement spending patterns of older Americans.

Don't forget to take inflation into account. Estimate high when calculating how much the prices of goods and services will rise by the time you retire (see Exhibit 14–4). Even a 3 percent rate of inflation will cause prices to double every 24 years.

Exhibit **14–3**

How "Average" Older (65-74 and 75+) Households Spend Their Money

Retired families spend a greater share of their income on food, housing, and medical care than nonretired families.

	AGE 65-74		AGE 75 & OLDER	
	Average $ Amount	**Percent**	**Average $ Amount**	**Percent**
Pretax Annual Income	$52,366	100	$35,467	100
Annual Expenditures	$48,855	100	$36,673	100
Housing	$15,838	32.4	$13,375	36.5
Food	$ 6,284	12.0	$ 4,349	11.9
Clothing	$ 1,417	2.9	$ 683	1.9
Transportation	$ 8,338	17.1	$ 5,091	13.9
Health Care	$ 5,456	12.2	$ 5,708	15.6
Entertainment	$ 2,988	6.1	$ 1,626	4.4
Pensions and Social Security	$ 2,788	5.7	$ 800	2.2
Other*	$ 6,074	11.6	$ 5,041	13.7

*Includes cash contributions, alcohol, tobacco, personal care products and services, reading, education, life and personal insurance, and miscellaneous expenses.

Source: Ann C. Foster, "A Closer Look at Spending Patterns of Older Americans," *Beyond the Numbers: Prices and Spending,* vol. 5, no. 4 (U.S. Bureau of Labor Statistics, March 2016).

Exhibit **14–4**

The Effects of Inflation over Time: The Time Value of Money

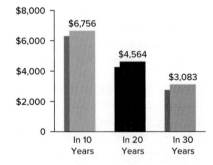

This chart shows you what $10,000 today will be worth in 10, 20, and 30 years, assuming a 4 percent rate of inflation.

The prices of goods and services rarely remain the same for any significant period of time because of inflation. How much will $10,000 be worth in 40 years, assuming a 4 percent rate of inflation? What can you do to counteract the effects of inflation?

PRACTICE QUIZ 14-1

1. What are the three assets you should review on a regular basis during retirement?

2. What expenses are likely to increase during retirement?

3. What expenses are likely to decrease during retirement?

Your Retirement Income

The four major sources of retirement income are employer pension plans, public pension plans, personal retirement plans, and annuities.

Employer Pension Plans

A pension plan is a retirement plan that is funded, at least in part, by an employer. With this type of plan, your employer contributes to your retirement benefits, and sometimes you contribute too. (See the nearby *Figure It Out!* feature.) These contributions and earnings remain tax-deferred until you start to withdraw them in retirement.

Private employer pension plans vary. If the company you work for offers one, you should know when you become eligible to receive pension benefits. You'll also need to know what benefits you'll receive. Ask these questions during your interview with a prospective employer and start participating in the plan as soon as possible. Most employer plans are one of two basic types: defined-contribution plans or defined-benefit plans.

DEFINED-CONTRIBUTION PLAN A **defined-contribution plan**, sometimes called an *individual account plan,* consists of an individual account for each employee to which the employer contributes a specific amount annually. This type of retirement plan does not guarantee any particular benefit. When you retire and become eligible for benefits, you simply receive the total amount of funds (including investment earnings) that have been placed in your account.

Several types of defined-contribution plans exist. With a money-purchase plan, your employer promises to set aside a certain amount of money for you each year. The amount is generally a percentage of your earnings. Under a stock bonus plan, your employer's contribution is used to buy stock in the company for you. The stock is usually held in a trust until you retire. Then you can either keep your shares or sell them. Under a profit-sharing plan, your employer's contribution depends on the company's profits.

In a **401(k) plan**, also known as a *salary-reduction plan,* you set aside a portion of your salary from each paycheck to be deducted from your gross pay and placed in a special account. Your employer will often match your contribution up to a specific dollar amount or percentage of your salary. For example, as one of the retirement benefits, McGraw-Hill Education (the publisher of your textbook) offers its employees a 401(k) savings plan. Under this plan, employees can contribute up to $19,500 in 2020. The company matches up to the first 6 percent of the employee's pretax contributions.

The funds in 401(k) plans are invested in stocks, bonds, and mutual funds. As a result, you can accumulate a significant amount of money in this type of account if you begin contributing to it early in your career. In addition, the money that accumulates in your 401(k) plan is tax-deferred, meaning that you don't have to pay taxes on it until you withdraw it.

In a 401(k) plan, your account balance will determine the amount of retirement income you will receive from the plan. While contributions to your account and the earnings on your investments will increase your retirement income, fees and expenses paid by your

LO14.2
Determine your planned retirement income and develop a balanced budget based on your retirement income.

ACTION ITEM

I'll need 70 to 90 percent of preretirement earnings to live comfortably during my retirement.

☐ **True**   ☐ **False**

defined-contribution plan
A plan—profit sharing, money purchase, Keogh, or 401(k)—that provides an individual account for each participant; also called an *individual account plan.*

401(k) plan A plan under which employees can defer current taxation on a portion of their salary; also called a *salary-reduction plan.*

Figure It Out!

Saving for Retirement

Calculate how much you would have in 10 years if you saved $2,000 a year at an annual compound interest rate of 10 percent, with the company contributing $500 a year.

	Contributions	10% Interest	Total
Annual contribution of 10% of a $20,000 salary	$2,000.00		
Company annual contribution matching $0.50 of 5% of the salary	500.00		
1st year			
2nd year			
3rd year			
4th year			
5th year			
6th year			
7th year			
8th year			
9th year			
10th year			
Total			

plan may substantially reduce the growth in your account, which will reduce your retirement income. The following example demonstrates how fees and expenses can impact your account.

> ### EXAMPLE: How 401(k) Fees Erode Your Retirement Savings
>
> Assume that you are an employee with 35 years until retirement and a current 401(k) account balance of $25,000. If returns on investments in your account over the next 35 years average 7 percent and fees and expenses reduce your average returns by 0.5 percent, your account balance will grow to $227,000 at retirement, even if there are no further contributions to your account. If fees and expenses are 1.5 percent, however, your account balance will grow to only $163,000. The 1 percent difference in fees and expenses would reduce your account balance at retirement by 28 percent.

If you're employed by a tax-exempt institution, such as a hospital or a nonprofit organization, the salary-reduction plan is called a Section 403(b) plan. As in a 401(k) plan, the funds in a 403(b) plan are tax-deferred. The amount that can be contributed annually to 401(k) and 403(b) plans is limited by law, as is the amount of annual contributions to money-purchase plans, stock bonus plans, and profit-sharing plans.

Employee contributions to a pension plan belong to you, the employee, regardless of the amount of time that you are with a particular employer. What happens to the contributions that the employer has made to your account if you change jobs and move to another company before you retire? One of the most important aspects of such plans is vesting. **Vesting** is the right to receive the employer's pension plan contributions that you've gained, even if you leave the company before retiring. After a certain number of years with the company, you will become *fully vested,* or entitled to receive 100 percent of the company's contributions to the plan on your behalf. Under some plans, vesting may occur in stages. For example, you might become eligible to receive 20 percent of your benefits after three years and gain another 20 percent each year until you are fully vested.

vesting An employee's right to at least a portion of the benefits accrued under an employer pension plan, even if the employee leaves the company before retiring.

DEFINED-BENEFIT PLAN A **defined-benefit plan** specifies the benefits you'll receive at retirement age, based on your total earnings and years on the job. The plan does not specify how much the employer must contribute each year. Instead, your employer's contributions are based on how much money will be needed in the fund as each participant in the plan retires. If the fund is inadequate, the employer will have to make additional contributions.

defined-benefit plan A plan that specifies the benefits the employee will receive at the normal retirement age.

CARRYING BENEFITS FROM ONE PLAN TO ANOTHER Some pension plans allow *portability,* which means that you can carry earned benefits from one pension plan to another when you change jobs. Workers are also protected by the Employee Retirement Income Security Act of 1974, which sets minimum standards for pension plans. Under this act, the federal government insures part of the payments promised by defined-benefit plans.

Public Pension Plans

Another source of retirement income is Social Security, a public pension plan established by the U.S. government in 1935. The government agency that manages the program is called the Social Security Administration.

SOCIAL SECURITY Social Security is an important source of retirement income for most Americans. The program covers 97 percent of all workers, and almost one out of every six Americans currently collects some form of Social Security benefit. Social Security is actually a package of protection that provides benefits to retirees, survivors, and disabled persons. The package protects you and your family while you are working and after you retire. Nevertheless, you should not rely on Social Security to cover all of your retirement expenses. Social Security was never intended to provide 100 percent of your retirement income.

Who Is Eligible for Social Security Benefits? The amount of retirement benefits you receive from Social Security is based on your earnings over the years. The more you work and the higher your earnings, the greater your benefits, up to a certain maximum amount.

The Social Security Administration provides you an annual history of your earnings and an estimate of your future monthly benefits. The statement includes an estimate, in today's dollars, of how much you will get each month from Social Security when you retire—at age 62, full retirement age, or 70—based on your earnings to date and your projected future earnings.

CAUTION!

This chart shows the percentage of final earnings Social Security is estimated to replace. Will you have enough to make up the difference?

Your Retirement "Gap"		
Preretirement Salary	Percent of Income Replaced by Social Security	The "Gap" You and Your Employer Must Fill
$20,000	45%	35%
30,000	40	40
40,000	33	47
60,000	25	55
100,000	15	65

Source: TIAA-CREF

CAUTION!

Safeguard your Social Security card. You are limited to three replacement cards in a year and 10 during your lifetime.

money minute focus

Average 2020 monthly Social Security benefits were:

- $1,503 for a retired worker
- $2,531 for a retired couple
- $1,258 for a disabled worker
- $1,422 for a widow or widower

Source: Social Security Administration, **www.ssa.gov**, accessed March 22, 2020.

To qualify for retirement benefits, you must earn a certain number of credits. These credits are based on the length of time you work and pay into the system through the Social Security tax, or contribution, on your earnings. You and your employer pay equal amounts of the Social Security tax. Your credits are calculated on a quarterly basis. The number of quarters you need depends on your year of birth. People born after 1928 need 40 quarters to qualify for benefits.

Certain dependents of a worker may receive benefits under the Social Security program. They include a wife or dependent husband aged 62 or older; unmarried children under 18 (or under 19 if they are full-time students in grade 12 or lower); and unmarried, disabled children aged 18 or older. Widows or widowers can receive Social Security benefits earlier.

Social Security Retirement Benefits Most people can begin collecting Social Security benefits at age 62. However, the monthly amount at age 62 will be less than it would be if the person waits until full retirement age. This reduction is permanent.

In the past, people could receive full retirement benefits at age 65. However, because of longer life expectancy, the full retirement age is being increased in gradual steps. For people born in 1960 and later, the full retirement age will be 67. If you postpone applying for benefits beyond your full retirement age, your monthly payments will increase slightly for each year you wait, but only up to age 70.

Financial experts recommend that retirees delay taking Social Security to increase their lifetime income, but most of today's retirees took Social Security before their full retirement age. An estimated 72.8 percent took benefits before age 65, and only 14.1 percent took benefits the month they reached their full retirement.

When you start receiving Social Security benefits, certain members of your family may also qualify for benefits on your record. Benefits may be paid to:

- *Your spouse*—To qualify for benefits, your spouse must be age 62 or older or be taking care of your minor child. The Social Security Administration may ask for proof of marriage and dates of prior marriages, if applicable.
- *Your children*—To qualify for benefits, your eligible child can be your biological child, adopted child, or stepchild. You'll need their Social Security numbers and birth certificates.
- *Your adult child disabled before age 22*—To qualify for children's benefits under the disability program, your disabled adult child must meet Social Security's strict definition of disabled. A person is disabled under the Social Security Act if he or she can't work due to a severe medical condition that has lasted, or is expected to last, at least one year or result in death.
- *Your divorced spouse*—If you are divorced, even if you have remarried, your ex-spouse may qualify for benefits on your record. If you have a divorced spouse who qualifies for benefits, it will not affect the amount of benefits you or your family may receive.

When you work, some of the Social Security taxes you pay now go toward survivors benefits for your family. The benefit amount your family is eligible for depends on your average lifetime earnings. The more you earned, the more your family's benefits will be. You can visit Social Security's Benefits Planner to help them better understand Social Security's family benefits as they plan for their own financial futures.

Social Security Information For more information about Social Security, you can visit the Social Security website (**www.ssa.gov**). It provides access to forms and publications and

money minute focus

Over one-third of retirees claim their Social Security benefits at age 62, but your monthly payments can increase by as much as 75 percent if you wait and claim at age 70 instead of 62.

Source: Social Security Administration.

gives links to other valuable information. To learn more about the taxability of Social Security benefits, contact the Internal Revenue Service at 1-800-829-3676 and ask for Publication 554, *Social Security and Equivalent Railroad Retirement Benefits.*

OTHER PUBLIC PENSION PLANS Besides Social Security, the federal government provides several other special retirement plans for federal government workers and railroad employees. Employees covered under these plans are not covered by Social Security. The Veterans Administration provides pensions for survivors of people who died while in the armed forces. It also offers disability pensions for eligible veterans. Many state and local governments provide retirement plans for their employees as well.

Personal Retirement Plans

In addition to public and employer retirement plans, many people choose to set up personal retirement plans. Such plans are especially important to self-employed people and other workers who are not covered by employer pension plans. Among the most popular personal retirement plans are individual retirement accounts and Keogh accounts.

INDIVIDUAL RETIREMENT ACCOUNTS An **individual retirement account (IRA)** is a special account in which the person sets aside a portion of income for retirement. Several types of IRAs are available:

individual retirement account (IRA) A special account in which the employee sets aside a portion of his or her income; taxes are not paid on the principal or interest until money is withdrawn from the account.

- *Regular IRA:* A regular (traditional or classic) IRA lets you make annual contributions until age 70½. The contribution limit was $6,000 per year in 2020 and after ($7,000, if 50 or over). Depending on your tax filing status and income, the contribution may be fully or partially tax-deductible. The tax deductibility of a traditional IRA also depends on whether you belong to an employer-provided retirement plan. For example, in 2020, if you were covered by a retirement plan at work and you filed a joint return, then your tax-deductible contribution was reduced if your adjusted gross income was between $104,000 and $124,000.

- **Roth IRA***:* Annual contributions to a Roth IRA are not tax-deductible, but the earnings accumulate tax-free. You may contribute the amounts discussed above if you're a single taxpayer with an adjusted gross income (AGI) of less than $139,000. For married couples, the combined AGI must be less than $206,000. You can continue to make annual contributions to a Roth IRA even after age 70½. If you have a Roth IRA, you can withdraw money from the account tax-free and penalty-free after five years if you are at least 59½ years old or plan to use the money to help buy your first home. You may convert a regular IRA to a Roth IRA. Depending on your situation, one type of account may be better for you than the other.

Roth IRA Type of retirement account: contributions are not tax-deductible, but the earnings accumulate tax-free.

CAUTION! ⚠️

Withdrawals from a regular IRA prior to age 59½ may be subject to a 10 percent penalty. From a Roth IRA, contributions may be withdrawn at any age without penalty if the account has been open for five years.

- *Simplified Employee Pension (SEP) Plan:* A simplified employee pension (SEP) plan, also known as a SEP IRA, is an individual retirement account funded by an employer. Each employee sets up an IRA account at a bank or other financial institution. Then the employer makes an annual contribution of up to $57,000 in 2020. The employee's contributions, which can vary from year to year, are fully tax-deductible, and earnings are tax-deferred. A business of any size, even the self-employed, can establish a SEP IRA. The SEP IRA is the simplest type of retirement plan if a person is self-employed.

- *Spousal IRA:* A spousal IRA lets you make contributions on behalf of your nonworking spouse if you file a joint tax return. The contributions are the same as for the traditional and Roth IRAs. As with a traditional IRA, this contribution may be fully or partially tax-deductible, depending on your income. This also depends on whether you belong to an employer-provided retirement plan.

- *Rollover IRA:* A rollover IRA is a traditional IRA that lets you roll over, or transfer, all or a portion of your taxable distribution from a retirement plan or other IRA. You may move your money from plan to plan without paying taxes on it. To avoid taxes, however, you must follow certain rules about transferring the money from one plan to another. If you change jobs or retire before age 59½, a rollover IRA may be just what you need. It will let you avoid the penalty you would otherwise have to pay on early withdrawals.
- *Education IRA:* An education IRA, also known as a Coverdell Education Savings Account (Coverdell ESA), is a special IRA with certain restrictions. It allows individuals to contribute up to $2,000 per year toward the education of any child under age 18. The contributions are not tax-deductible. However, they do provide tax-free distributions for education expenses.

Exhibit 14–5 summarizes the various types of IRAs.

Whether or not you're covered by another type of pension plan, you can still make IRA contributions that are not tax-deductible. All of the income your IRA earns will compound tax-deferred until you begin making withdrawals. Remember, the biggest benefit of an IRA lies in its tax-deferred earnings growth. The longer the money accumulates tax-deferred, the bigger the benefit.

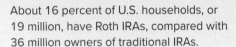

money minute focus

About 16 percent of U.S. households, or 19 million, have Roth IRAs, compared with 36 million owners of traditional IRAs.

IRA Withdrawals When you retire, you can withdraw the money from your IRA by one of several methods. You can take out all of the money at one time, but the entire amount will be taxed as income. If you decide to withdraw the money from your IRA in installments, you will have to pay tax only on the amount that you withdraw. A final alternative would be to place the money that you withdraw in an annuity that guarantees payments over your lifetime. See the discussion of annuities later in this section for more information about this option.

Exhibit **14–5**

Various Types of IRAs
IRAs can be a good way to save money for retirement.

Type of IRA	IRA Features
Regular IRA	• Tax-deferred interest and earnings • Annual limit on individual contributions • Limited eligibility for tax-deductible contributions
Roth IRA	• Annual limit on individual contributions • Withdrawals are tax-free in specific cases • Contributions do not reduce current taxes
Simplified Employee Pension Plan (SEP IRA)	• "Pay yourself first" payroll reduction contributions • Pretax contributions • Tax-deferred interest and earnings
Spousal IRA	• Tax-deferred interest and earnings • Both working spouse and nonworking spouse can contribute up to the annual limit • Limited eligibility for tax-deductible contributions
Rollover IRA	• Traditional IRA that accepts rollovers of all or a portion of your taxable distribution from a retirement plan • You can roll over to a Roth IRA
Education IRA	• Tax-deferred interest and earnings • 10 percent early withdrawal penalty is waived when money is used for higher-education expenses • Annual limit on individual contributions • Contributions do not reduce current taxes

KEOGH PLANS A **Keogh plan**, also known as an *H.R. 10 plan* or a *self-employed retirement plan,* is a retirement plan specially designed for self-employed people and their employees. Keogh plans have limits on the amount of annual tax-deductible contributions as well as various other restrictions. Keogh plans can be complicated to administer, so you should get professional tax advice before using this type of personal retirement plan.

REQUIRED MINIMUM DISTRIBUTIONS (RMDs) Required minimum distribution is the minimum amount you must withdraw from your account each year. With the exception of Roth IRAs, you cannot keep money in most tax-deferred retirement plans forever. Under the Setting Every Community Up for Retirement Enhancement Act (SECURE Act) of 2019, beginning in 2020, when you retire, or by age 72 at the latest, you must begin to receive "required minimum distributions," withdrawals from the funds you accumulated in the plan. The amount of the distributions is based on your life expectancy at the time the distributions begin. If you don't withdraw the minimum distributions from a retirement account, the IRS will charge you a penalty.

Exhibit 14-6 presents the timeline for retirement planning,

Keogh plan A plan in which tax-deductible contributions fund the retirement of self-employed people and their employees; also called an *H.R. 10 plan* or a *self-employed retirement plan.*

CAUTION!

If you turned age 70-1/2 prior to January 1, 2020, your required minimum distributions are based on age 70-1/2, not age 72.

> **WHAT WOULD YOU DO?** You have just been offered your dream job as a budget analyst for a recording studio. You majored in music business in college and were hoping you would find a job that would combine your love of music with your aptitude for finance. Now, as a single woman, you have many decisions to make. You will have to move to New York City; your new company will pay a lump sum of $20,000 to cover your moving expenses. You also have a variety of investment decisions to make. Although this is your first job, you know you should start investing for retirement now. Your new company offers a 401(k) plan as well as stock options. You have read about IRAs and think you should consider them. Because you have no experience with the various retirement options, how would you make a decision?

Age	Actions to take
50	Begin making catch-up contributions, an extra amount that those over 50 can add to 401(k) and other retirement accounts.
	Check your Social Security statement online every year for earnings accuracy and to learn what your estimated benefits will be.
59 1/2	No more tax penalties are levied on early withdrawals from employer-provided retirement savings plans such as 401(k) plans and other individual retirement accounts, but leaving money in means more time for it to grow.
	Also, withdrawals will be taxed as regular income.
62	The minimum age to receive Social Security benefits, but delaying claiming means a larger monthly benefit.
65	Eligible for Medicare
	Sign up for Medicare and Medicare Part D.
66-70	Receive Social Security full benefits, depending on your birth year.
	Earn Social Security Delayed Retirement Credits, which increase monthly benefits for each month claiming is delayed between the full retirement age and age 70.
72	Start taking minimum withdrawals from most retirement accounts by this age; otherwise, you may be charged heavy penalties in the future.

Exhibit 14–6

Timeline for Retirement Planning

Sources: U.S. Department of Labor, Social Security Administration, and Department of Health and Human Services, 2020.

Annuities

What do you do if you have funded your 401(k), 403(b), Keogh, and profit-sharing plans up to the allowable limits and you want to put away more money for retirement? The answer may be an annuity. You will recall from Chapter 10, an *annuity* is a contract purchased from an insurance company that provides for a sum of money to be paid to a person at regular intervals for a certain number of years or for life.

You might purchase an annuity with the money you receive from an IRA or company pension. You can simply buy an annuity to supplement the income you'll receive from either of these types of plans.

You can choose to purchase an annuity that has a single payment or installment payments. You will also need to decide whether you want the insurance company to send the income from your annuity to you immediately or begin sending it to you at a later date. The payments you receive from an annuity are taxed as ordinary income. However, the interest you earn from the annuity accumulates tax-free until payments begin.

Living on Your Retirement Income

As you plan for retirement, you'll estimate a budget or spending plan. When the time to retire arrives, however, you may find that your expenses are higher than you expected. If that's the case, you'll have some work to do.

First, you'll have to make sure that you're getting all the income to which you're entitled. Are there other programs or benefits for which you might qualify? You'll also need to think about any assets or valuables you might be able to convert to cash or sources of income.

You may have to confront the trade-off between spending and saving again. For example, perhaps you can use your skills and time instead of money. Instead of spending money on an expensive vacation, take advantage of free and low-cost recreation opportunities, such as public parks, museums, libraries, and fairs. Retirees often receive special discounts on movie tickets, meals, and more.

WORKING DURING RETIREMENT Some people decide to work part-time after they retire. Some even take new full-time jobs. Work can provide a person with a greater sense of usefulness, involvement, and self-worth. It may also be a good way to add to your retirement income.

DIPPING INTO YOUR NEST EGG When should you take money out of your savings during retirement? The answer depends on your financial circumstances, your age, and how much you want to leave to your heirs. (Your *heirs* are the people who will have the legal right to your assets when you die.) Your savings may be large enough to allow you to live comfortably on the interest alone. On the other hand, you may need to make regular withdrawals to help finance your retirement.

> ### EXAMPLE: Dipping into Your Nest Egg
>
> If you have $10,000 in savings that earns 5.5 percent interest, compounded quarterly, you could take out $68 every month for 20 years before reducing those savings to zero. If you have $40,000, you could withdraw $224 every month for 30 years.

If you dip into your retirement nest egg, you should consider one important question: How long will your savings last if you make regular withdrawals?

Whatever your situation is, once your nest egg is gone, it's gone. As shown in Exhibit 14–7, dipping into your nest egg is not wrong, but do so with caution.

Exhibit **14–7** Dipping into Your Nest Egg

| Starting Amount of Nest Egg | YOU CAN REDUCE YOUR NEST EGG TO ZERO BY WITHDRAWING THIS MUCH EACH MONTH FOR THE STATED NUMBER OF YEARS . . . | | | | | Or You Can Withdraw This Much Each Month and Leave Your Nest Egg Intact |
	10 Years	15 Years	20 Years	25 Years	30 Years	
$ 10,000	$ 107	$ 81	$ 68	$ 61	$ 56	$ 46
15,000	161	121	102	91	84	69
20,000	215	162	136	121	112	92
25,000	269	202	170	152	140	115
30,000	322	243	204	182	168	138
40,000	430	323	272	243	224	184
50,000	537	404	340	304	281	230
60,000	645	485	408	364	337	276
80,000	859	647	544	486	449	368
100,000	1,074	808	680	607	561	460

NOTE: Based on an interest rate of 5.5 percent per year, compounded quarterly.

Source: Select Committee on Aging, U.S. House of Representatives

WHAT WOULD YOU DO? You have worked hard for the same company for 45 years. Now, at age 67, you are about to retire. When you retire, you will be entitled to receive the $600,000 that has accumulated in your 401(k) plan. Now you have to decide what to do with the money. If you manage it wisely, it can help make your retirement years comfortable and rewarding. What would you do?

PRACTICE QUIZ 14–2

Sheet 42 Retirement Plan Comparison

Sheet 43 Forecasting Retirement Income

1. What are four major sources of retirement income?
2. What are the two basic types of employer pension plans?
3. What are the most popular personal retirement plans?
4. What is the major difference between a regular IRA and a Roth IRA?
5. What might you do if your expenses during retirement are higher than you expected?

Estate Planning

The Importance of Estate Planning

Many people think of estates as belonging only to the rich or elderly. The fact is, however, everyone has an estate. Simply defined, your **estate** consists of everything you own. During your working years, your financial goal is to acquire and accumulate money for both your current and future needs. Many years from now, as you grow older, your point of view will change. Instead of working to acquire assets, you'll start to think about what will happen to your hard-earned wealth after you die. In most cases, you'll want to pass that wealth along to your loved ones. That is where estate planning becomes important.

LO14.3

Analyze the personal and legal aspects of estate planning.

estate Everything one owns.

ACTION ITEM

I believe estate planning is only for the rich and famous.

☐ **True** ☐ **False**

estate planning A definite plan for the administration and disposition of one's property during one's lifetime and at one's death.

For example, identifying various kinds of wills and trusts will help you devise an estate plan that protects your interests as well as those of your family. Creating an effective estate plan will allow you to prosper during retirement and provide for your loved ones when you die.

What Is Estate Planning?

Estate planning is the process of creating a detailed plan for managing your assets so that you can make the most of them while you're alive and ensure that they're distributed wisely after your death. It's not pleasant to think about your own death. However, it is a part of estate planning. Without a good estate plan, the assets you accumulate during your lifetime might be greatly reduced by various taxes when you die.

Estate planning is an essential part of both retirement planning and financial planning. It has two phases. First, you build your estate through savings, investments, and insurance.

Second, you ensure that your estate will be distributed as you wish at the time of your death. If you're married, your estate planning should take into account the needs of your spouse and children. If you are single, you still need to make sure that your financial affairs are in order for your beneficiaries. Your *beneficiary* is a person you've named to receive a portion of your estate after your death.

When you die, your surviving spouse, children, relatives, and friends will face a period of grief and loneliness. At the same time, one or more of these people will probably be responsible for settling your affairs. Make sure that important documents are accessible, understandable, and legally proper.

Legal Documents

An estate plan typically involves various legal documents, one of which is usually a will. When you die, the person who is responsible for handling your affairs will need access to these and other important documents. The documents must be reviewed and verified before your survivors can receive the money and other assets to which they're entitled. If no one can find the necessary documents, your heirs may experience emotionally painful delays. They may even lose part of their inheritance. The important papers you need to collect and organize include:

- Birth certificates for you, your spouse, and your children.
- Marriage certificates and divorce papers.
- Legal name changes (especially important to protect adopted children).
- Military service records.
- Social Security documents.
- Veteran's documents.
- Insurance policies.
- Transfer records of joint bank accounts.
- Safe-deposit box records.
- Automobile registration.
- Titles to stock and bond certificates.

Sheet 44 Estate Planning Activities

PRACTICE QUIZ 14–3

1. What is estate planning?

2. What are the two stages in planning your estate?

3. List some important documents you will need to collect and organize.

Legal Aspects of Estate Planning

Wills

One of the most important documents that every adult should have is a written will. A **will** is the legal document that specifies how you want your property to be distributed after your death. If you die **intestate**—without a valid will—your legal state of residence will step in and control the distribution of your estate without regard for any wishes you may have had.

You should avoid the possibility of dying intestate. The simplest way to do that is to make sure that you have a written will. By having an attorney help you draft your will, you may forestall many difficulties for your heirs. Legal fees for drafting a will vary with the size of your estate and your family situation. A standard will costs between $300 and $400. Make sure that you find an attorney who has experience with wills and estate planning.

Types of Wills

You have several options in preparing a will. The four basic types of wills are the simple will, the traditional marital share will, the exemption trust will, and the stated amount will. The differences among them can affect how your estate will be taxed.

SIMPLE WILL A simple will leaves everything to your spouse. Such a will is generally sufficient for people with small estates. However, if you have a large or complex estate, a simple will may not meet your objectives. It may also result in higher overall taxation, since everything you leave to your spouse will be taxed as part of his or her estate.

TRADITIONAL MARITAL SHARE WILL The traditional marital share will leaves one-half of the adjusted gross estate (the total value of the estate minus debts and costs) to the spouse. The other half of the estate may go to children or other heirs. It can also be held in trust for the family. A **trust** is an arrangement by which a designated person, known as a *trustee,* manages assets for the benefit of someone else.

EXEMPTION TRUST WILL With an exemption trust will, all of your assets go to your spouse except for a certain amount, which goes into a trust. This amount, plus any interest it earns, can provide your spouse with lifelong income that will not be taxed. The tax-free aspect of this type of will may become important if your property value increases considerably after you die.

WILLS AND PROBATE The type of will that is best for your particular needs depends on many factors, including the size of your estate, inflation, your age, and your objectives. No matter what type of will you choose, it's best to avoid probate. **Probate** is the legal procedure of proving a valid or invalid will. It's the process by which your estate is managed and distributed after your death, according to the provisions of your will. A special probate court generally validates wills and makes sure that your debts are paid. You should avoid probate because it's expensive, lengthy, and public. As you will read later, a living trust avoids probate and is also less expensive, quicker, and private.

Formats of Wills

Wills may be either holographic or formal. A *holographic will* is a handwritten will that you prepare yourself. It should be written, dated, and signed entirely in your own handwriting. No printed or typed information should appear on its pages. Some states do not recognize holographic wills as legal.

A *formal will* is usually prepared with the help of an attorney. It may be typed, or it may be a preprinted form that you fill out. You must sign the will in front of two witnesses; neither person can be a beneficiary named in the will. The witnesses must then sign the will in front of you.

A *statutory will* is prepared on a preprinted form, available from lawyers, stationery stores, or Internet sites. Using preprinted forms to prepare your will presents serious risks. The form may include provisions that are not in the best interests of your heirs. Therefore, it is best to seek a lawyer's advice when you prepare your will.

Writing Your Will

Writing a will allows you to express exactly how you want your property to be distributed to your heirs. If you're married, you may think that all the property owned jointly by you and your spouse will automatically go to your spouse after your death. This is true of some assets, such as your house. Even so, writing a will is the only way to ensure that all of your property will end up where you want it.

executor Someone willing and able to perform the tasks involved in carrying out your will.

SELECTING AN EXECUTOR An **executor** is someone who is willing and able to perform the tasks involved in carrying out your will. These tasks include preparing an inventory of your assets, collecting any money due, and paying off your debts. Your executor must also prepare and file all income and estate tax returns. In addition, he or she will be responsible for making decisions about selling or reinvesting assets to pay off debt and provide income for your family while the estate is being settled. Finally, your executor must distribute the estate and make a final accounting to your beneficiaries and to the probate court.

money minute focus

Who can be an executor? Any U.S. citizen over 18 who has not been convicted of a felony can be named the executor of a will.

SELECTING A GUARDIAN If you have children, your will should also name a guardian to care for them in the event that you and your spouse die at the same time and the children cannot care for themselves. A **guardian** is a person who accepts the responsibility of providing children with personal care after their parents' death and managing the parents' estate for the children until they reach a certain age.

guardian A person who assumes responsibility for providing children with personal care and managing the deceased's estate for them.

ALTERING OR REWRITING YOUR WILL Sometimes you'll need to change the provisions of your will because of changes in your life or in the law. Once you've made a will, review it frequently so that it remains current. Here are some reasons to review your will:

- You've moved to a new state that has different laws.
- You've sold property that is mentioned in the will.
- The size and composition of your estate have changed.
- You've married, divorced, or remarried.
- Potential heirs have died, or new ones have been born.

codicil A document that modifies provisions in an existing will.

Don't make any written changes on the pages of an existing will. Additions, deletions, or erasures on a will that has been signed and witnessed can invalidate the will. If you want to make only a few minor changes, adding a codicil may be the best choice. A **codicil** is a document that explains, adds, or deletes provisions in your existing will.

A Living Will

living will A document that enables an individual, while well, to express the intention that life be allowed to end if he or she becomes terminally ill.

At some point in your life, you may become physically or mentally disabled and unable to act on your own behalf. If that happens, you'll need a living will. A **living will** is a document in which you state whether you want to be kept alive by artificial means if you become terminally ill and unable to make such a decision. Many states recognize living wills.

Exhibit 14–8 is an example of a typical living will.

To ensure the effectiveness of a living will, discuss your intention of preparing such a will with the people closest to you. You should also discuss this with your family doctor. Sign and date your document before two witnesses. Witnessing shows that you signed of your own free will.

Living Will Declaration

Declaration made this _____ day of _____ (month, year)

I, _____, being of sound mind, willfully and voluntarily make known my desire that my dying shall not be artificially prolonged under the circumstances set forth below, do hereby declare

If at any time I should have an incurable injury, disease, or illness regarded as a terminal condition by my physician and if my physician has determined that the application of life-sustaining procedures would serve only to artificially prolong the dying process and that my death will occur whether or not life-sustaining procedures are utilized, I direct that such procedures be withheld or withdrawn and that I be permitted to die with only the administration of medication or the performance of any medical procedure deemed necessary to provide me with comfort care.

In the absence of my ability to give directions regarding the use of such life-sustaining procedures, it is my intention that this declaration shall be honored by my family and physician as the final expression of my legal right to refuse medical or surgical treatment and accept the consequences from such refusal. I understand the full import of this declaration, and I am emotionally and mentally competent to make this declaration.

Signed _____

City, County, and State of Residence _____

The declarant has been personally known to me, and I believe him or her to be of sound mind.

Witness _____

Witness _____

Some people who become terminally ill cannot make decisions on their own behalf. What is the basic purpose of a living will?

Exhibit 14–8

A Living Will

Give copies of your living will to those closest to you, and have your family doctor place a copy in your medical file. Keep the original document readily accessible, and look it over periodically—preferably once a year—to be sure your wishes have remained unchanged. To verify your intent, re-date and initial each subsequent endorsement.

Most lawyers will do the paperwork for a living will at no cost if they are already preparing your estate plan. You can also get information from nonprofit advocacy groups, such as, **CompassionandChoices.org, aarp.org,** and **caregiver.org.** Working through end-of-life issues is difficult, but it can help avoid forcing your family to make a decision in a hospital waiting room—or worse, having your last wishes ignored.

SOCIAL MEDIA OR DIGITAL WILL Social media is part of daily life, so what happens to the online content that you created once you die? If you are active online, you should consider creating a statement of how you would like your online identity to be handled. You should appoint someone you trust as an online executor. This person will be responsible for the closure of your e-mail accounts, social media profiles, and blogs after you die. Take these steps to help you write a social media will:

- Review the privacy policies and the terms and conditions of each website where you have a presence.
- State how you would like your profile to be handled. You may want to completely cancel your profile or keep it up for friends and family to visit. Some sites allow users to create a memorial profile where other users can still see your profile but can't post anything new.
- Give the social media executor a document that lists all the websites where you have a profile, along with your usernames and passwords.
- State in your will that the online executor should have a copy of your death certificate. The online executor may need this as proof in order for websites to take any actions on your behalf.

power of attorney A legal document authorizing someone to act on one's behalf.

POWER OF ATTORNEY Related to the idea of a living will is power of attorney. A **power of attorney** is a legal document that authorizes someone to act on your behalf. If you become seriously ill or injured, you'll probably need someone to take care of your needs and personal affairs. This can be done through a power of attorney.

LETTER OF LAST INSTRUCTION In addition to a traditional will, it is a good idea to prepare a letter of last instruction. This document is not legally binding, but it can provide your heirs with important information. It should contain your wishes for your funeral arrangements as well as the names of the people who are to be informed of your death. Once your letter is complete, make several copies of it. Send one copy to your attorney or executor, attach another to your will, and keep one in a safe place at home. Update your letter periodically.

Trusts

Basically, a trust is a legal arrangement that helps manage the assets of your estate for your benefit or that of your beneficiaries. The creator of the trust is called the *trustor,* or *grantor.* The *trustee* might be a person or institution, such as a bank, that administers the trust. A bank charges a small fee for its services in administering a trust. The fee is usually based on the value of the assets in the trust.

Individual circumstances determine whether establishing a trust makes sense. Some of the common reasons for setting up a trust are to:

- Reduce or otherwise provide payment of estate taxes.
- Avoid probate and transfer your assets immediately to your beneficiaries.
- Free yourself from managing your assets while you receive a regular income from the trust.
- Provide income for a surviving spouse or other beneficiary.
- Ensure that your property serves a desired purpose after your death.

Types of Trusts

There are many types of trusts, some of which are described in detail in this section. You'll need to choose the type of trust that's most appropriate for your particular situation. An estate attorney can advise you about the right type of trust for your personal and family needs.

All trusts are either revocable or irrevocable. A *revocable trust* is one in which you have the right to end the trust or change its terms during your lifetime. An *irrevocable trust* is one that cannot be changed or ended. Revocable trusts avoid the lengthy process of probate, but they do not protect assets from federal or state estate taxes. Irrevocable trusts avoid probate and help reduce estate taxes. However, by law you cannot remove any assets from an irrevocable trust, even if you need them at some later point in your life.

CREDIT-SHELTER TRUST A credit-shelter trust is one that enables the spouse of a deceased person to avoid paying federal taxes on a certain amount of assets left to him or her as part of an estate. Perhaps the most common estate planning trust, the credit-shelter trust has many other names: bypass trust, "residuary" trust, A/B trust, exemption equivalent trust, or family trust. It is designed to allow married couples, who can leave everything to each other tax-free, to take full advantage of the exemption that allows $11.58 million (in 2020) in every estate to pass free of federal estate taxes. The surviving spouse's estate in excess of $23.16 million (in 2020) faces estate tax of 40 percent.

DISCLAIMER TRUST A disclaimer trust is appropriate for couples who do not yet have enough assets to need a credit-shelter trust but may have in the future. With a disclaimer

The Psychology of Living Trust Offers: Is It Ethical?

Misinformation and misunderstanding about estate taxes and the length or complexity of probate provide the perfect cover for unethical salespeople who have created an industry out of older people's fears that their estates could be eaten up by costs or that distribution of their assets could be delayed for years. Some unethical businesses are advertising seminars on living trusts or sending postcards inviting consumers to call for in-home appointments to learn whether a living trust is right for them. In these cases, it's not uncommon for the salesperson to exaggerate the benefits or appropriateness of the living trust and claim—falsely—that locally licensed lawyers will prepare the documents.

Other businesses are advertising living trust "kits": consumers send money for these do-it-yourself products but receive nothing in return. Still other businesses are using estate planning services to gain access to consumers' financial information and to sell them other financial products, such as insurance annuities.

What's a consumer to do? It's true that, for some people, a living trust can be a useful and practical tool. But for others, it can be a waste of money and time. Because state laws and requirements vary, "cookie-cutter" approaches to estate planning aren't always the most efficient way to handle your affairs. Before you sign any papers to create a will, a living trust, or any other kind of trust:

- Explore all your options with an experienced and licensed estate planning attorney or financial advisor. Generally, state law requires that an attorney draft the trust.

- Avoid high-pressure sales tactics and high-speed sales pitches by anyone who is selling estate planning tools or arrangements.

- Avoid salespeople who give the impression that AARP is selling or endorsing their products. AARP does not endorse any living trust products.

- Do your homework. Get information about your local probate laws from the clerk (or registrar) of wills.

- If you opt for a living trust, make sure it's properly funded—that is, that the property has been transferred from your name to the trust. If the transfers aren't done properly, the trust will be invalid, and the state will determine who inherits your property and serves as guardian for your minor children.

- If someone tries to sell you a living trust, ask whether the seller is an attorney. Some states limit the sale of living trust services to attorneys.

---

trust, the surviving spouse is left everything, but he or she has the right to disclaim, or deny, some portion of the estate. Anything that is disclaimed goes into a credit-shelter trust. This approach allows the surviving spouse to protect wealth from estate taxes.

LIVING TRUST A living trust, also known as an *inter vivos* trust, is a property management arrangement that goes into effect while you're alive. It allows you, as a trustor, to receive benefits during your lifetime. To set up a living trust, you simply transfer some of your assets to a trustee. Then you give the trustee instructions for managing the trust while you're alive and after your death. A living trust has several advantages:

- It ensures privacy. A will is a public record; a trust is not.
- The assets held in trust avoid probate at your death. This eliminates probate costs and delays.
- It enables you to review your trustee's performance and make changes if necessary.
- It can relieve you of management responsibilities.
- It's less likely than a will to create arguments between heirs upon your death.
- It can guide your family and doctors if you become terminally ill or unable to make your own decisions.

Read the nearby *Financial Literacy in Practice* feature to make sure that living trust offers are trustworthy.

Setting up a living trust costs more than creating a will. However, depending on your particular circumstances, a living trust can be a good estate planning option.

TESTAMENTARY TRUST A testamentary trust is one established by your will that becomes effective upon your death. Such a trust can be valuable if your beneficiaries are inexperienced in financial matters. It may also be your best option if your estate taxes will be high. A testamentary trust provides many of the same advantages as a living trust.

Taxes and Estate Planning

Federal and state governments impose various types of taxes that you must consider in estate planning. The four major types of taxes are estate taxes, estate and trust federal income taxes, inheritance taxes, and gift taxes.

ESTATE TAXES An estate tax is a federal tax collected on the value of a person's property at the time of his or her death. The tax is based on the fair market value of the deceased person's investments, property, and bank accounts, less an exempt amount of $11.58 million in 2020; this tax is due nine months after a death.

ESTATE AND TRUST FEDERAL INCOME TAXES In addition to the federal estate tax return, estates and certain trusts must file federal income tax returns with the Internal Revenue Service. Taxable income for estates and trusts is computed in the same manner as taxable income for individuals. Trusts and estates must pay quarterly estimated taxes.

smart money minute

Charitable gifts can be an important tool in estate planning. Giving to charity supports a cause and offers benefits such as reduced taxes and increased interest income. The National Philanthropic Trust is an independent public charity dedicated to increasing philanthropy in our society. For more information, visit **www.nptrust.org**.

INHERITANCE TAXES Your heirs might have to pay a tax for the right to acquire the property that they have inherited. An inheritance tax is a tax collected on the property left by a person in his or her will.

Only state governments impose inheritance taxes. Most states collect an inheritance tax, but state laws differ widely as to exemptions and rates of taxation. A reasonable average for state inheritance taxes would be 4 to 10 percent of whatever the heir receives.

GIFT TAXES Both the state and federal governments impose a gift tax, a tax collected on money or property valued at more than $15,000 (in 2020) given by one person to another in a single year. One way to reduce the tax liability of your estate is to reduce the size of the estate while you're alive by giving away portions of it as gifts. You're free to make such gifts to your spouse, children, or anyone else at any time. (Don't give away assets if you need them in your retirement!)

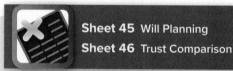

Sheet 45 Will Planning
Sheet 46 Trust Comparison

PRACTICE QUIZ 14–4

1. What is a will?

2. What are the four basic types of wills?

3. What are the responsibilities of an executor?

4. Why should you name a guardian?

5. What is the difference between a revocable and an irrevocable trust?

6. What are the four major types of trusts?

7. What are the four major types of taxes to consider in estate planning?

Road Map  to financial literacy

Retirement Planning

You Are Here

Checkpoint 1
- ☐ Evaluate your retirement and your estate planning goals to make sure they reflect what is important to you and your family.
- ☐ Consider information from several sources when making retirement and estate planning decisions.

Checkpoint 2
- ☐ Stop procrastinating and start your retirement and estate planning now.
- ☐ Starting savings small is better than not starting at all.

e value and present nputations to help ve your retirement e planning goals.

ur advance directives e you are still satisfied decisions.

Checkpoint 3

Checkpoint 4
- ☐ Revise your income distribution strategy.
- ☐ Find a living will executor who is willing and able to carry out your plans, should you be unable to.

Financial Security

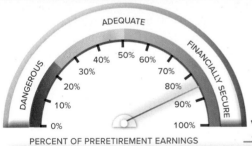

PERCENT OF PRERETIREMENT EARNINGS

your personal finance dashboard

Planning Retirement Income

You have several retirement savings opportunities available to you—from IRAs and SEPs to 401(k)s and 403(b)s. These options are especially important now that traditional pensions and other employer-funded retirement plans have become increasingly rare.

YOUR SITUATION: Have you figured out how much money you should save for retirement? Most financial advisors suggest that you will need 70 to 90 percent of preretirement earnings to live comfortably. Are you taking advantage of retirement savings programs at work, especially those where your employer matches contributions? Have you made sure that your investments are diversified?

LO14.1 The difference between your assets and your liabilities is your net worth. Review your assets to ensure they are sufficient for retirement. Then estimate your living expenses. Some expenses are likely to decrease while others will increase.

LO14.2 Your possible sources of income during retirement include employer pension plans, public pension plans, personal retirement plans, and annuities. If your income approximates your expenses, you are in good shape; if not, determine additional income needs and sources.

LO14.3 The personal aspects of estate planning depend on whether you are single or married. Never having been married does not eliminate the need to organize your financial affairs. Every adult should have a written will. A will is a way to transfer your property according to your wishes after you die.

LO14.4 The four basic types of wills are the simple will, the traditional marital share will, the exemption trust will, and the stated amount will. Types of trusts include the credit-shelter trust, the disclaimer trust, the living trust, and the testamentary trust.

Federal and state governments impose various types of estate taxes; you can prepare a plan for paying these taxes.

Key Terms

codicil 512

defined-benefit
 plan 503

defined-contribution
 plan 501

estate 509

estate planning 510

executor 512

401(k) plan 501

guardian 512

individual retirement
 account (IRA) 505

intestate 511

Keogh plan 507

living will 512

power of attorney 514

probate 511

Roth IRA 505

trust 511

vesting 503

will 511

Self-Test Problems

1. Beverly Foster is planning for her retirement. She has determined that her car is worth $10,000, her home is worth $150,000, her personal belongings are worth $100,000, and her stocks and bonds are worth $300,000. She owes $50,000 on her home and $5,000 on her car. Calculate her net worth.

2. Calculate how much money an average older (age 65-74) household with pretax annual income of $52,366 spends on food each year. (*Hint:* Use Exhibit 14–3.)

3. On December 31, 2020, George gave $15,000 to his son and $15,000 to his son's wife. On January 1, 2021, George gave another $15,000 to his son and another $15,000 to his son's wife. George made no other gifts to his son or his son's wife in 2020 and 2021. What was the gift tax?

Solutions

1.

Assets		Liabilities	
Car	$ 10,000	Mortgage	$ 50,000
Home	$150,000	Car	5,000
Personal belongings	$100,000	Total liabilities	$ 55,000
Stocks and bonds	$300,000		
Total assets	$560,000		

Net worth	=	Assets	−	Liabilities		
	=	$560,000	−	$55,000	=	$505,000

2. An average older household with an annual income of $52,366 spends about 12 percent of their income on food. Thus, $52,366 × 12 percent = $6,284.
3. There was no gift tax in 2020 or 2021 since George gifted $15,000 to his son and son's wife in each of the two years.

Financial Planning Problems

1. Shelly's assets include money in checking and saving accounts, investments in stocks and mutual funds, and personal property such as furniture, appliances, an automobile, a coin collection, and jewelry. Shelly calculates that her total assets are $165,200. Her current unpaid bills, including an auto loan, credit card balances, and taxes, total $21,300. Calculate Shelly's net worth. (LO14.1)

2. Prepare your net worth statement using the Assets – Liabilities = Net worth equation. (LO14.1)

3. Ted Riley owns a Lexus worth $40,000. He owns a home worth $275,000. He has a checking account with $800 in it and a savings account with $1,900 in it. He has a mutual fund worth $110,000. His personal assets are worth $90,000. He still owes $25,000 on his car and $150,000 on his home, and he has a balance on his credit card of $1,600. What is Ted's net worth? (LO14.1)

4. Calculate approximately how much money an older (age 65-74) household with an annual income of $45,000 spends on housing each year. (*Hint:* Use Exhibit 14–3.) (LO14.1)

5. Using Exhibit 14–3, calculate approximately how much money the household from Problem 4 spends on health care. (LO14.1)

6. Ruby is 25 and has a good job at a biotechnology company. She currently has $10,000 in an IRA, an important part of her retirement nest egg. She believes her IRA will grow at an annual rate of 8 percent, and she plans to leave it untouched until she retires at age 65. Ruby estimates that she will need $875,000 in her *total* retirement nest egg by the time she is 65 in order to have retirement income of $20,000 a year (she expects that Social Security will pay her an additional $15,000 a year). (LO14.2)
   a. How much will Ruby's IRA be worth when she needs to start withdrawing money from it when she retires? (*Hint:* Use Exhibit 1–A in the Chapter 1 Appendix.)
   b. How much money will she have to accumulate in her company's 401(k) plan over the next 40 years in order to reach her retirement income goal?

7. Gene and Dixie, husband and wife (ages 35 and 32), both work. They have an adjusted gross income of $95,000 in 2020, and they are filing a joint income tax return. Both have employer-provided retirement plans at work. What is the maximum IRA contribution they can make? How much of that contribution is tax-deductible? (LO14.2)

8. You have $100,000 in your retirement fund that is earning 5.5 percent per year, compounded quarterly. How many dollars in withdrawals per month would reduce this nest egg to zero in 20 years? How many dollars per month can you withdraw for as long as you live and still leave this nest egg intact? (*Hint:* Use Exhibit 14–7.) (LO14.2)

Problems 9, 10, and 11 are based on the following scenario:
   In 2019, Joshua gave $15,000 worth of Microsoft stock to his son. In 2020, the Microsoft shares were worth $23,000.

9. What was the gift tax in 2019? (LO14.4)
10. What was the total amount removed from Joshua's estate in 2020? (LO14.4)
11. What was the gift tax in 2020? (LO14.4)
12. In 2020, you gave a gift of $15,000 to a friend. What was the gift tax? (LO14.4)

Problems 13, 14, and 15 are based on the following scenario:
   Barry and Mary have accumulated over $3.5 million during their 50 years of marriage. They have three children and five grandchildren.

13. How much money can they gift to their children in 2020 without any gift tax liability? (LO14.4)

14. How much money can Barry and Mary gift to their grandchildren in 2020 without any gift tax liability? (LO14.4)

15. What is the total amount of estate removed from Barry and Mary's estate in 2020? (LO14.4)

16. Joe and Rachael are both retired. Married for 55 years, they have amassed an estate worth $4.4 million. The couple has no trust or other type of tax-sheltered assets. If Joe or Rachael died in 2020, how much federal estate tax would the surviving spouse have to pay, assuming that the estate is taxed at the 40 percent rate? (LO14.4)

 **To reinforce the content in this chapter, more problems are provided at connect.mheducation.com.**

FINANCIAL LITERACY PORTFOLIO. . .

RETIREMENT, ESTATE PLANNING

Competency

Develop a retirement/estate planning action plan.

Action Research

Based on this chapter, *Your Personal Financial Plan Sheets 42, 43, 44, 45* and *46*, online research, and conversations with others, create a personal retirement and estate planning action plan with 8 to 10 steps.

Outcome

Create a visual (photo flowchart, PowerPoint presentation, video, storyboard, or other visual format) that reports the steps and actions for your personal retirement and estate planning action plan. Describe your progress for each of the steps.

REAL LIFE PERSONAL FINANCE

PLANNING FOR RETIREMENT

Is a bad day fishing better than a good day at the office? Yes, according to a retired dad, Chuck. With his company pension, at least he didn't have to worry about money. In the good old days, if you had a decent job, you'd hang on to it, and then your company's pension combined with Social Security payments would be enough to live comfortably. Chuck's son, Rob, does not have a company pension and is not sure whether Social Security will even exist when he retires. So when it comes to retirement, the sooner you start saving, the better.

Take Maureen, a salesperson for a computer company, and Therese, an accountant for a lighting manufacturer. Both start their jobs at age 25. Maureen starts saving for retirement right away by investing $300 a month at 9 percent until age 65. But Therese does nothing until age 35. At 35, she begins investing the same $300 a month at 9 percent until age 65. What a shocking difference! Maureen has accumulated $1.4 million, while Therese has only $554,223 in her retirement fund. The moral? The sooner you start, the more you'll have for your retirement. Women especially need to start sooner because they typically enter the workforce later, have lower salaries, and, ultimately, have lower pensions.

Laura Tarbox, owner and president of Tarbox Equity, explains how to determine your retirement needs and how your budget might change when you retire. Tarbox advises that the old rule of thumb—that you need 60 to 70 percent of preretirement income—is too low an estimate. She cautions that most people will want to spend very close to what they were spending before retiring. There are some expenses that might be lower, however, such as clothing for work, dry cleaning, and commuting expenses. Other expenses, though, such as insurance, travel, and recreation, may increase during retirement.

Questions

1. In the past, many workers chose to stay with their employers until retirement. What was the major reason for employees' loyalty?

2. How did Maureen amass $1.4 million for retirement, while Therese could accumulate only $554,223?

3. Why do women need to start early to save for retirement?

4. What expenses may increase or decrease during retirement?

CONTINUING CASE

STARTING EARLY: RETIREMENT AND ESTATE PLANNING

Jamie Lee and Ross, now in their 50s, have plenty of time on their hands now that the triplets are away at college. They both realize that time has flown by; more than 24 years have passed since they married!

Looking back over the years, they realize that they have worked hard in their careers, Jamie Lee as the proprietor of a cupcake café and Ross, self-employed as a web page designer. They enjoyed raising their family and strived to be financially sound as they looked forward to a retirement that is just around the corner. They saved regularly and invested wisely over the years. They rebounded nicely from the recent economic crisis over the past few years, as they watched their investments closely and adjusted their strategies when they felt it necessary. They purchase vehicles with cash and do not carry credit card balances, choosing to use them for convenience only. The triplets are pursuing their master's degrees and have tuition covered through work-study programs at the university.

Jamie Lee and Ross are just a few short years from realizing their goals of retiring at 65 and purchasing the home at the beach!

Current Financial Situation

Assets *(Jamie Lee and Ross combined):*
Checking account, $5,500
Savings account, $53,000
Emergency fund savings account, $45,000
House, $475,000
IRA balance, $92,000
Life insurance cash value, $125,000
Investments (stocks, bonds), $750,000
Cars, $12,500 *(Jamie Lee)* and $16,000 *(Ross)*

Liabilities (Jamie Lee and Ross combined):
Mortgage balance, $43,000
Credit card balance, $0
Car loans, $0

Income:

Jamie Lee, $45,000 gross income ($31,500 net income after taxes)
Ross, $135,000 gross income ($97,200 net income after taxes)

Monthly Expenses
Mortgage, $1,225
Property taxes, $500
Homeowner's insurance, $300
IRA contribution, $300
Utilities, $250
Food, $600
Gas/Maintenance, $275
Entertainment, $300
Life insurance, $375

Questions

1. As Jamie Lee and Ross review their assets, can you tell them which will be valuable to them for income as retirement approaches?
2. Jamie Lee and Ross estimate that they will have $1 million in liquid assets to withdraw from at the start of their retirement. They plan to be in retirement for 30 years. Using Exhibit 14–7, how much do you think Jamie Lee and Ross can withdraw each month and still leave their nest egg intact? How much can they withdraw each month that will reduce their nest egg to zero?
3. Jamie Lee and Ross have been hearing many stories recently about acquaintances who are passing away without leaving a will, which made Jamie Lee and Ross anxious to review their estate plan with an attorney. They do not want to think about passing on, but they know it is an essential part to careful financial planning. It was suggested that they assemble all of their legal documents in a place where their heirs would be able to access them if necessary. What documents would you suggest that Jamie Lee and Ross make accessible?
4. Jamie Lee and Ross are now having the attorney draw up a will for each of them. What is the purpose of having a will? Do they need to have an attorney to draft a will? What type of will would you recommend they have, based on their marital/family status?

Spending Diary

"KEEPING TRACK OF MY DAILY SPENDING GETS ME TO START THINKING ABOUT SAVING AND INVESTING FOR RETIREMENT."

Directions The consistent use of a Daily Spending Diary can provide you with ongoing information that will help you manage your spending, saving, and investing activities. Taking time to reconsider your spending habits can result in achieving better satisfaction from your available finances. The Daily Spending Diary sheets are located at the end of Chapter 1 and in Connect Finance.

Analysis Questions

1. What portion of your available finances involve saving or investing for long-term financial security?
2. What types of retirement and estate planning activities might you start to consider at this point of your life?

Name: _____ **Date:** _____

Retirement Plan Comparison

Purpose: To compare benefits and costs for different retirement plans: 401(k), 403(b), 457, IRA, Roth IRA, SEP IRA, etc.

Financial Planning Activities: Analyze advertisements and articles, and contact your employer and financial institutions to obtain the information requested below. This sheet is also available in an Excel spreadsheet format in Connect Finance.

Suggested Websites: www.aarp.org, www.financialengines.com

Type of plan			
Name of financial institution or employer			
Address			
Phone			
Website			
Type of investments			
Minimum initial deposit			
Minimum additional deposits			
Employer contributions			
Current rate of return			
Service charges/fees			
Safety insured? By whom?			
Amount of coverage			
Payroll deduction available?			
Tax benefits			
Penalty for early withdrawal: • IRS penalty (10%) • Other penalties			
Other features or restrictions			

What's Next for Your Personal Financial Plan?

- Survey local businesses to determine the types of retirement plans available to employees.
- Talk to representatives of various financial institutions to obtain their suggestions for IRA investments.

Name: _____ **Date:** _____

Forecasting Retirement Income

Purpose: To determine the amount needed to save each year to have the necessary funds to cover retirement living costs.

Financial Planning Activities: Estimate the information requested below. This sheet is also available in an Excel spreadsheet format in Connect Finance.

Suggested Websites: www.ssa.gov, www.financialmentor.com, www.asppa.org

---

Estimated annual retirement living expenses

Estimated annual living expenses
if you retired today $ _____

Future value for _____ years until retirement at
expected annual income of _____% (use future
value of $1, Exhibit 1–A of Chapter 1 Appendix)   × _____

**Projected annual retirement living expenses
adjusted for inflation** .... (A) $ _____

Estimated annual income at retirement

Social Security income $ _____

Company pension, personal retirement account
income $ _____

Investment and other income $ _____

Total retirement income .... (B) $ _____

Annual shortfall of income after retirement (subtract B from A) .... (C) _____

**Additional amount required to fund the income
shortfall at retirement**

Expected annual rate of return on funds
before retirement   _____

Expected years in retirement   _____

Expected annual rate of return on invested
funds after retirement   _____

Additional amount needed at retirement to fund the shortfall .... (D) $ _____

Future value factor of a series of deposits for _____ years until
retirement and an expected annual rate of return before retirement
of _____ % (use Exhibit 1–Exhibit 1–B of Chapter 1 Appendix) equals   (E) $ _____

**Annual deposit required to accumulate the amount needed
(D ÷ E)** .... $ _____

What's Next for Your Personal Financial Plan?

- Survey retired individuals or people who are close to retiring to obtain information on their main sources of retirement income.
- Make a list that suggests the best investment options for an individual retirement account.

Name: _____ Date: _____

Estate Planning Activities

Purpose: To develop a plan for estate planning and related financial activities.

Financial Planning Activities: Respond to the following questions as a basis for making and implementing an estate plan. This sheet is also available in an Excel spreadsheet format in Connect Finance.

Suggested Websites: www.nolo.com, www.law.cornell.edu

YOUR PERSONAL FINANCIAL PLAN

Are your financial records, including recent tax forms, insurance policies, and investment and housing documents organized and easily accessible?	
Do you have a safe-deposit box? Where is it located? Where is the key?	
Where are your life insurance policies located? What is the name and address of each insurance company and agent?	
Is your will current? Where are copies of your will located? What is the name and address of your lawyer?	
What is the name and address of your executor?	
Do you have a list of the current value of assets owned and liabilities outstanding?	
Have any funeral and burial arrangements been made?	
Have you created any trusts? If so, what is the name and location of the financial institution(s)?	
Do you have any current information on gift and estate taxes?	
Have you prepared a letter of last instruction? Where is it located?	

What's Next for Your Personal Financial Plan?

- Talk to several individuals about the actions they have taken related to estate planning.
- Create a list of situations in which a will would need to be revised.

Suggested App:
- Tomorrow

McGraw Hill

Name: _____   **Date:** _____

Will Planning

Purpose: To compare costs and features of various types of wills.

Financial Planning Activities: Obtain information for the various areas listed based on your current and future situation; contact attorneys regarding the cost of various types of wills. This sheet is also available in an Excel spreadsheet format in Connect Finance.

Suggested Websites: www.estateplanninglinks.com, www.nnepa.com

Type of will	Features that would be appropriate for my current or future situation	Attorney, address, phone, cost

What's Next for Your Personal Financial Plan?

- Create a list of items that you believe would be desirable to include in a will.
- Obtain the cost of a will from a number of different sources.

Trust Comparison

Purpose: To identify features of different types of trusts.

Financial Planning Activities: Research features of various trusts to determine their value to your personal situation. This sheet is also available in an Excel spreadsheet format in Connect Finance.

Suggested Websites: www.massmutualtrust.com, www.legalzoom.com

Type of trust	Benefits	Possible value for my situation

Suggested App:
• Modern Trust

McGraw Hill

What's Next for Your Personal Financial Plan?

- Talk to legal and financial planning experts to contrast the cost and benefits of wills and trusts.
- Talk to one or more lawyers to obtain information about the type of trust recommended for your situation.

Index